PC WORLD

Paradox 3.5
Power Programming Techniques

By Gregory B. Salcedo
and Martin W. Rudy

Special Preface by
Richard Schwartz
Senior Vice President, Technology
Borland

Special Introduction by
Richard Landry
Editor-in-Chief
PC World

IDG Books Worldwide, Inc.
San Mateo, California 94402

PC World Paradox 3.5 Power Programming Techniques

Editor-in-Chief: Michael E. McCarthy
Associate Editor: Jeremy Judson
Production Manager: Lana Olson
Edited by Marie Scanlon, Publications Manager, Database Business Unit, Borland International
Technical edit by Judy Duncan, Duncan Engineering
Interior design by Mark Houts and Bill Hartman
Production by Hartman Publishing

Published by
IDG Books Worldwide, Inc.
155 Bovet Road, Suite 730
San Mateo, CA 94402
(415) 358-1250

Copyright © 1990 by IDG Books Worldwide, Inc. All rights reserved. No part of this book may be reproduced or transmitted in any form, by any means (electronic, photocopying, recording, or otherwise), except for the making of one backup copy of the attached diskette, without the prior written permission of the publisher. See last page for details on the appropriate use of the attached diskette.

Library of Congress Catalog Card No.: 90-84498

ISBN 1-878058-02-9

Printed in the United States of America

10 9 8 7 6 5 4 3 2

Distributed in the United States by IDG Books Worldwide, Inc.
Distributed in Canada by Macmillan of Canada, a Division of Canada Publishing Corporation.
For information on translations and availability in other countries, contact IDG Books Worldwide.
For sales inquiries and special prices for bulk quantities, write to the address above or call IDG Books Worldwide at (415) 358-1250.

Trademarks: Paradox is a registered trademark of Borland International. PAL, VROOMM, and TurboDrive are trademarks of Borland. All other Borland products are trademarks or registered trademarks of Borland International, Inc. All other brand names and product names used in this book are trademarks, registered trademarks, or trade names of their respective holders. IDG Books Worldwide and PC World are not associated with Borland International or any other product or vendor mentioned in this book. PC World is a trademark of PCW Communications, Inc.

Limits of Liability/Disclaimer of Warranty: The authors and publisher of this book have used their best efforts in preparing this book and its contents, and in testing the source code and utilities on the disk. Nevertheless, IDG Books Worldwide, Inc., PCW Communications, Inc., and the authors make no representation or warranties with respect to the accuracy or completeness of the contents of this book or the source code and programs and utilities on diskette included with it or the program listings given or the programming techniques described in the book, and specifically disclaim any implied warranties or merchantability or fitness for any particular purpose, and shall in no event be liable for any loss of profit or any other commercial damage, including but not limited to special, incidental, consequential, or other damages. See also the last page of this book for details regarding the included diskette.

Dedication

To our wives and families and to all those people who have made Paradox the success it is today.

Acknowledgements

We would like to thank the following people and organizations who have helped us with Paradox and with this book:

Borland International	Philippe Kahn
	Richard Schwartz
	Robert Wong
	Tony Lee
	Dan Putterman
	Marie Scanlon
Farpoint Systems Corp.	Joseph Fung
Kallista, Inc.	Dan Erhman
Softbite, Inc.	Kevin Smith

Special thanks for Kevin Smith's assistance with Chapter 12

Zenreich Systems, Inc.   Alan Zenreich

A very special thanks to Rusel DeMaria without whose continued literary mentorship and counsel this book would not have been possible.

The publishers also wish to thank Bill Murphy.

Read-me file excerpts provided courtesy of Borland International, Inc. Copyright © 1990. Used by permission. All rights reserved.

Screen displays were generated using Paradox, Paradox SQL Link, and Paradox Engine Products. Copyright © 1985-1990, Borland International, Inc. Used by permission.

Table of Contents

Preface	xiv
Special Introduction	xv
Introduction	xvi

1 A New Age in Programming: The Paradox Environment ... 1

The Paradox Database Environment	3
The Paradox Core	3
The Paradox User Interface and Internal Tools	4
The Paradox Objects	4
The Paradox Utilities and External Tools	5
Realistic versus Theoretical Development	6
The Internal versus the Third-Party Developer	7
Rapid Development Projects	9
Creating a Decision Process and Strategy	10
Business Knowledge	13
Vendor Support	13
Ready-to-go Solutions	13
Summary	15

2 The Application Life Cycle ... 17

Requirements Gathering	18
Logical Database Design	21
Physical Database Design	21
Program Design	26
Modular Coding	27
System Testing	31
Documentation	33
System Implementation: Turning the Application Over to the User	35
Summary	38

3 Normalizing Your Paradox Databases ... 39
Basic Terminology Review ... 40
Why You Should Normalize Your Data ... 40
Normalization: What Is It? ... 42
First Normal Form: Remove Repeating Groups ... 42
Second Normal Form ... 47
Third Normal Form ... 48
Denormalization: Should You DO_IT! ... 50
Summary ... 52

4 Prototyping with Paradox ... 53
Traditional Method of Development ... 54
KISS versus LAW ... 57
The Prototyping Model ... 58
How to Get Started: Involving the User ... 72
Creating the Conceptual Design ... 73
Physical Design ... 74
Program Development ... 74
Testing ... 74
Installation ... 75
Training ... 75
Post-installation Review ... 75
Paradox Prototyping Methodology Review ... 75
Summary ... 76

5 Paradox 3.5: What's New ... 77
Major Feature Overview ... 77
Paradox 3.5 Detailed Feature Set ... 78
Interactive Paradox ... 84
Borland Product Interoperability ... 85
New Commands ... 85
New Functions ... 87
Modified Commands ... 90
Modified Functions ... 91
Additional PAL Changes ... 92

Custom Configuration Program	94
The Personal Programmer	98
Compatibility with Previous Releases	99
SQL Link	100
Multi-Pack and User Counts	100
Product Line	101
Summary	101

6 Data Integrity ... 103

Data Integrity: What is it?	103
ValChecks: An Overview	107
Why ValChecks Alone are not Enough	107
Entering ValChecks	115
Master Picture Table	116
Basic Multitable Data Entry Code Example	122
Running the Basic Multitable Data Entry Program	126
Modifications to Script to Ensure Data Integrity	128
Enhanced Code for Field- and Record-Level Validation	129
Executing the Enhanced Integrity Checking Program	140
ValCheck Visibility Reporting	142

7 Building Procedures and Libraries ... 145

Procedures and Libraries: A Primer	146
What is a Procedure?	146
Defining Procedures	147
Global and Private Variables	151
Closed Procedures	152
What is a Procedure Library?	153
Creating Libraries	153
Storing Procedures in Libraries	154
Using Procedures	155
Explicit Procedure Loading	156
Autoloading Procedures from a Library	156
Library Contents Visibility	157
Debugging Procedures in Libraries	158

Procedures and Libraries Summary	160
Autolib, Swapping, and Releasing Procedures from Memory	161
Good Procedure versus Bad Procedure Construction	165
Optimal Procedure Size	169
Regular Procedures versus Closed Procedures	170
Different Methods for Creating Libraries	173
Multiple Small versus Single Large Libraries	177
Error Procedures	178
Summary	188

8 Creating and Enhancing the Paradox Interface ... 191

Building a Menu System	193
MAIN.SC Overview (Paradox-Style Main Menu)	195
Creating Stacking/Tiling Pop-up Menus	214

9 Viewing, Entering, and Editing Data ... 241

Generic View Script for Multiple Tables	242
Data Entry Methods	246
Edit versus CoEdit	249
Controlling Transaction Log in Edit Mode	253
Editing a Subset of a Table	259
Global Variables, Arrays, and Functions In Forms	272
Key Violations	275
Uniqueness Not Based on Key Field	286
Trapping for Field View	290
How to Get to DOS Within an Application and Ways to Prevent It	292
Summary	292

10 Running Advanced Queries ... 293

A Whole New Way of Asking Questions	294
QuerySave and PAL Commands	295
Queries in Scripts versus Libraries	301

Test Results	314
Test Analysis and Summary	322
A Better Mouse Trap?	323
Some Special Query Notes	327
Summary	330

11 Running Advanced Reports and Graphs ... 331

Reporting Techniques	331
Global Variables and Functions	341
Printer Control Characters	350
Graphs	352
Printing Multiple Graphs Per Page	356
Summary	358

12 Setting up a Multiuser Environment ... 359

Network Overview	359
Paradox Network Installation	361
More Installation and Network Information	364
Automatic (Implicit) Locking versus Explicit Locking	371
Editing/CoEditing Issues in the Multiuser Environment	371
A Special Network Problem	379
Summary	383

13 Using Paradox SQL Link ... 385

An Introduction to Client/Server Architecture	386
SQL Link Feature Overview	390
Installation	391
Interactive Access Connecting to a Server	393
Creating a Table on the Server	396
Entering Data into a Server Table	397
Querying a Server Table	398
Building a Report on a Server Table	406
Removing Data from a Server Table	406
SQL Menu Selection	406

Security	410
Existing Commands Enhanced by SQL Link	410
New PAL Commands with SQL Link	412
New PAL Functions with SQL Link	418
Error Handling in SQL Link	421
The SQL Setup Program	423
Automatic Menu Selection	424
Manual Menu Selection	429
UseSQL Menu Selection	431
ConnectList Menu Selection	432
The SQL Command Editor	435
Notes From READSQL Covering Each SQL Database Server Product	439
SQL Link Code Examples	441
Summary	460

14 Using the Paradox Engine ... 461

Engine Overview	462
Engine Requirements	462
PAL and the Engine: Major Differences	463
Compiling with Turbo C or Microsoft C	466
Engine Functions	468
Structure of an Engine Program	472
Getting the Engine Defaults	473
Initializing the Engine	474
Opening a Table	476
Printing Column Headings	477
Printing Records in a Table	477
Closing the Record Buffer and the Table	479
Terminating the Program	479
List Table Examples	480
What's Missing	491
Summary	492

15 Some Performance Tips 493
Memory 493
Table Design 496
Other Tips 499
Summary 500

16 Sample Applications 501
ABC Music Store 501
Personnel Application 535
Summary 543

17 Creating and Using Development Tools 545
Creating Paradox Tools 545
Using the Report Generator to write PAL 547
Database Selection Menu 549
Beeps 552
Display Paradox-Style Message in Window 553
Clearing Query Images on the Workspace 554
Exploding Window 554
Filled Window 557
Procedure to Test if Printer is Ready 558
ValCheck Reporting Program 559
Another Information Tool 564
Enhancing the PAL Editor 572
Summary 579

18 Integrating Data 581
Importing Information 581
Flimport 586
Exporting Data 588
Running Other Programs from Paradox 592
Data Modeling with Quattro Pro 593
Step-by-Step: Creating A Data Model Using Quattro Pro 595
Summary 602

19 Understanding and Managing Paradox Memory 603

How Paradox Looks at Memory 604
Protected Mode versus Real Mode 605
Paradox Graphics and Expanded Memory Conflicts 606
Getting More Memory Out of your 286 607
Running Caching Programs: Super PC Qwik,
    Lightning, Paul Mace 609
Running Paradox from Windows 610
Running Paradox from DESQview 611
Special Troubleshooting Notes 613
Summary 615

20 Getting More out of Paradox 617

Paradox Add-ons and Utilities 617
Script Editors 618
Documentation Tools 621
Other Paradox Add-ons 623
Training Organizations and Seminars 626
Other Books, Newsletters, and Support 627

21 More Information on PAL 629

PAL Commands and Functions 629
Special Functions 665
Summary 671

A Database Servers 673

Microsoft SQL Server 1.1 673
Oracle Server for OS/2 675
IBM OS/2 1.2 676
Database Server Comparison 678
Server Connection Information 678
Field Naming Conventions 679
SQL Link Queries that Lock Records with Autocommit=OFF 679

Supported Data Types	679
Database Server Limitations by Product	680

B Reference Charts 681

Glossary 719

Index 729

Preface

By Richard Schwartz
Senior Vice President, Technical
Borland International

In this book, Greg and Martin have set before you the manner and means to better understand and use Paradox. They bring with them years of experience in developing Paradox applications. This book contains many invaluable tips and insights that will help you with your own Paradox applications.

Paradox is more than PAL, more than QBE—it's a total development and user environment. Paradox contains all the tools you need to create sophisticated, efficient, and powerful applications. The better you understand and utilize the Paradox environment, the more you can take advantage of its power.

Paradox's approach to creation, maintenance, and manipulation of its tables, forms, and reports empowers the user to create applications. Application development naturally follows from interactive use. Think about the basic concepts for the application: the queries, the forms, the reports, and the menus. Build and refine them interactively, rapidly prototyping the basic components. Then use PAL to complete the framework and tie it together into an application.

Paradox brings programming and information together — it is for users and developers alike. Its very nature encourages cooperative development between user and programmer. *PC World Paradox 3.5 Power Programming Techniques* raises the art of Paradox programming to a new level.

Special Introduction

By Richard Landry
Editor-in-Chief & Associate Publisher
PC World

PC World Paradox 3.5 Power Programming Techniques marks the beginning of an important new line of books from PC World that will bring to the serious computer user a whole new level of practical, useful information.

Our books, like our magazine, are designed to be interesting to read and use — and to help you get the job done. Practical, and firmly fixed in the real world, our publications get straight to the point — getting the job done.

This book is aimed at the corporate or independent Paradox developer who has already gotten value from the interactive power of this advanced relational database, and who is ready to grow his or her Paradox programming knowledge to a new level of practical power. Our authors, developers for a major aerospace manufacturer, know what it means to work on projects in the real world, with the never-ending deadlines, and the constant tradeoffs between time and resources. Their practical experience and valuable insights will help you quickly harness even more of the power of Paradox.

We think of this as "the ultimate Paradox book." Like each new book in the PC World book line, it brings a special level of expertise to bear on the problems and opportunities of computing in the real world. We hope you enjoy the power.

Introduction

Welcome to *PC World Paradox 3.5 Power Programming Techniques*. You have before you a compilation of years of experience with Paradox. This book is a distillation of strategies, philosophies, and techniques for successful Paradox application efforts.

It begins with discussions of the strategy and philosophy of Paradox development. It then moves quickly to give you code that you can put to work immediately. At each step of the way, you are given information and code examples that will provide you with many solutions to problems you face in today's Paradox development environment. This book will open up the secrets, hidden or otherwise, to developing expert Paradox systems.

Why Paradox?

Once viewed as an end-user tool only, Paradox—powerful, flexible, and above all, easy to use—has become the DBMS environment of choice for successful developers throughout the world. The Paradox community has grown and matured and can now be found throughout the Fortune 1000. Paradox is no longer merely a hopeful candidate; it is now the foremost contender to the corporate and institutional microcomputer DBMS throne.

Paradox is truly one of the most powerful and easy-to-use information tools. It has lifted a whole generation of personal computer users out of the spreadsheet database doldrums and placed them in the bright light of the relational world. Paradox attempts to make the transition as easy as possible. Like a spreadsheet, there is a menu command interface, you can edit in a table (sheet mode) or in a form, and in addition, all the tools lacking from the spreadsheet are provided: form and report generators, a debugger, an application language, data type disciplines, validity checks, automatic lookup and fill, primary key and secondary index capability, and so on are provided for both the interactive user and developer alike.

Yet, even though the transition from spreadsheets to databases is smoothed by Paradox, the knowledge needed to take full advantage of a relational database is still just beginning to be understood by businesses and institutions. There is a need for a higher awareness of relational theory and good application design, as well as an increased ability to respond quickly to customers' rapidly changing business and information requirements. This book gives you the building blocks of relational theory in a practical, down-to-earth style that is immediately applicable to your current and future Paradox systems. The better you understand Paradox's environment, the better you are able to use it to its fullest extent.

Who Can Use This Book?

This book is dedicated to helping the Paradox developer deliver on the great potential of Paradox. It is written for every Paradox developer seeking discussions and examples of advanced Paradox programming—especially the corporate and institutional developer. Throughout the book, we try to bring an in-depth knowledge of Paradox application development, and present it in a straightforward, useful, easy-to-implement style.

More than just a book of programming examples, it guides you through issues ranging from database normalization to rapid prototyping. You'll learn how to get the most out of Paradox with the least effort.

The theory contained in this book is based on real-life, roll-up-the-shirt-sleeves experience. This book reflects, of course, our particular style and approach to software projects; our style is not necessarily better than another. We believe that you, as a developer, benefit from having many styles and resources at your fingertips, so you may draw upon styles and methods as necessary to create your solutions. It is in this spirit that the book is presented.

Whether you're just starting to develop in Paradox, or you have been doing so for years, you'll find this book an essential source of information for creating useful Paradox applications.

About Paradox 3.5 and Earlier Versions of Paradox

This book is based on Paradox 3.5. Paradox 3.5 contains features, functions, and capabilities not available in earlier versions. Among the new product features are additional functions in reports and forms, SQL Link (to access data in a client/server architecture), and VROOMM, Paradox's new memory management technique. Chapter 5 addresses the specific differences between version 3.5 and 3.01a in great detail. If you're presently using an earlier version of Paradox, we recommend you upgrade to the current version. This product will bring a substantial gain to your Paradox environment. If you do not upgrade, most of this book will still be useful to you but you may find that you'll have to skip certain chapters in the book.

What's in This Book?

In this book you will find all the information necessary to create efficient, productive, Paradox applications. The best way to read this book is with Paradox up and running. You'll want to try ideas and code as they are presented to you (every listing contained in this book, including complete accounting and personnel systems, are also provided on the disk that is bound into the back of this book). The best way to learn Paradox is to *Do_it!*

We begin with a discussion of common developer problems: How do you maximize you resources to cover all your customers? How do you shorten the development process? And what is the best way to approach the application life cycle? Next we provide a definitive comparison of the differences between Paradox 3.5 and Paradox 3.0. The middle sections of this book are devoted to valuable advanced tricks that will give your applications great features; we also warn of common traps to avoid. Later chapters devote themselves to supplying application code — the building blocks of a business application—in the form of an accounting, personnel, and other typical system modules (with code on disk). Finally, the book covers products that will aid your development efforts as well as help you gain optimum use of Paradox.

The first four chapters scan the issues surrounding developing Paradox applications.

> **Chapter 1** begins a discussion of realistic versus theoretical application development. It also contains a section outlining the roles of the user and developer with special attention given to the corporate developer.
>
> **Chapter 2** investigates the typical application life cycle and how it does or does not apply to Paradox applications.
>
> **Chapter 3** discusses how to normalize your Paradox databases, and elaborates on first, second, and third normal forms.

Chapter 4 shows how to rapidly develop applications using Paradox. This chapter lays the foundation for how Paradox programs should be constructed and methods that can be used to simplify the development process.

Chapter 5 gives an in-depth presentation of the new features in Paradox 3.5: functions in reports and forms, SQL Link, new memory management (VROOMM), and the new links to Borland's Quattro Pro. It cross-references the differences from Paradox 3.01a.

The next group begins with an overview of how Paradox handles data validation and ways to ensure data integrity. The topics in this section range from details on the proper procedure format to installing and optimizing *Paradox SQL Link*.

Chapter 6 details when and where Paradox's validity checking and data integrity are working for you and why they need to be augmented. In addition, this chapter gives routines to speed up the insertion of Validity Checks in your application.

Chapter 7 deals with proper procedural and library creating techniques and formats. In this chapter we examine what makes a *bad* procedure versus a *good* procedure, the optimal procedure size, and how to create error procedures.

Chapter 8 gives you code to build your pop-up menus, zoom up information screens, and add context-sensitive help to your application.

Chapter 9 provides routines for viewing, editing, and entering data. Special attention is given to multitable tricks and techniques (examples on how to create and load your own ValChecks and error procedures).

Chapter 10 covers advanced queries from QBE to SCANs, from SETs to special outer joins. This chapter also provides a method to benchmark which kind of query capability you should use and when you should use it.

Chapter 11 tackles advanced report generator concepts. You'll be lead step-by-step through the use of functions in reports, controlling the printer from the report format, and using the report generator to write PAL code.

Chapter 12 takes on multiuser issues and development. This chapter is devoted to walking you through the proper way to set up a local area network and workstations. Also, the tricks and traps surrounding running queries and reports in a network environment are thoroughly discussed.

Chapter 13 takes an in-depth look at the newest Paradox feature SQL Link. Here you'll see the proper way to approach the client/server architecture. You will inspect the nuances of three of the top database servers and how each should be set up to properly be utilized.

Chapter 14 delves into the Paradox Engine. What is it? Where can you use it? You'll learn how to use the Paradox Engine for basic table creation, and input and output of information in both single user and multiuser situations.

The final seven chapters get right to the heart of the matter. This section is devoted to examples of applications and includes the code to create Paradox applications.

Chapter 15 jumps right into performance tuning. How do you set the Paradox environment to provide it with all the resources it will need? Both single-user and multiuser workstations are addressed as well as how to evaluate your table structure size and the impact of record length on performance. This chapter provides a blueprint to review past and design future Paradox application environments.

Chapter 16 provides accounting, distribution, personnel, and manufacturing program code.

Chapter 17 presents routines and procedures that should be incorporated into every Paradox application. Backup, restore, and diagnostic and maintenance scripts are shown and discussed, line for line. Quick, useful scripts to help your report and form creation are also shown.

Chapter 18 explores exchanging and integrating Paradox data with other microcomputer applications. Here you'll see how to query a Paradox database from Quattro Pro.

Chapter 19 presents the new memory management scheme in Paradox 3.5 and what resources should be available to your system. Special attention is given to networking concerns.

Chapter 20 is a series of third-party product reviews that will enhance your Paradox application capabilities.

Chapter 21 is a command and function reference for certain commands and functions that need further explanation. This chapter is spiced up with code examples from the previous chapters' application code examples.

Sample Files on Disk

The examples and applications throughout this book can be found in the self-extracting archive file called POWERDOX.EXE on the enclosed disk. All the tables and scripts that you'll need to perform the examples are provided for you. We've also included a number of useful utilities including your own personal Paradox program editor.

Here is a brief overview of the examples included on the disk, where to find them and how to activate the scripts, if necessary:

Directories created:	Discussion
[drive]\powerdox	Once the disk has been installed you may erase the POWERDOX.EXE file to get back some drive space.
[drive]\powerdox\02	Chapter 2 The Application Life Cycle examples — no compiles are necessary, no startup scripts.
[drive]\powerdox\04	Chapter 4 Prototyping examples — no compiles are necessary, no startup scripts.
[drive]\powerdox\06	Chapter 6 Data Integrity examples — no compiles are necessary, no startup scripts.
[drive]\powerdox\07	Chapter 7 Procedure and Library examples — no compiles are necessary, no startup scripts.
[drive]\powerdox\08	Chapter 8 Pop-Up and other menu examples. Play the MAKELIB script to compile the procedures. Play MANIMENU to start the POP-UP menus, SMAIN for the static menus.
[drive]\powerdox\09	Chapter 9 View/Entry/Edit examples — no compiles are necessary, no startup scripts.
[drive]\powerdox\10	Chapter 10 Query examplesplay MAKELIB to compile the procedures. Look at Chapter 10 for how to proceed.
[drive]\powerdox\11	Chapter 11 Reports & Graphs examples — no compiles are necessary, no startup scripts.
[drive]\powerdox\12	Chapter 12 Multiuser development — no compiles are necessary, no startup scripts.

[drive]\powerdox\13	Chapter 13 SQL Link examples — no compiles are necessary, no startup scripts. Must have Paradox SQL Link to perform these examples.
[drive]\powerdox\14	Chapter 14 Paradox Engine examples — no compiles are necessary, no startup scripts. The "C" source code is provided for two listing examples.
[drive]\powerdox\16	Chapter 16 contains two applications. The ABC Music Store application includes invoicing, inventory management, class scheduling and purchase order management. To start the ABC MUSIC Store application play MAKE_ABC to start the application play MMAIN. The PERSONNEL application features basic human resource tracking and information. The procedures illustrate VALCHECK procedures, multitable reporting, and general error processing. The PERSONNEL application is compiled by playing MKPERSNL and MKUTIL. To start this application play STARTUP.
[drive]\powerdox\17	Chapter 17 provides you with various UTILITIES and Toolbox scripts that can help you with your application development. Here is a list of some of scripts and procedures your will find in this directory:

GETFLDS.SC	A script that returns the field names for a table.
STATSCRP.SC	A script that plays detective with your system and returns you information about the version of Paradox you're running, colors you have selected for your screens, how much drive space you have, how much memory and more!
DBSELECT.SC	This script provides you with Paradox MAIN MENU that allows you to quickly and efficiently switch between your Paradox applications/directories.
EXPLDWIN.SC	Shows you how to create an exploding window that will enhance the messages you present in your application.

... and more!

Also included are two complete utilities: EDITOR3 — your own personal Paradox Editor — and VCPGM, a VALCHECK documentation utility.

VCPGM.SC   Is a series of procedures that helps you document your Paradox tables, forms, and procedures.

To activate the VALCHECK catalog program play VCPGM.

SETEDIT3.SC   To compile EDITOR3 play SETEDIT3. To activate the editor play GO_EDIT3.

[drive]\powerdox\21   Chapter 21 shows examples of certain PAL nuances — no compiles are necessary, no startup scripts.

Tips, Traps, etc.

This book also contains hundreds of TIPS, HINTS, REMINDERS, and TRAPS to keep in mind during Paradox application development. Here is what to look for:

TIP
Tips give you inside information on how to best take advantage of PAL and the Paradox environment.

TRICK
Tricks are shortcuts we have learned over the years to save you time and trouble.

REMEMBER
Provide you with reminders of beginning-level Paradox concepts in order to set the stage for understanding the current topic.

NOTE
Notes are quick comments that guide you through a better understanding of the information currently being presented.

TRAP
These are the gems that help you avoid hours of wasteful effort. These bits of information not only save you time, they can help you avoid the loss of vital application data.

VARIABLES

Are found in italics. For example:

gc = **getchar()**

COMMANDS AND FUNCTIONS

Paradox commands and functions are shown in CAPITAL letters.

Summary

Martin and I hope you find this book helpful! Take a look at these examples. We encourage you to use the code contained on the disk as a starting point for your own Paradox development. These POWER techniques are provided for you to EMPOWER your applications. Enjoy! .... go forth and Do_it!

1 A New Age in Programming: The Paradox Environment

Paradox, without doubt, lives up to its name—it genuinely *is* a Paradox: simple to use for any end user, yet robust enough for the most sophisticated developer.

The advent of Paradox has heralded the exit of database management systems that require programming code to provide screens, reports, and simple table views.

```
*****************************************************************
*-- Command file Customer Input Form
*-- 8/27 GBS

CLEAR

@1,0 to 3,50
@11,0 to 17,50 Double

*----- Setup fields to edit
@2,1    SAY "Customer Number"
@2,17   GET Custid
@12,5   SAY "Current Balance"
@12,22  Get CurrBal
CLEAR GETS         && Release read
```

Figure 1-1 Old style of programming a form (using code)

A table of information now has a direct relationship with forms, reports, and validity checks. In Paradox, once a form is created, you don't have to worry about whether the form will *work* or not. Forms, reports, and other objects are always available to their associated table(s). Tables and their family of objects maintain a constant relationship with each other.

Because of Paradox's object-oriented philosophy, you spend less time building unnecessary code for screens, reports, and other basic system components. You now have the time to concentrate on solving the challenges of the application at hand.

Paradox brings more than a database to a developer's fingertips—it gives you a complete development environment. Understanding this environment is crucial. You must understand each and every component of Paradox to maximize its capabilities. This next section provides an overview of the Paradox environment, starting with the picture presented in Figure 1-2.

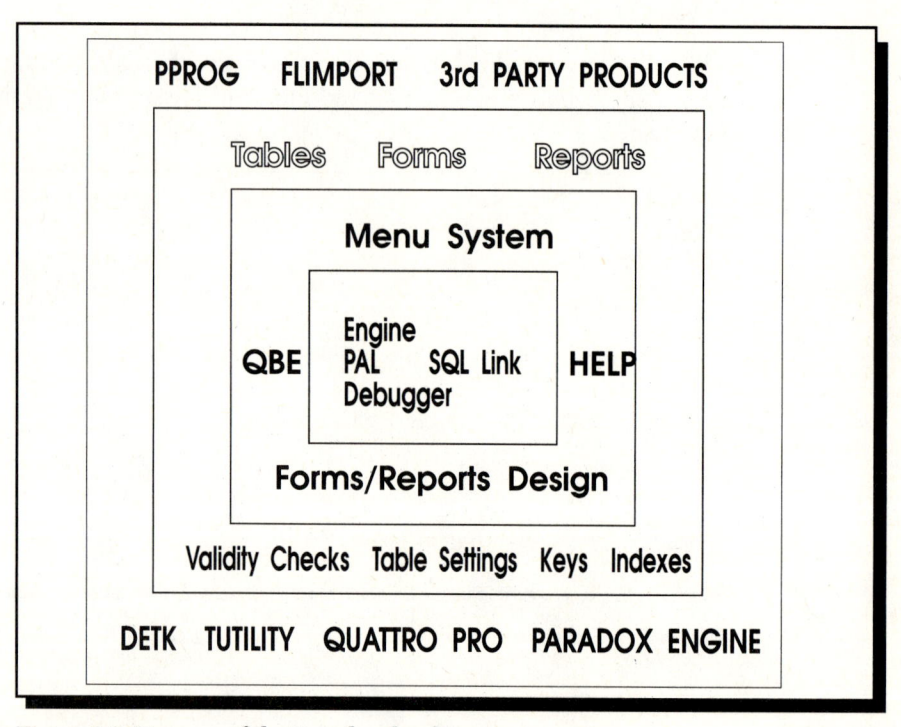

Figure 1-2 Diagram of the Paradox database environment

The Paradox Database Environment

The Paradox database environment is divided into four distinct groups:

- Core capabilities
- The user interface (UI) and internal tools
- Paradox objects
- Paradox utilities and external tools

The Paradox Core

Engine — The basic Paradox engine (not to be confused with the Paradox Engine 1.0) is the heart and soul of Paradox. With Paradox 3.5, the product takes a significant leap forward. First of all, the product is now written in Turbo C, so the database and language shops at Borland now literally and figuratively talk to each other. This is a very significant and welcome change to the core of the product. It bodes well for future product advances and provides synergy for tackling portability across platforms (Windows, OS/2 and Unix). Previous versions had trouble with numerical precision. This is (thankfully) no longer the case. We'll discuss this and other changes to the product in Chapter 5.

Debugger — Unlike other DBMS systems, Paradox's debugger is always available and working for you. Whether you are running PAL code or simply using the product interactively, the debugger steps in whenever a problem arises. The Paradox debugger is one of the more innovative aspects of Paradox, and when used properly, it's one of your key tools in rapidly developing high-quality information systems.

PAL — The Paradox Application Language (PAL) is the meat of the developer's meal. Command of this language set is essential for developing good applications.

SQL Link — The client/server architecture has come at last to the Paradox environment. With SQL Link, both the interactive user and the developer have a whole new world of information access to explore. With SQL Link, it no longer matters where data resides. You are now able to access powerful database engines like Microsoft's SQL Server, IBM's Extended Edition, and Oracle's Server.

The Paradox User Interface and Internal Tools

Menu — Paradox's heart lies with this component. Basically, if you don't know interactive Paradox, you'll be hard pressed to develop high-quality applications. If you haven't spent a lot of time with interactive Paradox, start doing so today.

QBE — If there is a fun part to Paradox, it has to be its query capability. Who would have thought that asking a database to answer complex questions could be so easy? QBE doesn't permit functions yet, but as the cat knows, skinning can be done various ways. We'll look into getting the most from queries and how to get around the function problem in Chapter 10.

Help — Every DBMS has to have a built-in help mechanism. Paradox does a fairly good job with help, but you need more than what's there. As a Paradox developer, you should build on Paradox's premise by including some sort of help facility in every system you build.

Generators — Paradox has built-in, fully-functional Report and Form generators. With Paradox 3.5, you can now use functions in forms and reports as calculated fields. This is certainly a welcome addition to the tool set and should eliminate a lot of PAL coding.

The Paradox Objects

Objects — Tables, forms, reports, validity checks, image settings, keys, as well as primary and secondary indexes are all physical objects that have a direct relationship to the table they are associated with. Each of these object files is date and time stamped as it is created and updated in order to establish and maintain relational integrity with the table each is associated with. If integrity is questioned, Paradox protects your information environment and won't let you continue with an operation until integrity is restored.

Many Paradox critics point to this as a cumbersome aspect of Paradox, but we prefer to think of it as one of its greatest strengths. How can you rely on forms and reports if their relationship to the associated tables is not valid? You simply can't. It is too cumbersome to code changes to a form as its application requirements change and far easier to keep the code as is and change the form when needed.

The Paradox Utilities and External Tools

PPROG The Paradox Personal Programmer (PPROG) is a very useful tool for an interactive user who is not ready for or doesn't want to deal with PAL programming. The only problem with this tool is that it tries to be all things to all people. Of course, no application generator can live up to that promise. We find that with PAL, we are able to create all the effects of PPROG, without the memory overhead and with fewer lines of code. Therefore, this Paradox component is not discussed in this book.

TUTILITY This is the save-the-bacon part of Paradox. Paradox 3.5 is a DOS product. As such, it must deal with the limitations of the DOS environment. TUTILITY is an essential tool for every Paradox developer, and, for that matter, interactive user as well. TUTILITY's job is to check, and if needed, rebuild, your tables if corruption occurs. TUTILITY is not a perfect product so it is good to have several alternative strategies to recover data. We'll discuss these alternatives in Chapter 17.

DETK The Paradox Data Entry Tool Kit (DETK) is one of the more innovative and yet misunderstood pieces of the Paradox development pie. While it can be the heart of a whole application, it is not intended to be! We are not heavy DETK users ourselves, relying more on DETK to show us the way rather than employing it directly. As with PPROG, we have chosen not to include a discussion on the DETK in this book, but we highly recommend that you delve into this tool to gain a better understanding of the kind of actions, effects, and routines you can create in Paradox.

FLIMPORT   This is the diamond in the data acquisition rough that many Paradox developers don't even know exists. This utility has been shipped with Paradox since version 3.0. It lets you take a flat, fixed-length file and parse it into a Paradox table. This is very useful when importing information from a large mainframe system. We discuss this tool more in Chapter 17.

Quattro Pro   Yes, Quattro Pro is now part of Paradox. Starting with 3.5, Paradox users can access Quattro Pro directly from their Paradox environment. Simply press [Ctrl][F10] or issue the new PAL command, TOQPRO, and you're in Quattro Pro, looking at your Paradox data. Now the whole range of Quattro Pro capabilities are accessible to Paradox users. We'll look into this further in Chapter 18.

Realistic versus Theoretical Development

Today's microcomputer database developer is facing an information crisis. Internal developers have to produce more in less time than they ever have before. Why? One of the reasons is Paradox itself. How many times have you delivered a system to a client and no matter how much time you spent developing requirements they say, "That's nice, but could we also add this capability?" Too often?

Paradox makes it so easy for users to deal with the information they control because it's such a visual product that users come to expect more and more from both you and the product.

Other reasons include the changing pressures of business itself. In order to remain competitive, data processing must be responsive to the ever-changing requirements of clients' business needs.

Good application development theory calls for you to take the time to engineer well-thought-out, reusable code. Too often a developer starts to create an application to solve a question that hasn't been fully developed or thought through.

Whatever the reason, how do you deal with this dilemma? You work smarter and faster. How? By learning as much as you can about the product you're using to develop your applications, and by creating a development environment complete with every tool you need to create quick, high-quality applications.

First of all, you have to develop a style that allows for quick prototyping. You must use an application cycle that plans for going back and laying in theoretical code constructs after you've dealt with the reality of delivering an application at any cost.

The Internal versus the Third-Party Developer

To understand the problems of developing for today's business environment, you first need to realize that there are two kinds of developers. No, we don't mean good and bad, though that problem certainly exists, even if the tool you develop with is excellent. What we really mean is that there are internal (corporate) and external (third-party) developers.

The third-party developer has many problems and certain advantages. As one of the best third-party Paradox developers in the country is fond of saying, "When you don't have a contract or job, you're simply unemployed. Call it what you like, but when you're not working, you can't make the house payment!" He's also quick to point out that the internal developer has choices that the third-party developer doesn't—the internal developer can walk away from a job (transfer or quit). The third-party developer has no other choice than to fulfill the purchase order or contract, or face possible legal as well as financial ramifications.

One advantage of being a third-party developer is that you can more or less pick your own clients. The demand for good Paradox developers and consultants simply outstrips the supply. In contrast, the internal developer must serve any or all clients within their business entity or institution. They are not afforded the luxury (from their view) of selecting which customers they wish to deal with.

Next, the third-party developer is usually able to negotiate a time of delivery that is commensurate with the challenge posed by the application to be developed. The internal developer is quite often expected to produce instant (measured in minutes and hours, not days and weeks) and accurate results. The internal developer often has little or no requirements and yet is expected to produce as if such requirements existed.

Finally, the third-party developer is less likely to face the dreaded creeping requirement. Face it, if you have to pay for a service, you're more likely to make sure that the service you desire is worth the money you pour out. The third-party developer must charge their client for changes that a user requests. Because data processing has few and at best, crude methods of billing back their internal customers, the internal developer is often asked to perform on the fly, with little or no guidance (or worse yet, no knowledge of the business task required).

Before we go any further, let's set some things straight. Relax—there is no war between third-party and internal developers. Obviously, both types of developers are needed in the application development community.

However, we are internal developers. As such, we have a special place in our hearts for the particular plights the internal developer faces. As we have just discussed, there are significant differences of approach and reality these two factions take.

In order for other internal developers to have an expanded view of their particular problems, let's look at the dilemma facing this faction from their perspective.

Today's internal developer is an often-overlooked, extremely important component of microcomputer application development. The internal developer is often a departmental PC guru—the super user of a software package or language, an analyst in a computing resource center or information systems development group. The internal developer is the first line of support in solving many of today's crucial business information problems. These are people who research, recommend, implement, develop, and support software products and applications in today's business. In addition, they participate in the selection of third-party products and outside contractors. Internal developers are a vital ingredient in delivering successful business systems.

Internal developers are directly or indirectly responsible for every dollar spent on microcomputer application development in corporate America. Whether programming and analytical services are delivered by third parties or developed internally, the corporation pays for software applications. Yet, software vendors frequently appear to overlook the importance of the in-house development staff.

Today's software vendor is primarily motivated to sell their product only. Their sales strategy targets business at the highest levels of management. The vendor presents the benefits of using their product to management. Next, they work to sell the business's upper management on the concept of their particular product.

Unfortunately, the people who are asked to use these products are too often left out of the decision-making process. This results in the acceptance of a product without any concrete idea of how it will be implemented (or if it can be implemented!) within the current system environment. Once the sale is made, the ISV (Independent Software Vendor) walks away—not so the internal developer.

This lack of participation in the product-selection process, as well as inadequate vendor support, is frustrating for the internal developer. What the internal developer requires is products and methods that shorten the development process. They need to create systems that are self-documenting, easy-to-use, and flexible enough to change as business requirements change.

Increased support from the ISV is essential to this process. ISV's must be willing to share inside information, power tips, and traps. The internal developer must be given more and better information on how to use the ISV's products. They must have the tools that help deliver the most cost-effective, dynamic solutions to today's business environment.

The bottom line is that business management needs to include the internal developer in the product-selection process. Business management, ISV's, and internal developers must work together more closely to provide successful solutions for business.

Rapid Development Projects

In rapid development projects, the internal developer does not have time to make every input a reusable variable. They do not have the luxury of always creating compact, precise procedures that fulfill many needs. In order to respond quickly, the internal developer must view the development effort as an iterative process.

The internal developer's first priority is to give the user a system that solves the user's problems. Once the system is delivered, the internal developer goes back and reviews the system, modifying it so that it is easier to maintain.

Written user requirements are always sparse, if they exist at all. To add to the complexity of a rapid development project, the user has little or no dedicated computing resources available. At best, the internal developer can count on one or two users who thoroughly understand the business requirements.

Solutions are needed quickly and they must be accurate, efficient, and productive. Internal developers are experts in data processing. They must equally become experts in the business. The more they know about their business, the better they can communicate with their users and respond more rapidly to quick programming projects.

The internal developer cultivates skills and tools that facilitate quick prototyping and allow for evolutionary solutions. Traditional in-house systems development groups aren't used to responding rapidly to changing business needs. A rapid project to them is three to six months, not two hours or three days.

In order to develop applications rapidly, the internal developer needs four resources:

- A development decision process and strategy
- A constantly expanding knowledge of the business
- Vendor hotline and other types of support
- Ready-to-use, tested solutions

Creating a Decision Process and Strategy

The internal developer is the Dirty Harry of application development. As such, they are constantly aware of their limitations. An internal developer faced with a rapid development project needs to quickly determine whether she or he can successfully complete the project. Here is a partial list of questions you should ask yourself when faced with this question.

- What is the crucial information that needs to be delivered?
  - Find out immediately what's the bottom line—what it will take to consider the project done and delivered.
  - Once you have determined the crucial tasks, decide whether you do or don't have the proper resources to complete the project successfully.

- If you believe you don't have the time or resources, let the user know right away. Next, help them find someone that can deliver for them now.
- If you do have the time and resources, ask your users, "If I deliver this crucial information in a system today, will it meet your information needs?"

◆ Are there existing reports that show what information is needed and how it should be expressed?
- Dig up the user's sources of information. Is the data available through a download from the mainframe? Do they re-key the data from several printed reports? Can the printed reports be made available electronically? If you're migrating a spreadsheet solution to a database, get the spreadsheet file. Look at the spreadsheet macros to help determine what the user requires. Use import and export capabilities of products to "cut" the data from its present product to its new environment.

◆ Is this project similar to past projects and if so, can code be borrowed from past projects and then customized?
- Have you created an application similar to the one at hand? Can portions of previous projects be used to speed up the development process?

◆ What business resources can the user make available to you?
- The user should provide someone, hopefully an expert, who knows the necessary business rules. How much time will you have to work with the end users of the application? How well do they (the users) understand the business rules?

◆ How knowledgeable are the users?
- Is the user already knowledgeable in the product that will be used for their project?
- If the user does have some knowledge, what portions of the project can be off-loaded to them?
- Can the user help the project by designing forms for viewing, editing, and entering data?
- Can the user develop some, if not all, of the reports?
- If the user does not have the product knowledge, how bullet-proof does the application need to be?

- What kind of training is available to bring the user up to speed?
- Are you expected to provide training?
- What kind of documentation will be expected? How detailed is the documentation? Can the user document parts of the system?
- In essence, what can you get the user to do so that you can concentrate on the critical parts of development?

◆ How much time do you have to complete the project? What other projects are you involved in currently?
- What is your schedule, and how much time will you be able to spend on the project? It is all too easy to formulate a solution and then be trapped with no time to devote to its successful development and implementation. Remember that somewhere in the process, continued support of the application becomes an issue.

◆ What kind of hardware will you be working with, and what is its configuration?
- The best intended and designed solution will not fly if you don't have the proper platform. Where will the system be installed? What items will need to be purchased, if any? Don't promise a solution that has no way of being installed. Conversely, if budgets are tight, don't give up on giving the user a solution.
- If a user doesn't have the means to buy the resources you need, be creative; design a solution with minimum cost and at least some of the functions they need.

◆ Who is the manager that will sign for delivery?
- Determine who actually accepts your work. Make sure that they agree with the crucial tasks you identify. Put your findings and the proposed solution in writing (even a quick memo will suffice), and get the manager to sign it. Get approval to start the project, and require a sign-off when you deliver the finished product.

Gathering answers to these questions is essential to delivering a successful and timely application. If you don't ask these questions up front, the missing information becomes issues that have to be solved later. The later you address project issues, the costlier the solution.

Business Knowledge

The internal developer must be given the opportunity to develop an intimate knowledge of the business as well as a comprehensive and in-depth knowledge of the products and tools used in the business. The questions here are how much is needed and how do you incorporate the knowledge into your solution base?

Vendor Support

The internal developer needs instant support resources. Software vendors must expand their knowledge beyond just their product. They must strive to know more about the customers they serve. The better the ISV's know a business, the better they can tailor support to help internal developers.

Ready-to-go Solutions

The internal developer must take the time to build a library of well-thought-out, easy-to-maintain procedures and code. Armed with this arsenal of finished goods, the internal developer can march forth and tackle many quick application projects, concentrating on creating the parts of the particular system that are not already built.

These "ready-to-go" solutions require an intimate knowledge of the business and of the technical environments of the corporation or institution they serve. In order to be effective, you need to get involved in technical architectural planning as well as keep abreast of future business goals.

There are a number of other key components to an internal developer's ability to provide rapid development capabilities. These include, but are not limited to:

Communication Edge An internal developer needs a patron. They must have an advocate in top management. Corporate America needs to be reminded constantly of the role they play.

Rapid Development Survey Form

DATE [/ /]

Critical Information Needed? _____
_____
_____

Existing Reports Avaliable? Samples? _____
_____
_____

Special Calculations? _____
_____

Special Reports Needed? _____
_____

Classification of Project _____
_____

Similar to Current/Existing Application ? _____
_____

User Expert Available? Times? _____
_____

Paradox Knowledge? (Level) _____
_____

Paradox Training Needed? _____
_____

Documentation required? _____
_____

Project Deadline? _____
_____

Hardware/Software Survey _____
_____

Person who approves project? _____

Figure 1-3 Rapid Development Project Questionnaire

There must be good communication with business top management to counter marketplace hype of software products. The hype needs to be tempered with software strategies that can truly be implemented. The internal developer must make today's solutions fit with yesterday's technology.

Information Strategies   The internal developer must constantly be aware of the business's information requirements and corporate goals. He or she must embrace the installed base of technology as well as future directions and information architecture.

Summary

In this chapter, we've discussed the basic Paradox database environment and its various components. Obviously, the more you know about Paradox, the better you'll be able to control it as you develop applications. We also looked at internal developers versus third-party developers and at each of their special needs and challenges. This book is for all developers. Because the internal developer is so often overlooked, we wanted to take a moment to bring their particular situation to light. The techniques presented throughout this book are geared to make any developer more efficient and productive. In the next chapter, you'll delve into a sometimes mysterious and certainly misunderstood part of application development—the application life cycle.

2 The Application Life Cycle

Certainly one of the most misunderstood and abused concepts in data processing is the application life cycle. In this chapter, you'll inspect each of the application life cycle components (see Figure 2-1) and how they apply in Paradox application development.

The components of the application life cycle are:

- Gathering requirements
- Logical database design
- Physical database design
- Program design
- Modular coding
- System testing
- Documentation
- System implementation

The application life cycle components are not necessarily sequential tasks. Some components can be performed simultaneously. Depending upon the user's needs and deadlines, one task might be performed before another. In some cases you'll find that it isn't necessary to spend time on a particular component. However, whether you complete every task or only a few of them, the application life cycle is integral to application development.

```
                    Gathering
                    Requirements
                         |
  Physical          Logical              Program Design and
  Database Design — Database Design  ——  Module Coding
                         |
  Tables                 |              Data Input
  Keys              Physical            Data Modification
  ValChecks         Design              Data Output
  Settings               |              Backup
  Forms                  |              Maintenance/Admn
  Reports           System              Menus
  Indexes           Testing             Procedures
                         |              Libraries
                         |
                    Documentation
                         |
                    System
                    Implementation
```

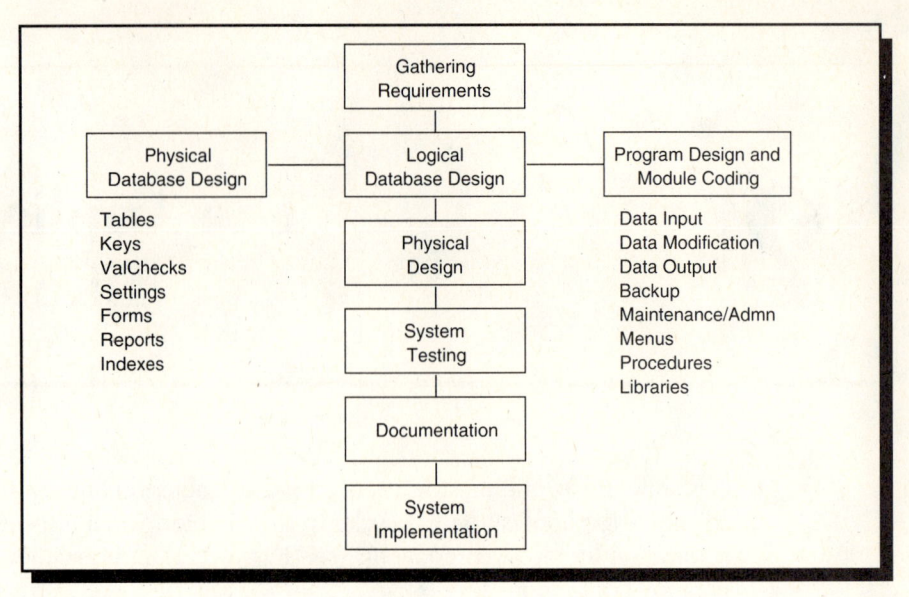

Figure 2-1 The application life cycle

There is constant interaction between user and developer during the application life cycle. In many cases, you can build a prototype of a portion of the application to help determine the best solution. The application life cycle for any database product starts when a client wants information or needs to automate a process. To determine whether a microcomputer solution is sufficient, you must gather the user's requirements.

Requirements Gathering

Requirements gathering rounds up information and determines the purpose and scope of the application. You must literally ask the user, "What do you want this system to do? What problem do you want the application to solve?" Start your information gathering with the existing system, whether it is manual or automated. Interview users (not just specifiers) of the current system and find out what is working and what isn't. How do they really use their current system? What work-arounds have they created to make it function? What pieces of information and methods have they added to accomplish their business tasks? This interview process gives insight into the real, especially the hidden, requirements of the application. Is the current system adequate, and if not, what changes need to be included in the new application?

The interview process can be either a one-on-one or a survey exercise. The interview/survey assists you in finding the requirements of the application. Following is a partial list of questions. (See Figure 2-2 for a sample form, like all samples and scripts, it is also on the disk that comes with this book.)

- What is the major purpose of the system? (What is the driving question or need that must be fulfilled?)
- Is the application used by more than one person at a time? (Is it a single or multi-user system?)
  - If multi-user, how many concurrent users?
  - What type of concurrent processing will be done?
  - To what level will there be insertions, updates, and queries?
  - What type and level of security is needed?
- What are the users' interface requirements? How do they want the system to look?
- What level of Help is required, and how should it be made available?
- What are the priorities of the application? What information and processes are crucial to the system's success?
- What kind of performance/response time does the user require?
- How well do the users know Paradox? What kind of ease-of-use features do they wish built into the system? Should the system be interactive, completely done in *PAL (Paradox Application Language)*, or a combination of both?
- What kind of ad-hoc query and reporting are required? Does the user want the ability to modify the programs?
- Must the proposed system be integrated with other systems?
- What kind of data validation and integrity is required? How should validation and integrity be applied?
- How large is the system? How much data will be stored? For how long will it be maintained? What is the volume of activity? How big are the records, and how many are anticipated at any given time?
- How is the data input? Data entry? Downloaded from a mini or mainframe system?
- Does the output need to be sent to other automated systems?
- Will the system be accessed seven days a week, twenty-four hours a day? Five days a week, eight hours a day?

Interview/Survey Questionnaire Form

◆ What is the major purpose of the system? (What is the driving question or need that must be fulfilled?)
◆ Is the application used by more than one person at a time? (Is it a single or multi-user system?)
◆ For multi-user systems:
  - How many concurrent users?
  - What type of concurrent processing will be done?
  - To what level will there be insertions, updates, and queries?
  - What type and level of security?
◆ What are the user's interface requirements? How *do* they want the system to look?
◆ What level of *HELP* features are required and how should they be made available?
◆ What are the priorities of the application? What information and processes are crucial to the systems success?
◆ What kind of performance/response time does the user require?
◆ How well does the user know *Paradox*?
◆ What kind of ease-of-use features do they wish built into the system?
◆ Should the system be interactive, completely done in *PAL,* or a combination of both.
◆ What kind of ad-hoc query and reporting are required?
◆ Does the user want the ability to modify the programs themselves?
◆ Must the proposed system be integrated with other systems? Which ones and how?
◆ What kind of data validation and integrity is required? How should validation and integrity be applied?
◆ How large is the system? How much data will be stored? For how long will it be maintained? What is the volume of activity? How big are the records and how many are anticipated at any given time?
◆ How does the data get inputted? Data entry? Is it downloaded from a mini or mainframe system?
◆ Does the output need to be sent to other automated systems.
◆ Will the system be accessed seven days a week, twenty-four hours a day? Five days a week, eight hours a day, etc?
◆ Will the system need an audit trail. How often will the system be audited? To what level?
◆ How often should backups and recovery be performed?
◆ Are there any special or mandatory rules and procedures (tax or state laws, etc.) or specific company policies that need to be taken into account?
◆ Is there any computing equipment currently in use and/or available? If so, will it handle the demands of the new system?

Figure 2-2 Sample interview/survey form

- Will the system need an audit trail? How often will the system be audited? To what level?
- How often should backups and recovery be performed?
- Are there any special or mandatory rules and procedures (tax or state laws, for example) or specific company policies that should be taken into account?
- Is there any computing equipment currently in use and/or available? If so, will it handle the demands of the new system?

Whether the current system is manual or automated, you must diagram its sources of input, manipulation of data, and output of information. The diagram provides a great picture of the business, and is very beneficial in analyzing the activities the application must perform. Look at the current input and update forms (or screens), inspect reports, analyze the data interchange occurring with other systems, and dig out current system documentation (if it exists). Look for special processing requirements. It is crucial that the developer understand the flows and processing necessary to the business. To implement the system a user wants, you must understand what things are not being addressed in the current process and include those missing items in the new system. Once you have the system's information requirements (the *requirements specification* or *requirements document*), you are ready to create the logical and physical design of the system.

Logical Database Design

In the design of a logical database model, entities and relationships, extended relational analysis, normalization, or other methods of analysis are used. No matter which technique you choose, the purpose of this phase in the application life cycle is to create the actual design of the database. In Paradox, this includes the tables and their relationships to other tables (primary keys and foreign keys). Keep in mind that smaller, narrower tables are more efficient than larger, wider tables. (See Figure 2-3, 2-4, and 2-5.)

Physical Database Design

Creating a database's physical design is the beginning of the real detail work. During this phase, each Paradox table and its family of forms and reports, validity checks, image settings, keys; and index is created, along with a design analysis of the program modules that will utilize each table.

Tables are created from your logical data model. As with many of today's relational databases, your Paradox physical databases may not exactly match your logical model. This is usually due to an absence of certain relational features or known performance enhancements that are gained through a change in the physical design. If limitations are known up front, fewer changes will be required later.

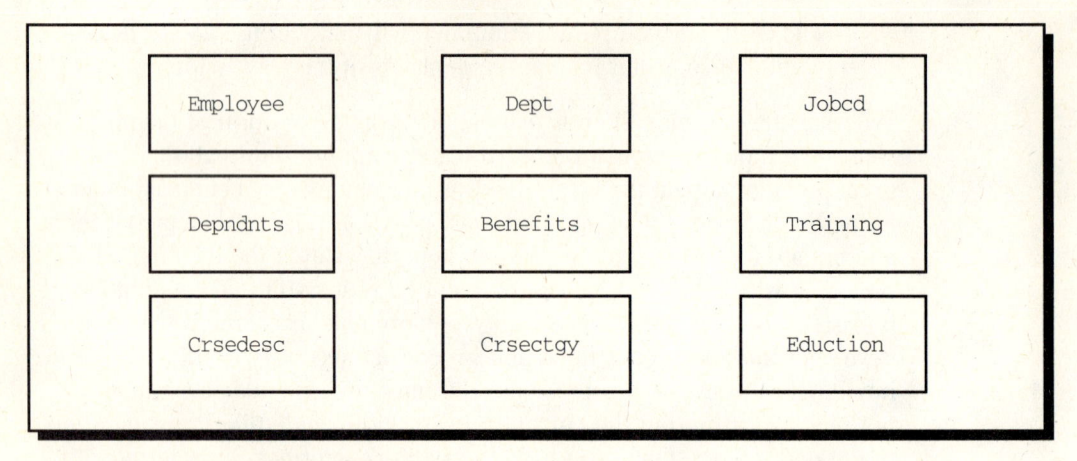

Employee	Dept	Jobcd
Depndnts	Benefits	Training
Crsedesc	Crsectgy	Eduction

Figure 2-3 A logical database design

When you create the physical design in Paradox, there are a few items you must take into account:

- Is there a requirement for a physical field to be located in the table to facilitate displaying values from a TableLookup?

TRICK: *Another option when dealing with One-to-One relationships is to display the information in a linked, DisplayOnly form.*

- Forms only support a two-level relationship. For example, there is a One-to-Many relationship between the master table and the detail table and a One-to-Many relationship between the detail table and another table.

TRICK: *Include in the master table any key field necessary to link to any of the desired detail tables.*

REMEMBER: *Forms are viewed from a master to a detail record. Reports are just the opposite. (See Figure 2-6.)*

The Application Life Cycle

```
         Dept                 Jobcd
      Employee
                           Department  A10*         Job Code           A3*
   Employee ID      S*      Manager     A20         Job Description    A40
   Last Name        A15                             Skills             A6
   First Name       A10                             Skills Description A40
   Date Hired       D         Depndnts              Security Level     A8
   Birth Date       D
   SSN              A11      Employee ID     S*       Benefits
   Department       A10      Dependents SSN  A11*
   Job Code         A3       Last Name       A15    Employee ID        S*
   Work Phone       A13      First Name      A10    Insurance Type     A12
   Salary           $        Birth Date      D      Life Insurance     $
   Exemptions       S                               Short Term Disab   A1
   Address          A25        Crsedesc             Long Term Disab    A1
   City             A20                             US Saving Bond     $
   State            A2       Course Number   A3*
   Zip              A5       Course Title    A40      Training
   Home Phone       A13      Course Length   S
   Marital Status   A8       Course Category A20    Employee ID        S*
   Sex              A1       Desc1           A240   Course Number      A3*
                             Desc2           A240   Course Title       A40
                             Desc3           A240   Date Attended      D
        Eduction

   Employee ID      S*        Crsectgy
   Item #           S*
   Year             A2       Course Category A20*
   School           A40
   Degree           A30
```

Figure 2-4 Logical database design (database tables)

After you create the tables, you can create the remaining Paradox objects. These include

- ValChecks (validity checks)
- Image settings
- Forms
- Reports
- Indexes

ValChecks are recorded in either DataEntry or Edit mode. ValChecks are a simple form of data validation but often need to be augmented to provide full data integrity.

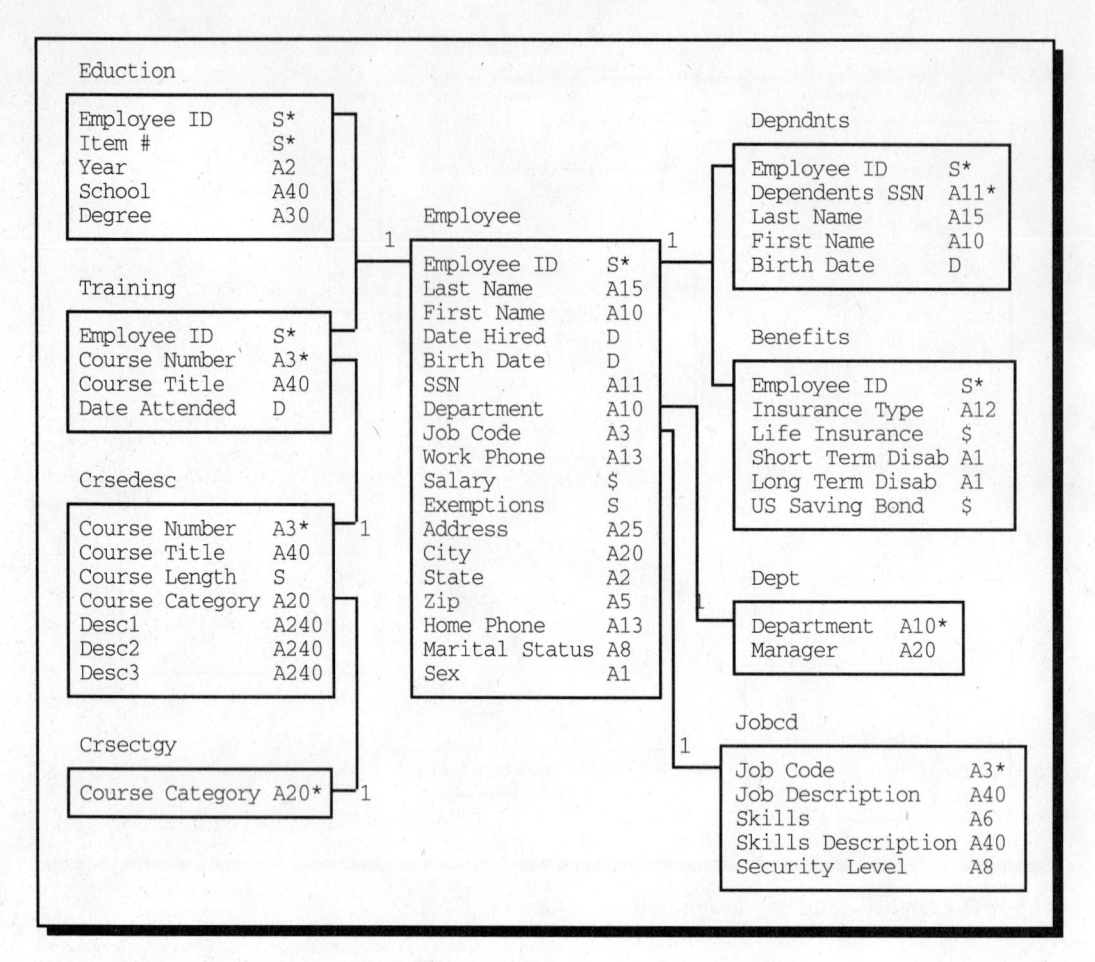

```
┌─────────────────────────────────────────────────────────────────────────┐
│  Eduction                                                               │
│  ┌─────────────────────┐                                                │
│  │ Employee ID    S*   │                                                │
│  │ Item #         S*   │                                                │
│  │ Year           A2   │                           Depndnts             │
│  │ School         A40  │                          ┌───────────────────┐ │
│  │ Degree         A30  │┐            Employee    ┌│ Employee ID   S*  │ │
│  └─────────────────────┘│          ┌────────────┐││ Dependents SSN A11*│ │
│                         ├─1      1 │Employee ID S*├│ Last Name     A15 │ │
│  Training               │          │Last Name A15 ││ First Name    A10 │ │
│  ┌─────────────────────┐│          │First Name A10││ Birth Date    D   │ │
│  │ Employee ID    S*   ││          │Date Hired  D │└───────────────────┘ │
│  │ Course Number  A3*  │┘          │Birth Date  D │  Benefits            │
│  │ Course Title   A40  │           │SSN        A11│ ┌───────────────────┐│
│  │ Date Attended  D    │           │Department A10│ │Employee ID    S*  ││
│  └─────────────────────┘           │Job Code    A3│ │Insurance Type A12 ││
│                                    │Work Phone A13│ │Life Insurance  $  ││
│  Crsedesc                          │Salary      $ │ │Short Term Disab A1││
│  ┌─────────────────────┐           │Exemptions  S │ │Long Term Disab A1 ││
│  │ Course Number  A3*  ├─1         │Address   A25 │ │US Saving Bond  $  ││
│  │ Course Title   A40  │           │City      A20 │ └───────────────────┘│
│  │ Course Length  S    │           │State      A2 │  Dept                │
│  │ Course Category A20 │           │Zip        A5 │ ┌───────────────────┐│
│  │ Desc1         A240  │           │Home Phone A13│ │Department   A10*  ││
│  │ Desc2         A240  │           │Marital Status A8│Manager      A20  ││
│  │ Desc3         A240  │           │Sex        A1 │ └───────────────────┘│
│  └─────────────────────┘           └────────────┘                        │
│                                                  1  Jobcd                │
│  Crsectgy                                         ┌───────────────────┐  │
│  ┌─────────────────────┐                          │Job Code      A3*  │  │
│  │ Course Category A20*├─1                        │Job Description A40│  │
│  └─────────────────────┘                          │Skills         A6  │  │
│                                                   │Skills Description A40│
│                                                   │Security Level  A8 │  │
│                                                   └───────────────────┘  │
└─────────────────────────────────────────────────────────────────────────┘
```

Figure 2-5 Logical database design (table relationships)

Next, if there are special viewing requirements for fields in a table, Image options are specified. These include:

Column Size   You can vary the width of a column from 1 to 255 characters.

Field Format   Date fields can be viewed as MM/DD/YY, DD-MON-YY or DD.MM.YY. Numeric and currency fields can be in *general*, *fixed*, *comma*, or *scientific* formats.

The Application Life Cycle

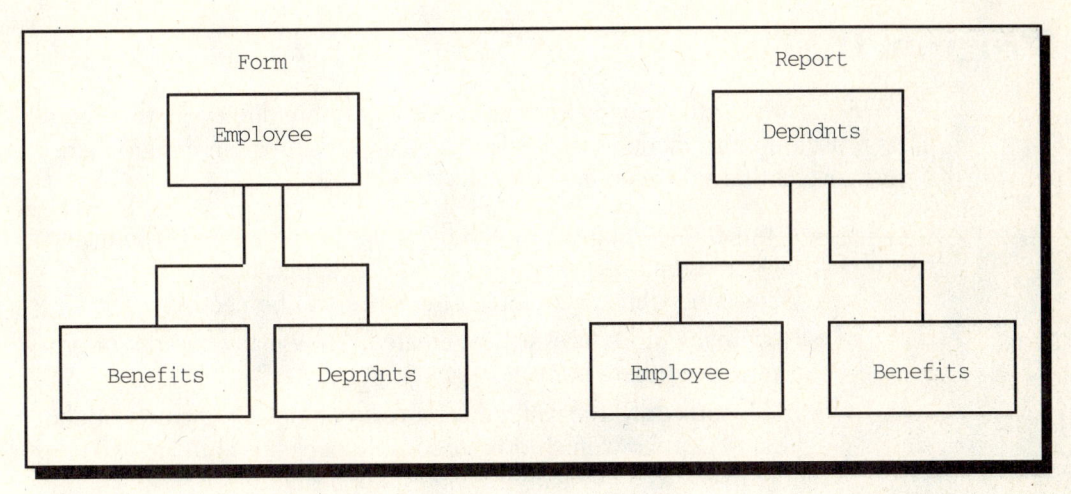

[Figure: Two boxed diagrams side by side. Left box labeled "Form" shows "Employee" at top connected to "Benefits" and "Depndnts" below. Right box labeled "Report" shows "Depndnts" at top connected to "Employee" and "Benefits" below.]

Figure 2-6 One-to-many relationships (forms versus reports)

Column Order	The order in which columns (fields) appear in a table view doesn't need to match the physical structure of the table.
Standard Form	Any form can be the default (standard form) for a table. Simply create a form, select it to view the table and choose *Menu {Image} {KeepSet}*. When you next view the table and press [F7] *Form Toggle*, the form you selected as the default appears.

Now create the table's forms and reports, both single and multitable. Final work will have to wait until test data is available to validate format and style.

Next, create the indexes needed to provide lookups, speed queries, and tune reports.

If a system is generating graphs, the *graph specification* files need to be created and saved for later use by the application. Graph specification files are Paradox objects that are not directly associated with any specific table. They are allowed to stand alone and can be used on any table. It is usually best to wait for test data before creating graph specification files.

Program Design

While analyzing the program design of the application life cycle, the system is broken up into modules. Before proceeding with program design, there are several things to keep in mind:

- Estimate the number of DOS files that will be created. Too many DOS files in a directory severely affects application performance. Determine whether multiple directories will be needed.
- How many procedures will be created? How many libraries of procedures will there be?
- If networked, where will the private directories for the network be located, and how much disk space is available? Will the available disk space accommodate the largest application need?

Identifying the major processes in an application determines the number of modules in a system. These modules actually form the building blocks of the application's menu structure. Typically, application modules include:

- Data input
- Data modification (changes and deletions)
- Data output (reports, graphs, ad-hoc queries, data export)
- Data backup and recovery
- Maintenance and/or administrative tasks

Now define the common processes used by each, and decide whether multiple modules can be consolidated. This helps eliminate coding separate modules and duplicate procedures that perform basically the same tasks. In so doing, you decrease the size of code to be created and maintained.

Next, decide on how you plan to handle errors that occur during processing. Paradox's error procedure capability lets you control many runtime errors and also lets you take specific action based on a particular error. Not all error conditions activate error procedures.

Runtime errors have to be dealt with in program code at the time they occur. Preparing a strategy for error processing results in an end-product that handles all potential problems. This creates a smooth, straightforward, easy-to-maintain application.

> **NOTE:** *Properly configuring Paradox with the Custom Configuration Program avoids many runtime errors and incorrect results. If you are creating an accounting system, blanks must equal zero. If the application is at all statistical in nature, blanks should not be zero. If your Paradox 3.5 system will be exchanging data with previous versions, you should not activate ImageOrder for your queries. Carefully consider the environment your application requires so that it functions properly.*

Modular Coding

Paradox provides three processes for creating modules:

- Interactive
- Interactive augmented with PAL
- Completely PAL

The following sections describe each of these, including examples of activities for each process.

Interactive Paradox

Record your keystrokes using *InstantRecord* ([Alt][F3]) or *{Scripts} {BeginRecord}*. Use *QuerySave* to store repeated queries.

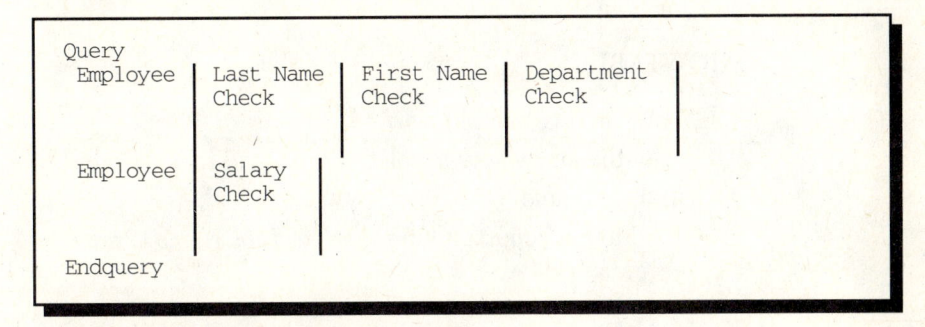

```
Query
   Employee  | Last Name | First Name | Department
             | Check     | Check      | Check
             |
   Employee  | Salary
             | Check
             |
Endquery
```

Figure 2-7 Record queries with QuerySave

Examples:
- Changeto, insert, delete, set, and select queries (QuerySave)
- Database backup to another drive
  Menu *{Tools} {Copy} {Table_A} {A:\\Table_A}*

- Output reports
  Menu {Report} {Output} {Table_A} {1} {Printer}
- Select a table, pick a form to view its information and go into Edit mode
  Menu {View} {Table_A} Menu {Image} {PickForm} {5} CoEditKey

Interactive Processes Augmented with PAL

Start by recording as much as possible interactively with *InstantScripts*. Next, rename and modify each script with PAL commands and functions to complete the necessary action.

```
While (true)
    Menu {View} {Table_A} Menu {Image} {PickForm} {5} EditKey
    Wait Table
    Prompt "When complete press [F2]"
    Until "F2","Esc"
    lookrv = retval
    if lookrv = "F2" or lookrv = "Esc" then
        quitloop
    endif
EndWhile
```

Create an InstantScript for *any activity* where a table can be selected by the user, such as:

SHOWTABLES

```
"C:\\paradox\\sample"
"Use the arrow keys to select a table and press [Enter]"
to TableName
    Menu {Report} {Output} select TableName {Printer}
```

Entirely PAL

Start with a blank script, or cut and paste from other scripts. It is still advantageous to use recorded keystrokes where there are no PAL commands for menu choice equivalents. For example, see Figures 2-8 and 2-9.

```
{Ask} {Employee} CheckPlus
```

Figure 2-8 Script to {Ask} a table (CheckPlus)

```
CLEAR
@ 5,5 ?? "Enter the department name: "
STYLE REVERSE
ACCEPT "A10" PICTURE "*!" TO dept
STYLE
```

Figure 2-9 Script to obtain a query selection for the {Ask} query

Other examples discussed later in this book include:

- User interaction with forms, queries, reports, graphs
- Ensuring data integrity checking for required fields, default values, and business rules not resolved using ValChecks
- Reports requiring PAL coding due to their complexity
- Auto-numbering
- Error procedures (how to handle errors)
- Explicit locking required in a networked environment. Checking for resource availability; setting retry periods; handling *livelocks*, form locks, and private directories, (switching to and from network drives if space is a problem)
- Help systems
- Assigning and changing private directories

Don't write unnecessary programs. Reuse programs as often as possible (see Figure 2-10). Reusing code cuts down the time it takes to add a procedure to handle a new application task, especially if it is similar to a procedure already created. Avoid treating each new program as a unique event. Instead of creating five edit routines to edit five different tables, create one edit routine that handles them all.

```
CLEAR
@ 5,5 ?? "Enter the department name: "
STYLE REVERSE
ACCEPT "A10" PICTURE "*!" TO dept
STYLE
MESSAGE "Selecting data, please wait!"
CANVAS OFF
{Ask} {Employee} CheckPlus
[Department] = dept
DO_IT!
```

Figure 2-10 The two scripts merged

Remember to think of your performance issues when coding the application. Paradox provides many ways to accomplish a task. Take the time to determine which is the most efficient method for the current activity. Prototype a proposed solution, then test it. This may increase the time you planned to complete the module, but in the long run the application will perform better and the user will be more satisfied with the end result. Here's an example: Even though Paradox supports queries using an unlimited number of tables, it is better to break down a six-table query into multiple steps. Use closed procedures, whenever possible, to maximize your memory resources (see Chapter 1). In regular procedures, use private variables. Memory space allocated for procedures using these techniques can be quickly regained after the procedure is no longer needed.

NOTE: *Edit requires disk space to store every modification to a table. CoEdit stores only the last change. Remember, for an Edit, data is not updated until DO_IT! is executed. While in CoEdit, a modification is posted after the cursor is moved off the record.*

TRICK: *SCAN does not use indexes; LOCATE does.*

Part of the process of planning and creating procedures is developing a strategy for creating your application libraries. Paradox supports multiple libraries, without any memory or performance penalty. A library holds a maximum of 300 procedures. For speed as well as good modular design, it is best to divide procedures into multiple libraries. This makes the application easier to change and maintain. Create separate libraries for each major section of the application. Separate your procedures into libraries for menus, help, utilities, and specific application processing. Or, if you prefer, divide libraries by type of activity. For example, in an accounting application, create a separate library for accounts receivable, accounts payable, general ledger, and other modules.

> **REMEMBER:** *Multiple libraries speed application development by dividing the system's tasks into predefined modules. It is not necessary to put all procedures into one library.*

Program security must be planned for up front, not as an afterthought. Security issues occur at multiple levels:

- Hardware
- Operating system
- LAN (for network environments)
- Database server (SQL Link applications)
- Paradox (Interactive and PAL)

Each one of these areas must be considered before incorporation into the overall application design.

Programs to handle backup and recovery depend entirely on the type of processes determined by the application requirements. These requirements can range from a task handled by system administrators to users backing up to floppy disks or tape. If the responsibility of backing up an application is left entirely in the hands of the user, it most likely won't be done. Your users/customers have little enough time to perform their normal work, let alone stop and backup the application's data. Build in a mechanism to track the last back up and notify the user when it's time to perform another. These backup and restore routines and other common system utilities are presented in Chapter 17.

System Testing

Testing a system is crucial to a successful implementation of an application. Test plans start with creating good test data. Multiple test scenarios must be created and run. Network applications must test and solve resource contentions. The key to any test plan is knowing what data to test and knowing how to identify when a process is not working correctly. You need a set of tools to assist in determining when results are not correct or are unacceptable.

Creating good test data is an art. You cannot simply take a subset of actual data and use it—you must ensure that you have anticipated all the situations the data and user will be facing. Create your test scenarios *with* the user. It is not important or necessary to have large volumes of data in fact, keep the number of records small. Know the expected results of performing each module in the application, then check and recheck your data after each phase of your application testing.

Network applications require additional steps in testing. Since resource contentions and concurrency issues can develop that are not problems in single user systems. Have at least two workstations (or better yet, three) in this phase of testing. Use two machines to access the same module of the system at the same time. While you are doing this, use the third machine to monitor the activity of the first two machines. The third machine can also be used to place explicit locks on resources to determine if the programs are handling all networking problems correctly. This is where the .NET configuration is tested, along with the private directory setups for each user.

Throughout testing, it is crucial to poll the information and resources built into Paradox that assist you in debugging your application. Just because a piece of code executes without a Cancel/Debug message or other error does not mean that the script or procedure did what was intended. For example, a query is started, and the DO_IT! command executed. Something is wrong in the query, and it never actually gets executed. If your next step in the program is to perform an activity on an *Answer* table and you don't check to see if you have a valid *Answer* table, the program will appear to complete successfully but actually will not have performed correctly or even at all. In interactive Paradox, you see a message stating the problem with the query. In a program, unless you test to see if the *Answer* table has been created, there is no way of knowing that a problem exists. Using the Paradox debugger and single-stepping through the code shows you whether your program is performing as expected.

Testing also verifies your design and determines whether you have included all the features the user requested.

> **TRAP:** *If your system will be distributed using Runtime, you need to test in the Runtime environment. Check the application under the conditions it will be expected to run to ensure that there are no differences in execution under the Runtime version of Paradox.*

Documentation

Documenting an application is often the most overlooked piece of the application life cycle—or at the very least, the component that is put off until the last moment. Create the appropriate documentation as pieces of the system are being designed and coded. The major types of documentation are:

- System documentation
- Application documentation
- User documentation

Products like ParaLex, ScriptView, and ParaTrak assist in developing the system documentation.

System documentation contains information on tables and objects used in the application. This part of the documentation also contains the data dictionary or system catalog. List the structure of each table and its family of objects. (See Figure 2-11.) You can easily perform this using Paradox (*Menu* {*Tools*} {*Info*} {*Structure*}). A better listing includes:

- Fields
- Keys
- Data types
- Indexes for each table

If there are any ValChecks or Image settings for fields, those specifications should also be listed. Figure 2-12 shows an example of this type of listing. The form and report layouts are also included.

Documenting your source code, *application documentation* is valuable for both you and anyone who modifies the application. Each script should have a *header* which includes the author, date created, and version number of the script. A revision log for each script is also important. Keep track of when the script was changed, what changes were made, and who made them. If some parts of a script are not active, create a "To Do" list and place it right in the script. This makes is easy to add, change, or delete functionality as each "To Do" is completed. Comment your scripts to help clarify special techniques or tricks that you employ to perform a particular task. Variable usage and the parameters unique to the script are also items that require explicit comments.

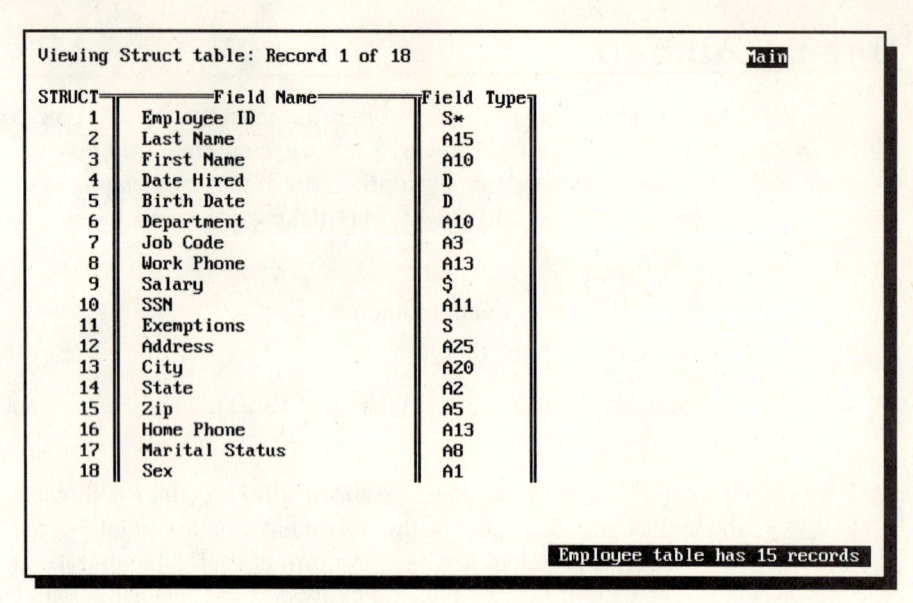

```
Viewing Struct table: Record 1 of 18                              Main
STRUCT     Field Name        Field Type
   1    Employee ID           S*
   2    Last Name             A15
   3    First Name            A10
   4    Date Hired            D
   5    Birth Date            D
   6    Department            A10
   7    Job Code              A3
   8    Work Phone            A13
   9    Salary                $
  10    SSN                   A11
  11    Exemptions            S
  12    Address               A25
  13    City                  A20
  14    State                 A2
  15    Zip                   A5
  16    Home Phone            A13
  17    Marital Status        A8
  18    Sex                   A1

                                        Employee table has 15 records
```

Figure 2-11 Table structure example

```
Viewing Family table: Record 1 of 20                              Main
FAMILY              Name                                    Date
   1    Employee                                         9/12/90
   2    Validity VAL                                     9/12/90
   3    Form F                                           9/09/90
   4    Form F1                                          9/09/90
   5    Form F2                                          9/12/90
   6    Form F4                                          9/09/90
   7    Form F9                                          9/09/90
   8    Form F10                                         9/09/90
   9    Form F11                                         9/09/90
  10    Report R2                                        9/11/90
  11    Report R3                                        9/09/90
  12    Report R4                                        9/09/90
  13    Report R5                                        9/09/90
  14    Report R6                                        9/09/90
  15    Report R7                                        9/09/90
  16    Report R9                                        9/09/90
  17    Report R13                                       9/09/90
  18    Report R14                                       9/09/90
  19    Speedup for Last Name [Maintained]               9/12/90
  20    Speedup for Department [Maintained]              9/12/90
```

Figure 2-12 Table family example

Following are examples of how to document scripts and procedures (Figures 2-13 through 2-16):

Last, but certainly not least, is the *user documentation*. The amount and level of user documentation depends on a number of things:

- Level of user knowledge
- Complexity of the system
- Amount of built-in help contained in the system

User documentation usually consists of:

- Configuration and installation instructions
- Overview of the system and menu structures
- Detailed description of each menu option
- Sample output (forms or report output)
- A complete listing of error messages and who to contact for help

System Implementation: Turning the Application Over to the User

The final component of the application life cycle is implementation. Install the system in the users' actual environment and begin final testing. This is typically white knuckle time. This is when you find out if you *did* or *didn't* give your users/customers what they requested. This phase of testing shakes out any oversights in the initial system testing and prevents unwanted surprises showing up when the application is put into production.

When system testing is complete, the users continue to work with the application and perform further testing. This is the time when the user becomes familiar with the application from your point of view. Running new and old systems in parallel is always desirable, if possible. If resources do not allow parallel testing, minimize the amount of duplication during the parallel process as much as possible.

Part of implementation is training the users to use all aspects of the system. This is where your user documentation is put to use. Training is minimized if your application design includes an interface that is intuitive, complete with a help system that answers most of the users' most common questions.

```
;   +---------------------------------------------------------------+
;   | Script Name:          Creation Date:  /  /    Author:         |
;   |                       Last Revision:  /  /    Revised By:     |
;   |---------------------------------------------------------------|
;   | Description:                                                  |
;   |                                                               |
;   |                                                               |
;   |                                                               |
;   |---------------------------------------------------------------|
;   | Called By: NONE                                               |
;   |---------------------------------------------------------------|
;   | Libraries: NONE                                               |
;   |---------------------------------------------------------------|
;   | Tables  | Forms  | Reports | Scripts | Procedures | External Pgms |
;   | NONE    | NONE   | NONE    | NONE    | NONE       | NONE          |
;   |                                                               |
;   |                                                               |
;   |---------------------------------------------------------------|
;   | Notes: NONE                                                   |
;   |                                                               |
;   +---------------------------------------------------------------+
;
```

Figure 2-13 Script header documentation example

```
;
;   +---------------------------------------------------------------+
;   |                    SCRIPT MAINTENANCE LOG                     |
;   |---------------------------------------------------------------|
;   | Date    | Description of the changes                          |
;   |         |                                                     |
;   |         |                                                     |
;   |         |                                                     |
;   |         |                                                     |
;   |         |                                                     |
;   |         |                                                     |
;   |         |                                                     |
;   |         |                                                     |
;   |---------------------------------------------------------------|
;   | Notes: NONE                                                   |
;   +---------------------------------------------------------------+
;
```

Figure 2-14 Revision log example

```
;
;
;       ┌─────────────────────────────────────────────────────────┐
;       │               TO DO LIST FOR THIS SCRIPT                │
;       ├─────────────────────────────────────────────────────────┤
;       │                                                         │
;       │                                                         │
;       │                                                         │
;       │                                                         │
;       │                                                         │
;       │                                                         │
;       │                                                         │
;       ├─────────────────────────────────────────────────────────┤
;       │Notes: NONE                                              │
;       │                                                         │
;       └─────────────────────────────────────────────────────────┘
;
```

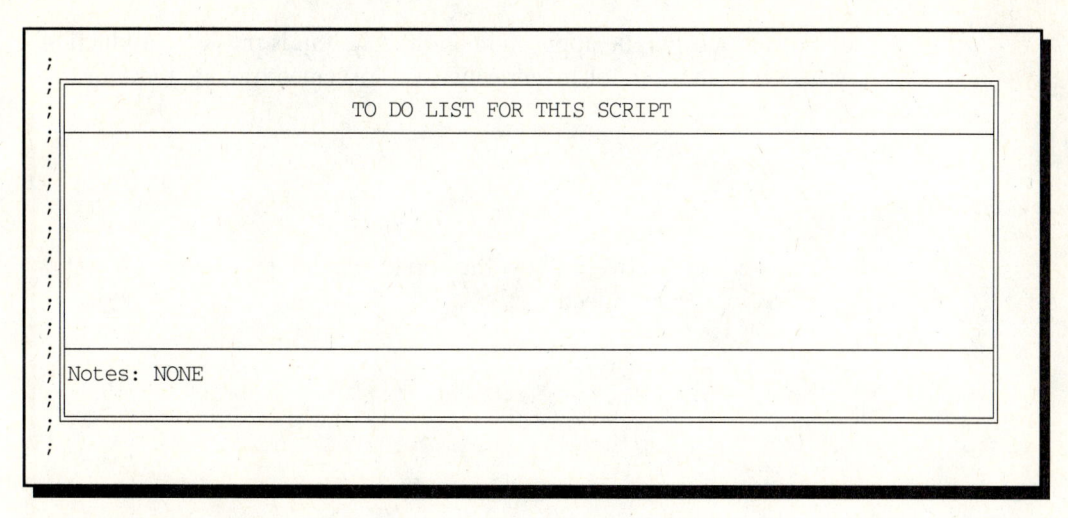

Figure 2-15 To Do list example

```
PROC ExplodeWindow(sr,er,sc,ec,clr,brdr,shdw)
  PRIVATE i, midr, midc, rcaspect, numofsteps
;
; Private variables
;    i           -  counter variable
;    midr        -  row midpoint value
;    midc        -  column midpoint value
;    rcaspect    -  row and column aspect ratio
;    numofsteps  -  number of steps to explode window
;
; Argument list
;
;    sr          -  starting row position
;    er          -  ending row position
;    sc          -  starting column position
;    ec          -  ending column position
;    clr         -  color to use for the window
;    brdr        -  border flag, "S" for single line, "D" for double line border
;    shdw        -  shadow flag, "Y" to include shadow
;
```

Figure 2-16 Procedure parameter list documentation example

Once the user accepts the application and the system is put into production, the project becomes one of maintenance, performance tuning, and enhancements.

Summary

In this chapter you discovered how the application life cycle occurs in a Paradox development project.

3 Normalizing Your Paradox Databases

Normalization is an area that everyone creating relational database applications has heard about but that many do not fully understand. Developers argue over the level of normalization required in the logical data model. Alternative design approaches such as the entity/relationship model or extended relational analysis are also used in defining the logical database model. It doesn't matter which approach you use, but you should use some approach that will help you design your database from the user's perspective as well as from the computer's perspective.

This chapter covers how to use the normalization method to create a data model consisting of the data elements defined in the requirements-gathering phase of application development. How should you structure the data? How should you group the data elements to create tables in a relational database? What tables should you create, and which fields should be defined in each table? What should the key be? What is a key? These are some of the questions you must answer when you begin the logical database design process.

From the logical design comes the physical design of the database. Before the physical database is created, the tables need to be normalized and the logical design completed. The process of developing a good physical design is what this chapter is all about. Many terms and definitions are used in this chapter. Table 3-1 lists those you'll need to be familiar with. The first section of this chapter reviews these definitions.

**Table 3-1
Key Terms**

Relational theory	Primary key	First Normal Form
Relational database	Foreign key	Second Normal Form
Relation	Concatenated key	Third Normal Form
Tuple	Referential integrity	Denormalization
Table	Domain	Repeating group
Record	Cardinality	Update anomalies
Row	Degree	Multifield key
Attribute	Candidate key	Non-key column
Column	Alternate key	Data redundancy
Field	Surrogate key	Realization

Basic Terminology Review

Before discussing normalization, let's define a few terms. A *relational database* is a collection of data elements perceived as a set of tables. Its logical representation is in row and column format, but the data is not physically stored in this structure. The logical and physical representation of the data do not match. The physical structure is known to the database management system, but users don't need to know how the data is stored.

Terms used in the relational model differ from those used in Paradox. Table 3-2 is a list of terms from the relational model, a brief definition, and the equivalent term in Paradox. Table 3-3 lists terms from the relational model that are not used in Paradox but that are used in this chapter to discuss certain points on normalization.

Why You Should Normalize Your Data

The result of the normalization process is a logical model that is a solid, stable database. Its structure provides correct answers for all access to data, including programmatic and ad-hoc queries, updates, inserts, and deletes. Modification anomalies are prevented. All relationships are determined and are combined to support previous statements. Normalization provides a method for taking the relational model and reducing the relations into the proper format for performance and maintainability. It should be noted, though, that this is based solely on the relational model. Actual implementation in relational products today vary because they have implemented only part of the relational model. Paradox is no exception. In discussing normal forms, we point out Paradox's weak points and show you where you might have to deviate from a fully normalized database.

Table 3-2
Terms used in Relational Model and equivalents in Paradox

Relational Model	Paradox	Description
Relation	Table	Collection of rows and columns, creating a two-dimensional representation of the data in tabular format.
Database	Directory	Collection of relations/tables.
Tuple	Row/Record	A row in a table.
Attribute	Column/Field	A single occurrence in a row representing one value.
Primary key	Primary key	One or more attributes used to uniquely identify a tuple in a relation. The values of the primary key prevent two rows from having the same value.
Foreign key	Foreign key	A column in a table whose value has to be a primary key in another table. A foreign key can be a primary key, part of a composite key, or a column in the table that is not already part of the primary key.
Concatenated key	Concatenated key	A primary key consisting of two or more columns. Also called a multifield key.
Referential Integrity	Referential Integrity	An assurance that no invalid foreign key value exists. In the relational model this is handled at the table level. In Paradox this is handled only through multitable forms and PAL programming.
Domain	Domain	This is a set of values for a column can have assigned to it.

Table 3-3
Additional terms from the Relational Model

Relational Model	Description
Cardinality	The number of tuples in the relation.
Degree	The number of attributes in a tuple.
Candidate key	An attribute in the relation that uniquely identifies a row. There can be multiple candidate keys for a relation. One has to be selected as the primary key.
Alternate key	Candidate keys not selected as the primary key.
Surrogate key	A system-generated primary key. These keys are meaningless to the end user and merely supply a unique way to identify a row with one field.

Normalization: What Is It?

Normalization is a set of rules and techniques based on relational theory to create tables that follow normal forms. These rules and techniques specify how to split data into separate tables, simplifying data input, modification, and retrieval. The original relational model included definitions for three normal forms. These are the most common normal forms and the ones discussed here in detail. Since the relational model was released, two additional normal forms have been defined. They are outside the scope of these examples. Information on all five normal forms is contained in most books on relational theory and normalization. You might think normalization is not for you; but, without it, your database design may suffer from poor implementation. Let's look at the first, second, and third normal forms and how your logical model benefits from using normalization.

We'll use a subset of a Personnel database to demonstrate the normalization process. Figure 3-1 is a flat file listing of the columns.

First Normal Form: Remove Repeating Groups

A table in First Normal Form (1NF) is defined as a normalized table. The properties of a normalized table are

- No duplicate rows

Normalizing Your Paradox Databases 43

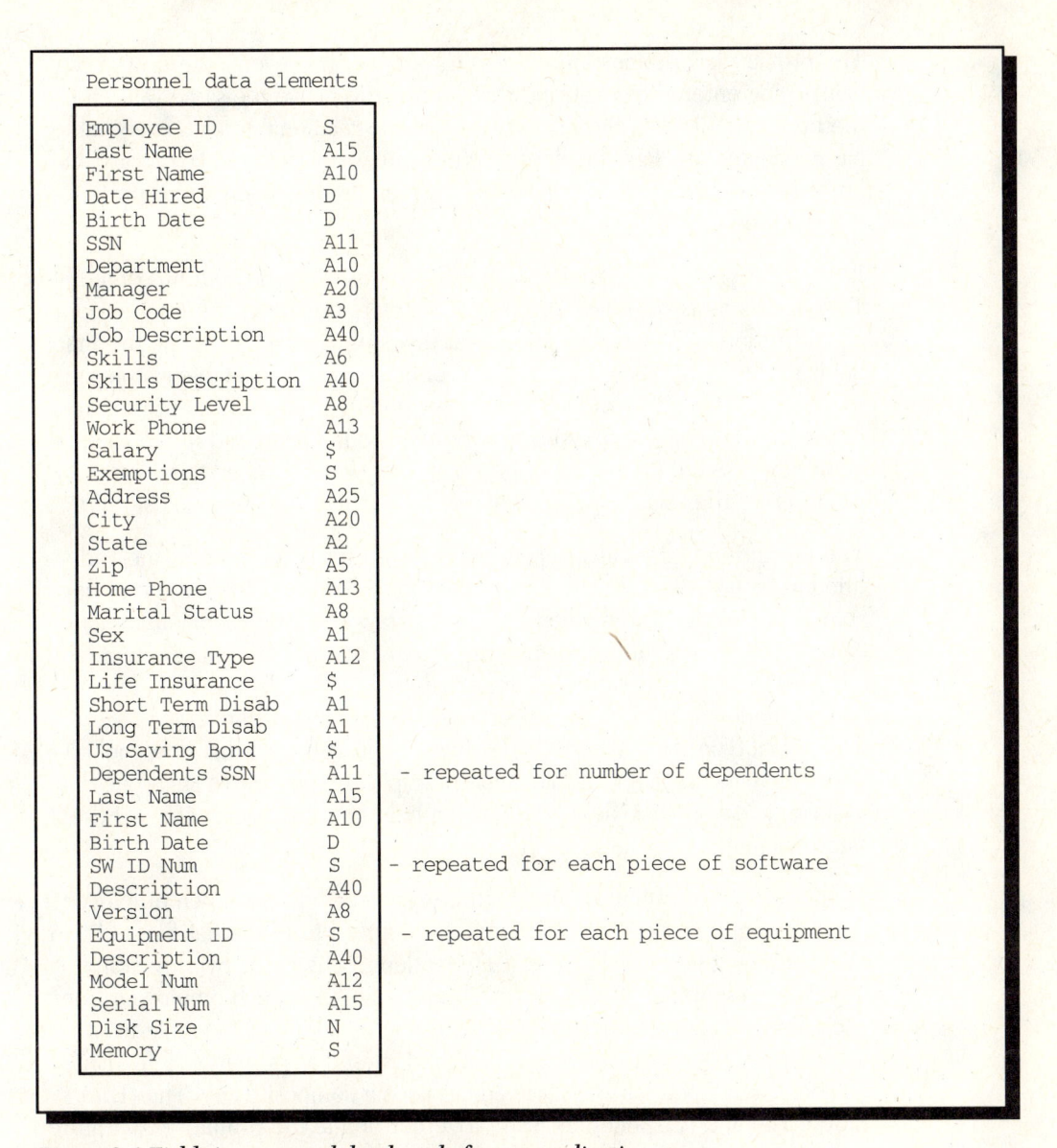

```
Personnel data elements
Employee ID          S
Last Name            A15
First Name           A10
Date Hired           D
Birth Date           D
SSN                  A11
Department           A10
Manager              A20
Job Code             A3
Job Description      A40
Skills               A6
Skills Description   A40
Security Level       A8
Work Phone           A13
Salary               $
Exemptions           S
Address              A25
City                 A20
State                A2
Zip                  A5
Home Phone           A13
Marital Status       A8
Sex                  A1
Insurance Type       A12
Life Insurance       $
Short Term Disab     A1
Long Term Disab      A1
US Saving Bond       $
Dependents SSN       A11   - repeated for number of dependents
Last Name            A15
First Name           A10
Birth Date           D
SW ID Num            S     - repeated for each piece of software
Description          A40
Version              A8
Equipment ID         S     - repeated for each piece of equipment
Description          A40
Model Num            A12
Serial Num           A15
Disk Size            N
Memory               S
```

Figure 3-1 Fields in personnel database before normalization

- Rows not ordered
- Columns not ordered
- No repeating groups

The primary key defines uniqueness for a table. It prevents duplicate rows from being entered by ensuring that no two rows have the same value for the field(s) defined as the primary key. In the relational model, every table has a primary key. Paradox doesn't require that you define a key for a table, but it is recommended. If you want to use multitable forms and reports, keys are required.

In the relational model, there is no order to the rows and columns of a table. To look at a table (or place a representation of one on paper) requires some type of ordering. Paradox requires that fields used as key fields be the first fields in the table. They must also be contiguous. A keyed table also forces row ordering based on the key. Field positioning is also crucial in multitable forms and reports. The physical position of the fields instead of the field names are used to link multiple tables. This is why you need to be careful not to move the relative position of any fields used as linking fields.

The fourth item eliminates repeating groups. This is the process most identified as being 1NF. Each record in the table must have the same number of columns. This is violated when there are arrays in a column or multi-value columns exist. To eliminate repeating groups, you need to make a separate table for each set of related columns and give each table a primary key. Since Paradox only supports a fixed number of fields within a table, there isn't a data type that supports repeating groups. A design that does violate 1NF is to concatenate multiple values and place them into a single field, or to have field 1, field 2, field 3, and so on hold multiple occurrences of the same data item.

In the personnel system there are three repeating groups. Each employee can have multiple dependents. They are removed from the flat file and two tables are created, Employee and Dependents. The other two repeating groups are equipment and software items assigned to each employee. For each of these tables, an identification number is added to the table to serve as a primary key. The [Employee ID] field is used as primary key for Employee. The Dependents table needs to have a composite key. The [Employee ID] and [Dependents SSN] together define the primary key. Figure 3-2 shows the database in first normal form.

You might be asking why repeating groups should be removed from the tables. The main reason is to eliminate update and retrieval anomalies. In the Personnel example, what happens if there is room for four dependents (as shown in Figure 3-3), each set of fields contains information on a dependent, and the employee increases the size of his/her family by one? You would have to add another field to the table. Then you would have to reorganize the database and modify all queries, forms, reports, data validation, and processing. Creating separate tables to hold any number of occurrences removes this requirement.

```
Employee                                Dependents

Employee ID          S*                 Employee ID          S*
Last Name            A15                Dependents SSN       A11*
First Name           A10                Last Name            A15
Date Hired           D                  First Name           A10
Birth Date           D                  Birth Date           D
SSN                  A11
Department           A10                Hardware
Manager              A20
Job Code             A3                 Employee ID          S*
Job Description      A40                Equipment ID         S*
Skills               A6                 Description          A40
Skills Description   A40                Model Num            A12
Security Level       A8                 Serial Num           A15
Work Phone           A13                Disk Size            N
Salary               $                  Memory               S
Exemptions           S
Address              A25
City                 A20                Software
State                A2
Zip                  A5                 Employee ID          S*
Home Phone           A13                SW ID Num            S*
Marital Status       A8                 Description          A40
Sex                  A1                 Version              A8
Insurance Type       A12
Life Insurance       $
Short Term Disab     A1
Long Term Disab      A1
US Saving Bond       $
```

Figure 3-2 Personnel tables in first normal form

There is also a problem with deletes and queries when repeating groups exist in a table. In the first place, you have to include selection criteria in each one of the repeated fields. For example, let's say you want to know how many dependents have a first name of John. [First Name 1], [First Name 2], [First Name 3], and [First Name 4] have to be checked for the value John. This is less cumbersome when a single field has to be checked, as in the Dependents table.

```
Dependents SSN 1     A11
Last Name 1          A15
First Name 1         A10
Birth Date 1         D
Dependents SSN 2     A11
Last Name 2          A15
First Name 2         A10
Birth Date 2         D
Dependents SSN 3     A11
Last Name 3          A15
First Name 3         A10
Birth Date 3         D
Dependents SSN 4     A11
Last Name 4          A15
First Name 4         A10
Birth Date 4         D
```

Figure 3-3 Number of fields required for four dependents before 1NF

All three new tables are tied to Employee by [Employee ID]. To allow multiple rows for each employee in Dependents, Hardware, and Software, the key must include at least one more field in the primary key. In the Dependents table, it is safe in most cases to use the dependent's SSN. This is not 100% unique since duplicate SSN's have been issued. To ensure uniqueness, a surrogate key (system assigned value) has to be used. The same situation applies to Hardware and Software. In both these cases a surrogate key is used in conjunction with [Employee ID].

NOTE: *Not all dependents have an SSN. Relational theory states that nulls are not allowed in the primary key. (However, Paradox allows nulls in both a single-field or composite primary key.) One suggestion is to always place a value in the field. In the scenario of no SSN for an employee's dependent, you could use 000-00-0000. This number won't create key violations with other employee's dependents because each record has a different [Employee ID]. The only situation where key conflicts arise is for the same employee. What if there are twins or triplets born? You could not use the same value. You have to adopt a scheme where more than one dummy SSN is input until the dependent gets an SSN.*

Another alternative is to use a surrogate key instead of the SSN. This will always be unique. If you need the value of the SSN for each dependent, make it a column in the table as is done for the Employee table.

Some relational purists recommend that each table have a single field as the primary key. In most cases this would be a surrogate key. This reduces the need for composite key support but increases the need for full foreign key support with referential integrity maintained at the table level. In Paradox this is more difficult to implement because multitable forms are the only place referential integrity is supported, and both forms and reports require links based strictly on the primary key. Therefore, in all logical and physical designs using Paradox, this philosophy cannot be implemented.

Second Normal Form

A table in second normal form (2NF) has to first of all be in 1NF. Second normal form deals with tables that have composite keys (multifield keys). If any column depends on only part of the composite key, it is removed and placed into a separate table. This means each column in the table must be tied to the entire key, not just a portion of it.

Looking at the personnel system in 1NF, there are three tables with composite primary keys: Dependents, Hardware, and Software. Looking at each non-key field of Dependents, you can see that they all depend on both [Employee ID] and [Dependents SSN]. Therefore, Dependents is already in 2NF. The Hardware and Software tables violate 2NF. All non-key columns in the Hardware table depend on the [Equipment ID], not the combination of [Employee ID] and [Equipment ID]. The same is true for Software. To satisfy 2NF, two new tables are created and the original tables are renamed to HW_Inv and SW_Inv. [Employee ID] is removed from these tables. Emp_SW contains two fields, the [Employee ID] and [SW ID Num]. Both fields combined comprise the primary key. Notice that there are no non-key fields in this table. The information in the Emp_SW table identifies each piece of software an employee has. The same is true for Emp_HW. The employee's ID and the ID number for the piece of equipment combine to make the primary key. Figure 3-4 shows the database in 2NF.

The division of Hardware and Software is necessary to ensure data is not lost when an employee is deleted. If an employee no longer exists in the system, the records for that employee are removed from the database. When the employee is removed from Hardware and Software, all information on the equipment and software assigned to the employee would also be deleted. This is not what you want to happen. By putting the data into separate tables, no matter whom the equipment and software is assigned to, you always have a record of what computer equipment and software you have.

```
Employee                            SW_Inv                         Emp_SW

Employee ID        S*               SW ID Num       S*             Employee ID   S*
Last Name          A15              Description     A40            SW ID Num     S*
First Name         A10              Version         A8
Date Hired         D
Birth Date         D                HW_Inv                         Emp_HW
SSN                A11
Department         A10              Equipment ID    S*             Employee ID   S*
Manager            A20              Description     A40            Equipment ID  S*
Job Code           A3                Model Num      A12
Job Description    A40              Serial Num      A15
Skills             A6               Disk Size       N
Skills Description A40              Memory          S
Security Level     A8
Work Phone         A13              Dependents
Salary             $
Exemptions         S                Employee ID     S*
Address            A25              Dependents SSN  A11*
City               A20              Last Name       A15
State              A2               First Name      A10
Zip                A5               Birth Date      D
Home Phone         A13
Marital Status     A8
Sex                A1
Insurance Type     A12
Life Insurance     $
Short Term Disab   A1
Long Term Disab    A1
US Saving Bond     $
```

Figure 3-4 Personnel tables in second normal form

Third Normal Form

Third normal form (3NF) requires separation of columns that are not dependent on the entire primary key. If a column does not contribute to a description of the key or is dependent on one of the other columns in the table, it is removed and a separate table is created. Each non-key field in a table is an attribute of the key and not information about any other non-key field.

Reviewing the 2NF model, the current Employee table has columns that are not directly related to [Employee ID]: the department manager and the description information for [Job Code]. The other tables are already in 3NF. Therefore, two additional tables result in the Personnel system from 3NF. They are Dept and Jobcd. Figure 3-5 shows the Personnel database in 3NF.

Normalizing Your Paradox Databases   49

```
Employee                              SW_Inv                                Emp_SW

  Employee ID          S*               SW ID Num           S*                Employee ID    S*
  Last Name            A15              Description         A40               SW ID Num      S*
  First Name           A10              Version             A8
  Date Hired           D                                                    Emp_HW
  Birth Date           D              HW_Inv
  SSN                  A11                                                    Employee ID    S*
  Department           A10              Equipment ID        S*                Equipment ID   S*
  Job Code             A3               Description         A40
  Work Phone           A13              Model Num           A12
  Salary               $                Serial Num          A15             Dept
  Exemptions           S                Disk Size           N
  Address              A25              Memory              S                 Department     A10*
  City                 A20                                                    Manager        A20
  State                A2
  Zip                  A5
  Home Phone           A13
  Marital Status       A8             Dependents                           Jobcd
  Sex                  A1
  Insurance Type       A12              Employee ID         S*                Job Code              A3*
  Life Insurance       $                Dependents SSN      A11*              Job Description       A40
  Short Term Disab     A1               Last Name           A15               Skills                A6
  Long Term Disab      A1               First Name          A10               Skills Description    A40
  US Saving Bond       $                Birth Date          D                 Security Level        A8
```

Figure 3-5 Personnel tables in third normal form

Putting tables into 3NF reduces data redundancy and the potential for data loss. Figure 3-6 shows a listing of data in Employee before 3NF. Notice the information for [Manager] is repeated for both employee 1003 and 1145. If these are the only two employees in the Finance department, when they are deleted, all record of the department disappears! In the real world this might be the case. If no employees are in the department, then the department does not exist. But that is a business rule decision, and database design is not the place to enforce it.

There is also an update anomaly. If the manager for a department changes, all records have to be changed for the employees in that department. A 3NF database would have to change the record in only one place.

A normalized database would create a department number and a department name in the Dept table instead of using the name as the primary key. In Paradox, displaying the name of the department number on a form cannot be done for each record unless you use an embedded form, which takes extra effort and is not really worth it. Many queries, reports, and graphs are created off the department name, and full normalization in this case is not justified. It is true that if a department name changes, both the Dept and Employee table have to be modified. This would happen so few times that the penalty of a department name change is worth it compared to always having to go to the Dept table to get the department name. The [Job Code] doesn't have the same implication; therefore the normalized design is maintained.

```
Employee ID  Last Name  First Name  Department  Manager        Job Code ...
1003         Smith      Jim         FINANCE     H. G. Jones    B34
1145         Jones      Harry       FINANCE     H. G. Jones    A99
1001         Wales      Jean        MIS         J. T. Binary   B23
1399         Barnes     Mary        SALES       J. B. Morgan   C22
```

Figure 3-6 Sample data for employee before 3NF

Denormalization - Should You DO_IT!

Going through the entire normalization process and then suggesting that you might want to denormalize seems to go against the grain. But it is an essential question when using Paradox. The previous section discussed one reason why you might not create a table that is fully normalized. There are other reasons why you might want to denormalize your design, some examples are:

- ◆ To improve performance. The narrower the tables, the better performance. If you can split tables because some columns of the table are used less frequently than others, it is better to create a one-to-one relationship between two tables. An example in Personnel is to split the employee's benefits into a separate table. This creates a new table as shown in Figure 3-7.

```
Benefits
  Employee ID         S*
  Insurance Type      A12
  Life Insurance      $
  Short Term Disab    A1
  Long Term Disab     A1
  US Saving Bond      $
```

Figure 3-7 Benefits table after denormalizing

- To display corresponding fields from a TableLookup.
- Because of multitable form restriction. Because detail tables can be linked in the form only via the primary key, you might have to change the design to create the one-to-one or one-to-many relationship required for multitable forms. In the Personnel system, this might be the case for the equipment and software information. If you want to look at all equipment and software assigned to an employee through a form and enter the information in that format, you need to denormalize to the tables in 1NF. *Be careful* if you do this. Remember, deleting an employee also deletes all detail records. This assumes the deletion is done via the multitable form. In this case, the hardware and software records must be assigned to someone else before the employee is deleted.
- Because of Paradox's limitation of 1,350 characters in a keyed table. If you have a wide table, you're forced to create multiple tables in a one-to-one relationship.

NOTE: *Some of these reasons to denormalize would be eliminated if Paradox included relational views and full primary key/foreign key support.*

Relational theory says that you don't have to denormalize and would, in fact, vote against it. To present both sides of the argument, here are reasons why you shouldn't denormalize:

- Data redundancy. This leads to increased use of disk space and potentially more I/O because additional records must be read or records are wider than necessary because of duplicate data.
- The design might be more difficult to understand, especially to those not familiar with Paradox's limitations.
- Maintaining the system's integrity is more difficult.
- Potential modifications to applications might be required as new features are implemented in future releases of Paradox.
- Data updates require extra work.
- Audit trails increase processing and disk space.

So, should you denormalize or not? There is no absolute or correct answer. Coming from the relational purist position, the response is obviously to avoid it as long as possible. This would be easy if Paradox, or any other relational database for that matter, implemented all 12 rules of the relational model. Since that is not the case, you need to weigh the advantages of completely following normalization versus providing the functionality your users want with the least amount of work. Therefore, *realization* might be a better design to work toward than normalization. Realization means a near-normalized database with minor modifications to take full advantage of Paradox features that make things easier for both the user and you.

Summary

In this chapter, we walked you through the process of normalizing a database and demonstrated examples of first, second, and third normal form. To review,

First Normal Form

- Each table must have a primary key.
- Remove repeating group to a separate table.

Second Normal Form

- Table is in 1NF.
- Table is in 2NF for single-valued primary key or no non-key fields exist.
- For composite primary key tables, each attribute must be dependent on the entire key, not a subset of the key.

Third Normal Form

- Table is in 2NF.
- No column is dependent on any other column besides the entire primary key.

In Paradox, fully normalized tables cause some constraints because of how certain features are implemented. You need to determine if maintaining a normalized design is worth the extra programming control or if you can live with some minor denormalization to gain performance benefits and reduce custom coding.

4 Prototyping with Paradox

In this chapter we'll examine various ideas for prototyping with Paradox. This chapter is meant for the Paradox user who is just starting to develop systems for other people. It's also meant to stimulate some thought in seasoned developers who want to speed up delivery of their systems.

Prototyping an application is a fairly foreign concept to large system developers and even small system developers. Data processing shops with "user-friendly, non-procedural 4GL programs" (such as Nomad and Focus) usually think of a quick project as one that is delivered in several weeks or months, not in days and certainly not in hours. Prototyping is a method that lets you deliver *as* you create your solution. It's a methodology that includes (as opposed to the more traditional *excludes*) the people who will actually use the system. In a prototyping methodology, the end user of the system is a vital resource in the process of developing the application. Prototyping is a method of application development that lets you build your system as you go. The system is divided into modules, and as each module is developed, the user tests and sometimes actually uses the prototype in their day-to-day business.

It was the desktop microcomputer that brought on a wider use of the prototyping technique. Programs like Paradox have accelerated a developer's ability to prototype quick solutions. The main criticism of using a prototyping method is that it appears too informal, without proper organization or discipline. How can you involve users so intimately in the design and implementation of a software application? They don't know how to program, do they? In truth, users know more than even they realize and prototyping is more involved and detailed than any other approach.

In order to succeed with prototyping methods, you must apply discipline, organization, and inspiration *as you go*. Prototyping developers need to know their resources intimately and utilize them correctly. They must prioritize their project into components of what's-needed-next steps. They must constantly re-evaluate their priorities. If in the course of developing an application, a situation crops up that requires that the developer drop a certain path of work in order to concentrate on newly discovered requirements or problems, the prototyping developer must be able to suspend current work and shift gears to the new area of concern. They must also be flexible enough to pick up exactly where they left off before they changed directions, without losing momentum or the context of what they were working on. Sound difficult? Well, there are a number of ways to streamline the process and make it easier to manage.

Traditional Method of Development

Before we go any further, we want to mention that traditional system development methodologies certainly have their place in data processing. Extremely large systems for banks, manufacturers, hospitals, and so forth—applications that require the manipulation of millions of records a day, million-dollar products, information vital to the well being of people—these types of applications need the proper time devoted to planning and executing a quality application. It doesn't matter whether you're designing for a large or small system, these projects need the discipline of more traditional system development approaches.

Now, let's take a moment to review the more traditional method of application development. As we quickly review the traditional process, recognize and realize that prototypers (developers) go through every step that traditional application developers go through—they merely compress the process. They tend to involve users more, even including them in creating parts of the application.

A Traditional System Development Sequence

The traditional approach to application development flow usually takes an eight-phase approach as shown in Figure 4-1. These phases are:

- User request
- Conceptual design

- Physical design
- Program development
- Testing
- Installation
- Training
- Post-implementation review

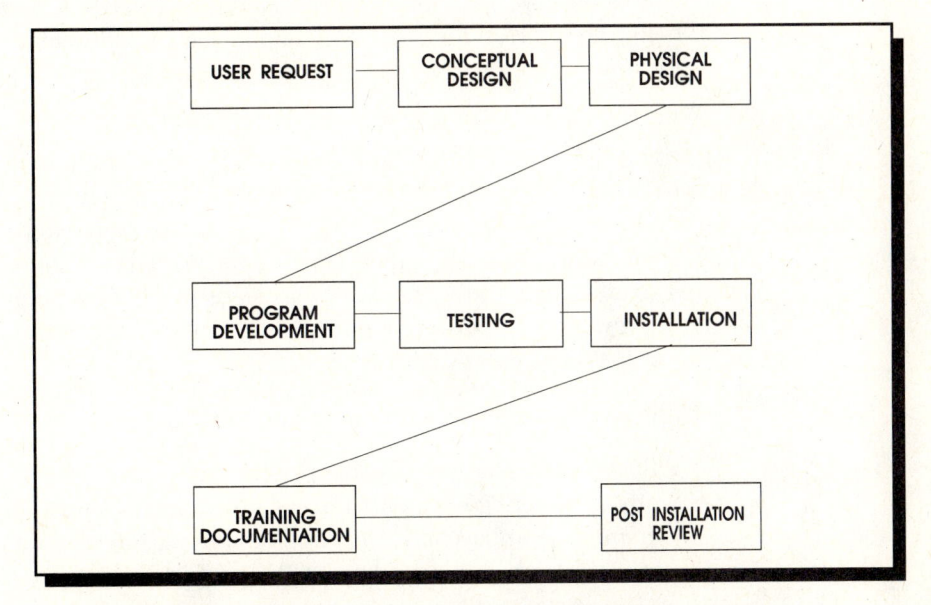

Figure 4-1 Phase and flow for a traditional system development project

Throughout the process (at the very least at the beginning, middle, and end of each phase), hold review meetings to analyze the past, present, and next phase of the work in process. This process takes time (usually lots of time), but is worth it in the end.

Too often, especially with microcomputers available, management wants an answer to an information problem *now*, not later. Sometimes a request for information doesn't warrant a rapid response.

More often than not, the problem or opportunity a business faces is the reason that a rapid response is demanded. In other words, if you can't get them the answer or respond to the opportunity in the frame of time demanded by the problem, they don't need you. How can you respond to the need for quick delivery when you're saddled with one and only one methodology? You simply can't; therefore—prototyping. Prototyping with Paradox is as challenging as with any other product; it's just faster and more fun!

We'll continue with the discussion of prototyping in just a moment. First, a commercial word for common sense. Before you approach prototyping, you first must accept the fact that by using a prototyping methodology, you're saying you don't have time for a more traditional approach. It means that you'd better have a plan for going back and taking care of details that you gloss over during the process, once you've delivered the prototype to your client.

Prototyping can be fun. If you don't keep some simple rules in place, it can also become hell on earth. The first rule and by far the foremost: *Common sense has not been displaced by the urgency of the users' request.* The last thing clients want you to do is fly off the handle and deliver some lame-brained solution that doesn't answer their needs just because they said they needed it yesterday. Producing a system that way would be a waste of your time as well as your clients' time.

What you need are a few rules and agreements to follow:

- Realize that unless you're the person who actually performs the process you're coding (you are a stock broker coding a trading program), or you have at least worked as the person who actually performs the job, you *don't* know more than your users.

  They obviously know their job better than you do—they were doing it before your solution (albeit slower and maybe not with automation).

  Make sure you create and maintain a good working relationship with the people who will use the application.

- You *can't* do everything at the same time! Make sure you're not over-committed with other programming projects. Assess whether you can take on another project.

  Remember those rapid development projects in Chapter 1? Once your client has asked you to help with a project, ask for the information you need. Ask all your questions. Find out who is buying the system. You have to be sure you know what the expectations are before you start, as you prototype, and after you've delivered the system.

If you can, spend some time working with your clients and doing their job. If this isn't possible, try to arrange an opportunity to observe the user at work. You don't have to actually perform every step of their job, just do enough to gain a better understanding of the context in which the system will be used.

Start your interview on their turf, not yours. Without a doubt, your client will *do* something they will not tell you about that is crucial to understanding the process to be automated. You can't get this kind of information by going back to the lab and coding the application—you've got to be there.

- Change your way of thinking! Don't use a KISS approach to your project; start living by the LAW!

KISS versus LAW

To understand where we're going with this train of thought, you should understand that we don't believe that the KISS (keep it simple and stupid) approach is ever a really good way to work. There are two reasons why we feel this way.

First, nothing is that simple!

What happened when you developed your first application for yourself in Paradox? Even when it was only you, the developer and the user, you looked at it and said, "This is great, but now that I can do this, how about adding this feature...hmmm... now how will I do that? ..." You'll always have a built-in problem—the creeping requirement. It doesn't matter how many written requirements you've managed to get your hands on. As you let your users see information on the screen they've never had easy access to before, as they run their reports, ask questions and are provided answers, they'll want one thing—more! This is why we say nothing is really simple—one thing always leads to another.

Second, nobody is stupid!

This is a conscious and necessary decision in how you choose to work. If you recall the old adage, "Don't judge a book by its cover," we've found that it really does apply, especially to rapid prototyping. You can't have any preconceived notions about your client or the work they do. You can have prior knowledge, you can know something about the subject, but do not develop preconceived ideas. If you enter into a rapid development project using a prototyping methodology and you can't rely on the fact that your clients know their business and work, you can't develop the system. There's no such thing as building a "dummy-proof" system using quick prototyping techniques. You just won't have enough time to build everything users need into the system, so you had better be able to rely on their knowledge of what it is they do. If you can't, step away—take a more traditional approach because quick prototyping simply isn't going to work.

If KISS isn't reality, then what is? There is another approach that works far better than KISS; and when you stop and think about it, you've probably been using it all along. Using this approach, you'll always build the best system possible. The approach is called the LAW.

> LAW stands for
> Least
> Amount (of)
> Work (possible)

When you build a system using the LAW, you don't waste time with unnecessary code, forms, or reports. When you can do things with one step instead of four, you do it in one—unless, of course, the process done in one step takes more time than it would take if you broke it down into four (or more) well-defined, very compact series of steps. Following the LAW means that you believe in the laws of physics. If it takes you less energy, time, or resources to do something one way versus another, you set yourself on course of least resistance and maximum benefit.

Don't do something the same way all the time simply because that's the way you do it! Look at the problem, logically, and determine which course will produce maximum results with the least amount of effort. We guarantee if you take on this attitude and approach, you'll always build a system that your client will find useful.

If you build with a KISS concept, you'll always overlook something. With LAW, you can deliver what a system requires and remain open to change as new facts and requirements present themselves. Now, back to our program.

The Prototyping Model

Prototyping is at its best when you involve users and show them the results of the questions they answer, quickly and as you go along. In order to accomplish this, you need several things:

- A general menu system that you can quickly change. As you define what it is the user wants automated, you'll be able to throw *their* system to the screen as you go. This will give them a sense of how the system will work and allow you to observe any styles you might need to use or changes you might need to make to satisfy your clients' requirements.
- An edit and view routine that deals with any table in at least a rudimentary way.
- A simple query program that lets your users pick and choose any field in a table and view the result.

Following are examples of these kinds of routines.

The main menu code shown next is a static-style menu. (We'll discuss menus in more depth in Chapter 8.) With this menu, you can quickly give users a feel for how their application will look.

NOTE: *The theory behind these scripts is discussed in Chapter 16.*

NOTE: *Using SETKEY lets you replay the menu as you go in and out of scripts with the user. This helps you avoid Menu {Scripts} {Play} {Main}.*

The Main Menu

```
Reset ClearAll
@0,0 Clear EOS

SetKey "F11" Play "Main"


While (true)
Release Procs All
Release Vars All
Reset ClearAll
AutoLib = "ProcLibr"
MenuColor=78
BegRow=5
BegCol=0
MarginInd = 10
Build_Main(MenuColor)
```

```
SETMARGIN MarginInd
Style Attribute MenuColor
@BegRow,BegCol

Text
                    1 - View a table
                    2 - Edit a table
                    3 - Run a report
                    4 - Perform a query
                    5 - Exit the App

EndText

Style Attribute 112
@begRow+1,MarginInd+BegCol+1 ?? format("W59,AC","Main Menu")


;@24,0 Clear EOL
CURSOR BOX
@24,30 ?? "Enter your selection "
CANVAS ON
gc = getchar()
CURSOR NORMAL
if gc < 0 then
          Cursor Off
          Style Attribute MenuColor+128
          @24,0 Clear EOL ?? format("W79,AC","Not a valid menu choice ")
          beep
          sleep 1000
          Cursor Normal
          loop
endif

sel = chr(gc)
Style Attribute MenuColor
?? sel

Switch
        case sel = "1" : action = "View" play "EditView"
        case sel = "2" : action = "Edit" play "EditView"
        case sel = "3" : play "ReptMenu"
        case sel = "4" : play "AskTable"
        case sel = "5" : quitloop
```

```
OtherWise: Cursor Off
          Style Attribute MenuColor+128
          @24,0 Clear EOL ?? format("W79,AC","Not a valid menu choice ")
          beep
          sleep 1000
          Cursor Normal
          loop

EndSwitch

EndWhile
```

Report Menu

```
; *********************************************
; **** ReptMenu                            ****
; ****                                     ****
; ****                                     ****
; ****                                     ****
; ****                                     ****
; ****Written by:G.Salcedo                 ****
; ****Date:                                ****
; *********************************************
;
; This menu always returns the main menu once a
; script has been played

While (true)
MenuColor=48

BegRow=BegRow+2
BegCol=BegCol+2
MarginInd = marginind+2
Build_Other_Menu(MenuColor)

SETMARGIN MarginInd
Style Attribute MenuColor
@BegRow,BegCol

Text

                    1 - Report # 1
                    2 - Report # 2
                    3 - Report # 3
                    4 - Report # 4
                    5 - Return to the Main Menu


EndText
```

```
Style Attribute 112
@BegRow+1,MarginInd+1 ?? format("W59,AC","Report Menu")


While (true)

CURSOR BOX
@24,30 ?? "Enter your selection "
CANVAS ON
gc = getchar()
CURSOR NORMAL
if gc < 0 then
          Cursor Off
          Style Attribute MenuColor+128
          @24,0 Clear EOL ?? format("W79,AC","Not a valid menu choice ")
          beep
          sleep 1000
          Cursor Normal
          loop
endif

sel = chr(gc)
Style Attribute MenuColor
?? sel

Switch

    case sel = "1" : repno = "R" play "RunRepts" quitloop; Change repno
    case sel = "2" : repno = "R" play "RunRepts" quitloop; as needed.
    case sel = "3" : repno = "R" play "RunRepts" quitloop; Add other reports
    case sel = "4" : repno = "R" play "RunRepts" quitloop; if needed.
    case sel = "5" : quitloop


OtherWise: Cursor Off
          Style Attribute MenuColor+128
          @24,0 Clear EOL ?? format("W79,AC","Not a valid menu choice ")
          beep
          sleep 1000
          Cursor Normal
          loop

EndSwitch
EndWhile

quitloop
EndWhile
```

The Edit Script (edits any table)

```
; *******************************************
; **** EditView                          ****
; ****                                   ****
; ****                                   ****
; ****                                   ****
; ****                                   ****
; ****Written by:G.Salcedo               ****
; ****Date: 8/1/90                       ****
; *******************************************

While (true)

ShowTables
        directory()
        "Select a table and press [ENTER]"
        to tablename

if tablename = "Esc" then
     quitloop
endif
if tablename = "None" then
   @24,0 Clear EOL ?? "No tables in the directory" style blink ?? "..." style
   beep
   sleep 1000
   quitloop
endif

View tablename

if action = "Edit" then
      CoEditkey
endif

While (true)   ; Keep doing UNTIL


Wait Table
Prompt "Press [F2] Save ... ",
       "Press [F7] Form Toggle .... [F9] Calc Total ... [F10] Other Function"
Until   "F2", "F7" ,-108, "Del", "DOS","DOSBIG","F10"
lookretval = retval


if lookretval = "DOS" or lookretval = "DOSBIG" then
       beep
       loop
endif
```

```
if lookretval = -108 then
      keypress -108
      While (true)
      WAIT FIELD
      Prompt "Press [F2] or [ENTER] to leave FIELDVIEW"
      UNTIL "F2","Enter","DOS","DOSBIG"
      fieldretval = retval
      if fieldretval = "DOS" or fieldretval = "DOSBIG" then
            NoDosExit("Bottom")
            loop
      endif
      if fieldretval = "F2" or fieldretval = "Enter" then
            quitloop
      endif
      EndWhile
      release vars fieldretval
      loop
endif

if lookretval = "Del" then
         @24,0 Clear EOL ?? "Do you really want to delete (Y/N) ? "
         Accept "A1" picture "{Y,N}" default "N" to answer
         if answer = "Y" then
               Del
               loop
         else
               loop
         endif
endif

if lookretval = "F7" then
      Formkey
      loop
endif

if lookretval = "F10" then
      @0,0 Clear EOL ?? format("AC,W79","No OTHER functions available")
      beep sleep 1000
      loop
endif

Reset
ClearAll

quitloop
Endwhile

quitloop
Endwhile
```

Generic Query Script

```
; *********************************************
; **** AskTable                            ****
; ****                                     ****
; ****                                     ****
; ****                                     ****
; ****                                     ****
; ****Written by:G.Salcedo                 ****
; ****Date: 8/1/90                         ****
; *********************************************

While (true)

ShowTables
        directory()
        "Select a table and press [ENTER]"
        to tablename

if tablename = "Esc" then
      quitloop
endif
if tablename = "None" then
 @24,0 Clear EOL ?? "No tables in the directory" style blink ?? "..." style
 beep
 sleep 1000
 quitloop
endif

Menu {ask} select tablename

While (true)   ; Keep doing UNTIL

Wait Table
Prompt "Press [F2] to run query"
Until   "F2", -108, "Del", "DOS","DOSBIG","F6","F36","F26"
lookretval = retval

if lookretval = "DOS" or lookretval = "DOSBIG" then
       beep
       loop
endif

; Check and checkplus
if lookretval = "F6" or lookretval = "F26" or lookretval = "F36" then
      keypress lookretval
      loop
endif
```

```
; Field view
if lookretval = -108 then
      keypress -108
      While (true)
      WAIT FIELD
      Prompt "Press [F2] or [ENTER] to leave FIELDVIEW"
      UNTIL "F2","Enter","DOS","DOSBIG"
          fieldretval = retval
          if fieldretval = "DOS" or fieldretval = "DOSBIG" then
              NoDosExit("Bottom")
              loop
          endif
          if fieldretval = "F2" or fieldretval = "Enter" then
              quitloop
          endif
          EndWhile
          release vars fieldretval
          loop
endif

if lookretval = "Del" then
      @24,0 Clear EOL ?? "Do you really want to delete (Y/N) ? "
      Accept "A1" picture "{Y,N}" default "N" to answer
      if answer = "Y" then
             Del
             loop
      else
             loop
      endif
endif

if lookretval = "F10" then
      @0,0 Clear EOL ?? format("AC,W79","No OTHER functions available")
      beep sleep 1000
      loop
endif

Reset
ClearAll

if istable("answer") = true then
      action = "View" play "editview"
endif

quitloop
Endwhile

quitloop
Endwhile
```

Report Script

```
; ******************************************
; **** RunRepts                         ****
; ****                                  ****
; ****                                  ****
; ****                                  ****
; ****                                  ****
; ****Written by:G.Salcedo              ****
; ****Date:                             ****
; ******************************************
;
; Runs a report for any table in the current directory
; if the report number is not valid, it runs the standard report
;

While (true)


ShowTables
        directory()
        "Select a table and press [ENTER]"
        to tablename

if tablename = "Esc" then
     quitloop
endif
if tablename = "None" then
  @24,0 Clear EOL ?? "No tables in the directory" style blink ?? "..." style
  beep
  sleep 1000
  quitloop
endif


@24,0 Clear EOL ?? format("AR,W50","Continue and run report
for table "),tablename
accept "A1" required picture "{Y,N}" default "Y" to answer

if isassigned(answer) = false then
     quitloop
endif
if answer = "N" then
     quitloop
endif

testrepno = tablename+"."+repno

if isfile(testrepno) = false then
     repno = "R"
endif
```

```
While (true)
        ShowMenu
              "Printer": "Send Report to the Printer",
              "Screen" : "Send Report to the screen",
              "Quit"   : "Don't run the Report"

              default "Printer" to sel

        Switch

        case sel = "Printer" :
         if printerstatus() = false then
              CURSOR OFF
              STYLE ATTRIBUTE (MENUCOLOR+128)
              @24,0 Clear EOL ?? format("AC,W80","PRINTER NOT READY ...")

              style ATTRIBUTE MENUCOLOR
              CURSOR NORMAL
              loop
         endif

         STYLE ATTRIBUTE (MENUCOLOR+128)

         @24,0 Clear EOL ?? format("AC,W79","PRINTING REPORT")

         REPORT tablename repno

         @24,0 Clear EOL

         case sel = "Screen": Menu {Report}{OutPut} select tablename
                              select repno select sel
                              CURSOR OFF
                              style attribute menucolor+128
                              @24,0 Clear EOL ?? format("AC,W80","ONE MOMENT")
                              style attribute menucolor
                              CURSOR NORMAL
         case sel = "Quit"  : quitloop

         OtherWise:beep

         EndSwitch
quitloop
EndWhile

quitloop
EndWhile
```

Prototyping with Paradox

Procedure Library (builds background for menus)

```
CreateLib "ProcLibr"

Proc Closed Build_Main(MenuColor)
UseVars BegRow,BegCol,MarginInd

Private Offset1,Offset2

Offset1 = MarginInd
Offset2 = MarginInd+1

CANVAS OFF
@0,0 Clear EOS

PAINTCANVAS FILL " " Attribute 112
0,0,24,79

PaintCanvas Fill "█" Attribute (Int(MenuColor/16)*16)
BegRow+1,Offset2,BegRow+10,71

PaintCanvas Attribute MenuColor
BegRow,offset1,BegRow+9,70

EndProc

Proc Closed Build_Other_Menu(MenuColor)
UseVars BegRow,BegCol,MarginInd

Private Offset1,Offset2

Offset1 = MarginInd
Offset2 = MarginInd+1

CANVAS OFF
PaintCanvas Fill "█" Attribute (Int(MenuColor/16)*16)
BegRow+1,Offset2,BegRow+10,75

PaintCanvas Attribute MenuColor
BegRow,offset1,BegRow+9,72
CANVAS ONEndProc
WriteLib "ProcLibr"
Build_Main,Build_Other_Menu
```

Figure 4-2 shows how the Main menu looks when you play MAIN.SC:

Figure 4-3 shows how the Report menu looks when you select the third option from the Main menu:

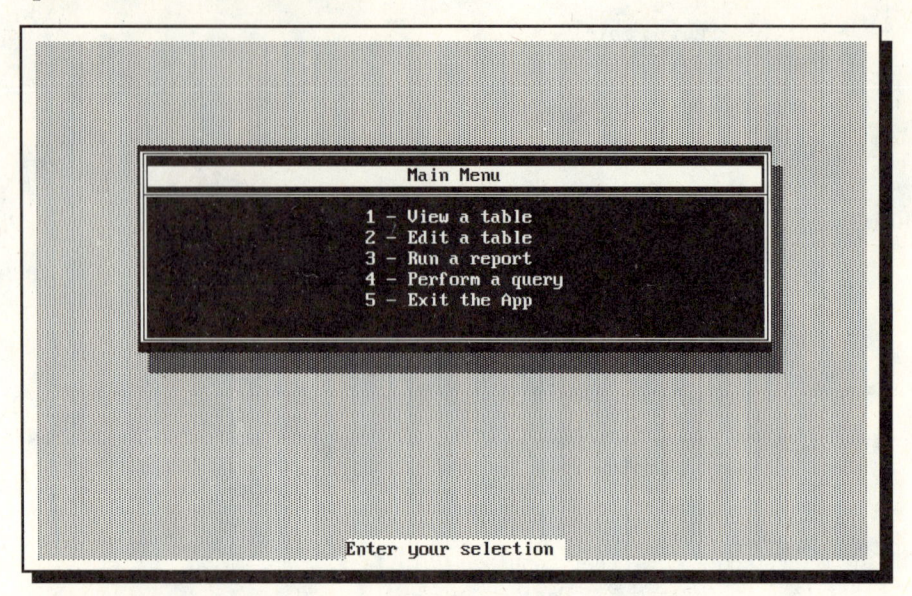

Figure 4-2 Prototype code for the Main menu

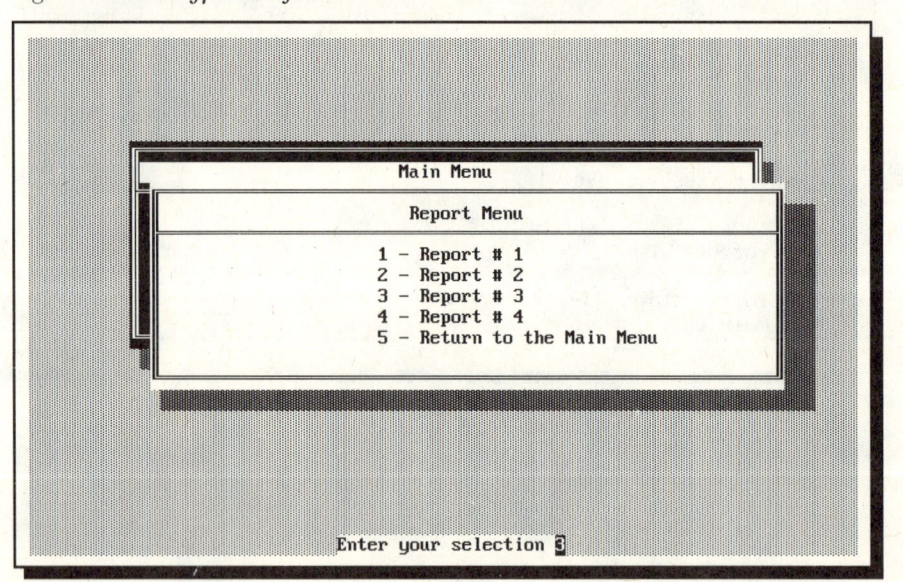

Figure 4-3 Report menu

Prototyping with Paradox 71

Figures 4-4 and 4-5 show you how the ASKTABLE.SC script looks when the fourth option is selected from the Main menu.

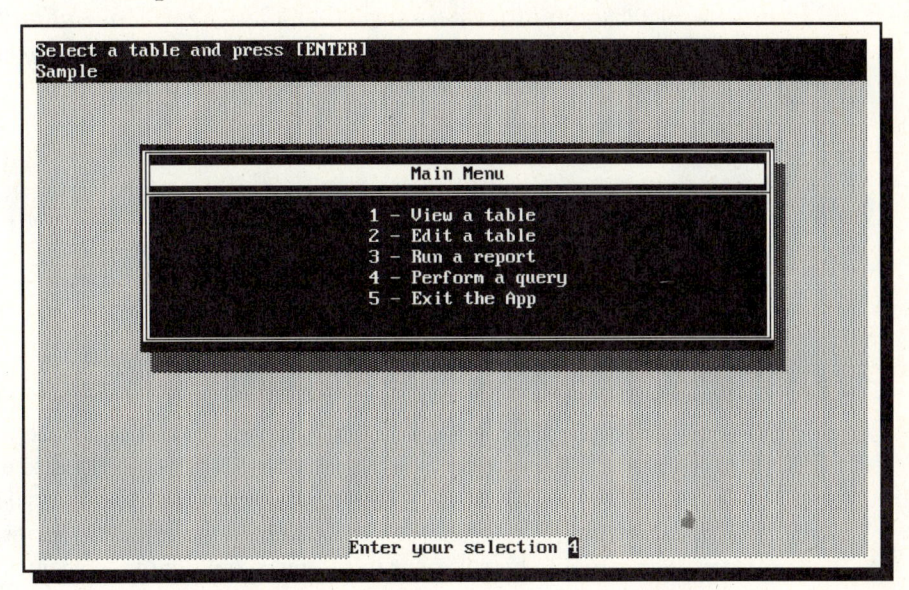

```
Select a table and press [ENTER]
Sample
                    ┌─────────── Main Menu ───────────┐
                    │         1 - View a table        │
                    │         2 - Edit a table        │
                    │         3 - Run a report        │
                    │         4 - Perform a query     │
                    │         5 - Exit the App        │
                    └─────────────────────────────────┘



                             Enter your selection 4
```

Figure 4-4 Table select for the AskTable script

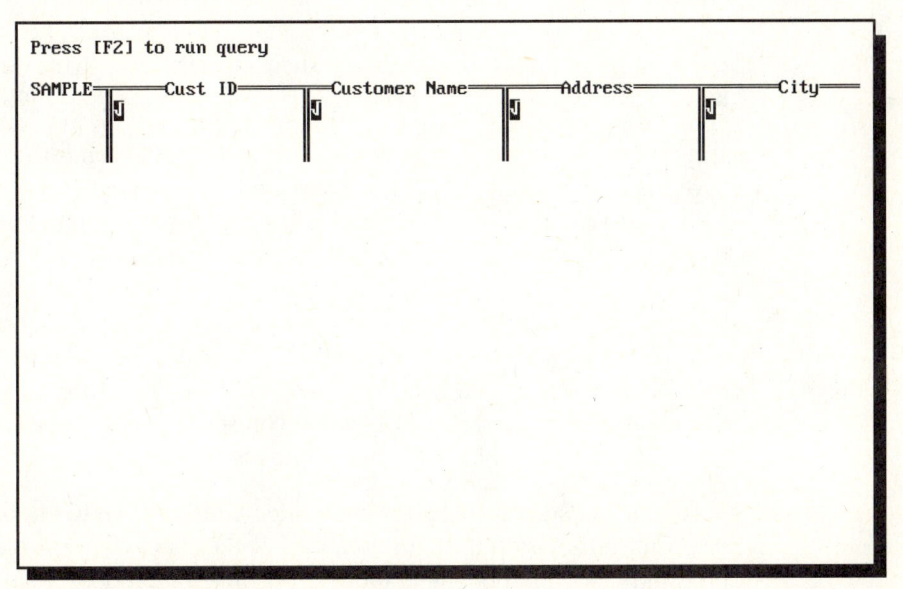

```
Press [F2] to run query
SAMPLE┬──── Cust ID ────┬──── Customer Name ────┬──── Address ────┬──── City ────
      │√│               │√│                     │√│               │√│
```

Figure 4-5 Selecting fields for the query

> **NOTE:** *If you are just starting Paradox and running ASKTABLE from the Main menu for the first time, you return to the Main menu if no Answer table results from your query. Otherwise, you're sent to the EDITVIEW.SC script, even if the table is empty. Also, if any error in the query occurs and an Answer table is not created, the script returns to the Main menu.*

How to Get Started: Involving the User

Armed with questions such as those contained in the rapid development questionnaire and with your simple prototyping scripts in hand, you are now ready to proceed.

To be a successful prototyper, you need to be part detective, part emergency room doctor (meatball surgery mentality), part kamikaze (you've got to plunge in the pool to get wet), part cheerleader (you need to encourage your users to take you through their process without sounding like a TV evangelist) and part negotiator (as you start to build tables, forms, and reports, you need to be sure that what you're building meets your client's approval).

You've already got the user request; now you need to define it in terms that you can understand. The first step is to determine what the heck it is the users want. To help you understand their process, have them walk you step-by-step through their job.

If the job includes processing paper, get a sample of each form they use and have them fill out one as it is normally used. If the data is not sensitive in nature, make copies of the forms that have already been filled out for further reference information. If a blank in a form can have more than one answer, for example, "Relationship to employee," make sure you know all the valid responses. This isn't as trivial as it seems. If a paper form allows multiple entries, and only those entries, you want to know every iteration the field in the form can take. You need to know this up front so that you can include it in your validity checks when you start creating your tables (validity checking is discussed in detail in Chapter 6).

If the current system is already automated you still have to ask the user to take you step-by-step through each part of the process. Ask if there is any user and/or system documentation. If documentation does exist, it can really speed up your investigative process.

If the application is brand new (it's not currently being done), think about visiting other businesses or organizations with the user to find out how they do it. Many organizations are glad to open their doors and share information as long as they don't have to give away a competitive edge. If this isn't possible or desirable, take a piece of paper and start scratching out a form or roll it through the typewriter and start creating it there.

Of course, you could jump right in and ask the user to give you names of fields to create. If you're going to start with the typewriter keyboard, be sure you have some expertise in the subject matter. If you don't have any knowledge in the user's subject area, there's no getting around doing a little brainstorming.

Whether the process is new or existing, look to existing reports to guide you in determining what the user wants as an end result.

> **TIP:** *Find the user's favorite, most frequently used, or most important form and report. Ask them what it is that they like about it and what it does for them. Be sure also to ask what is missing or needs to be changed. Listen and ask about anything you're not familiar with.*

Speaking of brainstorming, it's the next step.

Creating the Conceptual Design

This is blackboard (erasable white board) time. Find a room or area where you can spread out the forms and reports you've dug up and give your user a picture of what you've found so far. Let the client jump in anytime in the process and correct, add, or subtract from your understanding of the process. Once you and the client agree that you have a clear and valid picture of what's required, show how you intend to create the application. You can do this interactively on an easel, blackboard, or even with a computer (kill many birds with one stone) if the resource is available to you.

Once you know the user understands what you intend and you agree upon a course of action, go away and analyze how long it's going to take. If time doesn't permit this analysis, make an estimate on the spot (add a caveat that this is only an estimate and may be subject to change later if new requirements pop up). State what you intend to do for the customer and how much time it's going to take. If the user agrees to your proposal, *write it up!* Even if it's a only a quick note, be sure that you have the understanding in writing.

If time allows, send your client a letter or memo with a recap of your proposal. *Make sure the user who will accept delivery of the application signs off on your proposal, indicating their approval.* Once you have this agreement, you're ready for the next step.

Physical Design

Here's where Paradox prototyping departs from the more traditional system development process.

If your user knows Paradox, get them to help you create the necessary tables. If they don't know Paradox, start to teach them the product by getting them to create the tables and forms.

It's important to involve the user in this process. If the previous application was performed by a spreadsheet, you'll undoubtedly have to change the way some of the information is portrayed or processed. This is where you can confirm your conceptual design and make changes together as necessary.

Program Development

Ah, at last! This is the part you've been waiting for. This is where you take off to the lab and invent the solution. But don't go too far. Make sure that you let the user peek under the door every once in a while to confirm that what you're building is meeting their expectations.

> **NOTE:** *In Chapter 20, we discuss a number of tools that can help you document this process. Some of the tools will actually help in creating the application.*

Testing

We wish we could say that this process is so bullet-proof that there isn't a need for testing, but we can't. Prototypes should be run through interactively with your clients. You really want them to test each component and each added capability as you add and create it. This is another large difference between the prototype approach and the traditional approach, and it results in a big benefit. Involve users as you build the system, and you'll have tested it as you build it.

Installation

This is the nail-biting time of the project. Now you must test whether it works at your users' location. Be ready to make last-minute allowances or changes now that the users back on their turf. Remember the creeping requirement? Expect it! Handle it by getting the current capabilities in, and making a list of other desired features for later consideration.

Training

The beauty of this phase when you prototype is that if you have involved users throughout the process, they're already partially if not totally trained. If other people you've worked with need training, enlist your clients in training fellow workers.

This goes for creating documentation too. Remember, you didn't have time to develop with a traditional approach. You hardly have the time to sit down and type up a document telling the users to do what they already know how to do. Get the users to at least share any documentation requirements with you.

Post-installation Review

Make sure that you keep in contact with the client. Again, if you chose a prototyping method to create the application, as users get to know the system better they will usually want more or need to make some changes. Plan and prepare for it.

Paradox Prototyping Methodology Review

- Build your tables first.
- Build a master form and report for each of the tables that let you access all the fields. Look for existing paper or electronic forms to give you a clue as to how it should look. Let the user see the form as you build it. If you can, have your users build the form. Do the same thing with the master report for each table.

- Use your basic prototype code as shown above to create an application effect. This will give the user a feel for how the process will work.
- Change, add, and create your application based on a continuing interview and creation process. Show your user the work as you go.

Summary

In this chapter, we looked at some building blocks that let you create some fast Paradox prototypes. Prototyping is a partnership process. Neither your client nor you can accomplish the task without the other. In the next chapter, we'll take an in-depth look at a comparison of Paradox version 3.5 and Paradox version 3.01A.

5 Paradox 3.5: What's New

Paradox 3.5 expands your ability to fully utilize your hardware and your connectivity requirements. Paradox 3.5's new features are easy to incorporate into existing applications, and if you choose not to use the new options, your current systems will run in 3.5 without changes.

This chapter covers new features and options, enhancements to existing commands and functions, and other miscellaneous differences between Paradox 3.5 and Paradox 3.0. We'll also discuss changes to the Paradox product line.

Major Feature Overview

With the release of Paradox 3.5, there are actually three new products:

- Paradox 3.5
- Paradox SQL Link
- Paradox Multi-Pack

Paradox 3.5

There are four major areas of enhancement in Paradox 3.5:

- Memory Management
  Virtual Runtime Object-Oriented Memory Management (VROOMM) optimizes Paradox's use of memory.

- TurboDrive

    Real and protected mode operation on 286 and higher machines, including use of up to 16MB of extended memory.
- Variables and functions in forms and reports

    Global variables and some PAL functions can be used in form and report expressions.
- Connectivity

    Access to SQL database servers and improved interoperability with other Borland products.

Paradox SQL Link

SQL Link provides transparent connections to SQL database servers. The following are the three initial servers supported:

- IBM OS/2 Extended Edition Database Manager version 1.2
- Microsoft SQL Server version 1.0 and 1.1
- Oracle Server version 6.0

Paradox Multi-Pack

- Replaces the Paradox Lan Pack.

Paradox 3.5 Detailed Feature Set

Memory Management

A new memory management facility called the Virtual Runtime Object-Oriented Memory Manager (VROOMM) has been incorporated into Paradox 3.5. It is a faster and more efficient memory manager than that used in previous versions of Paradox. The major concept of VROOMM is the ability to quickly load small sections of code into memory based on the requested action. Paradox is broken down into small modules requiring less memory for the kernel. More memory is available for Paradox objects, procedures, and processing. This gives you improved performance for larger tables and memory-intensive operations.

TurboDrive

Paradox 3.5 has built-in intelligence to run optimally on 286 or higher machines with TurboDrive. Any 286, 386, or 486 machine with more than 1MB of extended memory runs Paradox in protected mode. This extension to VROOMM gives you full access to all available memory in your machine. If you're one of the fortunate few with 16MB of memory, TurboDrive lets you use it all. This will improve sorts, single-table queries, multitable queries, scrolling through large tables, as well as PAL application performance. Paradox automatically configures itself to the type of machine on which it is installed. You can customize the configuration to run in real or protected mode or use a command-line prompt (discussed later).

TurboDrive is meant for 286, 386, and 486 machines. This does not mean Paradox 3.5 will not work on an 8088 or 8086 machine. On the contrary, with VROOMM, the life of the XT-class machine is extended because Paradox 3.5 not only works within 640K, but it works better than many of its competitors (who seem to need more memory with each new release). Paradox 3.5 actually works on a 512K machine (but this is not recommended). The one thing you'll not be able to use with an XT-class machine is SQL connectivity, which requires the protected mode of a 286 or higher machine.

Variables and Functions in Forms and Reports

The new memory management scheme in 3.5 opens the door for Borland to support global variables and a subset of PAL functions in forms and reports. Expressions that define calculated fields accept any global variable, array element, and any of the functions listed in Table 5-1. If there's a syntax problem with the expression, Paradox won't let you place the field until it's syntactically correct. The result of an expression is always a character field with a maximum length of 255. Any global variable has to exist before the form or report is used. If it doesn't, Paradox considers the variable invalid. If this occurs or there is an incorrect data type for a parameter in a function, you get a runtime error.

A new configuration option and PAL command, CALCDEBUG, is available to handle these situations. This new feature lets you specify what is to be placed in the field to indicate some type of data error. CALCDEBUG also gives you the capability to turn the option On or Off in an application, overriding the configuration file setting.

Table 5-1
PAL functions allowed in form and report expressions

Function	Description
ABS	Absolute value of a number
ACOS	Arc cosine of a number
ASC	Converts a character to an ASCII value
ASIN	Arc sine of a number
ATAN	Arc tangent of a number
ATAN2	Four quadrant arc tangent
CAVERAGE	Averages of all records for one column in a table
CCOUNT	Count of the values for a column in a table
CHR	Converts an ASCII value to a character
CMAX	Maximum value for a column in a table
CMIN	Minimum value for a column in a table
CNPV	Net present value for a column in a table
COS	Cosine of an angle
CSTD	Standard deviation of the values for a column in a table
CSUM	Sum of the values for a column in a table
CVAR	Variance of the values for a column in a table
DATEVAL	Converts a date value to a string value
DAY	Numeric value of the day of the month for a date value
DOW	Three-letter string of the day of the week for a date value
EXP	Exponential value of a number
FILL	Returns a repeated character string
FORMAT	Formats date, numeric, text, and logical data types
FV	Future values of a series of cash flows
INT	Integer portion of a number
LEN	Length of a character string
LN	Natural log of a number
LOG	Base 10 log of a number
LOWER	Converts a text string to lowercase
MAX	Largest of two numeric values
MIN	Smallest of two numeric values

Table 5-1—continued

Function	Description
MOD	Modulus function
MONTH	Numeric value of the month for a date value
MOY	Three-character value of the month for a date value
NRECORDS	Number of records in a table
NUMVAL	Converts a text string to a number
PI	Value of Pi
PMT	Amortized mortgage payment
POW	Raises a number to a power
PV	Present value of a series of payments
RAND	Random number
ROUND	Rounds a number
SEARCH	Position of a substring
SIN	Sine of an angle
SQRT	Square root
STRVAL	Converts an expression to a string
SUBSTR	Returns a substring
TAN	Tangent of an angle
TIME	Current system time
TODAY	Current system date
UPPER	Converts a text string to uppercase
USERNAME	Current user's name
YEAR	Year of a date value

Access to variables and functions greatly expands the capabilities of forms and expressions. The list of things you can do is almost endless. Here are a few ideas on the types of functionality this feature adds to your applications:

- Custom report titles
- Floating dollar sign
- Formatting of both N and $ data types in forms
- Calculations using aggregates of an entire table
- All date and time functions

- Full day and month spelling, with an array defined before using the form or report and DAY() or MONTH() function
- Rotated bar graph in reports
- Generic printer escape sequences for bold, italics, underline, and so forth
- Line-drawing characters for word-wrapped fields
- Multiplication factors determined at runtime

Using functions and variables in expressions provides the capability to modify forms and reports at runtime. You no longer have to embed a dummy table in forms to display miscellaneous information or link a dummy table in a report to simulate access to global variables.

▽ **TRAP:** *Along with this new capability comes a major problem when certain functions are used with blank values. The CALCDEBUG function does not ensure that the return value is always the same when there is a runtime error in an expression. You can actually have one of four different values returned depending on the function you used. Table 5-2 lists each function and what type of value is returned for each function. You need to account for this in your applications. We hope this problem will be corrected in a future release.*

Multitable Forms and Reports

The number of embedded tables allowed in multitable forms has been increased to nine. Each embedded form still has to be either linked to the master or be an unlinked table. The same Paradox 3.0 restrictions apply:

- You cannot link multitable forms
- Multirecord master forms cannot contain embedded forms

This doesn't resolve the problem of more than two levels on related tables but does increase the number of tables that can be accessed in a single form.

Reports have no additional features outside of the use of variables and functions. Even though the number of embedded tables has increased for forms, that is not the case for reports. The limit is still five.

Table 5-2
Values returned for a null value with CALCDEBUG On

Function	N/A	Blanks	CalcDebug Value	"Garbage"	Zeros
ABS			X		
ACOS			X		
ASC			X		
ASIN			X		
TAN			X		
TAN2			X		
CAVERAGE					X
CCOUNT			X		
CHR			X		
CMAX				Error	
CMIN				Error	
CNPV					X
COS			X		
CSTD					X
CSUM					X
CVAR					X
DATEVAL				Error	
DAY				8	
DOW			X		
EXP			X		
FILL			X		
FORMAT		X			
FV			X		
INT			X		
LEN					X
LN			X		
LOG			X		
LOWER		X			
MAX			X		
MIN			X		
MOD			X		

Table 5-2—continued

Function	N/A	Blanks	CalcDebug Value	"Garbage"	Zeros
MONTH				1	
MOY				Jan	
NRECORDS					X
NUMVAL				Error	
PI	X				
PMT			X		
POW			X		
PV			X		
RAND	X				
ROUND			X		
SEARCH		X			
SIN			X		
SQRT				Error	
STRVAL		X			
SUBSTR		X			
TAN			X		
TIME	X				
TODAY	X				
UPPER		X			
USERNAME		X			
YEAR				1881	

Interactive Paradox

The only menu option that has changed in Paradox 3.5 is {QuerySpeedUp} from the {Tools} menu. It has been shortened to {QuerySpeed}. If you used {Tools}{QuerySpeedUp} in any of your previous scripts or procedures, you do not have to change them. Paradox 3.5 recognizes both {QuerySpeedUp} and {QuerySpeed}.

Selecting menu options is now easier when there is more than one option with the same starting letter. You can narrow the choices by typing a second letter, then a third letter, and so on until a unique option is found or you select the option with [Enter]. As soon as you use the arrow keys to move the highlight bar, the narrowing of selections using a character is disabled. This feature is called incremental menu selection. It works whenever a Paradox menu is displayed (during SHOWMENU, SHOWARRAY, SHOWTABLES, and SHOWFILES). Because of this new feature, you might not get the same results with TYPEIN and KEYPRESS in Paradox 3.5 as you did in 3.0.

You can no longer copy a corrupt object when copying the family of a table. Prior to 3.5, any corrupt or out-of-date family objects were copied with {Tools}{Copy}{JustFamily}.

Reporting of form locks is improved when you use {Tools}{Info}{Lock}. The value shown is "Form Lock-WL." The second record that was included in the List table (indicating that the table is write-locked) is omitted.

Borland Product Interoperability

Interaction with other Borland products is one of the major new features of 3.5. To start with, you can now export directly to Quattro Pro and import data from a Quattro Pro spreadsheet (although this isn't often necessary as Quattro Pro 1.0 can directly read and write a Paradox table).

If you have Quattro Pro 2.0, you can run it from within Paradox 3.5. With a single keystroke, Quattro Pro automatically loads a spreadsheet based on a Paradox table. This capability expands application functionality by allowing data to be modified in the database or in a spreadsheet. You can even use the advanced graphics capability of Quattro Pro with no user interaction. To use this feature, you will need a 286 or higher machine and a minimum of 2MB of memory.

You also have access to SQL database servers when combining Paradox 3.5 and SQL Link. This is covered in detail in Chapter 13.

New Commands

There are two new commands in Paradox 3.5, even though the *Upgrade Guide* says that there are four. Two of the commands listed in the *Upgrade Guide* were available in 3.0 but were not documented. CALCDEBUG and SAVETABLES are the new commands, RESYNCKEY and UNDO are the newly-documented commands.

CALCDEBUG toggles the way Paradox handles runtime errors for calculated field error messages. Figure 5-1 shows the syntax for this command.

CALCDEBUG { ON | OFF } *String*

Figure 5-1 CALCDEBUG syntax

Expressions in PAL statements, forms, and reports are checked only for the correct number of arguments. If one of the arguments is an incorrect data type, it isn't identified until the expression is evaluated at runtime. In interactive mode, Paradox displays a message in the lower-right corner of the screen when this occurs. You can disable the message window with CALCDEBUG OFF "". To have a constant set of text displayed for all fields with an error, include the characters inside the double quotes. For example, CALCDEBUG ON "^^^^^^" displays up to six ^ in each field that contains invalid data.

SAVETABLES flushes table buffers to ensure they are written to disk. It is executed without any arguments. In previous versions, RESET was one of the only ways to force changes to disk but was problematic because you lost all your locks and were returned to Main mode (which cancels any other mode and clears the workspace). SAVETABLES prevents you from having to perform workarounds for these problems.

RESYNCKEY is the equivalent of [Ctrl][L], which re-synchronizes the master and detail records in a multitable form. This only works for forms in a one-to-one or one-to-many relationship when there has been a change to the linking fields in the master table.

UNDO is the equivalent of *Menu {Undo}* in Edit and DataEntry mode, and the equivalent of [Ctrl][U] in Edit, CoEdit, and DataEntry mode. This command is used to reverse the last modification made to the table. In CoEdit, you can reverse only one modification. In Edit and DataEntry you can incrementally reverse, all modifications.

▽ **TRAP:** *The Paradox documentation states that a transaction starts with [Ins] and ends when you move off the record, indicating that you can reverse the insertion and the input to the record with one UNDO. This is not the case in CoEdit. In this case, you must execute two UNDO statements. The first reverses the changes to the unposted record and the* *second reverses the inserted blank record. Only a single UNDO is necessary in Edit and DataEntry.*

There is also a difference in how UNDO works in 3.5 and how it used to work in 3.0. It now takes two UNDO statements to back up in a multitable form after a form toggle.

New Functions

There are three new functions in Paradox 3.5: FORMTYPE, RECORDSTATUS, and RMEMLEFT.

FORMTYPE is used to test the type of form the cursor is currently in. Figure 5-2 shows the syntax. This function is useful in determining what activity is allowed within a form as you move from one table to another.

FORMTYPE(*String*)

where *String* is "MultiRecord", "Linked", "Detail", or "DisplayOnly"

Capitalization of the string is not required.

Figure 5-2 FORMTYPE syntax

In some cases, you need to execute FORMTYPE multiple times to get the correct picture of the type of multitable form and current table. Table 5-3 lists the possible form type and what FORMTYPE returns for each of the four parameters.

RECORDSTATUS is used to test the status of the current record for one of four conditions: new, locked, modified, and a key violation. Figure 5-3 shows the syntax. True or False is returned depending on the status of the current record for the condition tested.

RECORDSTATUS (*String*)

where *String* is "New", "Locked", "Modified", or "KeyViol"

Capitalization of the string is not required.

Figure 5-3 RECORDSTATUS syntax

Table 5-3
Return values for FORMTYPE

Form Type	Multi-Record	Linked	Detail	Display Only
Standard form or multitable master	False	False	False	False
Multirecord single table	True	False	False	False
Unlinked detail	False	False	True	False
DisplayOnly master	False	False	False	True
Unlinked multirecord detail	True	False	True	False
Linked detail	False	True	True	False
DisplayOnly unlinked detail	False	False	True	True
Multirecord linked detail	True	True	True	False
Multirecord unlinked DisplayOnly detail	True	False	True	True
Linked DisplayOnly detail	False	True	True	True

The use of RECORDSTATUS is restricted to CoEdit mode. This is necessary because the record has to be saved (or an attempt to save the record has to be made) before Paradox knows if the record violates an existing key. CoEdit is the only mode that supports this requirement. Table 5-4 lists each of the possible conditions a record can have and the value returned by RECORDSTATUS for each of the parameters to test.

All four conditions can be tested. This requires executing the function once for each test condition. You will have to perform multiple checks in some cases to accurately determine the state of a record. For example, testing the result of RECORDSTATUS("Modified") indicates if a change has been made to the record but does not tell you if it is an existing record or a new one. Table 5-5 lists the multiple tests necessary to evaluate the status of the record for each possible condition.

The first three RECORDSTATUS options, New, Locked, and Modified, do not require you to attempt to post the record. Checking for a key violation does. This potentially forces the cursor to leave the record if the type of posting executed puts the record in its proper place in the table. You should also be aware that Paradox locks the existing record in addition to the record that violates the key. If a TableLookup is executed, RECORDSTATUS("Modified") always returns True even if no change is made to the record. RESYNCKEY for many-to-one and many-to-many multitable forms posts the master record so that RECORDSTATUS("Modified") returns False.

Table 5-4
Return values for status of a record

Record status	New	Locked	Modified	KeyViol
New, blank record	True	False	False	False
New record after input	True	False	True	False
New record; key violation when attempting to post	True	True	True	True
Existing record, unchanged	False	False	False	False
Existing record, locked but unchanged	False	True	False	False
Existing record, modified	False	True	True	False
Existing record, modified; key violation when attempting to post	False	True	True	True

Table 5-5
Multiple conditions to test for full evaluation of record status

Record status	New	Locked	Modified	KeyViol
New, blank record	True		False	
New record after input	True	False	True	
New record, key violation after attempt to post	True			True
Existing record, unchanged	False	False		
Existing record, locked but unchanged		True	False	
Existing record, changed	False		True	False
Existing record, changed, key violation after attempt to post	False	True		

REMEMLEFT is the third new function in 3.5. It returns the amount of free memory in the code pool. The numeric value returned corresponds to the memory Paradox uses to store its own program code. This portion of memory is used by VROOMM. You can use a portion of the code pool before error code 44 is set. However, you do not want your application to invade the code pool.

Modified Commands

The *Upgrade Guide* states that three commands from Paradox 3.0 have been modified: COPYFROMARRAY, RUN, and SHOW. This is partially true. The option for the SHOW commands that is presented as new actually existed in 3.0 but was not documented and was not reliable, but these problems have been fixed. There is also a change to the PRINT FILE command.

COPYFROMARRAY is now supported in linked detail tables. You can now copy the contents of an array to a detail record as long as the values of the array for the key fields of the detail record match the values of the linking field(s) of the master table. This constraint ensures referential integrity between the master and detail tables.

The RUN command now has a new parameter, NOSHELL. This option prevents Paradox from loading another copy of COMMAND.COM when a RUN is executed. (Prior to 3.5 this always occurred.) More memory is available to the external program with this option. You can also interrogate the DOS return code after the execution of the external program. The system variable *retval* contains a return code between 0 and 255. A drawback to using NOSHELL is that you cannot execute a .BAT file because this requires another copy of COMMAND.COM.

> **NOTE:** *When executing RUN, the new memory manager might not release the same amount of memory as in previous versions of Paradox. Therefore, you need to test for this in your applications. Following is a section of the Paradox 3.5 README file that discusses RUN and RUN BIG:*
>
> "Paradox 3.5 uses Borland's VROOMM *memory management, which loads modules of program code into memory dynamically as they are needed. As a result, the amount of memory available when you execute PAL's RUN or RUN BIG command (or their keyboard equivalents, [Ctrl][O] and [Alt][O]) will vary more in the course of a session than it*

did in Paradox 3.0. Exactly how much memory is available depends on many factors, but neither RUN nor RUN BIG will always give you as much memory as Paradox 3.0 did. In both real and protected mode, RUN always gives 140K or more; if it can't free up that much, Paradox automatically converts the RUN to a RUN BIG. In real mode, RUN BIG can usually free up all but about 25K of the memory available when you started Paradox. In protected mode, it can usually free up all but about 75K of the memory available at Paradox startup.

For most users, RUN and RUN BIG will work just as before. If you are using RUN BIG to run a memory-intensive program from within Paradox, check that the operation will still work in your configuration. If you are using RUN to execute a program that needs 150-200K and Paradox is forced to convert the RUN command to RUN BIG, it will be slightly faster if you change the RUN to a RUN BIG."

Each of the four show commands, SHOWARRAY, SHOWFILES, SHOWMENU, and SHOWTABLES now have two additional documented parameters: UNTIL and KEYTO. Figure 5-4 shows the syntax for these four commands. UNTIL is the functional equivalent of the UNTIL in the WAIT command, while you list keystrokes you want to end the SHOW command (in addition to [Esc] and the menu values). One typical keystroke to add is [F1]. If this is also in your WAIT commands (to access Help), you increase consistency in the menu interface.

PRINT FILE performs better because output is buffered and Paradox keeps the file open as long as possible. Paradox intelligently knows when to open and close the file. Commands such as RUN, EXIT, PRINT to different file, FILESIZE on the print file name, and so forth close the file.

Modified Functions

The only function the documentation states as being changed is MEMLEFT and, for those with SQL Link, ERRORCODE. The change to MEMLEFT really deals with the new memory manager. MEMLEFT now returns the memory available in the central memory pool. ERRORCODE now also returns SQL errors and is used in conjunction with SQLERRORCODE. See Chapter 13 for more information on SQL errors.

> **SHOWARRAY** *Array1 Array2*
> [**UNTIL** *Keycodlist* [**KEYTO** *VarName1*]
> [**DEFAULT** *Choice*]
> **TO** *VarName2*
>
> **SHOWFILES** [**NOEXT**] *DOSPath Prompt*
> [**UNTIL** *Keycodlist* [**KEYTO** *VarName1*]
> **TO** *VarName2*
>
> **SHOWMENU** *MenuItemList*
> [**UNTIL** *Keycodlist* [**KEYTO** *VarName1*]
> [**DEFAULT** *Choice*]
> **TO** *VarName2*
>
> **SHOWTABLES** [**NOEXT**] *DOSPath Prompt*
> [**UNTIL** *Keycodlist* [**KEYTO** *VarName1*]
> **TO** *VarName2*

Figure 5-4 SHOW commands syntax

Additional PAL Changes

There are three additional changes that you will probably want to utilize. The first is the ability to retrieve the last entry for either a {*MiniScript*} or {*Value*} selection using the PAL Menu or Debugger. This is an excellent time saver. How many times have you typed in a long MiniScript only to spell a word wrong? Pressing [Ctrl][E] at either of these prompts returns the last entry for editing. This also works if you get an error and Paradox prompts you with the error message. A [Ctrl][E] reissues the {*MiniScript*} or {*Value*} menu selection and enters the string for you to modify.

The other two changes concern the information returned from the [Alt][=] and [Alt][-] screens. Figure 5-5 and 5-6 show examples of the new screens. The meaning of each is beyond the scope of this chapter. Stay tuned to CompuServe, user group newsletters, and various other publications. They will cover these screens as more information is discovered about using the information displayed.

```
Paradox 3.5 - English Version (308f  07/13/90 )  Serial #:
Memory  Utilization - hit any key to continue

  Job Cnt Total   Lo   Hi  Mov  Swp  Pur  HiC File  EMS  PUR LowC
    0 238   864    0    0  864  798  798   64    0    0  692  108
    1  10   121    0    0  121    0    0   70    0    0    0   51
    4   4     8    0    0    8    0    0    0    0    0    0    8
    5   4     8    0    0    8    0    0    0    0    0    0    8
    6   2     4    0    0    4    0    0    0    0    0    0    4
    8   1     1    0    0    1    0    0    1    0    0    0    0
 Free   5   288    0    0  288    0    0    0    0    0    0  288
  Sum 264  1294    0    0 1294  798  798  135    0    0  692  467

heap 1, temp 2, proc 3, stack 4, hash 5, menu 6, cache 8
Numeric Coprocessor: EMULATED
MemLeft  231
descrnum 1101
```

Figure 5-5 [ALT][=] screen example

```
                         D D D D A U U U U J F F F
                         l R D F L D D D A F D D D
 Net Compatibility       k L R L k L R D L L L R D FileName
< Not on Network       > 1 0 0 0 1 0 0 0 0 0 0 0 0 d:\PDX35\PARADOX.DIR
1 registered files
user
network     SingleUser
session     0
net control file:
form lock

Never used stack: 5164 bytes
  257 Hash Table Size
   96 Cache Table Size
    0 Kbytes Allocated
    0 Kbytes Loaded
    0 Kbytes Purgeable
    0 Number of Reads
    0 Read Hits
    0 Number of Writes
    0 Write Hits
    0 Number of Vfd Flushes
    0 Number of Collisions
>
```

Figure 5-6 [Alt][-] screen examples

Have you ever wanted to know the names of the Borland employees who work very hard to deliver the Paradox product? The answer is right at your fingertips. When you press [Alt][-] as soon as you enter Paradox 3.5, the screen looks like that shown in Figure 5-6. Notice the > at the bottom of the screen. This is like a prompt. If you type the letters c, r, e, d, i, t, s, the screen changes to that shown in Figure 5-7, a list of Borlanders who made Paradox 3.5 possible.

Custom Configuration Program

The Custom Configuration Program has some additions and some deletions from its menus. The first thing you'll notice is that the Main menu has a new option, {*Tune*}. Its submenu is {*MachineInfo*} and {*ProtectMode*}. {*MachineInfo*} creates a {*Basic*} or {*Detailed*} report of the hardware you are currently using. Figure 5-8 is an example of the output of a detailed report.

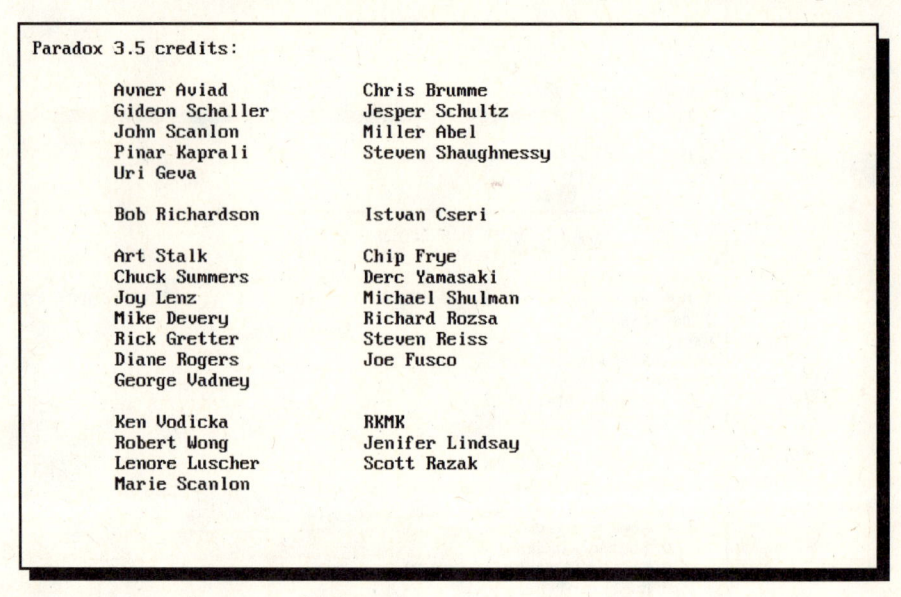

```
Paradox 3.5 credits:

        Avner Aviad            Chris Brumme
        Gideon Schaller        Jesper Schultz
        John Scanlon           Miller Abel
        Pinar Kaprali          Steven Shaughnessy
        Uri Geva

        Bob Richardson         Istvan Cseri

        Art Stalk              Chip Frye
        Chuck Summers          Derc Yamasaki
        Joy Lenz               Michael Shulman
        Mike Devery            Richard Rozsa
        Rick Gretter           Steven Reiss
        Diane Rogers           Joe Fusco
        George Vadney

        Ken Vodicka            RKMK
        Robert Wong            Jenifer Lindsay
        Lenore Luscher         Scott Razak
        Marie Scanlon
```

Figure 5-7 Paradox 3.5 credits listing

Paradox 3.5: What's New

```
Detailed Machine Information     Copyright (c) 1990 Borland International
============================
DOS Version:    3.30
BIOS Version:   Not Found
BIOS ID String:

CPU Type:     Intel 80386
Coprocessor: None Detected
Paradox is currently running in protected mode

Total Main Memory:            654,336 bytes
Extended Memory: Used by Paradox in protected mode
Expanded Memory: Not being used by Paradox

Display Adapter 1: VGA
      Monitor 1:    PS/2-compatible color display

Mouse Driver Version:   6.26
Configuration signature:
db_entry 003h 003h 004h 00000h 00000h 084227084h 000h 00000h 00000h

Disk Drive Information
======================
Boot Drive: C:
    Drive   Total Bytes       Free Bytes     Local?  Type (Floppy Only)
    -----   -------------     -------------  ------  ----------------------
      A:              0                 0      Y     3.5 inch 1.44MB 80 Track
      B:              0                 0      Y     5.25 inch 360K 40 Track
      C:     24,297,472         1,128,448      Y
      D:     20,101,120           911,360      Y

    Contents of CONFIG.SYS
    ----------------------
FILES=20
BUFFERS=20

DEVICE=C:\mouse.sys

    Contents of AUTOEXEC.BAT
    ------------------------
prompt $p$g
PATH d:\pdx35;c:\paradox3;c:\tc;c:\tc\lib;c:\dos33;c:\utils;c:\batch;c:\qpro;c:\
cls
```

Figure 5-8 MachineInfo detailed report

The {*ProtectMode*} options let you configure your machine to run in protected mode. If you have a 386 and more than 1MB of memory, Paradox automatically runs in protected mode.

The {Video} {Colors} selection has a totally new menu subsystem. The new options are:

Design	Create a new color setting
Change	Modify a color setting
PickSetting	Select from one of ten saved color settings
Tools	Rename, copy, or delete a color setting
Help	Color customization help
Return	Return to Main menu

Establishing the color scheme for your Paradox environment is completely different in 3.5 than in 3.0. For one thing, you do it all on one screen now. With every setting shown on one screen, you simply move your cursor to the area of Paradox you want to set colors for, press [Enter] to invoke the color palette and select foreground and background colors. Selecting {Do-It!} from the menu or pressing [F2] saves the data. This is a big improvement over the 3.0 color setting process.

The {PAL} menu choice has one new option. {CalcDebug} lets you set the default on how to handle errors in expressions. The error message window can be turned off and you can specify the characters that are to be displayed as the value of the expression.

Command-Line Override Options

Many of the defaults specified in the configuration file set with the Custom Configuration Program (CCP) have overrides that can be used when starting Paradox. These change the default for the current session only, they do not affect the configuration file. The options are listed and explained in Table 5-6.

One or more of these overrides can be used when you start Paradox. For example, to start the system in protected mode and turn the SQL option off, you would enter *paradox -prot -sql off* at the system prompt. The commands are not case sensitive. Each additional option you include is separated by a space. When there is an argument required for the option, it also requires a space before the argument.

Table 5-6
Command-line override options

Option	Example	Description
-b&w	c:\>paradox -b&w	Tells Paradox to use a monochrome monitor with color adapter.
-cachek *n*	c:\>paradox -cachek 128	Sets the size of cache in K, this example sets it to 128K.
-color	c:\>paradox -color	Use a color monitor with CGA, EGA, or VGA adapter.
-emk *n*	c:\>paradox -emk 512	Specifies the amount of expanded memory Paradox can use.
-extk *n*	c:\>paradox -extk 1024	Used when machines have extended memory that cannot run in protected mode to create a swap device.
-mono	c:\>paradox -mono	Tells Paradox to use a monochrome monitor with a monochrome adapter.
-net *path*	c:\>paradox -net g:\netfile\	Changes the location of PARADOX.NET from the setting in PARADOX.SOM. Note: the ending backslash is required.
-prot	c:\>paradox -prot	Runs Paradox in protected mode if the machine is 286 or higher with at least 1MB of memory.
-real	c:\>paradox -real	Runs Paradox in real mode.
-share	c:\>paradox -share	Lets you share files on a standalone machine as if you were on a network. This is necessary if you run Paradox in Windows or DESQView. It is also required if you are using a non-dedicated server.
-snow	c:\>paradox -snow	Eliminates the interference when an IBM Color/Graphics Adapter is used.

Table 5-6—continued

Option	Example	Description
-sql on/off	c:\>paradox -sql off	If SQL Link is installed, this is used to enable or disable SQL connectivity. It is only necessary to turn SQL off because the default is always on.
-stack *n*	c:\>paradox -stack 48	This increases the amount of stack space available to your PAL programs. The default is 8K in real mode and 8K or 16K for protected mode, depending on the amount of memory. The maximum value is 64K.
-tablek *n*	c:\>paradox -tablek 48	This sets the minimum allocation for table buffers.
-username *name*	c:\>pardox -username mary	This sets the user name for the current session.

The Personal Programmer

There are no major changes to the Personal Programmer (PPROG) outside of VROOMM, which should improve performance. Network and SQL applications cannot be built using the Personal Programmer. There is now one limitation for network users. If you previously configured your machine to run the Personal Programmer from the network, you no longer can do this. You cannot run PPROG from a network drive or access any data located on your network drives. This limitation requires that you install PPROG locally and copy the data and Paradox objects you need for your PPROG applications to your local machine to create the application. Maybe in a future release this will be corrected.

Compatibility with Previous Releases

In general, Paradox 3.5 is completely compatible with previous versions. Applications created in earlier versions will run in 3.5. One of the first changes you'll notice is how to start 3.5:

c:\>paradox

Any batch file or menu system that starts Paradox must be changed accordingly. There are some other changes that you should be aware of:

- Default table block size has changed. You'll get better performance if you restructure your tables in 3.5. If these tables are to be used in an earlier version as well, they'll require more memory when they're placed on the workspace. (Up to 2K for each table and index might be necessary.)
- Libraries from previous versions can be read by 3.5, but previous versions cannot read 3.5 libraries. You cannot write from Paradox 3.5 to a library created in an earlier version. This is the same situation Paradox users had when upgrading from 2.0 to 3.0.
- Procedure sizes are smaller in 3.5 than in earlier versions. This is not a problem, but your memory utilization is potentially less as you nest procedures.
- Forms and reports created in 3.5 that use functions and variables might work in previous releases, although you can't rely on this.
- There are minor changes to error and informational messages, mostly in spelling. Any tests in your applications for specific text in the message window might have to be changed.
- Field values generated with Changeto queries or PAL statements in 3.01a or earlier versions potentially have a numerical accuracy problem. This requires that you scrub for it to work properly in 3.5. To convert to 3.5's method of determining accuracy, export and import that data or write a PAL script to re-enter the data to correct this problem.

SQL Link

Paradox SQL Link works transparently with Paradox 3.5 to connect Paradox to multiple SQL database servers. At the same time, it doesn't require you to know SQL. You still create and execute queries using QBE. When you tell Paradox to execute a query, it converts it into the proper SQL dialect for the server you're connected to and transmits the SQL statements. The data satisfying your request is returned. Just as in regular Paradox, the result is stored in an Answer table. You cannot perform all Paradox operations on SQL database servers, but you can perform the following (in addition to querying):

- Create, delete, and empty tables
- Design forms and reports (on a single table only)
- Add data using {*Tools*}{*More*}{*Add*}
- Copy a table to or from the database server
- Perform data entry to a single table
- Embed SQL statements in a PAL program

In addition, full security is available at the Paradox level and the database server level. Transaction commit and rollback is implemented. A new menu choice {*SQL*} (from the {*Tools*} menu) provides interactive access to these features. Many new PAL commands and functions provide the same functionality as the menu choices, along with other SQL capabilities needed in programs.

An in-depth discussion of SQL Link can be found in Chapter 13 of this book.

Multi-Pack and User Counts

The Paradox Multi-Pack replaces the Paradox Lan Pack. It provides the same functionality but spans the spectrum of all Paradox products and versions. Each copy of Paradox 3.5 and SQL Link includes a license for one user to access data. A Multi-Pack increases the number of licenses by 5. It provides additional user counts for Paradox 2.0, 3.0, 3.5, and SQL Link.

> **NOTE:** *Paradox Lan Pack's serial numbers are not upwardly compatible. They will not increase the user counts for Paradox 3.5 or SQL Link.*

In a network environment, each license lets an additional user access centralized data. You can mix and match packages to come up with the user count you need in specific situations. Connecting to a SQL database server with SQL Link requires an extra user count. (For each user on the network who is connected to a SQL database server, two user counts are used.) There isn't a distinction between Paradox and SQL Link user counts—they can be used in any combination.

Product Line

The list of Paradox products changes with the release of 3.5. The performance benefits and hardware utilization of Paradox 386 is rolled into Paradox 3.5. If you have a 386 machine and are a user of Paradox 386, you now have full access to the 3.0 feature set. If you are a user of Paradox OS/2 there are no changes (it remains at the 2.0 feature set). The Paradox Lan Pack has been replaced by the Multi-Pack. The new Paradox family of products is:

- Paradox 3.0
- Paradox 3.5
- Paradox SQL Link
- Paradox Multi-Pack
- Paradox OS/2
- Paradox Engine

Summary

At first glance, you might not think the 3.5 upgrade is as major as going from 2.0 to 3.0. The impact of the changes on paper may seem minimal, but this is misleading. Functions and variables in forms and reports substantially expands your output formatting options. Interaction with Quattro Pro 2.0 expands visual presentation of your data and also provides fast access to a spreadsheet. VROOMM and TurboDrive greatly impact performance and application size for users of 286, 386, or 486 machines. SQL Link opens the door to additional data and transaction-oriented applications.

Paradox 3.5—immediate database power and more!

6 Data Integrity

Data integrity is a feature of database management that is much talked about, often misunderstood, and essential. This chapter shows how to ensure data integrity with built-in Paradox features. However, these features alone are not enough to ensure complete integrity and must be augmented to give the appropriate validation for specific situations. In this chapter, you'll see time-saving techniques for setting ValCheck options, traps to avoid to prevent invalid data from being entered, and ways to avoid losing or corrupting data.

Two code examples are used in this chapter to demonstrate how data integrity is handled. The first example shows the problem of relying solely on built-in validation features. The second code example enhances the first program example to provide complete data integrity checking. In both cases, a three-table data entry process is employed.

Data Integrity: What is it?

Data integrity refers to the accuracy or validity of the data in the database. This applies to data entry, data modification, and deletion of data. Table 6-1 lists the major data integrity types and how they are enforced in Paradox.

Entity integrity is one element that defines a relational database. Every table in the database has a key, and every row in the table is unique, based on the key. Paradox enforces uniqueness when a key is defined for the table. Even though Paradox does not require that a table be defined with a key, it is recommended that you create a key for each table so you can take advantage of additional benefits of keyed tables.

Table 6-1
Integrity types and how they are enforced in Paradox

Integrity Type	How Enforced
Entity	Paradox (via primary key)
Referential	Multitable forms and PAL (primary and foreign keys)
Concurrency	Paradox, PAL
Domain	ValChecks and PAL
Data types	Paradox
Business rules	PAL
Format	ValChecks and PAL

REMEMBER: *Benefits of keyed tables in Paradox are:*

- *Prevent duplicate records based on key values*
- *Improve performance when searching on first field in the key by using the primary index*
- *Display data in sorted order based on key value*
- *Required for multitable forms and reports*
- *Support secondary indexes that are incrementally maintained*

Referential integrity refers to the relationship between the primary key and the foreign keys. Whenever there is a foreign key in a table, it must match the primary key of a record in the table it references. Paradox supports this type of integrity through multitable forms by using keys (see Figure 6-1). This means that only the primary key/foreign key relationships defined via keyed tables are maintained automatically. If a foreign key is not part of the defined primary key for a table, as shown in Figure 6-2, PAL coding is required to enforce the integrity unless a table lookup can be used.

Data Integrity **105**

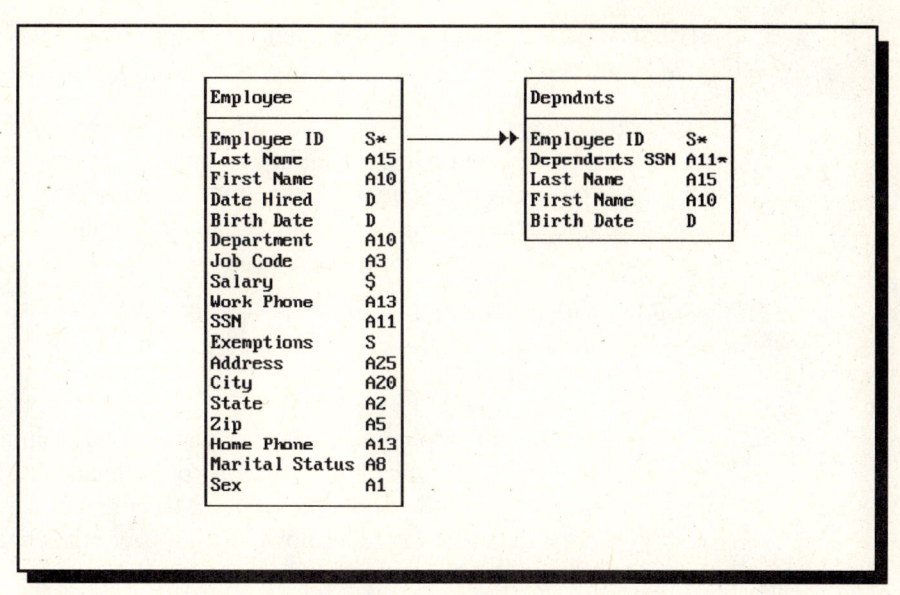

```
┌─────────────────────────────────────────────────────────────┐
│  ┌──────────────────────┐      ┌──────────────────────┐     │
│  │ Employee             │      │ Depndnts             │     │
│  ├──────────────────────┤      ├──────────────────────┤     │
│  │ Employee ID    S*    │─────▶▶│ Employee ID    S*    │     │
│  │ Last Name      A15   │      │ Dependents SSN A11*  │     │
│  │ First Name     A10   │      │ Last Name      A15   │     │
│  │ Date Hired     D     │      │ First Name     A10   │     │
│  │ Birth Date     D     │      │ Birth Date     D     │     │
│  │ Department     A10   │      └──────────────────────┘     │
│  │ Job Code       A3    │                                   │
│  │ Salary         $     │                                   │
│  │ Work Phone     A13   │                                   │
│  │ SSN            A11   │                                   │
│  │ Exemptions     S     │                                   │
│  │ Address        A25   │                                   │
│  │ City           A20   │                                   │
│  │ State          A2    │                                   │
│  │ Zip            A5    │                                   │
│  │ Home Phone     A13   │                                   │
│  │ Marital Status A8    │                                   │
│  │ Sex            A1    │                                   │
│  └──────────────────────┘                                   │
└─────────────────────────────────────────────────────────────┘
```

Figure 6-1 Primary key/foreign key relationship maintained via multitable form

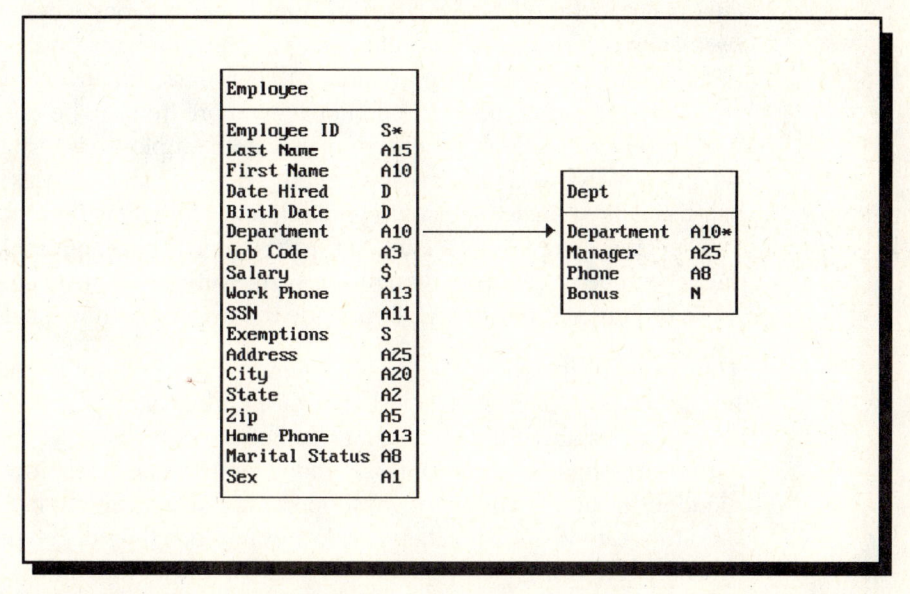

```
┌─────────────────────────────────────────────────────────────┐
│  ┌──────────────────────┐                                   │
│  │ Employee             │                                   │
│  ├──────────────────────┤                                   │
│  │ Employee ID    S*    │                                   │
│  │ Last Name      A15   │                                   │
│  │ First Name     A10   │                                   │
│  │ Date Hired     D     │      ┌──────────────────────┐     │
│  │ Birth Date     D     │      │ Dept                 │     │
│  │ Department     A10   │─────▶├──────────────────────┤     │
│  │ Job Code       A3    │      │ Department     A10*  │     │
│  │ Salary         $     │      │ Manager        A25   │     │
│  │ Work Phone     A13   │      │ Phone          A8    │     │
│  │ SSN            A11   │      │ Bonus          N     │     │
│  │ Exemptions     S     │      └──────────────────────┘     │
│  │ Address        A25   │                                   │
│  │ City           A20   │                                   │
│  │ State          A2    │                                   │
│  │ Zip            A5    │                                   │
│  │ Home Phone     A13   │                                   │
│  │ Marital Status A8    │                                   │
│  │ Sex            A1    │                                   │
│  └──────────────────────┘                                   │
└─────────────────────────────────────────────────────────────┘
```

Figure 6-2 Primary key/foreign key relationship maintained via TableLookup

REMEMBER: *TableLookup can only be used for keyed tables with one field in the key.*

Concurrency integrity is applicable in a multi-user environment where locking is required to prevent data loss. Paradox supports both implicit and explicit resource locking. Each menu choice implicitly places the level of lock appropriate for the task being performed. In an application, you must place locks to ensure access or prevent others from changing the state of the table.

Specifications that define the range of acceptable values for a field are called *domain integrity rules*. Domains are handled using Picture and TableLookup ValChecks along with PAL.

A *data type* is a specific implementation of domains. Each column in a table has one and only one data type, and it is enforced automatically by Paradox. For example, a date field only contains dates, and a currency column only contains numeric data. Paradox does not allow improper data to be input based on the data type assigned at table creation.

Every application and company has unique validation of data that requires checks not included in any of the previous integrity types. These are called *business rules*. For example, your bank's application has a business rule that says you cannot withdraw more money than is currently in your account. A receiving dock application should not allow more items to be rejected than were received. In a personnel system, when an employee is terminated, the records are archived rather than deleted. These are all examples of business rules. Any time an action can trigger additional activity within the database, or a specific value is entered into a record that prevents another field or value from being entered, then business rule integrity is invoked. All of these require you to use PAL to provide the necessary functionality.

The last integrity type in the list is *format*. While this is not found in most integrity type listings, it is included as a reminder that certain validation requirements necessitate that values conform to a format that does not fit within a reasonable list of values. Paradox Picture ValCheck provides tremendous flexibility and power to support data formatting. In fact, it can be used to create your own data types. For example, a time data type is not available but, using Pictures, you can create a format that only will allow valid time values to be entered. This picture clause is shown later in this chapter in the Master Picture table (see Table 6-9).

ValChecks: An Overview

Paradox ValChecks provide support for some of the integrity types already discussed. As data is entered into a field, Paradox automatically monitors the data entered and applies the ValCheck defined for each field. ValChecks can be defined in DataEntry or Edit mode only.

ValCheck options are:

- LowValue   Minimum value
- HighValue   Maximum value
- Default   Value entered if field left blank
- TableLookup   Values exist in another table
- Picture   Values conform to certain format or list of values
- Required   Value required in field

Why ValChecks Alone are Not Enough

Data validation should be applied at the field, record, table, and database level to ensure the entire system is complete and accurate. ValChecks are applied only at the field level, and only if the cursor is moved into the field. This means a ValCheck will not be tested if the user never moves into the field. This is a problem for fields with Default and Required ValChecks established. Both of these types of validations always need to be applied. Unless the cursor is moved to each field by the user, it is possible that some fields will not have the appropriate values. In addition, ValChecks do not support conditional validation between fields.

ValChecks are applied only during three modes that modify data in a table: DataEntry, Edit, and CoEdit. A table modified by Add, FormAdd, MultiAdd, an Insert or Changeto query, and Import cannot employ ValChecks.

This means that integrity checking at the record, table, and database level is not directly supported and field-level validation support is conditional (applied only if the cursor is moved into the field).

The solution to these problems is to augment ValChecks with PAL programming. With PAL, you can ensure that data is entered for required fields, values are placed in default fields, and conditional validation between fields is checked. Five tables from the Personnel database (three as entry tables and two used for lookups) are used in the following sections to show how to enforce data validation during data entry. Figure 6-3 shows the tables.

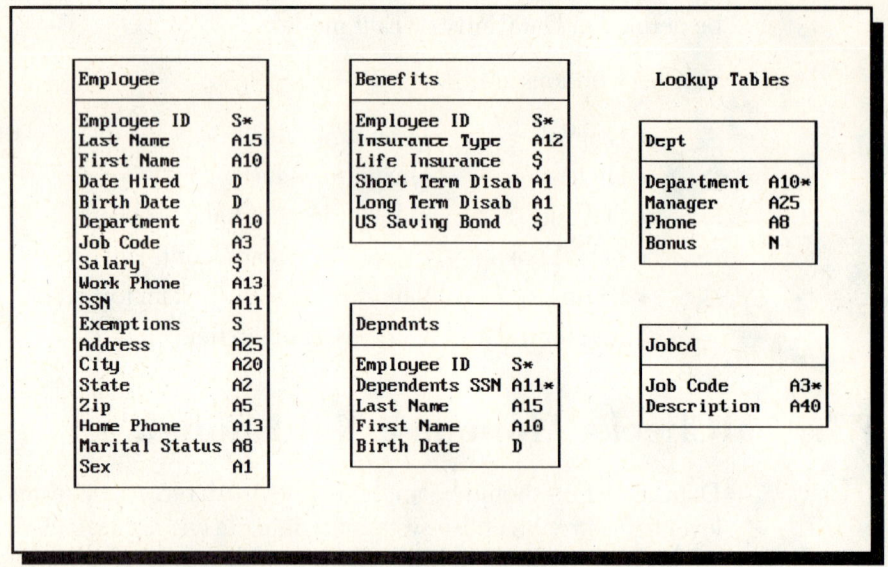

```
Employee                        Benefits                       Lookup Tables

Employee ID      S*             Employee ID      S*
Last Name        A15            Insurance Type   A12           Dept
First Name       A10            Life Insurance   $
Date Hired       D              Short Term Disab A1            Department    A10*
Birth Date       D              Long Term Disab  A1            Manager       A25
Department       A10            US Saving Bond   $             Phone         A8
Job Code         A3                                            Bonus         N
Salary           $
Work Phone       A13
SSN              A11            Depndnts
Exemptions       S
Address          A25            Employee ID      S*            Jobcd
City             A20            Dependents SSN   A11*
State            A2             Last Name        A15           Job Code      A3*
Zip              A5             First Name       A10           Description   A40
Home Phone       A13            Birth Date       D
Marital Status   A8
Sex              A1
```

Figure 6-3 Personnel database tables used for integrity validation program examples

Validation Requirements For Employee, Benefits, and Depndnts Tables

Defining the validation requirements for an application is part of the application life cycle (discussed in Chapter 2). To demonstrate data validation, the Employee, Benefits, and Depndnts tables in the Personnel application will be used in data entry mode. Validation requirements for each table are discussed, along with the methods Paradox uses to enforce them.

The structure of the Employee table is shown in Figure 6-4, and the validation requirements for this table are listed in Table 6-2. [Employee ID] is the unique identifier for each employee record. It must also be a sequential number. By establishing it as the key when the table is defined, Paradox can maintain its uniqueness. PAL is used to provide the sequential numbering.

This process also removes the burden from the user of inputting the key value. If the application assigns the key value, you don't have to check for key violations.

```
Viewing Struct table: Record 1 of 17                    Main
STRUCT         Field Name          Field Type
  1      Employee ID               S*
  2      Last Name                 A15
  3      First Name                A10
  4      Date Hired                D
  5      Birth Date                D
  6      Department                A10
  7      Job Code                  A3
  8      Salary                    $
  9      SSN                       A11
 10      Exemptions                S
 11      Address                   A25
 12      City                      A20
 13      State                     A2
 14      Zip                       A5
 15      Home Phone                A13
 16      Marital Status            A8
 17      Sex                       A1
```

Figure 6-4 Employee table structure

Two foreign keys exist in the Employee table. The [Department] field is a foreign key to the Dept table and [Job Code] is a foreign key to the Jobcd table. Both of these integrity types are handled using TableLookup ValChecks.

Both [Date Hired] and [Exemptions] are defined to have a default value. In each case, a Default ValCheck is defined and a PAL supplement is used. The Default ValCheck enters the value in the field if the user places the cursor on the field but does not enter anything, and the PAL process ensures the default value is entered even if the cursor is never moved into the field.

LowValue and HighValue ValChecks are used to restrict the [Salary] range between 18000 and 98000. Any time an entry falls outside this range, Paradox displays an error message indicating the valid range.

Table 6-2
Validation requirements for Employee table

Field Validation	Type	How Enforced
Unique sequential Employee ID uppercase	Entity	Primary key, PAL
First and Last Name initial	Format	ValCheck - Picture
Date Hired defaults to Today	Format	ValCheck - Default, PAL
Date Hired 16 years after Birth Date	Business Rule	PAL
Department in Dept table	Foreign Key	ValCheck - TableLookup
Job Code in Jobcd table	Foreign Key	ValCheck - TableLookup
Salary between 18000 and 98000	Domain	ValCheck - LowValue, HighValue
Automatic dash in SSN	Format	ValCheck - Picture
Exemptions defaults to 0	Domain	ValCheck - Default, PAL
Address and City uppercase	Format	ValCheck - Picture
State uppercase	Format	ValCheck - Picture
Zip digits only	Format	ValCheck - Picture
Home Phone and Work Phone digits only, area code optional	Format	ValCheck - Picture
Marital Status Single, Married, Divorced, or Widow	Domain	ValCheck - Picture
Sex = M or F	Domain	ValCheck - Picture

[Marital Status] and [Sex] fields both restrict the possible values using Picture clauses. The [Sex] field must be either M or F, while [Marital Status] must be either Single, Married, Divorced, or Widow.

The remaining fields need only special formatting. They all vary, but each format is handled by a Picture ValCheck. [Address] and [City] are converted to uppercase. [State] allows only two letters and is converted to uppercase. To further ensure correct data in the [State] field, a State Lookup table is required (this table is not included in this example). [Zip Code] is restricted to digits only. Both [Work Phone] and [Home Phone] include area code as an option. [SSN] is formatted to include the dashes. [First Name] and [Last Name] convert the first character to uppercase.

NOTE: *This is a problem when [Caps Lock] is activated. There is no ValCheck Picture option to convert to lowercase, and therefore it is possible that the user could input all uppercase letters. The only way to guarantee initial caps is to format the data before saving it, using the FORMAT function.*

TRAP: *Relying on the user to format uppercase and lowercase values could cause problems later in the application, especially in data selection. Because Paradox is case sensitive, queries return only those records that exactly match the selection criteria unless you use partial field searching. This type of query (using partial field searching) does not utilize keys or indexes and is much slower. Therefore, it is best to explicitly control the case of values as much as possible.*

Conditional validation is required to ensure that [Hire Date] is sixteen years after [Birth Date]. This is handled by PAL, because there isn't a ValCheck option is available to support this type of integrity check.

In addition to these validation requirements, certain fields require mandatory entry before the record can be saved. Review the list in Table 6-3. Notice that the enforcement of the required validation is through PAL coding instead of through a Required ValCheck. Performing the validation in this manner increases lines of code but prevents traps that are caused using Required ValCheck.

TRAP: *A Required ValCheck of "Yes" forces a value to be entered into the field before the cursor is moved off the field or any special key command is executed. This is a major trap and prevents customized help, canceling the data entry session, or any other special processing defined by pressing specific key combinations.*

Validation for the Benefits table is described in one word—defaults. [Employee ID] validation is automatically controlled by the multitable form. Each of the remaining fields in the table (see Figure 6-5) has a default value if none is entered. (Actually, even if the user never places the cursor in the table, a record needs to be entered with the default values. Both ValCheck Default and PAL code are used to ensure values in this instance, as described in Table 6-4.)

Table 6-3
Required fields for Employee table

Required Fields	How Enforced
Employee ID	PAL
First and Last Name	PAL
Date Hired	Implied via default
Birth Date	PAL
Salary	PAL
SSN	PAL
Department	PAL
Job Code	PAL
Work Phone	PAL

▽ **TRAP:** *Placing a Default ValCheck on all fields in a detail table in a one-one relationship with a master table prevents the detail and master record from being deleted within a multitable form. Paradox will always place a value in a field when the cursor moves off the field. Moving from a detail table to the master table would produce the same result. This creates a record in the detail table and, as long as a detail record exists, Paradox does not allow the master record to be deleted.*

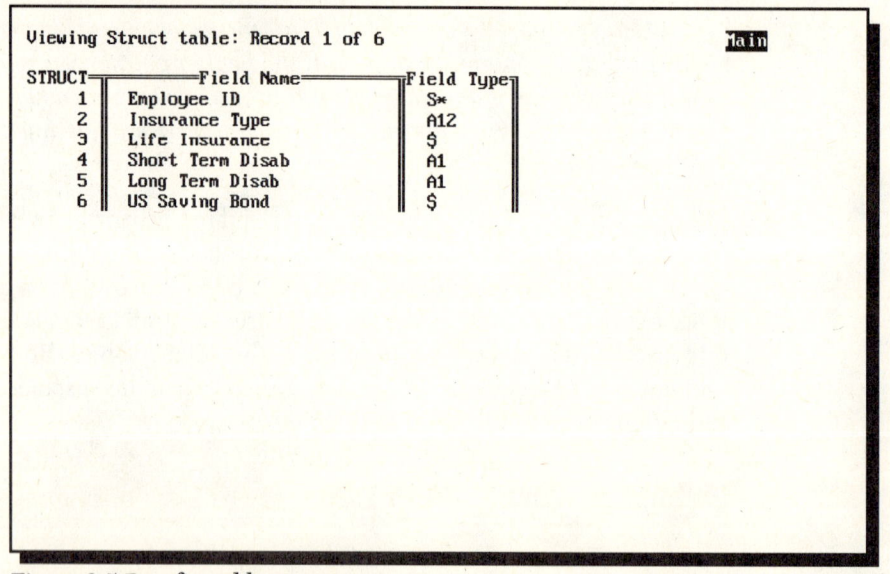

```
Viewing Struct table: Record 1 of 6                    Main
STRUCT┌─────────Field Name─────────┬─Field Type─┐
      1 ║    Employee ID           ║    S*
      2 ║    Insurance Type        ║    A12
      3 ║    Life Insurance        ║    $
      4 ║    Short Term Disab      ║    A1
      5 ║    Long Term Disab       ║    A1
      6 ║    US Saving Bond        ║    $
```

Figure 6-5 Benefits table structure

Table 6-4
Validation requirements for Benefits table

Field Validation	Type	How Enforced
Employee ID in Employee	Referential	Multitable Forms
Insurance Type defaults Aetna and must be Aetna, King County, or Group Health	Domain	ValCheck - Picture and Default, PAL
Life Insurance defaults to 0 or must be 50000,100000, 150000,200000,250000	Domain	ValCheck - Picture and Default, PAL
Short and Long Term Disab Y or N, default N	Domain	ValCheck - Picture and Default, PAL
Saving Bond defaults to 0 or must be 25,50,100,150,250,500	Domain	ValCheck - Picture and Default, PAL

Since each field will have a value entered even if the user doesn't enter anything, it is implied that every field is required, (as shown in Table 6-5). The [Employee ID] field is automatically entered by the multitable form.

Table 6-5
Required fields for Benefits table

Required Fields	How Enforced
Employee ID	Multitable Form
Insurance Type	Implied via defaults
Life Insurance	Implied via defaults
Short Term Disab	Implied via defaults
Long Term Disab	Implied via defaults
Saving Bond	Implied via defaults

The Depndnts table, like the Benefits table, has few validation requirements. The [Employee ID] field is automatically validated by the multitable form. Formatting for [First Name], [Last Name], and [SSN] is handled by a Picture format. As noted with the [First Name] and [Last Name] fields in Employee, the Picture clause cannot force lowercase (the same considerations are applied here). Validation requirements and the table structure for Depndnts are shown in Figure 6-6 and Tables 6-6 and 6-7.

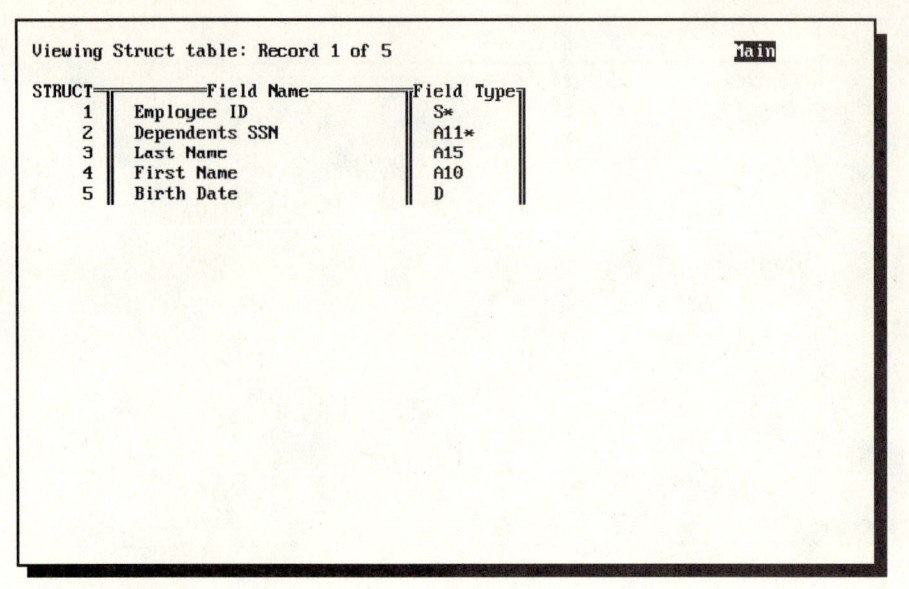

```
Viewing Struct table: Record 1 of 5                              Main
STRUCT┌─────────Field Name─────────┬─Field Type─┐
    1 ║ Employee ID                ║ S*
    2 ║ Dependents SSN             ║ A11*
    3 ║ Last Name                  ║ A15
    4 ║ First Name                 ║ A10
    5 ║ Birth Date                 ║ D
```

Figure 6-6 Depndnts table structure

Table 6-6
Validation requirements for depndnts table

Field Validation	Type	How Enforced
Employee ID in Employee	Referential	Multitable Forms
Automatic dash in SSN	Format	ValCheck - Picture
Uppercase 1st letter in First and Last Name	Format	ValCheck - Picture

Table 6-7
Required fields for depndnts table

Required Fields	How Enforced
Employee ID	Multitable
SSN	PAL
First and Last Name	PAL

Data Integrity   **115**

Entering ValChecks

Modifying a table in DataEntry, Edit, or CoEdit mode enables Paradox to automatically verify the data against the ValChecks created for the table. To define ValChecks, Paradox needs to be in DataEntry or Edit mode. If you have only one table to define the ValChecks on, either mode will work. If you're defining ValChecks for multiple tables, don't use DataEntry mode because only one table is available in tabular view. (A multitable form can be selected allowing access to a maximum of nine tables, but the forms have to be created first.) In Edit mode you can easily define ValChecks for as many tables as memory allows. By placing each table on the workspace (using View) and then changing to Edit mode ([F9]), you can define ValChecks for all your tables at the same time.

> *TRAP: There is no checking between ValChecks to ensure that one ValCheck does not invalidate another. Watch out for:*
>
> - *LowValue greater than HighValue and vice versa*
> - *Picture format outside range set by LowValue and HighValue*
> - *Picture format requiring more characters than defined for the field (for example, ###### for an A5 field)*
> - *TableLookup and a Picture format that conflict with each other*

Picture ValChecks are a very powerful option. While it could be said it is the one area of Paradox that closely resembles hieroglyphics, once you master the symbol logic, Picture ValChecks greatly enhance the usability of the system. Table 6-8 lists the pattern elements for defining a Picture format. Combining these elements provides the formatting and validation options to:

- Perform data validation
- Define your own data type
- Reduce keystrokes to enter values
- Automatically format entered values

> *TRICK: Use Paradox context-sensitive help to list the format symbols if you cannot remember them when defining a Picture format.*

**Table 6-8
Picture format symbols**

Picture Symbol	Description
#	Accept digits only
?	Accept upper- or lowercase letters
&	Accept only a letter and convert to uppercase
@	Accept any character
!	Accept any character and convert to uppercase
;	Use the next character in the format literally
*	Repetition counter
[ ]	Contents are optional
{ }	Grouping
,	Alternative value separator

Master Picture Table

A technique that assists in mastering the use of Picture elements is a Master Picture table. Creating a Paradox table that contains picture formats and using them each time they are needed eliminates the need to remember or recreate a format. Figure 6-7 shows the structure for the table and Table 6-9 lists commonly used formats.

To make the Master Picture table useful when defining Picture formats, place it on the workspace along with the tables you will be using to define ValChecks. You should also write two keyboard macros, described in Figure 6-8. In line 5, [Alt][P] is set to play the ALTP.SC script, which is a macro used to assign a Picture to a field in a table. Line 9 sets [Alt][M] to play ALTM.SC, which places a new entry in the Master Picture table.

Data Integrity   **117**

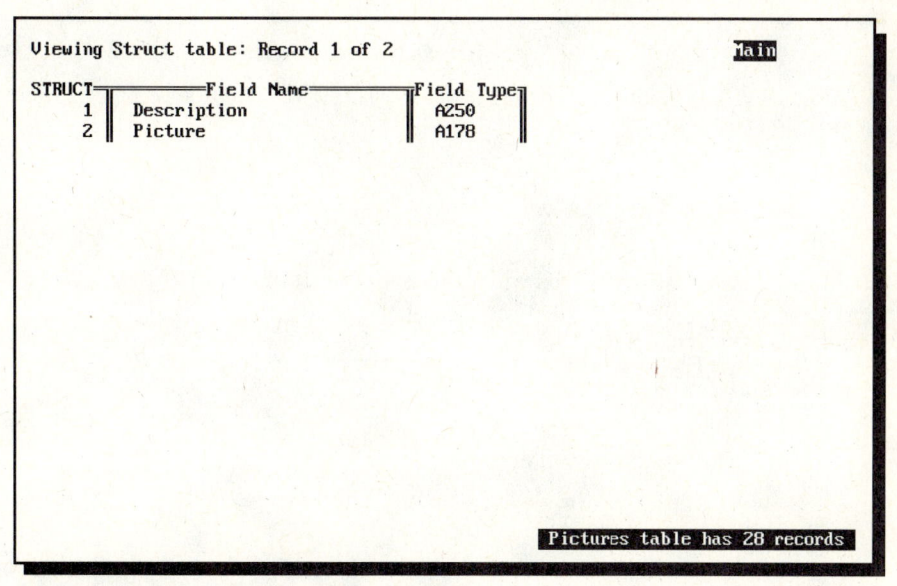

```
Viewing Struct table: Record 1 of 2                          Main
STRUCT      Field Name              Field Type
   1    Description                    A250
   2    Picture                        A178




                                            Pictures table has 28 records
```

Figure 6-7 Structure of Master Picture table

Table 6-9
Master Picture Table

Description	Picture
SSN with automatic fill-in of dashes	###-##-####
SSN with fill-in of dashes using space bar or dash	###{-}##{-}####
All characters uppercase	°!
Allow letters only, spaces not allowed	°?
Allow letters only and capitalize the first character	&°?
Allow letters only and capitalize all of them	°&
Capitalize the first letter of the field	!°@
Capitalize the first letter of every word, Example I	°[![°?][°]]
Capitalize the first letter of every word, Example II	!°[° !,@]
Capitalize the first letter of every word, Example III	°{ ,.}!°{{ ,.}°{ ,.}!,@}
Capitalize the first letter of every word after a period, comma, blank, or parentheses	!°[[,.,(,;,}°{ ,.,(,;,}!,@]
Simulate a Time data type with format of HH:MM:SS	{0#,1#,2{0,1,2,3}}:{0,1,2,3,4,5}#:{0,1,2,3,4,5}#

Table 6-9—continued

Description	Picture
Simulate a Time data type with format of HH:MM and :SS optional	{0#,1#,2{0,1,2,3}}:{0,1,2,3,4,5}#[:{0,1,2,3,4,5}#]
Description	*Picture*
Simulate a Time data type with format of HH:MMAM or HH:MMPM	{1{:,{0,1,2}:},{2,3,4,5,6,7,8,9}:}{0,1,2,3,4,5}#{AM,PM}
Phone Number, seven digits with automatic fill-in of dashes	###-####
Phone Number, seven digits with automatic fill-in of dashes and area code optional	[(###)]###-####
Phone Number, seven digits with automatic fill-in of dashes and area code, 1-800 optional	[{1-800-,(###)}]###-####
Date, allow only 01 for the day and have it filled in automatically	{##/01/##,#/01/##}
Date, allow only 01 for the day and have it filled in automatically. If year not entered, have year from system date entered, Example I	{##/01/[##],#/01[##]}
Date, allow only 01 for the day and have it filled in automatically and if year not entered, have year from system date entered, Example II	{1{/01/,{0,1,2}/01/},{2,3,4,5,6,7,8,9}/01/}}[##]
State codes	&&
ZIP Code	#####
ZIP Code with optional dash and 4 digits	#####[-####]
ZIP Code with optional dash and 4 digits, allows for Canadian & British postal codes	#####[-####],&#&#&#
3-letter month abbreviation	Feb,Sep,Oct,Nov,Dec,J{an,u{n,1}},Ma{r,y},A{pr,ug}
Marital status options	{Married,Single,Divorced,Widow}

```
1) ; Setkey.sc
2)
3) ; [Alt][P] - Insert Picture into current table
4)
5) SETKEY -25 PLAY "Altp"
6)
7) ; [Alt][M] - Insert Picture into Master Picture table
8)
9) SETKEY -50 PLAY "Altm"
```

Figure 6-8 Macros used for Master Picture table

Figure 6-9 lists the contents of ALTP.SC. Let's walk through how it works. Line 1 brings up the menu. It is assumed the system mode is Edit; therefore, line 4 will bring up the ValCheck menu and select the Picture option. To reduce the size of the macro, no error checking is performed. (If this macro is played in a mode other than Edit or DataEntry, a script error will occur.) The last line assigns the contents of the Picture field in the Pictures table to the Picture format. Using the SELECT command, if a Picture format already exists, it is overwritten with the new format and [Enter] is simulated to successfully define the Picture format.

```
1) ; Altp.sc
2)
3) MENU
4) {ValCheck} {Define} Enter {Picture}
5) SELECT [Pictures->Picture]
```

Figure 6-9 Macro for setting Picture format for current field

The script to place a new definition in the Master Picture table is shown in Figure 6-10. Here, ALTM.SC looks at the Picture format for the current field in line 3. Using the MENUCHOICE function, the text defining the format is placed in the variable *vchk*. Line 5 presses the Menu ([F10]) and [Esc] keys to cancel the change and put the cursor back in the current field on the workspace. Line 6 moves the cursor to the Pictures table and the next line opens up a new record at the end of the table. The contents of *vchk* is placed in the Pictures field in line 8, and line 9 moves the cursor to the Description field for entry of an explanation of the new format.

```
1) ; Altm.sc
2)
3) MENU {ValCheck} {Define} Enter {Picture}
4) vchk = MENUCHOICE()
5) MENU Esc
6) MOVETO "Pictures"
7) END DOWN
8) [Picture] = vchk
9) MOVETO [Description]
```

Figure 6-10 Macro for adding new Picture format to Master Picture table

Let's look at how these macros are used while defining ValChecks. After placing the tables on the workspace and putting the system in Edit mode, move the cursor to the record containing the desired Picture format. Now move to the field in each table the Picture is to be assigned, and press [Alt][P]. A new Picture format is defined for the current field. Let's walk through an example to put a Picture format in the [First Name] and [Last Name] fields for both the Employee and Depndnts table and the [SSN] field in both tables. The steps are:

1. Play the SETKEY script which defines [Alt][P] and [Alt][M] (if they have not already been set).
2. View Employee, Benefits, Depndnts, and Picture tables.
3. Press [F9] for Edit mode.
4. Move to the ninth record in the Picture table (this positions the cursor for the Picture format). The workspace looks as shown in Figure 6-11.
5. Move to the First Name field in Depndnts and press [Alt][P] (this assigns the Picture format !*[* !,@] to First Name).
6. Repeat step 5 for Last Name, and both First and Last Name in Employee.
7. Move to the Picture table and place the cursor in the record for the SSN format (record 1).

Data Integrity **121**

8. Move to the Dependent's SSN field in the Depndnts table and press [Alt][P]. The Picture format is set to ###-##-####.
9. Move to the SSN field in Employee and press [Alt][P].

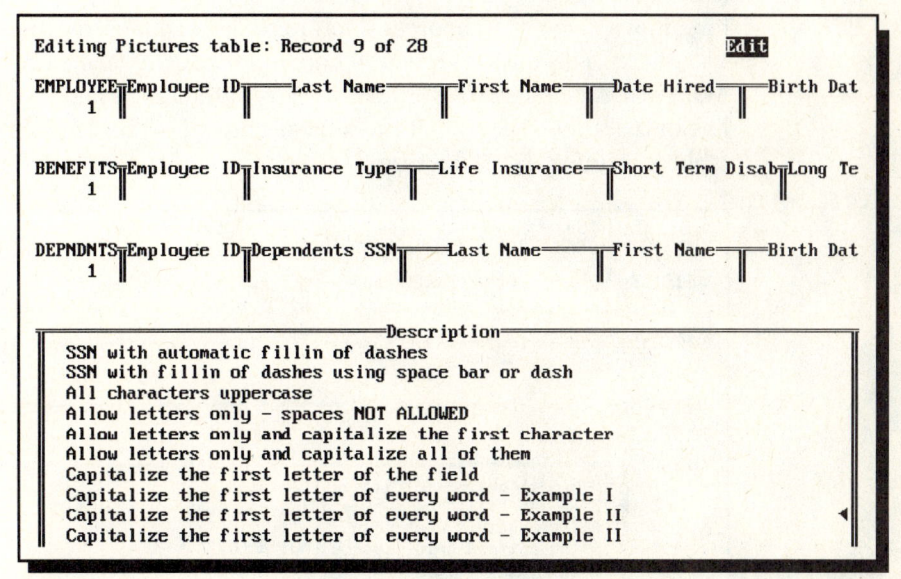

```
Editing Pictures table: Record 9 of 28                           Edit
EMPLOYEE─Employee ID────Last Name────────First Name────Date Hired────Birth Dat
      1

BENEFITS─Employee ID─Insurance Type───Life Insurance──Short Term Disab─Long Te
      1

DEPNDNTS─Employee ID─Dependents SSN────Last Name──────First Name───Birth Dat
      1
                          ┌─Description─────────────────────────────┐
                          │ SSN with automatic fillin of dashes      │
                          │ SSN with fillin of dashes using space bar or dash │
                          │ All characters uppercase                 │
                          │ Allow letters only - spaces NOT ALLOWED  │
                          │ Allow letters only and capitalize the first character │
                          │ Allow letters only and capitalize all of them │
                          │ Capitalize the first letter of the field │
                          │ Capitalize the first letter of every word - Example I │
                          │ Capitalize the first letter of every word - Example II │
                          │ Capitalize the first letter of every word - Example II │
                          └──────────────────────────────────────────┘
```

Figure 6-11 Workspace after selecting tables and positioning cursor in Pictures table

If a Picture format that you want to use is not in the Master Picture table but already exists in another field, use [Alt][M] to add it to the Master Picture table. Let's say the format for phone numbers with optional area code is not in the table and you want to add it. The steps to follow are:

1. Move to either the Work Phone or the Home Phone field in the Employee table.
2. Bring up the Picture option
   Menu [F10] {ValCheck} {Define} {Picture}
3. Type **[(###)]###-####** and press [Enter].
4. Test to see if it works. This is crucial. Always make sure it works before you add it to the Master Picture table.
5. Press [Alt][M] to add the format to Pictures.
6. Enter a description for the new format.

Before saving Picture formats or any other ValChecks, you need to take care of one crucial task. While you've been defining formats, establishing defaults, and testing, you've been adding records to the tables. If you press [F2] or choose Do_It! from the menu, these test records are saved. Therefore, move to each table, press [Del] to remove all records, then save the ValChecks. This ensures the tables are empty. A simple check, once back in Main mode, is to move the cursor to each of the tables and see if the first line of the screen shows that the table is empty (see Figure 6-12). The only table containing data is Pictures.

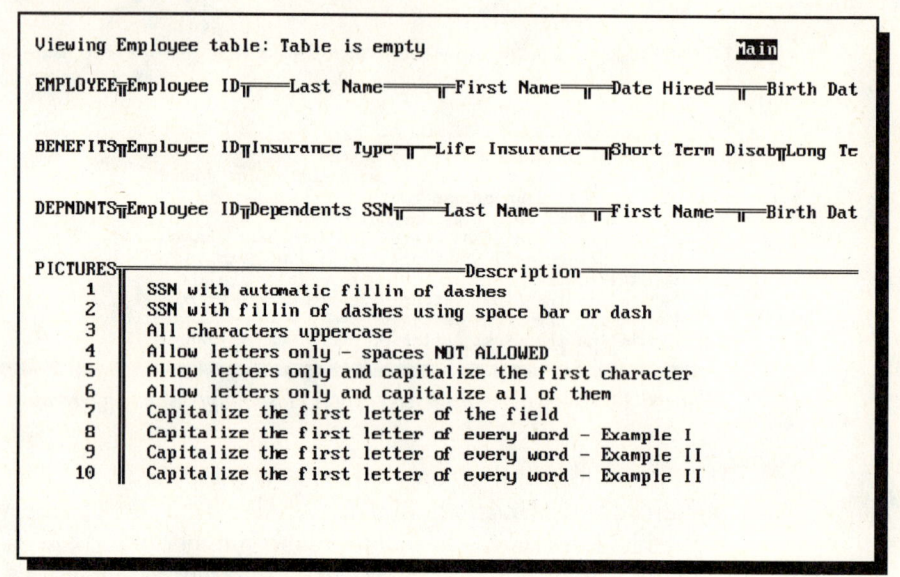

```
Viewing Employee table: Table is empty                                    Main
EMPLOYEE╥Employee ID╥══Last Name══════╥═First Name══╥══Date Hired══╥══Birth Dat

BENEFITS╥Employee ID╥Insurance Type╥══Life Insurance══╥Short Term Disab╥Long Te

DEPNDNTS╥Employee ID╥Dependents SSN╥══Last Name══════╥═First Name══╥══Birth Dat

PICTURES┬──────────────────────────────Description──────────────────────────
       1  │ SSN with automatic fillin of dashes
       2  │ SSN with fillin of dashes using space bar or dash
       3  │ All characters uppercase
       4  │ Allow letters only - spaces NOT ALLOWED
       5  │ Allow letters only and capitalize the first character
       6  │ Allow letters only and capitalize all of them
       7  │ Capitalize the first letter of the field
       8  │ Capitalize the first letter of every word - Example I
       9  │ Capitalize the first letter of every word - Example II
      10  │ Capitalize the first letter of every word - Example II
```

Figure 6-12 Workspace after saving ValChecks

Basic Multitable Data Entry Code Example

Let's take a look at ENTRDATA.SC in Listing 6-1. This script provides data entry capability in a multitable form and relies on ValChecks alone to provide data integrity. Lines 1 through 6 clear the PAL canvas, display a message in the message window, and turn the canvas off. This technique is used to place Paradox-style messages on the canvas while processing occurs on the workspace so the user doesn't see the background activity. The message remains on the screen until the canvas is turned on with CANVAS ON.

```
 1)   ; EntrData
 2)
 3)   CLEAR
 4)   CURSOR OFF                                    ;  Place informational message
 5)   MESSAGE "Loading form, Please wait"           ; on the screen while form is
 6)   CANVAS OFF                                    ; loading
 7)   IF ISEMPTY("Employee") THEN                   ;  If the table is empty, set
 8)     empid = 1001                                ; the id counter to 1001
 9)   ELSE                                          ; otherwise calculate the max
10)     empid = CMAX("Employee","Employee ID") + 1  ; id in the table and add 1.
11)   ENDIF                                         ; This is used to set Employee
12)   MENU {Modify} {DataEntry} {Employee}          ; ID.
13)   {Image} {Pickform} {1}
14)   [Employee ID] = empid
15)   empid = empid + 1
16)   CANVAS ON                                     ;  Need to turn canvas on!
17)   WHILE True
18)     WAIT RECORD
19)       PROMPT "Enter New Employee Information [F2]-Save/Exit [Esc]-Cancel",
20)              "[F3]-Employee Data    [F4]-Benefits Data    " +
21)              "[F5]-Dependents Data"
22)       UNTIL "F2","F3","F4","F5","Esc","PgDn","PgUp","End","Home"
23)     tblname = TABLE()
24)     SWITCH
25)       CASE retval = "F2" :
26)           CLEAR
27)           MESSAGE "Saving data, Please wait"
28)           CANVAS OFF
29)           DO_IT!                                ;  NOTE: need to check for
30)           QUITLOOP                              ;  key violations in Depndnts
31)       CASE retval = "F3" : MOVETO "Entry" LOOP   ;  Moveto Employee Table
32)       CASE retval = "F4" : MOVETO "Entry1" LOOP  ;  Moveto Benefits Table
33)       CASE retval = "F5" : MOVETO "Entry2" LOOP  ;  Moveto Depndnts Table
34)       CASE retval = "Esc" :
35)           SHOWMENU
36)             "No"  : "Return to Data Entry",
37)             "Yes" : "Cancel data entry"
38)           TO canceloption
39)           IF canceloption = "Yes" THEN
40)             CLEAR
41)             MESSAGE "Data Entry cancelled"
42)             CANVAS OFF
43)             CANCELEDIT
44)             QUITLOOP
45)           ENDIF
46)       CASE retval = "PgDn" :
47)           SWITCH
48)             CASE tblname = "Entry" :
49)                 PgDn                            ;  Moveto next Employee rcd
50)                 IF ISBLANK([Employee ID]) THEN  If this is a new record
```

Listing 6-1 Basic multitable data entry script

```
51)                    [Employee ID] = empid     ; set the Employee ID
52)                    empid = empid + 1
53)                 ENDIF
54)              CASE tblname = "Entry1" :        ; Only 1 record allowed for
55)                 BEEP LOOP                     ; Benefits table
56)              CASE tblname = "Entry2" :        ; Moveto next record in
57)                 DOWN CtrlHome                 ; Depndnts table
58)              ENDSWITCH
59)              LOOP
60)           CASE retval = "PgUp" :
61)              IF ATFIRST() THEN
62)                 BEEP
63)                 LOOP
64)              ENDIF
65)              IF tblname = "Entry1" THEN       ; Only 1 record allowed for
66)                 BEEP                          ; Benefits table
67)              ELSE                             ; For Employee and Depndnts
68)                 SKIP -1                       ; move to the previous
69)              ENDIF                            ; record
70)              LOOP
71)           OTHERWISE:
72)              KEYPRESS retval
73)           ENDSWITCH
74)     ENDWHILE
75)     CLEARALL
```

Listing 6-1 Basic multitable data entry script—continued

Sequential numbering initialization is handled in lines 7 through 11. The variable *empid* is used to contain the value of the next ID to be assigned. If the Employee table is empty, *empid* is set to 1001. If data exists in the table, *empid* is set to the maximum value of [Employee ID] plus one.

Selecting the Employee table and Form 1 are performed in the next two lines of code. Before the form is presented with the first record for input, the value for [Employee ID] is assigned, and *empid* is incremented by one for use by the next record added. CANVAS ON, line 16, is a must to show the form in the WAIT command. This is necessary because of the CANVAS OFF on line 6.

Data Integrity **125**

The major portion of code is between lines 17 and 76. A WHILE loop controls user interaction with the tables. A separate function key is defined to move to each of the three tables, [F3] for the Employee table, [F4] for the Benefits table, and [F5] for the Depndnts table. This provides the capability to move from the current table to any other table for the current employee record. This adds flexibility to the user interface. [PgDn] and [PgUp] are used to move between records, [F2] commits the data, [Esc] cancels the data entry session, [Home] takes you to the top of the table, and [End] takes you to the bottom of the table. WAIT RECORD is used to provide control at the record level, allowing the unique employee ID to be assigned. The PROMPT parameter of the WAIT command does not provide enough room to display all the potential keystrokes, so the top line of the form is used for additional information (see Figure 6-13).

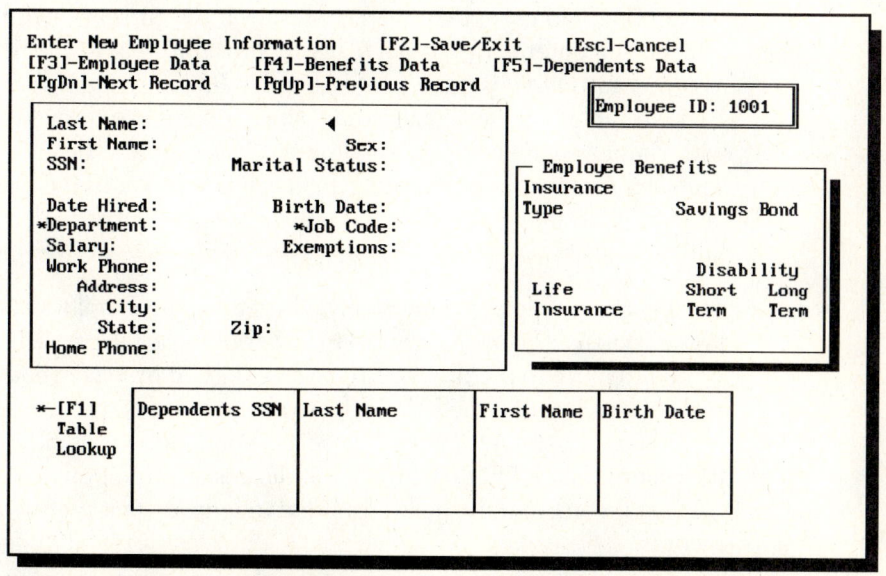

```
Enter New Employee Information    [F2]-Save/Exit    [Esc]-Cancel
[F3]-Employee Data    [F4]-Benefits Data    [F5]-Dependents Data
[PgDn]-Next Record    [PgUp]-Previous Record
                                             ┌─────────────────────┐
                                             │ Employee ID: 1001   │
  Last Name:              ◄
  First Name:         Sex:
  SSN:       Marital Status:
                                      ┌─ Employee Benefits ─────────┐
                                      │ Insurance                   │
  Date Hired:    Birth Date:          │ Type           Savings Bond │
 *Department:     *Job Code:          │                             │
  Salary:        Exemptions:          │                  Disability │
  Work Phone:                         │ Life           Short   Long │
      Address:                        │ Insurance      Term    Term │
         City:
        State:   Zip:
   Home Phone:

  *-[F1]     Dependents SSN  Last Name     First Name  Birth Date
   Table
   Lookup
```

Figure 6-13 Data Entry form for Employee, Benefits, and Depndnts Tables

The SWITCH command processes the keystroke used to exit the WAIT command. Notice lines 31, 32, and 33. Testing for the current table requires the comparison to Entry, Entry1, and Entry2. In data entry, input is not directly entered into the master tables. Paradox uses temporary tables to hold the data until it is committed.

The entire data entry session is cancelled by pressing the [Esc] key. Lines 34 through 45 process the [Esc] keypress. SHOWMENU is used to display a menu asking for confirmation and, if Yes is selected, the process is cancelled. This follows the Paradox implementation to ensure that the user wants the action taken when data loss is a possibility.

Moving between records is only applicable in the Employee and Depndnts tables. In Employee, the previous employee entered is displayed for [PgUp], and [PgDn] displays either a blank input screen allowing for a new employee record or the next employee record entered. Moving to a blank record requires the next [Employee ID] to automatically be entered before user interaction with the form. The SWITCH statement starting on line 47 first checks for the current table. If the current table is Entry (the Employee table), [PgDn] is executed to move to the next record. Checking the [Employee ID] field using ISBLANK indicates if the current record already has information entered or if it is a blank record. If it's blank, the next ID is assigned and *empid* is incremented by one. Pressing [PgDn] while in the Benefits table is an invalid keystroke since it has a one-to-one relationship with Employee. Since only a single Benefits record can be entered, BEEP sounds the system bell indicating an illegal keystroke. In the Depndnts table, [PgDn] moves to the next employee dependent record as handled in line 57.

Moving to a previous record is only allowed for the Employee and Depndnts tables. When a [PgUp] is pressed in either of these tables, SKIP -1 is executed to move to the previous record. A [PgUp] pressed while in the Benefits table will sound the bell. If the current record is the first in the table or restricted view, Paradox knows there are no more records and remains on the record. The ATFIRST function indicates an attempt to move beyond the first record, and the bell is sounded to indicate that there are no more records.

The OTHERWISE portion of the SWITCH command handles any valid keystrokes that are not explicitly resolved by a CASE command. The only two keystrokes not listed in the UNTIL clause are [End] and [Home]. If either of these two keys is pressed, the cursor is moved to the top or bottom of the table. For the Employee table, this moves the cursor to the first record entered or the last record entered during this data entry session. If in the Depndnts table, the cursor is moved to the first or last record for the current employee record. No movement is required when in the Benefits table because there is only one record.

Running the Basic Multitable Data Entry Program

Playing ENTRDATA.SC displays the multitable data entry form shown in Figure 6-13. [Employee ID] is automatically set to 1001 because the Employee table is empty. Pressing [PgDn] moves to the next record where the [Employee ID] is 1002. No data is entered in the first record. All data validation has been bypassed because the cursor is not moved into any of the fields under ValCheck control.

There is also another problem—pressing [Ctrl][O] or [Alt][O] displays the screen shown in Figure 6-14. The user is now in DOS. Major problems can occur if the user is not familiar with the feature in Paradox that suspends to the operating system. If "exit" is not entered to return to Paradox, all data input will be lost.

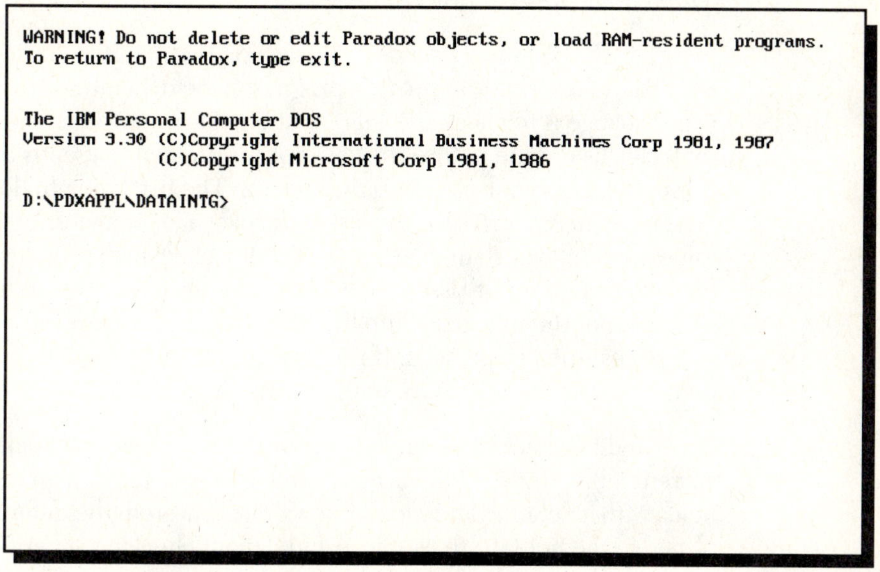

```
WARNING! Do not delete or edit Paradox objects, or load RAM-resident programs.
To return to Paradox, type exit.

The IBM Personal Computer DOS
Version 3.30 (C)Copyright International Business Machines Corp 1981, 1987
             (C)Copyright Microsoft Corp 1981, 1986

D:\PDXAPPL\DATAINTG>
```

Figure 6-14 Result of a [Ctrl][O] or [Alt][O]

▽ **TRAP**: *Be aware of the following options that should be checked for in a WAIT command:*

1. *[Ctrl][O] and [Alt][O] from WAIT TABLE, RECORD, and FIELD.*
2. *ZOOM or [Ctrl][Z]—a user can press [Ctrl][O] or [Alt][O] at the Zoom prompt and suspend to operating system. You need to include this command in UNTIL and explicitly control the ZOOM command and keystroke.*

Modifications to Script to Ensure Data Integrity

The basic data entry script shown earlier (Listing 6-2) proves that ValChecks alone cannot be relied upon to ensure the integrity of data. You have to provide the necessary checks that will guarantee the accuracy and completeness of the data entered. You also need to be aware of the built-in features of Paradox providing additional flexibility but also potential problems for users that are not familiar with their options. To do this, additional coding is required in the form of procedures.

Figure 6-15 shows in a pseudo-code fashion the modifications to the ENTRDATA script that provide programmatic data integrity checking. The major change is to check the validity of the data before moving from the record. This is done before the keystroke is pressed that ends the WAIT command. Let's look at lines 6 through 12. The first thing to do after the WAIT command is to save the last keystroke. This is necessary because the value of *retval* will change when the validity checking procedure is called. If the key pressed is not [Esc], execute the validity checking module. If there is an error, put the user back into the form, display an error message, and do not process the key pressed. If no errors are encountered, the keystroke is processed per the SWITCH statement.

The Validity Checking module is the nucleus of integrity checking. For the current table, required fields are tested to ensure they aren't empty. For fields with a default validation, if no value is entered, the default value is placed in the field. Both required and default checking is performed before conditional testing between fields is done. If the data has passed all of the above, True is returned to indicate that the data passes all the programmatic data validations. As soon as a field fails a test, further checking is halted, the error message is set, the cursor is moved to the field causing the error, and False is returned to prevent the key pressed by the user from being executed.

```
 1) Data Entry Module
 2) WHILE True
 3) WAIT RECORD
 4)   UNTIL acceptable key press list
 5)
 6) Save key pressed
 7) If key pressed not Esc then
 8)   perform Validity Checking Module (below)
 9)   If data does not pass validity checks then
10)     loop to WAIT command
11)   Else
12)     process key pressed
13)
14) ENDWHILE
15)
16)
17) Validity Checking Module
18)
19) For current table
20) Check required fields
21) Enter default values if fields empty
22) Check relational conditions between fields
23) If a test fails
24)   halt checking
25)   set message variable
26)   place cursor in field failing validation
26)   return False condition to indicate a test failed
27) Else
28)   return True to indicate ALL tests passed
```

Figure 6-15 Pseudo-code for programmatic data integrity checking

Enhanced Code for Field- and Record-Level Validation

Now that you have an overview of the processes used to ensure data integrity, let's look at how it is implemented. Six procedures are used, along with a start-up script and a script to create a library. Figure 6-16 shows the flow of processing after the library is created.

The first section of code is the main processing module. Listing 6-2 shows the complete script. It is the same as the basic data entry module discussed previously with the enhancements discussed next.

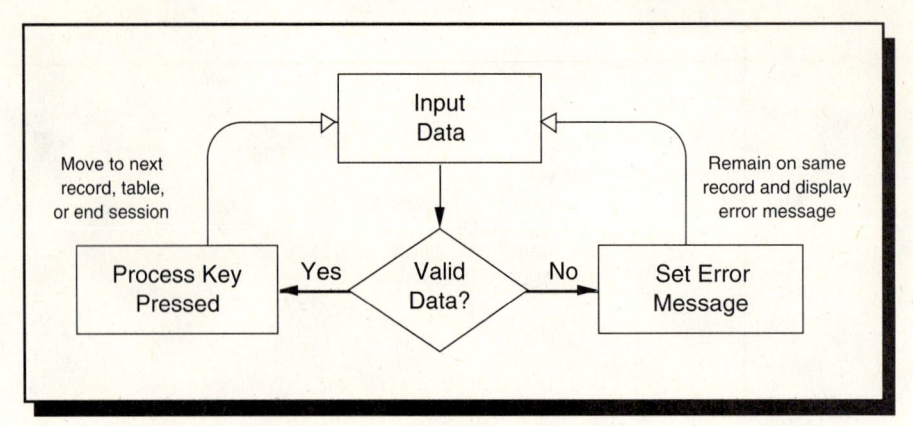

Figure 6-16 Processing flow for validation procedures

A global variable *msg* is used to hold any information or error message to be displayed on the screen. It is initialized in line 43. In the WHILE loop, *msg* is checked to see if it is not blank; if so, there is an error and the system bell is sounded (lines 46-48). SLEEP 100 between each BEEP pauses the system enough to give three distinct beeps, not one long beep.

```
46)   IF NOT ISBLANK(msg) THEN   ; If there is a message sound
47)         BEEP SLEEP 100 BEEP SLEEP 100 BEEP    ; the system bell
48)   ENDIF
```

The WAIT command includes two additions. Line 53 utilizes the MESSAGE parameter of the WAIT command to display an error message (when one exists). If *msg* is blank, no message is displayed. If a message is displayed, it remains onscreen until a key is pressed. (This is the same as in interactive Paradox.) The UNTIL parameter now traps for [Ctrl][O] and [Alt][O] to prevent suspending Paradox to DOS.

```
49)   WAIT RECORD
50)      PROMPT "Enter New Employee Information  [F2]-Save/Exit   [Esc]-Cancel",
51)            "[F3]-Employee Data    [F4]-Benefits Data       " +
52)            "[F5]-Dependents Data"
53)      MESSAGE msg
54)      UNTIL "F2","F3","F4","F5","Esc","PgDn","PgUp","End","Home", ; 15 - Ctrl O
55)            15,-24                                                ;-24 - Alt O
```

NOTE: *DOS and DOSBIG can be used in the UNTIL instead of 15 and -24 as in*

UNTIL "DOS","DOSBIG"

Data Integrity

The key pressed to end the WAIT command is saved in *retkey*. This is used instead of *retval* because calls to procedures set *retval* and the value of the key pressed would be lost. *Msg* is blanked to remove the last error message (if there was one).

```
56)     retkey = retval          ; Save the key pressed
57)     msg = ""                 ; Blank message variable
```

If any key in the UNTIL parameter other than [Esc] is pressed, the ValidityChecks procedure is called with the name of the current table. The return value is placed in *retprocval*.

REMEMBER: *Procedures should not be included in expressions that do not allow swapping. See Chapter 7, "Building Procedures and Libraries," for details.*

If an error occurred, data does not pass a validity check, the key pressed is not passed to the system, and processing loops to the beginning of the WHILE loop. If [Esc] was pressed, the code discussed earlier is executed.

```
59) IF retkey <> "Esc" THEN            ; If any key except Esc is
60)    retprocval = ValidityChecks(tblname)   ; pressed, check if data is
61)                                    ; valid.
62)    IF NOT retprocval THEN          ; If the proc returns False
63)       LOOP                         ; the data did not pass the
64)    ENDIF                           ; validation rule therefore do
65) ELSE                               ; not process the key pressed
66)    SHOWMENU
67)       "No"  : "Return to Data Entry",
68)       "Yes" : "Cancel data entry session"
69)    TO canceloption
70)    IF canceloption = "Yes" THEN
71)       CLEAR
72)       MESSAGE "Data Entry cancelled"
73)       CANVAS OFF
74)       CANCELEDIT
75)       QUITLOOP
76)    ENDIF
77)    LOOP
78) ENDIF
```

For each Employee record entered, a Benefits record needs to be entered even if the user never moves to the Benefits table. Because each field in the Benefits table has a default value, executing the programmatic validations ensures the default values are entered. This is required before moving off every employee record and saving the data. Lines 84-88 perform this requirement when [F2] is pressed. The same commands are executed for both [PgUp] and [PgDn] when in the Employee table.

```
84)    MOVETO "Entry1"
85)    retprocval = ValidityChecks("Entry1")
86)                                           ;  Ensure the default values
87)                                           ;  have been entered for
88)    MOVETO "Entry"                         ;  Benefits table.
```

The last section of code that changed is how [Ctrl][O] and [Alt][O] are handled. This is done with the OTHERWISE portion of the SWITCH command. If either of these keys is pressed, the system bell is sounded, the keystroke is ignored, and processing loops to the beginning of the WHILE loop. Trapping these two keystrokes in OTHERWISE forces a validation check before notifying the user they are illegal keystrokes. Explicit checking done earlier forces any other keystroke to always check for [Ctrl][O] and [Atl][O] first. This is not necessary, because the frequency of these two key combinations being pressed is minimal.

```
132)     OTHERWISE:
133)         IF retkey = 15 OR retkey = -24 THEN  ;  Beep is Alt or Ctrl O
134)            BEEP                              ;  is pressed
135)         ELSE
136)            KEYPRESS retkey
137)         ENDIF
138)  ENDSWITCH
```

In line 126, any other key listed in the UNTIL parameter that has not already been processed is passed to the system using the KEYPRESS command.

```
 1)  ; Enter2
 2)
 3)
 4)  ; *****************************************
 5)  ; *  Enter2 Procedure                     *
 6)  ; *****************************************
 7)  ;
 8)  ;  This script contains the procedure for entering data into a
 9)  ;  multitable form for the following three tables:
10)  ;      EMPLOYEE - Master table
11)  ;      BENEFITS - One-to-One relationship
12)  ;      DEPNDNTS - One-to-Many relationship
13)  ;  ValChecks are augmented with PAL to ensure the required fields are
14)  ;  entered, relational comparisons between fields are validated, and the
```

Listing 6-2 Enhanced multitable data entry driver script

```
15) ;    defaults are entered into a field if they are left blank. These
16) ;    checks are made before a user can move off the record.
17) ;       The following assumptions may require changes based on user needs:
18) ;           If the user does not move to the Benefits table the defaults are
19) ;           applied by calling the validation procedure for the table. If the
20) ;           cursor is never placed in the Depndnts table no validation is
21) ;           checked and the assumption is no data is to be entered.
22) ;           It should also be noted that in this code example, a user must
23) ;           enter data into a record once the data entry process has started
24) ;           unless the entire session is cancelled. An option can be added to
25) ;           this code to allow the user to cancel the entry for the entire
26) ;           session OR the current record.
27)
28) PROC Enter2()
29)    CLEAR
30)    CURSOR OFF                                   ;  Place informational message
31)    MESSAGE "Loading form, Please wait"          ; on the screen while form is
32)    CANVAS OFF                                   ; loading
33)    IF ISEMPTY("Employee") THEN                  ;  If the table is empty, set
34)       empid = 1001                              ; the id counter to 1001
35)    ELSE                                         ; otherwise calculate the max
36)      empid = CMAX("Employee","Employee ID") + 1 ; id in the table and add 1.
37)    ENDIF                                        ; This is used to set Employee
38)                                                 ; ID.
39)    MENU {Modify} {DataEntry} {Employee}
40)    {Image} {Pickform} {1}
41)    [Employee ID] = empid
42)    empid = empid + 1
43)    msg    = ""
44)    CANVAS ON                                    ; Need to turn canvas on!
45)    WHILE True
46)      IF NOT ISBLANK(msg) THEN                   ; If there is a message sound
47)        BEEP SLEEP 100 BEEP SLEEP 100 BEEP       ; the system bell
48)      ENDIF
49)      WAIT RECORD
50)        PROMPT "Enter New Employee Information   [F2]-Save/Exit   [Esc]-Cancel",
51)               "[F3]-Employee Data    [F4]-Benefits Data       " +
52)               "[F5]-Dependents Data"
53)        MESSAGE msg
54)        UNTIL "F2","F3","F4","F5","Esc","PgDn","PgUp","End","Home", ; 15 - Ctrl O
55)              15,-24                                                ;-24 - Alt O
56)      retkey = retval                            ; Save the key pressed
57)      msg = ""                                   ; Blank message variable
58)      tblname = TABLE()
59)      IF retkey <> "Esc" THEN                    ; If any key except Esc is
60)        retprocval = ValidityChecks(tblname)     ; pressed, check if data is
61)                                                 ; valid.
62)        IF NOT retprocval THEN                   ; If the proc returns False
63)          LOOP                                   ; the data did not pass the
64)        ENDIF                                    ; validation rule therefore do
65)      ELSE                                       ; not process the key pressed
66)        SHOWMENU
```

Listing 6-2 Enhanced multitable data entry driver script—continued

```
 67)              "No"  : "Return to Data Entry",
 68)              "Yes" : "Cancel data entry session"
 69)           TO canceloption
 70)           IF canceloption = "Yes" THEN
 71)             CLEAR
 72)             MESSAGE "Data Entry cancelled"
 73)             CANVAS OFF
 74)             CANCELEDIT
 75)             QUITLOOP
 76)           ENDIF
 77)         LOOP
 78)        ENDIF
 79)        SWITCH
 80)          CASE retkey = "F2" :
 81)             CLEAR
 82)             MESSAGE "Saving data, Please wait"
 83)             CANVAS OFF
 84)             MOVETO "Entry1"
 85)             retprocval = ValidityChecks("Entry1")
 86)                                         ;  Ensure the default values
 87)                                         ;  have been entered for
 88)             MOVETO "Entry"              ;  Benefits table.
 89)             DO_IT!                      ;   NOTE: need to check for
 90)             QUITLOOP                    ;  key violations in Depndnts
 91)          CASE retkey = "F3" : MOVETO "Entry"  LOOP ;  Moveto Employee Table
 92)          CASE retkey = "F4" : MOVETO "Entry1" LOOP ;  Moveto Benefits Table
 93)          CASE retkey = "F5" : MOVETO "Entry2" LOOP ;  Moveto Depndnts Table
 94)          CASE retkey = "PgDn" :
 95)             SWITCH
 96)               CASE tblname = "Entry" :
 97)                  MOVETO "Entry1"
 98)                  retprocval = ValidityChecks("Entry1")
 99)                                         ;  Ensure the default values
100)                                         ;  have been entered for
101)                  MOVETO "Entry"         ;  Benefits table.
102)                  PgDn                   ;   Moveto next Employee rcd
103)                  IF ISBLANK([Employee ID]) THEN ; If this is a new record
104)                     [Employee ID] = empid ; set the Employee ID
105)                     empid = empid + 1
106)                  ENDIF
107)               CASE tblname = "Entry1" :  ;  Only 1 record allowed for
108)                  BEEP LOOP               ;  Benefits table
109)               CASE tblname = "Entry2" :  ;   Moveto next record in
110)                  DOWN CtrlHome           ;  Depndnts table
111)             ENDSWITCH
112)          CASE retkey = "PgUp" :
113)             IF ATFIRST() THEN
114)                BEEP
115)                LOOP
116)             ENDIF
117)             SWITCH
118)               CASE tblname = "Entry" :
119)                  MOVETO "Entry1"
```

Listing 6-2 Enhanced multitable data entry driver script—continued

```
120)                     retprocval = ValidityChecks("Entry1")
121)                                           ;  Ensure the default values
122)                                           ;  have been entered for
123)                     MOVETO "Entry"        ;  Benefits table.
124)                     SKIP -1               ;   Moveto previous Employee
125)                                           ;  record.
126)              CASE tblname = "Entry1" :    ;   Only 1 record allowed for
127)                     BEEP LOOP             ;  Benefits table
128)              CASE tblname = "Entry2" :    ;   Moveto previous record in
129)                     SKIP -1               ;  Depndnts table
130)              ENDSWITCH
131)              LOOP
132)         OTHERWISE:
133)              IF retkey = 15 OR retkey = -24 THEN   ;  Beep is Alt or Ctrl O
134)                 BEEP                              ;  is pressed
135)              ELSE
136)                 KEYPRESS retkey
137)              ENDIF
138)       ENDSWITCH
139)     ENDWHILE
140)     CLEARALL
141)  ENDPROC
142)
143)  WRITELIB "Intgrty" Enter2
144)  RELEASE PROCS Enter2
```

Listing 6-2 Enhanced multitable data entry driver script—continued

The ValidityChecks procedure is the validity checking control program, shown in Listing 6-3. It calls the appropriate procedure based on the name of the current table. ValidityChecks requires one parameter, the name of a table. Based on the value of that parameter, the validation function is called for that table. If all validations are successful, *retprocval* will be assigned True; otherwise, it will be assigned False, indicating an error was encountered. In either case, the value returned from the function call is passed back to the calling procedure. Take special note of the values *tblname* is evaluated against in the CASE statements. The current process is a data entry session. Paradox always names the tables Entry, Entry1, and so on up to Entry9, based on the number of tables in the multitable form. In order for this procedure to work in both an entry and modification program, the CASE statement should be changed to include the appropriate Entry name and the actual table name.

CASE tblname = "Entry" OR tblname = "Employee" : ; Employee table

The OTHERWISE portion is included to catch situations where the procedure is called with an incorrect set of tables. In this code example, it is never executed.

Listing 6-4 lists the contents of RQDFLDS.SC. This script includes four procedures, a generic procedure for testing if a field is blank, and a separate procedure to test each table for data validation.

FldBlank is a generic procedure used to determine if the field passed as *fldnm* is blank. It is shown in lines 6-29 in Listing 6-4. The second parameter, *fldtxt*, is used as the name of the field in the error message if the field contains no value. An EXECUTE command creates a dynamic statement testing the contents of the field. If it is blank, the global variable *msg* is set to *fldtxt* plus "must be entered." and FldBlank returns True. For example, if the field being tested is [Last Name] and it is empty, *msg* equals "Last Name must be entered." FldBlank returns False if the field is not blank.

A separate procedure is created for each table's validity checks. All data validation not ensured by ValChecks is coded here. The basic process is:

1. Call FldBlank for each required field. Pass the name of the field and the text used on the form to identify the field.
2. Use ISBLANK for each field defined to have a default value. If it is blank, place the default value in the field.

```
1)   ; VldtyChk           Validity Checks script
2)
3)   ; Processes the validation required for the current table
4)
5)   PROC ValidityChecks(tblname)
6)     PRIVATE retprocval
7)
8)     SWITCH
9)       CASE tblname = "Entry" :            ; Employee table
10)          retprocval = RqdRulesEmp()
11)          RETURN retprocval
12)       CASE tblname = "Entry1" :           ; Benefits table
13)          retprocval = RqdRulesBenefits()
14)          RETURN retprocval
15)       CASE tblname = "Entry2" :           ; Depndnts table
16)          retprocval = RqdRulesDepndnts()
17)          RETURN retprocval
18)       OTHERWISE:
19)          msg = "Table not found, call programmer to fix"
20)          RETURN False
21)     ENDSWITCH
22)   ENDPROC
23)
24)   WRITELIB "Intgrty" ValidityChecks
25)   RELEASE PROCS ValidityChecks
```

Listing 6-3 *ValidityChecks procedure*

3. Process the conditional validation between fields. If an error occurs, halt checking, set error message, move to field considered in error, and return False to calling program.

> **NOTE:** *When two or more fields are compared, a decision is made at code creation time as to which field will most likely be in error, and the cursor is placed in that field. In this example, it is assumed [Birth Date] is entered correctly. Therefore [Hire Date] is considered in error.*

If all of these conditions are passed, no errors exist, and True is returned to calling procedure.

```
1)  ; RqdFlds.SC
2)
3)  ;  This script contains the procs used for the validation rules on each
4)  ;  table. A separate procedure is used for each table.
5)
6)  ; *****************************************
7)  ; * FldBlank Procedure                    *
8)  ; *****************************************
9)  ;
10) ; Procedure to test if the field passed as a parameter is blank. If the
11) ; field is blank the procedure returns True, otherwise False is returned.
12)
13) PROC FldBlank(fldnm,fldtxt)
14)   PRIVATE fldblnk
15)
16) ; fldnm   - Field name as defined in the table
17) ; fldtxt  - Text to be inserted into the global variable "msg" that is
18) ;           displayed to the user if the field is blank
19) ; fldblnk - Variable for the logical result of the ISBLANK function
20)
21)   EXECUTE "fldblnk = ISBLANK(["+fldnm+"])" ;  Create a PAL statement to
22)   IF fldblnk THEN                          ;  test if the field is blank. If it
23)     MOVETO FIELD fldnm                     ;  is empty, move to the field, set
24)     msg = fldtxt+" must be entered"        ;  the msg variable and return
25)     RETURN True
26)   ELSE
27)     RETURN False
28)   ENDIF
29) ENDPROC
30)
31) WRITELIB "Intgrty" FldBlank
32) RELEASE PROCS FldBlank
33)
34)
35) ; *****************************************
36) ; * RqdRulesEmp Procedure                 *
37) ; *****************************************
```

Listing 6-4 Contents of RqdFlds

```
38) ;
39) ;   Employee Table procedure that checks for the required fields,
40) ;   inserts default values if the field is left blank, and makes
41) ;   necessary comparison between fields in the table for valid entries.
42) ;   Tests are performed sequentially. At the first failure, the procedure
43) ;   returns False. A True is returned if all tests are passed. The order
44) ;   of the required fields is based on the order they appear on the form.
45)
46) PROC RqdRulesEmp()
47)   IF FldBlank("Last Name","Last Name") THEN      ; Required Last Name
48)     RETURN False
49)   ENDIF
50)   IF FldBlank("First Name","First Name") THEN    ; Required First Name
51)     RETURN False
52)   ENDIF
53)   IF FldBlank("SSN","SSN") THEN                  ; Required SSN
54)     RETURN False
55)   ENDIF
56)   IF FldBlank("Birth Date","Birth Date") THEN    ; Required Birth Date
57)     RETURN False
58)   ENDIF
59)   IF FldBlank("Department","Department") THEN    ; Required Department
60)     RETURN False
61)   ENDIF
62)   IF FldBlank("Job Code","Job Code") THEN        ; Required Job Code
63)     RETURN False
64)   ENDIF
65)   IF FldBlank("Salary","Salary") THEN            ; Required Salary
66)     RETURN False
67)   ENDIF
68)   IF FldBlank("Work Phone","Work Phone") THEN    ; Required Home Phone
69)     RETURN False
70)   ENDIF
71)   IF ISBLANK([Date Hired]) THEN                  ; Default Hire Date
72)     [Date Hired] = TODAY()
73)   ENDIF
74)   IF ISBLANK([Exemptions]) THEN                  ; Default Exemptions
75)     [Exemptions] = 0
76)   ENDIF
77)   IF [Date Hired] < [Birth Date] + (16 * 365) THEN ; Check if Date Hired
78)                                                  ; is 16 years after Birth Date
79)     msg = "Birth Date and Hire Date must be 16 years apart"
80)     MOVETO [Date Hired]
81)     RETURN False
82)   ENDIF
83)   RETURN True
84) ENDPROC
85)
86) WRITELIB "Intgrty" RqdRulesEmp
87) RELEASE PROCS RqdRulesEmp
88)
89)
90) ; *****************************************
```

Listing 6-4 Contents of RqdFlds—continued

```
 91) ;  * RqdRulesBenefits Procedure            *
 92) ;  *******************************************
 93) ;
 94) ;  Benefits Table procedure that inserts default values if the field is left
 95) ;  blank. Since each field has a default, there are no required fields.
 96)
 97) PROC RqdRulesBenefits()
 98)    IF ISBLANK([Insurance Type]) THEN         ; Default Insurance Type
 99)       [Insurance Type] = "Aetna"
100)    ENDIF
101)    IF ISBLANK([Life Insurance]) THEN         ; Default Life Insurance
102)       [Life Insurance] = 0
103)    ENDIF
104)    IF ISBLANK([Short Term Disab]) THEN       ; Default Short Term Disab
105)       [Short Term Disab] = "N"
106)    ENDIF
107)    IF ISBLANK([Long Term Disab]) THEN        ; Default Long Term Disab
108)       [Long Term Disab] = "N"
109)    ENDIF
110)    IF ISBLANK([US Saving Bond]) THEN         ; Default US Saving Bond
111)       [US Saving Bond] = 0
112)    ENDIF
113)    RETURN True
114) ENDPROC
115)
116) WRITELIB "Intgrty" RqdRulesBenefits
117) RELEASE PROCS RqdRulesBenefits
118)
119)
120) ;  *******************************************
121) ;  * RqdRulesDepndnts Procedure            *
122) ;  *******************************************
123) ;
124) ;  Benefits Table procedure that checks for the required fields. Tests
125) ;  are performed sequentially. At the first failure, the procedure
126) ;  returns False. A True is returned if all tests are passed. The order
127) ;  of the required fields is based on the order they appear on the form.
128)
129)
130) PROC RqdRulesDepndnts()
131)    IF FldBlank("Dependents SSN","Dependents SSN") THEN; Required Dependents SSN
132)       RETURN False
133)    ENDIF
134)    IF FldBlank("Last Name","Last Name") THEN       ; Required Last Name
135)       RETURN False
136)    ENDIF
137)    IF FldBlank("First Name","First Name") THEN     ; Required First Name
138)       RETURN False
139)    ENDIF
140)    RETURN True
141) ENDPROC
142)
143) WRITELIB "Intgrty" RqdRulesDepndnts
144) RELEASE PROCS RqdRulesDepndnts
```

Listing 6-4 Contents of RqdFlds—continued

A library is created for all of these procedures by playing MAKELIB.SC. Listing 6-5 lists the contents of the script. A message is displayed onscreen while the library is being created. The contents of the library are displayed by executing INFOLIB "Intgrty" in line 14. An informational message is displayed in the message window along with the contents of the library using the QUIT command.

```
 1)   ; Makelib
 2)   ;  This script creates the Data Integrity library
 3)
 4)
 5)   CURSOR OFF
 6)   CLEAR
 7)   MESSAGE "Creating Intgrty library, Please wait"
 8)   CANVAS OFF
 9)   CREATELIB "Intgrty"
10)   PLAY "Enter2"
11)   PLAY "Rqdflds"
12)   PLAY "Vldtychk"
13)   ; List the contents of the library
14)   INFOLIB "Intgrty"
15)   QUIT "Intgrty library created, contents listed above"
```

Listing 6-5 Script to create Intgrty library

Executing the Enhanced Integrity Checking Program

```
1)   ; Start-up
2)
3)   CLEAR
4)   CLEARALL
5)   autolib = "Intgrty"
6)   Enter2()
7)   RELEASE VARS ALL
```

Listing 6-6 Start-up script

Listing 6-6 lists the script to run the enhanced data entry process. After clearing the workspace and canvas, line 5 establishes INTGRTY as the library to use when a procedure is called. Initially, executing the enhanced

Data Integrity **141**

program looks exactly the same as running ENTRDATA.SC. The change is evident when you attempt to move off a record without completing the required entries or enter an unacceptable value. For example, pressing [PgDn] before entering any data now displays the message "Last Name must be entered" as shown in Figure 6-17. Before the enhancements, the next record would be displayed. A [PgDn] does not move to the next employee record until all validations have been satisfied. The same thing occurs for any keystroke that moves the cursor off the record (with the exception of [Esc], which cancels the session).

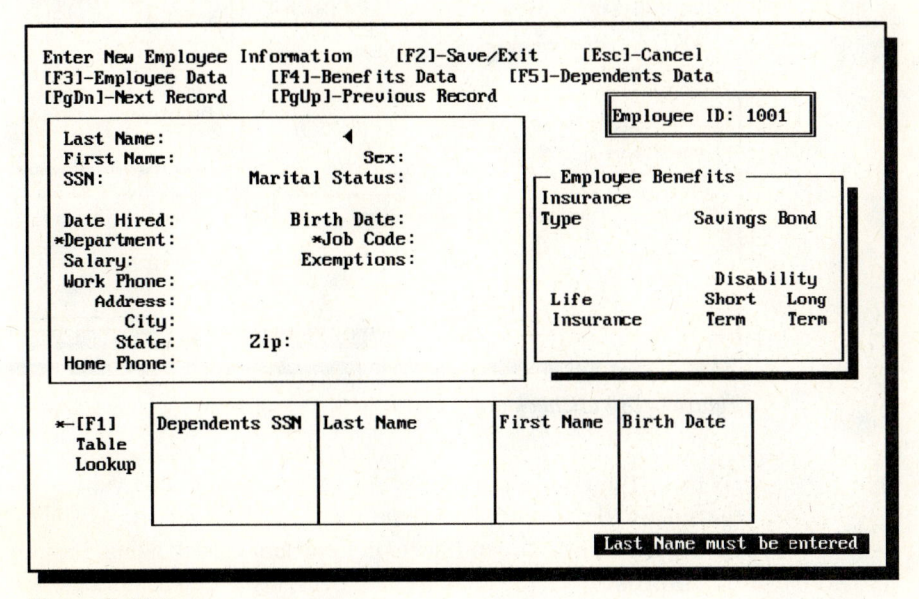

```
Enter New Employee Information    [F2]-Save/Exit    [Esc]-Cancel
[F3]-Employee Data    [F4]-Benefits Data    [F5]-Dependents Data
[PgDn]-Next Record    [PgUp]-Previous Record
                                                    Employee ID: 1001
  Last Name:              ◀
  First Name:              Sex:
       SSN:        Marital Status:         ┌─ Employee Benefits ──────┐
                                           │ Insurance                │
 Date Hired:           Birth Date:         │ Type         Savings Bond│
*Department:            *Job Code:         │                          │
     Salary:            Exemptions:        │                 Disability│
 Work Phone:                               │ Life         Short    Long│
    Address:                               │ Insurance    Term     Term│
       City:                               └──────────────────────────┘
      State:  Zip:
 Home Phone:

*─[F1]    Dependents SSN  Last Name    First Name  Birth Date
  Table
  Lookup


                                              Last Name must be entered
```

Figure 6-17 Custom error message

All ValChecks automatically display the appropriate error message without interaction from the program. Figure 6-18 shows the error message displayed when the value entered in [Salary] is outside the range set by LowValue and HighValue.

The one option that is visible to interactive users (but not while a program is running) is the message on the second line about performing a table lookup on a field. This is handled by placing an asterisk next to the fields supporting a table lookup and placing an information message on the form. Using a different foreground and background color than the form highlights this option. Another option is to change the prompt to indicate the current field has lookup help. Providing this option requires field-level movement and checking versus record-level checking. Another option along the same lines would be to use a global variable, place it on the form as an informational line, and set it at the appropriate time.

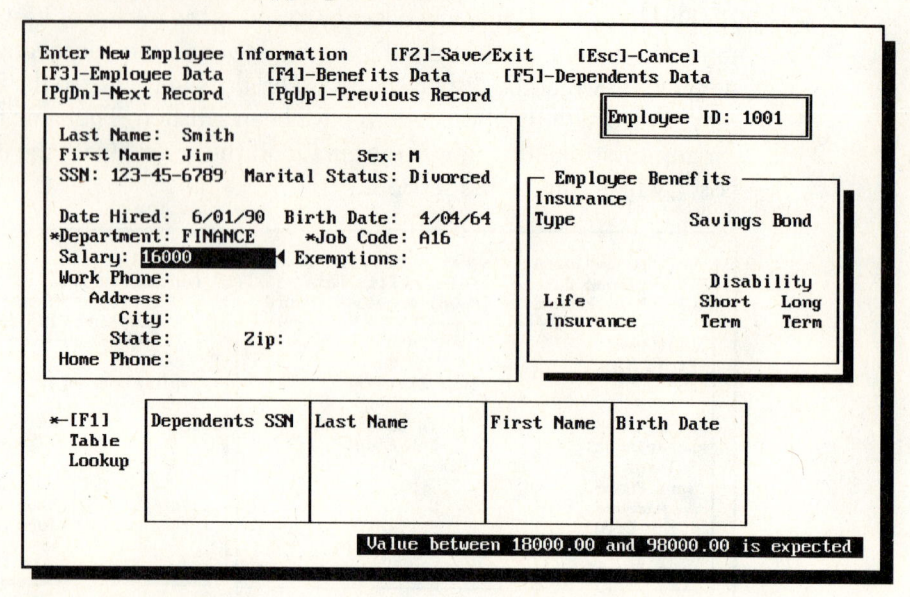

```
Enter New Employee Information    [F2]-Save/Exit    [Esc]-Cancel
[F3]-Employee Data    [F4]-Benefits Data    [F5]-Dependents Data
[PgDn]-Next Record    [PgUp]-Previous Record
                                                    ┌─────────────────┐
                                                    │Employee ID: 1001│
  Last Name: Smith                                  └─────────────────┘
  First Name: Jim              Sex: M
  SSN: 123-45-6789  Marital Status: Divorced   ┌─ Employee Benefits ──┐
                                               │ Insurance            │
  Date Hired:  6/01/90  Birth Date:  4/04/64   │ Type      Savings Bond│
  *Department: FINANCE   *Job Code: A16        │                      │
  Salary: 16000         ◄ Exemptions:          │            Disability│
   Work Phone:                                 │ Life      Short   Long│
      Address:                                 │ Insurance Term    Term│
         City:                                 └──────────────────────┘
        State:      Zip:
   Home Phone:

  *-[F1]  │Dependents SSN│Last Name│First Name│Birth Date│
   Table  │              │         │          │          │
   Lookup │              │         │          │          │
          │              │         │          │          │
                                   Value between 18000.00 and 98000.00 is expected
```

Figure 6-18 ValCheck error message

By using both ValChecks and PAL to limit acceptable values, check for required and default fields, and perform conditional processing between fields, you ensure the integrity of your data during a data entry or modification process.

ValCheck Visibility Reporting

Visibility of ValChecks defined for each field is part of the system documentation discussed in Chapter 2. Unfortunately, there is no built-in feature to provide viewing ValChecks except moving to each field during an Edit session, selecting the ValCheck menu choice, and manually viewing each ValCheck option. This is a time-consuming and tedious task.

There are three ways to get ValCheck. Third-party products are available that create the information for you. ParaLex is one product available that provides this capability (discussed in Chapter 20). The second solution is to

Data Integrity **143**

write your own. PAL provides the ability to write a ValCheck reporting program. The third solution is to use one of the freeware scripts that are available from a Paradox BBS or use the ValCheck Catalog Program included here.

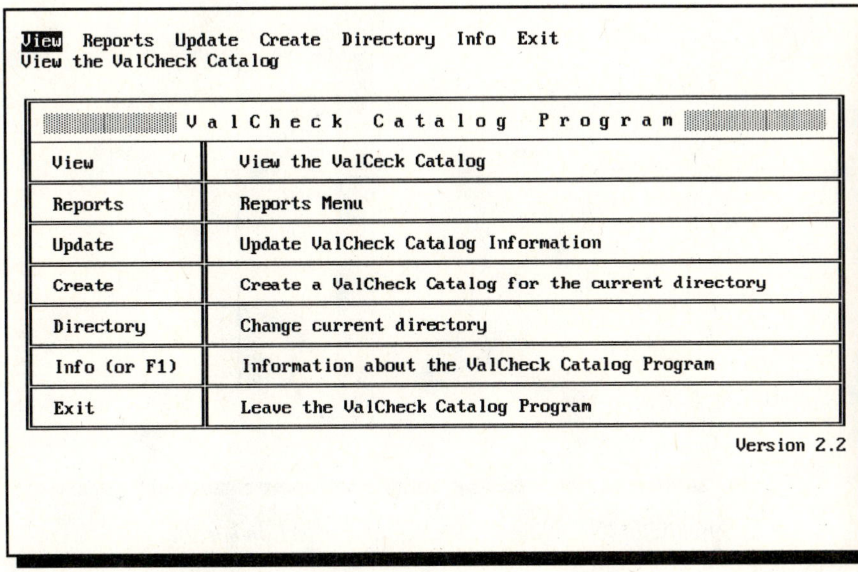

```
View  Reports  Update  Create  Directory  Info  Exit
View the ValCheck Catalog
```

ValCheck Catalog Program	
View	View the ValCeck Catalog
Reports	Reports Menu
Update	Update ValCheck Catalog Information
Create	Create a ValCheck Catalog for the current directory
Directory	Change current directory
Info (or F1)	Information about the ValCheck Catalog Program
Exit	Leave the ValCheck Catalog Program

Version 2.2

Figure 6-19 ValCheck Catalog Main menu

Figure 6-19 displays the ValCheck Catalog Main menu. Selecting Create starts the initialization process and creates a list of tables in the current directory. Each table to be included is selected using the form shown in Figure 6-20. After processing the data on each table, the results are viewed by ˡecting View from the Main menu. Figure 6-21 shows the display for the ᵉfits table. Multiple reports are available using the Reports menu
 ion.

chapter we looked at different ways to bring improved data integrity
 Paradox applications. While Paradox has good interactive validity
 capabilities, most applications will need to supplement Paradox's
ities with data integrity procedures that will ensure the validity of
ddition, you got a preview of the ValCheck Catalog program that is
ented in more detail in Chapter 17.

PC World Paradox 3.5—Power Programming Techniques

Next we will dig into building different kinds of procedures and libraries focusing on memory and error procedures.

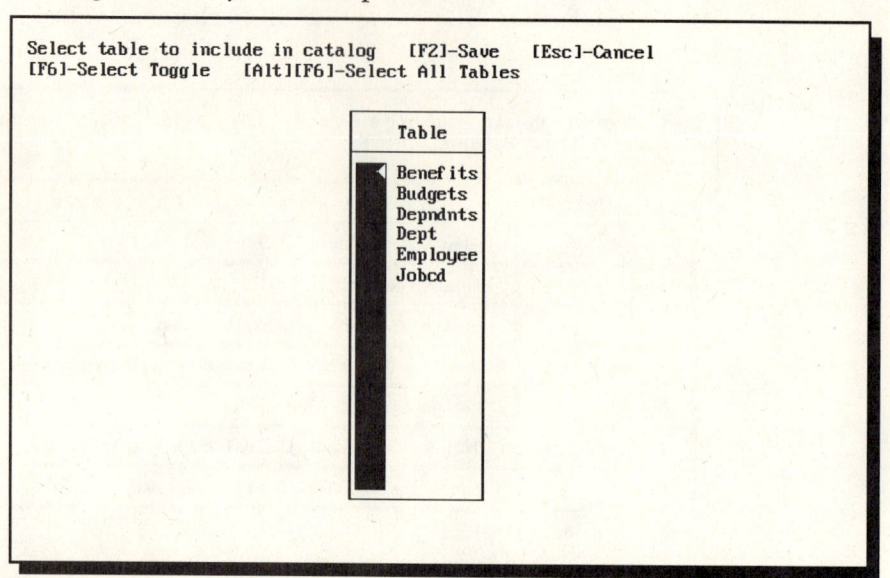

```
Select table to include in catalog   [F2]-Save    [Esc]-Cancel
[F6]-Select Toggle    [Alt][F6]-Select All Tables

                          Table
                        ◄ Benefits
                          Budgets
                          Depndnts
                          Dept
                          Employee
                          Jobcd
```

Figure 6-20 ValCheck Catalog table selection screen

```
Viewing ValCheck Catalog
Press F2 when finished

   Table Name: Benefits

Fld              Fld  Low   High        Table                      R
 #  Field Name  Type Value Value Deflt Lookup  Picture              q
 1  Employee ID  S*                                                 N
 2  Insurance Type A12          Aetna           Aetna,King C        N
 3  Life Insurance $             0.00           {50000,1{000        N
 4  Short Term Disab A1          N              Y,N                 N
 5  Long Term Disab  A1          N              Y,N                 N
 6  US Saving Bond   $           0.00           {2{5[0]},1{0        N
```

Figure 6-21 Viewing ValCheck Catalog information

7

Building Procedures and Libraries

Procedures and libraries are essential tools for the Paradox developer. The benefits of faster execution, protected code, defining your own set of functions, and utilizing built-in memory management streamline application creation, performance, and maintenance.

The first section of this chapter covers procedure and library fundamentals. After the what, why, and how of procedures, we'll show you what to watch out for in autoloading and swapping procedures, how to reuse the system variable *autolib*, what makes a good procedure versus a bad procedure, how to use closed procedures, how to write error procedures (and potential problems when combining these with closed procedures), and how to enable automatic procedure swapping.

Table 7-1 lists key terms, commands, and functions discussed in this chapter.

Table 7-1
Procedure terminology

Procedures	Swapping	ERRORCODE()	Central memory pool
Libraries	SETSWAP	ERRORMESSAGE()	Code pool
Private variables	READLIB	ERRORUSER()	Cache
Global variables	WRITELIB	Error procedure	
Closed procedure	INFOLIB	*errorproc*	
Autoloading	*autolib*	Debbuger	

145

Procedures and Libraries: A Primer

The following sections cover the basics of procedures and libraries. Topics include:

- Defining procedures
- Differences between procedures and scripts
- Global and private variables
- Closed procedures
- Creating a library
- Adding procedures to a library
- Listing the contents of a library

If you are comfortable with procedures and libraries, you can skip these sections. If you're a new PAL programmer or you want a quick refresher, this information prepares you for the topics discussed later in the chapter.

What is a Procedure?

A procedure is a collection of interactive Paradox menu choices and PAL commands combined into a single RAM-resident package. One way to describe procedures is to compare them to scripts. Following are the major areas that differentiate procedures from scripts:

- Procedures are pre-parsed, syntax-checked, memory-resident programs, and thus provides performance benefits. When stored in libraries, Paradox automatically pages procedures in and out of RAM as memory requirements dictate. Scripts are read from a file and interpreted a line at a time. This is slower, especially within looping command structures and when a script is called repetitively, because each line of code is interpreted and the syntax is checked before execution.
- Procedures can include parameters in their declaration that are passed from the calling procedure or script. Parameters cannot be passed when a script is played.
- Procedures utilize expanded and extended memory. Scripts do not benefit from extra memory.

- Procedures can return a value and thus be treated like Paradox functions. A script can return a value but cannot be treated as a function.
- Procedures can also be thought of as subroutines, further enhancing the modularity necessary in applications and allowing you to create generic code that is portable among applications. While scripts can do somewhat the same thing using global variables, they aren't as convenient.
- Procedures provide the option to declare variables as private to the procedure and any procedure subordinate to it. Variables created in a script are global to the application.
- Procedures can be treated as self-contained modules and thus assist in PAL's built-in memory management facility. This facility automatically releases resources as procedures complete. Scripts require that you explicitly release the resources used.
- Procedures can be nested (you can define procedures within procedures). There is no limit to nesting procedures except when using closed procedures.
- Procedures can be grouped into libraries, providing a quick-loading mechanism and reducing the number of DOS files distributed with an application. This also protects the source code from being modified by a user. Scripts, unless password protected, are open to modification and increase the number of files distributed with the application.
- Procedures support recursion.
- Procedures provide the flexibility and functionality available in languages such as C and Pascal.

Defining Procedures

Scripts are transformed into procedures simply by placing the command PROC <procedure name> at the top of the script and ENDPROC at the end of the script. The basic syntax is:

```
PROC procname()
    body of the procedure
ENDPROC
```

The PROC statement tells Paradox to parse the statements following it until an ENDPROC statement is encountered and store them in memory. The procedure is now defined to Paradox. Once a procedure is defined, all subsequent PROC statements for the same procedure name are ignored. A procedure remains in memory until:

- The program terminates
- All script play ends
- The procedure is explicitly released
- Paradox swaps the procedure out to make room for additional procedures or when SETSWAP changes the memory swapping threshold
- A closed procedure terminates (which automatically removes the procedure from memory)

Naming conventions for procedures are the same as for variables and arrays. They are:

- Maximum 132 characters

NOTE: *We recommend keeping name less than 32 characters.*

- First character must be a letter
- Remaining characters must be letters, digits, or the characters ., $, !, or _
- Spaces and tabs are not allowed
- Names are not case sensitive
- Cannot be a Paradox reserved word (command, function, command keyword, or a system variable)
- Should not duplicate the name of any Paradox object

Parentheses are required following the procedure name. Spaces are allowed between the procedure name and the parentheses but should not be used. Listing 7-1 shows a basic procedure that sounds the system bell with three distinct beeps (they are distinct because of the SLEEP 100 between each BEEP command). This procedure is called as follows:

Beeps()

```
; Beeps.sc

PROC Beeps()
   BEEP SLEEP 100 BEEP SLEEP 100 BEEP
ENDPROC
```

Listing 7-1 Beep procedure

TIP: *Placing PROC procname() at the beginning of a script and ENDPROC after the last line of the script performs syntax checking on the entire script. In a script, syntax checking is performed for each line before it is executed.*

The PROC command includes options to expand procedure usability. Listing 7-2 shows the various syntax options. Values are passed to the procedure by including arguments within the parentheses.

NOTE: *Arrays cannot be passed as arguments, but an array element can be used.*

Procedures can return a value (just like Paradox functions) by using the RETURN command followed by the value. The value must be a constant, variable, or expression. The procedure is terminated when RETURN is executed. When a procedure returns a value, the system variable *retval* is set to the returned value. Procedures can return only a single value.

NOTE: *To modify multiple variables using a procedure, use global variables or closed procedures.*

```
PROC procname(parameter_1,parameter_2,..., parameter_n)
   PRIVATE varname_1, varname_2,..., varname_n

   body of the procedure

   RETURN value
ENDPROC
```

Listing 7-2 Syntax options for defining procedures

Listing 7-3 is an example of a procedure with an argument list. DisplayMsg is a procedure for displaying text on the canvas at a specific row and column position. Three arguments are passed: the row position, the column position, and the text to be displayed. This is a simple example of a procedure that uses arguments but it is generic enough that it can be called any time to place information on the screen.

```
; DsplMsg.sc

PROC DisplayMsg(r,c,txt)

  ; Parameters passes are:
  ;   r   - row position
  ;   c   - column position
  ;   txt - text to be displayed
  ;
  @ r,c ?? txt
ENDPROC
```

Listing 7-3 Procedure with an argument list

An example of a procedure used to return a value is shown in Listing 7-4. In this procedure, CreateID, the values of three fields are passed and the expected result is an ID for the record. Typically, the first name, last name, and middle initial are the fields used. The first three characters of the last name and first name are concatenated with the middle initial and a random three-digit number. To ensure that there are always the appropriate number of characters, the letter Z is used as a filler when a value is blank or shorter in length. An expression is used with the RETURN command to return the calculated ID in uppercase characters.

```
; CreateID.sc

PROC CreateID(fld1,fld2,fld3)
  PRIVATE id1, id2, id3, id4

   ; Parameters passes are:
   ;   fld1 - field from table, typically Last Name
```

Listing 7-4 Procedure that returns a value

```
;     fld2 - field from table, typically First Name
;     fld3 - field from table, typically Middle Initial
;
; Private variables are:
;     id1 - subset of id based on fld1
;     id2 - subset of id based on fld2
;     id3 - subset of id based on fld3
;     id4 - subset of id generated by RAND function limited
;           to 3 digits
;
id1 = SUBSTR(fld1,1,3)
id1 = id1 + FILL("Z",3-LEN(id1))
id2 = SUBSTR(fld2,1,3)
id2 = id2 + FILL("Z",3-LEN(id2))
IF ISBLANK(fld3) THEN
  id3 = "Z"
ELSE
  id3 = fld3
ENDIF
id4 = STRVAL(INT(RAND()*1000))
RETURN UPPER(id1 + id2 + id3 + id4)
ENDPROC
```

Listing 7-4 Procedure that returns a value—continued

Global and Private Variables

Procedures support both global and private variables. Global variables retain their value throughout the application and are accessible in every procedure and script. Private variables exist only for the life of the procedure. Variables are declared private to the procedure and any subordinate procedures by listing them after the keyword PRIVATE. They are private to the procedure and can be changed in the procedure without modifying a global variable of the same name. The memory used by these variables is released when the procedure completes. We recommended that you declare all variables used solely within a procedure as private. This prevents accidently changing a global variable or one declared in the calling procedure.

NOTE: *Any variable declared in a procedure that is not in the PRIVATE variable list is defined as a global variable and exists after the procedure completes.*

Paradox uses call-by-value for parameters passed to a procedure. This means that the value of the argument is passed and the variable names created or remains for the life of the procedure. If the values of these variables change in the procedure, they do not change the values in the calling procedure or script. If you want a procedure to modify multiple variables, use global variables. This differs from other programming languages where you can call-by-reference, passing variable addresses and allowing changes to any variable in the argument list.

Closed Procedures

A closed procedure is a special type of procedure that is treated as a self-contained module. Listing 7-5 shows the syntax for closed procedures. CLOSED is the reserved word that identifies the procedure as being a closed procedure. All global variables used within a closed procedure must be identified with the USEVARS parameter.

```
PROC CLOSED procname(parameter_1,parameter_2,..., parameter_n)
  USEVARS varname_1, varname_2,..., varname_n

    body of the procedure

    RETURN value
ENDPROC
```

Listing 7-5 Closed procedure syntax

Closed procedures have the following requirements and limitations:

- ◆ All global variables and procedures currently defined to Paradox are forgotten. This includes the system variables *autolib* and *errorproc*. To include these variables, use:
  USEVARS autolib, errorproc
- ◆ Additional global variables included as arguments in USEVARS retain their values outside the closed procedure if changed within the closed procedure.
- ◆ An error procedure is not defined in a closed procedure until you explicitly read it (just like you have to at the beginning of an application). Include the following line after the USEVARS:
  READLIB *"libname" errorprocname*

- It isn't necessary to use RELEASE PROCS and RELEASE VARS inside a closed procedure. All procedures, variables, and arrays defined within a closed procedure are removed from memory upon termination of the procedure.
- Closed procedures can only be called from a library. The CLOSED parameter cannot be used on a procedure in a script and then immediately make a call to the procedure.
- You can nest closed procedures six levels.
- All procedures called within a closed procedure are also closed.

What is a Procedure Library?

A procedure library is a collection of procedures stored in a single file. These procedures are stored in a pre-parsed format so that they can be loaded quickly into memory. Procedure libraries provide multiple benefits:

- Load faster than procedures stored in scripts
- Are easier to manage than multiple scripts
- Protect source code (you distribute only the library, not the scripts creating the procedures)
- Swap automatically
- Provide an easy method to store often-used macros for productivity enhancements
- Automatically use available expanded/extended memory

Creating Libraries

You create procedure libraries using the CREATELIB command. The syntax is:

CREATELIB libname

or

CREATELIB libname SIZE numofprocs

The library name can be a maximum of 8 characters in length, the same as any DOS file. If a library already exists with the same name, it is automatically overwritten.

NOTE: *You should test for the existence of a library (using the ISFILE function) before executing a CREATELIB statement:*

```
libname = "Abclib"
answr = ""
IF ISFILE(libname+".lib") THEN
  BEEP
  @ 5,5 ?? "Library " + libname + " already exists, Replace? (Y/N) "
  ACCEPT "A1" PICTURE "Y,N" TO answr
  IF answr <> "Y" THEN
    MESSAGE "Library creation cancelled"
    SLEEP 2000
    RETURN
  ENDIF
ENDIF
MESSAGE "Creating library, Please wait"
CREATELIB libname
```

The number of procedures stored in a library defaults to 50. Using the SIZE option, the maximum number of procedures can be set to 300. The overhead storage for each procedure is 44 bytes. Therefore, the larger the SIZE option, the more disk space required. Each library also uses 24 bytes for file overhead. A library with 50 procedures requires 2224 bytes, one with 300 procedures requires 13,224 bytes.

Storing Procedures in Libraries

Procedures are placed into a library using the WRITELIB command. Syntax for WRITELIB is:

>WRITELIB "libraryname" procname
>
>   or
>
>WRITELIB "libraryname" procname_1, procname_2, ..., procname_n

You must first define a procedure before writing it to a library.

REMEMBER: *A procedure is defined when it is loaded in memory.*

A WRITELIB command can place a single procedure in a library or multiple procedures (separate each procedure name with a comma). If the procedure already exists in the library, it is replaced with the new definition.

The space in the library used by the previous version of the procedure is not used for the new version, it is appended to the procedure library and creates dead space. Continued insertion of existing procedures increases disk space requirements and reduces performance. Let's look at an example. Figure 7-1 shows a diagram of the size and contents of a procedure library before and after writing a duplicate procedure to the library.

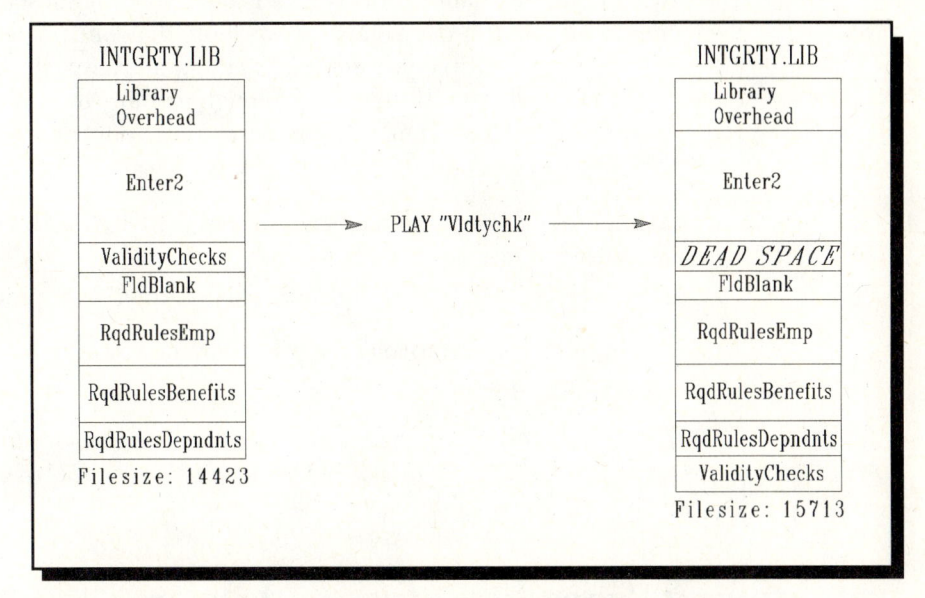

```
INTGRTY.LIB                                    INTGRTY.LIB
Library                                        Library
Overhead                                       Overhead

Enter2                                         Enter2
                  PLAY "Vldtychk"
ValidityChecks                                 DEAD SPACE
FldBlank                                       FldBlank

RqdRulesEmp                                    RqdRulesEmp

RqdRulesBenefits                               RqdRulesBenefits

RqdRulesDepndnts                               RqdRulesDepndnts
                                               ValidityChecks
Filesize: 14423
                                               Filesize: 15713
```

Figure 7-1 Dead space created by inserting an existing procedure

> **NOTE:** *Procedures cannot be removed from a library using a Paradox command. The only way to remove a procedure is to recreate the library and omit the procedure from the new library.*

Using Procedures

Procedures are used by defining them in a script or by loading them from a library. Executing from a script does not take advantage of autoloading and swapping. Using a library, procedures are loaded either explicitly or automatically if a library is identified to the system.

Explicit Procedure Loading

Procedures are read into memory on demand using READLIB. The syntax for READLIB is:

> READLIB "libname" proc_1, proc_2, ..., proc_n

The procedure library name informs Paradox which library to search to find the names in the list. READLIB also allows more than one procedure to be loaded. If there are multiple procedures listed, Paradox expects to find all of them in the named library. If there isn't enough memory to load all the procedures, Paradox will load as many procedures as memory allows and then load the remaining procedures automatically as they are referenced.

> IMMEDIATE is an optional parameter of the READLIB command and is used as in
>
> READLIB IMMEDIATE "libname" proc_1, proc_2, ..., proc_n

This keyword tells Paradox to load the procedure now, without concern for low-memory conditions.

▽ | **TRAP:** *You'll get a script error if there isn't enough memory to load the procedure. Therefore, we do not recommend using the IMMEDIATE keyword.*

Autoloading Procedures from a Library

Procedure libraries let Paradox automatically load a procedure into memory from a file if the procedure is not already defined. Paradox looks for PARADOX.LIB in the current directory to search for the named procedure. If the library doesn't exist, a script error occurs unless the system variable *autolib* is defined. *Autolib* contains the name or names of libraries to search when a call is made to a procedure not in memory. This example establishes a single library to search:

> *autolib = "Intgrty"*

Any call to a procedure not found in memory would initiate a search of the INTGRTY library catalog to see if the procedure exists in the library. If it does, the procedure is quickly loaded into memory for execution. A script error occurs if the procedure is not found. Multiple libraries can be searched by setting autolib as follows:

autolib = "Intgrty,Utils,Menus"

In this case, the libraries are searched in the order they are listed until the procedure is located or until all libraries have been searched. Fully qualified path names can also be included:

autolib = "c:\\paradox3\\dataintg\\Intgrty"

NOTE: *You can change the value of* autolib *within an application to use a different library, even as a private variable (it will exist only for duration of the procedure).*

The order of precedence when looking for a procedure is:

1. Central memory pool
2. Cache memory
3. On disk in the library from which it was originally read
4. On disk in the current autoload library or libraries

Library Contents Visibility

Procedures contained in a library and the number of bytes used by each procedure is stored in the List table using the INFOLIB command:

INFOLIB "libname"

This is executed from a script or from the *MiniScript* option on the PAL Menu.

Figure 7-2 displays the result of an INFOLIB command for the INTGRTY library.

NOTE: *Only 31 characters are placed in the [Procedure] field in List.db.*

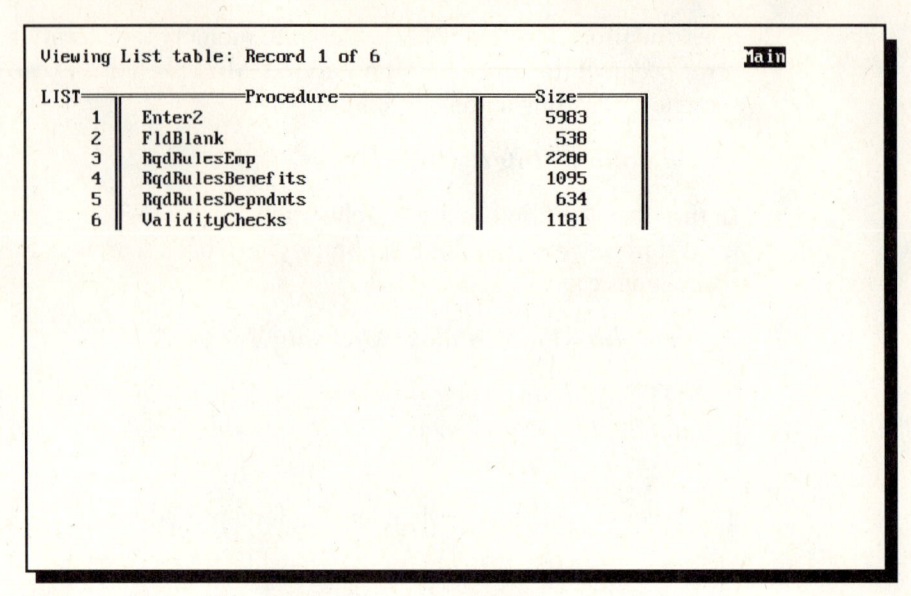

```
Viewing List table: Record 1 of 6                                    Main
 LIST          Procedure                      Size
    1    Enter2                                5983
    2    FldBlank                               538
    3    RqdRulesEmp                           2200
    4    RqdRulesBenefits                      1095
    5    RqdRulesDepndnts                       634
    6    ValidityChecks                        1181
```

Figure 7-2 List table containing contents of a library

Debugging Procedures in Libraries

If you're like most developers, you'll probably make at least one mistake somewhere in one of your modules. The Paradox Debugger is an excellent tool to help you track down the problem. Using procedure libraries doesn't complicate the process. The only requirement is that the script that generated the procedure for the library has to be available to the debugger. Since the full path name for the script is stored in the library along with the procedure, the Debugger has the correct navigational information to find the script. To debug the script, two things are required: the script must be available in the drive and directory it was written from, and the script cannot change from when it was written to the library. If the Debugger cannot find the script, the following message is displayed:

```
Could not find script MAINMNU containing text of procedure MainMenu
```

This means either the script is missing from the directory or the directory path does not exist. You are most likely to get this message when you're moving an application from your machine to a user's machine, unless you place the application scripts and libraries in the exact directory structure as your machine. A simple technique to avoid this problem is to create the library on your user's machine in whatever directory the files exist. Of course, this is only valid if the user gets the libraries and scripts.

If the script was modified since it was written to the library, the Debugger displays the message:

```
Script MAINMNU of procedure MainMenu has changed since library was created
```

When this occurs, play the script to rewrite the procedure in the library and run the application performing the same tasks. You can then debug the procedure.

In both cases, if the scripts are in a directory other than the current working directory, the full path name is included with the script name.

There are multiple ways to invoke the Paradox Debugger. The one we're all familiar with is via the Cancel/Debug menu displayed when an error occurs. However, this is exactly what you do not want to occur when the application is running at a customer's site. While testing an application, you'll need to see exactly what's happening on the workspace. Invoking the Debugger in one of the following ways gives you this capability:

1. Include the DEBUG command within your application code.
2. Start the application using the {Debug} menu selection from the PAL Menu.
3. Press [Ctrl][Break] while the application is running. If you're in a WAIT command, you'll need to press one of the keys in the UNTIL clause before Paradox displays the Cancel/Debug menu.
4. Return a 2 from the error procedure. Error procedures are discussed at the end of the chapter.

▽ **TRAP:** *{Value} from the Debug menu creates a script using the RETURN command and sets retval. If your application is using retval for comparison, do not execute {Value} before performing the test. If you do, the value of retval will not be what you expected and you might think something is wrong with your application or with Paradox.*

The {Where} menu selection on the Debug menu is an option every developer should use. It shows the current nesting of procedures and scripts, and displays the values for all procedure parameters and private variables. Figure 7-3 shows an example of this. {Where} is a handy tool to help you track where your application is and to examine the contents of variables. The one thing {Where} doesn't provide is a listing of the values for global variables.

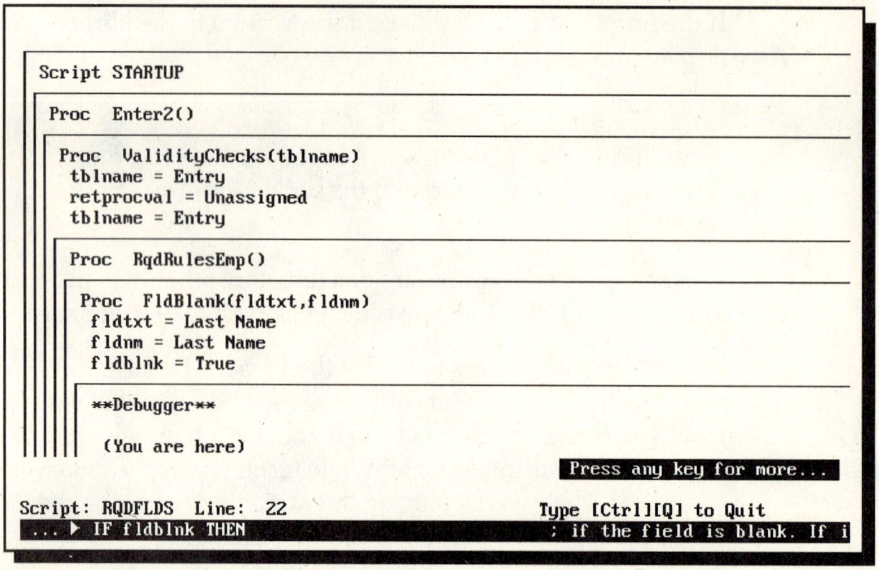

```
Script STARTUP
 Proc  Enter2()
  Proc  ValidityChecks(tblname)
   tblname = Entry
   retprocval = Unassigned
   tblname = Entry
   Proc  RqdRulesEmp()
    Proc  FldBlank(fldtxt,fldnm)
     fldtxt = Last Name
     fldnm = Last Name
     fldblnk = True

    **Debugger**
    (You are here)
                                                 Press any key for more...
Script: RQDFLDS  Line:  22                       Type [Ctrl][Q] to Quit
...  ▶ IF fldblnk THEN                           ; if the field is blank. If i
```

Figure 7-3 Script and procedure nesting display using {Where} option

TIP: *Have you ever wanted to look at the contents of multiple variables while in the Debug without having to use the {Value} option multiple times? One way to view all variables is to select {MiniScript} from the Debug menu and enter SAVEVARS ALL. This creates a script named Savevars containing the current variables. If you shell out to the operating system you can look at the script with an editor (you could even use TYPE to display the script on the screen).*

CAUTION: *Do not use PRINT unless it has already been loaded.*

Procedures and Libraries Summary

Transforming scripts into procedures and libraries is a relatively simple task if you know the appropriate sequence in which to execute the necessary tasks. The steps for turning scripts into procedures and placing them into libraries are:

1. Create your script.
2. Add PROC and the procedure name followed by () before your first line of code and ENDPROC after your last line of code.
3. Create a library using CREATELIB.
4. Write your procedure to the library with WRITELIB.

Using procedures depends on a couple of things. If the procedures were defined using a script, you can call them as long as all script execution has not completed. If you store procedures in a library, you can either explicitly or implicitly load them. Explicitly load them using READLIB. Paradox automatically loads procedures if they're in PARADOX.LIB or if you set the system variable *autolib* to the name of the library. Using libraries enables the autoloading feature of Paradox. The SETSWAP command is used to force procedures to swap at a given point and leave the specified amount of memory available to the application. For performance reasons, put as much of the application code as possible into procedures to fully benefit from the memory management features of Paradox.

Autolib, Swapping, and Releasing Procedures from Memory

The system variable *autolib* designates a library or libraries to search for a called procedure not in memory. This variable must be set or Paradox searches only PARADOX.LIB. Like any other variable, *autolib* can be changed anytime during an application. This lets you dynamically change the libraries searched depending on what section of the application is being executed.

Procedure swapping is handled automatically by Paradox if procedures are either loaded automatically from a library or if READLIB is used. Swapping refers to the ability to swap procedures in and out of memory whenever memory requirements dictate. A least-recently-used algorithm determines which procedures are swapped. The current procedure is never swapped out. In order for the calling procedure to be swapped or for those earlier on the call chain to be swapped, they must be used in one of two ways:

1. As a standalone command
   Proc1()

2. Assigning the result of a procedure to a variable
   varname = Proc1()

Any other use of a procedure inhibits swapping. Let's look at some of the common incorrect uses of procedure calls and some commands that prevent swapping.

1. Assigning a variable to a procedure used in an expression:
   varname = Proc1() + 101
2. Using NOT before a procedure call:
   varname = NOT Proc1()
3. Using a procedure in a control structure (IF, WHILE, FOR, SCAN):
   IF Proc1() THEN
      OR
   WHILE Proc1()
4. Assigning a field to the result of a procedure:
   [Fieldname] = Proc1()

NOTE: *To solve these problems, simply use a variable. Assign the result of the procedure to a variable and use the variable instead of the procedure name in the expression or command:*

varname = Proc1()
varname = varname + 101
varname = NOT varname
IF varname THEN
WHILE varname

5. Calling a script within a procedure. This prevents not only the calling procedure from being swapped, but any procedures the script calls as well.
6. Using the EXECUTE command. All procedure swapping is disabled when an EXECUTE statement is active within the call chain. Once EXECUTE is no longer on the call chain, swapping is enabled.

> **NOTE:** *EXECUTE is necessary in some applications to provide a dynamic statement to be executed. Most often this is an assignment statement setting a variable to the result of a function or expression. While this does prevent swapping, the statement generally does not require additional memory and will not cause an out-of-memory condition. Once the EXECUTE script completes, if the amount of memory is less than the swap point, procedures are swapped to satisfy the SETSWAP setting.*

7. Using either {MiniScript} or {Value} from the Debug menu. {MiniScript} uses the EXECUTE command to create the statement to run. {Value} creates a script that uses RETURN.

> **NOTE:** *The EXECPROC command does not inhibit swapping based on our testing so it isn't included in this list. However, the Paradox documentation states that if EXECPROC is used, the calling procedure cannot be swapped. This did not happen in the tests we ran. As a reminder, only procedures that don't have arguments can be used with EXECPROC.*

Automatic swapping of procedures alone is not enough to ensure that there won't be a memory problem. For each procedure loaded, enough memory must be available to establish memory variables and place images on the workspace. SETSWAP is used to adjust the minimum amount of memory maintained in the central memory pool before swapping begins, which is called the swap point. When this threshold is crossed, Paradox begins swapping procedures from the central memory pool. The memory amount is the same as the value returned by the function MEMLEFT(). To set the swap point, indicate the number of bytes as follows:

SETSWAP 20000

This sets the swap point at 20,000 bytes. This is a good swap point to use in general. With only 8K to 10K of memory, Paradox can't place a table on the workspace. This implies that SETSWAP 10000 doesn't do too much for you. To load certain modules (like the Graphics module to change titles or page output) you need 35,000 bytes. There are other times when 50K is needed. What this means is that you must dynamically set the swap point. You can issue SETSWAP multiple times in an application to set the amount of memory to reserve.

You don't want to set the swap point too high because it will cause unnecessary swapping and slow down your application. The reverse is also true. A low swap point can cause low memory conditions and might force Paradox (version 3.5) to use the code pool. This is not a good practice! If you use too much of the code pool's memory, error 44 is set and your error procedure is triggered. Testing for this condition is discussed later in this chapter.

> **NOTE:** *You don't have to use SETSWAP for Paradox to swap procedures. When there isn't enough memory for a procedure to be loaded, Paradox begins swapping. This doesn't mean that SETSWAP is unnecessary. On the contrary, just because Paradox automatically swaps procedures doesn't guarantee that there will be enough memory to load tables or forms and perform the processing defined in the procedure. You should always have some swap point set within your applications and adjust it as tasks require.*

> **TRICK:** *Want to keep a procedure in memory and not have it be swapped out? Use PROC...ENDPROC around a script. This keeps the script in memory until it's explicitly released so it won't be affected by the swapping mechanism.*

As discussed previously, the {Where} selection on the Debug menu displays the procedure nesting level and indicates if a procedure has been swapped. Figure 7-4 shows a nesting level map. Notice that the first two procedures have been swapped, which indicates that there wasn't enough memory to load all procedures so Paradox swapped based on the least-recently-used algorithm (SETSWAP was not used).

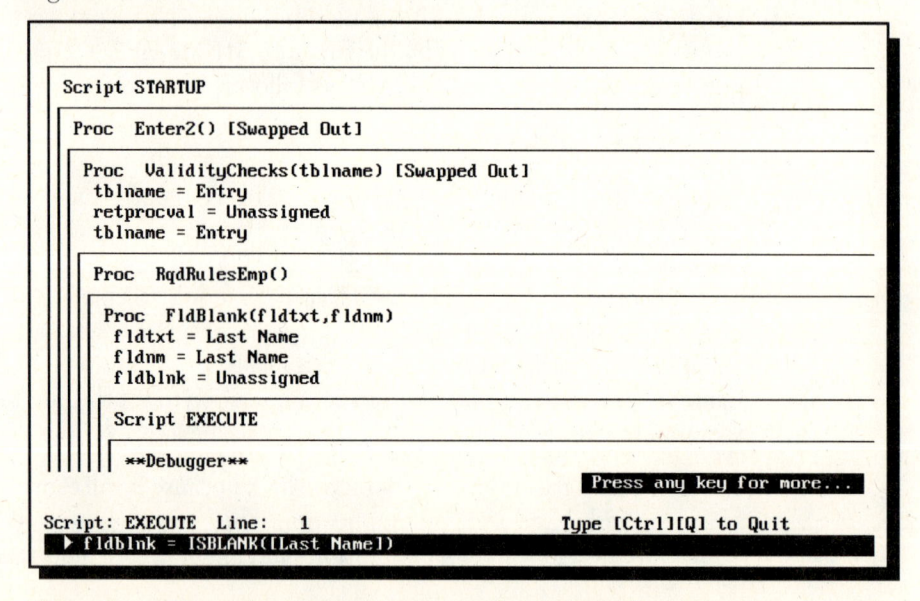

```
Script STARTUP
  Proc  Enter2() [Swapped Out]
    Proc  ValidityChecks(tblname) [Swapped Out]
      tblname = Entry
      retprocval = Unassigned
      tblname = Entry
      Proc  RqdRulesEmp()
        Proc  FldBlank(fldtxt,fldnm)
          fldtxt = Last Name
          fldnm = Last Name
          fldblnk = Unassigned
        Script EXECUTE
          **Debugger**
                                              Press any key for more...
Script: EXECUTE  Line:   1            Type [Ctrl][Q] to Quit
  ▶ fldblnk = ISBLANK([Last Name])
```

Figure 7-4 Script and procedure nesting display using {Where} option

Good Procedure versus Bad Procedure Construction

What makes a good procedure? What makes a bad procedure? A bad procedure is obviously one that doesn't work, either due to a syntax error or a logic error. Along with these two errors, the items mentioned previously in this chapter that prevent swapping are considered bad practice. Following are some ideas to help write good procedures:

- Do not use READLIB and RELEASE PROCS.

    Use Paradox's automatic loading and swapping of procedures. READLIB is required only when defining an error procedure. Paradox doesn't automatically load the procedure defined in *errorproc*. One area where it is advantageous to explicitly load a procedure is in a data entry/modification process where separate procedures are used for various error checks. If the procedures aren't explicitly loaded first, there's a slight delay while the procedures are loaded and executed the first time they are called. Loading the procedures before presenting the form to the user prevents this delay.

- Use private variables.

    Private variables prevent accidentally changing to a global variable and are removed from memory when the procedure completes.

    REMEMBER: *Any variable declared in a procedure that isn't on the PRIVATE list is a global variable and exists after the procedure completes.*

- Reduce the number of Paradox functions called repetitively.

    Change the following code:

    ```
    FOR cntr FROM startpt TO endpt
      IF TABLE() = "Firstone" THEN
          DoSomeThing1()
      ELSE
          DoSomeThing2()
      ENDIF
    ENDFOR
    ```

    To:

    ```
    tblname = TABLE()
    FOR cntr FROM startpt TO endpt
      IF tblname = "Firstone" THEN
          DoSomeThing1()
      ELSE
          DoSomeThing2()
      ENDIF
    ENDFOR
    ```

- Create generic procedures.
- Use recursive calls sparingly.

  If you get a message stating that you're out of stack space, the first thing to look for is a recursive call.

Paradox provides multiple ways to create a set of commands that produce the same results. Some perform faster than others and some produce larger procedures than others. Let's look at an example of a three-table query to see how both performance and procedure size are affected. Figure 7-5 shows the workspace with the query forms linked and fields checked. The four procedures discussed were created in the following ways:

1. QuerySave (Listing 7-6)
2. QuerySave and remove unnecessary lines (Listing 7-7)
3. Programming the menu selections and cursor movements (Listing 7-8)
4. Recording the interactive process of creating the query (Listing 7-9)

The menu selections {*Scripts*} {*QuerySave*} {*Q3tbls*} creates the lines shown between PROC and ENDPROC in Listing 7-6. Each of the three tables on the workspace, along with any checked field, example element, or selection criteria is included.

```
√ [F6] to include a field in the ANSWER; [F5] to give an Example      Main
   EMPLOYEE ─┬─Employee ID─┬─┬─Last Name─┬─┬─First Name─┬─┬─Department
             │     id      │ │     √     │ │     √     │ │     √
             │             │ │           │ │           │ │
             │             │ │           │ │           │ │
   BENEFITS ─┬─Employee ID─┬─┬─Life Insurance─┬─US Saving Bond─┬─Insurance Ty
             │     id      │ │       √        │       √        │
             │             │ │                │                │
             │             │ │                │                │
   DEPNDNTS ─┬─Employee ID─┬─┬─Last Name─┬─┬─First Name─┬─┬─Birth Date
             │     id      │ │     √     │ │     √     │ │
             │             │ │           │ │           │ │
             │             │ │           │ │           │ │
```

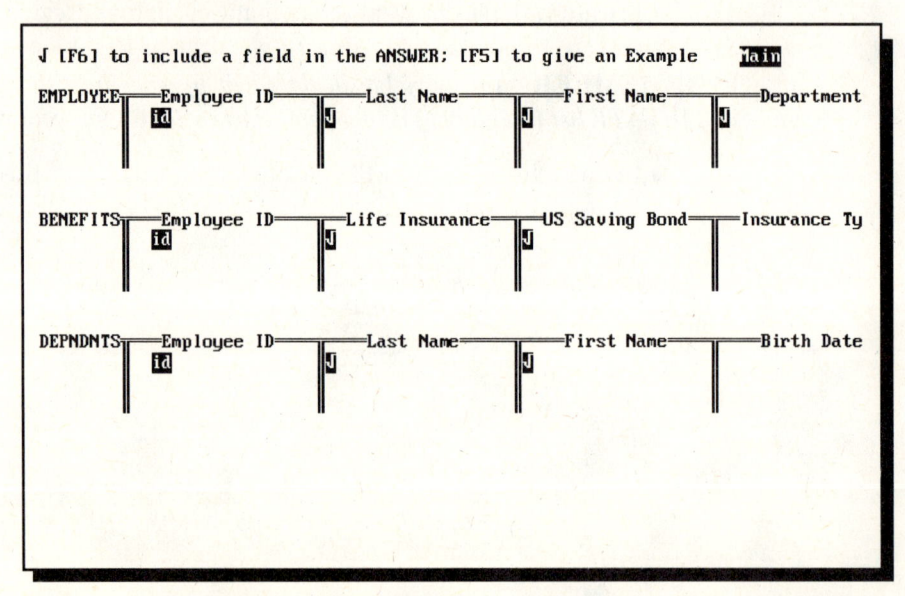

Figure 7-5 Three-table query example

```
PROC Qry3Tbls()
Query
  Employee | Employee ID | Last Name | First Name | Department
           | _id         | Check     | Check      | Check

  Employee |             |           |            |


  Benefits | Employee ID | Life Insurance | US Saving Bond |
           | _id         | Check          | Check          |

  Depndnts | Employee ID | Last Name | First Name |
           | _id         | Check     | Check      |

Endquery
ENDPROC
WRITELIB "Qrytest" Qry3Tbls
```

Listing 7-6 Three-table query script created using QuerySave

In Listing 7-7, the same process as in the previous example was used to create the procedure, except the "blank lines" in the query image are removed. Paradox always includes a minimum of three lines for each table in a QuerySave. This is equivalent to the three lines initially available when you place a query form on the workspace. Any line that doesn't contain information used in the query can be deleted from the script. As you'll see later, this reduces the size of the procedure.

The third example, Listing 7-8, uses PAL commands. Here we explicitly move to each field to place the examples, checkmarks, and data selection criteria.

```
PROC Qry3Tbls2()
Query

  Employee  | Employee ID | Last Name | First Name | Department  |
            | _id         | Check     | Check      | Check       |
  Benefits  | Employee ID | Life Insurance | US Saving Bond  |
            | _id         | Check          | Check           |
  Depndnts  | Employee ID | Last Name | First Name |
            | _id         | Check     | Check      |

Endquery
ENDPROC

WRITELIB "Qrytest" Qry3Tbls2
```

Listing 7-7 Three-table query script created using QuerySave with excess lines removed

```
PROC Qry3Tbls3()
{Ask} {Employee}
MOVETO [Employee ID] EXAMPLE "id"
MOVETO [Last Name]    CHECK
MOVETO [First Name]   CHECK
MOVETO [Department]   CHECK
{Ask} {Benefits}
MOVETO [Employee ID] EXAMPLE "id"
MOVETO [Life Insurance] CHECK
MOVETO [US Saving Bond] CHECK
{Ask} {Depndnts}
MOVETO [Employee ID] EXAMPLE "id"
MOVETO [Last Name]    CHECK
MOVETO [First Name]   CHECK
ENDPROC

WRITELIB "Qrytest" Qry3Tbls3
```

Listing 7-8 Three-table query script with programmed menu selection and cursor movement

The last example uses keystroke recording (choose {*Scripts*} {*BeginRecord*} and enter the script name). You could also use [Alt][F3] for instant script recording or the PAL Menu, [Alt][F10] {*BeginRecord*} {*scriptname*}. In all three cases, each keystroke, keypress, and cursor movement is recorded in the script as shown in Listing 7-9.

```
PROC Qry3Tbls4()
{Ask} {Employee} Enter Example  "id" Enter Check Enter Check
Enter Enter Enter Check Menu {Ask} {Benefits} Enter Example
"id" Enter Enter Check Enter Enter Enter Check Menu {Ask}
{Depndnts} Enter Example  "id" Enter Enter Check Enter Check
ENDPROC

WRITELIB "Qrytest" Qry3Tbls4
```

Listing 7-9 Table query script created by keystroke recording

The result of each of these procedures is exactly the same. They all place a query form for three tables on the workspace, check the appropriate fields, and link the tables with an example element. Performance is the same, as each takes about 4 seconds on a 16 Mhz IBM Model 80. The difference is:

1. Procedure size

   Figure 7-6 shows the result of an INFOLIB "Qrytest" command. Qry3Tbls2 is clearly the winner for the minimum number of bytes. The other three queries are essentially the same size.

2. Maintainability

   Both Qry3Tbls and Qry3Tbls2 are the easiest procedures to modify. Simply executing either procedure places the query forms on the workspace so that the query can be modified. QuerySave captures the query in script form which in turn replaces the existing QUERY...ENDQUERY for the procedure. This process also ensures that the query syntax is correct (provided you have tested the query before you save it).

   The last two procedures are more difficult to change. Qry3Tbls3 requires that each new field included in the query have a MOVETO and CHECK command added. Qry3Tbls4 is simply too cumbersome to modify. It would be better to record the entire process than attempt to modify the code.

Optimal Procedure Size

What is the maximum procedure size? This question is inevitably asked by every Paradox developer. Like asking what time it is at a train station, many different answers are given, depending on which source you ask. The Paradox *Network Administrator's Guide* says that procedures shouldn't be larger than 4K. Various articles on the subject have set 12K as the maximum size. You need to decide the largest amount of memory you want swapped out, keeping in mind that the smaller the better. We recommend that you keep your procedures between 6K and 8K.

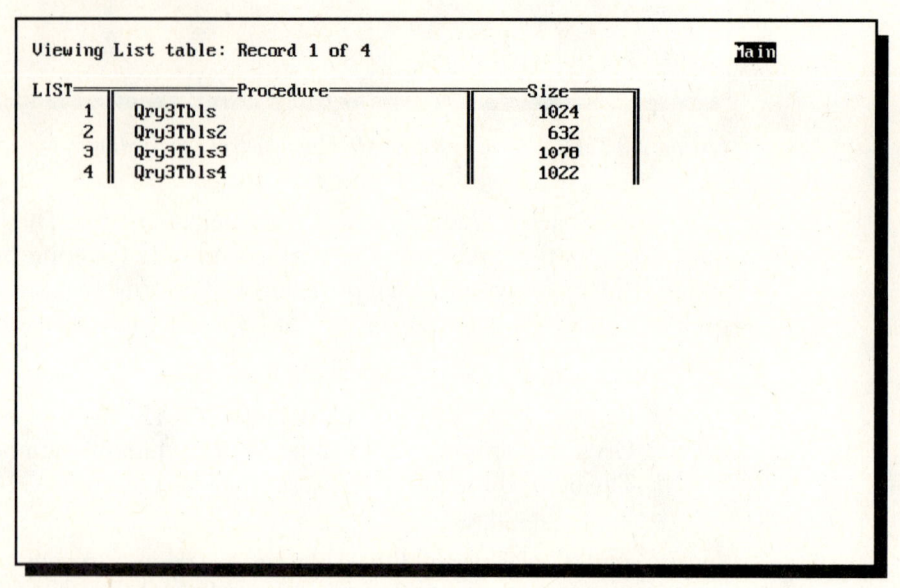

```
Viewing List table: Record 1 of 4                              Main
 LIST            Procedure              Size
    1     Qry3Tbls                      1024
    2     Qry3Tbls2                      632
    3     Qry3Tbls3                     1078
    4     Qry3Tbls4                     1022
```

Figure 7-6 Procedure sizes for three-table query examples

Regular Procedures versus Closed Procedures

To close a procedure or not to close a procedure? This question also invariably comes up many times during code development. Whether a procedure is closed or not depends on what action is occurring and how far down on the call chain the action is performed. To help you decide whether to create a closed procedure or not, let's look at how procedures and closed procedures compare in the following areas:

- Private variables
- Global variables
- SAVEVARS command
- Calling other procedures
- Using an error procedure

- Utilizing memory
- Nesting levels
- Returning values

**Table 7-2
Procedures vs. closed procedures**

Procedures	*Closed Procedures*
Private variables: Using the PRIVATE parameter after the procedure name with a list of variable names tags each variable as being defined only to that procedure and any procedure below it on the call chain.	The same options for private variables exist for closed procedures. The need to declare isn't as important because a closed procedure is treated as a self-contained unit.
Global variables: All global variables are accessible to expressions and can be modified.	Global variables are not accessible unless they've been included in the USEVARS parameter. This includes both *autolib* and *errorproc*. The concern of reassigning the value of a global variable in a procedure if the variable name is left off the PRIVATE list is not applicable.
SAVEVARS command: All global and private variables are included in SAVEVARS.SC when SAVEVARS ALL is executed.	Only the variables defined in the current scope are included in SAVEVARS.SC when SAVEVARS ALL is executed. Global variables not included in USEVARS are not written to SAVEVARS.SC unless an explicit list of variables is used instead of SAVEVARS ALL.

Table 7-2—continued

Procedures	*Closed Procedures*
Calling other procedures: Any procedure currently defined can be called. A call to an undefined procedure loads the procedure into memory.	Closed procedures treat all procedures defined to Paradox at the time a closed procedure is executed as unknown. If a procedure is to be executed within a closed procedure, it must be read into memory. This means a second copy of the procedure is in memory if it was defined before the closed procedure was called.
Use of an error procedure: If a runtime error occurs and an error procedure and *errorproc* are defined, it is executed.	An error procedure defined at the beginning of an application isn't available to a closed procedure. Error procedures, like any other procedure, must be explicitly read into memory inside a closed procedure.
Memory utilization: The size of the procedure, number of variables, number of objects, and the system mode determine the amount of memory needed to successfully execute the procedure. Any variable not included in the PRIVATE list is defined as global and remains after the procedure is finished. All private variables are placed on a separate variable stack and released when the procedure completes. Unless explicitly released from memory after it's called, the procedure remains defined, residing in memory, until swapped or explicitly released later.	Closed procedures require the same amount of memory as regular procedures plus the additional memory for the "second copy" of any procedures that were previously defined. The most common procedure this applies to is the error procedure. It would also apply to any utility procedures such as message handlers, exploding windows, and multi-purpose generic routines. When the closed procedure ends, all memory used during its execution is returned to the central memory pool.

Table 7-2—continued

Closed Procedures	*Closed Procedures*
Nesting levels: There is no limit to the nesting levels of procedures except the amount of memory. Correct usage of procedure swapping alleviates this.	There is a six-level limit for nesting.
Returning values: Procedures return only one value. If multiple variables or arrays need to be changed, they have to be used as global variables in the procedure.	Only a single-value is returned from a closed procedure. With the USEVARS parameter, returning multiple values is accomplished with global variables. This is like call-by-reference for the variables instead of call-by-value.

The bottom line is that closed procedures don't provide an overwhelming advantage over regular procedures. Performance is about the same for both. Closed procedures can alleviate memory problems but require an extra error procedure to be loaded for each level executed. If you have a large error procedure, this reduces available memory. (This is discussed further later in this chapter.) Closed procedures are best used for the top-level of major modules in a system. This ensures that the memory used by all called procedures is returned when the module completes.

Different Methods for Creating Libraries

To create a procedure library, you always start with CREATELIB. From there on, the options for inserting procedures into the library vary considerably. Style and personal choice determine what is best for you. The following section demonstrates various methodologies for adding procedures to a library.

The first method could be called the all or nothing method. A single script is used to define each procedure and a single WRITELIB is used to incorporate them into a library. Listing 7-10 shows an outline of this method.

```
CREATELIB "libname"

PROC p1()
    body of the procedure
ENDPROC

PROC p2()
    body of the procedure
ENDPROC

PROC p3()
    body of the procedure
ENDPROC

PROC p4()
    body of the procedure
ENDPROC

WRITELIB "libname" p1, p2, p3, p4
RELEASE PROCS ALL
```

Listing 7-10 Creating a library and inserting procedures with a single WRITELIB

This method works only if enough memory exists for all procedures to be defined before the WRITELIB statement is executed. Small applications (total size of procedures in bytes less than available memory) are about the only situation in which this approach to library creation will work. If you see the message,

```
Resource limitation: Not enough memory to complete operation
```

the first thing to think of is "out of memory, too many procedures still defined." This leads us to the second methodology.

When the total size of the procedures in an application is larger than the amount of memory in your machine, you need to reduce the number of procedures defined before they're written to the library. Listing 7-11 displays such a script. For each procedure there is a WRITELIB and RELEASE PROCS statement. This method removes the possibility of running out of memory (providing that no procedures or variables are currently defined and Paradox has full access to the majority of the machine's memory).

The problem with this method is one of maintenance. What happens if procedure p3 needs to be updated? The script is changed, played, and the entire library and all procedures are reproduced. This is time-consuming when there are more than a few procedures and modifications are frequent. This leads us to the third methodology.

```
CREATELIB "libname"

PROC p1()
    body of the procedure
ENDPROC

WRITELIB "libname" p1
RELEASE PROCS p1

PROC p2()
    body of the procedure
ENDPROC

WRITELIB "libname" p2
RELEASE PROCS p2

PROC p3()
    body of the procedure
ENDPROC

WRITELIB "libname" p3
RELEASE PROCS p3

PROC p4()
    body of the procedure
ENDPROC

WRITELIB "libname" p4
RELEASE PROCS p4
```

Listing 7-11 Creating a library and inserting procs with a single WRITELIB

The third method of creating libraries and inserting procedures is to have a separate script for creating the library and for each procedure, as shown in Listing 7-12. Script 1 is played to create the library. A separate script is played for each procedure placed in the library. This method is easy to maintain because you can change any procedure without having to reprocess all procedures. But as in the previous examples, there is one drawback: remembering all the script names! If the library is lost or damaged, all the scripts have to be played to recreate the library. What if you forget one of them? This leads to the fourth methodology for creating and populating a library.

```
;Script 1
CREATELIB "libname"

;Script p1.sc
PROC p1()
   body of the procedure
ENDPROC

WRITELIB "libname" p1
RELEASE PROCS p1

;Script p2.sc
PROC p2()
   body of the procedure
ENDPROC

WRITELIB "libname" p2
RELEASE PROCS p2

;Script p3.sc
PROC p3()
   body of the procedure
ENDPROC

WRITELIB "libname" p3
RELEASE PROCS p3

;Script p4.sc
PROC p4()
   body of the procedure
ENDPROC

WRITELIB "libname" p4
RELEASE PROCS p4
```

Listing 7-12 Creating library with multiple scripts

The final example of creating a library uses a control script, commonly called a *makelib* script. Listing 7-13 displays the structure for this methodology. The MAKELIB script controls the name of the library by using a variable name and playing the appropriate scripts defining the procedures that should be in the library. The library name variable is used in each script to name the library.

WRITELIB libraryname p1

In addition, annotation for each script played provides documentation on the contents of the scripts executed. This makes it easier to maintain the application. When a single procedure needs modification, just that script is played after the changes, and only a single procedure is updated in the library.

```
;MAKELIB.SC

libraryname = "libname"

CREATELIB libraryname

PLAY "p1"      ; p1 does ...
PLAY "p2"      ; p2 does ...
PLAY "p3"      ; p3 does ...
PLAY "p4"      ; p4 does ...
```

Listing 7-13 Creating a library with a MAKELIB script

There are still two areas of weakness in this methodology. The variable *libraryname* must be set before playing one of the scripts writing to the library. The second weakness is that with each successive execution of one of the scripts, dead space is created in the library, requiring that you either run a condensing program to reclaim the space or execute MAKELIB to create a condensed library.

Depending on the situation, you'll probably use one of these methods to create your libraries. Just be aware of each method's pros and cons, and explore other approaches to creating and maintaining libraries. These are four of the more common methodologies used. The key is to use the one that best suits your needs.

Multiple Small versus Single Large Libraries

To conserve memory in Paradox 2.0, you had to create libraries with no more than 50 procedures. Beginning with Paradox 3.0, the memory problem was fixed. The decision on how many procedures to place into a library became one more concerned with maintenance than performance. There is a slight performance penalty when Paradox searches the libraries specified in *autolib*. But using multiple libraries lets you logically separate libraries for utilities, help systems, menus, and main modules and use them in multiple applications. To reduce library maintenance, multiple libraries are recommended.

Error Procedures

Paradox provides a special procedure called an error procedure to control your application when a run error occurs. This procedure is executed whenever a command cannot be executed due to missing or invalid information or resources. The system variable *errorproc* contains the name of the procedure to invoke. Like *autolib*, *errorproc* can be changed for different modules in your application.

You must do three things to incorporate error procedures into your system:

1. Set variable *errorproc* to the name of your error procedure.
   errorproc = "ErrorHandler"
2. Create the error procedure in the same fashion as any other procedure. Error procedures cannot take any arguments.
3. Explicitly define your procedure using READLIB.
   READLIB *"Libname"* ErrorHandler

You define what action to take from within the error procedure. Possible actions are:

1. Re-execute the command causing the error.
2. Skip the command causing the error and execute the next command.
3. Tell Paradox to cause a script error.
4. Exit the application.

The first three options are handled by returning a 0, 1, or 2 respectively, from your error procedure. The fourth option requires an EXIT command.

Use the ERRORCODE and ERRORMESSAGE functions to diagnose the error that occurred. ERRORCODE returns an integer code for the error. ERRORMESSAGE returns the text for the error message. Table 7-3 lists the possible error codes and messages.

It is highly recommended that you do not rely heavily on an error procedure to control error conditions in your applications. You should explicitly program for potential conditions for each task being performed. Error procedures are your safety net, just in case something unexpected occurs.

With this in mind, the next question is "What should I include in an error procedure?" Conditions such as printer not ready, resource locked, floppy drive unavailable, and so on should be coded in the modules where they're likely to occur. Conditions such as corruption, out of disk or stack space, and low memory conditions are types of errors to trap for. The error procedure is also used to give you a snapshot of the system and assist you in debugging the problem. Having all available information on tables used, system mode, current memory, current disk space, and so forth is beneficial in tracking down the problem. Most users aren't able to tell you this type of information so it's best to have the application provide this level of visibility.

Table 7-3
Paradox 3.5 Error Code List

Code	Meaning
0	No error (for example, record was not changed or key was found)

File or directory errors

1	Drive not ready
2	Directory not found
3°	Table in use by another user
4°	Full lock placed on table by another user
5	File not found
6	File corrupted
7	Index file corrupted
8	Object version mismatch
9°	Record locked by another user
10	Directory in use by another user
11°	Directory is private directory of another user
12	No access to directory at operating system level
13	Index inconsistent with sort order
14	Multi-user access denied
15	PARADOX.NET file conflict

General script errors

20	Invalid context for operation
21	Insufficient password rights
22	Table is write-protected
23	Invalid field value
24	Obsolete procedure library

° For this code, ERRORUSER() returns the name of the user who locked the resource

Table 7-3—continued

Code	Meaning
25	Insufficient image rights
26**	Invalid PAL context

Code	Meaning
27	Operation not completed
28	Too many nested closed procedures
29	Table is remote (on an SQL server)

Argument errors

30	Data type mismatch
31	Argument out of range
32	Wrong number of arguments
33	Invalid argument
34	Variable or procedure not assigned
35	Invalid menu command

Resource errors

40**	Not enough memory to complete operation
41	Not enough disk space to complete operation
42**	Not enough stack space to complete operation
43	Printer not ready
44	Low memory warning

Record-oriented operation errors

50**	Record was deleted by another user
51**	Record was changed by another user
52**	Record was inserted by another user
53**	Record with that key already exists
54**	Record or table was not locked
55**	Record is already locked by you
56**	Lookup key not found

Multitable operation errors

60	Referential integrity check
61	Invalid multitable form
62**	Form locked
63	Link locked

** This code does not invoke a designated error procedure

Listing 7-14 is an example of an error procedure that captures the status of the workspace and environment before halting the system. In any error procedure, the system variable *errorproc* must be either declared private or set to another value (besides the name of the error procedure) to prevent a recursive call if an error occurs within the error procedure. Formatting the error message screen is performed by lines 5 through 50. Lines 45 through 48 place the name of the person to contact and a phone number on the screen. This gives the users someone they can call to get assistance when a problem occurs. Both *contactperson* and *contactphn* are considered global variables and are typically initialized at system start up. Line 52 calls ErrorPrint. This procedure prints an error log containing information on the status of the workspace, memory, disk space, and other environmental data. (This procedure is discussed later in this chapter.)

After the error log is printed, the system is halted. If the mode is other than Main, the RESET in line 58 cancels the mode and returns to Main mode. You can give your user the option to attempt to execute the command that caused the error or skip the command by having the error procedure return a 1 or 0. A SHOWMENU is typically used to give the user this option when it is a requirement of the error procedure.

Printing the error log information is handled by the ErrorPrint procedure shown in Listing 7-15. This procedure checks to see if there is disk space before it prints. Because a user sometimes likes to run the same process multiple times to see if an error always occurs, the procedure looks to see if there are any error log files on disk. The file extension is used as a counter.

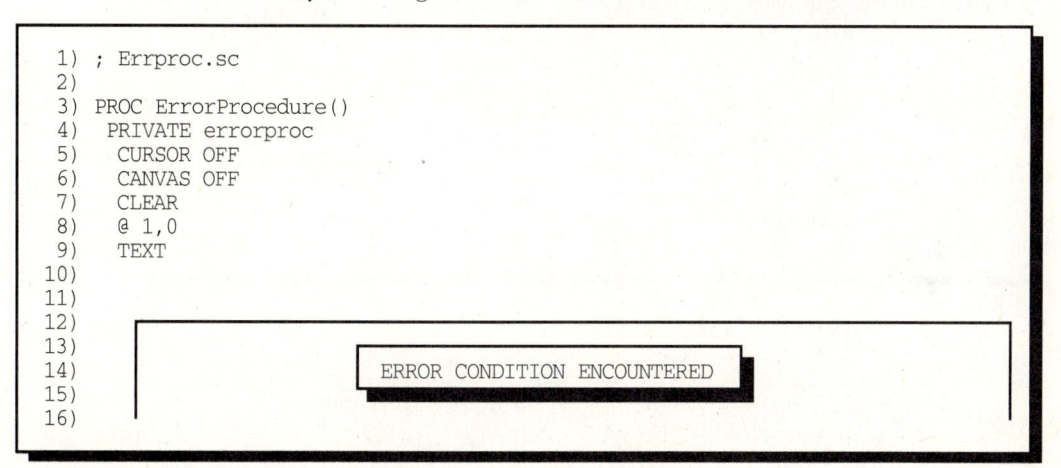

```
 1)  ; Errproc.sc
 2)
 3)  PROC ErrorProcedure()
 4)    PRIVATE errorproc
 5)    CURSOR OFF
 6)    CANVAS OFF
 7)    CLEAR
 8)    @ 1,0
 9)    TEXT
10)
11)
12)
13)
14)                   ERROR CONDITION ENCOUNTERED
15)
16)
```

Listing 7-14 Error procedure script

```
17)             Error Message
18)
19)
20)
21)             Error Code:
22)
23)
24)
25)
26)
27)
28)
29)
30)   ENDTEXT
31)   PAINTCANVAS ATTRIBUTE 116 0,0,24,79       ; Red on Gray
32)   PAINTCANVAS ATTRIBUTE 79  4,22,6,52       ; White on Red
33)   PAINTCANVAS ATTRIBUTE 127 7,23,7,53       ; White on Gray
34)   PAINTCANVAS ATTRIBUTE 127 4,53,6,53       ; White on Gray
35)
36)   BEEP SLEEP 100 BEEP SLEEP 100 BEEP
37)   STYLE ATTRIBUTE 79                        ; White on Red
38)   @ 10,5 ?? ERRORMESSAGE()
39)   @ 12,17 ?? ERRORCODE()
40)   ;
41)   ; Place the name of the person responsible for the application and
42)   ; their phone number on the screen. The variables 'contactperson' and
43)   ; 'contactphn' are global variables assigned earlier in the application.
44)   ;
45)   IF ISASSIGNED(contactperson) AND ISASSIGNED(contactphn) THEN
46)      @ 16,10 ?? "Contact " + contactperson + " on " + contactphn +
47)               " for assistance."
48)   ENDIF
49)   STYLE
50)   CANVAS ON
51)   ; Write system status information to error log file
52)   ErrorPrint()
53)   PAINTCANVAS ATTRIBUTE 116 22,0,22,79
54)   CANVAS ON
55)   MESSAGE "System will now be shut down, press any key to continue!"
56)   kp = GETCHAR()
57)   IF SYSMODE() <> "Main" THEN
58)      RESET
59)   ENDIF
60)   EXIT
61) ENDPROC
```

Listing 7-14 Error procedure script—continued

The extension with the largest number is the file that was the last to print. Starting with line 31, PAL functions are used to capture information about the current status of the workstation (the date, time, error code and message, available memory, and so on).

```
17) IF DRIVESPACE(SUBSTR(DIRECTORY(),1,1)) < 3000 THEN
18)    CANVAS ON
19)    BEEP SLEEP 100 BEEP SLEEP 100 BEEP
20)    MESSAGE "Not enough disk space to write error log, process cancelled!"
21)    SLEEP 4000
22) ENDIF
23) cntr = 1
24) filenam = PRIVDIR() + "ERRLOG.001"         ;  Find the name of last log file
25) WHILE ISFILE(filenam)                      ;  Find the name of last log file
26)    cntr = cntr + 1                         ;  printed
27)    filenam = PRIVDIR() + "ERRLOG." +
28)             SUBSTR(FORMAT("w4,ez",cntr),2,3)
29) ENDWHILE
30)
31) PRINT FILE filenam "Error log file:  ",filenam,"\n\n"
32) PRINT FILE filenam "Current Date:    ",TODAY(),"\n"
33) PRINT FILE filenam "Current Time:    ",TIME(),"\n"
34) PRINT FILE filenam "Error Code:      ",ERRORCODE(),"\n"
35) PRINT FILE filenam "Error Message:   ",ERRORMESSAGE(),"\n"
36) PRINT FILE filenam "Error User:      ",ERRORUSER(),"\n"
37) PRINT FILE filenam "Central Memory:  ",MEMLEFT(),"\n"
38) PRINT FILE filenam "Code Pool Memory:",RMEMLEFT(),"\n"
39) PRINT FILE filenam "Menu Choice:     ",MENUCHOICE(),"\n"
40) IF MENUCHOICE() <> "Error" THEN            ;  If cursor is at a menu need to
41)    MENU ESC                                ;  cancel the menu selection
42) ENDIF
43) PRINT FILE filenam "Monitor Type:    ",MONITOR(),"\n"
44) PRINT FILE filenam "Network Type:    ",NETTYPE(),"\n"
45) PRINT FILE filenam "System Mode:     ",SYSMODE(),"\n"
46) smode = SYSMODE()
```

If a menu is currently active on the workspace, attempting to execute some functions causes errors. Lines 40 through 42 remedy this problem by executing MENU to take the system to the Main menu for the current mode, and ESC cancels the menu.

```
40) IF MENUCHOICE() <> "Error" THEN            ;  If cursor is at a menu need to
41)    MENU ESC                                ;  cancel the menu selection
42) ENDIF
```

Problems also occur when attempting to execute functions in certain system modes. Some functions will either cause a script error or won't return accurate information. For example, if the application is currently in Graph mode, Table creates a script error. This code in lines 62 through 68 remedies this problem. It also points out how some modes require a {*Cancel*} {*Yes*} while others only need {*Cancel*} without confirmation of the menu selection.

```
62) IF smode = "Create" OR smode = "Restructure" OR smode = "Sort" THEN
63)    MENU {Cancel}
64) ENDIF
65) IF smode = "Form" OR smode = "Report" OR smode = "Password" OR
66)    smode = "Graph" THEN
67)       CANCELEDIT
68) ENDIF
```

If there are images on the workspace, their names and types are printed starting with the code in line 92. Information on the current image, form, multitable form, and current field is printed in lines 96 through 110. For each image on the workspace, lines 111 through 119 print the image name and image type (Query or Display). The last thing this procedure does is to save the currently defined variables using SAVEVARS ALL. You might want to change or modify this if your system relies on SAVEVARS.SC or if you want to track each iteration of error (as the error log file does) by renaming SAVEVARS.SC to a different name.

```
92)  IF IMAGETYPE() <> "None" THEN
93)
94)     PRINT FILE filenam "Current Table:   ",TABLE(),"\n"
95)     PRINT FILE filenam "Table Shared: ",FORMAT("LY",ISSHARED(TABLE())),"\n"
96)     IF IMAGETYPE() = "Display" THEN
97)        IF ISFORMVIEW() THEN
98)           PRINT FILE filenam "View Type:        Form\n"
99)           PRINT FILE filenam "Form #:           ",FORM(),"\n"
100)          PRINT FILE filenam "MultiTable Form:  ",
101)                   FORMAT("LY",ISMULTIFORM(TABLE(),FORM())),"\n"
102)          FORMKEY                          ; Put into Table View
103)       ELSE
104)          PRINT FILE filenam "View Type:        Table\n"
105)       ENDIF
106)       PRINT FILE filenam "Current Image #:  ",IMAGENO(),"\n"
107)       PRINT FILE filenam "Current Field:    ",FIELD(),"\n"
108)       PRINT FILE filenam "Cur View Rcd #:   ",RECNO(),"\n"
109)       PRINT FILE filenam "Cur Table Rcd #:  ",[#],"\n"
110)    ENDIF
111)    IF NIMAGES() > 0 THEN              ; Print name and type of each
112)                                       ; image on the workspace
113)       PRINT FILE filenam "Tables placed on the workspace:\n"
114)       FOR i from 1 to NIMAGES()
115)          MOVETO i
116)          PRINT FILE filenam " Table # ",FORMAT("w3",i),":     ",TABLE();
117)                    " - ",IMAGETYPE(),"\n"
118)       ENDFOR
119)    ENDIF
120) ENDIF
121) SAVEVARS ALL                          ; This should be done only for
122)                                       ; versions 3.0 and above
```

```
1) ;ErrPrnt.sc
2)
3) PROC ErrorPrint()
4)   PRIVATE errorproc, cntr, smode
5)   ;
6)   ; Private variables:
7)   ;  errorproc  - this is a private variable to prevent infinite loop if
```

Listing 7-15 Error procedure error log printing routine

```
 8) ;                there is an error in this procedure
 9) ;   cntr       - counter variable to determine the file extension for the
10) ;                error log file
11) ;   smode      - contains the result of SYSMODE so multiple calls to the
12) ;                function do not have to be made
13) ;
14) CANVAS ON
15) MESSAGE "Printing error log file, Please wait!"
16) CANVAS OFF
17) IF DRIVESPACE(SUBSTR(DIRECTORY(),1,1)) < 3000 THEN
18)   CANVAS ON
19)   BEEP SLEEP 100 BEEP SLEEP 100 BEEP
20)   MESSAGE "Not enough disk space to write error log, process cancelled!"
21)   SLEEP 4000
22) ENDIF
23) cntr = 1
24) filenam = PRIVDIR() + "ERRLOG.001"    ; Find the name of last log file
25) WHILE ISFILE(filenam)                 ; Find the name of last log file
26)   cntr = cntr + 1                     ; printed
27)   filenam = PRIVDIR() + "ERRLOG." +
28)             SUBSTR(FORMAT("w4.ez",cntr),2,3)
29) ENDWHILE
30)
31) PRINT FILE filenam "Error log file: ",filenam,"\n\n"
32) PRINT FILE filenam "Current Date:    ",TODAY(),"\n"
33) PRINT FILE filenam "Current Time:    ",TIME(),"\n"
34) PRINT FILE filenam "Error Code:      ",ERRORCODE(),"\n"
35) PRINT FILE filenam "Error Message:   ",ERRORMESSAGE(),"\n"
36) PRINT FILE filenam "Error User:      ",ERRORUSER(),"\n"
37) PRINT FILE filenam "Central Memory:  ",MEMLEFT(),"\n"
38) PRINT FILE filenam "Code Pool Memory:",RMEMLEFT(),"\n"
39) PRINT FILE filenam "Menu Choice:     ",MENUCHOICE(),"\n"
40) IF MENUCHOICE() <> "Error" THEN       ;  If cursor is at a menu need to
41)   MENU ESC                            ; cancel the menu selection
42) ENDIF
43) PRINT FILE filenam "Monitor Type:    ",MONITOR(),"\n"
44) PRINT FILE filenam "Network Type:    ",NETTYPE(),"\n"
45) PRINT FILE filenam "System Mode:     ",SYSMODE(),"\n"
46) smode = SYSMODE()
47) ;
48) ;  If the process is in modes other than in a table on the workspace
49) ; certain workspace informational functions either cause a script
50) ; error or the return erroneous information. Therefore, the current
51) ; mode needs to be Main, Edit, CoEdit, or DataEntry. If it is not
52) ; one of these modes then the current mode is cancelled. Some modes
53) ; require the {Cancel} {Yes} options. These are cancelled using
54) ; CANCELEDIT. The other modes only need {Cancel}, there is no Yes/No
55) ; menu option.
56) ;
57) ; NOTE:  If the current table is in form view, returning from Create,
58) ;        Graph, Password, Restructure, and Sort puts the table in
59) ;        Table View so the functions below testing for type of
```

Listing 7-15 Error procedure error log printing routine—continued

```
60)    ;         form will not be a true indicator of the workspace status.
61)    ;
62)    IF smode = "Create" OR smode = "Restructure" OR smode = "Sort" THEN
63)      MENU {Cancel}
64)    ENDIF
65)    IF smode = "Form" OR smode = "Report" OR smode = "Password" OR
66)       smode = "Graph" THEN
67)      CANCELEDIT
68)    ENDIF
69)    PRINT FILE filenam "Directory:        ",DIRECTORY(),"\n"
70)    PRINT FILE filenam "Diskspace:        ",
71)                      DRIVESPACE(SUBSTR(DIRECTORY(),1,1)),"\n"
72)    PRINT FILE filenam "Is Runtime        ",FORMAT("LY",ISRUNTIME()),"\n"
73)    PRINT FILE filenam "Is Blank Zero     ",FORMAT("LY",ISBLANKZERO()),"\n"
74)    PRINT FILE filenam "Private Directory:",PRIVDIR(),"\n"
75)    PRINT FILE filenam "User Name:        ",USERNAME(),"\n"
76)    PRINT FILE filenam "Script Directory: ",SDIR(),"\n"
77)    PRINT FILE filenam "Query Order:      ",QUERYORDER(),"\n"
78)    PRINT FILE filenam "Sort Order:       ",SORTORDER(),"\n"
79)    PRINT FILE filenam "Version:          ",VERSION(),"\n"
80)    IF ISASSIGNED(procname) THEN
81)      PRINT FILE filenam "Cur Proc:         ",procname,"\n"
82)    ELSE
83)      PRINT FILE filenam "Cur Proc:         ** Not Set **\n"
84)    ENDIF
85)    ;
86)    ; NOTE: The above is here to save the name of the current PROC being
87)    ;       executed. This will only work if procname is set at the
88)    ;       beginning of every procedure and it is a global variable
89)    ;
90)    PRINT FILE filenam "# of images:      ",NIMAGES(),"\n"
91)    PRINT FILE filenam "Image Type:       ",IMAGETYPE(),"\n"
92)    IF IMAGETYPE() <> "None" THEN
93)
94)      PRINT FILE filenam "Current Table: ",TABLE(),"\n"
95)      PRINT FILE filenam "Table Shared: ",FORMAT("LY",ISSHARED(TABLE())),"\n"
96)      IF IMAGETYPE() = "Display" THEN
97)        IF ISFORMVIEW() THEN
98)          PRINT FILE filenam "View Type:       Form\n"
99)          PRINT FILE filenam "Form #:          ",FORM(),"\n"
100)         PRINT FILE filenam "MultiTable Form: ",
101)                     FORMAT("LY",ISMULTIFORM(TABLE(),FORM())),"\n"
102)         FORMKEY                           ; Put into Table View
103)       ELSE
104)         PRINT FILE filenam "View Type:       Table\n"
105)       ENDIF
106)       PRINT FILE filenam "Current Image #: ",IMAGENO(),"\n"
107)       PRINT FILE filenam "Current Field:   ",FIELD(),"\n"
108)       PRINT FILE filenam "Cur View Rcd #:  ",RECNO(),"\n"
109)       PRINT FILE filenam "Cur Table Rcd #: ",[#],"\n"
110)     ENDIF
```

Listing 7-15 Error procedure error log printing routine—continued

```
111)      IF NIMAGES() > 0 THEN                  ;  Print name and type of each
112)                                             ;  image on the workspace
113)        PRINT FILE filenam "Tables placed on the workspace:\n"
114)        FOR i from 1 to NIMAGES()
115)           MOVETO i
116)           PRINT FILE filenam " Table # ",FORMAT("w3",i),":      ",TABLE(),
117)                         " - ",IMAGETYPE(),"\n"
118)        ENDFOR
119)      ENDIF
120)    ENDIF
121)    SAVEVARS ALL                             ;  This should be done only for
122)                                             ; versions 3.0 and above
123) ENDPROC
```

Listing 7-15 Error procedure error log printing routine—continued

Figure 7-7 is an example of the output from ErrorPrint. You can see that the error here was an attempt to select an invalid menu choice. This most likely means a coding problem. Look at the line that says **# of images**. You'll see it says 7. But now look at the bottom of the output, which says there are only 5 images on the workspace (one Query and four Display). This seems to be an error but it isn't. The current image, Employee, was in a multitable form. At the time that Niamges was executed, the table was in Form view. To print the images on the workspace, the procedure toggled to Table view to move between all the images.

The two error processing procedures discussed here provide a lot of information necessary for you to track down problems that arise in applications. You gain this capability for a price though—ErrorProcedure is about 4K and ErrorPrint is just under 10K using Paradox 3.5. The procedure size might cause problems depending on your application. These should definitely not be combined into a single procedure. Reducing the size of both procedures can be accomplished by eliminating unnecessary pieces from each. It might also be feasible to execute ErrorPrint as a script.

The size of an error procedure is more critical when you're using a closed procedure. Using the size of the above error procedure, you lose 4K for each closed procedure you implement. Four levels of closed procedure nesting requires an additional 16K (4K for the error procedure at each level). Why? Remember, a closed procedure doesn't have access to any procedure defined outside of the closed procedure, including any error procedure. This requires that you explicitly read the error procedure with each nesting level.

To conserve memory, create an error procedure that has a single statement to call your error procedure. Listing 7-16 is an example.

```
;   ErrHndlr.sc
PROC ErrorHandler()
   Private errorproc
     ErrorProcedure()
ENDPROC
```

Listing 7-16 Minimal size error procedure

Paradox 3.5 adds the requirement to check for a low-memory condition within the error procedure, especially if you use the error procedure driver mentioned above. VROOMM introduces the central memory pool, which is basically the available memory returned by MEMLEFT() and the code pool. The code pool is memory shared between Paradox and your applications. Paradox uses this memory to swap in code modules depending on the command, function, or menu choice your application requests. If conditions arise where MEMLEFT() becomes 0, your application can invade the code pool. If too much of the code pool is used, error code 44 indicates this as a low-memory warning and causes a script error.

There is no best way to handle code pool invasions. You can track the code pool memory using RMEMLEFT() and when it starts to shrink, free up some memory. If you trap for error code 44 in your error procedure, you need to be aware that if your error procedure calls another procedure, there might not be enough memory to load it. If you write a single error procedure large enough to handle all situations (including low-memory conditions) you erode memory as you use closed procedures. So the answer to "How do I handle using too much of the code pool?" is "It depends."

Summary

In this chapter, we covered procedures and libraries. The first section walked you through the basics of procedures and then moved on to how to write and use libraries. We explained the concept of swapping and showed you what disables swapping. We discussed good and bad procedures and how to improve your procedures. We covered four different methods of creating procedures, along with the pros and cons of each method. And lastly, we covered error procedures.

```
Error log file: ERRLOG.005

Current Date:      9/06/90
Current Time:      14:00:41
Error Code:        35
Error Message:     Not a possible menu choice
Error User:
Central Memory:    235520
Code Pool Memory:  68608
Menu Choice:       Format
Monitor Type:      Color
Network Type:      SingleUser
System Mode:       CoEdit
Directory:         d:\PDXAPPL\ZDB\
Diskspace:         2002944
Is Runtime         No
Is Blank Zero      Yes
Private Directory:
User Name:
Script Directory: d:\PDXAPPL\ZDB\
Query Order:       ImageOrder
Sort Order:        ascii
Version:           3.5
Cur Proc:          ModifyTable
# of images:       7
Image Type:        Display
Current Table:     Employee
Table Shared:      No
View Type:         Form
Form #:            1
MultiTable Form:   Yes
Current Image #:   5
Current Field:     Last Name
Cur View Rcd #:    1
Cur Table Rcd #:   1
Tables placed on the workspace:
 Table #   1:      List - Query
 Table #   2:      List - Display
 Table #   3:      Comps - Display
 Table #   4:      Crsectgy - Display
 Table #   5:      Employee - Display
; ErrHndlr.sc
PROC ErrorHandler()
 PRIVATE errorproc
  ErrorProcedure()
ENDPROC
```

Figure 7-7 Output of ErrorPrint

8 Creating and Enhancing the Paradox Interface

Developers and users alike are demanding SAA features (System Application Architecture) in their applications. While interactive Paradox doesn't have pull-down menus, PAL provides many programming presentation tools and capabilities.

Paradox's ability to present menus and information has barely been tapped by PAL developers. Your user's perception of how easy your application is to use often depends on your application's menu system and user interface. The basic building blocks of a user interface are:

- Menu system
- Help system
- Process and application message system

Paradox gives you all the tools you need to create your own pop-up menus, messages, and help screens without the aid of any utility software program and with very little memory. This chapter presents some superb ways to enhance the Paradox interface. Most of the routines in this chapter require only a minimum of 4K and a maximum of 25K of memory for a five-to-six level menu driven system! Why build your menus with some third-party product when PAL can do it all, saving the expense and memory it takes (48K-128K) to run those programs?

Creating a customized interface in Paradox is relatively simple. Table 8-1 lists a number of terms and functions you need to be familiar with to fully manipulate Paradox's presentation capabilities.

Table 8-1
Key Terms and Concepts

SHOWMENU	SHOWARRAY	SHOWFILE
SHOWTABLE	Proc	Closed Proc
Private variable	UseVars	FOR/ENDFOR
WHILE/ENDWHILE	Array	ASCII Ext. Character
SWITCH/ENDSWITCH	IsAssigned	RETURN
Re-entrant	Re-useable code	Event
Static menu	Paradox-style Menus	Pop-up Menus

In this chapter, you'll examine three styles of presenting menus and information:

- Paradox-style menus
- Static-style menus
- Pop-up menus

As you begin to create your user interface, your menus must be totally re-entrant. When you launch a routine (for example, an edit routine) the routine must return to the menu it came from without requiring you to direct the program how to return. This is basically done by issuing a WHILE...ENDWHILE that encircles the entire routine. Each routine is exited by either a conscious selection from the user or by the process control that you establish in the program. Figure 8-1 illustrates the re-entrant concept. Notice that the EDIT routine quits back to the routine it was launched from only when the user presses [F2]. You don't have to tell the routine to go back, it simply re-enters the previous script at the line below where the current script was launched.

REMEMBER: *Every menu system must have Help available. Interactive Paradox designates [F1] for Help. Make your system's menu help facility context sensitive to the current menu and choice. Allow users to get help by pressing the [F1] key (an SAA concept).*

Always tell the user what's going on. Let the user know that a query is being processed, that a report or form is being copied, that the system is scanning records and editing data. Provide informational messages at appropriate times and places throughout your application.

```
Routine 1           Routine 2           Routine 3           Edit
MainMenu            Modify Menu         Play "Edit"         Edit Data
 While (true)
                     While (true)
                                         While (true
                                                             Edit "table"
                                                             Wait Table
   play "ModiMenu"    play "edit"                            Until "F2"
                                                             if retval="F2"
                                                                Do_it!
                                                             endif
                                                             quitloop
                                         EndWhile
                     EndWhile
 EndWhile
```

Figure 8-1 Re-entrant Program Design

Building a Menu System

Because there are so many ways to create a user interface in Paradox, no one way is right or wrong. Which style or styles you select is based on your own tastes and the desires of the people who use your system.

The first step in building a menu system is to experiment with your users. Show them several styles of menus and ask them which one they like. The second step is to make the menu structure simple and direct. This doesn't mean your menus can't be sophisticated and stylish, it simply means that your user should always know:

- Where they are in the system
- What choices they can make
- How to return to where they came from
- What to do if they need help

SHOWMENU

Let's start by examining Paradox's SHOWMENU command. SHOWMENU creates a Paradox-style ring menu. A SHOWMENU is a horizontal menu consisting of the following properties.

- **Top-row commands**: A row of one- or two-word menu selections.
- **Menu annotations**: A longer explanation of each menu selection. These annotations appear on the second line of your screen, below the top-row commands.
- **Menu choice selection**: Users make menu selections by using the direction keys to move to the desired menu selection and then pressing [Enter].
  OR
- Users select a menu command by pressing the first letter and any successive letters of the desired menu selection until SHOWMENU is able to determine which menu selection the user desires.

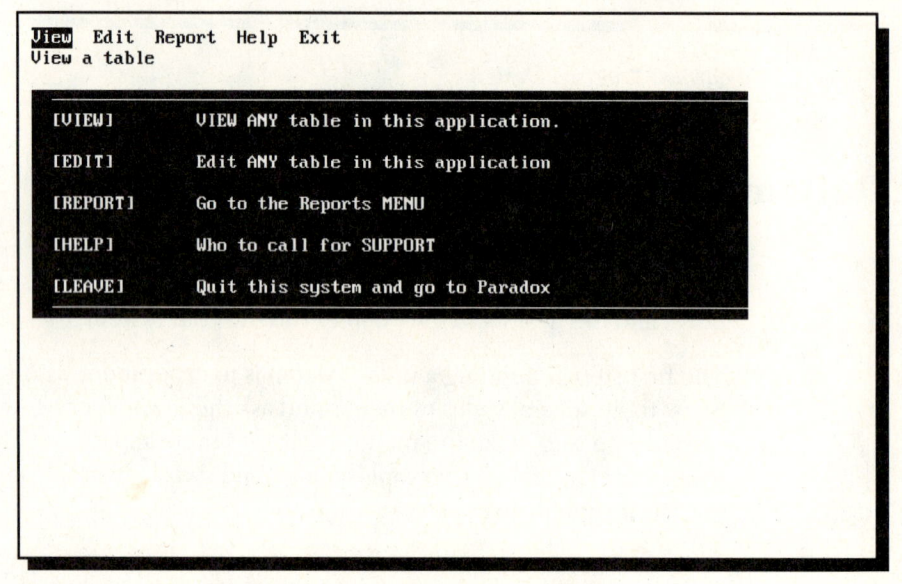

```
View  Edit  Report  Help  Exit
View a table

    [VIEW]      VIEW ANY table in this application.
    [EDIT]      Edit ANY table in this application
    [REPORT]    Go to the Reports MENU
    [HELP]      Who to call for SUPPORT
    [LEAVE]     Quit this system and go to Paradox
```

Figure 8-2 A Paradox ring menu using SHOWMENU

Figure 8-2 is a typical SHOWMENU routine. Listing 8-1 (MAIN.SC) shows how to create the menu.

MAIN.SC performs the following:

- Allows the user to play a View script
- Allows the user to play an Edit script
- Goes to a Report menu

- Provides more information about the system
- Lets the user leave the application

MAIN.SC Overview (Paradox-style main menu)

Lines 1-2	Reset memory, clear the screen and workspace.
Lines 4 & 35	Combine to create an *event* that continues processing until the user chooses to leave.
Line 5	Plays an external script that clears the screen and fills in the space below the Paradox SHOWMENU with a longer, more definitive explanation of each menu choice.
Lines 7-14	The SHOWMENU itself. Any selection the user makes is assigned to a variable *sel* (line 14).
Lines 16-33	Once the user makes a selection, this SWITCH…ENDSWITCH processes the choice.

As in all Paradox menus, users select a menu choice by pressing the first letter and successive letters of the menu item or by using the arrow keys to highlight their selection and then pressing [Enter]. Notice that the menu choice "Leave" initiates another SWITCH…ENDSWITCH. In either of the SWITCH…ENDSWITCH statements, if the user presses any key except the direction keys, [Enter], or the first letter of one of the menu choices, the system beeps at them and waits for the user to make a correct selection.

```
1    Reset Clear
2    ClearAll
3
4    While (true)
5    play "MSplash"
6
7        ShowMenu
8           "View":     "View a table",
9           "Edit":     "Edit a table",
10          "Report":   "Go to the Reports Menu",
11          "Help":     "Help on this system",
12       "Exit":    "Leave the system"
13
14       to sel
```

Listing 8-1 MAIN.SC (the Main menu of an application using SHOWMENU)

```
15
16    Switch
17       case sel = "View":    play "View"
18       case sel = "Edit":    play "Edit"
19       case sel = "Report:   play "ReptMenu"
20       case sel = "Help":    play "MainHelp"
21       case sel = "Exit":    ShowMenu
22                  "Leave":"Leave the system"
23                  "Return":"Go back to the Main Menu"
24                  to subsel
25
26                  Switch
27                     case subsel = "Leave":
28                        QuitLoop
29                        Otherwise:Loop
30                  EndSwitch
31       OtherWise:Loop
32
33    EndSwitch
34
35    EndWhile
```

Listing 8-1 MAIN.SC *(the Main menu of an application using SHOWMENU)—continued*

```
 1    @0,0 Clear EOS
 2
 3    Style Attribute 48
 4    @3,0
 5    Text
 6    -------------------------------------------------
 7    [VIEW]     VIEW ANY table in this application.
 8
 9    [EDIT]     Edit ANY table in this application
10    [REPORT]   Go to the Reports MENU
11
12    [HELP]     Who to call for SUPPORT
13
14    [LEAVE]    Quit this system and go to Paradox
15    -------------------------------------------------
16    EndText
```

Listing 8-2 MSPALSH.SC *(splash screen for MAIN.SC)*

SHOWARRAY

You can create an elaborate system of menus using SHOWMENU. The advantage of SHOWMENU is that it's quick and consistent with interactive

Paradox. The disadvantages are that the user must be told how they arrived at the menu and how to return to where they came. Help is limited and maintenance is high as your system becomes more complex.

SHOWMENU's primary purpose is to build a menu. Two other PAL commands, SHOWARRAY and SHOWFILE, also build Paradox-style menus.

In SHOWARRAY, two arrays must be declared, one for the top row of commands and the second to provide a description for each choice. The arrays are declared prior to the SHOWARRAY statement. Once the arrays have been declared and values assigned to each array element, the SHOWARRAY command is invoked. From this point, the SHOWARRAY functions exactly like the SHOWMENU command. (See Listing 8-3.)

MSARRAY.SC overview (Paradox-style menu)

Lines 1-2	Reset all memory, clear the screen and workspace.
Lines 3 & 48	Combine to create an *event* that continues processing until the user chooses to leave.
Lines 4-22	Establish and record values for the two arrays needed for the SHOWARRAY.
Lines 23-46	Once the user makes a selection, the SWITCH...ENDSWITCH processes the choice. If the user tries to type any letter other than the first letter of each of the DeptAbbrev array elements, the routine displays an error message, beeps and returns to the top of WHILE...ENDWHILE.

```
1   Reset ClearAll
2   @0,0 Clear EOS
3   While (true)
4
5   Array DeptAbbrev[6]
6   Array DeptDescr[6]
7
8   DeptAbbrev[1] = "ACCT"
9   DeptAbbrev[2] = "SALES"
10  DeptAbbrev[3] = "MKTG"
11  DeptAbbrev[4] = "MFG"
12  DeptAbbrev[5] = "DIST"
13  DeptAbbrev[6] = "RETURN"
```

Listing 8-3 MSARRAY.SC (example of a Paradox-style menu using SHOWARRAY)

```
14
15    DeptDescr[1] = "Accounting and Administration"
16    DeptDescr[2] = "Foreign and Domestic Sales"
17    DeptDescr[3] = "Corporate Marketing"
18    DeptDescr[4] = "Manufacturing and Quality Assurance"
19    DeptDescr[5] = "Shipping, Receiving and  Trans Depts"
20    DeptDescr[6] = "Return to the previous menu"
22
23    SHOWARRAY DeptAbbrev DeptDescr
24
25       Default choice
26
27       to sel
28
29
30    Switch
31
32       case sel = "ACCT"  : play "ACCTRept"
33       case sel = "SALES" : play "SALERept"
34       case sel = "MKTG"  : play "MKTGRept"
35       case sel = "DIST"  : play "MFG_Rept"
36       case sel = "MFG"   : play "DISTRept"
37       case sel = "RETURN": quitloop
38
39    Otherwise:@24,0 Clear EOL ?? format("W79,AR","Not a valid choice")
40       Style blink ?? "..." style
41       sleep 1000
42       @24,0 Clear EOL
43       beep
44       loop
45
46    EndSwitch
47
48    EndWhile
```

Listing 8-3 MSARRAY.SC *(example of a Paradox-style menu using SHOWARRAY)—continued*

Figure 8-3 illustrates a SHOWARRAY menu.

SHOWFILE

SHOWFILE lets you create another type of Paradox-style menu. SHOWFILE is used to present a list of DOS files. Once the list is presented, the user selects a file or presses [Esc] (to avoid selecting a file). After you declare a SHOWFILE, you determine whether you want file extensions

```
View  Edit  Report  Help  Exit
View a table
```

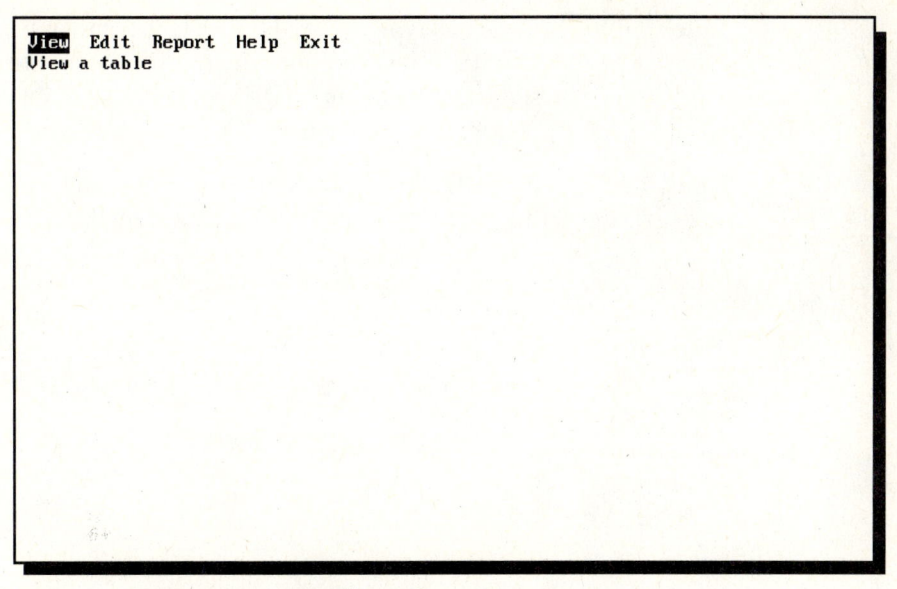

Figure 8-3 SHOWARRAY Paradox-style menu

to be shown or not (NOEXT). Next you enter the DOSPATH where the files exist and what kind of prompt or message you want displayed. Finally, you declare a variable to store the user's selection. This code is shown in Listing 8-4.

MSFILE.SC overview (Paradox-style menu)

Lines 1-2   Reset all memory, clear the screen and workspace.

Lines 3 & 26 Combine to create an *event* that continues processing until the user chooses to leave.

Line 5   Establishes the directory and file type (*.SC) for the path statement required in the SHOWFILES command. In this example, the PAL function DIRECTORY() is invoked to return the value of the current directory.

Lines 7-11 Once you type in the SHOWFILE command and DOSPATH, determine whether file extensions are to be shown in the menu (NOEXT). Next, tell Paradox what directory to search and the file type (line 5).

Lines 12-22 Once the user makes a selection, the routine checks to see if the variable *filename* has been assigned a value. If a value has been assigned to *filename*, the routine continues, otherwise it quits out of the current WHILE…ENDWHILE. In addition, if the value of *filename* is "Esc", the routine quits out of the current WHILE…ENDWHILE otherwise, the routine plays the script that has been selected by the user.

```
1   Reset ClearAll
2   @0,0 Clear EOS
3   While (true)
4
5   dospath = directory()+".sc"
6
7   SHOWFILE NOEXT
8     dospath
9   "Use the direction keys to highlight your selection, then press [[Enter]]"
10
11    to filename
12
13  if isassigned(filename) = false then
14     quitloop
15  endif
16
17  if filename = "Esc" then
18     quitloop
19  endif
20
21
22
23  play filename
24
25  quitloop
26  EndWhile
```

Listing 8-4 MSFILE.SC (example of a Paradox-style menu using SHOWFILE)

Figure 8-4 illustrates a SHOWFILE menu.

```
ACCT  SALES  MKTG  MFG  DIST  RETURN
Foreign and Domestic Sales
```

Figure 8-4 SHOWFILE Paradox-style menu

Static-style menus

Static-style menus act much like their Paradox-style counterparts. They are very useful when a system requires a main menu and no submenus. Figure 8-5 illustrates a static-style menu generated by Listing 8-5.

Static-style menus require very little memory. They are limited in their help capability and do little to help identify where a user may be in the system. Therefore, it is usually best to limit static-style menus to one or two levels.

SMAIN.SC overview (static-style menu)

Lines 1-2	Reset all memory, clear the screen and workspace.
Line 4	Sets the [Shift][F1] combination of keys to PLAY the SMAIN.SC script. Once SMAIN.SC is played, SETKEY allows the developer or user to toggle back and forth between interactive Paradox and the application's main menu.

```
Use the direction keys to highlight your selection, then press [ENTER]
Main  Mainmenu  Makelib  Menuhelp  Menus  Mesglibr  Msarray  Msfile  Msplash ▶
```

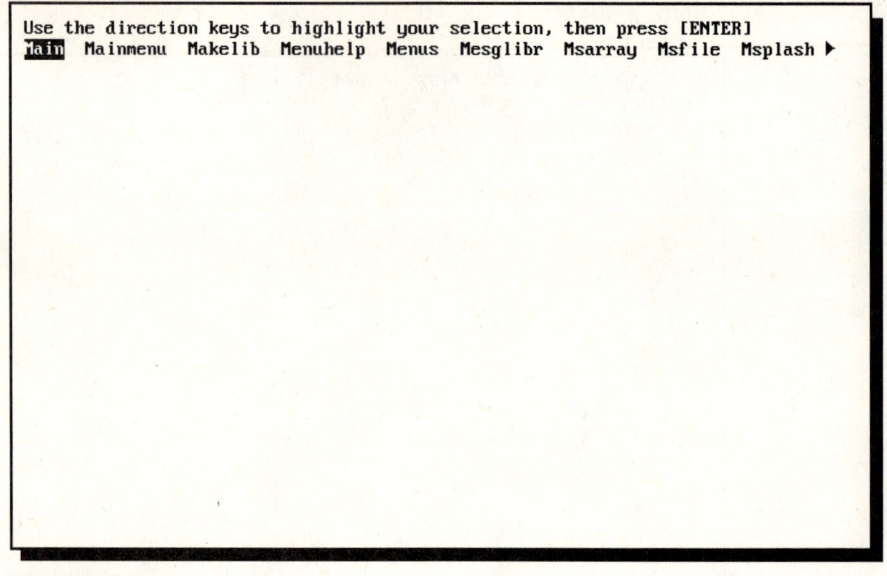

Figure 8-5 Static-style menu

Lines 7 & 79   Combine to create an *event* that continues processing until the user chooses to leave (keep this menu until directed to another script or until the user chooses to leave the application).

Lines 8-10   Release all variables and procedures, and recover any DOS memory that was used by variables and procedures.

Line 14   Establishes a variable *MenuColor* (78=yellow text on red background).

Lines 16-35   Paint a shadow menu on the screen. The two PAINTCANVAS statements overlay each other to create the shadow effect.

Line 20   Uses SETMARGIN to move the left border of the screen to column 10.

Lines 24-35   Type the TEXT…ENDTEXT menu to the screen using the MENUCOLOR.

Lines 37-44 Place a title bar on the main menu, present a selection prompt at the bottom of the screen, and pause the script, waiting for the user to press a key (user's key press is assigned to a variable *gc*).

Lines 46-54 Evaluate the variable *gc*. The PAL GETCHAR() function stores the key the user presses as a code (for example, 13 for [Enter], -59 [F1], -83 [Delete]). If *gc* is less than 0, then the user has pressed the incorrect key. **Not a valid menu choice** is displayed onscreen, the user hears a beep, and the routine LOOPS, returning to the top of the WHILE…ENDWHILE.

Lines 56-58 Assign the *gc* variable to the variable *sel*, converting *gc* to a character with the PAL function CHR(character). Line 58 displays the converted *sel* back to the screen.

Lines 60-76 The SWITCH…ENDSWITCH processes the user's selection. If the key the user presses has a value greater than zero (it passed the IF…ENDIF in lines 46-54), and it doesn't match any of the CASE statements, the user sees the same message found in lines 47-52 and is returned to the top of the WHILE…ENDWHILE. Otherwise, the SWITCH…ENDSWITCH launches the next step in the application.

TIP: *Line 16 ensures that the shadow border always has the screen attribute of the selected color as a background and black text in the foreground. Screen attributes for a DOS machine range from 0-15, black text to intense white text on whatever background is selected. To get a shadow border with a background the same as the current menu and black text in the foreground, obtain the integer value of the MENUCOLOR divided by 16 and multiply this result by 16.*

TIP: *Lines 48 and 69 provide a blinking message in the same color as the current menu. To accomplish this, simply add 128 to the current MENUCOLOR attribute.*

TRAP: *Make sure that you turn the blinking attribute off! If you don't, anything displayed onscreen from that point on will blink until overridden by some other STYLE statement.*

```
 1  Reset ClearAll
 2  @0,0 Clear EOS
 3
 4  SetKey "F11"  Play "SMain"
 5
 6
 7  While (true)
 8  Release Procs All
 9  Release Vars All
10  Reset ClearAll
11
12  CANVAS OFF
13  @0,0 Clear EOS
14  MenuColor = 78
15
16  PaintCanvas Fill "█" Attribute (Int(MenuColor/16)*16) 6,11,15,71
17
18  PaintCanvas Attribute MenuColor 5,10,14,70
19
20  SETMARGIN 10
21  Style Attribute MenuColor
22  @5,0
23
24  Text
25
26    ┌────────────────────────────┐
27    │                            │
28    │ 1 - View/Edit tables       │
29    │ 2 - Import Download File   │
30    │ 3 - Reports Menu           │
31    │ 4 - Utilities Menu         │
32    │ 5 - Exit the App           │
33    │                            │
34    └────────────────────────────┘
35  EndText
36
37  Style Attribute 112
38  @6,11 ?? format("W30,AC","Main Menu")
39  Style
40
41  @24,0 Clear EOL
42  @24,30 ?? "Enter your selection "
43  CANVAS ON
44  gc = getchar()
45
46  if gc < 0 then
47          Cursor Off
48          Style Attribute MenuColor+128
49          @24,0 Clear EOL ?? format("W79,AC","Not a valid menu choice ")
50          beep
51          sleep 1000
52          Cursor Normal
53          loop
```

Listing 8-5 SMAIN.SC *(the Main menu of an application using a STATIC MENU)*

```
54    endif
55
56    sel = chr(gc)
57    Style Attribute MenuColor
58    ?? sel
59
60    Switch
61            case sel = "1" : play "View"
62            case sel = "2" : play "Import"
63            case sel = "3" : play "Reports"
64            case sel = "4" : play "UtilMenu"
65            case sel = "5" : quitloop
66
67
68    OtherWise: Cursor Off
69            Style Attribute MenuColor+128
70            @24,0 Clear EOL ?? format("W79,AC","Not a valid menu choice ")
71            beep
72            sleep 1000
73            Cursor Normal
74            loop
75
76    EndSwitch
77
78
79    EndWhile
```

Listing 8-5 SMAIN.SC (the Main menu of an application using a STATIC MENU)—continued

To give the appearance of stacking successive menus (each menu indented, one over the other) the following routine is copied, customized, and played from SMAIN.SC. Listing 8-6 shows a typical report menu.

REPORTS.SC overview (static-style menu)

The REPORTS.SC overview is exactly like the SMAIN.SC listing with the following exceptions:

Line 13   Plays an external script named BACK. The BACK script paints the screen to give the appearance that the main menu is still in the background. This is especially important after a script that has been launched by this menu returns. This will give the user the effect of being in the second of a two-level menu system.

Line 14	Establishes a variable *MenuColor* (48=black text on a cyan background).
Lines 16-35	Paint a shadow menu on the screen. The two PAINTCANVAS statements overlay each other to create the shadow effect. (The values have been incremented to give the "down and over" effect of stacking.)
Line 20	Uses SETMARGIN to move the left border of the screen to column 11.
Lines 24-35	Type the TEXT...ENDTEXT menu to the screen using the MENUCOLOR starting at row 8.
Lines 37-44	Place a title bar on the reports menu starting at row 9, present a selection prompt at the bottom of the screen, and pause the script, waiting for the user to press a key (the user's key press is assigned to a variable *gc*).

NOTE: *If the user selects "6", the main menu is redisplayed.*

TIP: *The* gc = getchar() *portion of the static-style menus is an excellent alternative to the standard ACCEPT statement. ACCEPT forces the user to press [Enter] to continue while this routine does not.*

Try combining static-style menus with SHOWMENUS, SHOWARRAYS, and SHOWFILE for an easy-to-create and easy-to-maintain user interface.

```
 1
 2
 3
 4
 5
 6
 7  While (true)
 8  Release vars all
 9  Release procs all
10  Reset ClearAll
11
12  CANVAS OFF
13  play "back"
14  MenuColor = 48
15
```

Listing 8-6 REPORTS.SC (a second menu launched from SMAIN.SC)

```
16   PaintCanvas Fill "█" Attribute (Int(MenuColor/16)*16) 9,12,18,72
17
18   PaintCanvas Attribute MenuColor 8,11,17,71
19
20   SETMARGIN 11
21   Style Attribute MenuColor
22   @8,0
23
24   Text
25
26
27
28   1 - Inventory Report
29   2 - Sales Report File
30   3 - Customer Listing
31   4 - Price Book
32   5 - Print Sales Orders
33   6 - Return to the Main Menu
34
35   EndText
36
37   Style Attribute 112
38   @9,12 ?? format("W30,AC","Reports Menu")
39   Style
40
41   @24,0 Clear EOL
42   @24,30 ?? "Enter your selection "
43   CANVAS ON
44   gc = getchar()
45
46   if gc < 0 then
47            Cursor Off
48            Style Attribute MenuColor+128
49            @24,0 Clear EOL ?? format("W79,AC","Not a valid menu choice ")
50            beep
51            sleep 1000
52            Cursor Normal
53            loop
54   endif
55
56   sel = chr(gc)
57   Style Attribute MenuColor
58   ?? sel
59
60   Switch
61            case sel = "1" : play "PrntInv
62            case sel = "2" : play "PrntSale"
63            case sel = "3" : play "PrntCust"
64            case sel = "4" : play "PrntBook"
65            case sel = "5" : play "PrntOrdr"
66            case sel = "6" : quitloop
```

Listing 8-6 REPORTS.SC *(a second menu launched from SMAIN.SC)—continued*

```
67
68   OtherWise: Cursor Off
69             Style Attribute MenuColor+128
70             @24,0 Clear EOL ?? format("W79,AC","Not a valid menu choice ")
71             beep
72             sleep 1000
73             Cursor Normal
74             loop
75
76   EndSwitch
77
78
79   EndWhile
 1   CANVAS OFF
 2   @0,0 Clear EOS
 3   MenuColor = 78
 4
 5   PaintCanvas Fill "▌" Attribute (Int(MenuColor/16)*16) 6,11,15,71
 6
 7   PaintCanvas Attribute MenuColor 5,10,14,70
 8
 9   SETMARGIN 10
10   Style Attribute MenuColor
11   @5,0
12
13   Text
14
15
16
17
18
19
20
21
22
23
24   EndText
25
26   Style Attribute 112
27   @6,11 ?? format("W30,AC","Main Menu")
28   Style
```

Listing 8-6 REPORTS.SC *(a second menu launched from SMAIN.SC)—continued*

Pop-up menus

Pop-up menus are simple to create using PAL. Paradox's Data Entry ToolKit provides the ability to create pop-up menus (and more), but you don't need the DETK to create this style of menus. In order to understand the components of pop-up menus, you need to understand each component of this menu style and its purpose.

The elements of a pop-up system are

- Menu choices and long descriptions
- Position of the menu on the screen
- Desired width of the menu
- The color of the menu
- The menu name

The pop-up routines in this chapter provide the

- Ability to draw a pop-up box
- Method to [Enter] and SELECT menu choices
- Capability to show Help on the menu
- Capability to have the user see where they are. (As a user goes from one menu to the next, menus stack in front of each other, leaving a trail of selections for the user to see.)
- Non-destructive method of restoring previous menus
- Ability to request a table or list of tables

To help you understand the pop-up procedures, read the following definition of variables, terms, and procedures used in Listing 8-7.

MAINMENU.SC overview (pop-up menu)

BeginX	Upper-left row coordinate for the pop-up menu.
BeginY	Upper-left column coordinate for the menu.
NumberChoices	The number of menu items to be displayed by the pop-up menu.
PopWidth	Determines how wide to make the menu box.
Color	Selects a color based on the ASCII attribute codes for the menu.
MenuName	Establishes the name of the current menu, displayed at the top of the pop-up menu.
PrevX	An array that stores a history of the upper-left row coordinates for the previous pop-up menus.

PrevY   An array that stores a history of the upper-left column coordinates for the previous pop-up menus.

PrevNC   An array that stores a history of the number of choices for each of the previous pop-up menus.

PrevPW   An array that stores a history of the widths of the previous pop-up menus.

PrevCL   An array that stores a history of the colors of the previous pop-up menus.

PrevML   An array that stores a history of the menu titles for each of the previous pop-up menus.

PrevN   An array that stores a history of the previous choice selected for each of the previous pop-up menus.

AutoLib   A variable that declares one or more library of procedures as the default(s) to search through when a procedure call is made.

ProcName()   Calls a procedure.

MAINMENU.SC overview

To understand each section of this routine, overview comments are placed in appropriate places in the script.

Lines 1-10   Establish [Shift][F1] as a quick method of running the MAINMENU script.

Lines 12 & 128   Start of the MAINMENU event.

Lines 13-19   Clear and recover all memory and establish (or if returning, re-establish) the AutoLib. This is essential as you re-enter the MAINMENU after quitting from another menu or process. This release and recovery of memory ensures that the maximum amount of memory is available when the user enters or returns to MAINMENU. If you don't refresh and grab back DOS memory periodically throughout your application, your memory will slowly diminish and the system might halt with a Cancel/Debug.

Lines 20-27	Establish arrays for variables that will be used to create the pop-up menu.
Lines 28-31	Tell the procedure that it's at the first level of the menu system (MAINMENU) and that the menu should highlight the first menu selection (*n*).
Lines 32-38	Declare, record, and archive, in a set of arrays, the values for the MAINMENU.
Lines 39-48	Activate the values stored in the arrays as the current values to use when drawing the pop-up menu. (Important when you re-enter the MAINMENU from another process.)
Lines 49-68	Declare arrays for the menu choices and descriptions. Arrays are created in the MENUS library (arrays *SC* and *SD*) that build top-bar versions of the pop-up menu of information (Arrays *C* and *D*). In addition, the system records the first letter of each of the menu choices to allow the user to press the first letter to process their menu selection (Array *NICK*).
Lines 69-89	Record the values for each menu choice and the description that is associated with each.
Lines 90-102	Check to see if the variable *n* has been declared with a value. If it has been declared, let it stand; otherwise assign it the number 1. Line 96 determines how large the array *C* is and loads a variable last with the size of the array *C*.
Lines 103-105	Turn the CANVAS ON and call the MENUS library that builds the pop-up menu.
Line 104	Activates the FillMenu procedure in the MENUS library. This procedure takes all declared variables and creates the pop-up menu.
Line 105	Activates the SelMenu procedure. This procedure lets the user move up and down in the pop-up menu. Once the user makes a selection, this procedure processes the request.

Lines 109-129   Process the user's selection of ESC (quit the menu) or menu item. Plays a script or provides information based on the user's selection.

```
1  ;
2  ;Script [MainMenu] Type [FirstMenu]  Called from [   ]
3  ;
4  ;Description [This is the main Menu for a system]
5  ;
6  ;
7  ;Created [07/31/90] By [G.Salcedo ]
8  ;
9
10  setkey "F11" play "MainMenu"
11
12  While (true)
13  CANVAS OFF
14  Release Procs All
15  Release Vars All
16  Reset
17  Clear
18  ClearAll
19  Autolib = "Menus,MesgLibr,MenuHelp"
20
21  Array  Prevx[10]
22  Array  Prevy[10]
23  Array PrevNC[10]
24  Array PrevPW[10]
25  Array PrevCL[10]
26  Array  PrevN[10]
27  Array PrevML[10]
28
29  Level = 1
30      n = 1
31
32   Prevx[Level] = 3
33   Prevy[Level] = 25
34  PrevNC[Level] = 5
35  PrevPW[Level] = 20
36  PrevCL[Level] = 31
37  PrevML[Level] = format("W18,AC","Main Menu"
38
39         BeginX = Prevx[Level]
40         BeginY = Prevy[Level]
41  NumberChoices = PrevNC[Level]
42       Popwidth = PrevPW[Level]
43          Color = PrevCL[level]
43          Color = PrevCL[level]
44       MenuName = PrevML[level]
45
46
47
```

Listing 8-7 MAINMENU.SC *(the Main menu of an application using MENUS.LIB)*

```
48  ;
49  ;You must declare the following:
50  ;
51  ;         C[n]  = menu items (the possible choices)
52  ;         D[n]  = descriptions of the menu items
53  ;        SC[n]  = "top bar" representation of menu item
54  ;        SD[n]  = "top bar" description
55  ;      NICK[n]  = first letter of menu items
56
57
58  Array          C[NumberChoices]
59  Array          D[NumberChoices]
60  Array         SC[NumberChoices]
61  Array         SD[NumberChoices]
62  Array       NICK[NumberChoices]
63
64
65
66
67
68
69  C[1] = "View/Modify"
70  D[1] = "Go to the MODIFY menu"
71
72
73  C[2] = "Reports"
74  D[2] = "Go the Report Menu"
75
76
77  C[3] = "Utilities"
78  D[3] = "Go to the Utilities Menu"
79
80
81  C[4] = "Info"
82  D[4] = "More information on system"
83
84
85  C[5] = "Quit"
86  D[5] = "Exit the System"
87
88
89
90  if isassigned(n) = false then
91       n = 1
92  else
93       n = n
94  endif
95
96  last = arraysize(c)
97
```

Listing 8-7 MAINMENU.SC (the Main menu of an application using MENUS.LIB)—continued

```
 98
 99
100
101
102
103     CANVAS ON
104     FillMenu()
105     SelMenu()
106
107     Reset
108
109     if sel = "Esc" then
110          @24,0 Clear EOL ?? format("w79,ac","One moment please ...")
111          quitloop
112
113     else
114
115
116     switch
117             case sel = "Esc" : level = level -1
118                                quitloop
119             case sel = c[1]  : play "modimenu"
120             case sel = c[2]  : play "reptmenu"
121             case sel = c[3]  : play "utilmenu"
122             case sel = c[4]  : HelpMenu(sel)
123             case sel = c[5]  : quitloop
124
125     EndSwitch
126     endif
127
128     EndWhile
129
```

Listing 8-7 MAINMENU.SC *(the Main menu of an application using MENUS.LIB)—continued*

Creating Stacking/Tiling Pop-up Menus

To give the appearance of stacking successive menus (with the menus indented and overlayed over the previous menus), copy, customize and play the following script (Listing 8-8) from any other menu script. (This listing is a generic listing.)

NEXTMENU.SC overview (static-style menu)

NEXTMENU.SC acts exactly like MAINMENU.SC with the following exceptions:

Lines 11-16   Store the previous menu's values.

Lines 18-22   Establish the new default menu choice and increment the variable *level* by 1, thus opening up this *level's* array elements for new values. The values for the beginning coordinates are incremented to make the current menu indent in front of the previous menu.

Lines 94-108 Process if the user selects "Esc". The variable *level* is reduced by 1 and the values stored in the *PREV* series of arrays are retrieved and made available to the previous routine.

```
1  ;
2  ;Script [NextMenu] Type [2nd/3rd Level] Call [AnyMenu]
3  ;
4  ;Description [This is a sample menu.]
5  ;
6  ;
7  ;Created [07/31/90] By [G.Salcedo ]
8  ;
9
10
11    Prevx[Level]  = BeginX
12    Prevy[Level]  = BeginY
13   PrevNC[Level]  = NumberChoices
14   PrevPW[Level]  = PopWidth
15   PrevCL[Level]  = Color
16    PrevN[Level]  = n
17
18             n = 1
19         level = level + 1
20
21        BeginX = Prevx[Level-1]+(n)
22        BeginY = Prevy[Level-1]+2 ;
23
24   NumberChoices = 5
25        PopWidth = 20
26           Color = 32
27   MenuName =   format("AC,W18","Next Menu")
28
29    Prevx[Level] = BeginX
30    Prevy[Level] = BeginY
```

Listing 8-8 *NEXTMENU.SC (pop-up menu launched from any other pop-up menu)*

```
31    PrevNC[Level] = NumberChoices
32    PrevPW[Level] = PopWidth
33    PrevCL[Level] = Color;
34     PrevN[Level] = n
35    PrevML[Level] = MenuName
36
37
38    While (true)
39
40
41    ; this sets up arrays for all menu choices and the
42    ; corresponding messages.
43    ;
44    ;         C[n] = menu items (the possible choices)
45    ;         D[n] = descriptions of the menu items
46    ;        SC[n] = "top bar" representation of menu item
47    ;        SD[n] = "top bar"  description
48    ;      NICK[n] = first letter of menu items
50
51    Array        C[NumberChoices]
52    Array        D[NumberChoices]
53    Array     NICK[NumberChoices]
54
55
56    ; These are the menu choices and the corresponding "wide"
bar (top) display.
57    ; Be sure to enclose the menu item in quotes. The number of characters in the
58    ; menu items should not exceed PopWidth-2. Example "View".
59
60    C[1] = "Next Choice 1"
61    D[1] = "Perform Next #1"
62
63
64    C[2] = "Next Choice 2"
65    D[2] = "Perform Next #2"
66
67
68    C[3] = "Next Choice 3"
69    D[3] = "Perform Next #3"
70
71
72    C[4] = "Next Choice 4"
73    D[4] = "Perform Next #4"
74
75
76    C[5] = "Quit"
77    D[5] = "Exit to the MAIN Menu"
78
79
80
81    if isassigned(n) = false then
82        n = 1
```

Listing 8-8 NEXTMENU.SC (pop-up menu launched from any other pop-up menu)—continued

Creating and Enhancing the Paradox Interface

```
 83  else
 84       n = n
 85  endif
 86
 87  last = arraysize(c) ; Lets the procedure know the 'bottom' menu choice.
 88
 89  ; This sets up the ability to graphically display the present menu level.
 90
 91
 92  FillMenu()
 93  SelMenu()
 94  if sel = "Esc" then
 95       @24,0 Clear EOL ?? format("w79,ac","One moment please ...")
 96
 97            Level = Level - 1
 98           BeginX = Prevx[Level]
 99           BeginY = Prevy[Level]
100    NumberChoices = PrevNC[Level]
101         PopWidth = PrevPW[Level]
102            Color = PrevCL[Level]
103         MenuName = PrevML[Level]
104                n = PrevN[Level]
105
106       @24,0 Clear EOL
107       reset
108       quitloop
109  else
110
111
112  switch
113            case sel = "Esc" :        Level = Level - 1
114                                     BeginX = Prevx[Level]
115                                     BeginY = Prevy[Level]
116                               NumberChoices = PrevNC[Level]
117                                    PopWidth = PrevPW[Level]
118                                       Color = PrevCL[Level]
119                                           n = PrevN[Level]
120                                             reset
121                                             quitloop
122            case sel = c[1]  : play "next1"
123            case sel = c[2]  : play "next2"
124            case sel = c[3]  : play "next3"
125            case sel = c[4]  : play "next4"
126            case sel = c[5]  :        Level = Level - 1
127                                     BeginX = Prevx[Level]
128                                     BeginY = Prevy[Level]
129                               NumberChoices = PrevNC[Level]
130                                    PopWidth = PrevPW[Level]
131                                       Color = PrevCL[Level]
132                                           n = PrevN[Level]
133                                             reset
134                                             quitloop
135
```

Listing 8-8 NEXTMENU.SC (pop-up menu launched from any other pop-up menu)—continued

```
136
137    EndSwitch
138    endif
139
140
141    EndWhile
142
```

Listing 8-8 NEXTMENU.SC (pop-up menu launched from any other pop-up menu)—continued

Complete Pop-up Menu Listings with Message and Menuhelp Libraries

```
 1   ;
 2   ;Script [MainMenu] Type [FirstMenu]  Called from [    ]
 3   ;
 4   ;Description [This is the main Menu for a system]
 5   ;
 6   ;
 7   ;Created [07/31/90] By [G.Salcedo ]
 8   ;
 9
10   setkey "F11" play "MainMenu"
11
12   While (true)
13   CANVAS OFF
14   Release Procs All
15   Release Vars All
16   Reset
17   Clear
18   ClearAll
19   Autolib = "Menus,MesgLibr,MenuHelp"
20
21   Array   Prevx[10]
22   Array   Prevy[10]
23   Array PrevNC[10]
24   Array PrevPW[10]
25   Array PrevCL[10]
26   Array   PrevN[10]
27   Array PrevML[10]
28
29   Level = 1
30       n = 1
31
32    Prevx[Level] = 3
33    Prevy[Level] = 25
34   PrevNC[Level] = 5
35   PrevPW[Level] = 20
```

Listing 8-9 MAINMENU.SC (first routine for pop-up menus)

```
36       PrevCL[Level] = 31
37       PrevML[Level] = format("W18,AC","Main Menu")
38
39              BeginX = Prevx[Level]
40              BeginY = Prevy[Level]
41       NumberChoices = PrevNC[Level]
42            Popwidth = PrevPW[Level]
43               Color = PrevCL[level]
44            MenuName = PrevML[level]
45
46
47
48  ;
49  ;You must declare the following:
50  ;
51  ;         C[n] = menu items (the possible choices)
52  ;         D[n] = descriptions of the menu items
53  ;        SC[n] = "top bar" representation of menu item
54  ;        SD[n] = "top bar" description
55  ;      NICK[n] = first letter of menu items
56
57
58  Array          C[NumberChoices]
59  Array          D[NumberChoices]
60  Array         SC[NumberChoices]
61  Array         SD[NumberChoices]
62  Array       NICK[NumberChoices]
63
64
65
66
67
68
69  C[1] = "View/Modify"
70  D[1] = "Go to the MODIFY menu"
71
72
73  C[2] = "Reports"
74  D[2] = "Go the Report Menu"
75
76
77  C[3] = "Utilities"
78  D[3] = "Go to the Utilities Menu"
79
80
```

Listing 8-9 MAINMENU.SC *(first routine for pop-up menus)—continued*

```
 81   C[4] = "Info"
 82   D[4] = "More information on system"
 83
 84
 85   C[5] = "Quit"
 86   D[5] = "Exit the System"
 87
 88
 89
 90   if isassigned(n) = false then
 91        n = 1
 92   else
 93        n = n
 94   endif
 95
 96   last = arraysize(c)
 97
 98
 99
100
101
102
103   CANVAS ON
104   FillMenu()
105
106   SelMenu()
107   Reset
108
109   if sel = "Esc" then
110        @24,0 Clear EOL ?? format("w79,ac","One moment please ...")
111        quitloop
112
113   else
114
115
116   switch
117            case sel = "Esc" : level = level -1
118                               quitloop
119            case sel = c[1]  : play "modimenu"
120            case sel = c[2]  : play "reptmenu"
121            case sel = c[3]  : play "utilmenu"
122            case sel = c[4]  : HelpMenu(sel)
123            case sel = c[5]  : quitloop
124
125   EndSwitch
126   endif
127
128   EndWhile
129
```

Listing 8-9 MAINMENU.SC *(first routine for pop-up menus)—continued*

```
 1;
 2;Script [NextMenu] Type [2nd/3rd Level] Call [AnyMenu]
 3;
 4;Description [This is a sample menu.]
 5;
 6;
 7;Created [07/31/90] By [G.Salcedo ]
 8;
 9
10
11   Prevx[Level] = BeginX
12   Prevy[Level] = BeginY
13  PrevNC[Level] = NumberChoices
14  PrevPW[Level] = PopWidth
15  PrevCL[Level] = Color
16   PrevN[Level] = n
17
18            n = 1
19        level = level + 1
20
21       BeginX = Prevx[Level-1]+(n)
22       BeginY = Prevy[Level-1]+2 ;
23
24  NumberChoices = 5
25       PopWidth = 20
26          Color = 32
27  MenuName =  format("AC,W18","Next Menu")
28
29   Prevx[Level] = BeginX
30   Prevy[Level] = BeginY
31  PrevNC[Level] = NumberChoices
32  PrevPW[Level] = PopWidth
33  PrevCL[Level] = Color;
34   PrevN[Level] = n
35  PrevML[Level] = MenuName            ;
36
37
38  While (true)
39
40
41  ; this sets up arrays for all menu choices and the
42  ; corresponding messages.
43  ;
44  ;        C[n] = menu items (the possible choices)
45  ;        D[n] = descriptions of the menu items
46  ;       SC[n] = "top bar" representation of menu item
47  ;       SD[n] = "top bar"  description
48  ;     NICK[n] = first letter of menu items
50
51   Array       C[NumberChoices]
52   Array       D[NumberChoices]
53   Array    NICK[NumberChoices]
54
```

Listing 8-10 NEXTMENU.SC (any other menu in pop-up menu system)

```
55
56    ;These are the menu choices and the corresponding "wide" bar (top) display.
57    ;Be sure to enclose the menu item in quotes. The number of characters in the
58    ;menu items should not exceed PopWidth-2. Example "View".
59
60    C[1] = "Next Choice 1"
61    D[1] = "Perform Next #1"
62
63
64    C[2] = "Next Choice 2"
65    D[2] = "Perform Next #2"
66
67
68    C[3] = "Next Choice 3"
69    D[3] = "Perform Next #3"
70
71
72    C[4] = "Next Choice 4"
73    D[4] = "Perform Next #4"
74
75
76    C[5] = "Quit"
77    D[5] = "Exit to the MAIN Menu"
78
79
80
81    if isassigned(n) = false then
82         n = 1
83    else
84         n = n
85    endif
86
87    last = arraysize(c)  ; Lets the procedure know the 'bottom' menu choice.
88
89    ; This sets up the ability to graphically display the present menu level.
90
91
92    FillMenu()
93    SelMenu()
94    if sel = "Esc" then
95         @24,0 Clear EOL ?? format("w79,ac","One moment please ...")
96
97              Level = Level - 1
98              BeginX = Prevx[Level]
99              BeginY = Prevy[Level]
100        NumberChoices = PrevNC[Level]
101          PopWidth = PrevPW[Level]
```

Listing 8-10 NEXTMENU.SC (any other menu in pop-up menu system)—continued

```
102                  Color = PrevCL[Level]
103              MenuName = PrevML[Level]
104                     n = PrevN[Level]
105
106       @24,0 Clear EOL
107       reset
108       quitloop
109  else
110
111
112  switch
113            case sel = "Esc" :         Level = Level - 1
114                                      BeginX = Prevx[Level]
115                                      BeginY = Prevy[Level]
116                                NumberChoices = PrevNC[Level]
117                                    PopWidth = PrevPW[Level]
118                                       Color = PrevCL[Level]
119                                           n = PrevN[Level]
120                                           reset
121                                           quitloop
122            case sel = c[1]  : play "next1"
123            case sel = c[2]  : play "next2"
124            case sel = c[3]  : play "next3"
125            case sel = c[4]  : play "next4"
126            case sel = c[5]  :         Level = Level - 1
127                                      BeginX = Prevx[Level]
128                                      BeginY = Prevy[Level]
129                                NumberChoices = PrevNC[Level]
130                                    PopWidth = PrevPW[Level]
131                                       Color = PrevCL[Level]
132                                           n = PrevN[Level]
133                                           reset
134                                           quitloop
135
136
137  EndSwitch
138  endif
139
140
141  EndWhile
142
```

Listing 8-10 NEXTMENU.SC *(any other menu in pop-up menu system)—continued*

Listing 8-11 MENUS.SC (library of menu and file procedures for pop-up menu system)

MENUS.SC is the heart of the pop-up menu system. These routines provide all the tools to create and recreate your application's menus.

Procedures contained in this library include:

FillMenu	Draws and fills in the pop-up menu.
DrawPopBox	Alternative method to FillMenu.
PaintBox	Alternative method to FillMenu.
SelMenu	This procedure provides the mechanism to move around the menu and make selections. It also provides help by calling the Helpmenu procedure from the MENUHELP library. If more than one menu choice starts with the same letter, it calls SubMenu to help the user process their selection.
SubMenu	Presents a Paradox-style menu using SHOWARRAY for all the choices that start with the same letter. For example, if a menu had both a REPORTS and REVIEW selection, a tie-breaker menu would be created at the top of the screen and the user directed to select the menu choice they desire.
PopFileBox	Procedure that draws a box and allows the user to type in a table selection. If the user presses [Enter], a SHOWTABLE command is processed and the user is prompted to make a selection from the list.
CheckTable	Procedure usually called by EDIT or COEDIT routines. This procedure checks to see whether a table exists and if so, whether it has any records.
CleanScreen	Cleans up the current menu as you go back to the previous menu.
ReDrawPopBox	Procedure placed and called from the bottom of a script that has been launched from a pop-up menu. ReDrawPopBox rebuilds the previous menus, giving the user the effect that they are back to the menu choice they selected from the current menu.
NoDosExit	Routine that displays a special message for VIEW/EDIT/COEDIT/DATAENTRY routines. If one of the above routines prevents the user from going to DOS

([Ctrl][O] or [Alt][O]), this message is displayed to let the user know that access to DOS is not allowed in the routine.

```
1   CreateLib "Menus"
2   @24,0 Clear EOL ?? "Creating MENUS library "
3   Style blink ?? "..."
4   style
5
6   Proc Closed PaintBox ()
7   UseVars BeginX,BeginY,Numberchoices,PopWidth,Color
8
9   Setmargin Beginy
10
11  Style attribute color
12  @Beginx,Beginy ?? "┌"+fill("=",Popwidth-2)+"┐"
13
14  for paintit from 1 to (Numberchoices-1) step 1
15      @Beginx+Paintit,Beginy ?? "║"+fill(" ",Popwidth-2)+"║"
16  endfor
17
18  @beginx+NumberChoices,beginy ?? "└"+fill("=",Popwidth-2)+"┘"
19  SETMARGIN 0
20  EndProc
21
22  Proc Closed DrawPopBox ()
23
24  UseVars HelpMenu,MesgLibr,sel,n,Nick,C,D,last,nick,
25          Beginx,BeginY,Numberchoices,Popwidth,Color,MenuName
26
27   UpLCr = "┌"  F_Hchar = "="   UpRCr = "┐"
28                F_VChar = "║"
29  LowLCr = "└"                  LowRCr = "┘"
30
31    NumberLines = NumberChoices + 2
32  FillHLn = fill(F_Hchar,PopWidth-2)
33  FillBox = F_VChar + spaces(PopWidth-2) + F_VChar
34  m = beginy+2
35
36  Cursor Off
37
38  Style Attribute Color
39  @BeginX,BeginY ?? UpLCr + FillHLn + UpRCr
40  EndProc
41
42  Proc Closed FillMenu()
43
44  Usevars
                Beginx,beginy,m,PopWidth,Nick,Numberchoices,
                MenuName,c,d,last,nick,color,autolib,level,
                prevx,prevy,prevpw,prevnc
45
```

Listing 8-11 *MENUS.SC (library of menu and file procedures for pop-up menu system)*

```
46  CANVAS OFF
47  CleanScreen()
48
49  TR = beginx+1
50  LC = beginy+2
51  BR = beginx+2+last
52  RC = beginy+1+popwidth
53
54  PAINTCANVAS Fill "▓" Attribute 113
55  TR,LC,BR,RC
56
57  Style Attribute Color
58      m = beginy+2
59
60  FillBox = "║"+spaces(PopWidth-2)+"║"
61  FillHLn = fill("=",PopWidth-2)
62
63  for CntBLine from 1 to NumberChoices step 1
64      @BeginX+CntBLine,BeginY ?? FillBox
65      if isassigned(C[CntBLine]) = true then
66          @BeginX+CntBLine,m ?? C[CntBLine]
67          NICK[CntBline] = substr(c[CntBLine],1,1)
68      endif
69  Endfor
70  @BeginX+CntBLine,BeginY ?? "╚" + FillHLn + "╝"
71
72  lenmenu = len(MenuName)
73
74  if len(MenuName) < PopWidth-2 then
75      padmenu = spaces((PopWidth-2)-lenmenu)
76  else
77      padmenu = ""
78  endif
79
80  MenuName = MenuName+PadMenu
81  MenuName = format("AC,PopWidth-2",MenuName)
82
83  MenuLine = "╔"+format("AL,PopWidth",MenuName)+"╗"
84
85  @BeginX,BeginY ?? MenuLine
86  style
87
88  CANVAS ON
89  EndProc
90
91  Proc Closed SelMenu ()
92  Usevars n,BeginX,Beginy,sel,m,color,c,d,last,level,Autolib,nick,popwidth
93
94  While (true)
95
96  ; The following displays the menu item and description as top bars
97  ; and highlights the item in the bar menu.
98
```

Listing 8-11 MENUS.SC *(library of menu and file procedures for pop-up menu system)—cont.*

```
 99    padchoice = fill(" ",(Popwidth-4)-len(c[n]))
100
101    style attribute 112      @0,0 ?? format("w79,ac",C[n])
102    style Attribute color    @1,0 ?? format("w79,ac",D[n])
103    style attribute 112      @beginx+n,beginy+2 ?? c[n],padchoice
104
105    ; wait for the "user" to type a letter
106      gc = getchar()
107    ; evaluate the character and perform based on which character was chosen
108
109    Switch
110
111    CASE gc = -59 : sel = C[n]
112                    HelpMenu(sel)
113                    loop
114
115    CASE gc >= 48 and gc <= 122 :style attribute color
116                                 @beginx+n,beginy+2 ?? c[n],padchoice
117                                 SubMenu()
118                                 padchoice = fill(" ",(Popwidth-4)-len(c[n]))
119                                 sel = c[n]
120                                 style attribute 112
121
122                                 @beginx+n,beginy+2 ?? c[n],padchoice
123                                 quitloop
124
125    CASE gc = 27 :sel = "Esc"
126             quitloop
127
128    CASE gc = 13 :@beginx+n,Beginy+2 ?? c[n],padchoice
129             sel = c[n]
130             quitloop
131
132    CASE gc = -71:Style attribute color       ; Home key is pressed
133             @BeginX+n,m ?? c[n],padchoice
134             n = 1
135             loop
136
137    CASE gc = -79:                            ; End key is pressed
138             Style attribute color
139             @BeginX+n,beginy+2 ?? c[n],padchoice
140             n = last
141             loop
142
143    CASE gc = -72:                            ; Up key is pressed
144             if n = 1 then
145                   Style attribute color
146                   @beginx+n,beginy+2 ?? c[n],padchoice
147                   n = last
148                   loop
149             else
150                   Style attribute color
151                   @beginx+n,beginy+2 ?? c[n],padchoice
```

Listing 8-11 MENUS.SC (library of menu and file procedures for pop-up menu system)—cont.

```
152                         n = n - 1
153                         loop
154                 endif
155
156     CASE gc = -80:                          ; Down key is pressed
157             if n = last then
158                     Style Attribute color
159                     @beginx+n,beginy+2 ?? c[n],padchoice
160                     n = 1
161                     loop
162             else
163                     Style Attribute color
164                     @beginx+n,beginy+2 ?? c[n],padchoice
165                     n = n + 1
166                     loop
167             endif
168
169     OtherWise:Loop
170
171     EndSwitch
172
173     quitloop
174     Endwhile
175
176     endproc
177
178     Proc Closed SubMenu()
179     UseVars last,gc,c,d,sc,sd,nick,n,color,beginx,beginy
180     Private SubMa,SubMB,countit,look
181
182     While (true)
183
184     Array submA[last]
185     Array submB[last]
186
187     if gc > 90 then
188          gc = gc - 32
189     endif
190
191     countit = 0
192
193     for look from 1 to last step 1
194          if asc(nick[look]) = gc then
195                n = look
196                RETURN look
197                countit = countit + 1
198                subma[countit] = c[look]
199                submB[countit] = d[look]
200          endif
201          n = look
202     endfor
203
204     if isassigned(subma[1]) = false then
```

Listing 8-11 MENUS.SC (library of menu and file procedures for pop-up menu system)—cont.

```
205         quitloop
206 endif
207
208 if countit = 1 then
209
210
211         style reverse            @0,0 ?? SC[n]
212         style Attribute color    @1,0 ?? SD[n]
213         style reverse       @beginx+n,beginy+2 ?? c[n]
214         sel = subma[countit]
215         quitloop
216 endif
217
218 Array SubA[countit]
219 Array SubB[countit]
220
221 for assign from 1 to countit
222         suba[assign] = subma[assign]
223         subb[assign] = submb[assign]
224         style reverse            @0,0 ?? SC[n]
225         style Attribute color    @1,0 ?? SD[n]
226         style reverse            @beginx+n,beginy+2 ?? c[n]
227 endfor
228
229
230 showarray
231            subA subB
232
233 to sel
234
235 quitloop
236 endwhile
237 RETURN sel
238 endproc
239
240 Proc PopFileBox()
241
242
243 style attribute 79
244 @Beginx+n+1,m+2 ?? "┌───File───┐"
245 @Beginx+n+2,m+2 ?? "│          │"
246 @Beginx+n+3,m+2 ?? "└──────────┘"
247
248 Style Reverse
249 @Beginx+n+2,m+4 ??
250 Accept "a8" to tablename
251
252 if isassigned(tablename) = false then
253         RETURN tablename
254 endif
255
256 if tablename = "Esc" then
257         RETURN tablename
```

Listing 8-11 MENUS.SC (library of menu and file procedures for pop-up menu system)—cont.

```
258  endif
259
260  if tablename = "" or tablename = "?" then
261       @0,0 Clear EOL
262       @1,0 Clear EOL
263       ShowTables
264       Directory()
265   format("W79,AC","Use the \017- -\016 keys...press \017|| to select table")
266       to tablename
267       @Beginx+n+2,m+4 ?? tablename
268  endif
269
270  if tablename = "Esc" then
271
272       RETURN tablename
273
274  endif
275
276  RETURN tablename
277
278  endproc
279
280  Proc Closed CheckTable(tablename)
281
282  if istable(tablename) = false then
283       @24,0 Clear EOL ?? "No records in ",tablename
284       beep
285       sleep 500
286       @24,0 Clear EOL
287       tablename = "Escape"
288       RETURN
289  endif
290
291  if nrecords(tablename) = 0 then
292       @24,0 Clear EOL ?? "No records in ",tablename
293       beep
294       sleep 500
295       @24,0 Clear EOL
296       tablename = "Escape"
297       RETURN
298  endif
299  endproc
300
301  Proc Closed CleanScreen ()
302  Usevars PopWidth, Beginx, numberchoices, beginy, level, prevx, prevy, prevnc, prevpw
303
304  if level > 1 then
305       @PrevX[level-1],Prevy[level]+PrevPW[level]+1 Clear EOS
306       @PrevX[level-1]+PrevNC[level-1]+1,PrevY[level] Clear EOS
307
308  endif
309  RETURN
```

Listing 8-11 MENUS.SC (library of menu and file procedures for pop-up menu system)—cont.

```
310
311   EndProc
312
313   Proc ReDrawPopBox (level)
314
315
316   @0,0 Clear EOS
317
318     UpLCr = "┌"  F_Hchar = "═"   UpRCr = "┐"
319                  F_VChar = "║"
320   LowLCr = "└"                  LowRCr = "┘"
321   StopReDraw = level;-1
322
323   for counter from 1 to StopReDraw step 1
324          BeginX =    Prevx[Counter]
325          BeginY =    Prevy[Counter]
326   NumberChoices =    PrevNC[Counter]
327       PopWidth =     PrevPW[Counter]
328          Color =     PrevCL[Counter]
329      MenuName =      PrevML[counter]
330             n =      PrevN[Counter]
331
332     NumberLines = NumberChoices + 2
333   FillHLn = fill(F_Hchar,PopWidth-2)
334   FillBox = F_VChar + spaces(PopWidth-2) + F_VChar
335
336   Cursor Off
337
338   Style Attribute Color
339   @BeginX,BeginY ?? UpLCr + FillHLn + UpRCr
340
341   for CntBLine from 1 to NumberChoices step 1
342          @BeginX+CntBLine,BeginY ?? FillBox
343   Endfor
344
345          @BeginX+CntBLine,BeginY ?? LowLCr + FillHLn + LowRCr
346
347          lenmenu = len(MenuName)
348
349          if len(MenuName) < PopWidth-2 then
350              padmenu = spaces((PopWidth-2)-lenmenu)
351          else
352              padmenu = ""
353          endif
354
355          MenuName = MenuName+PadMenu
356          MenuName = format("AC,PopWidth-2",MenuName)
357
358          MenuLine = UpLCr+format("AL,PopWidth",MenuName)+UpRCr
359
360          @BeginX,BeginY ?? MenuLine
361
362   endfor
```

Listing 8-11 MENUS.SC (library of menu and file procedures for pop-up menu system)—cont.

```
363                       level = counter-1
364                      BeginX = Prevx[Level]
365                      BeginY = Prevy[Level]
366               NumberChoices = PrevNC[Level]
367                    PopWidth = PrevPW[Level]
368                       Color = PrevCL[Level]
369                           n = PrevN[Level]
370                    MenuName = PrevML[Level]
371
372   EndProc
373
374   Proc Closed NoDosExit(Pos)
375
376   NoDosMsg = format("AC,w79","Exit to DOS not allowed here")
377
378   if pos = "Top" then
379        @0,0 Clear EOL ?? NoDosMsg
380        beep sleep 1000
381        RETURN
382   endif
383   if pos = "Bottom" then
384        @24,0 Clear EOL ?? NoDosMsg
385        beep sleep 1000
386        RETURN
387   endif
388   if pos <> "Top" or pos <> "Bottom" then
389        message NoDosMsg
390        beep sleep 1000
391        RETURN
392   endif
393
394   EndProc
395
396   WriteLib "Menus" DrawPopBox, SubMenu, PopFileBox, CheckTable, CleanScreen, ReDrawPopBox,
397                   SelMenu,FillMenu,PaintBox,NoDosExit
```

Listing 8-11 MENUS.SC (library of menu and file procedures for pop-up menu system)—cont.

Listing 8-12 MESGLIBR.SC (library that provides routines that display messages for any process during application)

MESGLIBR routines provide you with a way of informing the user about the processes and actions as they are run by your application. Presenting process messages helps the user understand what is going on in the background. For example, you should display a message to the screen so the user knows that a query is in process or that a report is being sent to a printer. Never make the user guess what is going on. Give your user the appearance that your application is in motion.

Besides the message capability in this library, a percent bar function is provided. The PerCentbar procedure displays a grid starting at 0 and ending with 100. As a routine is processed, the user sees an expanding bar below the grid that indicates how much of the process has been completed.

Two types of messages are available here. If a message is assigned to a message number less than 97, the message is displayed and the user is required to press a key to continue. If the message number is 97 or greater, the message displays until it is replaced by another message or the screen is cleared by some other routine.

Procedures contained in this library include:

Messgbox — Creates a pop-up message box that can be called anytime in the application. As it is called, it requires a message number to function correctly.

Percentbar — Simple procedure that paints a 0-100 scale on the screen.

Scale — Procedure that paints an active, moving bar below the 0-100 scale placed on the screen by Percentbar.

Clearmsg — This procedure requires that you pass it a row number *TR* before clearing the message from the screen.

NOTE: You enter the message text into one of the IF...ENDIF statements in the MESGLIBR.SC script. In this routine, each message line should not exceed 55 characters per line. You are allowed 3 lines for each message. If you need more messages than presented, add the appropriate number of IF...ENDIF statements, assigning each new message a unique message number.

```
1
2 ;Script [MesgLibr] Type [Help    ] Called from [Menus   ]
3 ;
4 ;Description [Provides Help for all Menu Choices]
5 ;
6 ;
7 ;Created [07/31/90] By [G.Salcedo ]
8
9
10   @24,0 Clear EOL ?? "Compiling MesgLibr"
11   Style Blink ?? "..."
```

Listing 8-12 MESGLIBR.SC

```
12    Style
13
14    createlib "MesgLibr"
15
16    Proc MessgBox(Msg)
17    Private TR,LC,BR,RC
18
19    CURSOR OFF
20
21    TR = 19
22    LC = 10
23    BR = 22
24    RC = 66
25
26    PaintCanvas Attribute Color
27    TR,LC,BR,RC
28
29
30
31
32
33
34
35
36
37    PAINTCANVAS Fill "▓" Attribute 113
38    TR+1,LC+2,TR+4,RC+2
39
40
41 ;....+...10....+...20....+....30....+...40....+...50....+.
42    if msg = 1 then
43            MLine1 = "To select a TABLE, type in the TABLE name and press ◁┘"
44            MLine2 = ""
45            MLine3 = "To see a list of all tables press " and then SELECT"
46    endif
47
48    if msg = 2 then
49            MLine1 = ""
50            MLine2 = ""
51            MLine3 = ""
52    endif
53
54    if msg = 3 then
55            MLine1 = ""
56            MLine2 = ""
57            MLine3 = ""
58    endif
59
60    if msg = 4 then
61            MLine1 = ""
62            MLine2 = ""
63            MLine3 = ""
64    endif
```

Listing 8-12 MESGLIBR.SC —continued

Creating and Enhancing the Paradox Interface

```
 65
 66  if msg = 5 then
 67          MLine1  = ""
 68          MLine2  = ""
 69          MLine3  = ""
 70  endif
 71
 72  if msg = 6 then
 73          MLine1  = ""
 74          MLine2  = ""
 75          MLine3  = ""
 76  endif
 77
 78  if msg = 7 then
 79          MLine1  = ""
 80          MLine2  = ""
 81          MLine3  = ""
 82  endif
 83
 84  if msg = 8 then
 85          MLine1  = ""
 86          MLine2  = ""
 87          MLine3  = ""
 88  endif
 89
 90  if msg = 9 then
 91          MLine1  = ""
 92          MLine2  = ""
 93          MLine3  = ""
 94  endif
 95
 96  if msg = 10 then
 97          MLine1  = ""
 98          MLine2  = ""
 99          MLine3  = ""
100  endif
101
102  if msg = 96 then
103          MLine1  = ""
104          MLine2  = ""
105          MLine3  = ""
106  endif
107
108  if msg = 97 then
109          MLine1  = ""
110          MLine2  = "ONE MOMENT PLEASE"
111          MLine3  = ""
112  endif
113
114  if msg = 98 then
115          MLine1  = ""
116          MLine2  = "PERFORMING BACKUP AND ANALYSIS"
117          MLine3  = ""
```

Listing 8-12 MESGLIBR.SC —continued

```
118  endif
119  if msg = 99 then
120          MLine1  = ""
121          MLine2  = "UNABLE to PERFORM BACKUP/COPY"
122          MLine3  = "CALL [SUPPORT]"
123  endif
124
125  Style Attribute Color
126  @TR+1,LC+2 ?? format("W55,AL",MLine1)
127  @TR+2,LC+2 ?? format("W55,AL",MLine2)
128  @TR+3,LC+2 ?? format("W55,AL",MLine3)
129
130  Style
131
132  if msg < 90 then
133        gc = getchar()
134        @20,0 Clear EOS
135  else
136        sleep 500
137  endif
138
139  CURSOR NORMAL
140
141  Release vars Mline1,Mline2,Mline3,gc,Msg
142
143  endproc
144  Proc PerCentBar()
145
146  @20,0 Clear EOS
147
148  Style Attribute Color
149  @21,12 ?? "  0   10   20   30   40   50   60   70   80   90  100"
150  @22,12 ?? " |---+---+---+---+---+---+---+---+---+---| "
151  style
152  endproc
153
154  Proc Scale(Eval)
155
156  scalechar = ">"
157
158      Style Attribute (Int(Color/16)*16))
159      fillbar = int(eval/2)
160      @23,13 ?? fill(scalechar,fillbar)
161      style
162
163  endproc
164
165  Proc ClearMsg(TR)
166          @TR,0 Clear EOS
167  EndProc
168
169
170  Style
```

Listing 8-12 MESGLIBR.SC —*continued*

```
171  @24,0 Clear EOL
172  Clear
173
174  writelib "MesgLibr" MessgBox, PerCentBar, Scale, ClearMsg
175
```

Listing 8-12 MESGLIBR.SC —continued

Listing 8-13 MENUHELP.SC (library of routines that provide context sensitive help pop-up menu system)

MENUHELP routines provide you with a way of informing the user about the choices on the pop-up menu. This information is usually not obvious or can't be adequately expressed by the top bar descriptions. When the user presses [F1], the routine records which menu selection is currently being highlighted. The routine then passes that menu value to the HelpMenu procedure. If Help exists for the menu value, it is displayed at the bottom of the screen. Of course, in order to receive help on a menu choice, you must first enter help text for the menu choice in the MENUHELP library.

To return to the menu, the user presses any key. Notice that the MENU-HELP routine presents Help in the same color as the current menu.

NOTE: *You enter the help text for each menu item into one of the IF...ENDIF statements in the MENUHELP.SC script. In this routine, each help line should not exceed 55 characters per line. You are allowed 3 lines of help for each menu choice.*

```
 1 ;
 2 ;Script [MenuHelp] Type [Help    ] Called from [Menus   ]
 3 ;
 4 ;Description [Provides Help for all Menu Choices]
 5 ;
 6 ;
 7 ;Created [04/12/90] By [G.Salcedo ]
 8 ;
 9
10   @24,0 Clear EOL ?? "Compiling MenuHelp "
11   Style Blink ?? "..."
12   Style
13
```

Listing 8-13 MENUHELP.SC

```
14  createlib "MenuHelp"
15
16  Proc Closed HelpMenu(Sel)
17  Usevars Color
18  Private TR,LC,BR,RC
19
20  CANVAS OFF
21  CURSOR OFF
22
23  TR = 19
24  LC = 10
25  BR = 22
26  RC = 66
27
28  PaintCanvas Attribute Color
29  TR,LC,BR,RC
30
31
32  PAINTCANVAS Fill "▌" Attribute 113
33  TR+1,LC+2,TR+4,RC+2
34
35
36  ;....+...10....+...20....+....30....+...40....+...50....+.
37  if sel = "View" then
38          HLine1 = "SELECT View to browse thru tables and to perform minor"
39          HLine2 = "editing. SUGGESTION: for MAJOR editing SELECT EDIT"
40          HLine3 = ""
41  endif
42  if sel = "View/Modify" then
43          HLine1 = "This choice allows you to go the View/Modify Menu"
44          HLine2 = "You may View or Edit any file in the current"
45          HLine3 = "directory."
46  endif
47  if sel = "Choice #1" then
48          HLine1 = "                                                    "
49          HLine2 = "                                                    "
50          HLine3 = "                                                    "
51  endif
52  if sel = "Reports" then
53          HLine1 = ""
54          HLine2 = "              Go to the REPORTS Menu"
55          HLine3 = ""
56  endif
57
58  if sel = "Utilities" then
59          HLine1 = "BACKUP, Recovery, System Utilities       "
60          HLine2 = "RUN OTHER PROGRAMS                       "
61          HLine3 = "EXPORT/IMPORT data                       "
62  endif
63  if sel = "Info" then
64       HLine1 = "This is where GENERAL INFORMATION about the system is    "
65       HLine2 = "placed. [F1] will bring up context sensitive HELP for    "
66       HLine3 = "a menu choice if it is available."
```

Listing 8-13 MENUHELP.SC—*continued*

Creating and Enhancing the Paradox Interface 239

```
 67  endif
 68  if sel = "Edit" then
 69          HLine1  = "Choose this function to perform MAJOR editing"
 70          HLine2  = ""
 71          HLine3  = ""
 72  endif
 73  if sel = "DataEntry"      then
 74          HLine1  = "Allows you to perform initial and batch entries of"
 75          HLine2  = "data.          "
 76          HLine3  = "                              "
 77  endif
 78  if sel = "Choice #2" then
 79          HLine1  = "                              "
 80          HLine2  = "                              "
 81          HLine3  = "                              "
 82  endif
 83  if sel = "Choice #3" then
 84          HLine1  = "                                      "
 85          HLine2  = "                                      "
 86          HLine3  = "                                      "
 87  endif
 88  if sel = "Choice #4" then
 89          HLine1  = "                                      "
 90          HLine2  = "                                      "
 91          HLine3  = "                                      "
 92  endif
 93  if sel = "More" then
 94          HLine1  = ""
 95          HLine2  = "    More SELECTIONS"
 96          HLine3  = ""
 97  endif
 98  if sel = "Next Choice 1" then
 99          HLine1  = ""
100          HLine2  = "              No Help Available"
101          HLine3  = ""
102  endif
103  if sel = "Next Choice 2" then
104          HLine1  = ""
105          HLine2  = "              No Help Available"
106          HLine3  = ""
107  endif
108  if sel = "Next Choice 3" then
109          HLine1  = ""
110          HLine2  = "              No Help Available"
111          HLine3  = ""
112  endif
113  if sel = "Backup" then
114          HLine1  = ""
115          HLine2  = "     BACKUP a SINGLE or all FILES to DISK"
116          HLine3  = ""
117  endif
118  if sel = "Date/Time" then
119          HLine1  = "                 EXIT to DOS"
```

Listing 8-13 MENUHELP.SC—continued

```
120             HLine2 = "         RESET the SYSTEM Date and/or Time"
121             HLine3 = ""
122     endif
123     if sel = "System/Analysis" then
124             HLine1 = ""
125             HLine2 = "   Run Statistics on the SYSTEM to evaluate Performance"
126             HLine3 = ""
127     endif
128     if sel = "Quit" then
129             HLine1 = ""
130             HLine2 = "    Select this to GO BACK to the Previous Menu or to"
131             HLine3 = "                    QUIT the SYSTEM                    "
132     endif
133
134     if isassigned(Hline1) = false and isassigned(Hline2) = false and
135        isassigned(Hline3) = false then
136             HLine1 = ""
137             HLine2 = "                   HELP NOT AVAILABLE"
138             HLine3 = ""
139     endif
140
141     CANVAS ON
142
143     Style Attribute Color
144     @TR+1,LC+2 ?? format("W55,AL",HLine1)
145     @TR+2,LC+2 ?? format("W55,AL",HLine2)
146     @TR+3,LC+2 ?? format("W55,AL",HLine3)
147
148     style
149
150     gc = getchar()
151
152     @19,0 Clear EOS
153
154     CURSOR NORMAL
155
156     endproc
157
158     writelib "MenuHelp" HelpMenu
```

Listing 8-13 MENUHELP.SC—*continued*

9 Viewing, Entering, and Editing Data

Entering data, modifying it later, and viewing the contents of a table are the backbone of an application. In interactive use, Paradox provides easy access to data at the table level and prompts interactive users immediately when it detects a problem with their actions. In an application, however, you have to trap for these problems and take the appropriate action. Areas such as key violations require tremendous effort and a good understanding of the Paradox environment to ensure that all potential problems are handled.

This chapter presents tips and techniques for viewing, entering, and modifying data in an application. In some examples, multiple solutions are presented simply to demonstrate different methods. There are also situations where two different techniques must be used to obtain sightly different results. The various topics covered in this chapter include:

- Generic view script for multiple tables
- Data entry methods
- Edit versus CoEdit
- Controlling a transaction log in Edit mode
- Editing a subset of a table
- Global variables, arrays, and functions in forms
- Key violations
- Uniqueness not based on key field
- Trapping for Field view
- How to get to DOS within an application (and ways to prevent it)

Generic View Script for Multiple Tables

Viewing a table is one of the easiest commands to execute in Paradox. To place a table on the workspace (in Main mode) in an application, use either VIEW tablename or {View} {tablename} followed by a WAIT command. In some cases, multiple images of the same tables or different tables are required on the workspace. Listing 9-1 is a generic routine simulating some of the features available for table viewing in interactive Paradox.

```
 1) PROC ViewTbls()                           ; Viewtbls.sc
 2) WHILE True
 3)    numofimages = NIMAGES()                ;  Save the number of images in a
 4)                                           ;  variable to prevent repeated
 5)                                           ;  calls the NIMAGES()
 6)
 7)    IF numofimages = 1 THEN                ;  Use two different WAIT TABLE
 8)                                           ;  statements depending on the
 9)                                           ;  number of images on the workspace
10)       WAIT TABLE
11)          PROMPT "Viewing Single Table   [F2]-Exit   [F10]-Table Menu",
12)                 "[F7]-Form/Table View Toggle"
13)          UNTIL "F7","F2","F10","DOS","DOSBIG","ZOOM","ZOOMNEXT"
14)    ELSE
15)       WAIT TABLE
16)          PROMPT "Viewing Table " + STRVAL(IMAGENO()) + " of " +
17)                 STRVAL(numofimages) + "   [F2]-Exit   [F10]-Table Menu    " +
18)                 "[T]-Size Image",
19)                 "[F3]-Next Table   [F4]-Previous Table   " +
20)                 "[F7]-Form/Table View Toggle"
21)          UNTIL "F3","F4","F10","T","t","F7","F2","DOS","DOSBIG","ZOOM","ZOOMNEXT"
22)    ENDIF
23)    SWITCH
24)       CASE retval = "F3"        : UPIMAGE           LOOP
25)       CASE retval = "F4"        : DOWNIMAGE         LOOP
26)       CASE retval = "ZOOM"      : ZoomMenu()        LOOP
27)       CASE retval = "ZOOMNEXT:  : ZoomNextProc()    LOOP
28)       CASE retval = "F10"       : ViewTblsMenu()    LOOP ; Get another table
29)       CASE retval = "F7"        : FORMKEY           LOOP
30)       CASE retval = "T" OR                       ;  Allow user to size the
31)            retval = "t"         :                ;  the number of rows shown
32)          WHILE (true)                           ;  for the current table
33)             Menu {Image} {TableSize}
34)             WAIT TABLE
35)                PROMPT "Use UpArrow to decrease the table by one row;" +
36)                       " DownArrow to increase by one row...",
37)                       "then press Enter when finished"
38)                UNTIL "ENTER","DOS","DOSBIG"
39)                IF retval = "ENTER" THEN QUITLOOP ENDIF
40)          ENDWHILE
```

Listing 9-1 *Generic procedure for viewing tables*

```
41)            ENTER                              ; Ends TableSize command
42)            LOOP
43)       CASE retval = "F2"    : QUITLOOP
44)       OTHERWISE              : BEEP LOOP
45)    ENDSWITCH
46)  ENDWHILE
47)  CLEARALL
48)  CLEAR
49)  RETURN
50) ENDPROC
```

Listing 9-1 Generic procedure for viewing tables—continued

Let's analyze this procedure in detail. Two WAIT commands are used based on the number of images on the workspace. The difference between the two is the ability to size the number of rows displayed in Table view. If only one table is available for viewing, the first WAIT is executed. The second WAIT command is processed for multiple images. This is not a Paradox requirement but is included in this procedure as an example of multiple WAIT statements that depend on the status of the workspace. The UNTIL statements also differ by including "F3" and "F4" in the multiple-table WAIT. These two keys do not affect the workspace when only one table is viewed, but are used to move between tables when two or more tables are viewed. If you want the option to always size the table, use only the second WAIT and remove the IF condition in line 7.

The prompt line for multiple tables on the workspace indicates the current image number and the total number of tables. The expression STRVAL(IMAGENO()) displays the current image number. STRVAL(numofimages) displays the total number of tables on the workspace.

```
16)     PROMPT "Viewing Table " + STRVAL(IMAGENO()) + " of " +
17)            STRVAL(numofimages) + "    [F2]-Exit   [F10]-Table Menu   " +
18)            "[T]-Size Image",
19)            "[F3]-Next Table   [F4]-Previous Table   " +
20)            "[F7]-Form/Table View Toggle"
```

The SWITCH statement in lines 23-45 processes the last keystroke. You'll notice that there isn't a separate set of CASE statements for each WAIT. Even though there is a different set of keystrokes that end the different WAIT commands, a single SWITCH examines *retval* and takes the appropriate action. ZOOM and ZOOMNEXT invoke procedures instead of passing the keystroke to Paradox.

Sizing the table is controlled by lines 30-42. If a "T" or "t" is pressed, a WHILE loop is executed until [Enter] is pressed. Since all activity is in View mode, using a letter does not interfere with data input. (A function key would have to be used in any other mode.) Line 33 initiates the interactive TableSize option. A WAIT TABLE lets you press the up and down arrows to visually size the table. "DOS" and "DOSBIG" are trapped to prevent you from suspending to DOS. Only [Enter] ends the process.

```
23)     SWITCH
24)         CASE retval = "F3"        : UPIMAGE              LOOP
25)         CASE retval = "F4"        : DOWNIMAGE            LOOP
26)         CASE retval = "ZOOM"      : ZoomMenu()           LOOP
27)         CASE retval = "ZOOMNEXT:  : ZoomNextProc()       LOOP
28)         CASE retval = "F10"       : ViewTblsMenu()       LOOP    ; Get another table
29)         CASE retval = "F7"        : FORMKEY              LOOP
30)         CASE retval = "T" OR                                     ; Allow user to size the
31)              retval = "t"         :                              ; the number of rows shown
32)             WHILE (true)                                         ; for the current table
33)                 Menu {Image} {TableSize}
34)                 WAIT TABLE
35)                   PROMPT "Use UpArrow to decrease the table by one row;" +
36)                          " DownArrow to increase by one row...",
37)                          "then press Enter when finished"
38)                   UNTIL "Enter","DOS","DOSBIG"
39)                   IF retval = "Enter" THEN QUITLOOP ENDIF
40)             ENDWHILE
41)             ENTER                                                ; Ends TableSize command
42)             LOOP
43)         CASE retval = "F2"        : QUITLOOP
44)         OTHERWISE                 : BEEP LOOP
45)     ENDSWITCH
```

As of this writing, there is a slight problem with this technique. When you size the table interactively, the cursor style changes to a box (■). Normally the cursor returns to an underscore upon completion, but in this code it remains a box, and CURSOR NORMAL has no effect. This isn't a problem in this code but might not be desired in another application. An alternative to this code is to ask for the number of rows to display and programmatically change the number of rows displayed.

TIP: *Using the [Home] key while setting the number of rows always reduces the table display to two records. This is a quick way to size the table for only a couple of rows.*

Place additional tables on the workspace by pressing [F10], which executes ViewTblsMenu, a procedure that displays the tables in the current directory (see Listing 9-2). If there are no tables in the current directory, Paradox does not display a menu and sets *tblname* to "None." If this condition exists

Viewing, Entering, and Editing Data

or [Esc] is pressed at the menu, the procedure returns "None" to the calling routine.

NOTE: *In this example, there is no checking for encrypted tables. The ISENCRYPTED() function is used to test if a table is password protected.*

```
1)  PROC ViewTblsMenu()
2)    PRIVATE tblname
3)    SHOWTABLES                                  ; Select from the tables in
4)      DIRECTORY()                               ; the current directory
5)      "Select table to view, [Esc] to Cancel"
6)    TO tblname
7)    IF tblname = "Esc" OR tblname = "None" THEN ; If there are not tables
8)      RETURN "None"                             ; in current directory or
9)    ELSE                                        ; Esc pressed return None
10)     MESSAGE "Loading ",tblname                ; Otherwise, view the table
11)     VIEW tblname                              ; and return the table name
12)     RETURN tblname
13)   ENDIF
14) ENDPROC
```

Listing 9-2 Generic table section menu for view mode

The code in Listing 9-3 uses the same procedure as in Listing 9-1 to view data. A message is displayed if ViewTblsMenu returns "None" to indicate that either no tables exist in the current directory or that [Esc] was pressed. Otherwise, ViewTbls is executed.

```
1) CURSOR OFF
2) ViewTblsMenu()
3) IF retval <> "None" THEN
4)   ViewTbls()
5) ELSE
6)   MESSAGE "No tables available or selected, program terminated!"
7)   SLEEP 3000
8) ENDIF
```

Listing 9-3 Viewing data

Data Entry Methods

Paradox provides three modes for keyboard input into a table: DataEntry, Edit, and CoEdit. Each mode has its advantages and disadvantages. You must determine which is best for your application, based on its input demands. Before looking at examples, let's review the pros and cons of each mode. Table 9-1 lists the major needs during data entry and how each mode addresses those needs. A more detailed discussion of Edit and CoEdit follows this section on data entry.

Table 9-1
Data entry requirements

DataEntry	*Edit*	*CoEdit*
Key Violation		
Key violations are not found until data is posted to the master table. If any record duplicates an existing record, a Keyviol table is created to store such records.	There is no indication of key violations. Any record input that duplicates an existing record replaces it.	A record cannot be saved that duplicates an existing key. You are notified when you attempt to save the record.
Posting		
Data is not saved until Do-It! is executed from the menu or [F2] is pressed.	Edit is the same as DataEntry.	Input is saved on a record-by-record basis.
Undo		
Incremental Undo is available for all data input.	Edit is the same as DataEntry.	Only the change to the last record can be reversed.

Table 9-1—continued

DataEntry	Edit	CoEdit
Cancel Session Because no data is added to the permanent table until it is posted, all input for the session can be cancelled.	Similar to DataEntry: no changes affect the table until posted, so all changes in the session can be reversed. NOTE: This excludes any data saved with EDITLOG.	Records are posted as entered. Can cancel (Undo) only the last change.
Audit Trail DataEntry provides an audit trail of the records added in the Entry table. In a multitable form, Entry1 through Entry9 are used for detail tables.	No automatic audit trail is provided and it is cumbersome to program.	Like Edit, there is no automatic audit trail. The RECORDSTATUS function can be used to program an audit trail facility.
Save Activity and Not Post The {KeepEntry} menu selection saves the data in Entry table(s) without posting to the permanent table. This allows further processing on the data before saving.	There is no option to capture the data and not affect the original data.	CoEdit is the same as Edit.
Validity Checks Validity Checks are applied during DataEntry. They are defined interactively in this mode.	Edit is the same as DataEntry.	Validity Checks are applied during CoEdit but you cannot define or change them.

Table 9-1—continued

DataEntry	Edit	CoEdit
Network Usage Entry tables are placed in private directories. This prevents locking contention when multiple users are entering data.	A full lock is placed on the table to prevent any other user from accessing the table.	CoEdit supports multiple users accessing the same table as long as a full lock is not required. Only the current record is locked. During data entry, the record does not exist in the table until it is posted.
Access To Other Records There is no access to records currently in the table. Input is placed into Entry tables.	Explicit control required to prevent access to existing records.	CoEdit is the same as Edit.

As you can see, each mode provides different features for entering data. One mode alone cannot provide all capabilities. Edit mode is the most restrictive in a network environment because of the full lock placed on the table. It also doesn't handle key violations gracefully. These two limitations make Edit the least attractive of the three.

CoEdit provides the best option for evaluating key violations online. Trapping at the time the record is entered gives immediate feedback as to the success or failure of a record being entered. This is one of the major benefits of using CoEdit.

DataEntry is the only option with an audit trail. The records in the Entry tables provide a history of the activity for each data entry session. Edit and CoEdit do not provide an automatic audit trail, but one can be coded. Using a table with the same structure, entering data into it, and adding it to the master table provides the same functionality. You could also use COPY-TOARRAY before leaving the record, move to a table with the same structure, and use COPYFROMARRAY to get the same effect. DataEntry mode is commonly used when the system assigns the value of the key. Whether in a stand-alone or multiuser environment, key violations are not a concern because the application controls contention. Sequential numbering schemes lend themselves to this mode. An example of this type of entry process is discussed in Chapter 6. A three-table input process is used to explain data validation and a technique for multitable input. Examples using CoEdit are discussed later in this chapter.

Edit versus CoEdit

In addition to entering data using Edit and CoEdit, you can also modify data using a form in either of these modes. Each mode provides a different set of features and limitations, and there are advantages and disadvantages to using one or the other. The major differences that separate the two commands are:

- When changes are saved
- Ability to cancel all changes for the session
- Ability to undo changes
- How key violations are handled
- Number of concurrent users on a network
- Disk space required
- Effect on indexes
- Data manipulation in multitable forms
- Establishing ValChecks

Table 9-2 lists the characteristics of each command for each of these areas.

Just as you would consider certain factors in choosing a data entry mode, you should consider some of the same factors in choosing how to modify data. In most applications, CoEdit is used because it doesn't lock the entire table, it gives immediate notification of key violations, it maintains primary and secondary indexes, and it supports multitable processing. Edit is primarily used in single-user, single-table operations. The following section demonstrates how to use Edit and how to control the transaction log using EDITLOG.

**Table 9-2
Command characteristics**

Edit	*CoEdit*
When changes are saved	
No changes are saved in the table until the entire session is committed by selecting {*Do-It!*} from the Edit menu or pressing [F2].	Changes are saved on a record-by-record basis.
Ability to cancel all changes for the session	
All changes made to the table are reversed by selecting {*Cancel*} {*Yes*} from the Edit menu. The PAL command CANCELEDIT is the short form equivalent. NOTE: [Ctrl][Break] also ends an Edit session if it has not been disabled using the Custom Configuration Program.	Only the last change to the table can be reversed. In a network environment, *Undo* reverses the last change made by the user issuing *Undo*.
Ability to undo changes	
A transaction log is maintained of all changes and insertions of new records made to the table. This permits the reversal of actions taken during an Edit session incrementally (in the reverse order they occurred). Each entry in the transaction log is used to return the record to the state before the modification. All changes can be reversed. This is the same as cancelling the session.	A transaction log is maintained of only the last change made by the user. Because each record is posted when the cursor leaves the record, incremental Undo is not available. The *Cancel* option is also omitted from the CoEdit menu.

Table 9-2—continued

Edit	CoEdit
How key violations are handled	
Adding new records that duplicate a key or changing the key of a record to that of an existing key is not handled until the session is committed, and then it is too late to do anything about it. In both cases, the last record entered or modified for a key value is the record saved in the table. You are not informed of the decision; Paradox does it automatically. You can think of Edit mode as a batch update modification process. All input is entered into the table; once committed, all records with duplicate keys are processed, with the last record winning out by staying in the table.	Key violations are handled in real time. Because Paradox commits on a record-by-record basis, the duplication of a key is checked when posting is attempted. If a key violation occurs, you are notified immediately and the record is not saved until the key is unique or you indicate that the current record should update the existing record.
Number of concurrent users on a network	
A full lock is placed on a table in Edit mode (no other user can access the data in the table). This means no viewing, queries, reports, graphs, exporting, and so on. All other users are completely prohibited from using the table.	CoEdit supports multiple users modifying one table in a network environment with record-level locking. The table is also available for other actions such as reports, queries, and graphs. Only actions by other users requiring a full lock are prohibited.
Disk space required	
Additional disk space is required for the transaction log. For each record changed, an entry is recorded in the log. If every record in the table is changed, the transaction log would be at least as large as the original table.	No transaction log is maintained; therefore, additional disk space is not required.

Table 9-2—continued

Edit	*CoEdit*
Effect on indexes	
All indexes, primary and secondary, are marked out-of-date with the first change to the table. Commands such as LOCATE and ZOOM, which are faster if an index exists, have to perform a sequential search. The primary index and maintained secondary indexes are updated when the session is cancelled or committed. Non-maintained indexes in either case are no longer current and have to be updated.	Primary and maintained secondary indexes are updated with each change to the table. Non-maintained indexes are not current and have to be updated.
Data manipulation in multitable forms	
Multitable forms work in Edit mode but, because all modifications are batched and processed at once, you can overwrite a master record and lose all the detail associated with it for one-to-one and one-to-many relationships.	Multitable forms used in CoEdit ensure there is no data loss in the linked detail tables. CoEdit is the recommended mode for use with multitable forms, especially when users are entering and modifying the key.
Establishing ValChecks	
ValChecks can be defined, changed, and removed in Edit mode.	ValChecks cannot be defined while in CoEdit mode.
Special Note:	
EDITLOG is an option in Edit mode to save changes, update indexes, and provide rollback-like features while still editing the table. This provides some of the features found in CoEdit. An EDITLOG example is discussed in the next section.	

Controlling Transaction Log in Edit Mode

Use EDITLOG for increased control over the transaction log maintained during an Edit session. Four parameters specify the action to apply to the transaction log:

MARK — Places a marker in the transaction log for future reference.

REVERT — Reverses the changes in the table back to the last marker.

INDEX — Updates primary and maintained secondary indexes.

PERMANENT — Commits all changes, updates indexes, and removes transaction log. This is the same as a Do_It! but you stay in the Edit mode.

Many of the features in CoEdit are provided with EDITLOG. EDITLOG INDEX and EDITLOG PERMANENT improve ZOOM and LOCATE commands because indexes are used instead of a sequential search. A full lock is still applied to all tables on the workspace, making Edit less useful in a multiuser application.

NOTE: *In Edit mode, indexes are not maintained during editing. Indexes are updated only after changes are saved. This means that LOCATE, ZOOM, or ZOOMNEXT have to perform a sequential search. Take special note of non-maintained secondary indexes; they are always marked "out of date" after an edit session (even when the session is cancelled).*

Listing 9-4 is a sample procedure demonstrating the EDITLOG command. This procedure is intended to modify a table in Table view (not Form view). During editing, any one of the four parameters of EDITLOG is available for execution either by selecting it from the menu ([F10]) or the specific function key assigned to the desired option.

```
1) PROC EditLogAnyTbl(tblname,nokeys)
2)    PRIVATE choice,msg
3)
4)    ; Procedure parameters:
5)    ;    tblname - name of the table to edit
6)    ;    nokeys  - flag to indicate update access to table
7)    ;              If True, then IMAGERIGHTS set to UPDATE otherwise no
8)    ;              prevention taken to preserve key values. This also
9)    ;              disables insert and delete actions for the table.
```

Listing 9-4 The EDITLOG command

```
10)   ;
11)   ; Private variables:
12)   ;   choice - holds SHOWMENU selection
13)   ;   msg    - variable for information message display in WAIT command
14)   ;
15)   EDIT tblname
16)   IF nokeys = True THEN
17)     IMAGERIGHTS UPDATE                ; Prevent modification to key fields
18)   ENDIF
19)   msg = ""
20)   WHILE True
21)     WAIT TABLE
22)       PROMPT "EditLog Routine    [F2]-Save    [F10]-Menu",
23)              "[F3]-Mark   [F4]-Revert   [F5]-Index   [F6]-Permanent"
24)     MESSAGE msg
25)     UNTIL "Esc","F2","F3","F4","F5","F6","F10",
26)           "DOS","DOSBIG","ZOOM","ZOOMNEXT"
27)     msg = ""
28)     IF retval = "F10" THEN
29)       SHOWMENU
30)         "Mark"      : "Set a marker in the transaction log",
31)         "Revert"    : "Undo all changes back to the latest MARK",
32)         "Index"     : "Re-index current changes",
33)         "Permanent" : "Commit current changes and remain editing the table",
34)         "Do-It!"    : "Commit current changes and end edit session",
35)         "Cancel"    : "Cancel the edit session"
36)       TO choice
37)       IF choice = "Esc" THEN
38)         LOOP
39)       ENDIF
40)     ELSE
41)       choice = retval
42)     ENDIF
43)     SWITCH
44)       CASE choice = "F3" OR choice = "Mark"      :
45)         MESSAGE "Setting marker, Please wait"
46)         EDITLOG MARK
47)         msg = "Marker has been placed"
48)       CASE choice = "F4" OR choice = "Revert"    :
49)         MESSAGE "Reverting to previous marker, Please wait"
50)         EDITLOG REVERT
51)         msg = "Table is reverted to previous marker"
52)       CASE choice = "F5" OR choice = "Index"     :
53)         MESSAGE "Re-indexing current changes, Please wait"
54)         EDITLOG INDEX
55)         msg = "Indexes have been updated"
56)       CASE choice = "F6" OR choice = "Permanent" :
57)         MESSAGE "Committing changes, Please wait"
58)         EDITLOG PERMANENT
59)         msg = "Changes have been committed"
60)       CASE choice = "F2" OR choice = "Do-It!"    :
61)         MESSAGE "Saving changes, Please wait"
62)         CANVAS OFF
```

Listing 9-4 The EDITLOG command—continued

```
63)            DO_IT!
64)            QUITLOOP
65)      CASE choice = "Cancel"   :
66)            SHOWMENU
67)              "No"  : "Return to form and continue editing",
68)              "Yes" : "Cancel editing process and discard all changed"
69)            TO choice
70)            IF choice = "Yes" THEN
71)              CLEAR
72)              MESSAGE " Edit canceled, Please wait . . . "
73)              CANVAS OFF
74)              CANCELEDIT
75)              QUITLOOP
76)            ENDIF
77)            LOOP
78)      OTHERWISE                :
79)            BEEP
80)      ENDSWITCH
81)   ENDWHILE
82)   IF nokeys = True THEN
83)      IMAGERIGHTS                   ;  Remove update access only set at
84)   ENDIF                            ;  start of procedure
85)   CLEARIMAGE
86) ENDPROC
```

Listing 9-4 The EDITLOG command—continued

Let's walk through the code. Four private variables are used: *tblname* is the name of the table passed to the procedure, *nokeys* is a flag used to set the table update access level, *choice* is the variable used in the SHOWMENU command, and *msg* contains text placed on the canvas in the WAIT command for status information.

```
1) PROC EditLogAnyTbl(tblname,nokeys)
2)   PRIVATE choice,msg
3)
4) ; Procedure parameters:
5) ;   tblname  - name of the table to edit
6) ;   nokeys   - flag to indicate update access to table
7) ;               If True, then IMAGERIGHTS set to UPDATE otherwise no
8) ;               prevention taken to preserve key values. This also
9) ;               disables insert and delete actions for the table.
10) ;
11) ; Private variables:
12) ;   choice - holds SHOWMENU selection
13) ;   msg    - variable for information message display in WAIT command
14) ;
```

If *nokeys* is set to True, insert and delete operations are disabled, along with the ability to modify key fields by executing IMAGERIGHTS UPDATE (line 17). IMAGERIGHTS lets you set access rights to a table without having to set a password on the table. If there is a password on the table, access rights cannot be increased with IMAGERIGHTS (only further restriction can be applied). Before setting the access level, an image must be on the workspace. The name of the table passed as an argument is placed on the workspace in Edit mode in line 15. Variable *msg* is initialized to blank in line 19.

```
15)     EDIT tblname
16)     IF nokeys = True THEN
17)        IMAGERIGHTS UPDATE            ; Prevent modification to key fields
18)     ENDIF
19)     msg = ""
```

A WAIT TABLE is used inside a WHILE loop to give you access to the table. The keys trapped in UNTIL are [F3] through [F6] (for the four parameters of EDITLOG), [F10] to present a menu to select actions from, and the usual key commands that allow suspension to the operating system. The MESSAGE parameter displays the contents of *msg* in the lower right corner of the screen (like messages displayed during interactive Paradox usage). If *msg* is blank, nothing is displayed. The variable *msg* is blanked out after the WAIT—the next time through the loop, nothing is displayed if no information text is assigned for the current key press.

```
21)     WAIT TABLE
22)     PROMPT "EditLog Routine    [F2]-Save    [F10]-Menu",
23)            "[F3]-Mark    [F4]-Revert    [F5]-Index    [F6]-Permanent"
24)     MESSAGE msg
25)     UNTIL "Esc","F2","F3","F4","F5","F6","F10",
26)           "DOS","DOSBIG","ZOOM","ZOOMNEXT"
27)     msg = ""
```

NOTE: *If you want to be able to insert and delete records, both keystrokes have to be included in UNTIL. You also need to have a CASE statement for each.*

When [F10] is pressed, the application displays the menu defined in lines 29-36. This provides access to each EDITLOG parameter in addition to saving the changes with Do-It! and cancelling the entire selection with Cancel. This is an example of how to create your application to closely follow the Paradox interface (by always having [F10] display a menu to assist the user). This provides a consistent interface to anyone familiar with interactive Paradox. If [Esc] is pressed instead of a menu selection, you return to editing the table the same as you would in Paradox. If [F10] is not the key pressed, line 41 sets *choice* to *retval*. This allows a single variable to be evaluated for the action to take based on the key pressed.

```
28)     IF retval = "F10" THEN
29)       SHOWMENU
30)         "Mark"      : "Set a marker in the transaction log",
31)         "Revert"    : "Undo all changes back to the latest MARK",
32)         "Index"     : "Re-index current changes",
33)         "Permanent" : "Commit current changes and remain editing the table",
34)         "Do-It!"    : "Commit current changes and end edit session",
35)         "Cancel"    : "Cancel the edit session"
36)       TO choice
37)       IF choice = "Esc" THEN
38)         LOOP
39)       ENDIF
40)     ELSE
41)       choice = retval
42)     ENDIF
```

The SWITCH statement in lines 43-80 processes the key you pressed. A separate CASE statement is used for each option available. Because an option is selected either by function key or menu selection, both are checked in each CASE statement. MESSAGE is used for all options to display an informational message as to the activity occurring while processing. For each of the EDITLOG parameters, *msg* is set when the command is completed and is displayed on the screen when control returns to the WAIT command. This technique keeps you informed as to the status of the processing. If [Esc] is entered, you are prompted to confirm that you really want to cancel changes. The DOS, DOSBIG, etc., keystrokes are handled by the OTHERWISE clause. If any of these keys are pressed no action is taken except to sound the system bell indicating an illegal keystroke. Unless [F2] is pressed, you loop back to the top of the WAIT and continue editing the table or select another function key or menu option.

```
43)     SWITCH
44)       CASE choice = "F3" OR choice = "Mark"      :
45)         MESSAGE "Setting marker, Please wait"
46)         EDITLOG MARK
47)         msg = "Marker has been placed"
48)       CASE choice = "F4" OR choice = "Revert"    :
49)         MESSAGE "Reverting to previous marker, Please wait"
50)         EDITLOG REVERT
51)         msg = "Table is reverted to previous marker"
52)       CASE choice = "F5" OR choice = "Index"     :
53)         MESSAGE "Re-indexing current changes, Please wait"
54)         EDITLOG INDEX
55)         msg = "Indexes have been updated"
56)       CASE choice = "F6" OR choice = "Permanent" :
57)         MESSAGE "Committing changes, Please wait"
58)         EDITLOG PERMANENT
59)         msg = "Changes have been committed"
60)       CASE choice = "F2" OR choice = "Do-It!"    :
61)         MESSAGE "Saving changes, Please wait"
62)         CANVAS OFF
```

```
63)            DO_IT!
64)            QUITLOOP
65)      CASE choice = "Cancel"   :
66)            SHOWMENU
67)               "No"  : "Return to form and continue editing",
68)               "Yes" : "Cancel editing process and discard all changed"
69)            TO choice
70)            IF choice = "Yes" THEN
71)               CLEAR
72)               MESSAGE " Edit canceled, Please wait . . . "
73)               CANVAS OFF
74)               CANCELEDIT
75)               QUITLOOP
76)            ENDIF
77)            LOOP
78)      OTHERWISE
79)            BEEP
80)      ENDSWITCH
```

Lines 82-85 are the closing statements that clean up the workspace before returning. If IMAGERIGHTS UPDATE is executed at the beginning of the procedure, those restrictions are cleared by executing IMAGERIGHTS by itself. This makes the current password level of access apply to any object. The last action to take is to remove the table placed on the workspace, using CLEARIMAGE. (This is not necessary, but the idea of leaving the environment the way it was when the procedure began is applied in this example.)

```
82)   IF nokeys = True THEN
83)      IMAGERIGHTS              ; Remove update access only set
84)   ENDIF                       ; at start of procedure
85)   CLEARIMAGE
```

To execute the procedure, you must pass a valid table name. No checking is done for an invalid table name, encrypted table, or write-protected table. The following code presents a list of available tables in the current directory. If there are no tables in the directory *tblname* is assigned "None". If this is the case or you press [Esc], the process is halted; otherwise, EditLogAnyTbl is called with the selected table.

```
CLEAR
SHOWTABLES
   DIRECTORY()
   "Select the table to edit"
TO tblname
IF tblname = "Esc" or tblname = "None" THEN
   QUIT
ENDIF

;  Check here for encrypted and write protected table. Table name is valid
; because SHOWTABLES is used to present list to select from.

EditLogAnyTbl(tblname)
```

Editing a Subset of a Table

Many applications require users to provide criteria to select a subset of data and then allow editing of the records satisfying the selection criterion. In Paradox, this is not a simple, straightforward task. There is no option in Edit or CoEdit to include a WHERE clause (stipulating the rows to modify). Using either of these commands provides access to all data in every table on the workspace. Therefore, a programmatic approach is necessary to perform subset editing.

There are many approaches to subset editing. Which approach you choose depends on the type of access you need and whether you need to scroll forward and backward through the data. The approach also depends on the number of records that will be returned. If only a single record matches the criteria, a different solution is used than if multiple records are expected to be returned.

Single-record subsets are the easiest to control. In most instances the selection is based on the key or on a field that has a one-to-one correspondence with the key. For a single-field selection, cursor access is required to the field. In Table view there isn't a problem, but in a form, the field cannot be DisplayOnly (this is most likely to occur to protect the key field). Therefore, to search when there is no access in a form, you need to toggle to Table view, perform the search, then return to the form. In either case, the LOCATE command is the most common method used. The algorithm for a single-column selection is:

1. Get value to search for.
2. Move to the column in the table (may have to use Table view if field in form is DisplayOnly).
3. Search for the value using LOCATE.
4. If the value is found, present data to user to modify.
5. If the value is not found, display message.

Listing 9-5 shows the procedure to perform this process.

EditDeptData provides access to data in the Dept table. A prompt requests department name. Listing 9-6 shows the code for GetOneDept.

```
 1) PROC EditDeptData()
 2) VIEW "Dept"
 3) MOVETO [Department]
 4) WHILE True                                      ;  Get the dept to edit. If
 5)   dept = GetOneDept()                           ; user pressed Esc, cancel
 6)   IF dept = False THEN                          ; processing. Otherwise
 7)     CLEARIMAGE                                  ; loop until a valid dept
 8)     RETURN "No data selected"                   ; is entered or Esc is
 9)   ELSE                                          ; pressed.
10)     MESSAGE "Searching for ",dept," department, please wait!"
11)     CANVAS OFF
12)   ENDIF
13)   LOCATE dept
14)   IF retval = False THEN
15)     CANVAS ON
16)     MESSAGE dept + " department does not exist!"
17)   ELSE
18)     QUITLOOP
19)   ENDIF
20) ENDWHILE
21) COEDITKEY
22) PICKFORM 3                                      ;  Form 3 has [Department]
23) CANVAS ON                                       ; as DisplayOnly field
24) msg = ""
25) WHILE True
26)   WAIT RECORD
27)     PROMPT "Edit Department Information [F2]-Save/Exit [F7]-New Department"
28)     MESSAGE msg
29)     UNTIL "F2","F7","DOS","DOSBIG","ZOOM","ZOOMNEXT"
30)   msg = ""
31)   SWITCH
32)     CASE retval = "F7" :                        ;  F7 used to search
33)         dept = GetOneDept()                     ; for different dept
34)         IF dept = False OR ISBLANK(dept) THEN   ;  If an Esc or Enter
35)           msg = "No department selected!"       ; pressed at prompt, no
36)         ELSE                                    ; data entered so leave
37)           FORMKEY                               ; cursor on current dept
38)           MOVETO [Department]                   ; otherwise search for
39)           LOCATE dept                           ; dept entered. If not
40)           IF retval = False THEN                ; found, display message.
41)             msg = dept +                        ; NOTE: need to toggle
42)               " department does not exist!"    ; to Table view to
43)           ENDIF                                 ; move cursor to
44)           FORMKEY                               ; [Department] for LOCATE
45)         ENDIF                                   ; to work
46)         LOOP
47)     CASE retval = "F2" :
48)         QUITLOOP
49)     OTHERWISE         :
```

Listing 9-5 Subset editing

```
50)         BEEP
51)      ENDSWITCH
52)   ENDWHILE
53)   MESSAGE "Editing complete!"
54)   CANVAS OFF
55)   DO_IT!
56)   CLEARIMAGE
57) ENDPROC
```

Listing 9-5 Subset editing—continued

```
1)  PROC GetOneDept()                    ;Get1Dept.sc
2)    PRIVATE dept
3)    dept = ""
4)    @ 0,0 CLEAR EOL                    ; Clear the top two lines
5)    @ 1,0 CLEAR EOL                    ; of the screen
6)    ?? "Enter department to edit (Esc to Cancel): "
7)    STYLE REVERSE                      ; Set style for area of
8)    ACCEPT "A10" PICTURE "*!" TO dept  ; canvas used to input dept
9)    STYLE                              ; IMPORTANT: turn style off
10)   IF retval = False OR ISBLANK(dept) THEN  ; If Esc entered, dept = ""
11)      RETURN False                    ; return False
12)   ELSE                               ; otherwise return value
13)      RETURN dept                     ; entered
14)   ENDIF
15) ENDPROC
```

Listing 9-6 Locating data for one department

Subset editing where multiple records meet the criteria or multiple fields are used to define the subset introduces additional concerns. The first question is how to get a subset. Queries seem to be the obvious choice, but they always return an Answer table. LOCATE works in some situations but not all. There are many ways to provide subset editing on multiple records; each has its own benefits and problems depending on your editing requirements. As examples, four different solutions are presented here along with the potential pitfalls associated with each. The four solutions include

- Using SCAN with the FOR parameter.
- A query selecting the records and all the fields to allow copying the form to the Answer table.
- Using LOCATE to sequentially find records.

- A query selecting the key field(s) of the records matching the selection criteria, and copying a form with embedded tables to give access to all the fields.

Each of these examples uses the Employee table from the personnel system. Record selection is done based on the department the employees are in. A multitable form provides access to the fields in Employee, Benefits, and Depndnts. A separate procedure (Listing 9-7) is used to prompt for the name of the department. Let's look at the code for GetDept before discussing the four examples.

```
1)  PROC GetDept()        ; GetDept.sc
2)    PRIVATE dept
3)    CLEAR
4)    dept = ""
5)    @ 5,0 ?? "Enter department to edit, RETURN (\17\217) for lookup table: "
6)    STYLE REVERSE
7)    ACCEPT "A10" PICTURE "*!" TO dept
8)    STYLE
9)    IF retval = False THEN
10)      RETURN False
11)   ELSE
12)     IF ISBLANK(dept) THEN
13)       MOVETO "Dept"
14)       WHILE True
15)         WAIT TABLE
16)           PROMPT "Move cursor to Department to select",
17)                  "[F2]-Select     [Esc]-Cancel"
18)           UNTIL "F2","Esc","DOS","DOSBIG","ZOOM","ZOOMNEXT"
19)         SWITCH
20)           CASE retval = "F2"   : dept = [Department] QUITLOOP
21)           CASE retval = "Esc"  : dept = False        QUITLOOP
22)           OTHERWISE            : BEEP
23)         ENDSWITCH
24)       ENDWHILE
25)     ENDIF
26)   ENDIF
27)   RETURN dept
28) ENDPROC
```

Listing 9-7 *GetDept procedure*

GetDept returns a valid department from the Dept table or returns False, indicating no department was selected. The private variable *dept* is defined and initialized to blank in line 4. A prompt is placed on the screen in line 5 and ACCEPT is used to accept the department entered. The PICTURE parameter ensures that the characters entered are uppercase. (This is necessary because all departments in the table are uppercase.) Line 6 issues STYLE REVERSE. This paints a ten-character area onscreen (as defined by "A10"). The reverse video style is turned off in line 8. If [Esc] is pressed, *retval* is set to False, and the procedure returns False in line 10.

```
3)      CLEAR
4)      dept = ""
5)      @ 5,0 ?? "Enter department to edit, RETURN (\17\217) for lookup table: "
6)      STYLE REVERSE
7)      ACCEPT "A10" PICTURE "*!" TO dept
8)      STYLE
9)      IF retval = False THEN
10)        RETURN False
11)     ELSE
```

> **TIP:** *ACCEPT does not allow [F1] to be pressed to display the values in a table. If the LOOKUP parameter is used with ACCEPT, it validates only entries. A technique to provide table lookup capability is to place the table on the workspace and check for [Enter] being pressed at the prompt without entering a value. Then display the table and wait for an [F2] to select the data or [Esc] to cancel. This process is used in lines 12-25. If dept is blank, it signals that [Enter] was pressed at the ACCEPT statement but no value was entered. This requires the variable to be initialized as in line 4. The cursor is moved to the Dept table and a WAIT TABLE is executed until an [Esc] or [F2] is pressed. The department of the current record is returned if [F2] is pressed; otherwise, False is returned.*

```
12)        IF ISBLANK(dept) THEN
13)           MOVETO "Dept"
14)           WHILE True
15)              WAIT TABLE
16)                 PROMPT "Move cursor to Department to select",
17)                        "[F2]-Select    [Esc]-Cancel"
18)                 UNTIL "F2","Esc","DOS","DOSBIG","ZOOM","ZOOMNEXT"
19)              SWITCH
20)                 CASE retval = "F2"  : dept = [Department] QUITLOOP
21)                 CASE retval = "Esc" : dept = False         QUITLOOP
22)                 OTHERWISE           : BEEP
23)              ENDSWITCH
24)           ENDWHILE
25)        ENDIF
```

Using SCAN with the FOR Parameter

Listing 9-8 shows the procedure for using the SCAN FOR command. This method allows you to move through the records in a sequential fashion from top to bottom. Once you move to the next record you cannot move back. This is an easy method to program but it is a slow performer. The SCAN command does not use primary or secondary indexes to match the selection criteria. Paradox starts at the first record of the table and checks to see if it matches the FOR condition. If it does, the statements following the SCAN are executed. This process requires each record in the table to be checked. In a large table where only a few records match the conditions, the delay between records presented for editing will vary noticeably. You will also see a delay if no records match the condition. Therefore, SCAN is good for quickly providing subset editing for small tables only.

TRAP: *Using the SCAN command without FOR and having a FOR i FROM command as the first statement inside the SCAN causes a script error.*

```
SCAN
   FOR i FROM 1 TO 10
```

Paradox assumes the word FOR is part of the SCAN command. To prevent the syntax from being misinterpreted, include a PAL statement between the two. A simple solution is to set a variable to some value.

```
SCAN
   i = 0
   FOR i FROM 1 TO 10
```

```
1)  PROC EditEmpByDept()                      ; Ssedit01.sc
2)    PRIVATE dept,anyrcdflag
3)  ;
4)  ; Private variables:
5)  ;    dept         - department to edit
6)  ;    anyrcdflag   - flag to indicate if any records where found in scan
7)  ;
8)    VIEW "Dept"
9)    dept = GetDept()                        ;  Get name of department to edit
10)   CLEAR
11)   IF dept = False THEN                    ;  If no department selected
12)     MESSAGE "No department selected"
13)     SLEEP 3000
14)   ELSE
15)     MESSAGE "Selecting employees in ",dept," department, please wait"
16)     COEDIT "Employee"
17)     PICKFORM 1
18)     anyrcdflag = 1
19)     SCAN FOR [Department] = dept
20)       anyrcdflag = 0                      ;  Set flag to indicate at least
21)       WHILE True                          ;  one record exists
```

Listing 9-8 SCAN command used for subset editing

```
22)          WAIT RECORD
23)            PROMPT "Edit record       [F2]-Save/Exit      [F3]-Next Table    " +
24)                   "[PgDn]-Next Record"
25)            UNTIL "F3","PgDn","F2","DOS","DOSBIG","ZOOM","ZOOMNEXT"
26)            SWITCH
27)              CASE retval = "F3"    : DOWNIMAGE LOOP
28)              CASE retval = "PgDn"  :
29)                 SWITCH
30)                    CASE TABLE() = "Employee" : QUITLOOP
31)                    CASE TABLE() = "Benefits" : BEEP LOOP
32)                    CASE TABLE() = "Depndnts" : SKIP 1 LOOP
33)                 ENDSWITCH
34)              CASE retval = "F2"    : QUITLOOP
35)              OTHERWISE             : BEEP
36)            ENDSWITCH
37)         ENDWHILE
38)         IF retval = "F2" THEN
39)            QUITLOOP
40)         ENDIF
41)      ENDSCAN
42)      IF anyrcdflag = 1 THEN              ;  If not records matched dept
43)         MESSAGE "No employees in ",dept," department"
44)      ELSE
45)         MESSAGE "Editing complete"
46)      ENDIF
47)      SLEEP 3000
48)      DO_IT!
49)   ENDIF
50) ENDPROC
51)
52) RELEASE VARS ALL
53) RESET
54) EditEmpByDept()
55) CLEARALL
```

Listing 9-8 SCAN command used for subset editing—continued

Subset Editing Using a Query to Select All Fields

The second example for editing a subset of a table is to create an Answer table containing the records matching the selection criteria. The code is shown in Listing 9-9. All fields are selected, allowing the form to be copied to the Answer table from the master table. GetSubset is the procedure executed to perform the query. If there are employees in the requested department, the procedure returns True. If there are no records returned from the query, the procedure returns False.

This technique works fine in a standalone environment, but there is a delay during the actual query. The length of the delay depends on whether the primary or secondary indexes are used. This technique should not be used in a multiuser environment because each user has his own copy of the Answer table and updates would overwrite each other.

```
1)  PROC GetSubset()                       ; GetSub01.sc
2)    {Ask} {Employee} CHECK [Department] = dept
3)    DO_IT!
4)    IF ISEMPTY("Answer") THEN
5)      RETURN False
6)    ELSE
7)      RETURN True
8)    ENDIF
9)  ENDPROC
```

Listing 9-9 Query subset editing

```
1)  PROC EditEmpByDept()                   ; Ssedit02.sc
2)    PRIVATE dept
3)  ;
4)  ; Private variables:
5)  ;    dept        - department to edit
6)  ;
7)    VIEW "Dept"
8)    dept = GetDept()                     ; Get name of department to edit
9)    CLEAR
10)   IF dept = False THEN                 ; If no department selected
11)     MESSAGE "No department selected"
12)     SLEEP 3000
13)   ELSE
14)     MESSAGE "Selecting employees in ",dept," department, please wait"
15)     CANVAS OFF
16)     retprocval = GetSubset()           ; Select data to edit
17)     IF retprocval = False THEN         ; No records for dept
18)       CANVAS ON
19)       MESSAGE "No employees in ",dept," department"
20)       SLEEP 3000
21)       RETURN
22)     ENDIF
23)     COPYFORM "Employee" "1" "Answer" "1"
24)     COEDIT "Answer"
25)     PICKFORM 1
26)     msg = ""
27)     CANVAS ON
28)     WHILE True
29)       WAIT RECORD
```

Listing 9-10 Program example that calls Listing 9-9

Viewing, Entering, and Editing Data

```
30)            PROMPT "Edit record     [F2]-Save/Exit      [F3]-Next Table",
31)                   "[PgDn]-Next Record    [PgUp]-Previous Record"
32)            MESSAGE msg
33)          UNTIL "F3","PgDn","PgUp","F2","DOS","DOSBIG","ZOOM","ZOOMNEXT"
34)       msg = ""
35)       SWITCH
36)         CASE retval = "F3"    :
37)              DOWNIMAGE
38)              LOOP
39)         CASE retval = "PgDn" :
40)              SWITCH
41)                CASE TABLE() = "Answer"    : ;Employee  records are in Answer
42)                     SKIP                    ;  Move to next record. If
43)                     IF EOT() THEN           ; this is the last record
44)                        BEEP                 ; notify the user.
45)                        msg = "No more " + dept + " records!"
46)                     ENDIF
47)                     LOOP
48)                CASE TABLE() = "Benefits" :
49)                     BEEP
50)                     LOOP
51)                CASE TABLE() = "Depndnts" :
52)                     SKIP
53)                     LOOP
54)              ENDSWITCH
55)         CASE retval = "PgUp" :
56)              SWITCH
57)                CASE TABLE() = "Answer"    :
58)                     SKIP -1                 ;  Move to next record. If
59)                     IF BOT() THEN           ; this is the last record
60)                        BEEP                 ; notify the user.
61)                        msg = "This is the first " + dept + " record!"
62)                     ENDIF
63)                     LOOP
64)                CASE TABLE() = "Benefits" :
65)                     BEEP
66)                     LOOP
67)                CASE TABLE() = "Depndnts" :
68)                     SKIP
69)                     LOOP
70)              ENDSWITCH
71)         CASE retval = "F2"   : QUITLOOP
72)         OTHERWISE            : BEEP
73)       ENDSWITCH
74)     ENDWHILE
75)     MESSAGE "Editing complete"
76)     SLEEP 3000
77)     DO_IT!
78)     ADD "Answer" "Employee"
79)   ENDIF
80) ENDPROC
```

Listing 9-10 Program example that calls Listing 9-9—continued

Using LOCATE to Find Records

The LOCATE command supports subset editing if the selection criteria are based on a single field or on the first field in the table. Since LOCATE uses primary and secondary indexes, performance is very good when finding the first and subsequent records. Listing 9-11 shows code using LOCATE. This method, like the one using SCAN, does not provide backward scrolling. It simply provides forward access through the table for each matching record. If no records match the selection criteria, you are notified immediately (if an index field is used). This works for both standalone and network applications.

```
1)  PROC EditEmpByDept()                        ; Ssedit03.sc
2)    PRIVATE dept
3)    ;
4)    ; Private variables:
5)    ;    dept        - department to edit
6)    ;
7)      VIEW "Dept"
8)      dept = GetDept()                        ; Get name of department to edit
9)      CLEAR
10)     IF dept = False THEN                    ; If no department selected
11)       MESSAGE "No department selected"
12)       SLEEP 3000
13)     ELSE
14)       MESSAGE "Selecting employees in ",dept," department, please wait"
15)       CANVAS OFF
16)       VIEW "Employee"
17)       MOVETO [Department]
18)       LOCATE dept                           ; Find the first dept
19)       IF retval = False THEN                ; If not records for dept
20)         CANVAS ON
21)         MESSAGE "No employees in ",dept," department"
22)         SLEEP 3000
23)         RETURN
24)       ENDIF
25)       COEDITKEY
26)       PICKFORM 1
27)       CTRLHOME                              ; Move to first field on form
28)       CANVAS ON
29)       msg = ""                              ; Initialize msg variable
30)       WHILE True
31)         WAIT RECORD
32)           PROMPT "Edit record    [F2]-Save/Exit    [F3]-Next Table   " +
33)                  "[PgDn]-Next Record"
34)           MESSAGE msg
35)         UNTIL "F3","PgDn","F2","DOS","DOSBIG","ZOOM","ZOOMNEXT"
36)         msg = ""
```

Listing 9-11 Using LOCATE for subset editing

```
37)      SWITCH
38)        CASE retval = "F3"    :
39)             DOWNIMAGE
40)             LOOP
41)        CASE retval = "PgDn" :
42)          SWITCH
43)            CASE TABLE() = "Employee" :
44)              SKIP                    ; Move to next record. If this is
45)              IF EOT() THEN           ; the last record notify the user.
46)                msg = "No more " + dept + " records!"
47)              ELSE
48)                MOVETO [Department]
49)                LOCATE NEXT dept       ; Find the next record
50)                IF retval = False THEN ; No more records, put cursor
51)                  SKIP -1              ; on last record that matched
52)                  msg = "No more " + dept + " records!"
53)                ENDIF
54)                CTRLHOME              ; Move to first field on form
55)              ENDIF
56)              LOOP
57)            CASE TABLE() = "Benefits" :
58)              BEEP
59)              LOOP
60)            CASE TABLE() = "Depndnts" :
61)              SKIP
62)              LOOP
63)          ENDSWITCH
64)        CASE retval = "F2"    :  QUITLOOP
65)        OTHERWISE              :  BEEP
66)      ENDSWITCH
67)     ENDWHILE
68)     MESSAGE "Editing complete"
69)     SLEEP 3000
70)     DO_IT!
71)   ENDIF
72) ENDPROC
73)
74)
75) RELEASE VARS ALL
76) RESET
77) CURSOR OFF
78) EditEmpByDept()
79) CLEARALL
```

Listing 9-11 Using LOCATE for subset editing—continued

Subset Editing Using a Query to Select Key Fields

This last method uses a query to select the key field(s) of the records matching the selection criteria. It then copies a form with embedded tables to provide access to all the fields. Listing 9-12 shows the code for the query as used in Listing 9-13. Unlike the second example shown earlier, only the key field is checked here. The Answer table contains the keys to each of the records selected and is used as a navigational tool through the master table.

```
1)  PROC GetSubset()                    ; Getsub02.sc
2)    {Ask} {Employee} [Department] = dept
3)    MOVETO [Employee ID]  CHECK
4)    DO_IT!
5)    IF ISEMPTY("Answer") THEN
6)      RETURN False
7)    ELSE
8)      RETURN True
9)    ENDIF
10) ENDPROC
```

Listing 9-12 *Query subset editing*

The multitable form copied to the Answer table from the Empshdw table contains Employee, Benefits, and Depndnts as embedded tables. This provides access to all the data and allows forward and backward movement through the selected records. If many records are selected, there is a noticeable pause. This technique works for both single and multiuser environments. (Network implementation requires explicit locking to ensure access to the records.)

```
1)  PROC EditEmpByDept()                ; Ssedit04.sc
2)    PRIVATE dept
3)  ;
4)  ; Private variables:
5)  ;   dept       - department to edit
6)  ;
7)    VIEW "Dept"
8)    dept = GetDept()                  ; Get name of department to edit
9)    CLEAR
10)   IF dept = False THEN              ; If no department selected
11)     MESSAGE "No department selected"
12)     SLEEP 3000
13)   ELSE
14)     MESSAGE "Selecting employees in ",dept," department, please wait"
15)     CANVAS OFF
16)     retprocval = GetSubset()        ; Select data to edit
17)     IF retprocval = False THEN      ; No records for dept
18)       CANVAS ON
```

Listing 9-13 *Query subset editing on key only*

```
19)        MESSAGE "No employees in ",dept," department"
20)        SLEEP 3000
21)        RETURN
22)     ENDIF
23)     COPYFORM "Empshdw" "1" "Answer" "1"
24)     COEDIT "Answer"
25)     PICKFORM 1
26)     msg = ""
27)     CANVAS ON
28)     WHILE True
29)        IF TABLE() = "Answer" THEN      ;  If F3 press to move to next
30)           MOVETO "Employee"            ;  table and it is Anser, move
31)        ENDIF                           ;  cursor to Employee table
32)        WAIT RECORD
33)           PROMPT "Edit Employee Information      [F2]-Save/Exit    " +
34)                  "[F3]-Next Table",
35)                  "[PgDn]-Next Record      [PgUp]-Previous Record"
36)           MESSAGE msg
37)           UNTIL "F2","F3","PgDn","PgUp","DOS","DOSBIG","ZOOM","ZOOMNEXT"
38)        msg = ""
39)        SWITCH
40)           CASE retval = "F3"    :
41)                DOWNIMAGE
42)                LOOP
43)           CASE retval = "PgDn" :
44)                SWITCH
45)                   CASE TABLE() = "Employee" :
46)                        MOVETO "Answer"
47)                        SKIP                ;  Move to next record. If
48)                        IF EOT() THEN       ;  this is the last record
49)                           BEEP             ;  notify the user.
50)                           msg = "No more " + dept + " records!"
51)                        ENDIF
52)                        LOOP
53)                   CASE TABLE() = "Benefits" :
54)                        BEEP
55)                        LOOP
56)                   CASE TABLE() = "Depndnts" :
57)                        SKIP
58)                        LOOP
59)                ENDSWITCH
60)           CASE retval = "PgUp" :
61)                SWITCH
62)                   CASE TABLE() = "Employee" :
63)                        MOVETO "Answer"
64)                        SKIP -1             ;  Move to next record. If
65)                        IF BOT() THEN       ;  this is the last record
66)                           BEEP             ;  notify the user.
67)                           msg = "This is the first " + dept + " record!"
68)                        ENDIF
69)                        LOOP
70)                   CASE TABLE() = "Benefits" :
```

Listing 9-13 Query subset editing on key only—continued

```
71)                       BEEP
72)                       LOOP
73)            CASE TABLE() = "Depndnts" :
74)                       SKIP -1
75)                       LOOP
76)            ENDSWITCH
77)         CASE retval = "F2"   : QUITLOOP
78)         OTHERWISE             : BEEP
79)       ENDSWITCH
80)     ENDWHILE
81)     MESSAGE "Editing complete"
82)     SLEEP 3000
83)     DO_IT!
84)   ENDIF
85) ENDPROC
```

Listing 9-13 *Query subset editing on key only—continued*

The four techniques described in this section all support editing a subset of a table when multiple records satisfy the selection criteria. If you don't need to provide forward and backward scrolling between records, the best solution is to use the LOCATE command—unless the selection criteria are not based on a single field or the first fields in the table, in which case you must use one of the other solutions.

Global Variables, Arrays, and Functions In Forms

Paradox 3.5 enhances expressions in forms by supporting global variables, arrays, and a subset of PAL functions. You can include these in expressions using {Field} {Place} {Calculated}. The result of the expression is an alphanumeric field with a maximum length of 255 characters. Before Paradox lets you place the expression, it checks the syntax of the expression to ensure there are no errors. Table 9-3 lists the functions that can be used.

Let's look at some examples of expressions using variables and functions. Figure 9-1 shows a form based on the Employee table. It has six expressions:

- Number of records in the entire table
- Current day of the week and date
- Employee's age
- Employee's years of service
- A rotated bar graph showing employee's salary
- A rotated bar graph showing the employee's average salary

Table 9-3
PAL functions allowed in form expressions

ABS	Absolute value of a number
ACOS	Arc cosine of a number
ASC	Converts a character to an ASCII value
ASIN	Arc sine of a number
ATAN	Arc tangent of a number
ATAN2	Four-quadrant arc tangent
CAVERAGE	Averages of all records for a column in a table
CCOUNT	Count of the values for a column in a table
CHR	Converts an ASCII value to a character
CMAX	Maximum value for a column in a table
CMIN	Minimum value for a column in a table
CNPV	Net present value for a column in a table
COS	Cosine of an angle
CSTD	Standard deviation of the values for a column in a table
CSUM	Sum of the values for a column in a table
CVAR	Variance of the values for a column in a table
DATEVAL	Converts a date value to a string value
DAY	Numeric value of the day of the month for a date value
DOW	Three-letter string of the day of the week for a data value
EXP	Exponential value of a number
FILL	Returns a repeated character string
FORMAT	Formats date, numeric, text, and logical data types
FV	Future values of a series of cash flows
INT	Integer portion of a number
LEN	Length of a character string
LN	Natural log of a number
LOG	Base 10 log of a number
LOWER	Converts a text string to lowercase
MAX	Largest of two numeric values
MIN	Smallest of two numeric values
MOD	Modulus function

Table 9-3—continued

MONTH	Numeric value of the month for a date value
MOY	Three-character value of the month for a date value
NRECORDS	Number of records in a table
NUMVAL	Converts a text string to a number
PI	Value of Pi
PMT	Amortized mortgage payment
POW	Raises a number to a power
PV	Present value of a series of payments
RAND	Random number
ROUND	Rounds a number
SEARCH	Position of a substring
SIN	Sine of an angle
SQRT	Square root
STRVAL	Converts an expression to a string
SUBSTR	Returns a substring
TAN	Tangent of an angle
TIME	Current system time
TODAY	Current system date
UPPER	Converts a text string to uppercase
USERNAME	Current user's name
YEAR	Year of a date value

The syntax for each of the expressions is as follows:

- FORMAT("w5.0,ar",NRECORDS("Employee"))
- DOW(TODAY()) + " " + FORMAT("d2",TODAY())
- INT((TODAY() - [Birth Date]) / 365.25)
- INT((TODAY() - [Date Hired]) / 365.25)
- FILL(barsymbol,INT([Salary] / 1000))
- FILL(barsymbol,INT(CAVERAGE("Employee","Salary") / 1000))

You must set the variable *barsymbol* so that the formula evaluates correctly. In this example, *barsymbol* is set to "\223". Remember, if an expression cannot be evaluated, the result placed on the form depends on the function used, whether or not the data is blank, and the result of CALCDEBUG. Refer to the notes in Chapter 5 for a description of the known problems with functions.

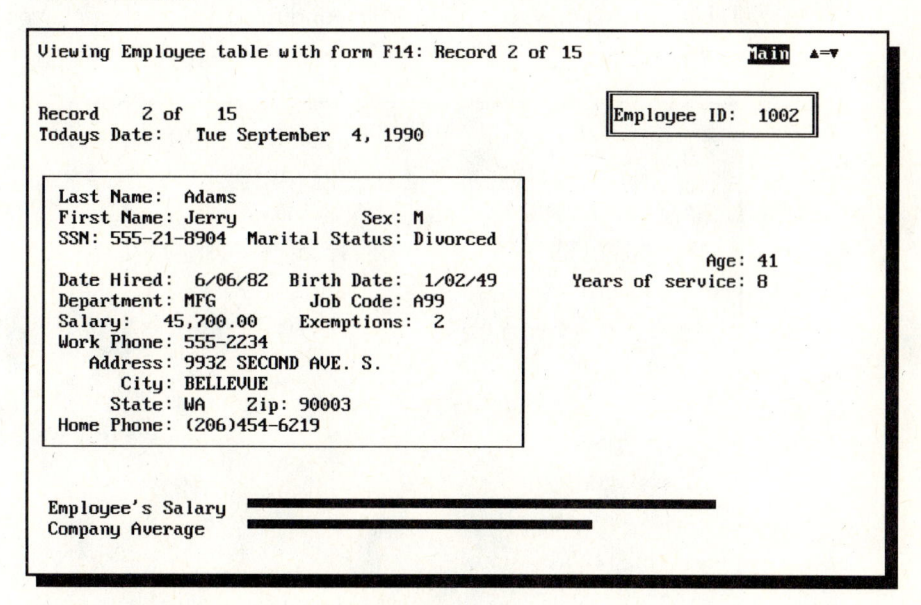

```
Viewing Employee table with form F14: Record 2 of 15        Main  ▲=▼

  Record    2 of   15                        ┌─────────────────────┐
  Todays Date:   Tue September  4, 1990      │ Employee ID:  1002  │
                                             └─────────────────────┘
  ┌──────────────────────────────────────────┐
  │ Last Name:  Adams                        │
  │ First Name: Jerry            Sex: M      │
  │ SSN: 555-21-8904  Marital Status: Divorced│
  │                                          │            Age: 41
  │ Date Hired:  6/06/82  Birth Date: 1/02/49│  Years of service: 8
  │ Department: MFG         Job Code: A99    │
  │ Salary:     45,700.00  Exemptions:  2    │
  │ Work Phone: 555-2234                     │
  │    Address: 9932 SECOND AVE. S.          │
  │       City: BELLEVUE                     │
  │      State: WA     Zip: 90003            │
  │ Home Phone: (206)454-6219                │
  └──────────────────────────────────────────┘


  Employee's Salary   ████████████████████████
  Company Average     █████████████████
```

Figure 9-1 Form using variables and functions

Key Violations

Creating a key for a table ensures that no duplicate records are added to the table, as determined by the values of the key. Interactive Paradox presents a message in the lower-right corner of the screen when a key violation occurs. In an application, it isn't as easy to determine that a key violation occurred. Paradox does not support a function to test the current record to see if another record exists with the same key. Unfortunately, this puts the burden on you to write this code yourself.

Paradox 3.5 includes a new function, RECORDSTATUS, that assists in coding a procedure as a key violation handler. Use RECORDSTATUS to test the status of the current record for one of four conditions: new, locked, modified, or key violation. A True or False is returned depending on the status of the current record for the condition tested. The syntax is as follows:

    RECORDSTATUS (String)
        where String is "New", "Locked", "Modified", or "KeyViol"

> **NOTE:** *Capitalization of the string is not required.*

Table 9-4 lists each of the possible conditions a record can have and the value returned by RECORDSTATUS for each parameter.

Table 9-4
Return values for status of a record

Record status	New	Locked	Modified	KeyViol
New, blank record	True	False	False	False
New record after input	True	False	True	False
New record; key violation when attempting to post	True	True	True	True
Existing record, unchanged	False	False	False	False
Existing record, locked but unchanged	False	True	False	False
Existing record, modified	False	True	True	False
Existing record, modified; key violation when attempting to post	False	True	True	True

All four conditions can be tested if you execute the function once for each test condition. You must perform multiple checks in some cases to accurately determine the state of a record. For example, testing the result of RECORDSTATUS("Modified") indicates if a change has been made to the record but does not tell you if it is an existing record or a new one. Table 9-5 lists the multiple tests necessary to evaluate the status of the record for each possible condition.

The first three RECORDSTATUS options, New, Locked, and Modified, don't require that you attempt to post the record. Checking for a key violation does. This potentially forces the cursor to leave the record if the type of posting executed puts the record in its proper place in the table. You should also be aware that Paradox locks the existing record in addition to the record that violates the key. There is one other note of importance: if a TableLookup is executed, RECORDSTATUS("Modified") always returns True even if no change is made to the record. With this in mind, let's look at multiple ways to check for key violations.

Table 9-5
Multiple conditions to test for full evaluation of record status

Record status	New	Locked	Modified	KeyViol
New, blank record	True		False	
New record after input	True	False	True	
New record, key violation after attempt to post	True			True
Existing record, unchanged	False	False		
Existing record, locked but unchanged		True	False	
Existing record, changed	False		True	False
Existing record, changed, key violation after attempt to post	False			True

There is no single command or set of commands that tell you the current record is a key violation. You must handle new records differently than existing records. The only way to know the record violates an existing record in real time is to use CoEdit for both data entry and for modifications. Four techniques are presented here to handle key violations. They include:

- Copying the record to an array, deleting the record, copying data from the array.
- Setting the key to itself.
- Using RECORDSTATUS and arrays for new records or comparing the key before and after modification for existing records.
- Relying on the error procedure.

Paradox's ability to place the contents of a record into an array is used in the first technique. When a new record is inserted during CoEdit, the data resides only in memory until it is posted. You have to post the record before Paradox checks for a key violation. In interactive Paradox, you have the option to press [Alt][K] to see the existing record or [Alt][L] to replace the existing record. In an application you need to post the record using LOCKRECORD. If the record duplicates a key, the error code is 53. At this point you want to inform your user of the problem and let them fix it. You also need to change the status of the record back to that of entering a new record. If you don't, the next LOCKRECORD or UNLOCKRECORD acts the same as [Alt][L]—it replaces the existing record. The following resets the status of the record for you:

> COPYTOARRAY temp.rcd
> DEL
> INS
> COPYFROMARRAY temp.rcd

The contents of the current record is stored in array *temp.rcd*, thus retaining the values for the current record. By deleting the record and executing INS, a new, unposted record is available. The COPYFROMARRAY places the values from *temp.rcd* into the empty record for you to present to your user with a message indicating there is a duplicate key. The next time you attempt to post the record, it will not overwrite the existing record if no change has been made to the key.

This method works well for new records, but not for existing records. Multitable forms don't let you delete the master record when detail records exists. If the workstation loses power or the network goes down after executing, the data is lost. If you support the Undo feature in your code, using this technique also destroys data. Before Paradox 3.5, there was also a problem with COPYFROMARRAY for detail tables in a multitable form—it could not be done. On a network, confusion could arise as one user is viewing data and sees their screen refreshed with the row they were looking at removed, then a few seconds later it reappears. Anytime existing data is deleted then reinserted you run the risk of data loss. The method works, but we feel it should only be used for new records.

The second technique is somewhat similar to the first. It is for new records only. After attempting to post the record, the status of the record is returned to a new, unposted record if you set the key field to itself. If there is a multi-field key, any field that is part of the key can be used. This is not as generic as the previous method, as you are required to know which field to use. Following is a generic solution:

```
COPYTOARRAY temp.rcd
COPYFROMARRAY temp.rcd
```

Copying the data to an array and copying it back to the record resets the record status. This works for a single or multi-field key. Once again, this is for new records only, it does not work for existing records.

The next example of a key violation handler (Listing 9-15) uses RECORDSTATUS along with other functions to determine if the current record violates an existing key. It checks for key violations when you're in table view, form view for a single table, and in multitable view for both master and detail tables. Each one of these requires a different type of test (there is no one way to check for a duplicate key). This method also requires the contents of the record to be stored in an array before any changes are made. An example program using this method is shown in Listing 9-16.

```
1)   ; KeyVioln.sc
2)
3)   ; If in a multitable form and in master record, cannot use KEYLOOKUP but
4)   ; RESYNC key will set ERRORCODE to 53 indicating a duplicate key.
5)   ;  If in a detail table, issuing a KEYLOOKUP will set ERRORCODE to 56
6)   ; indicating there is no key violations otherwise the errorcode is not set
7)   ; indicating a duplicate key exists and KEYLOOKUP is executed again to return
8)   ; the data back to the original state. BUT!!!  Anytime you change any non-key
9)   ; fields in record, KEYLOOKUP returns a 0 and there are two records with the
10)  ; same key, one with the data before the changes, and one with the changes.
11)  ; Using an array for the before and an array for the after, checking the
12)  ; elements of the array for the number of key fields determines if the
13)  ; changes were to the key fields or non-key fields.
14)  ;
15)  ; NOTE: This procedure needs the array rcd.old to be created and contain
16)  ;       the contents of the record before any changes were made.
17)  ;
18)  ;  Using this method, there is no "temporary" loss of data by copying to an
19)  ; array, delete the record, insert, copy from an array. An UNDO works with
20)  ; this process without loss of data.
21)
22)
23)  PROC AnyKeyViol()
24)    PRIVATE rcd.temp, i
25)    IF RECORDSTATUS("New") THEN            ; Test if for new record in table
26)      LOCKRECORD
27)      IF RECORDSTATUS("KeyViol") THEN
28)        msg = "Record duplicates an existing value, renter"
29)        COPYTOARRAY rcd.temp
30)        COPYFROMARRAY rcd.temp
31)        RETURN True
32)      ELSE
33)        RETURN False
34)      ENDIF
35)    ELSE
36)      IF RECORDSTATUS("Modified") THEN
37)        IF ISFORMVIEW() THEN
38)          IF ISMULTIFORM(TABLE(),FORM()) THEN
39)            IF LINKTYPE() = "None" THEN       ; Must be in master table
40)              RESYNCKEY
```

Listing 9-15 Key violation handler

```
41)             IF ERRORCODE() = 53 THEN          ; Duplicate key
42)               msg = "Record duplicates an existing value, renter"
43)               RETURN True
44)             ELSE
45)               RETURN False
46)             ENDIF
47)           ENDIF
48)         ENDIF
49)       ENDIF
50) ;
51) ;  If the following code is executed, must be one of the following:
52) ;    - not in a form
53) ;    - if in a form, it is a single table form
54) ;    - if in a form and it is a multitable form, must be in a detail table
55) ;
56)       KEYLOOKUP
57)       IF ERRORCODE() = 56 THEN          ; No duplicate key found
58)         RETURN False
59)       ELSE
60)         KEYLOOKUP                       ; Return record to values entered
61)         COPYTOARRAY rcd.temp
62)         FOR i FROM 1 to NKEYFIELDS(TABLE())
63)           IF rcd.old[1+i] <> rcd.temp[1+i] THEN
64)             msg = "Record duplicates an existing value, renter"
65)             RETURN True
66)           ENDIF
67)         ENDFOR
68)         RETURN False
69)       ENDIF
70)     ELSE                                ; The record was not changed
71)       RETURN False
72)     ENDIF
73)   ENDIF
74) ENDPROC
75)
76) PROC SaveRcd()
77)   COPYTOARRAY rcd.old
78) ENDPROC
79)
```

Listing 9-15 Key violation handler—continued

```
1) ; Modtbl.sc
2)
3) PROC ModifyTbl(tbl,formnum)
4)   PRIVATE retprocval, msg
5)   ShowMsg("Loading information, Please wait!","OFF","Y",0)
6)   COEDIT tbl
7)   PICKFORM formnum
```

Listing 9-16 Program example using key violation handler

```
8)     msg = ""
9)     SaveRcd()
10)    CANVAS ON
11)    WHILE True
12)      IF NOT ISBLANK(msg) THEN
13)        BEEP SLEEP 100 BEEP SLEEP 100 BEEP
14)      ENDIF
15)      WAIT RECORD
16)        PROMPT "Editing information",
17)               "[F2]-Save/Exit   [F3]-Next Table   [Ctrl][U]-Undo"
18)        MESSAGE msg
19)        UNTIL "PgDn","PgUp","F3","UNDO","F2","DOS","DOSBIG","ZOOM","ZOOMNEXT"
20)      retkey = retval
21)      msg = ""
22)      IF FORMTYPE("DisplayOnly") = False THEN  ; Check for keyviolations and
23)        IF RECORDSTATUS("New") = False THEN   ; and validity checks only if
24)          IF retkey <> "UNDO" THEN            ; current table is not
25)            retprocval = AnyKeyViol()         ; DisplayOnly and the table
26)            IF retprocval THEN                ; has data. Some detail may
27)              LOOP                            ; be empty.
28)            ENDIF
29)          ENDIF
30)          EXECPROC TABLE()+"VldtyChk"         ;  Check validation rules for
31)          IF retval = False THEN              ; current table, if the fail, loop
32)            LOOP                              ; to WAIT, otherwise process
33)          ENDIF                               ; keystroke
34)        ENDIF
35)      ENDIF
36)      SWITCH
37)        CASE retkey = "PgDn"  : SKIP
38)        CASE retkey = "PgUp"  : SKIP -1
39)        CASE retkey = "F3"    : DOWNIMAGE
40)        CASE retkey = "UNDO"  : UNDO
41)        CASE retkey = "F2"    : QUITLOOP
42)        OTHERWISE             : BEEP LOOP
43)      ENDSWITCH
44)      SaveRcd()                               ;  Save data of next record
45)    ENDWHILE
46)    ShowMsg("Saving data, Returning to Modify Menu, Please wait!","OFF","Y",0)
47)    DO_IT!
48)    CLEARALL
49) ENDPROC
```

Listing 9-16 Program example using key violation handler—continued

As you can see, it isn't as simple as the earlier two examples. Paradox reacts differently to certain commands depending on whether you're using a form and on what type of form you're using. The comments at the beginning of Listing 9-15 explain the types of checking required.

RECORDSTATUS tells you if you're in a new record. If you are, LOCKRECORD attempts to post the record. RECORDSTATUS is used a second time to check for a key violation. If a True is returned, the COPYTOARRAY/COPYFROMARRAY method resets the status of the current record (lines 25 through 34, Listing 9-15).

```
25)    IF RECORDSTATUS("New") THEN              ; Test if for new record in table
26)       LOCKRECORD
27)       IF RECORDSTATUS("KeyViol")  THEN
28)          msg = "Record duplicates an existing value, renter"
29)          COPYTOARRAY rcd.temp
30)          COPYFROMARRAY rcd.temp
31)          RETURN True
32)       ELSE
33)          RETURN False
34)       ENDIF
35)    ELSE
```

If the record is not new, and it was modified, multiple tests are made to determine how to check for a key violation. When you're using a multitable form and you're in the master table, RESYNCKEY sets the error code to 53 when a key violation exists (lines 36 through 49, Listing 9-15).

```
36)       IF RECORDSTATUS("Modified") THEN
37)          IF ISFORMVIEW() THEN
38)             IF ISMULTIFORM(TABLE(),FORM()) THEN
39)                IF LINKTYPE() = "None" THEN       ; Must be in master table
40)                   RESYNCKEY
41)                   IF ERRORCODE() = 53 THEN       ; Duplicate key
42)                      msg = "Record duplicates an existing value, renter"
43)                      RETURN True
44)                   ELSE
45)                      RETURN False
46)                   ENDIF
47)                ENDIF
48)             ENDIF
49)          ENDIF
```

If you're not in a form, in a single table form, or in a detail table of a multitable form, lines 56 through 69 are executed. KEYLOOKUP sets error code to 56 if there is no duplicate key, otherwise the error code is 0. This occurs if you change a key field so that it duplicates the key of another record or if you modify a non-key field in the record. Paradox maintains two records when non-key fields are modified, one before the modification and one containing the changes. KEYLOOKUP is executed again to return the changed values to the record and store them in *rcd.temp*. The array containing the record before any changes were made is now used. A loop is executed comparing the array elements of the before record to the after record for the number of key fields (determined by NKEYFIELDS). If there is no difference, there is no key violation. If the array elements don't match, the record violates an existing key.

```
56)       KEYLOOKUP
57)       IF ERRORCODE() = 56 THEN            ;  No duplicate key found
58)          RETURN False
59)       ELSE
60)          KEYLOOKUP                        ;  Return record to values entered
61)          COPYTOARRAY rcd.temp
62)          FOR i FROM 1 to NKEYFIELDS(TABLE())
63)             IF  rcd.old[1+i] <> rcd.temp[1+i] THEN
64)                msg = "Record duplicates an existing value, renter"
65)                RETURN True
66)             ENDIF
67)          ENDFOR
68)          RETURN False
69)       ENDIF
```

This is a lengthy process but does support the different CoEdit options without data loss (no record is ever deleted). You don't risk data loss if you add the undo feature to your application.

The second solution uses an error procedure along with a key violation checking procedure. The key violation script is shown in Listing 9-17 and the error procedure in Listing 9-18. In this example, an attempt has to be made to move off the record or save the data in order to force Paradox to do the checking. Some commands cause the error procedure to be invoked at this point. The error procedure checks for the key violation error code of 53. If it is a duplicate record, the error procedure sets the global variable *msg* and returns a 1, causing the command to be skipped. At that point, the AnyKeyViol procedure is called. This procedure first checks to see if the global variable is set. If not, it checks if error code 53 has been set. This catches the commands that don't invoke the error procedure. An example using these procedures is shown in Listing 9-19.

```
1)  ; KeyViol2.sc
2)
3)  PROC AnyKeyViol()
4)     IF NOT ISBLANK(msg) THEN
5)        RETURN True
6)     ELSE
7)        IF ERRORCODE() = 53 THEN
8)           msg = "Record duplicates an existing value, renter"
9)           RETURN True
10)       ENDIF
11)    ENDIF
12)    RETURN False
13) ENDPROC
```

Listing 9-17 Second key violation handler

```
1)  PROC ErrProc()
2)    IF ERRORCODE() = 53 THEN
3)      msg = "Record duplicates an existing value, renter"
4)      RETURN 1
5)    ENDIF
6)    CLEAR
7)    @ 5,5 ?? "ERROR OCCURED"
8)    ? "Error code:" + ERRORCODE()
9)    ? ErrorMessage()
10)   ;
11)   ; Error handling code goes here
12)   ;
13)   kp = getchar()                          ; For test purposes only
14) ENDPROC
```

Listing 9-18 Error procedure used in conjunction with key violation handler

```
1)  errorproc = "ErrProc"
2)  COEDIT "Employee"
3)  PICKFORM 9
4)  msg = ""
5)  WHILE True
6)    IF NOT ISBLANK(msg) THEN
7)      BEEP SLEEP 100 BEEP SLEEP 100 BEEP
8)    ENDIF
9)    WAIT RECORD
10)     PROMPT "Modify Data    [F2]-Exit   [Ctrl][U]-Undo  [Ins]-Add Record",
11)            "[PgDn]-Next Record     [PgUp]-Previous Record"
12)     MESSAGE msg
13)     UNTIL "PgDn","Down","PgUp","Up","Undo","F2","Ins",
14)           "DOS","DOSBIG","ZOOM","ZOOMNEXT",
15)           -129,"F3"
16)   msg = ""
17)   retkey = retval
18)   SWITCH
19)     CASE retkey = "F3" :
20)          DOWNIMAGE
21)          AnyKeyViol()
22)     CASE retkey = "PgDn" OR retkey = "Down" :
23)          SKIP 1
24)          AnyKeyViol()
25)     CASE retkey = "PgUp" OR retkey = "Up" :
26)          SKIP -1
27)          AnyKeyViol()
28)     CASE retkey = "F2"  :
29)          DO_IT!
30)          retprocval = AnyKeyViol()
31)          IF retprocval THEN
32)            LOOP
```

Listing 9-19 Program example using error procedure in conjunction with key violation handler

```
33)              ELSE
34)                  QUITLOOP
35)              ENDIF
36)         CASE retkey = "Ins" :
37)              INS
38)              AnyKeyViol()
39)         CASE retkey = "Undo" :
40)              UNDO
41)         OTHERWISE             :
42)              BEEP
43)      ENDSWITCH
44)  ENDWHILE
45)  CLEARALL
```

Listing 9-19 program example using error procedure—continued

The last two methods detect key violations for new records and modifications to existing records when the key fields are accessible. Besides the code differences, they also perform differently when you use a routine that lets you scroll forwards and backwards in a form when inserting new records. This involves the fly-away problem.

When tables are keyed, Paradox always displays them in the order of the key field(s). In CoEdit mode, once the record is posted it moves to its proper location. This is fine if you're entering a single record or modifying only one record. But when you're processing multiple records based on selection criteria, you want to move to the next record in the sequence even if you change the key value. If your cursor moves to the new location in the table, you run the risk of missing records. The third key violation example always moves with the record. If you change the key so the record moves from the first to the last in the table, your cursor goes with the record. The last method lets the record fly away if you move from one master record to the next. If you insert a record or change the key of the master and move to a detail table, Paradox automatically locks the record and places it in the proper location in the table. This, too, causes problems for code that scans the data.

As you've seen, coding for key violations is not trivial. Because there is no single command or function to use in every situation, you have to be aware of when a duplicate record can be entered and if you're in Form view or Table view. Maybe in the near future Paradox will include a simple function to test if the key is valid.

Uniqueness Not Based on Key Field

In some situations, another field in the table besides the key field(s) has to be unique. There is no ValCheck or other menu selection to use for defining this type of validation. It is up to you to incorporate this type of data integrity into the application. To demonstrate this, let's consider the following table and validation requirements.

- The table contains names of business licenses within the state.
- Each business has a unique number assigned.
- There cannot be two businesses with the same name.

These requirements allow for two fields to be used to identify the record: the numerical ID or the name of the business. One of the rules for establishing a key is to make it short, so a business name doesn't qualify. Therefore, the business ID is the key and uniqueness is ensured by Paradox. Ensuring that no two companies have the same name becomes the developer's responsibility.

Listing 9-20 is a script containing all the procedures used in this example. Let's take a quick overview of each procedure.

Line 3-5	Beep is used to make three distinct sounds of the system bell.
Line 8-22	ShowMsg is a generic procedure used to place a message in the lower right corner of the screen. This follows the style used by interactive Paradox.
Line 26-37	FldBlnk is used by RqdComps. (This procedure is discussed in Chapter 6.)
Line 40-66	RqdComp is the procedure to validate the data. This is where the uniqueness test on the company name is tested.
Line 70-134	EnterComps is the main procedure for entering companies.

Viewing, Entering, and Editing Data

```
 1)  ; EntrComp.sc
 2)
 3)  PROC Beeps()
 4)     BEEP SLEEP 100 BEEP SLEEP 100 BEEP
 5)  ENDPROC
 6)
 7)
 8)  PROC ShowMsg(inmsg,ca,clr,slp)
 9)     ; inmsg   -  message to be displayed
10)     ; ca      -  after message CANVAS option
11)     ; clr     -  if = Y then CLEAR before message
12)     ; slp     -  number for use with SLEEP command
13)     CANVAS ON
14)     IF clr = "Y" THEN
15)        CLEAR
16)     ENDIF
17)     MESSAGE inmsg
18)     IF ca = "OFF" THEN
19)        CANVAS OFF
20)     ENDIF
21)     SLEEP slp
22)  ENDPROC
23)
24)
25)
26)  PROC FldBlnk(fldnm,fldtxt)
27)
28)     EXECUTE "fldblnk = ISBLANK(["+fldnm+"])"
29)     IF fldblnk THEN
30)        MOVETO FIELD fldnm
31)        msg = fldtxt+" must be entered"
32)        Beeps()
33)        RETURN True
34)     ELSE
35)        RETURN False
36)     ENDIF
37)  ENDPROC
38)
39)
40)  PROC RqdComps()
41)     PRIVATE cname,rcd.temp
42)     IF FldBlnk("Name","Business Name") THEN
43)        RETURN False
44)     ENDIF
45)     IF FldBlnk("State","State") THEN
46)        RETURN False
47)     ENDIF
48)     ; Check for duplicate name
49)     cname = [Name]
50)     COPYTOARRAY rcd.temp
51)     DEL
```

Listing 9-20 Program example demonstrating uniqueness not based on key

```
52)    MOVETO [Name]
53)    LOCATE cname
54)  ; If LOCATE is successful, then the name of the business is a duplicate
55)    IF retval = True THEN
56)       msg = "This business name already exits"
57)       INS
58)       COPYFROMARRAY rcd.temp
59)       Beeps()
60)       RETURN False
61)    ELSE
62)       INS
63)       COPYFROMARRAY rcd.temp
64)    ENDIF
65)    RETURN True
66) ENDPROC
67)
68)
69)
70) PROC EnterComps()
71)    CURSOR OFF
72)    ShowMsg("Loading form, Please wait","OFF","N",0)
73)
74)  ; check for empty table
75)    IF ISEMPTY("Comps") THEN
76)       compid = 101
77)    ELSE
78)       compid = CMAX("Comps","Business ID") + 1
79)    ENDIF
80)    COEDIT "Comps"
81)    MENU "IP" {1}
82)    INS
83)  ;  READLIB "Prime" RqdComps
84)    [Business ID] = compid
85)    compid = compid + 1
86)    msg = ""
87)    CANVAS ON
88)    WHILE TRUE
89)       WAIT RECORD
90)          PROMPT "Enter New Company Information [F2]-Save/Exit [Esc]-Cancel" +
91)                 "/Exit",
92)                 "[PgDn]-New Company   "
93)          MESSAGE msg
94)          UNTIL "F2","PgDn","FieldView","Esc",
95)                "DOS","DOSBIG","ZOOM","ZOOMNEXT"
96)       msg = ""
97)       SWITCH
98)          CASE retval = "F2" :
99)             retprocval = RqdComps()
100)            IF retprocval THEN
101)               msg = "Saving information, Returning to Main Menu"
102)               QUITLOOP
103)            ENDIF
```

Listing 9-20 Program example demonstrating uniqueness not based on key—continued

Viewing, Entering, and Editing Data

```
104)        CASE retval = "PgDn" :
105)             retprocval = RqdComps()
106)             IF retprocval THEN
107)               INS                           ; move to new record
108)               CtrlHome                      ; move to first field on form
109)               [Business ID] = compid
110)               compid = compid + 1
111)             ENDIF
112)        CASE retval = "PgUp" :
113)             retprocval = RqdComps()
114)             IF retprocval THEN
115)               CtrlPgUp
116)             ENDIF
117)        CASE retval = "Esc" :
118)             SHOWMENU
119)               "No"  : "Do not cancel input for this record",
120)               "Yes" : "Cancel input for this record, Return to Main Menu"
121)             TO cancelchoice
122)             IF cancelchoice = "Yes" THEN
123)               DEL
124)               msg = "Cancelling input for current record, Returning to Main Menu"
125)               QUITLOOP
126)             ENDIF
127)             LOOP
128)      ENDSWITCH
129)    ENDWHILE
130)    ShowMsg(msg,"OFF","Y",0)
131)    DO_IT!
132)    CLEARALL
133)    RETURN
134) ENDPROC
135)
136)
137) EnterComps()
```

Listing 9-20 Program example demonstrating uniqueness not based on key—continued

The core piece of this example is in RqdComps. Lines 48-64 check for a duplicate name. Before each new record is posted, the validation requirements have to be met. To check for a duplicate name, the business name is stored in *cname*. Line 50 copies the data into an array. Because this is a new record, it is deleted without having to worry about detail records. LOCATE is used in line 53 to see if the name already exists. If it does, the global variable *msg* is set, indicating the record duplicates an existing business name.

```
48)   ; Check for duplicate name
49)   cname = [Name]
50)   COPYTOARRAY rcd.temp
51)   DEL
52)   MOVETO [Name]
53)   LOCATE cname
```

```
54)    ; If LOCATE is successful, then the name of the business is a duplicate
55)    IF retval = True THEN
56)       msg = "This business name already exits"
57)       INS
58)       COPYFROMARRAY rcd.temp
59)       Beeps()
60)       RETURN False
61)    ELSE
62)       INS
63)       COPYFROMARRAY rcd.temp
64)    ENDIF
```

Trapping for Field View

Editing a field requires that you use Field view ([Ctrl][F] or [Alt][F5]). You don't have to trap for these keys in a WAIT TABLE or WAIT RECORD, but you're asking for trouble if you don't.

Keystrokes affect cursor movement differently while in Field view than normal field editing. Table 9-6 lists the various keys used and the effect they have on the cursor in Field view, Edit/CoEdit, and a menu prompt.

Table 9-6
Keystroke effects in Field view, Edit/CoEdit, and menu prompts

Key	Field View Effect	Edit/CoEdit Effect	Menu Prompt Effect
← and →	Move between characters	Move between fields	No effect
Home, End	Move to start or end of the field	Move to start or end of the table	No effect
Del	Deletes character at cursor	Deletes current record	No effect
Ins	Insert/Overstrike toggle	Inserts new record	No effect
Backspace	Deletes character to the left of the cursor	Deletes character to the left of the cursor	Deletes character to the left of the cursor
Ctrl-Backspace	Deletes all characters	Deletes all characters	Deletes all characters
Enter	Ends Field View	Moves to next field	Accepts value
↑ and ↓	Move to next line	Moves between records	No effect
Ctrl ←, Ctrl →	Moves between words in field	Moves one screen left or right	No effect

As shown in this table, keystrokes have different effects depending on when they're used. If you're in Field view and press a key included in the UNTIL statement, you might not get the desired action. For example, in a WAIT RECORD, trapping for the Ins, Del, Up, or Down keystrokes ends a Field view operation. To resolve potential conflicts, it is best to trap for Field view in the WAIT command. Adding "FieldView" to the UNTIL traps for both [Alt][F5] and [Ctrl][F]. The following fragment is an example of the CASE statement used to process either of these keystrokes.

```
CASE retval = "FieldView"   :          ;  Executes for both [Alt][F5]
     WHILE True                        ;  and [Ctrl][F]
        FIELDVIEW                      ;  FIELDVIEW is done in WHILE loop
        WAIT FIELD                     ;  to ensure field level editing in
                                       ;  case F2, DOS or DOSBIG pressed
           PROMPT "Editing current field",
                  "Press Enter (\017\217) when finished"
           UNTIL "Enter","F2","DOS","DOSBIG"
        IF retval = "Enter" THEN       ;  End FieldView and return to
           QUITLOOP                    ;  to main processing loop
        ELSE
           BEEP                        ;  Beep if F2, DOS or DOSBIG pressed
        ENDIF
     ENDWHILE
```

You must use a WHILE loop for Field view control because [F2] (in addition to [Enter]) ends field editing. With [F2] being a common keystroke in data entry and edit modules, it's possible that [F2] will be pressed here accidentally. [Ctrl][O] and [Alt][O], like in most other places, suspend Paradox to the operating system while in Field view. Therefore, both these keystrokes have to be included in the UNTIL portion of the WAIT RECORD statement (along with [Enter] and [F2]).

The FIELDVIEW command must be inside the WHILE loop. If it isn't, pressing any of the keys in the UNTIL (except [Enter]) continues in the loop but ends Field view. Even when you trap for these unwanted keystrokes, the cursor is still placed at the end of the field after looping. If it was in another position prior to ending the WAIT command, you have to reposition the cursor before continuing to modify the field.

Explicitly trapping for Field view in this manner alleviates the contention with other keystrokes commonly used in other entry and edit modes. This is the safest way to ensure accurate control over interaction with data in an application.

How to Get to DOS Within an Application and Ways to Prevent It

In many of the examples in this chapter and throughout the book, you have seen UNTIL statements containing the keystrokes "DOS," "DOSBIG," and "ZOOM." There is a good reason for making this part of your WAIT statements—your users could accidentally get to the operating system prompt. Some users would read and understand the screen displayed by Paradox (a warning not to delete objects and to type "exit" to return to Paradox). Others wouldn't know what has happened and might decide it's time to reboot the system! This is an open door for corruption, and it is therefore essential that you trap for these situations to create a tighter application.

As of this writing, the following are the known areas of Paradox where you can press [Ctrl][O] and [Alt][O] to suspend Paradox:

- Within a WAIT command (TABLE, RECORD, and FIELD)
- At the ZOOM prompt
- While in an ValCheck TableLookup ([F1])

The first two are the easiest to control. Including "DOS" and "DOSBIG" in the UNTIL statement determines whether to pass the keystroke to Paradox or disallow the action. Trapping for "ZOOM" prevents the prompt "Value:" from being displayed. If your application requires the Zoom feature, it is best to include a separate CASE statement for a customized search option.

The area which is harder to control is when a ValCheck is defined for a field providing TableLookup access (by pressing [F1]). While the lookup table is displayed, both [Ctrl][O] or [Alt][O] suspend Paradox. This eliminates using TableLookup if you're concerned about your user accidentally getting to DOS. The Paradox Data Entry Toolkit includes a script (LOOKSLCT.SC) which provides basic access from a WAIT command. The concept presented in that script is the basis for the code necessary to provide TableLookup functionality and also trap for [Ctrl][O] and [Alt][O].

Summary

Viewing, entering, and modifying data in an application requires custom programming not only to handle complex data manipulation requirements, but also to provide the same user-friendly interface Paradox users are accustomed to on the interactive side. You might have to jump through hoops to get the result you need, but PAL provides the means to handle most situations.

10 Running Advanced Queries

Queries are one of Paradox's strongest features. Even so, changing, fetching, adding, and deleting table information is still frustrating to implement in an application with any product—even Paradox.

While Paradox 3.5 brings many new features with its SQL Link capability, in this chapter we'll concentrate on Paradox's native ability to produce queries. This chapter assumes that you have a basic understanding of how to create a query. This chapter is not intended as a reference on the different types of queries you can produce; rather it is a collection of key concepts on how Paradox's query mechanism actually works. In order to determine what kind of query is best for certain applications, we'll also look at several approaches to asking questions on Paradox tables and ways to test, record, and optimize queries. Let's start by reviewing some basic QBE concepts.

Table 10-1
Key terms and concepts

Answer table	AS	Calculation fields
CHANGETO	Check Descending	Checkmark
DELETE	Example element	Example
Filter	FIND	Image order
INSERT	Logical AND	Logical OR
NOT	QBE	Multiple lines
Query By Example	Query Form	Query operators
Query script	Query Statement	QuerySave
Rename (table)	Rotate(Ctrl-R)	SCAN
SET queries	Script/Play	Wildcards

A Whole New Way of Asking Questions

QBE (Query By Example) is an extremely powerful mechanism. While simple in concept, QBE can be complex. Sometimes it's just downright tough to implement certain types of queries.

Paradox changed the way people talk to databases. By presenting a form-based approach using the actual table structure and allowing users to select fields with a press of a key, Paradox started a revolution in database query capabilities (see Figure 10-1). Paradox pioneered QBE. Its basic premise is that you don't have to be a programmer to ask a table a question. While QBE is simple, there are still some things it cannot do, which we'll discuss towards the end of the chapter.

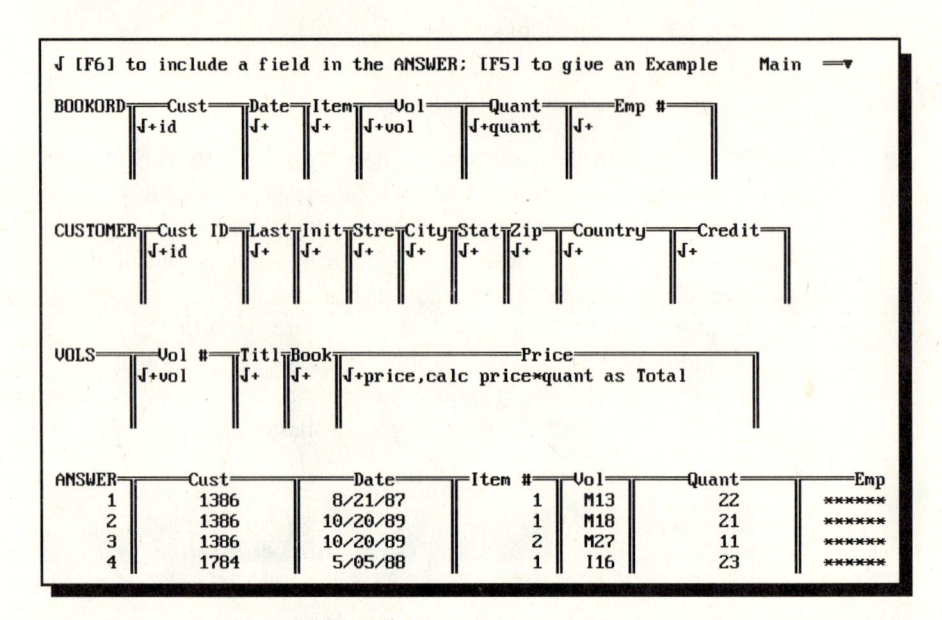

```
√ [F6] to include a field in the ANSWER; [F5] to give an Example    Main  ▼
BOOKORD┬──Cust──┬──Date─┬─Item─┬──Vol──┬──Quant──┬──Emp #─┐
       │ √+id   │ √+    │ √+   │ √+vol │ √+quant │ √+     │




CUSTOMER┬─Cust ID─┬─Last─┬─Init─┬─Stre─┬─City─┬─Stat─┬─Zip─┬─Country─┬──Credit──┐
        │ √+id    │ √+   │ √+   │ √+   │ √+   │ √+   │ √+  │ √+      │          │




VOLS─┬──Vol #─┬─Titl─┬─Book┬────────────Price──────────────┐
     │ √+vol  │ √+   │ √+  │ √+price,calc price*quant as Total │




ANSWER─┬────Cust────┬─────Date─────┬─Item #─┬──Vol──┬──Quant──┬──Emp────┐
   1   │    1386    │   8/21/87    │   1    │  M13  │   22    │ ******  │
   2   │    1386    │   10/20/89   │   1    │  M18  │   21    │ ******  │
   3   │    1386    │   10/20/89   │   2    │  M27  │   11    │ ******  │
   4   │    1784    │   5/05/88    │   1    │  I16  │   23    │ ******  │
```

Figure 10-1 The Paradox query form

Here's a quick review of the terms and capabilities available in Paradox's QBE function.

Summary Operators

    AVERAGE   Average of the values in a column
    COUNT   Number of values in a column
    MAX   Highest value in a column

MIN	Lowest value in a column
SUM	Sum of the values in a column

Set Operators

ONLY	Table B is a subset of Table A
NO	Sets are disjoint. (There are records in Table A that do not exist in Table B and vice versa.)
EVERY	Table A is a subset of Table B
EXACTLY	Table B is equal to Table A

Special Operators

OR	This expression versus another expression
AS	Rename a selected field name in the Answer table
!	Inclusion operator. (Include all items from a table regardless if they match or not.)

Matching Patterns

LIKE	Find a match even though the pattern isn't exact
..	Wildcard, any character in a group
@	Any single character in a single position
TODAY	Match today's date against date values in a column
BLANK	Find all the records that have blank values in a column

Reserved Words

CALC	Calculate a new field
INSERT	Insert records from Table A into Table B
DELETE	Remove selected records from the table
CHANGETO	Change values in selected records to other values
FIND	Locate selected records
SET	Used only for SET queries

QuerySave and PAL Commands

You can record queries in QuerySave statements, or you can enter them through PAL. To illustrate, following are examples of QuerySave and of PAL commands for each of the summary operators. In each QuerySave, the "Do_it! Reset ClearAll" commands have been added. This is one example of how there are different methods for asking the same question.

AVERAGE

QuerySave

```
Query
  Masterbk |              Total              |
           | calc average all as "Average" |
           |                               |
           |                               |
  Masterbk |
           |
           |
           |

Endquery
Do_it!
Reset
ClearAll
```

PAL

```
Menu {ask} {bookord}
    moveto[total]
    typein "calc average all as "Average of Values""
    Do_it!
```

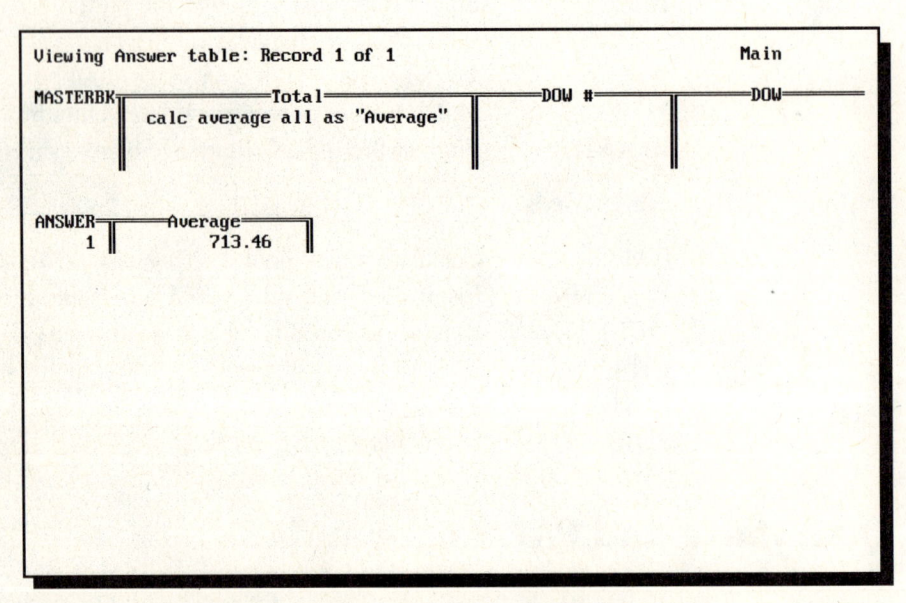

Figure 10-2 Examples of summary operators—AVERAGE

COUNT

QuerySave

```
Query
  Masterbk |            Total            |
           | calc count all as "Total Count" |
           |                             |
           |                             |
  Masterbk |
           |
           |
           |
Endquery
Do_it!
Reset
ClearAll
```

PAL

```
Menu {ask} {bookord}
    moveto[total]
        typein "calc count all as "Total Count""
        Do_it!
```

```
Viewing Answer table: Record 1 of 1                              Main
MASTERBK┬────────Total────────┬────────DOW #────────┬────────DOW═══
        │ calc count all as "Total Count"           │             │
        │                                           │             │
        │                                           │             │

ANSWER┬─Total Count─┐
   1  │    128      │
```

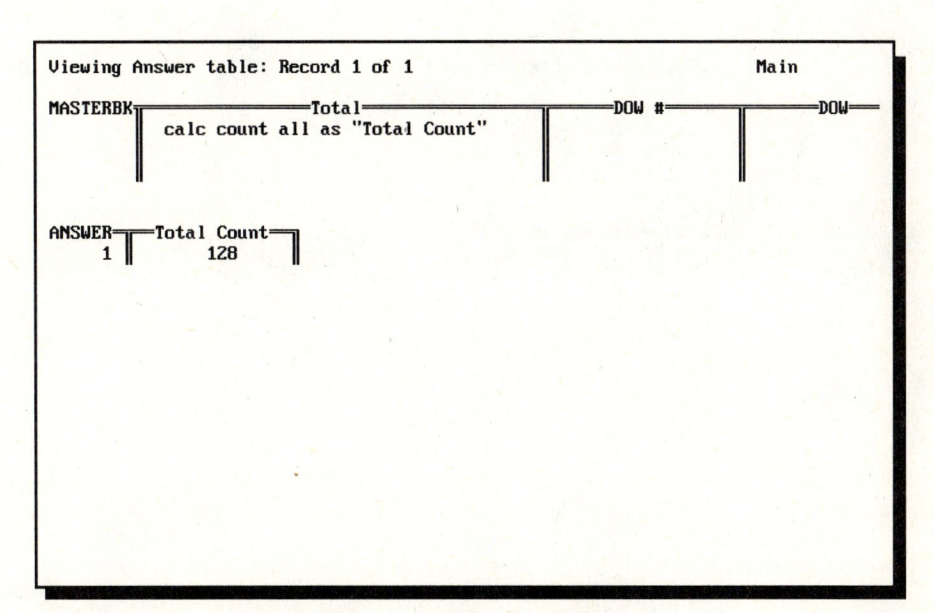

Figure 10-3 Examples of summary operators—COUNT

MAX

QuerySave

```
Query
  Masterbk |                  Total              |
           | calc max all as "Maximum Value" |
           |                                     |
           |                                     |
  Masterbk |
           |
           |
           |
Endquery
Do_it!
Reset
ClearAll
```

PAL

```
Menu {ask} {bookord}
    moveto[total]
    typein "calc max all as "Maximum Value""
    Do_it!
```

```
Viewing Answer table: Record 1 of 1                              Main
MASTERBK╤═══════════Total═══════════╤══════DOW #══════╤══════DOW══
        │ calc max all as "Maximum Value" │             │
        │                                 │             │


ANSWER╤══Maximum Value══╗
   1  ║     2,878.40    ║
```

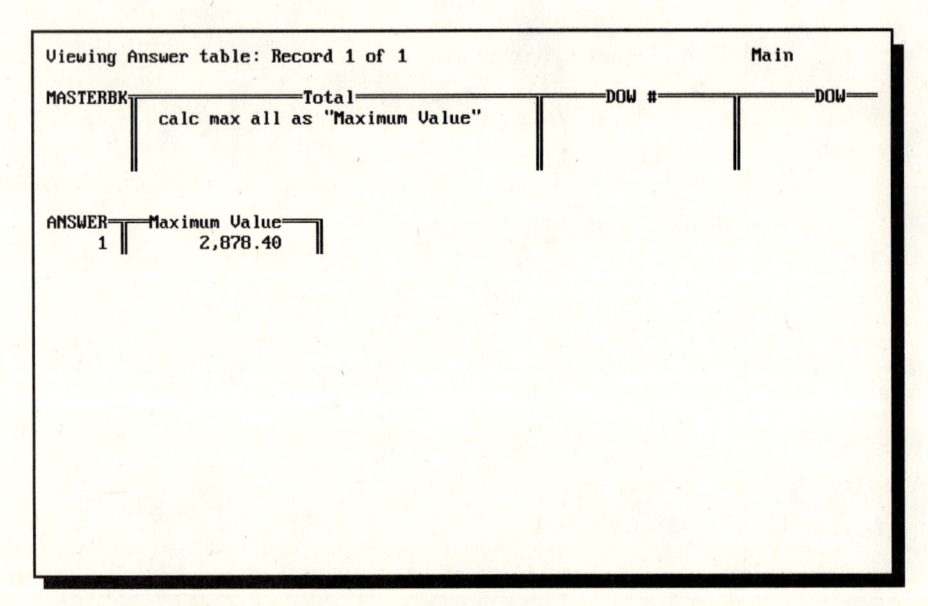

Figure 10-4 Examples of summary operators—MAX

MIN

QuerySave

```
Query
  Masterbk |              Total             |
           | calc min all as "Minimum Value" |
           |                                 |
           |                                 |
  Masterbk |
           |
           |
           |
Endquery
Do_it!
Reset
ClearAll
```

PAL

```
Menu {ask} {bookord}
    moveto[total]
    typein "calc min all as "Minimum Value""
    Do_it!The lowest value in a column
```

```
Viewing Answer table: Record 1 of 1                          Main
MASTERBK═══════════Total═══════════════════DOW #═══════════DOW═
            calc min all as "Minimum Value"



ANSWER═══Minimum Value═
    1          29.95
```

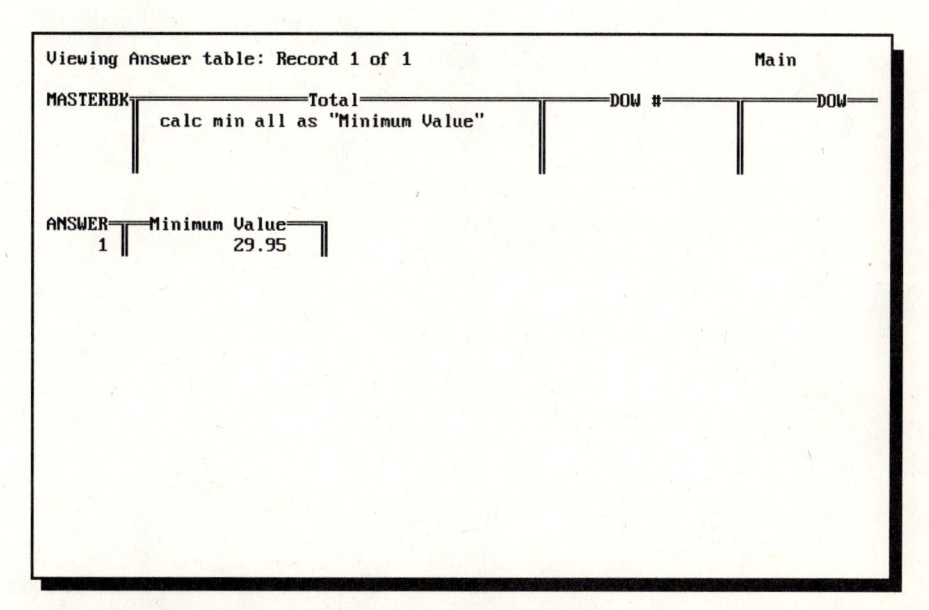

Figure 10-5 Examples of summary operators—MIN

SUM

QuerySave

```
Query
  Masterbk |         Total         |
           | calc sum all as "Total" |
           |                       |
           |                       |
  Masterbk |
           |
           |
           |

Endquery
Do_it!
Reset
ClearAll
```

PAL

```
Menu {ask} {bookord}
    moveto[total]
    typein "calc sum all as "Total""
    Do_it!
```

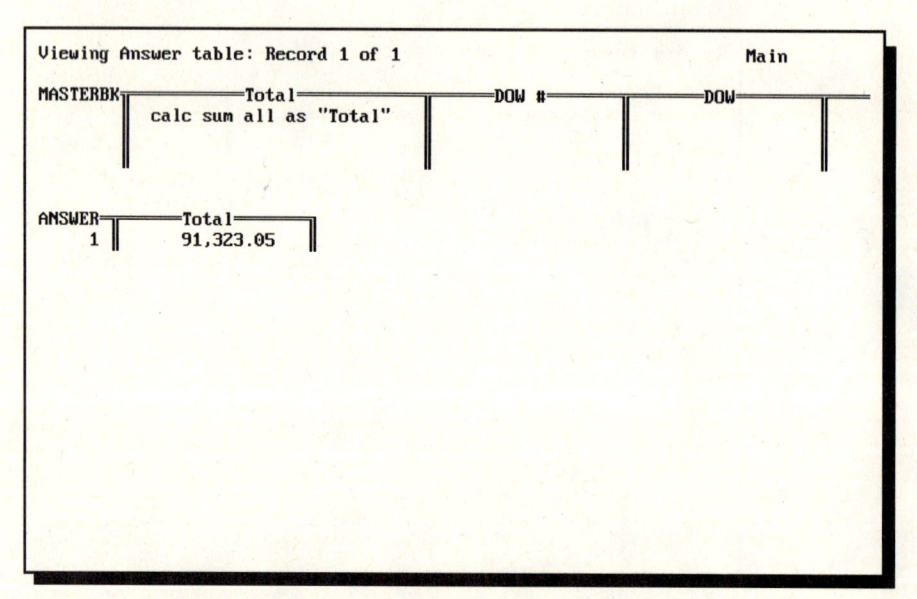

```
Viewing Answer table: Record 1 of 1                              Main
MASTERBK┬────────Total────────┬────────DOW #────────┬────────DOW────────
        │ calc sum all as "Total" │                     │
        │                     │                     │


ANSWER┬────Total────┐
    1 ║    91,323.05 ║
```

Figure 10-6 Examples of summary operators—SUM

Now that we've reviewed what QBE can do, which methods are better than others? Let's explore a way of quantifying some test results and take a closer look at how Paradox queries function.

Queries in Scripts versus Libraries

Is it better to save a Paradox query in a script or in a library as a procedure? Developing a strategy for and style of creating, storing, and executing queries is essential to every application. The correct strategy to use isn't always as obvious as you might think. It really depends on what you're after in the way of performance and control over your application. It also depends on whether you're doing a rapid prototype or you have the time to test which method is better. To help examine this issue we'll create a query demonstration.

This demonstration serves two purposes. First, it shows the effects of storing and retrieving queries as scripts or procedures, with procedures in several flavors. It also shows how to build query tests and how these tests can record their own results as part of your design process.

To test whether queries should be saved as scripts or procedures, the five summary operator scripts shown in Figures 10-2 through 10-6 have each been converted to a procedure and compiled into several libraries. Listing 10-1 shows how the scripts look in a library. The first set of procedures in QUERYLB1 library (Query1-Query6) contains QuerySave where the extra vertical lines still appear in the query form. The second set of procedures have had the extra rows removed (Query1a-Query6a). The next set of procedures are the PAL command equivalents of the same summary operator queries (Query1b-Query6b). Finally, we include a series of queries that develop the information for Table 10-2. These queries are included to illustrate a CHANGETO query.

NOTE: *The tests were conducted on an AST Premium 286 with 2MB RAM, QRAM, and a 40MB hard drive with Paradox running in protected mode. These tests do not address the SETSWAP problems that PLAY and EXECPROC present when running the queries. The tests are meant to give an overview of how a series of queries behave in the Paradox environment.*

```
LibName = "QueryLb1"
@24,0 Clear EOL ?? "Creating ",LibName
Style blink ?? "..."
style
CreateLib LibName
Proc Query1 ()
Query
 Bookord |      Cust      |    Date     |   Item #    |     Vol       |
         | CheckPlus _id  | CheckPlus   | CheckPlus   | CheckPlus _vol |
         |                |             |             |               |
         |                |             |             |               |
 Bookord |     Quant      |   Emp #     |
         | CheckPlus _quant | CheckPlus |
         |                |             |
         |                |             |
 Customer |    Cust ID    |  Last Name  |    Init     |    Street     |
          | CheckPlus _id | CheckPlus   | CheckPlus   | CheckPlus     |
          |               |             |             |               |
          |               |             |             |               |
 Customer |     City      |   State     |     Zip     |   Country     |   Credit    |
          | CheckPlus     | CheckPlus   | CheckPlus   | CheckPlus     | CheckPlus   |
          |               |             |             |               |             |
          |               |             |             |               |             |
 Vols |   Vol #       |  Title    |   Book    |       Price                          |
      |CheckPlus _vol|CheckPlus|CheckPlus|CheckPlus _p,calc _p*_q as Total            |
      |               |           |           |                                      |
      |               |           |           |                                      |
Endquery
Do_it!
EndProc
Proc Query2()
Query
 Masterbk |             Total              |
          | calc average all as "Average"  |
          |                                |
          |                                |
 Masterbk |
          |
          |
          |
Endquery
Do_it!
EndProc
Proc Query3()
Query
 Masterbk |             Total                |
          | calc count all as "Total Count"  |
          |                                  |
          |                                  |
 Masterbk |
          |
          |
```

Listing 10-1 *QueryLb1*

```
               |
Endquery
Do_it!
EndProc
Proc Query4()
Query
  Masterbk |           Total            |
           | calc max all as "Maximum Value" |
           |                            |
           |                            |
  Masterbk |
           |
           |
           |

Endquery
Do_it!
EndProc
Proc Query5()
Query
  Masterbk |           Total            |
           | calc min all as "Minimum Value" |
           |                            |
           |                            |
  Masterbk |
           |
           |
           |

Endquery
Do_it!
EndProc
Proc Query6()
Query
  Masterbk |           Total            |
           | calc sum all as "Total"    |
           |                            |
           |                            |
  Masterbk |
           |
           |
           |

Endquery
Do_it!
EndProc
Proc Query1a()
Query
  Bookord  |    Cust       |    Date       |   Item #   |     Vol         |
           | CheckPlus _id | CheckPlus     | CheckPlus  | CheckPlus _vol  |
  Bookord  |    Quant      |    Emp #      |
           | CheckPlus _quant | CheckPlus  |
  Customer |    Cust ID    |  Last Name    |   Init     |    Street       |
           | CheckPlus _id | CheckPlus     | CheckPlus  | CheckPlus       |
  Customer |    City       |    State      |    Zip     |   Country     | Credit |
```

Listing 10-1 *QueryLb1—continued*

```
            | CheckPlus  | CheckPlus  | CheckPlus  | CheckPlus  | CheckPlus    |
  Vols  |   Vol #       |   Title      |    Book      | CheckPlus  |   Price      |
        |CheckPlus _vol| CheckPlus    |CheckPlus     |CheckPlus _p,calc _p*_q as Total |
Endquery
Do_it!
EndProc
Proc Query2a()
Query
  Masterbk |          Total            |
           | calc average all as "Average" |
  Masterbk |
           |
Endquery
Do_it!
EndProc
Proc Query3a()
Query
  Masterbk |          Total            |
           | calc count all as "Total Count" |
  Masterbk |
           |
Endquery
Do_it!
EndProc
Proc Query4a()
Query
  Masterbk |          Total            |
           | calc max all as "Maximum Value" |
  Masterbk |
           |
Endquery
Do_it!
EndProc
Proc Query5a()
Query
  Masterbk |          Total            |
           | calc min all as "Minimum Value" |
  Masterbk |
           |
Endquery
Do_it!
EndProc
Proc Query6a()
Query
  Masterbk |          Total            |
           | calc sum all as "Total"   |
  Masterbk |
           |
Endquery
Do_it!
EndProc
Proc Query1b()
```

Listing 10-1 QueryLb1—continued

```
menu {ask} {bookord}
CheckPlus
moveto[cust]
Example "id"
moveto[vol]
Example "vol"
moveto[quant]
Example "quant"
menu {ask} {customer}
CheckPlus
moveto[cust id]
Example "id"
menu {ask} {vols}
CheckPlus
moveto[vol #]
CheckPlus
Example "vol"
moveto[price]
Example "price"
",calc "
Example "price"
"*"
Example "quant"
" as Total"
Do_it!
EndProc
Proc Query2b()
menu {ask} {masterbk}
moveto[total]
"calc average all as \"average\""
Do_it!
EndProc
Proc Query3b()
menu {ask} {masterbk}
moveto[total]
"calc count all as \"Total Count\""
Do_it!
EndProc
Proc Query4b()
menu {ask} {masterbk}
moveto[total]
"calc max all as \"Maximum Value\""
Do_it!
EndProc
Proc Query5b()
menu {ask} {masterbk}
moveto[total]
"calc min all as \"Minimum Value\""
Do_it!
EndProc
Proc Query6b()
menu {ask} {masterbk}
```

Listing 10-1 *QueryLb1—continued*

```
moveto[total]
"calc sum all as \"Total\""
Do_it!
EndProc
Proc CalcDiff()
Query
 Listproc | QueryForm | QueryForm Trimmed |    Diff % Query/Trimmed     |
          |    _a     |      _b            | changeto (1-(_b/_a))*100*-1 |
          |           |                    |                             |
          |           |                    |                             |
 Listproc | QueryForm PAL |   Diff % Query/PAL       |    Diff % Trimmed/PAL      |
          |    _c    | changeto (1-(_c/_a))*100*-1 | changeto (1-(_c/_b))/_b*100*-1 |
          |          |                             |                              |
          |          |                             |                              |
Endquery
Do_it!
EndProc
Proc CalcDiffa()
Query
 Listproc | QueryForm | QueryForm Trimmed |    Diff % Query/Trimmed     |
          |    _a     |      _b            | changeto (_b-_a)/_a*100*-1  |
 Listproc | QueryForm PAL |   Diff % Query/PAL   |   Diff % Trimmed/PAL    |
          |    _c    | changeto (_c-_a)/_a*100*-1 | changeto (_c-_b)/_b*100*-1 |
Endquery
Do_it!
EndProc
Proc CalcDiffb()
menu {ask} {listproc}
Right Right
Right Right Example "a"
Right Example "b"
Right Right Example "c"
Left
"changeto ("
Example "b"
"-"
Example "a"
")/"
Example "a"
"*100*-1"
Right Right
"changeto ("
Example "c"
"-"
Example "a"
")/"
Example "a"
"*100*-1"
Right
"changeto ("
Example "c"
"-"
```

Listing 10-1 QueryLb1—continued

```
Example "b"
")/"
Example "b"
"*100*-1"
Do_it!
EndProc
Proc CalcDiffc()
menu {ask}{listProc}
moveto[queryform] Example "a"
moveto[queryform trimmed] Example "b"
moveto[diff % query/trimmed];Right
"changeto (1-("
Example "b" "/"
Example "a"
"))*100*-1"
moveto[queryform pal];Right
Example "c"
moveto[diff % query/pal];Right
"changeto (1-("
Example "c" "/"
Example "a"
"))*100*-1"
moveto[diff % trimmed/pal] ;Right
"changeto (1-("
Example "c" "/"
Example "b"
"))*100*-1"
Do_it!
EndProc
Proc CalcDiffd()
menu {ask}{listProc}
moveto[queryform] Example "a"
moveto[queryform trimmed] Example "b"
Right
"changeto (1-("
Example "b" "/"
Example "a"
"))*100*-1"
Right
Example "c"
Right
"changeto (1-("
Example "c" "/"
Example "a"
"))*100*-1"
Right
"changeto (1-("
Example "c" "/"
Example "b"
"))*100*-1"
Do_it!
EndProc
```

Listing 10-1 *QueryLb1—continued*

```
WriteLib LibName Query1,Query2,Query2,Query3,Query4,Query5,Query6,
Query1a,Query2a,Query2a,Query3a,Query4a,Query5a,Query6a,
Query1b,Query2b,Query2b,Query3b,Query4b,Query5b,Query6b,
CalcDiff,CalcDiffA,CalcDiffb,CalcDiffc,CalcDiffd
```

Listing 10-1 QueryLb1—continued

Table 10-2 lists Paradox's interesting and sometimes confusing stats on how it has stored each query. If you look at Query1-Query6, you see that procedures storing untrimmed query forms take up more space than their trimmed counterparts. The PAL statements take even less space than the trimmed queries. Yet as we'll see next, there appears to be no (or only a negligible) difference in performance in one method versus another. Also, the Calcdiff series of queries actually occupy more space than their query-form counterparts, yet there isn't any degradation in speed (there's actually an improvement).

Table 10-2
Size of queries when stored in procedures

	SIZE			PERCENTAGE DIFFERENCE		
Procedure	Form	Query Trimmed	PAL	Query Form vs Trimmed	Query Form vs PAL	Trimmed vs PAL
Query1	1690	1166	1149	-31.01	-32.01	-1.46
Query2	422	318	284	-24.64	-32.70	-10.69
Query3	424	320	286	-24.53	-32.55	-10.62
Query4	424	320	243	-24.53	-42.69	-24.06
Query5	424	320	243	-24.53	-42.69	-24.06
Query6	416	312	278	-25.00	-33.17	-10.90
CalcDiff	817	633	1450	-22.52	77.48	129.07
CalcDiffB	817	633	1228	-22.52	50.31	94.00
CalcDiffC	817	633	1105	-22.52	35.25	74.57

Let's continue to examine this phenomena by creating a query test. Here we'll run and record the results on how the different query methods perform.

RUN_TEST.SC

First you need an overall control script to launch each series of tests. Listing 10-2 is a listing of the RUN_TEST.SC script that serves as a control script. Notice that all variables, procedures, and tables are cleared from memory before and after each test.

TESTCALC   Queries stored in scripts
TESTCAL1   Queries stored in procedures as normal procs
TESTCAL2   Queries stored in procedures using closed procs

```
;**************************************************
;*** Run_Test                                   ***
;***                                            ***
;***                                            ***
;*** G.Salcedo 8/25/90                          ***
;**************************************************
;Control Script for running TestCalc,TestCal1,TestCal2
;
Release Vars All
Release Procs All
Reset ClearAll
print file "testimr.sc" "StartTest1",time(),"\n"
play "testcalc"
print file "testimr.sc" "EndTest1",time(),"\n"
Release Vars All
Release Procs All
Reset ClearAll
print file "testimr.sc" "StartTest2",time(),"\n"
play "testcal1"
print file "testimr.sc" "EndTest2",time(),"\n"
Release Vars All
Release Procs All
Reset ClearAll
print file "testimr.sc" "StartTest3",time(),"\n"StartTest3 = time()
play "testcal2"
print file "testimr.sc" "EndTest3",time(),"\n"
beep beep beep beep beep beep
```

Listing 10-2 RUN_TEST.SC

TESTCALC.SC

The TESTCALC script (Listing 10-3) pulls in seven QuerySave scripts stored in individual script files. As each script is played, start and end times, as well as before and after available memory, are stored and printed along with the script name to a log named TCRESULTS.SC.

```
;****************************************************
;*** TestCalc                                      ***
;***                                               ***
;***                                               ***
;*** G.Salcedo 8/25/90                             ***
;****************************************************
;
;Tests the various forms of producing summary
;queries. Prints to a file TCResult.sc"
;
While (true)
@0,0 Clear EOS
;
;
;
Release Vars All
Release Procs All
Reset ClearAll
if isfile("tcresult.sc") = true then
     Menu {Tools} {Delete} {Script} {tcresult} {OK}
endif
;
;
;
Menu {Tools} {Info} {Inventory} {Files} {10*.sc}
;
;
;
Array TestScript[nrecords("list")]
moveto[name]
@0,0 Clear EOL ?? "Working "
Scan
                 element = [#]
         TestScript[element] = substr([],1,search(".",[])-1)
         ?? "."
EndScan
?? "Script=TestCalc"
;
;
;
;
stoptest = arraysize(testscript)
;
;
;
;
```

Listing 10-3 TESTCALC.SC

```
for counter from 1 to stoptest step 1
reset clearall
      membefore = " MStart="+strval(memleft())
      ScriptName = testscript[counter]
      @1,0 Clear EOL ?? "Executing ",ScriptName," ",counter," of ",stoptest
      style blink ?? "..."
      style
      Starttime = " Start="+time()
      play scriptname
      EndTime = " End="+time()
      memafter = " MEnd="+strval(memleft())
      RecordResult = ScriptName+"\t"+StartTime+"\t"+EndTime+
                     "\t"+membefore+"\t"+memafter
      print file "tcresult.sc" RecordResult,"\n"
      release vars membefore,procname,starttime,endtime,memafter,recordresult
endfor
quitloop
EndWhile
```

Listing 10-3 TESTCALC.SC—continued

TESTCAL1

The TESTCAL1 script (Listing 10-4) pulls in the same Query1-Query6 scripts plus an additional 17 procedures all stored in a library named QUERYLB1. As the procedures are played, start and end times, as well as before and after available memory, are stored and printed along with the procedure name to a log named TCRES_1.SC.

```
;*************************************************
;*** TestCal1                                  ***
;***                                           ***
;***                                           ***
;*** G.Salcedo 8/25/90                         ***
;*************************************************
;
;Tests the various forms of producing summary
;queries. Prints to a file TCRes_1.sc"
;
While (true)
@0,0 Clear EOS
;
;
;
Release Vars All
```

Listing 10-4 TESTCAL1

```
Release Procs All
Reset ClearAll
if isfile("tcres_1.sc") = true then
      Menu {Tools} {Delete} {Script} {tcres_1} {OK}
endif
;
;
;
LibName = "QueryLb1"
AutoLib = LibName
infolib(libname)
;
;
;
Array TestProc[nrecords("list")]
moveto[procedure]
@0,0 Clear EOL ?? "Working "
Scan
                    element = [#]
          TestProc[element] = []
        ?? "."
EndScan
?? "Script=TestCal1"
;
;
;
;
stoptest = arraysize(testproc)
;
;
;
;
for counter from 1 to stoptest step 1
reset
       membefore = " MStart="+strval(memleft())
       ProcName = testproc[counter]
       @1,0 Clear EOL ?? "Executing ",procname," ",counter," of ",stoptest
       style blink ?? "..."
       style
       Starttime = " Start="+time()
       execproc procname
       EndTime = " End="+time()
       memafter = " MEnd="+strval(memleft())
       RecordResult = Procname+"\t"+StartTime+"\t"+EndTime+
                   "\t"+membefore+"\t"+memafter
       print file "tcres_1.sc" RecordResult,"\n"
          release vars membefore,procname,starttime,endtime,memafter,recordresult
endfor
quitloop
EndWhile
```

Listing 10-4 TESTCAL1—*continued*

TESTCAL2

The TESTCAL2 script (Listing 10-5) pulls in 23 procedures stored in a library called QUERYLB2. As each procedure is played, start and end times, as well as before and after available memory, are stored and printed along with the procedure name to a log named TCRES_2.SC.

The only real difference between TESTCAL1 and TESTCALC2 is that TESTCAL2 is pulling closed procedures from QUERYLB2.

```
;*************************************************
;*** TestCal2                                  ***
;***                                           ***
;***                                           ***
;*** G.Salcedo 8/25/90                         ***
;*************************************************
;
;Tests the various forms of producing summary
;queries. Prints to a file TCRes_2.sc"
;
While (true)
@0,0 Clear EOS
;
;
;
Release Vars All
Release Procs All
Reset ClearAll
if isfile("tcres_2.sc") = true then
     Menu {Tools} {Delete} {Script} {tcres_2} {OK}
endif
;
;
;
LibName = "QueryLb2"
AutoLib = LibName
infolib(libname)
;
;
;
Array TestProc[nrecords("list")]
moveto[procedure]
@0,0 Clear EOL ?? "Working "
Scan
                 element = [#]
          TestProc[element] = []
          ?? "."
```

Listing 10-5 TESTCAL2

```
EndScan
?? "Script=TestCal2"
;
;
;
;
stoptest = arraysize(testproc)
;
;
;
;
for counter from 1 to stoptest step 1
reset clearall
      membefore = " MStart="+strval(memleft())
      ProcName = testproc[counter]
      @1,0 Clear EOL ?? "Executing ",procname," ",counter," of ",stoptest
      style blink ?? "..."
      style
      Starttime = " Start="+time()
      execproc procname
      EndTime = " End="+time()
      memafter = " MEnd="+strval(memleft())
      RecordResult = Procname+"\t"+StartTime+"\t"+EndTime+
                    "\t"+membefore+"\t"+memafter
      print file "tcres_2.sc" RecordResult,"\n"
      release vars membefore,procname,starttime,endtime,memafter,recordresult
endfor
quitloop
EndWhile
```

Listing 10-5 TESTCAL2—*continued*

Test Results

TESTIMR.SC overview

Remember, the purpose of each series of tests is to determine which method of storing, retrieving, and playing scripts is superior. Each series of scripts or procedures performs each of the following:

- A three-table join with calculation
- A summary AVERAGE script
- A summary COUNT script
- A summary MAX script

- A summary MIN script
- A summary SUM script

TESTCALC, TESTCAL1, and TESTCAL2 run one after the other and execute in an elapsed time of 7 minutes, 35 seconds, allowing for time to reclaim memory before and after each test is executed. The overall results:

TESTCALC results—TCRESULT.SC

StartTest1   23:57:42
EndTest1   23:58:21

Elapsed Time = 1 minute 39 seconds

StartTest2   23:58:33
EndTest2   00:01:28

Elapsed Time = 2 minutes 57 seconds

StartTest3   00:01:35
EndTest3   00:04:34

Elapsed Time = 2 minutes 59 seconds

TESTCAL1 results—TC_RES1.SC

Procedure	Time Start	Time End	Memory Start	Memory End	Time Diff
10-1	23:57:42	23:57:54	140288	140288	7 sec
10-2	23:57:55	23:57:59	140288	140288	4 sec
10-3	23:58:00	23:58:05	140288	140288	5 sec
10-4	23:58:05	23:58:10	140288	140288	5 sec
10-5	23:58:10	23:58:16	140288	140288	6 sec
10-6	23:58:16	23:58:21	140288	140288	5 sec

Elapsed time = 1 minute 39 seconds   Working time = 32 sec

| 10-diff | 23:58:22 | 23:58:28 | 140288 | 140288 | 6 sec |

TESTCAL2 results—TC_RES2.SC

Procedure	Time Start	Time End	Memory Start	Memory End	Time Diff
Query1	23:58:33	23:58:42	140288	128000	9 sec
Query2	23:58:46	23:58:52	136192	132096	6 sec
Query3	23:58:53	23:58:59	136192	131072	6 sec
Query4	23:59:01	23:59:06	135168	131072	5 sec
Query5	23:59:08	23:59:13	135168	130048	5 sec
Query6	23:59:15	23:59:20	134144	130048	5 sec

Elapsed Time = 47 seconds overall   Working Time = 36 sec

Query1a	23:59:22	23:59:31	134144	124928	8 sec
Query2a	23:59:34	23:59:39	133120	128000	5 sec
Query3a	23:59:41	23:59:46	132096	128000	5 sec
Query4a	23:59:48	23:59:54	132096	128000	6 sec
Query5a	23:59:55	00:00:01	132096	126976	6 sec
Query6a	00:00:03	00:00:08	131072	126976	5 sec

Elapsed Time = 46 seconds overall   Working Time = 35 sec

Query1b	00:00:09	00:00:18	131072	121856	9 sec
Query2b	00:00:20	00:00:25	130048	124928	5 sec
Query3b	00:00:27	00:00:32	129024	124928	5 sec
Query4b	00:00:34	00:00:39	129024	124928	5 sec
Query5b	00:00:41	00:00:46	129024	124928	5 sec
Query6b	00:00:48	00:00:53	129024	123904	5 sec

Elapsed Time = 44 seconds overall   Working Time = 34 sec

CalcDiff	00:00:54	00:01:01	128000	122880	7 sec
CalcDiffa	00:01:02	00:01:08	126976	122880	6 sec
CalcDiffb	00:01:09	00:01:14	126976	120832	5 sec
CalcDiffc	00:01:16	00:01:21	124928	119808	5 sec
CalcDiffd	00:01:23	00:01:28	123904	118784	5 sec

Elapsed Time = 34 seconds overall   Working Time = 28 sec

TESTCAL3.SC

Procedure	Time Start	Time End	Memory Start	Memory End	Time Diff
Query1	00:01:35	00:01:46	140288	132096	11 sec
Query2	00:01:50	00:01:56	140288	136192	6 sec
Query3	00:01:58	00:02:04	140288	136192	6 sec
Query4	00:02:05	00:02:10	140288	136192	5 sec
Query5	00:02:12	00:02:18	140288	136192	6 sec
Query6	00:02:20	00:02:25	140288	136192	5 sec

Elapsed time = 50 seconds   Working Time = 39 sec

Query1a	00:02:27	00:02:38	140288	132096	11 sec
Query2a	00:02:41	00:02:46	140288	136192	5 sec
Query3a	00:02:48	00:02:54	140288	134144	6 sec
Query4a	00:02:55	00:03:00	138240	134144	5 sec
Query5a	00:03:02	00:03:07	138240	134144	5 sec
Query6a	00:03:09	00:03:14	138240	134144	5 sec

Elapsed time = 47 seconds   Working Time = 37 sec

Query1b	00:03:16	00:03:25	138240	130048	9 sec
Query2b	00:03:27	00:03:32	138240	134144	5 sec
Query3b	00:03:34	00:03:38	138240	134144	4 sec
Query4b	00:03:40	00:03:45	138240	134144	5 sec
Query5b	00:03:47	00:03:51	138240	134144	4 sec
Query6b	00:03:54	00:04:00	138240	134144	6 sec

Elapsed time = 44 seconds   Working Time = 33 sec

CalcDiff	00:04:02	00:04:08	138240	134144	6 sec
CalcDiffa	00:04:10	00:04:15	138240	134144	5 sec
CalcDiffb	00:04:16	00:04:21	138240	134144	5 sec
CalcDiffc	00:04:22	00:04:27	138240	134144	5 sec
CalcDiffd	00:04:29	00:04:34	138240	134144	5 sec

Elapsed time = 32 seconds   Working Time = 26 sec

Before we analyze these tables, here's another thought—all of these scripts required us to calculate elapsed and working time. To automate the test more, Listing 10-6 shows an identical test approach to the one used in TESCAL2, except that elapsed times have been calculated and recorded as the test runs.

```
;*************************************************
;*** TestCal3                                  ***
;***                                           ***
;***                                           ***
;*** G.Salcedo 8/25/90                         ***
;*************************************************
;
;Tests the various forms of producing summary
;queries. Prints to a file TCRes_3.sc"
;
While (true)
@0,0 Clear EOS
;
;
;
Release Vars All
Release Procs All
Reset ClearAll
if isfile("tcres_3.sc") = true then
     Menu {Tools} {Delete} {Script} {tcres_3} {OK}
endif
;
;
;
LibName = "QueryLb2,Time"
AutoLib = LibName
infolib("QueryLb2")
;
;
;
;
Array TestProc[nrecords("list")]
moveto[procedure]
@0,0 Clear EOL ?? "Working "
Scan
               element = [#]
          TestProc[element] = []
          ?? "."
EndScan
?? "Script=TestCal3"
;
;
;
;
stoptest = arraysize(testproc)
;
```

Listing 10-6 TESTCAL3.SC

```
;
;
;
for counter from 1 to stoptest step 1
reset clearall
        membefore = " MStart="+strval(memleft())
        ProcName = testproc[counter]
        @1,0 Clear EOL ?? "Executing ",procname," ",counter," of ",stoptest
        style blink ?? "..."
        style
        D=today()
        SW=time()
        Stime = CalcTime(D,SW)
        Starttime = " Start="+SW
        execproc procname
        D=today()
        SW=time()
        ETime =  CalcTime(D,SW)
        Endtime = " End="+SW
        memafter = " MEnd="+strval(memleft())
        Interval =ETime-STime
        Trans_int(Interval)
        Elapsed = "Elapsed="+ret_interval
        RecordResult = Procname+"\t"+StartTime+"\t"+EndTime+
                  "\t"+membefore+"\t"+memafter+"\t"+Elapsed
        print file "tcres_3.sc" RecordResult,"\n"
        release vars membefore,procname,starttime,endtime,memafter,recordresult
         release vars elapsed,S,SW,Interval
          release procs CalcTime,Trans_int
endfor
quitloop
EndWhile
```

Listing 10-6 TESTCAL3.SC—continued

TESTCAL3 results

Procedure	Time Start	Time End	Memory Start	Memory End	Time Diff
Query1	10:06:26	10:06:36	139264	132096	00:00:10
Query2	10:06:40	10:06:45	138240	136192	00:00:05
Query3	10:06:48	10:06:53	138240	136192	00:00:05
Query4	10:06:56	10:07:01	138240	136192	00:00:05
Query5	10:07:04	10:07:10	138240	136192	00:00:06
Query6	10:07:12	10:07:17	138240	136192	00:00:05

Elapsed time = 51 seconds   Working Time = 36 seconds

Procedure	Time Start	Time End	Memory Start	Memory End	Time Diff
Query1a	10:07:20	10:07:29	138240	132096	00:00:09
Query2a	10:07:32	10:07:39	138240	136192	00:00:07
Query3a	10:07:41	10:07:46	138240	136192	00:00:05
Query4a	10:07:49	10:07:53	138240	136192	00:00:04
Query5a	10:07:56	10:08:01	138240	136192	00:00:05
Query6a	10:08:04	10:08:09	138240	136192	00:00:05

Elapsed time = 49 seconds   Working Time = 35 seconds

Procedure	Time Start	Time End	Memory Start	Memory End	Time Diff
Query1b	10:08:11	10:08:21	138240	132096	00:00:10
Query2b	10:08:25	10:08:30	138240	136192	00:00:05
Query3b	10:08:33	10:08:38	138240	134144	00:00:05
Query4b	10:08:41	10:08:46	136192	134144	00:00:05
Query5b	10:08:48	10:08:53	136192	134144	00:00:05
Query6b	10:08:55	10:08:59	136192	134144	00:00:04

Elapsed time = 48 seconds   Working Time = 34 seconds

Procedure	Time Start	Time End	Memory Start	Memory End	Time Diff
CalcDiff	10:09:02	10:09:08	136192	134144	00:00:06
CalcDiffa	10:09:11	10:09:17	136192	134144	00:00:06
Calcdiffb	10:09:19	10:09:23	136192	134144	00:00:04
CalcDiffc	10:09:26	10:09:31	136192	134144	00:00:05
CalcDiffd	10:09:33	10:09:37	136192	134144	00:00:04

Elapsed time = 35 seconds   Working Time = 25 seconds

To automatically calculate the time, use the script shown in Listing 10-7 (CALCTIM7.SC), which creates a library called TIME. This library is then added to the AUTOLIB statement in TESTCAL3.

There are three procedures in this library:

CalcTime(D,SW)
> A procedure that acts like a stopwatch and converts the split into a serialized number.

Trans_int(Interval)
> Translates the difference between the two splits (expressed as serialized number) into an elapsed time—the difference between split 1 and split 2.

Record_int(FileName,Phrase,Interval)
Lets you print the results of the elapsed time to a file.

```
;****************************************************
;*G.Salcedo      ParaDocs      03/01/90               *
;*                                                    *
;*This Library provides for calculations of time intervals *
;****************************************************
CreateLib "time"
Proc Closed CalcTime(D,SW)
timecalc = (D-1/1/00) +    (numval(substr(sw,1,2))/24)+
                           ((numval(substr(sw,4,2))/60)/24)+
                           (((numval(substr(sw,7,2))/60)/60)/24)
Return timecalc
EndProc
Proc Trans_Int(Interval)
if interval < 1 and interval >-1 then
        nodays = 0
      evaltime =interval
else
        nodays = int(interval)
      evaltime = interval-nodays
endif
    ndays = (nodays)
NoSecsDay = 86400
NoTotSecs = round(evaltime * NoSecsDay,0)
NoTotMins = int(mod(nototsecs/60,60))
NoTotHrs  = int(mod(nototsecs/3600,60));round(NoTotSecs/3600,0)
     Hrs  = format("W3,EZ",NoTotHrs)
     Sec  = format("W3,EZ",mod(NoTotSecs,60))
if mod(NoTotSecs,60) > 0 then
     Mnn = format("W3,EZ",round(NoTotMins+.49,0))
else
     Mnn = format("W3,EZ",round(NoTotMins+.49,0))
endif
Ret_interval = format("W5,SP",Ndays)+" days and "+substr(Hrs,2,2)+":"+
                                                 substr(Mnn,2,2)+":"+
                                                 substr(Sec,2,2)
Return Ret_interval
EndProc
Proc Record_Int(FileName,Phrase,Interval)
if interval < 1 and interval >-1 then
        nodays = 0
      evaltime =interval
else
        nodays = int(interval)
      evaltime = interval-nodays
endif
    ndays = nodays
NoSecsDay = 86400
NoTotSecs = round(evaltime * NoSecsDay,0)
NoTotMins = int(mod(nototsecs/60,60))
```

Listing 10-7 CALCTIM7

```
NoTotHrs  = int(mod(nototsecs/3600,60));round(NoTotSecs/3600,0)
     Hrs  = format("W3,EZ",NoTotHrs)
     Sec  = format("W3,EZ",mod(NoTotSecs,60))
if mod(NoTotSecs,60) > 0 then
     Mnn = format("W3,EZ",round(NoTotMins+.49,0))
else
     Mnn = format("W3,EZ",round(NoTotMins+.49,0))
endif
Rectime  = substr(Hrs,2,2)+":"+
           substr(Mnn,2,2)+":"+
           substr(Sec,2,2)
Ret_interval = format("w5,EP",Ndays)+" days and "+Rectime
           Print File FileName  Phrase,",",Ndays,",",RecTime,"\n\r"
Return Ret_interval
EndProc
writelib "time" CalcTime,Trans_Int,Record_int
```

Listing 10-7 CALCTIM7—*continued*

Test Analysis and Summary

When you sit back and analyze these tests, it's apparent that while it is running, the speed of the query is not really affected by how it is stored. In fact, if you're not careful, you could conclude that storing queries in scripts outperforms storing queries in procedures. But notice the overall elapsed times: the scripts took 1 minute, 39 seconds to perform Query1-Query6 plus 10-Diff, while the proc and closed proc queries took only 53-57 seconds to perform the same tasks (Query1-Query6 plus Calcdiff). What is causing this difference?

The first factor is that each query stored in scripts must deal with DOS file reads. The second is that the script must be compiled and then executed. The third is that in order to return memory to Paradox, the workspace must be entirely cleared. These manipulations take more time.

Procedures are handled more efficiently in the Paradox environment because the queries are already parsed (interpreted) into machine language and are therefore already compiled. There are fewer DOS file reads, and in the case of closed procs, memory is automatically returned to the Paradox environment as each proc is completed.

> **NOTE:** *TESTCAL3 is interesting in itself because it demonstrates a more accurate reading of the working time of each query. Notice that the elapsed time is longer than in TESTCAL2. This is because it takes extra steps to mark and record time, as well as to release those procedures used to calculate the time intervals. The lesson this routine teaches is to be sure what you want to measure—overall performance or the individual times of each component.*
>
> *The point is to have some mechanism to do this kind of testing, not only for queries but for every component and module of your application. Unless you are purposely pausing (WAIT, GETCHAR(), and so on) you should know the run times of each of the major parts of your application, as well as all key steps. This way you'll be able to fine-tune performance for an individual or isolated process, rather than trying to rebuild the whole thing every time.*

A Better Mouse Trap?

We mentioned earlier that we would talk about some things QBE can't do. Well for one, it can't think for you. There is nothing that can replace some good common sense in understanding and dealing with Paradox's query mechanism. To understand the problem, let's take a look at the peanut butter theory of programming.

The Peanut Butter Theory

Simply presented, the peanut butter theory states that even though peanut butter looks nice, smells great, and tastes fantastic, if you try to swallow too much at one time you'll choke! You may even die!

Paradox doesn't know when to discard a table it no longer needs. When you ask it to join one table with another table or several other tables, Paradox keeps a matrix of all the potential combinations in memory (even if those combinations are not actually possible) until it has completed the query. This means that the query runs slower, takes up more disk space for temporary tables, and may indeed run out of disk space (die) before it completes. If Paradox could know that it no longer needed a table and then discard it, it could perform more efficiently.

The second feature lacking from Paradox is the ability to apply functions in QBE. It would be nice to apply multiple levels of IF statements to avoid query multiple times.

Let's bring both of these problems home with another test that shows how the peanut butter theory affects our Paradox queries. In order to see its effects, we'll try three methods of querying a table and inspecting its results. Each of these tests uses the Masterbk table included on disk with this book.

Three-level Query (10-PB-1)

The first approach attempts a three-level query. On the first level, those records where STATE=CA are identified and their prices are increased 10% (sorry California residents). The second level of the query then recomputes a new total. The third and final level adds a sales tax by multiplying the new total by 1.08. The advantages of this query is that it's easy to construct, store, and play. The disadvantages: it isn't very efficient if you're on a network, and it's the slowest of all the methods (see Listing 10-8).

```
;****************************************************
;*** 10-PB-1                                      ***
;***                                              ***
;***                                              ***
;*** G.Salcedo 8/25/90                            ***
;****************************************************
;
;Tests the various forms of producing summary
;queries. Prints to a file PB-1.sc"
;
if isfile("pb-1.sc") = true then
     Menu {tools} {delete} {script} {pb-1} {ok}
     beep
endif
Reset
Stime = time()
Query
  Masterbk | State |         Price         | Quant |         Total          |
           | CA    | _pr,changeto _pr*1.1  |       |                        |
           | CA    | _pr                   | _q    | changeto _pr*_q        |
           | CA    |                       |       | _t,changeto _t*1.08    |
  Masterbk |
           |
           |
           |
Endquery
Do_it!
ETime=time()
Print file "pb-1.sc" "start=",stime," end =",etime,"\n"
```

Listing 10-8 10-PB-1

The Three-step Query (10-PB-2)

The second approach is somewhat like the first except that it breaks each level into a separate query. The advantages are that it's still easy to create and it performs faster than the three-level query. The disadvantages are that it's still not very efficient if you're on a network and it's still not the fastest method to perform the query (see Listing 10-9).

```
;***************************************************
;*** 10-PB-2                                     ***
;***                                             ***
;***                                             ***
;*** G.Salcedo 8/25/90                           ***
;***************************************************
;
;Tests the various forms of producing summary
;queries. Prints to a file PB-2.sc"
;
if isfile("pb-2.sc") = true then
     Menu {tools} {delete} {script} {pb-2} {ok}
     beep
endif
Reset
Stime = time()
Query
 Masterbk | State |       Price              |
          | CA    | _pr,changeto _pr*1.1     |
 Masterbk |
          |
Endquery
Do_it!
Query
 Masterbk | State |  Price  | Quant |       Total         |
          | CA    | _pr     | _q    | changeto _pr*_q     |
 Masterbk |
          |
Endquery
Do_it!
Reset
Query
 Masterbk | State |        Total            |
          | CA    | _t,changeto _t*1.08     |
 Masterbk |
          |
Endquery
Do_it!
ETime=time()
Print file "pb-2.sc" "start=",stime," end =",etime,"\n"
```

Listing 10-9 10-PB-2

A PAL Query (10-PB-3)

The third approach uses a SCAN with COEDIT to search for STATE=CA, using an IF statement. Once the record has been identified as a California record, the calculations are performed—otherwise, the SCAN passes the record and moves on to the next record. This is an excellent approach if you're querying or editing on a network, because it reduces the amount of data that has to be sent over the network cable, thus speeding the operations. This is by far the fastest of the three methods (see Listing 10-10).

```
;****************************************
;*** 10-PB-3                          ***
;***                                  ***
;***                                  ***
;*** G.Salcedo 8/25/90                ***
;****************************************
;
;Tests the various forms of producing summary
;queries. Prints to a file PB-3.sc"
;
if isfile("pb-3.sc") = true then
      Menu {tools} {delete} {script} {pb-3} {ok}
      beep
endif
Reset
Stime = time()
CoEdit "Masterbk"
moveto[total]
Scan
        if [state] = "CA" then
              [price] = [price]*1.1
              [] = [quant]*[price]
              [] = []*1.07
        endif
EndScan
Do_it!
ETime=time()
Print file "pb-3.sc" "start=",stime," end =",etime,"\n"
```

Listing 10-10 *A PAL query*

Peanut Butter Test Results

10-PB-1 took 36 seconds to complete, 10-PB-2 took only 26 seconds, and 10-PB-3 came in at 14 seconds. In other words, scanning the table and performing a filter/calcuation was 72% faster than a three-level QBE and 50% faster than a three-step QBE. The three-step QBE out-performed the three-level query by 27%.

Yes, there is more than one way to skin a cat. Take a look at the way you're currently performing your queries. Here's a quick check list:

- See if you can sub-select your data to minimize the number of records that Paradox must deal with.
- Explore building a rule-based (IF...THEN...ELSE...ENDIF or SWITCH...CASE...ENDSWITCH) SCAN that can perform the query in a single pass rather than in multiple passes.
- Place your queries in closed procedures to ensure that maximum resources are available to Paradox at any given time.
- If you're on a network, avoid as much as possible anything that dictates moving a lot of data (changes, adding, deleting, and so forth).

Some Special Query Notes

Paradox's SET queries have some very nice features, but you should use caution when it comes to the NO keyword. If you're not careful, it can give you fits and sometimes, the wrong answer.

To illustrate, look at Figure 10-7. Tablea and Tableb are both single-field keyed tables. As long as the field being queried in combination with the field being grouped by are unique, you get the correct answer.

This is also true for looking at the value description fields, as shown in Figure 10-8, which returns all fields (Tablec is an exact copy of Tableb except that the value descriptions are not all unique.)

Problems start when you have a field that isn't unique and you use GROUPBY on it (see Figure 10-10). The only way to navigate around this problem is to use the COUNT=0 method shown in Figure 10-11.

While the NO SET query can perform some great tasks, if you need to see the field value for the field you are linking on and you want to make sure that you are returned a true NO SET, COUNT=0 is your safest bet.

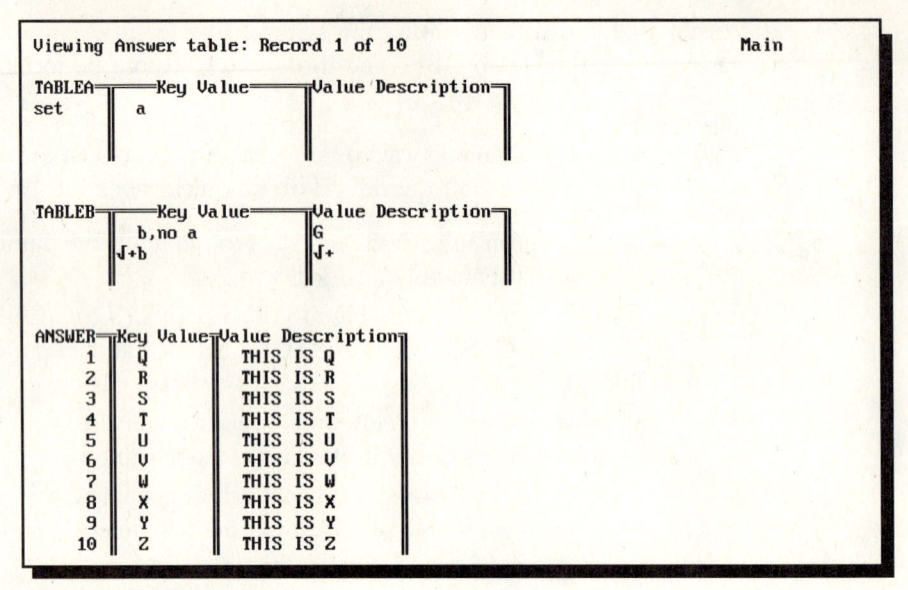

```
Viewing Answer table: Record 1 of 10                          Main
┌TABLEA─┬──Key Value──┬─Value Description─┐
│set    │ a           │                   │
│       │             │                   │
└───────┴─────────────┴───────────────────┘

┌TABLEB─┬──Key Value──┬─Value Description─┐
│       │ b, no a     │ G                 │
│       │ √+b         │ √+                │
└───────┴─────────────┴───────────────────┘

┌ANSWER─┬Key Value┬Value Description┐
│   1   │ Q       │ THIS IS Q       │
│   2   │ R       │ THIS IS R       │
│   3   │ S       │ THIS IS S       │
│   4   │ T       │ THIS IS T       │
│   5   │ U       │ THIS IS U       │
│   6   │ V       │ THIS IS V       │
│   7   │ W       │ THIS IS W       │
│   8   │ X       │ THIS IS X       │
│   9   │ Y       │ THIS IS Y       │
│  10   │ Z       │ THIS IS Z       │
└───────┴─────────┴─────────────────┘
```

Figure 10-7 NO SET query

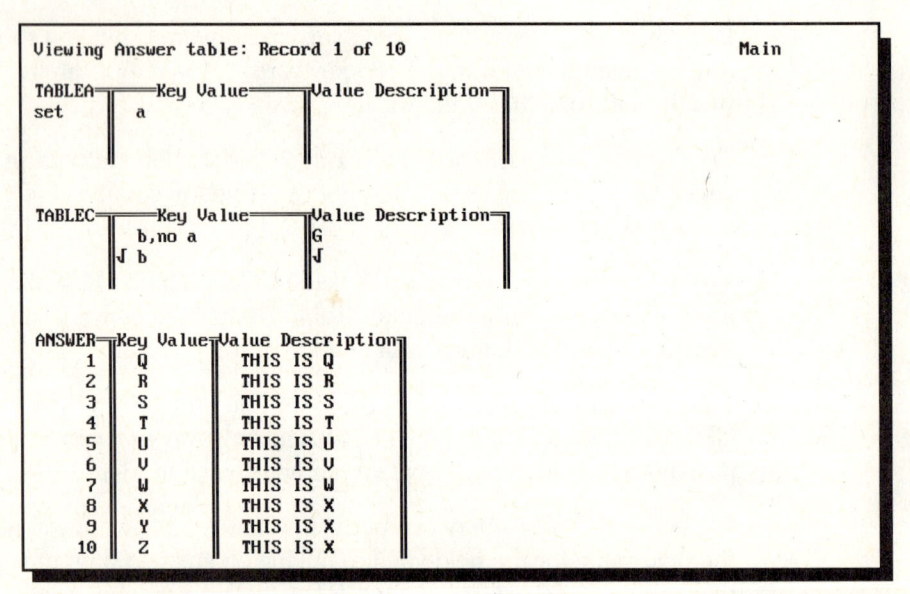

```
Viewing Answer table: Record 1 of 10                          Main
┌TABLEA─┬──Key Value──┬─Value Description─┐
│set    │ a           │                   │
│       │             │                   │
└───────┴─────────────┴───────────────────┘

┌TABLEC─┬──Key Value──┬─Value Description─┐
│       │ b, no a     │ G                 │
│       │ √ b         │ √                 │
└───────┴─────────────┴───────────────────┘

┌ANSWER─┬Key Value┬Value Description┐
│   1   │ Q       │ THIS IS Q       │
│   2   │ R       │ THIS IS R       │
│   3   │ S       │ THIS IS S       │
│   4   │ T       │ THIS IS T       │
│   5   │ U       │ THIS IS U       │
│   6   │ V       │ THIS IS V       │
│   7   │ W       │ THIS IS W       │
│   8   │ X       │ THIS IS X       │
│   9   │ Y       │ THIS IS X       │
│  10   │ Z       │ THIS IS X       │
└───────┴─────────┴─────────────────┘
```

Figure 10-8 NO SET query of value description field

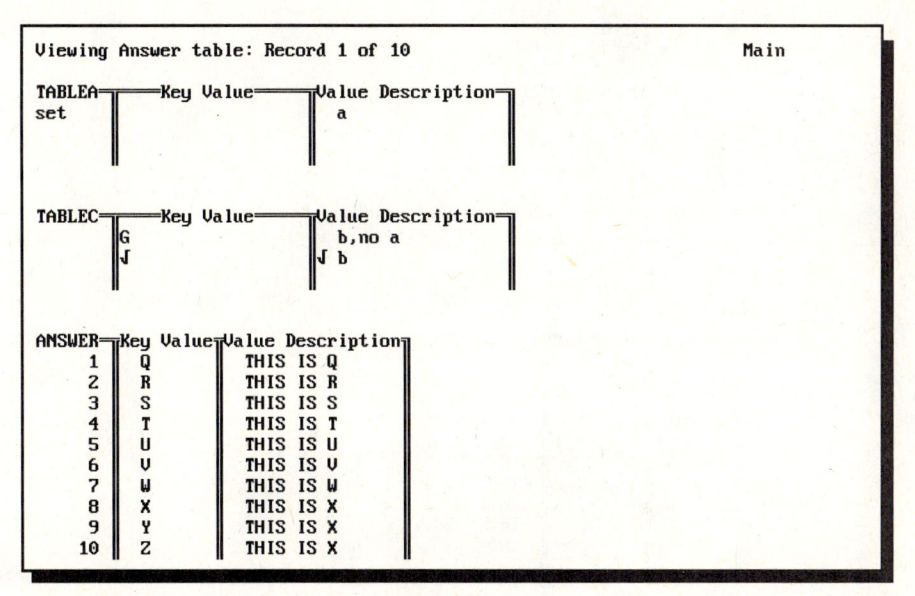

```
Viewing Answer table: Record 1 of 10                          Main
TABLEA┬─────Key Value─────┬─Value Description─┐
set   │                   │ a                 │
      │                   │                   │
      │                   │                   │

TABLEC┬─────Key Value─────┬─Value Description─┐
      │ G                 │ b,no a            │
      │√                  │√b                 │
      │                   │                   │

ANSWER┬Key Value┬Value Description┐
   1  │ Q       │ THIS IS Q       │
   2  │ R       │ THIS IS R       │
   3  │ S       │ THIS IS S       │
   4  │ T       │ THIS IS T       │
   5  │ U       │ THIS IS U       │
   6  │ V       │ THIS IS V       │
   7  │ W       │ THIS IS W       │
   8  │ X       │ THIS IS X       │
   9  │ Y       │ THIS IS X       │
  10  │ Z       │ THIS IS X       │
```

Figure 10-9 NO SET query, return all fields

```
√ [F6] to include a field in the ANSWER; [F5] to give an Example   Main
TABLEA┬─────Key Value─────┬─Value Description─┐
set   │ a                 │                   │
      │                   │                   │

TABLED┬─────Key Value─────┬─Value Description─┬─Another Desription─┐
      │ b,no a            │                   │ G                  │
      │√b                 │√                  │√                   │
```

Figure 10-10 COUNT=0, NO SET query

```
Viewing Answer table: Record 1 of 10                        Main
TABLEA─┬─Value Description─┬─┬─Key Value─┬─
       │   a,count=0       │ │           │


TABLEC─┬─Key Value─┬─Value Description─┬─
       │  √        │ √ a!              │


ANSWER─┬─Key Value─┬─Value Description─┐
   1   │    Q      │    THIS IS Q
   2   │    R      │    THIS IS R
   3   │    S      │    THIS IS S
   4   │    T      │    THIS IS T
   5   │    U      │    THIS IS U
   6   │    V      │    THIS IS V
   7   │    W      │    THIS IS W
   8   │    X      │    THIS IS X
   9   │    Y      │    THIS IS X
  10   │    Z      │    THIS IS X
```

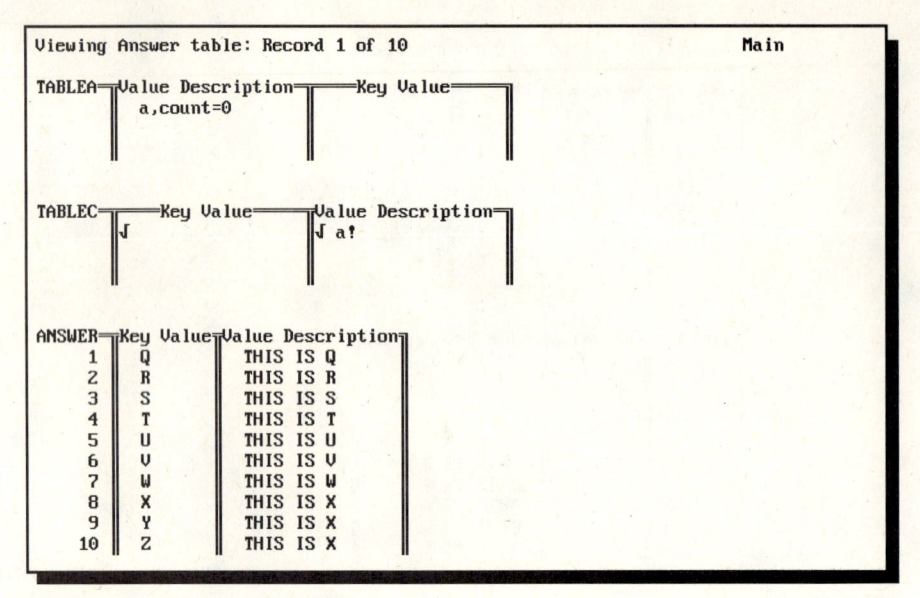

Figure 10-11 Wrong NO SET

Summary

In this chapter, we have examined different methods to store, retrieve, and execute Paradox queries. The method that is right for your application depends on the way you're developing the application and how you need to control your system resources. Remember that SCAN is another form of a query that can out-perform QBE in the right situation.

Looking ahead to the next chapter, we'll discuss a number of tricks and traps in dealing with functions in reports. In addition, we'll take a stab at enhancing the look of your reports.

11 Running Advanced Reports and Graphs

Reports and graphs are the most common methods of formatting output. Paradox's built-in support for columnar and free-form reports makes it relatively easy to generate output from a table (or multiple tables if they have a one-to-one or one-to-many relationship). Graphs follow the same basic philosophy as single-table reports. Most applications require reports created with data from multiple tables. This is where your database structure might push Paradox's report writer to its limits.

In this chapter we present various methods for generating reports. We'll show you how to use variables and functions to extend the type of information you present in reports. We'll cover creating reports from a subset of a table and from multiple tables. We'll show you an example of using a multitable form to generate a report from six tables, including PAL code. We'll also give you valuable tips on generating graphs from applications, including graph size parameters for printing multiple graphs on one page.

Reporting Techniques

You can generate reports from three different groupings of data:

- The entire table
- A subset of a table
- Multiple tables

Each of these situations requires a different level of effort to create the output. To generate a report from the entire table, simply design the report and execute it. To report on a subset of a table requires two steps: extracting the data and running the report. The most common technique is to use a table that matches the structure of the Answer table. Include the report design you want to print as part of this report table's Family. Each time you want to print a subset of a table, extract the data, copy the report to the Answer table, and output the data. (If the extract contains all columns from the table, there is no need for the report table. Simply design the report on the master table and copy it to the Answer table.)

Reports from multiple tables is where the effort to output the data increases, depending on the relationships between the tables. Creating reports from multiple tables works well for tables in a one-to-one or one-to-many relationship. When you have two or more tables on the many side, the report generator can't directly support report output. You have to either generate two reports based on each table on the many side of the relationship, or use PAL. Following are three techniques to solve this problem:

- Query each subset and print the report
- Write the entire report in PAL
- Use a multitable form in conjunction with PAL to output the data

The first two options are probably not new to you, but the third technique is one that you may not have thought of. Using tables from the personnel system, let's look at how you'd do this. The output we want to produce is a one page report for each employee, listing their personnel information. This requires data in six tables:

- Employee
- Jobcd
- Benefits
- Depndnts
- Eduction
- Training

Each of these tables contains information required in the report. Figure 11-1 lists these tables and their fields.

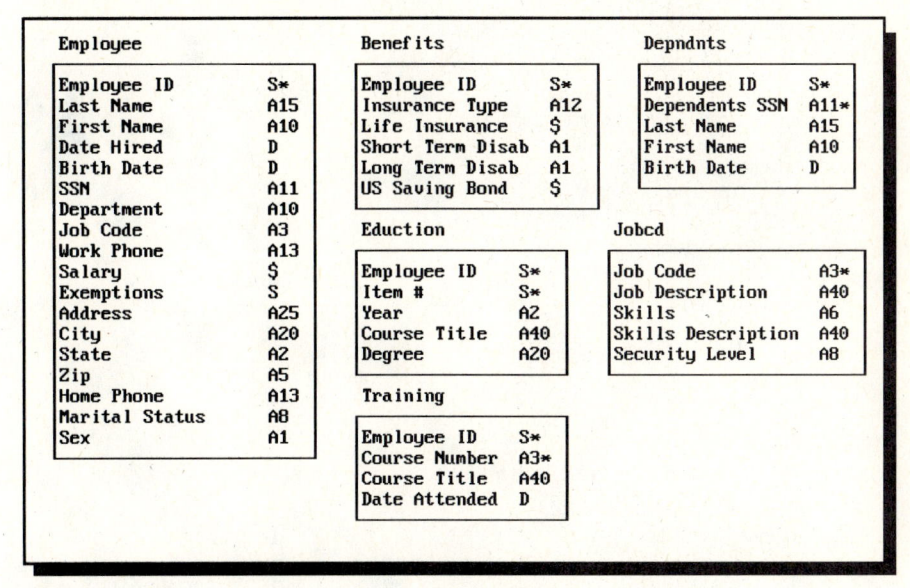

```
Employee                          Benefits                         Depndnts

Employee ID        S*             Employee ID        S*            Employee ID        S*
Last Name          A15            Insurance Type     A12           Dependents SSN     A11*
First Name         A10            Life Insurance     $             Last Name          A15
Date Hired         D              Short Term Disab   A1            First Name         A10
Birth Date         D              Long Term Disab    A1            Birth Date         D
SSN                A11            US Saving Bond     $
Department         A10                                             Jobcd
Job Code           A3             Eduction
Work Phone         A13                                             Job Code           A3*
Salary             $              Employee ID        S*            Job Description    A40
Exemptions         S              Item #             S*            Skills             A6
Address            A25            Year               A2            Skills Description A40
City               A20            Course Title       A40           Security Level     A8
State              A2             Degree             A20
Zip                A5
Home Phone         A13            Training
Marital Status     A8
Sex                A1             Employee ID        S*
                                  Course Number      A3*
                                  Course Title       A40
                                  Date Attended      D
```

Figure 11-1 Personnel tables used in multitable report example

You first need to create a multitable form on the Employee table, linking each of the remaining tables as detail tables. The form doesn't have to be one that is used for viewing, entry, or editing. It just needs to include all the fields necessary for the report. Figure 11-2 shows an example of the output for one employee.

Using a form lets Paradox do all the work and gather data on each employee. Paradox automatically provides access to each employee's data using a multitable form. Since any linked detail table has to be keyed, searching for the linking records is instantaneous. Building the form is the easy part—creating the PAL code takes some extra thinking. Code is necessary to ensure that page and group headings, line spacing, and page formatting are handled correctly no matter how much data exists. Listing 11-1 lists all the procedures used in this example. Let's look at each procedure starting with the main procedure, PrintDriver.

```
            ********** Confidential **********
9/03/90          Employee Personnel Information              Page:   1
Name: Peter Smith   ID:     1004
Department: FINANCE   Job Title: ACCOUNTANT
Employee Benefits
Insurance Type         : King County
Life Insurance         : $75,000.00
Short Term Disability: N
Long Term Disability : Y
U.S. Saving Bonds      : $250.00
Employee Dependents
Name                       SSN            Birth Date
-------------------------  -------------  ----------
Jane Smith                 388-22-3771    12/02/49
Timothy Smith              838-38-1937    6/06/74
Tana Smith                 838-38-1938    6/06/74
Thomas Smith               838-38-1939    6/06/74
Roger Smith                887-63-2322    4/21/72
Janice Smith               912-38-3282    3/02/71
Mike Smith                 993-92-1883    1/03/70
Employee Education History
Year  School                                 Degree
----  --------------------------------------  ------------------------
75    University of Miami                     B.A. Accounting
Employee Company Training History
 #    Course Title                           Date Attended
---   --------------------------------------  -------------
129   Getting to Know Your PC                 2/08/85
139   Quattro Pro Introduction                8/08/89
154   Paradox Introduction                    7/09/87
155   Paradox Intermediate                    9/07/89
156   PAL I                                   2/05/90
157   PAL II                                  4/05/90
158   MultiUser Paradox                       5/23/90
159   Paradox Workshop                        7/06/90

            ********** Confidential **********
```

Figure 11-2 Employee personnel information report

```
1)  ; MTRpts.sc
2)
3)  PROC StartOfPage()
4)    PRINT "\n",boldon,FORMAT("w80,ac","********** Confidential **********") +
5)          boldoff,"\n\n"
6)    PRINT FORMAT("D1",TODAY()) + boldon +
7)          FORMAT("w64,ac","Employee Personnel Information") + boldoff +
8)          "Page: " + FORMAT("w4,al",pgnum) + "\n\n"
9)    linenumber = linenumber + 5
10) ENDPROC
11)
12) PROC EndOfPage()
13)   WHILE linenumber < pagesize - pagefooter
14)     PRINT "\n"
15)     linenumber = linenumber + 1
16)   ENDWHILE
17)   PRINT boldon,FORMAT("w80,ac","********** Confidential **********"),
18)         boldoff,"\f"
19)   pgnum = pgnum + 1
20)   linenumber = 1
21) ENDPROC
22)
23) PROC AddLineNumber(incrmnt)
24)   IF linenumber + incrmnt > pagesize - pagefooter THEN
25)      EndOfPage()
26)      StartOfPage()
27)   ELSE
28)      linenumber = linenumber + incrmnt
29)   ENDIF
30) ENDPROC
31)
32) PROC AddBlankLines(numoflines)
33)   PRIVATE i
34)   AddLineNumber(numoflines)
35)   FOR i From 1 TO numoflines
36)     PRINT "\n"
37)   ENDFOR
38) ENDPROC
39)
40) PROC PrintEmployee()
41)   AddLineNumber(3)
42)   PRINT boldon,"Name: ",boldoff,
43)         [First Name] + " " + [Last Name],gap,
44)         boldon,"ID: ",boldoff,
45)         FORMAT("w8,ar",[Employee ID]),gap,"\n\n"
46)   PRINT boldon,"Department: ",boldoff,
47)         [Department],gap,
48)         boldon,"Job Title: ",boldoff,
49)         [Jobcd->Job Description],"\n"
50) ENDPROC
51)
52) PROC PrintBenefits()
```

Listing 11-1 Program for multitable reporting using a form

```
53)     MOVETO "Benefits"
54)     PRINT boldon,underlineon,"Employee Benefits",underlineoff,boldoff,"\n\n"
55)     AddLineNumber(5)
56)     PRINT boldon,"Insurance Type       : ",boldoff,[Insurance Type],"\n"
57)     PRINT boldon,"Life Insurance       : ",boldoff,
58)          FORMAT("w12.2,al,e$c",[Life Insurance]),"\n"
59)     PRINT boldon,"Short Term Disability: ",boldoff,[Short Term Disab],"\n"
60)     PRINT boldon,"Long Term Disability : ",boldoff,[Long Term Disab],"\n"
61)     PRINT boldon,"U.S. Saving Bonds    : ",boldoff,
62)          FORMAT("w10.2,al,e$c",[US Saving Bond]),"\n"
63) ENDPROC
64)
65) PROC PrintDepndnts()
66)   PRIVATE numofdetail
67)   MOVETO "Depndnts"
68)   numofdetail = NIMAGERECORDS()
69)   IF numofdetail = 0 THEN
70)      RETURN
71)   ELSE
72)     AddLineNumber(numofdetail+4)
73)     PRINT boldon,underlineon,"Employee Dependents",underlineoff,boldoff,"\n\n"
74)     PRINT boldon,FORMAT("w26","Name"),gap,FORMAT("w11","SSN"),gap,
75)           "Birth Date","\n"
76)     PRINT FILL("-",26),gap,FILL("-",11),gap,FILL("-",10),boldoff,"\n"
77)     SCAN
78)       PRINT FORMAT("w26",[First Name] + " " + [Last Name]),gap,
79)             [Dependents SSN],gap,
80)             [Birth Date],"\n"
81)     ENDSCAN
82)   ENDIF
83) ENDPROC
84)
85) PROC PrintEducation()
86)   PRIVATE numofdetail
87)   MOVETO "Eduction"
88)   numofdetail = NIMAGERECORDS()
89)   IF numofdetail = 0 THEN
90)      RETURN
91)   ELSE
92)     AddLineNumber(numofdetail+4)
93)     PRINT boldon,underlineon,"Employee Education History",
94)           underlineoff,boldoff,"\n\n"
95)     PRINT boldon,FORMAT("w4","Year"),gap,FORMAT("w40","School"),gap,
96)           "Degree","\n"
97)     PRINT FILL("-",4),gap,FILL("-",40),gap,FILL("-",20),boldoff,"\n"
98)     SCAN
99)       PRINT FORMAT("w4",[Year]),gap,
100)           FORMAT("w40",[School]),gap,
101)           [Degree],"\n"
102)    ENDSCAN
103)  ENDIF
104) ENDPROC
```

Listing 11-1 Program for multitable reporting using a form—continued

```
105)
106) PROC PrintTraining()
107)   PRIVATE numofdetail
108)   MOVETO "Training"
109)   numofdetail = NIMAGERECORDS()
110)   IF numofdetail = 0 THEN
111)     RETURN
112)   ELSE
113)     AddLineNumber(numofdetail+4)
114)     PRINT boldon,underlineon,"Employee Company Training History",
115)           underlineoff,boldoff,"\n\n"
116)     PRINT boldon,FORMAT("w3","#"),gap,FORMAT("w40","Course Title"),gap,
117)           "Date Attended","\n"
118)     PRINT FILL("-",3),gap,FILL("-",40),gap,FILL("-",13),boldoff,"\n"
119)     SCAN
120)       PRINT FORMAT("w3",[Course Number]),gap,
121)             FORMAT("w40",[Course Title]),gap,
122)             [Date Attended],"\n"
123)     ENDSCAN
124)   ENDIF
125) ENDPROC
126)
127) PROC PrintDriver()
128)   PRIVATE linenumber, pagefooter, gap, pgnum
129)   linenumber  = 1
130)   pagefooter = 2
131)   gap = "  "
132)   VIEW "Employee"
133)   PICKFORM 11
134)
135)   SCAN
136)     pgnum = 1
137)     StartOfPage()                    ;  Print page headings
138)     PrintEmployee()                  ;  Print Employee information
139)     AddBlankLines(2)
140)     PrintBenefits()                  ;  Print Benefits information
141)     AddBlankLines(1)
142)     PrintDepndnts()                  ;  Print Depndnts information
143)     AddBlankLines(1)
144)     PrintEducation()                 ;  Print Eduction information
145)     AddBlankLines(1)
146)     PrintTraining()                  ;  Print Training information
147)     EndOfPage()                      ;  End the current page
148)     MOVETO "Employee"                ;  Ensure cursor in Employee Table
149)   ENDSCAN
150)   CLEAR
151)   CLEARALL
152) ENDPROC
```

Listing 11-1 *Program for multitable reporting using a form—continued*

PrintDriver is the controlling procedure. It begins by initializing the variables for the starting line number (*linenumber*) and the number of lines to reserve for the page footer (*pagefooter*). Next, the Employee table is placed on the workspace and form 11 is selected. This is the multitable form, including all of the necessary tables as detail tables. The processing performed on each Employee record prints the information from the Employee table, then moves to each of the other tables and prints the information found if any records exist (the SCAN in lines 135 through 149). A separate procedure is used for each table in the form. At the start of each employee record, the page headings are printed by StartOfPage. The procedure AddBlankLines advances the printer the number of lines specified in the argument list. In each call in this example, the printer is advanced two lines. When all of the information is printed for the employee, the last procedure, EndOfPage, prints the page footer and advances the page for the next employee record.

```
127)  PROC PrintDriver()
128)    PRIVATE linenumber, pagefooter, gap, pgnum
129)    linenumber  = 1
130)    pagefooter = 2
131)    gap = " "
132)    VIEW "Employee"
133)    PICKFORM 11
134)
135)    SCAN
136)      pgnum = 1
137)      StartOfPage()         ; Print page headings
138)      PrintEmployee()       ; Print Employee information
139)      AddBlankLines(2)
140)      PrintBenefits()       ; Print Benefits information
141)      AddBlankLines(1)
142)      PrintDepndnts()       ; Print Depndnts information
143)      AddBlankLines(1)
144)      PrintEducation()      ; Print Eduction information
145)      AddBlankLines(1)
146)      PrintTraining()       ; Print Training information
147)      EndOfPage()           ; End the current page
148)      MOVETO "Employee"     ; Ensure cursor in Employee Table
149)    ENDSCAN
150)    CLEAR
151)    CLEARALL
152)  ENDPROC
```

StartOfPage prints headings, a date, and a page number at the start of every page. Global variables are used to handle printer control sequences and are set before PrintDriver is called. The variables *boldon* and *boldoff* contain the escape sequences to turn the bold option on and off. These variables are printed before and after the sections of the header that are to appear boldface type.

```
 3) PROC StartOfPage()
 4)   PRINT "\n",boldon,FORMAT("w80,ac","********** Confidential **********") +
 5)         boldoff,"\n\n"
 6)   PRINT FORMAT("D1",TODAY()) + boldon +
 7)         FORMAT("w64,ac","Employee Personnel Information") + boldoff +
 8)         "Page: " + FORMAT("w4,al",pgnum) + "\n\n"
 9)   linenumber = linenumber + 5
10) ENDPROC
```

There are two utility procedures used in this example, AddLineNumber and AddBlankLines. AddLineNumber controls what line number the print head is on and ensures that the number of lines to be printed fit on the current page. In this example, if there isn't enough room for a section, it is printed on the next page. Line 24 compares the summation of current line number plus the number of lines to print to see if it is less the page size minus the size of the page footer. If there isn't enough room, page footer (line 25) and header (line 26) processing is performed. If there is enough room on the page, the line number is added to the next line after printing the current section. AddBlankLines creates spaces between sections. It has one parameter, the number of lines to advance the printer head. It also calls AddLineNumber to see if there is enough room on the page before printing blank lines.

```
23) PROC AddLineNumber(incrmnt)
24)   IF linenumber + incrmnt > pagesize - pagefooter THEN
25)       EndOfPage()
26)       StartOfPage()
27)   ELSE
28)       linenumber = linenumber + incrmnt
29)   ENDIF
30) ENDPROC
31)
32) PROC AddBlankLines(numoflines)
33)   PRIVATE i
34)   AddLineNumber(numoflines)
35)   FOR i From 1 TO numoflines
36)     PRINT "\n"
37)   ENDFOR
38) ENDPROC
```

Each table has a separate procedure for printing the data. The Benefits table is in a one-to-one relationship with Employee. Each field from the table is printed using PrintBenefits. Each section has a separate heading. Global variables are used to print a bold, underlined heading (line 54). The Benefits information always exists for an employee, so no checking is done for blank fields. Line 55 checks to see if there is enough room to print the five lines. (In this example, this check is not really necessary. To make the code shorter, most of the fields from the Employee table are not printed. Therefore, there will always be room for the Benefits information.)

```
52) PROC PrintBenefits()
53)    MOVETO "Benefits"
54)    PRINT boldon,underlineon,"Employee Benefits",underlineoff,boldoff,"\n\n"
55)    AddLineNumber(5)
56)    PRINT boldon,"Insurance Type          : ",boldoff,[Insurance Type],"\n"
57)    PRINT boldon,"Life Insurance          : ",boldoff,
58)          FORMAT("w12.2,a1,e$c",[Life Insurance]),"\n"
59)    PRINT boldon,"Short Term Disability:  ",boldoff,[Short Term Disab],"\n"
60)    PRINT boldon,"Long Term Disability :  ",boldoff,[Long Term Disab],"\n"
61)    PRINT boldon,"U.S. Saving Bonds       : ",boldoff,
62)          FORMAT("w10.2,a1,e$c",[US Saving Bond]),"\n"
63) ENDPROC
```

The remaining tables can potentially contain multiple records for each employee. Since the processing is the same for Depndnts, Eduction, and Training, let's look at only one of the procedures, PrintDepndnts. Line 69 checks each table for detail records. If there are no detail records, the section is not printed (if the number of detail lines = 0, the procedure ends). If there is at least one record, the next check is to see if there is enough room on the page for all the detail lines (and the section header lines) by calling AddLineNumber in line 72. (Printing all or nothing is the easy way out. An enhancement to this code would be to check for each line, not the entire section. If this is done, a procedure to handle carryover is required.) The section headers are printed in lines 73 through 76, before processing each detail record. A SCAN is used to move through the detail and print each field. When all the records are printed, control returns to PrintDriver.

```
65) PROC PrintDepndnts()
66)    PRIVATE numofdetail
67)    MOVETO "Depndnts"
68)    numofdetail = NIMAGERECORDS()
69)    IF numofdetail = 0 THEN
70)       RETURN
71)    ELSE
72)       AddLineNumber(numofdetail+4)
73)     PRINT boldon,underlineon,"Employee Dependents",underlineoff,boldoff,"\n\n"
74)       PRINT boldon,FORMAT("w26","Name"),gap,FORMAT("w11","SSN"),gap,
75)             "Birth Date","\n"
76)       PRINT FILL("-",26),gap,FILL("-",11),gap,FILL("-",10),boldoff,"\n"
77)       SCAN
78)         PRINT FORMAT("w26",[First Name] + " " + [Last Name]),gap,
79)               [Dependents SSN],gap,
80)               [Birth Date],"\n"
81)       ENDSCAN
82)    ENDIF
83) ENDPROC
```

Before printing this report, certain variables have to be set. Listing 11-2 contains the commands necessary to initiate the report. Global variables for the page size and printer escape sequence have to be initialized before PrintDriver is called. The printer escape sequence for turning bold and underline styling on and off must also be set.

```
pagesize = 60              ; Set the page length
boldon =     "\27(s3B"     ; Bold on escape sequence for laser printer
boldoff=     "\27(s0B"     ; Bold off escape sequence for laser printer
underlineon = "\27&dD"     ; Underline on escape sequence for laser printer
underlineoff = "\27&d@"    ; Underline off escape sequence for laser printer
PrintDriver()
```

Listing 11-2 Starter script for multitable reporting using a form

As you can see, this is an involved process, but you only have to do it once. Any multitable report can use the same basic code, just change the procedures for each table's information. Until Paradox supports multi-level structures in the report generator, you have to use techniques like this.

Global Variables and Functions

One of the new features in Paradox 3.5 is the ability to use global variables, arrays, and some PAL functions in report expressions. This removes the need to preprocess the data in cases where functions had to be used to output the correct information. The result of any expression using a function is always a text string with a maximum length of 255 characters. Table 11-1 lists the functions that can be used in report expressions.

▽ **TRAP:** *In the first release of Paradox 3.5, there are problems with functions used in report and form expressions. Chapter 5 details the problems when you use null (blank) fields as parameters for functions. In writing this chapter, we discovered (and Borland confirmed) additional problems that restricted the usage of some functions in certain situations. Where possible, these problems are noted. If the failure of the function caused the example to be withdrawn from this chapter, the problem is identified as a trap.*

**Table 11-1
Functions allowed in report expressions**

ABS	Absolute value of a number
ACOS	Arc cosine of a number
ASC	Converts a character to an ASCII value
ASIN	Arc sine of a number
ATAN	Arc tangent of a number
ATAN2	Four-quadrant arc tangent
CAVERAGE	Averages of all records for one column in a table
CCOUNT	Count of the values for a column in a table
CHR	Converts an ASCII value to a character
CMAX	Maximum value for a column in a table
CMIN	Minimum value for a column in a table
CNPV	Net present value for a column in a table
COS	Cosine of an angle
CSTD	Standard deviation of the values for a column in a table
CSUM	Sum of the values for a column in a table
CVAR	Variance of the values for a column in a table
DATEVAL	Converts a date value to a string value
DAY	Numeric value of the day of the month for a date value
DOW	Three letter string of the day of the week for a date value
EXP	Exponential value of a number
FILL	Returns a repeated character string
FORMAT	Formats date, numeric, text, and logical data types
FV	Future values of a series of cash flows
INT	Integer portion of a number
LEN	Length of a character string
LN	Natural log of a number
LOG	Base 10 log of a number
LOWER	Converts a text string to lowercase
MAX	Largest of two numeric values
MIN	Smallest of two numeric values

Table 11-1—continued

MOD	Modulus function
MONTH	Numeric value of the month for a date value
MOY	Three-character value of the month for a date value
NRECORDS	Number of records in a table
NUMVAL	Converts a text string to a number
PI	Value of Pi
PMT	Amortized mortgage payment
POW	Raises a number to a power
PV	Present value of a series of payments
RAND	Random number
ROUND	Rounds a number
SEARCH	Position of a substring
SIN	Sine of an angle
SQRT	Square root
STRVAL	Converts an expression to a string
SUBSTR	Returns a substring
TAN	Tangent of an angle
TIME	Current system time
TODAY	Current system date
UPPER	Converts a text string to uppercase
USERNAME	Current user's name
YEAR	Year of a date value

Formatting and styling options are available with variables and functions. The following examples show you some of the things that can now be done in Paradox 3.5, such as formatting data, generic report titles, graphical displays, and other creative solutions.

Have you ever wanted to have the day of the week or current month spelled out in a report? Did you find a function to do this for you? Well, it doesn't exist. With Paradox 3.5, there is a solution that doesn't require pre-processing the data. You can use arrays to spell out the month and day, and functions to retrieve the correct element.

To demonstrate this technique, a trivial example is used which lists the employees, the date they were hired, and a text string spelling out the day of the week and the month, day, and year. Figure 11-3 lists the report output.

```
 9/02/90             Array Example for Month and Day                Page    1

 Employee Name       Date Hired   Text String For Date Hired
 -----------------   ----------   ------------------------------------------
 Adams, Jerry         6/06/82     Sunday     June 6 in the year 1982
 Barnaby, Raymond     6/16/84     Saturday   June 16 in the year 1984
 Barnes, Dorothy      9/02/83     Friday     September 2 in the year 1983
 Barth, Jim          10/02/87     Friday     October 2 in the year 1987
 Brown, Bubba        10/11/82     Monday     October 11 in the year 1982
 Brown, John          3/10/83     Thursday   March 10 in the year 1983
 Charles, Anthony    10/19/83     Wednesday  October 19 in the year 1983
 Garth, Timothy       2/28/84     Tuesday    February 28 in the year 1984
 Harris, Jean         3/12/84     Monday     March 12 in the year 1984
 Jones, Mike          5/05/83     Thursday   May 5 in the year 1983
 McCarthy, Jennifer   2/22/85     Friday     February 22 in the year 1985
 Owens, Lucy          9/19/83     Monday     September 19 in the year 1983
 Smith, Peter        12/12/82     Sunday     December 12 in the year 1982
 Walls, Ingrid        1/01/82     Friday     January 1 in the year 1982
 Williams, Bill       1/12/85     Saturday   January 12 in the year 1985
```

Figure 11-3 Full spelling for day of the week and month report example

You have to create two arrays to use this technique: one to contain the full spelling for the months and another to contain the full spelling for the days. Following are the PAL statements to create the array for the months:

```
ARRAY Full.Month[12]
Full.Month[1]  = "January"
Full.Month[2]  = "February"
Full.Month[3]  = "March"
Full.Month[4]  = "April"
Full.Month[5]  = "May"
Full.Month[6]  = "June"
Full.Month[7]  = "July"
Full.Month[8]  = "August"
Full.Month[9]  = "September"
Full.Month[10] = "October"
Full.Month[11] = "November"
Full.Month[12] = "December"
```

The MONTH function returns the numeric value for the month of a date value. This allows an expression to be created that returns the full spelling:

Full.Month[MONTH([Date Hired])]

Supporting the full spelling of the weekday has to be handled differently. Paradox doesn't have a function that returns the day of the week as a number. Using the DOW function, you get the three-letter spelling of the weekday. You can still use this function by creating a table that contains the values for each weekday with the column names matching the values returned by DOW. The structure of the table and its contents are shown in Figure 11-4.

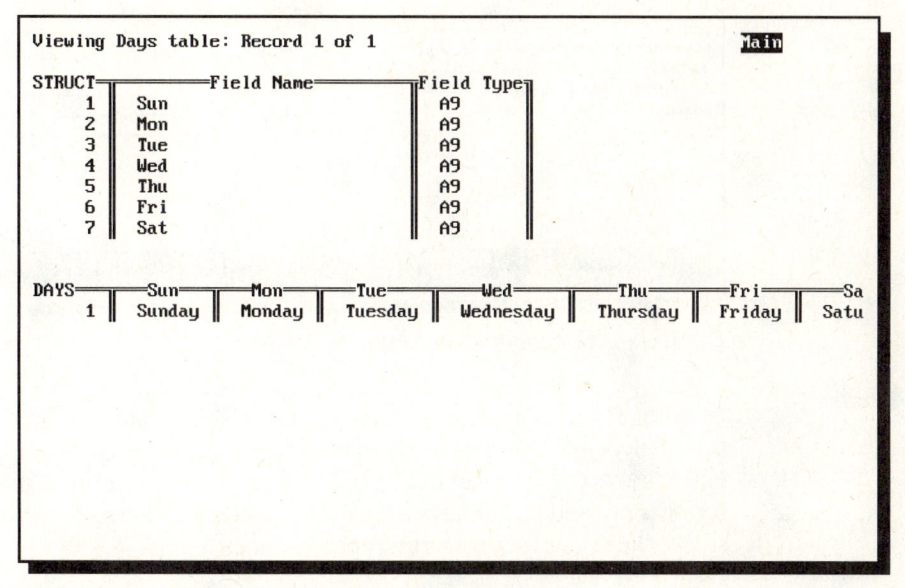

```
Viewing Days table: Record 1 of 1                                    Main
STRUCT    Field Name          Field Type
   1    Sun                   A9
   2    Mon                   A9
   3    Tue                   A9
   4    Wed                   A9
   5    Thu                   A9
   6    Fri                   A9
   7    Sat                   A9

DAYS    Sun       Mon       Tue       Wed        Thu       Fri      Sa
   1    Sunday    Monday    Tuesday   Wednesday  Thursday  Friday   Satu
```

Figure 11-4 Structure and content of Days table

Before running the report, the Days table is placed on the workspace and COPYTOARRAY is used to create the Full.Day array containing the days off the week. Using the DOW function to subscript the array, the appropriate full week spelling is returned:

Full.Day[DOW([Date Hired])]

Using this technique, the next step is to create the report. Figure 11-5 displays the final report layout. At the bottom of the screen is the complete syntax for the expression placed as the last field in the Table Band. For expressions that are longer than the available space on the line, use the FIELDINFO function with the cursor on a field so that Paradox returns the definition of the field in the message window.

```
Changing report R7 for Employee table                      Report    1/1
FORMAT("w10",Full.Day[DOW([Date Hired])])+Full.Month[MONTH([Date Hired])]+" "+ST
....+...10....+...20....+...30....+...40....+...50....+...60....+...70....+...8*
─▼page─────────────────────────────────────────────────────────────────────────

mm/dd/yy                    Array Example for Month and Day         Page 999

  ──▼group Last Name────────────────────────────────────────────────────────
  ┌▼table──────────────┬───────────┬───────────────────────────────────────┐
  Employee Name         Date Hired  Text String For Date Hired
  ──────────────────── ─────────── ────────────────────────────────────────
  AAAAAAAAAAAAAAAAAAAA mm/dd/yy    AAAAAAAAAAAAAAAAAAAAAAAAAAAAAAAAAAAAAAAA
  └▲table──────────────┴───────────┴───────────────────────────────────────┘
  ──▲group Last Name────────────────────────────────────────────────────────
─▲page─────────────────────────────────────────────────────────────────────────




FORMAT("w10",Full.Day[DOW([Date Hired])])+Full.Month[MONTH([Date Hired])]+"
"+STRVAL(DAY([Date Hired]))+" in the year "+STRVAL(YEAR([Date Hired]))
```

Figure 11-5 Company Roster report layout

Running this report without defining both Full.Month and Full.Day arrays prints incorrect information. Depending on the setting of CalcDebug, you'll either get no data or the text string defined for CalcDebug. Therefore, a script is needed to guarantee that both arrays are defined. Listing 11-3 shows the script that runs the report correctly.

As stated earlier, this is a trivial example, but it demonstrates some of the new features of 3.5. Both arrays and functions can expand the formatting capabilities of the report generator. This is just the beginning of using the new features of 3.5. Let's look at some other examples.

Figure 11-6 displays a typical Paradox multitable report based on tables in a one-to-many relationship. The two tables used here are the Dept and Employee tables. Because Employee is on the many side of the relationship, it's the table the report is based on, while the Dept table is linked to the report. This report prints the roster of all employees by department and subtotals their salaries. The manager for the department, is taken from the Dept table. All fields in the Table Band are expressions except the SSN. The expressions are:

    Employee Name   [Last Name] + ", " + [First Name]
    Years   INT((TODAY() - [Date Hired]) / 365.25)

Wage	[Salary] / 2080
Yearly Salary	FORMAT("w12.2,e$c",[Salary])

```
; RptFnct1.sc
ARRAY Full.Month[12]
Full.Month[1]   = "January"
Full.Month[2]   = "February"
Full.Month[3]   = "March"
Full.Month[4]   = "April"
Full.Month[5]   = "May"
Full.Month[6]   = "June"
Full.Month[7]   = "July"
Full.Month[8]   = "August"
Full.Month[9]   = "September"
Full.Month[10]  = "October"
Full.Month[11]  = "November"
Full.Month[12]  = "December"
VIEW "Days"
COPYTOARRAY Full.Day
CLEARIMAGE
MENU {Report} {Output} {Employee} {7} {Screen}
RELEASE VARS Full.Month, Full.Day
```

Listing 11-3 Script to run full month and day spelling example

```
Changing report R2 for Employee table                        Report    1/1
Table Band                              [Last Name] + ", " + [First Name]
....+...10....+...20....+...30....+...40....+...50....+...60....+...70....+...8*
─▼page─
   M o n t h dd, yyyy            Company Roster              Page 999
   ──▼group Department──────────────────────────────────────────────
   Dept: AAAAAAAAAA    Mgr: AAAAAAAAAAAAAAAAAA
         ──▼group Last Name───────────────────────────────────────
            ──▼group First Name────────────────────────────────────
   ┌▼table─
   Employee Name          SSN         Years   Wage    Yearly Salary
   ─────────────          ───         ─────   ────    ─────────────
   AAAAAAAAAAAAAAAAAAAAAA AAAAAAAAAA  AAA     99.99   AAAAAAAAAAAA
   └▲table─
            ──▲group First Name────────────────────────────────────
         ──▲group Last Name───────────────────────────────────────
   Total salary for AAAAAAAAAA                       AAAAAAAAAAAA
         ──▲group Department──────────────────────────────────────
                                                    ==============
   Total Company Salary                              AAAAAAAAAAAA
```

Figure 11-6 Company Roster report layout

Both *Employee Name* and *Wage* were supported before Paradox 3.5. The other two expressions show new capabilities of 3.5. *Years* is a calculation displaying the number of years the employee has worked for the company based on the date of hire. FORMAT is used in *Yearly Salary* to display a floating dollar sign.

▽ **TRAP:** *To keep with the same style, both the subtotal for each department and the report total should have a floating dollar sign. The expressions for each are:*

Department subtotal FORMAT("w13.2,e$c,sum([Salary],group))
Report total FORMAT("w13.2,e$c,sum([Salary]))

This is where we found a problem. Extraneous characters were placed by Paradox at the end of each of these expressions, varying from extra zeroes to other letters and even extended ASCII characters. The only way to solve this problem was to shrink the size of the displayed field. If you use this format option, you might have to test different sizes to get the correct output.

Variables and functions can also be used to produce rotated bar charts in reports. Figure 11-7 shows a report with this type of output. The report lists each employee grouped by department, their salary as a numeric value, and a line showing their salary relative to other employees.

Figure 11-8 shows the report layout for this output. The expression that calculates the bar graph is:

FILL(barsymbol,INT([Salary] / 1000) -10)

The expression divides the Salary field by 1000 to fit it on the scale (10 is subtracted from the result because the scale starts at 10,000). The integer of the result is used as a parameter to the FILL command for the number of characters to return. The global variable *barsymbol* populates the output for the size of the salary. Using a global variable allows this report to work on any printer. For this example, ASCII 223 is the value of *barsymbol*. This doesn't work on some printers (like certain dot matrix models).

▽ **TRAP:** *We found some serious problems in creating a rotated bar example. We initially wanted to show a salary summary by department and have a bar graph of the percentage of total salary for each department. The first expression tested was*

sum([Salary],group) / CSUM("Employee","Salary")

Running Advanced Reports and Graphs 349

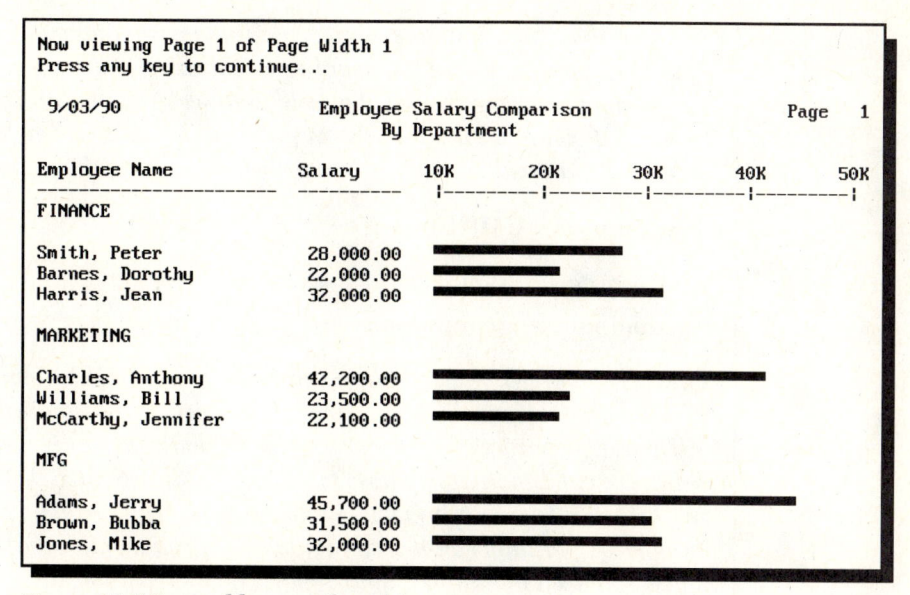

```
Now viewing Page 1 of Page Width 1
Press any key to continue...

 9/03/90              Employee Salary Comparison            Page   1
                          By Department

Employee Name           Salary     10K     20K     30K     40K     50K
------------------------ ---------- |-------|-------|-------|-------|
FINANCE

Smith, Peter            28,000.00  ███████████████
Barnes, Dorothy         22,000.00  ███████████
Harris, Jean            32,000.00  ████████████████████

MARKETING

Charles, Anthony        42,200.00  ████████████████████████████
Williams, Bill          23,500.00  █████████████
McCarthy, Jennifer      22,100.00  ███████████

MFG

Adams, Jerry            45,700.00  ██████████████████████████████
Brown, Bubba            31,500.00  █████████████████████
Jones, Mike             32,000.00  ██████████████████████
```

Figure 11-7 Rotated bar graph within a report

```
Changing report R4 for Employee table              Report  Ins 1/1
Table Band                      FILL(barsymbol,INT([salary] / 1000)-10)
....+...10....+...20....+...30....+...40....+...50....+...60....+...70....+...8*
─▼page─

mm/dd/yy             Employee Salary Comparison            Page 999
                         By Department

Employee Name          Salary     10K     20K     30K     40K     50K
------------------------ ---------- |-------|-------|-------|-------|
     ──▼group Department──
AAAAAAAAAA

  ┌▼table─
  AAAAAAAAAAAAAAAAAAAAAAA  (99,999.99)  AAAAAAAAAAAAAAAAAAAAAAAAAAAAAAAAAA
  └▲table─

    ──▲group Department──
──▲page──
```

Figure 11-8 Rotated bar graph report layout

This was disastrous. An unexpected condition occurred with a message **End of summary chain — Leaving Paradox.** *Needless to say, this is something no developer or end user likes to see! You can prevent this problem if you don't use the CSUM function. Instead, use a global variable created outside the report writer before running the report, such as*

salsum = CSUM("Employee", "Salary")

The report expression then becomes:

sum([Salary],group) / *salsum*

Creating a bar graph using this expression and the FILL command uncovered another problem. Any time a summary expression is used with FILL, extra characters are appended or the entire result is garbage (an arbitrary combination of characters, usually the extended ASCII characters). This, along with previous problems, leads us to believe that using summary operations with certain functions produces unpredictable results. You need to fully test your reports if you have this type of requirement. You're probably better off waiting until these problems are fixed in a future release.

Printer Control Characters

Report output is enhanced by using printer options for underlining, boldface type, various fonts, italics, and other options that vary depending on the type of printer you can access. Paradox 3.5 includes a new appendix that covers printer setup strings for many popular printers. Support for using printer escape sequences is accomplished using one of three methods:

- Calculated fields
- PAL TYPEIN command
- Global variables

Calculated fields let you enter the printer escape sequence as a text string and place it like any other field in your report. The entire text of the escape sequence is enclosed in double quotes and can be concatenated with other text fields. Most control codes require an ASCII 27 as the first character (represented as "\27"). For example, to turn boldface type on for an HP Laserjet, the escape sequence is "\27(s3B". Each character printed after this

is printed in bold type. Each of these calculated fields takes up space on
your report layout, which might mean you have to adjust field placement.
Each calculated field placed that contains printer control characters is represented by A's in the layout. Figure 11-9 shows an example using bold type
for the report title. The only way you'll know that a field contains escape
codes is to place your cursor on the field and look at the status line at the top
of the screen.

```
Changing report R13 for Employee table                     Report     1/1
Page Header                             "\27(s3B" + "Company Roster" + "\27(s0B"
....+...10....+...20....+...30....+...40....+...50....+...60....+...70....+...8*
─▽page─
                                                                      Page 999
                        AAAAAAAAAAAAAAAAAAAAAAAAA
        ─▽group Department─
Dept: AAAAAAAAA     Mgr: AAAAAAAAAAAAAAAAAA
            ─▽group Last Name─
                ─▽group First Name─
  ┌▽table─                                  ┬       ┬
   Employee Name              SSN          Years   Wage      Yearly Salary
   ─────────────              ───          ─────   ────      ─────────────
   AAAAAAAAAAAAAAAAAAAAAAA   AAAAAAAAAA    AAA     99.99     AAAAAAAAAA
  └▲table─
            ─▲group First Name─
                ─▲group Last Name─
                                                             ──────────────
 Total salary for AAAAAAAAA                                  AAAAAAAAAAAA
        ─▲group Department─
                                                             ==============
 Total Company Salary                                        AAAAAAAAAAAA
```

Figure 11-9 Printer escape sequence using calculated field

You can also place printer control codes in your report using TYPEIN. To
do this, select {*MiniScript*} from the PAL Menu and enter TYPEIN *string*.
Using the previous example to set bold type, the entry would be *TYPEIN
"\27(s3B"*. Paradox then types the characters at the current cursor location
in your report. Before you start this process, position the cursor in the correct location and make sure there is either enough room for the characters
to be entered in overstrike mode or toggle on insert mode. You'll also notice
a difference in the screen. Figure 11-10 shows a report layout using this
technique. Instead of A's for the placed field, you see the ASCII representation of the escape sequence on each side of the report title. Using this technique gives you immediate visibility for any printer control codes in a report
layout.

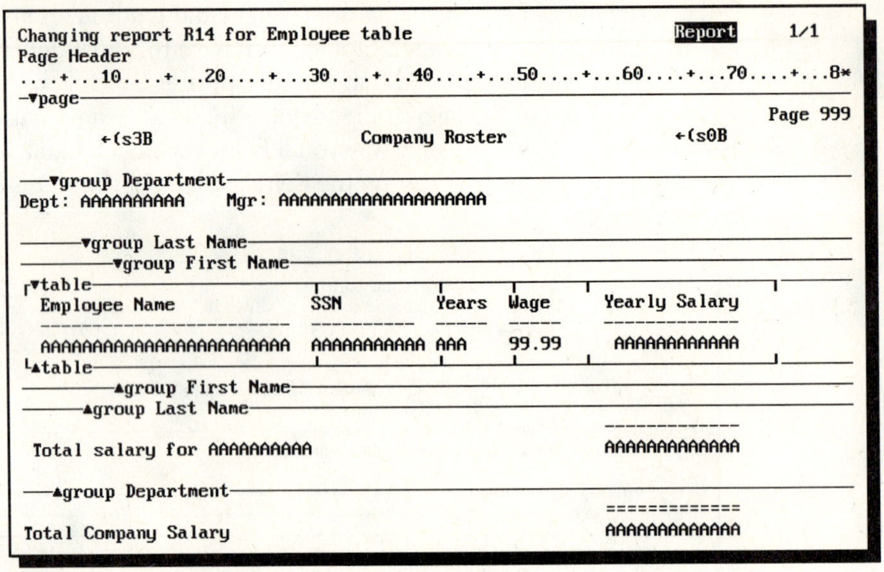

```
┌─────────────────────────────────────────────────────────────────────────┐
│ Changing report R14 for Employee table                    Report   1/1  │
│ Page Header                                                             │
│ ....+...10....+...20....+...30....+...40....+...50....+...60....+...70....+...8*│
│ ─▼page──────────────────────────────────────────────────────────────    │
│                                                                Page 999 │
│         ←(s3B                  Company Roster         ←(s0B             │
│   ──▼group Department──────────────────────────────────────────         │
│   Dept: AAAAAAAAA    Mgr: AAAAAAAAAAAAAAAAAA                            │
│                                                                         │
│   ────▼group Last Name─────────────────────────────────────────         │
│     ──▼group First Name──────────────────────────────────────           │
│   ┌▼table──────────────────────────────────────────────────┐            │
│   │ Employee Name          SSN        Years  Wage   Yearly Salary │     │
│   │ ───────────            ─────────  ─────  ─────  ───────────── │     │
│   │ AAAAAAAAAAAAAAAAAAAAAA AAAAAAAAA AAA   99.99  AAAAAAAAAAA   │     │
│   └▲table──────────────────────────────────────────────────┘            │
│     ──▲group First Name──────────────────────────────────────           │
│   ────▲group Last Name─────────────────────────────────────────         │
│                                                          ─────────────  │
│   Total salary for AAAAAAAAAA                            AAAAAAAAAAA    │
│   ──▲group Department──────────────────────────────────────────         │
│                                                          ============= │
│   Total Company Salary                                   AAAAAAAAAAA    │
└─────────────────────────────────────────────────────────────────────────┘
```

Figure 11-10 Printer escape sequence using TYPEIN

The third technique is by far the most generic and is made possible by using global variables. In both of the previous methods, you have to hard code a report for a specific type of printer. If your users have a variety of printers, some with laser printers and others with dot matrix printers, you have to code two different report layouts. With global variable support, you initialize the variables with the appropriate escape sequence based on the type of printer before the report is printed. Continuing with the same example, to bold the report title, the expression is *"boldon + [Field Name] + boldoff"*. Here *boldon* and *boldoff* are the variable names. Figure 11-11 shows an example. The one thing you do have to consider is that different printers have different escape code lengths. On one printer, turning bold on may take three characters while on another machine it may take five characters. This difference may affect the number of spaces you have to leave for the field placed in the report.

Graphs

Graphical output from a Paradox table can be output in one of eleven styles:

- Stacked bar
- Regular bar graph
- 3-D bar

```
Changing report R3 for Employee table                        Report      1/1
Page Header                            boldon + rpttitle + boldoff, center
....+...10....+...20....+...30....+...40....+...50....+...60....+...70....+...8*
 ─▼page──────────────────────────────────────────────────────────────────────
                                                                    Page 999
 AAAAAAAAAAAAAAAAAAAAAAAAAAAAAAAAAAAAAAAAAAAAAAAAAAAAAAAAAAAAAAAAAAAAAAAAAAAAA
   ──▼group Department─────────────────────────────────────────────────────
 Dept: AAAAAAAAA      Mgr: AAAAAAAAAAAAAAAAAA
      ──▼group Last Name──────────────────────────────────────────────────
       ──▼group First Name────────────────────────────────────────────────
      ┌▼table─────────────────┬──────────────┬──────┬──────┬───────────────┐
        Employee Name           SSN            Years  Wage   Yearly Salary
       ─────────────────────   ──────────────  ─────  ─────  ───────────────
        AAAAAAAAAAAAAAAAAAAA   AAAAAAAAAA AAA         99.99  AAAAAAAAAAA
      └▲table─────────────────┴──────────────┴──────┴──────┴───────────────┘
       ──▲group First Name────────────────────────────────────────────────
      ──▲group Last Name──────────────────────────────────────────────────
                                                         ───────────────
 Total salary for AAAAAAAAA                              AAAAAAAAAAAAA
   ──▲group Department─────────────────────────────────────────────────────
                                                         ===============
 Total Company Salary                                    AAAAAAAAAAAAA
```

Figure 11-11 Printer escape sequence using global variables

- Rotated bar
- Line
- Markers
- Combined lines and markers
- X-Y graph
- Pie graph
- Area graph
- Combinations of the above

Creating graphs is well documented in the *Presenting Paradox Data* manual and we will not reiterate it here. If you need to learn how to create a chart, look at Chapters 6 and 7 of that book.

Certain elements of charts vary from application to application, just like reports. Titles, minimum and maximum values for the Y-Axis, outputting to different devices, and the number of graphs per printed page are items that you might want to give your user the option to set. All of these require that you enter the graphics module to modify the current settings. Let's look at how these are handled.

Listing 11-4 is a procedure used to change graph titles dynamically within an application. The SetGraphTitle procedure has two arguments, text for line one of the graph and text for line two. This procedure expects the current system mode to be Graph. Line 1 changes the graph entry screen to that for titles. The cursor is always placed initially on the entry for the first line of the titles. A CTRLBACKSPACE is required to remove the value in the field if there is one. SELECT does not work for this option. Line 6 enters the first parameter. Line 7 moves the cursor two fields down so the second title line text can be entered.

```
1) ; GrphTitl.sc
2)
3) PROC SetGraphTitle(title1text,title2text)
4)    MENU {Overall} {Titles}
5)    CTRLBACKSPACE
6)    TYPEIN title1text
7)    Enter Enter CTRLBACKSPACE
8)    TYPEIN title2text
9) ENDPROC
```

Listing 11-4 Procedure to set graph titles

In some applications, you might want to let the user set the upper and lower limits of the Y-Axis. In cases where they see the data before it is charted, it is feasible for them to set the range so the value spread is less. SetGraphAxis, Listing 11-5, provides this capability. Three parameters are necessary for this procedure:

axistype	M for Manual or A for Automatic scaling
ymimval	Minimum value if Manual specified
ymaxval	Maximum value if Manual specified

If axis type is "M," the scaling is set to manual in line 5. The minimum and maximum value is set in line 6. Just like changing the graph titles, you have to clear out the existing value using **CTRLBACKSPACE**. If automatic scaling is requested, line 8 changes the scaling to automatic. If there are values in the minimum and maximum fields, they are ignored.

```
 1) ; GrphAxis.sc
 2)
 3) PROC SetGraphAxis(axistype,yminval,ymaxval)
 4)    IF axistype = "M" THEN
 5)       MENU {Overall} {Axes} RIGHT "M" DOWN CTRLBACKSPACE
 6)       TYPEIN yminval DOWN CTRLBACKSPACE TYPEIN ymaxval
 7)    ELSE
 8)       MENU {Overall} {Axes} RIGHT "A"
 9)    ENDIF
10) ENDPROC
```

Listing 11-5 Procedure to set graph Y-Axis scaling

You have two choices when sending a graph to a device other than the screen, a printer or a file. Paradox supports four different printer settings, defined in the Custom Configuration Program. If you output to a file, there are three selections:

CurrentPrinter	File format based on current printer (.GRF)
EPS	Encapsulated PostScript format (.EPS)
PIC	Lotus PIC format (.PIC)

SetGraphDevice, Listing 11-6, selects the output device for either printer or file based on the first parameter, *outdev*. If the device is a file, line 6 selects one of the three formats. If the output device is a printer, line 8 chooses the printer specified. TYPEIN is used instead of SELECT because the parameter sent is a 1, 2, 3, or 4. (This is to shorten the value sent—entering a "2" is much easier than entering "2ndPrinter.")

```
 1) ; GrphDev.sc
 2)
 3) PROC SetGraphDevice(outdev,devparam2)
 4)    MENU {Overall} {Device} SELECT outdev    ; Select either Printer or File
 5)    IF UPPER(outdev) = "FILE" THEN           ; For File device, need to
 6)       SELECT devparam2                      ; set the file type of
 7)    ELSE                                     ; CurrentPrinter, EPS, or PIC
 8)       TYPEIN devparam2                      ; For Printer, need to enter
 9)    ENDIF                                    ; printer 1, 2, 3, or 4
10) ENDPROC
```

Listing 11-6 Procedure to set graph titles

GRPHDEV.SC (Listing 11-6) outputs the graph to a specified device. Listing 11-7 shows the code for the OutputGraph procedure. Graphs can be viewed from either Main mode or Graph mode. In either mode, you have to first of all be in the menu (line 4). When in Main mode, {*Image*} {*Graph*} has to be selected. If in Graph mode, you're at the proper menu location. The next selection in either mode is {*ViewGraph*} and the device. This is handled in line 8. This works for screen, printer, and file output. If the output is to a file, the name is specified in line 10. There is the possibility that the file already exists, so MENUCHOICE is used in line 11. If a menu is displayed and the current selection is "Cancel," the file exists on disk. In this procedure, the user is not prompted and the file is automatically replaced. Once the graph is created, control is returned to the calling procedure.

```
1)  ; GrphOut.sc
2)
3)  PROC OutputGraph(outdev,gfilename)
4)     MENU
5)     IF SYSMODE() <> "Graph" THEN         ;  Not in Graph Mode
6)        {Image} {Graph}                   ;    Select {Image} {Graph} from
7)     ENDIF                                ;    from Main Menu
8)     {ViewGraph} SELECT outdev            ;  Select output device
9)     IF UPPER(outdev) = "FILE" THEN       ;  If output device is a file,
10)       SELECT gfilename                  ;  then enter the file name
11)       IF MENUCHOICE() = "Cancel" THEN
12)          {Replace}                      ;    If graph file exists, replace it
13)       ENDIF
14)    ENDIF
15) ENDPROC
```

Listing 11-7 *Procedure to output a graph*

Printing Multiple Graphs Per Page

Graphs provide a quick, visible measure of your data. In some cases, it is easier to analyze the data with multiple charts on the same piece of paper. This is possible when printing to a laser printer or a plotter. If your output device is a dot matrix printer, there are limitations on placing multiple graphs on a single page. The following example provides information on printing up to six graphs per page on a laser printer.

Running Advanced Reports and Graphs   357

The first thing to decide is how many graphs you want on a page. This determines the maximum size of each graph. The dimensions vary depending on whether the orientation of the page is landscape or portrait. The examples shown here deal only with a landscape orientation.

Specify dimensions and orientation of the graph in the Customize Graph Layout for Printing screen (Figure 11-12). To print multiple graphs per page, the Left and Top Margins, Graph Height and Width, Orientation, and Break Page must be set. Separate settings need to be defined for each graph printed on the page. Access this screen from the Main menu as follows:

{Image} {Graph} {Modify} [F10] {Overall} {PrinterLayout}.

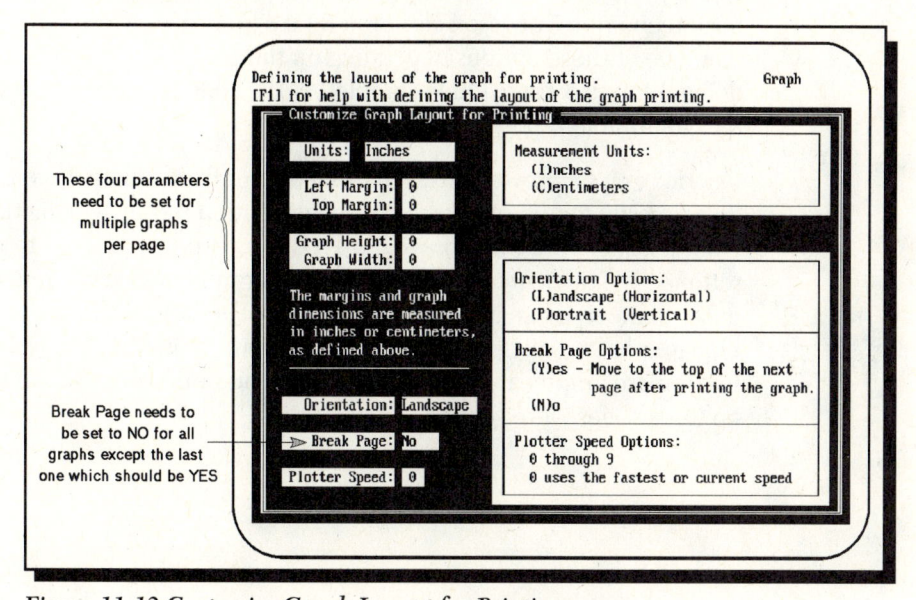

```
                    Defining the layout of the graph for printing.           Graph
                    [F1] for help with defining the layout of the graph printing.
                    ┌─ Customize Graph Layout for Printing ─────────────────────┐
                    │                                                            │
                    │   ┌Units:  Inches ┐      ┌Measurement Units:            ┐ │
These four parameters│                         │  (I)nches                    │ │
  need to be set for │   ┌Left Margin: 0 ┐     │  (C)entimeters               │ │
    multiple graphs  │   └Top Margin:  0 ┘     └──────────────────────────────┘ │
       per page      │                                                          │
                     │   ┌Graph Height: 0 ┐                                     │
                     │   └Graph Width:  0 ┘                                     │
                     │                         ┌Orientation Options:          ┐ │
                     │   The margins and graph │  (L)andscape (Horizontal)    │ │
                     │   dimensions are measured│ (P)ortrait  (Vertical)      │ │
                     │   in inches or centimeters,└────────────────────────────┘│
                     │   as defined above.                                      │
                     │                         ┌Break Page Options:           ┐ │
                     │                         │  (Y)es - Move to the top of  │ │
                     │   ┌Orientation: Landscape│     the next page after    │ │
 Break Page needs to │   └                    ┘│     printing the graph.     │ │
  be set to NO for all│  ▶┌Break Page: No ┐    │  (N)o                       │ │
  graphs except the last│ └              ┘     └──────────────────────────────┘│
  one which should be YES│                                                     │
                      │   ┌Plotter Speed: 0 ┐   ┌Plotter Speed Options:       ┐│
                      │   └                ┘    │ 0 through 9                 ││
                      │                         │ 0 uses the fastest or       ││
                      │                         │   current speed             ││
                      │                         └─────────────────────────────┘│
                      └────────────────────────────────────────────────────────┘
```

Figure 11-12 Customize Graph Layout for Printing screen

> **NOTE:** For Paradox 3.0 users, the options for Break Page are reversed. Yes means no, and No means yes. This was fixed in version 3.01a.

You can create separate graph files for each graph position or dynamically set them in an application. To save the graph settings, choose {Image} {Graph} {Save} from the Main menu and enter a filename. To use the saved settings, choose {Image} {Graph} {Load} and enter the filename before creating the graph.

Summary

In this chapter, we discussed multiple ways to present data. Both reports and graphs are used to convert data in tables to information that can be used to make decisions. Using functions and variables in reports greatly enhances report generation; even though there are some problems with the first release of 3.5, they will be fixed. Paradox's report writer is very robust as long as your data conforms to certain relationships.

Multiple table reporting for relationships other than one-to-many require different solutions than the report writer. Whether you write the process entirely in PAL, combine PAL code with the report generator, or use the form technique discussed earlier, it'll take time. You might have to use more than one of these options depending on the application. The hard part is doing it the first time. Once completed, the code becomes a model for further multitable reports.

Paradox graphs provide basic charting output from a data driven standpoint. Dynamically modifying graphs in an application requires using the graphics module. There are no abbreviated PAL commands to change the various settings. We presented some of the typical graph options as generic procedures to incorporate into you applications. The last area covered was multiple graphs per single page of printed output. Many times it is much easier to compare graphical output if they're on the same page. Graph settings for up to six pages were shown.

12 Setting up a Multiuser Environment

Setting up a multiuser environment is a daunting task for any developer. Paradox helps though, as it handles multiuser applications in a number of unique ways. In this chapter, we cover the important issues concerning writing Paradox network applications.

**Table 12-1
Key terms and concepts**

File server	User configuration	PARADOX.CFG
PARADOX.NET	Directory	Subdirectory
Network printer	Locks	Form Lock
Prevent Full Lock	Write Lock	SETRESTARTCOUNT
SETRETRYPERIOD	SETPRIVDIR	SETDIR
LOCKRECORD	LOCKSTATUS	RECORDSTATUS

Network Overview

Paradox deals with network installations in a very straightforward way, and doesn't try to be everything to everybody. Even though Paradox installation leads you to think otherwise, there isn't a special version for Novell, 3Com, PC LAN, and so on. Paradox doesn't lock files differently on one network that it does on any other; it basically lets the network itself handle file manipulation and handles only key operations itself.

Let's begin this overview with a some of the most often asked questions.

Question — How do I tell Paradox to configure itself correctly for each workstation (assuming some have different hardware configurations)?

Answer — After you install Paradox on your network, use the Custom Configuration Program (CCP) to create a PARADOX.CFG file for each user (*Menu* {*Scripts*} {*Play*} {*Custom*}). Store the PARADOX.CFG file in each user's private directory (discussed more later). Each user must start Paradox from their private directory.

Question — How does Paradox determine how many users are using Paradox at any given time?

Answer — When you installed Paradox, you told it where to create and maintain a file called PARADOX.NET (stored in a shared Read/Write directory). This file maintains a list of current Paradox users on the network.

Question — How does Paradox keep my Answer table from interfering with other network users' Answer tables?

Answer — Paradox uses two concepts to keep network users from destroying each other's data: a working directory and a private directory.

A working directory is usually a network directory where all users have equal access (they have rights, unless otherwise coded or password protected, to read and write Paradox objects). This directory is where all users sharing the same PARADOX.NET file have common access to network data.

A private directory is used to store each user's unique configuration file, temporary Paradox objects like Answer and Changed tables, and instant scripts. This is also where Paradox performs table restructures and sorts.

Question — How does Paradox keep track of access to working and private directories?

Answer — A file called PARADOX.LCK is created in each user's private directory each time they start Paradox on the network. This lock file blocks other user's access to the tables and objects in that directory. When User2 tries to access

User1 data in User1's private directory, Paradox detects the PARADOX.LCK placed for User1 and doesn't allow User2 to access data.

In addition, another PARADOX.LCK file is created in the working directory. This file prevents users from making the working directory their own private directory.

Question **What are locks?**

Answer   Locks come in different varieties, each serving a specific purpose, but in general they are the mechanism used to ensure data integrity during concurrent use of Paradox objects. There are table locks, form locks, object locks, link locks, and many more. (We'll discuss locks in greater detail later.)

Question **Should my private directory be located on my local or network drive?**

Answer   That depends on the following issues:
- What type of network do you have?
- How fast is the transport of data (cabling)?
- How much local drive space do you have?
- How much network traffic exists?
- How many users does your network support?
- What are your response time requirements?

We'll explore the answers to most of these questions later in the chapter.

Before we proceed any further, let's review a general installation configuration.

Paradox Network Installation

Network installations vary from one type of LAN to another. Some networks are "true blue" (pun-intended) DOS networks. As such, they have a number of the same file limitations and quirks that single-user DOS stations experience. Other networks employ proprietary operating systems and file configurations that aren't shackled by DOS conventions. While these networks have their advantages, they have their special problems to deal with as well. Some networks deal with physical and logical drives and others only deal with one or the other.

No matter what the network, there is a conceptual view that networks should all share, whether they are physical implementations of the concepts or merely logical. These three components are integral to installing Paradox on a network:

- Placement and access to Paradox (.EXE, and so on)
- User configuration
- Common data and PARADOX.NET access

Paradox Programs

Paradox system files should be stored on a separate logical or physical drive from data and user directories. The Paradox system directory should have read-only privileges for all users except the network administrator.

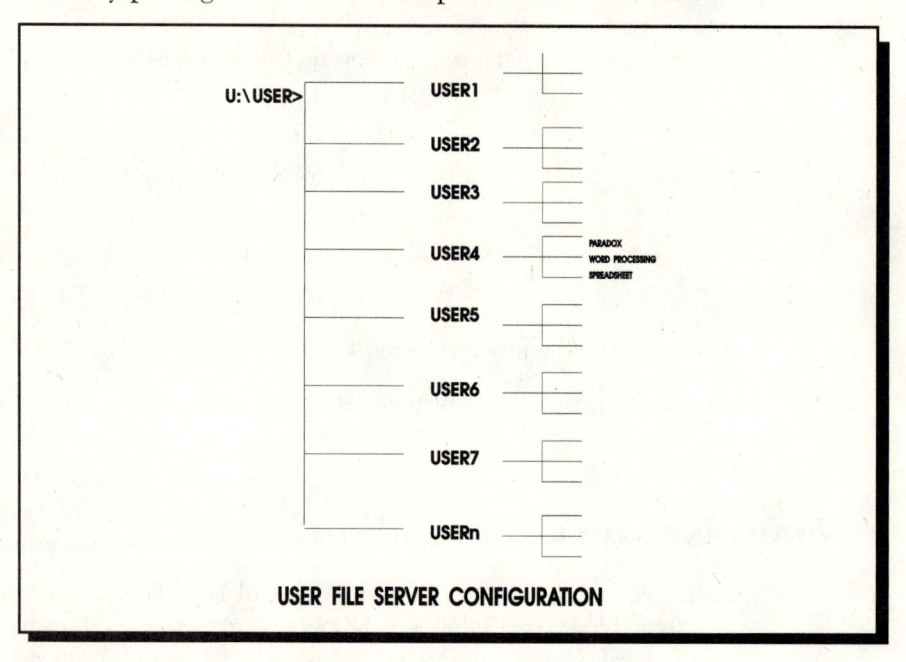

```
U:\USER>     USER1
             USER2
             USER3
             USER4 ── PARADOX
                      WORD PROCESSING
                      SPREADSHEET
             USER5
             USER6
             USER7
             USERn

        USER FILE SERVER CONFIGURATION
```

Figure 12-1 Where to store Paradox system files

Paradox Network Workstation Configuration

If possible, each workstation needs a local private directory and a network private directory. If you have both, store PARADOX.CFG in both private directories.

Even if you're going to use the user's local drive as their private directory, we recommend that the user start Paradox from the network first and then use *Menu {Tools} {Net} {Setprivate} private directory name* or SETPRIVDIR "\\directory name" to make the current directory one on the local drive. This strategy lets you control and update user's PARADOX.CFG files from the network. It also provides a pre-designated private directory for the user to switch to if their local drive doesn't have sufficient drive space to perform a particular operation (many-table query or large table restructure).

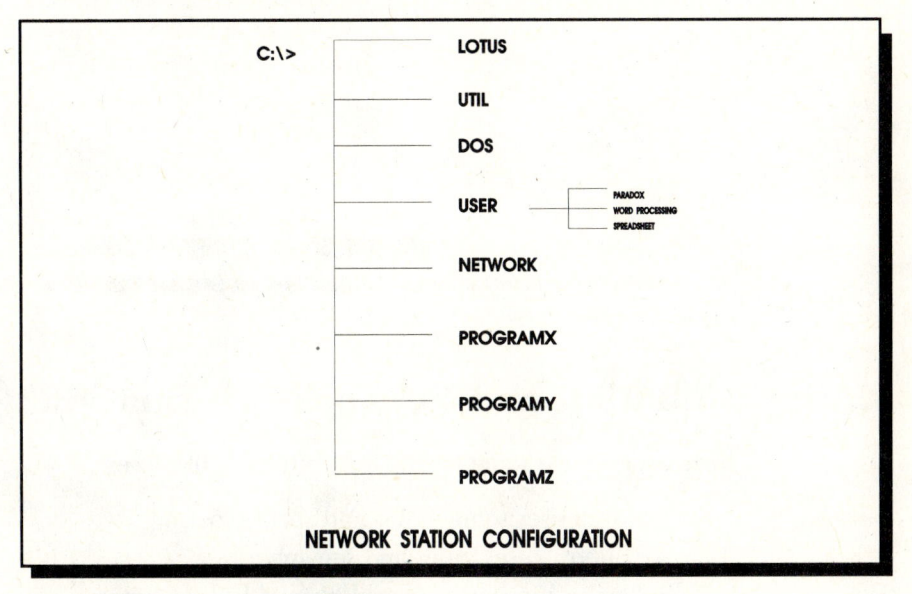

```
C:\>──┬── LOTUS
      │
      ├── UTIL
      │
      ├── DOS
      │
      ├── USER ──┬── PARADOX
      │          ├── WORD PROCESSING
      │          └── SPREADSHEET
      │
      ├── NETWORK
      │
      ├── PROGRAMX
      │
      ├── PROGRAMY
      │
      └── PROGRAMZ

       NETWORK STATION CONFIGURATION
```

Figure 12-2 Workstation configuration

The File Server

The file server should be configured so that there is a distinct and separate user area, with private directories for each network product. Rarely is Paradox the sole product being used on the network. Plan a sensible strategy for tracking and controlling network configurations and other product's temporary file needs by developing a network philosophy that can be used with any product.

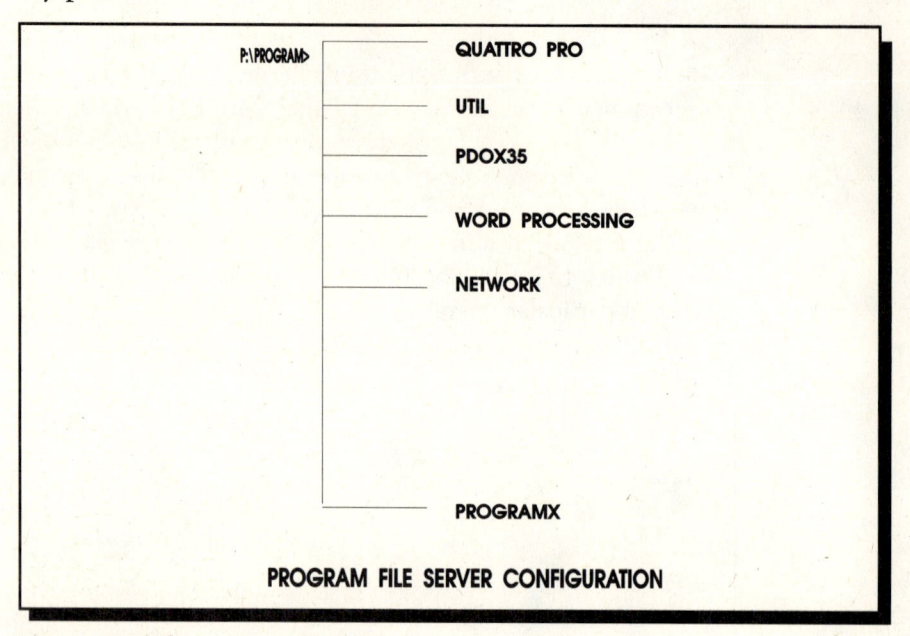

```
P:\PROGRAM>
              ┬──── QUATTRO PRO
              ├──── UTIL
              ├──── PDOX35
              ├──── WORD PROCESSING
              ├──── NETWORK
              │
              └──── PROGRAMX

       PROGRAM FILE SERVER CONFIGURATION
```

Figure 12-3 File server configuration

More Installation and Network Information

All networks have some facility for controlling file access.

- Novell uses semaphores and special locking
- MS-NET uses pipes and semaphores
- Banyan Vines uses special file and locking systems

Paradox makes little or no use of how a particular network handles locking.

DOS versions 3.1 and higher provide operating system level support for controlling file access. However, Paradox uses DOS file locking in only two cases:

- To control access to PARADOX.NET
- To control access to any *.LCK files

All lock files are really controlled by Paradox. DOS provides a sufficient, albeit crude, level of operating system support for manipulating simultaneous access to network files. This DOS capability makes it easier to run Paradox on a wide variety of networks.

> **NOTE:** *Paradox does not place physical locks on data.*

How Paradox Controls Access to Tables

Paradox controls access to tables in a multiuser environment by creating its own control files. These control files help Paradox keep track of what is going on while you're working with it. It does this by manipulating two types of files: PARADOX.NET and .LCK files.

PARADOX.NET

The PARADOX.NET file contains one entry for each user who is currently using Paradox. Each entry consists of:

- User name
- Product code (Paradox 3.5, 386, 2.x, and so on)
- Session number (arbitrary number set by Paradox to keep track of different users)
- Other special control information

When you first start Paradox, it tries to locate the PARADOX.NET file as designated by the PARADOX.SOM file. If the PARADOX.NET file is not present, Paradox creates one. Once Paradox has created the PARADOX.NET file, it stores the information for the first user accessing Paradox in PARADOX.NET. Paradox then adds any subsequent users as new entries to the PARADOX.NET file. As users exit Paradox, their PARADOX.NET entry is removed. When the last user exits Paradox, the PARADOX.NET file is not erased; it remains on disk, waiting for the next network user to start Paradox.

*.LCK files

*.LCK files have one entry for each user that has placed a *logical* lock on an object. When a *.LCK file is created, it records the location of

PARADOX.NET (the logical drive/path of PARADOX.NET). Each entry in the *.LCK file contains:

- User name (derived from PARADOX.NET)
- Session number (also from PARADOX.NET)
- Lock type (FullLock, WriteLock, RecordLock, FormLock, and so on)
- Other control information about the lock needed for Paradox to manipulate the object properly

*.LCK files come in two flavors:

- PARADOX.LCK
- Tablename.LCK (where tablename is the name of the table this file controls)

A PARADOX.LCK file is created in two places on the network for each user:

- The first place is in the working directory. A PARADOX.LCK file stored here tells any other Paradox user that they can't make that directory their private directory. The type of lock placed here is a Prevent Full Lock.
- The second place is in a private directory. Paradox places a Write Lock on this file so no one else can access the Paradox tables in your private directory.

NOTE: *Because Paradox must place a PARADOX.LCK file in each directory being accessed by a user, all users must have read/write/create access to any directories they need to access.*

When a Paradox user changes directories with either:

Menu {*Tools*} {*More*} {*Directory*}
{*Tools*} {*Net*} {*SetPrivate*}
SETDIR "\\dirname"
SETPRIVDIR "\\privname"

the PARADOX.LCK files in the old working and private directories are removed and new PARADOX.LCK files are stored in the new directories.

NOTE: *As users exit Paradox, the PARADOX.LCK files are removed (assuming users exit properly). If a user is thrown out of Paradox with an "unexpected condition" or other abnormal problem, the *.LCK files are not removed. You must remove these *.LCK prior to restarting Paradox in order to avoid future problems.*

Tablename.LCK is stored in the same directory as the table it controls. It records who is actively using which Paradox objects and what kind of lock they are applying.

Paradox discerns a shared from a non-shared drive and does not write *.LCK files to non-shared drives.

Paradox *.LCK lock types include:

- FL (Full Lock)
  Prevents other users from placing any type of lock on the table.
- WL (Write Lock)
  Prevents other users from placing a FL or PWL on the table.

NOTE: *Placing a WL on a table doesn't prevent other users from placing a WL on the same table.*

- RL (Record Lock)
  Prevents other uses from placing a RL on the record you are locking.

NOTE: *Placing a RL on any record in the table makes Paradox try and place a PWL on the table first. If the PWL fails, the RL is not attempted.*

- PFL (Prevent Full Lock)
  Prevents other users from placing a FL on a table.
- PWL (Prevent Write Lock)
  Prevents other users from placing a FL or WL on a table.
- FrmL (Form Lock)
  Prevents other users from placing a PWL on the table.

These *.LCK files can only be read and written to by Paradox. PAL and interactive Paradox have no direct access to the information contained in these files. You might think of these files as special Paradox tables.

How PARADOX.NET and *.LCK Files Interact

Each time an entry is written to a *.LCK file, the PARADOX.NET file is accessed. The user name, session number, and so on, are read from PARADOX.NET and written to a *.LCK file.

> **NOTE:** *You can't share the same table from two different Paradox sessions unless all users needing access to the table are logged into the same PARADOX.NET.*

PARADOX.NET Errors and Problems

When you see the message **Can't lock PARADOX.NET** you have probably run into one of the following problems.

- Your PARADOX.SOM (created by INSTALL or NUPDATE) points to a logical drive and directory that doesn't exist.
- Your PARADOX.SOM (created by INSTALL or NUPDATE) points to a logical drive and directory that exists, but you don't have sufficient rights to share, read, write, or create files in that directory.
- You have loaded a local-drive copy of Paradox and want to share data on the network but you haven't logged in yet.
- The first user into the system starts Paradox and then does a *Menu {Tools} {Net} {Setprivate} working directory* or SETPRIVDIR "\\working directory". This places a PARADOX.LCK such that no other user can access the working directory.

Following are a few tips for preventing these problems.

- Novell networks:

  Make sure that the drive letter for PARADOX.NET specified in PARADOX.SOM is mapped to the same disk volume name for each user.

  Be sure that the full path name for PARADOX.NET is stored in PARADOX.SOM.

  Ensure that each Paradox user has share/read/write/create rights in the directory where PARADOX.NET is stored.

- DOS-based networks (3Com, IBM PC LAN, and so on)

    Make sure the drive letter for PARADOX.NET specified in PARADOX.SOM is linked to the same disk volume and subdirectory for each network user.

    Ensure that only the drive letter for PARADOX.NET is stored in PARADOX.SOM.

    Ensure that each Paradox user has share/read/write/create rights in the directory where PARADOX.NET is stored.

Another error you might see is **R:\PDOXDATA controlled by .NET in U:\NETFILE** (your .NET is P:\NETFILE). This message appears when Paradox is trying to write to a PARADOX.LCK file (to secure your access to that directory) and finds a PARADOX.LCK file already there that points to a different logical drive and path than exists for you.

When this message appears, there are always two (or more) PARADOX.NET files in use.

REMEMBER: *Each PARADOX.NET file must have exclusive use of any directory in which it will be placing lock files.*

Following are some causes of this error.

- You have installed Paradox on a workstation and supplied PARADOX.SOM with the wrong location of PARADOX.NET.
- On 3Com or IBM PC LAN (where the location of the PARADOX.NET file is usually specified as just a drive letter), you have linked the wrong directory to the logical drive.

In either of these situations, Paradox creates PARADOX.NET in the directory it's told to use if it doesn't already find one there.

A somewhat similar problem occurs when two or more different PARADOX.NET files attempt to access the same directory. On many networks, such as 3Com and IBM PC LAN, you can link drive letters as symbolic names for directories.

For example, if H: is linked to PDOXDATA, a user doesn't necessarily know the path to PDOXDATA and neither does Paradox.

REMEMBER: *The PARADOX.NET network commandment:*

"When PARADOX.NET is using a directory, all others are locked out!"

On the DOS-based networks described earlier, this can't be enforced. In this scenario, two or more PARADOX.NET files think they have control of the same directory. The following situation then develops:

> Paradox User1 writes Tablename.LCK normally and then Paradox User2, using a different physical PARADOX.NET, tries to use the same table.
>
> Paradox sees Tablename.LCK and thinks it is obsolete (since none of its current users wrote the lock) so it deletes it. This results in:
>
> > **Unexpected condition** (missing Tablename.LCK for at least one of the users) or data corruption.

Paradox on Non-dedicated Servers

We generally recommend that you don't run Paradox on non-dedicated servers as a multiuser application. We think these systems should be used to exchange files rather than run database applications. Networks that support a non-dedicated server include:

- PC LAN
- Torus Tapestry
- LanLink
- InvisibleNet
- LanTastic
- Alloy's PC Salve
- 10-Net

Your application may run perfectly fine on these type of networks, so before you exclude them from your possible network choices, check out the difference between each and determine what your multiuser application will do. Set up a test with the dealer to see if your application will succeed or not.

> **NOTE:** *Novell Netware ELS I and II use the term non-dedicated. However, because of the proprietary nature of Novell NetWare and the particular way it maps drives, Paradox doesn't appear to have problems when running on Novell NetWare ELS.*

Common errors that occur when running Paradox as a multiuser application on non-dedicated servers are **Unexpected condition** errors and data corruption.

REMEMBER: *If you're using a non-dedicated sever you must start Paradox with:*

paradox -share

so that Paradox knows that what looks like a local drive is actually a shared drive. This helps alleviate some of these problems but doesn't eliminate numerous other non-dedicated server problems.

NOTE: *Using the -share command-line option tells Paradox to write *.LCK files when accessing tables from any drive.*

Automatic (Implicit) Locking versus Explicit Locking

A key issue in creating a multiuser application is developing a strategy for resolving simultaneous access to shared data. Here are some things you should keep in mind as you develop this strategy:

- Don't lock shared resources longer than required.
- Apply a "least lock" rule. That is, don't place a Full Lock on a table when a Prevent Full Lock will do.

Paradox performs numerous locking activities during normal operation. In general, Paradox applies the "least lock" rule. Even when Paradox places the minimum lock required to perform the requested task, it can still pose a dilemma for other Paradox users on the network. For a list of specific locks placed automatically, refer to Table 2-5 in the *Paradox User's Guide*.

Although Paradox provides automatic locking for each of its operations, you probably won't want to rely on automatic locking for your multiuser applications. Using explicit locks (using the LOCK command) lets you control the actions of your network applications in a more disciplined and predictable manner.

Editing/CoEditing Issues in the Multiuser Environment

Users can always edit tables that are stored in their private directory. A simple trick to temporarily place a table in your private directory is to rename it Entry*nnn* or copy it, naming the new file Entry*nnn*, where *nnn* is a number from 1 to 999. We suggest you start with 999 and count backwards in assigning file names. This will make it less likely that you'll accidentally interfere with a data entry Entry table created by Paradox itself. Remember, gaining exclusive rights to a table using this method actually removes the table from the working directory and moves it to your private directory. This method works with any temporary Paradox table name (Answer, Changed, Deleted, and so on), but is best suited for Entry*nnn*.

> **REMEMBER:** *The Answer, Changed, and Deleted tables are overwritten the next time an action demanding the resultant table is initiated.*

Editing Tables

While users can safely edit tables in their private directory, editing in the working directory places a full lock on the table and all family members. Attempting to edit while another user is already using the table or object results in a script error. Therefore, we recommend that you test the table to see if you have sufficient access rights before you need to edit it. You can do this with a simple:

```
While (true)
LOCK tablename FL
if retval = false then ; the lock failed
    beep
    @24,0 Clear EOL ?? "Table is in use by "+erroruser()
    sleep 1500
else
    EDIT tablename
    Wait Table
    Prompt "Press F2" when completed"
    Until "F2","Esc"
    lookretval = retval
    if lookretval = "F2" then
       Do_it!
    else
       CANCELEDIT
    endif
    endif
endif
quitloop
EndWhile
```

If the lock is successful (*retval*=true), then you can edit the table. If not, you get a message stating who's already using it.

CoEditing Tables

CoEdit lets more than one user access, add, update, and delete records in the working directory. It does this by automatically locking records when any change is made to a record. While User1 is updating a particular record, other users cannot access the record for editing.

> **NOTE:** *If User1 is merely viewing a record that User2 has locked, User1 sees the record as it existed before User2 began making changes. When User2 moves from the record, User1's view is refreshed (unless Refresh has been turned off for User1).*

CoEdit places an implicit Prevent Full Lock on a table. As a record is edited, a record lock is created. If User1 has started to edit record 5 and User2 attempts to edit the same record a moment later, User2 is sent a message:

Record in use by User1

Once User1 moves from record 5, User2 can then attempt to make changes (after the refresh has occurred).

Handling Key Values

Network users shouldn't be allowed to change key values unless you take special precautions to ensure that you don't lose records when a key violation occurs. Listing 12-1 shows an approach to handle this problem:

```
tablename = "Parts"
formno = "2"
keyf="part number"
CoEdit tablname
While (true)
   Wait table
   Prompt "Ins-Add, F2-End CoEdit"
   Until "Ins","F2", "Del"
   lookretval=retval
   if lookretval = "Ins" then
      keypress -82
      pickform formno
      moveto field keyf
      retval = ""
      While retval <> "F2"
         Wait Field
         Prompt "Enter new PART Number, ... press ENTER"
```

Listing 12-1 Handling key values

```
                Until "Enter","Esc","Lockkey"
            msg = ""
;This section trys to lock the new value in the table
;If it is successful it continues to allow you to enter
;the other record information, otherwise it removes the key
;violation problem with the []=[] and loops
            if retval = "Enter" and NOT isblank([]) then
                LOCKRECORD
                   if retval = false then
                        beep
                        []=[]
                        message "ID already assigned"
                        loop
                    endif
                ImageRights UPDATE
                Enter
                Wait Record
                Prompt "Add other part info"
                Until "F2"
            endif
        Quitloop
        EndWhile
        loop
    endif
    if lookretval = "Del" then
        LOCKRECORD
        if retval = false then
             beep
             mesage "Record in use by",erroruser()
             sleep 1000
             loop
        else
            SHOWMENU
                "Yes":"Delete the record",
                "No": "Don't delete the record"
            to del_sel
            Switch
                case sel = "Yes": kepyress -83
                case sel = "No" : UNLOCKRECORD
            EndSwitch
            release vars del_sel
            loop
        endif
    endif
    if retval = "F2" then
        Do_it!
    endif
quitloop
EndWhile
```

Listing 12-1 Handling key values—continued

The special []=[] technique to let you exit key violation mode can actually be done two additional ways:

1. COPYTOARRAY temp (store the current information to memory)
2. Del (delete the attempted insert)
3. Ins (try it again)
4. COPYFROMARRAY temp (restore the information from memory)

or,

1. COPYTOARRAY temp
2. COPYFROMARRAY temp

Form Lock Theory versus Reality

The Paradox manuals tell us that Paradox places a special lock on each of the tables involved in certain types of multitable form edit operations. This special lock (a Form Lock) is in place during the CoEdit of one-to-many and one-to-one table relationships. Paradox's purpose for this lock is to protect data integrity.

In reality, the Form Lock is a shortcut that Paradox takes to avoid the potential problem of corrupting the referential integrity of the detailed data involved. Paradox has no other way to protect the detail records so it uses the Form Lock.

Physically, a Form Lock's entry in the *.LCK file is different than any other lock. This type of lock blocks the use of any form other than the embedded form being used in the current master table to edit the detail table's records. This is a considerable restriction to avoid. The following sections describe some workarounds.

Form Lock Workaround #1: Shadow Keys and Tables

The first workaround involves creating a shadow key. The shadow key is placed somewhere in the table (usually at the end) and links the master and detail tables as a group rather than as a one-to-many relationship. This removes the Form Lock problem. The problem with this method is that you must build in a mechanism to update the shadow key [Keyfield] = [shadow key field] in order to maintain integrity.

```
; part editing script
CoEdit "part"
msg.text = ""
WHILE true
   CtrlHome Right      ; move to first field in table view
   ImageRights READONLY
   WAIT TABLE
      PROMPT FORMAT("AL,W6",UserName())+"  F9: Edit partdesc info ;Esc: Leave"
      MESSAGE msg.text
   UNTIL "F9","Esc"
   ImageRights
   msg.text = ""
   SWITCH
      CASE RETVAL = "F9"  :
         PICKFORM "2"    ; go to the multi-table form
         LockRecord
         IF RETVAL = false THEN
            BEEP
            msg.text = "Record is in use by "+UserName()
         ELSE
            MOVETO "partdesc" ; moveto the detail table
            WAIT TABLE
               PROMPT "Make changes, additions and deletions; Press F2 when done"
            UNTIL "F2"
            UnLockRecord
            UnLockRecord              ; destroy key violations
            IF NImageRecords() = 1 AND
               IsBlank([date]) THEN ; there is only one, blank rec in table
               DEL
            ENDIF
            MOVETO "part"          ; go up to the master table
            UnLockRecord            ; unlock the master record
         ENDIF
         FormKey           ; back to table view

      CASE RETVAL = "Esc" :
         QUITLOOP

   ENDSWITCH
ENDWHILE
Do_It!
ClearAll
RELEASE VARS msg.text
```

Listing 12-2 *Form lock workaround #1: Shadow keys and tables*

Shadow Key Workaround #2

The principle of this next solution is to link the detail table to a shadow table, one record at a time. The shadow table is an unkeyed, one-record-at-a-time copy of the master table. As you need to process a record in the master table, you select it and then transfer the information to the shadow table. Special caution is taken so that the user can't change the key once in the shadow table. The advantage of this solution is that Paradox doesn't apply a Form Lock and no extra fields are required (as they are in workaround #1).

```
; part editing script
VIEW "partdesc"
CoEdit "part"
msg.text = ""
WHILE true
   CtrlHome Right      ; move to first field in table view
   FirstShow
   ImageRights READONLY
   WAIT TABLE
      PROMPT FORMAT("AL,W6",UserName())+" F9: Edit part info ;Ins: Add new part",
      "          Esc: Leave            ;    Del: Delete part"
      MESSAGE msg.text
   UNTIL "F9","Ins","Del","Esc","Lockkey"
   ImageRights
   msg.text = ""
   SWITCH
      CASE RETVAL = "F9" :
         LockRecord
         IF RETVAL = false THEN
            BEEP
            msg.text = "Record is in use by "+UserName()
         ELSE
            PICKFORM "1"
            ImageRights UPDATE
            WAIT RECORD
               PROMPT "Make changes, Press F2 when done"
            UNTIL "F2"
            UnLockRecord
            FormKey           ; back to table view
         ENDIF
      CASE RETVAL = "Ins" :
         Ins
         PICKFORM "1"
         MOVETO FIELD "PART ID"
         msg.text = ""
         WHILE true
            WAIT FIELD
               PROMPT "Enter new ID, then press Enter",
               "Press Esc to return"
               MESSAGE msg.text
            UNTIL "Enter","Esc","LockKey"
            msg.text = ""
            IF RETVAL = "Enter" AND NOT IsBlank([]) THEN
               LockRecord
               IF RETVAL = false THEN
```

Listing 12-3 Shadow key workaround #2

```
                    BEEP
                    [] = []  ; assign the key field to itself, leave KeyViol mode
                    msg.text = "That ID is already in use - use another"
                    LOOP
                ENDIF
                ImageRights UPDATE
                Enter    ; execute the Enter operation, bring user to 2nd field
                WAIT RECORD
                    PROMPT "Add complete record, Press F2 when done"
                UNTIL "F2"
                LockRecord      ; post the record to the table, then lock it
                UnLockRecord    ; unlock the record
            ELSE; Esc was pressed, or ID was not filled in
                DEL     ; un-insert the record - "close up the row"
            ENDIF
            FormKey     ; back to table view
            QUITLOOP
        ENDWHILE
     CASE RETVAL = "Del" :
        LockRecord ; lock the record in preparation to delete it
        IF RETVAL = false THEN
            BEEP
            msg.text = "Record is in use by "+UserName()
            UnLockRecord
        ELSE
            part.id = [PART ID]
            MOVETO "PARTDESC" ; moveto detail table (it's in TableView)
            MOVETO FIELD "PART ID"
            LOCATE part.id       ; see if there are any detail records
            MOVETO "PART" ; move back to table being edited
            IF RETVAL = true THEN
                BEEP
                msg.text = "Cannot delete part record - PARTDESC still exist"
                UnLockRecord
            ELSE
                SHOWMENU
                "Oops!":"Do not delete the record",
                "Delete":"Delete the record"
                TO delete.ok
                IF delete.ok = "Delete" THEN
                    DEL
                    msg.text = "Record deleted - Press Ctrl-U to get it back"
                ELSE; user did not want to delete
                    UnLockRecord
                ENDIF
            ENDIF
        ENDIF
     CASE RETVAL = "Esc" :
        QUITLOOP
   ENDSWITCH
ENDWHILE
Do_It!
ClearAll
RELEASE VARS msg.txt, delete.ok, part.id
```

Listing 12-3 Shadow key workaround #2—continued

> **NOTE:** *A special script that builds a shadow table configuration is included on disk with this book.*

A Special Network Problem

Developing system-assigned keys like invoice numbers, purchase order numbers, or any unique identifiers for records poses a particular type of problem. How do you ensure that the next number you assign will be correct? The problem is more complex when you look at it from the requirement where the assignment takes place after you post the record instead of before. The following scripts (Listings 12-4 and 12-5) address this problem.

```
; EntrData
PROC UnlockEmpID()
  PRIVATE empid
     moveto "Empid"
;     lockrecord
;     while retval = False
;        sleep 50
;        lockrecord
;     endwhile
     empid = [Next Emp ID]
     [Next Emp ID] = empid + 1
     unlockrecord
     moveto "Employee"
;     UNLOCK "empid" WL, "Empid" PWL
     UNLOCK ALL
ENDPROC
PROC LockEmpID()
  WHILE True
     LOCK "Empid" WL, "Empid" PWL
     IF retval THEN
        RETURN
     ENDIF
     SLEEP 200
  ENDWHILE
ENDPROC
CLEAR
CURSOR OFF               ;  Place informational message
MESSAGE "Loading form, Please wait"   ; on the screen while form is
CANVAS OFF                   ; loading
MENU {Modify} {CoEdit} {Employee}   ; ID.
END DOWN
{Image} {Pickform} {1}
CANVAS ON                ;  Need to turn canvas on!
WHILE True
   WAIT RECORD
      PROMPT "Enter New Employee Information    [F2]-Save/Exit    [Esc]-Cancel",
            "[F3]-Employee Data    [F4]-Benefits Data      " +
```

Listing 12-4 System-assigning keys method #1: After the record is posted

```
            "[F5]-Dependents Data"
     UNTIL "F2","F3","F4","F5","Esc","PgDn","PgUp"
tblname = TABLE()
SWITCH
   CASE retval = "F2" :
         CLEAR
         MESSAGE "Saving data, Please wait"
         CANVAS OFF
         IF ISBLANK([Employee ID]) THEN     ;  If this is a new record
            LockEmpID()
            REFRESH
            [Employee ID] = [Empid->Next Emp ID]
            UnlockEmpID()
         ENDIF
         DO_IT!                             ;  NOTE: need to check for
         QUITLOOP                           ;  key violations in Depndnts
   CASE retval = "F3" : MOVETO "Employee"   ;  Moveto Employee Table
   CASE retval = "F4" : MOVETO "Benefits"   ;  Moveto Benefits Table
   CASE retval = "F5" : MOVETO "Depndnts"   ;  Moveto Depndnts Table
   CASE retval = "Esc" :
         SHOWMENU
             "No"  : "Return to Data Entry",
             "Yes" : "Cancel data entry"
         TO cancELoption
         IF canceloption = "Yes" THEN
            CLEAR
            MESSAGE "Data Entry cancelled"
            CANVAS OFF
  ;         CANCELEDIT
            DO_IT!
            QUITLOOP
         ENDIF
     CASE retval = "PgDn" :
         SWITCH
            CASE tblname = "Employee" :
                  IF ISBLANK([Employee ID]) THEN   ;  If this is a new record
                     LockEmpID()
                     REFRESH
                     [Employee ID] = [Empid->Next Emp ID]
                     UnlockEmpID()
                  ENDIF
                  PgDn       ;  Moveto next Employee rcd
            CASE tblname = "Benefits" : ; Only 1 record allowed for BEEP LOOP
                                                 ; Benefits table
            CASE tblname = "Depndnts" :       ;  Moveto next record in
                  DOWN CtrlHome               ;  Depndnts table
         ENDSWITCH
     CASE retval = "PgUp" :
         SWITCH
            CASE tblname = "Employee" :
                     IF ISBLANK([Employee ID]) THEN   ;  If this is a new record
                        LockEmpID()
                        REFRESH
```

Listing 12-4 System-assigning keys method #1: After the record is posted—continued

```
                    [Employee ID] = [Empid->Next Emp ID]
                    UnlockEmpID()
                 ENDIF
                 SKIP -1                        ; Moveto prev Employee rcd
           CASE tblname = "Benefits" :          ; Only 1 record allowed for
              BEEP LOOP                         ; Benefits table
           CASE tblname = "Depndnts" :          ; Moveto next record in
              SKIP -1                           ; Depndnts table
         ENDSWITCH
     OTHERWISE:
        KEYPRESS retval
   ENDSWITCH
ENDWHILE
CLEARALL
```

Listing 12-4 *System-assigning keys method #1: After the record is posted—continued*

System-Assigned Keys Method #2

This next method assigns the key prior to posting the record.

```
; EntrData
PROC GetEmpID()
 PRIVATE id
    moveto "Empid"
    lockrecord
    while retval = False
       sleep 50
       lockrecord
    endwhile
    id = [Next Emp ID]
    [Next Emp ID] = id + 1
    unlockrecord
    moveto "Employee"
    RETURN id
;    UNLOCK "empid" WL, "Empid" PWL
;    UNLOCK ALL
ENDPROC
PROC LockEmpID()
  WHILE True
    LOCK "Empid" WL, "Empid" PWL
    IF retval THEN
      RETURN
    ENDIF
    SLEEP 200
  ENDWHILE
ENDPROC
```

Listing 12-5 *System-assigned keys method #2*

```
PROC Autonum2()
CLEAR
CURSOR OFF                                       ;  Place informational message
MESSAGE "Loading form, Please wait"              ; on the screen while form is
CANVAS OFF                                       ; loading
MENU {Modify} {CoEdit} {Employee}                ; ID.
{Image} {Pickform} {1}
empid = GetEmpID()
INS
[Employee ID] = empid
CANVAS ON                                        ; Need to turn canvas on!
WHILE True
  WAIT RECORD
    PROMPT "Enter New Employee Information    [F2]-Save/Exit    [Esc]-Cancel",
           "[F3]-Employee Data    [F4]-Benefits Data    " +
           "[F5]-Dependents Data"
    UNTIL "F2","F3","F4","F5","Esc","PgDn","PgUp"
  tblname = TABLE()
  SWITCH
    CASE retval = "F2" :
         CLEAR
         MESSAGE "Saving data, Please wait"
         CANVAS OFF
         DO_IT!                                  ; NOTE: need to check for
         QUITLOOP                                ; key violations in Depndnts
    CASE retval = "F3" : MOVETO "Employee"       ; Moveto Employee Table
    CASE retval = "F4" : MOVETO "Benefits"       ; Moveto Benefits Table
    CASE retval = "F5" : MOVETO "Depndnts"       ; Moveto Depndnts Table
    CASE retval = "Esc" :
         SHOWMENU
            "No"  : "Return to Data Entry",
            "Yes" : "Cancel data entry"
         TO canceloption
         IF canceloption = "Yes" THEN
           CLEAR
           MESSAGE "Data Entry cancelled"
           CANVAS OFF
;          CANCELEDIT
           DO_IT!
           QUITLOOP
         ENDIF
    CASE retval = "PgDn" :
         SWITCH
           CASE tblname = "Employee" :
                LOCKRECORD
                UNLOCKRECORD
                IF ATLAST() THEN
                  empid = GetEmpID()
                  INS
                  [Employee ID] = empid
                ELSE
                  PgDn                           ; Moveto next Employee rcd
```

Listing 12-5 System-assigned keys method #2—continued

```
                    ENDIF
            CASE tblname = "Benefits" :        ;  Only 1 record allowed for
                BEEP LOOP                      ;  Benefits table
            CASE tblname = "Depndnts" :        ;  Moveto next record in
                DOWN CtrlHome                  ;  Depndnts table
          ENDSWITCH
      CASE retval = "PgUp" :
        SWITCH
            CASE tblname = "Employee" :
                LOCKRECORD
                UNLOCKRECORD
                SKIP -1                        ;  Moveto prev Employee rcd
            CASE tblname = "Benefits" :        ;  Only 1 record allowed for
                BEEP LOOP                      ;  Benefits table
            CASE tblname = "Depndnts" :        ;  Moveto next record in
                SKIP -1                        ;  Depndnts table
          ENDSWITCH
      OTHERWISE:
          KEYPRESS retval
    ENDSWITCH
ENDWHILE
CLEARALL
ENDPROC
Autonum2()
```

Listing 12-5 System-assigned keys method #2—continued

All in all, automatically assigning keys is no trivial task.

Summary

In this chapter we delved into the nuances of running Paradox in a multiuser environment. The shadow table approach is highly recommended when dealing with data integrity and concurrency in a multiuser application. The particular method that is right for your application depends on how your users need to access their information.

To enhance your network's performance, don't step around the problem—be willing to throw some money at it. Network workstations need at least 2-4MB of RAM as well as 40MB of storage (more if you can swing it). Look into setting up RAM disks to copy Paradox and your application files. Above all, set up stress tests to determine if the application will perform satisfactorily—before you install it, not after!

The next chapter takes a look at one of the exciting new features of Paradox 3.5: SQL Link. This connectivity feature has opened up a whole new world of data access to the Paradox user.

13 Using Paradox SQL Link

SQL database servers introduce a new environment to PC application developers. Database servers based on Structured Query Language (SQL) provide a structured approach to accessing data outside the local product. These database servers are the core of client/server architecture, one of the latest trends in the computing industry.

Paradox SQL Link is Borland's offering for this new world. SQL Link expands the capability of Paradox so you can access SQL databases within a Paradox application. You can now tap the power of these SQL database products and gain improved performance and transaction capabilities not currently available in Paradox. As you will see, SQL Link enhances applications currently written in Paradox—it doesn't replace the current Paradox architecture.

This chapter serves as an introduction to SQL Link. A detailed discussion of programming in SQL, client/server architecture, and Paradox SQL Link are beyond what we can cover in one chapter of a book. Following is a list of what we feel are important introductory concepts.

- An introduction to client/server architecture
- Some of the advantages and disadvantages of this architecture
- Overview of SQL Link
- Installing SQL Link
- How to connect to a database server
- Using the new and modified menu selections with SQL Link
- Review of the type of SQL statements Paradox's QBE generates
- Brief explanation of new and enhanced commands and functions

- Description of two new utilities, the SQL Setup Program and the SQL Command Editor
- A few code examples using the new features
- A subset of the SQL Link READSQL file

There are many new terms and concepts that you need to understand before entrenching yourself in this new architecture. Table 13-1 lists many of these that are used or explained in this chapter. As this technology grows and more users experiment with it, the features and capabilities of the environment will also grow. If you are new to SQL databases, some of the concepts discussed will be unfamiliar. If you have been using Paradox for any length of time, you'll notice the sound SQL foundation upon which Paradox is built.

Table 13-1
Key terms and concepts in this chapter

Client/server architecture	Transaction processing	Security
Structured Query Language	Commit	GRANT/REVOKE
SQL	Rollback	Database Administrator
Front-end	Unit of work	Access privileges
Back-end	Local table	User name
Data Control Language	Remote table	Host
Data Definition Language	Replica table	Database name
Data Manipulation Language	Server connection	Server messages
File servers	SQL cursors	SQL dialect
Print servers	FETCH	
Database servers	Pending query	

An Introduction to Client/Server Architecture

Client/server architecture has two major elements, a server component and a client component. A server is a computer that provides processing and services to other computers. These machines can be mainframes, minis, or personal computers. A client is a workstation accessing the server over a network. The main task of the server is to provide access to the data and control the database. The storage of the data, as well as security, integrity, dictionary and catalog maintenance, query optimization, logging and recovery, and locking are the responsibility of the database server. The client provides the interface to the server. Forms design, querying, reporting, and graphing are all done at the workstation.

Sometimes the terms front end and back end are used in describing client/server architecture. A client is more than a workstation accessing information on another machine. It also has the tools to work with a server in addition to processing data in its own format.

Client/server architecture attempts to provide the best of both worlds, a mix of mainframe and mini strengths (performance, data centralization, integrity, and security) with the workstation's ease-of-use, tools, and low cost. The objective is to use the best component for the task. The server has the power, the client the intelligent interface.

SQL is the foundation that client/server architecture is built upon. SQL provides a language to create, manipulate, and access data. It is becoming the industry standard for relational databases. An unfortunate problem with SQL as a standard is each database management system uses a different dialect. This makes portability and communication between different vendor offerings a problem. SQL statements must be translated from one dialect to another. There is at least some commonality between the products, so this still makes SQL an attractive and viable offering.

A database server differs from a file server. Figure 13-1 shows a file server environment and what occurs when a Paradox query uses a table stored on the server. All processing is performed on the local workstation. Think of the file server as an extension to the hard disk on the workstation. Each record from the table must be shipped across the network so the local CPU can determine if the record is included in the result of the query. This increases the amount of network traffic and doesn't use the power of the file server's CPU.

A database server uses the processing power of the server machine. All database processing is performed on the database server. Data validation, security administration, transaction processing, query optimization, data reduction, and so forth are performed on the database server. Contrast the file-server picture to that of a database server in Figure 13-2. When Paradox SQL Link requests data from a database server, the SQL statement is sent to the server and only the data satisfying the request is returned. This reduces the amount of network traffic and makes it cost effective to have a 386 or 486 as a server. You still use the local machine to format the data.

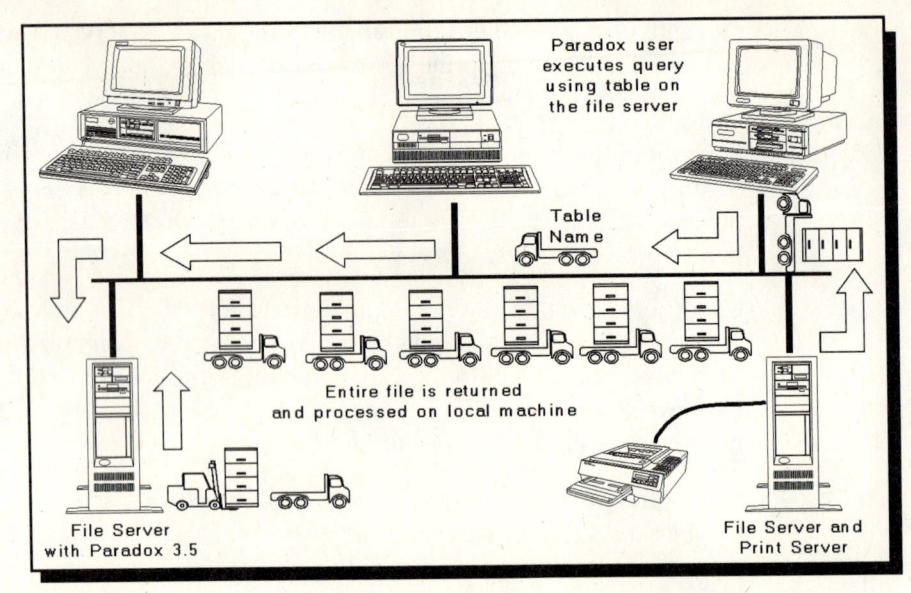

Figure 13-1 File server technology

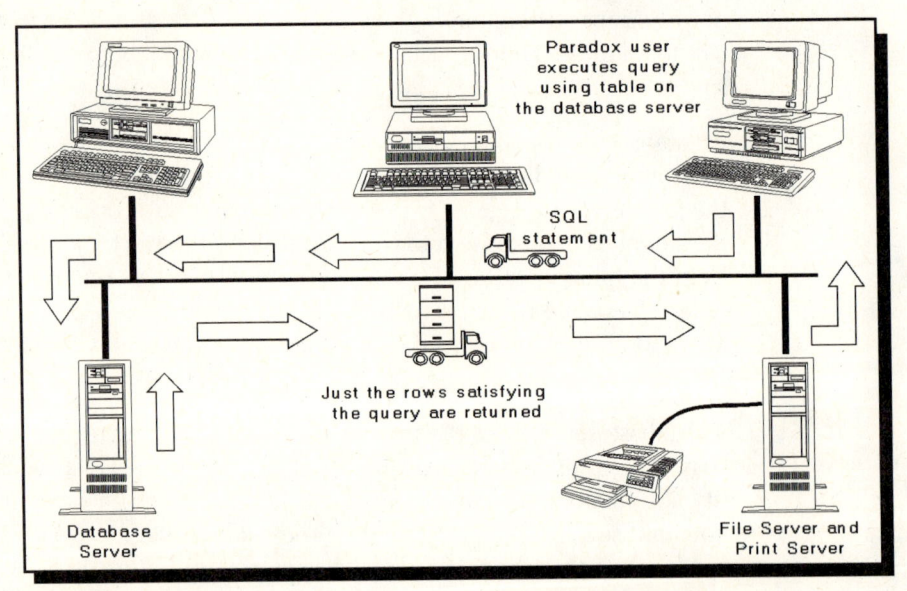

Figure 13-2 Database server technology

All of this sounds good doesn't it? Well, like everything else, there are advantages and disadvantages to a client/server architecture.

Advantages

- Eliminates the need to re-key or import mainframe/mini data.
- Eliminates data redundancy.
- Reduces network traffic.
- Improves the security and integrity of the data with centralized control.
- Expands capacity and improves performance.
- Provides greater data accessibility, both locally and across multiple vendor solutions.
- Provides transaction processing.
- Expands available data types.
- Provides data dictionary and system cataloging.
- Enhances backup and recovery.
- Reduces cost.
- Builds on familiarity with current workstation tools/products.
- Retains current investment in time, resources, and training.

Disadvantages

- The integration of enterprise-wide data is not as seamless as vendors imply.
- SQL is not the same in every DBMS, different dialects require at least minimal modification. SQL is also not a panacea for all ills. It has problems and can't do everything. If it did, it probably wouldn't need so many dialects and extensions!
- Database administration is a must. Modifying the structure of a table is not as simple as {*Modify*} {*Restructure*}. Backup, recovery, and logging maintenance must be managed on a set schedule.
- Client products don't map 100% to the data types supported by the servers. You're limited by the data type support provided by the client product. For example, Paradox doesn't support the long text and image data types of server products.
- Many features available in client products are not available when you're using server data. The TableLookup feature in Paradox is one example of this. When working with a remote table (one stored on a server), you cannot press [F1] on a field and browse through a table of possible values.

Implementing client/server architecture requires changes not only in application development but also in how you think about developing applications. SQL is a transaction-oriented environment, Paradox is not. The nice thing about most of the SQL database offerings today is that they support both decision-support applications and transaction-oriented applications. SQL Link offers you the choice as to which pieces to develop on the server and which pieces to leave to Paradox.

SQL Link Feature Overview

Paradox SQL Link works transparently with Paradox 3.5 to connect Paradox to multiple SQL database servers. SQL Link release 1.0 provides access to three SQL database servers:

- Oracle Server version 6.0
- Microsoft SQL Server version 1.0 and 1.1
- IBM OS/2 Extended Edition Database Manager version 1.2

SQL Link lets you work with Paradox tables, called local tables, and data stored on the database server, called remote tables. To provide the same type of access to remote tables that you have for local tables, Paradox uses a replica table. Replica tables do not store any data, they are used solely to inform Paradox of the structure of the remote table. Forms and reports for the remote table are attached to their replica tables. Replicas are treated like Paradox tables for the actions SQL Link supports on remote tables.

You don't have to know SQL to use SQL Link. You create queries and execute them using QBE. Paradox converts the query into the proper SQL dialect for the server you are connected to and transmits the SQL statement. The data satisfying the query is returned and placed in an Answer table (the same as queries using Paradox tables). You cannot perform all Paradox operations on remote tables, but you can perform the following in addition to querying:

- Create, delete and empty tables
- Design forms and reports (on a single table only)
- Add data using {*Tools*} {*More*} {*Add*}
- Copy a table, to or from the database server
- Perform data entry
- Embed SQL statements in a PAL program

Full security is available at both the Paradox level and the database server level. Transaction commit and rollback is implemented. A new menu choice {*SQL*} has been added to the {*Tools*} menu, providing interactive access to these features. Many new PAL commands and functions provide the same functionality as the menu choices, as well as other SQL capabilities.

Any menu choice that displays a list of tables indicates a table is remote by placing the database server name on the first line of the screen. Figure 13-3 shows an example.

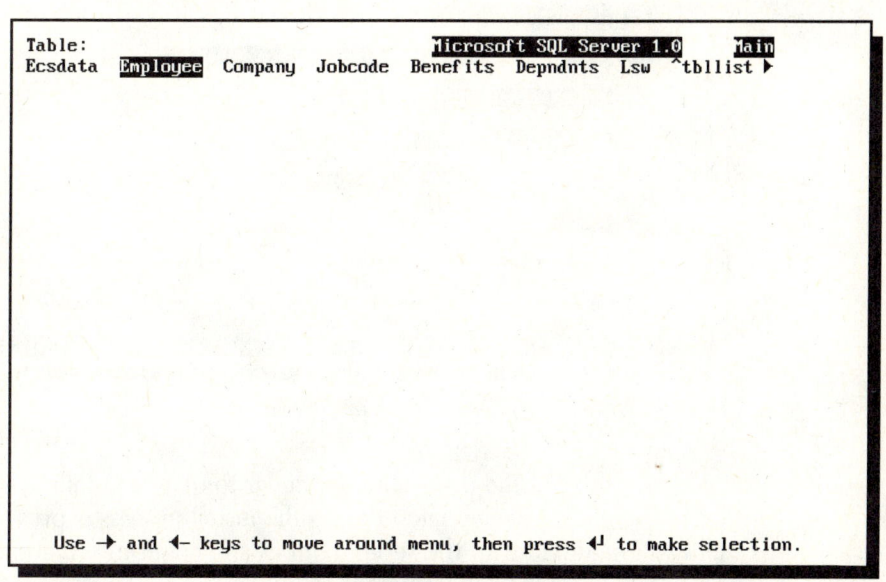

```
Table:                           Microsoft SQL Server 1.0      Main
Ecsdata  Employee  Company  Jobcode  Benefits  Depndnts  Lsw  ^tbllist ▶




















      Use → and ← keys to move around menu, then press ↵ to make selection.
```

Figure 13-3 Remote table highlighted example

Installation

Like Paradox 3.5, SQL Link has an installation program that guides you through the setup procedure. With the SQL Link Installation Disk in drive A, enter

>**A:SQLINST**

The installation options are displayed next, as shown in Figure 13-4. You can install one or all of the products. Once a product is chosen, you are prompted for a source drive (where to copy the SQL Link program from) and the destination drive (where to copy the program to). You must install SQL Link in the same directory where you installed Paradox 3.5. Make sure the destination drive you enter is where Paradox 3.5 is installed.

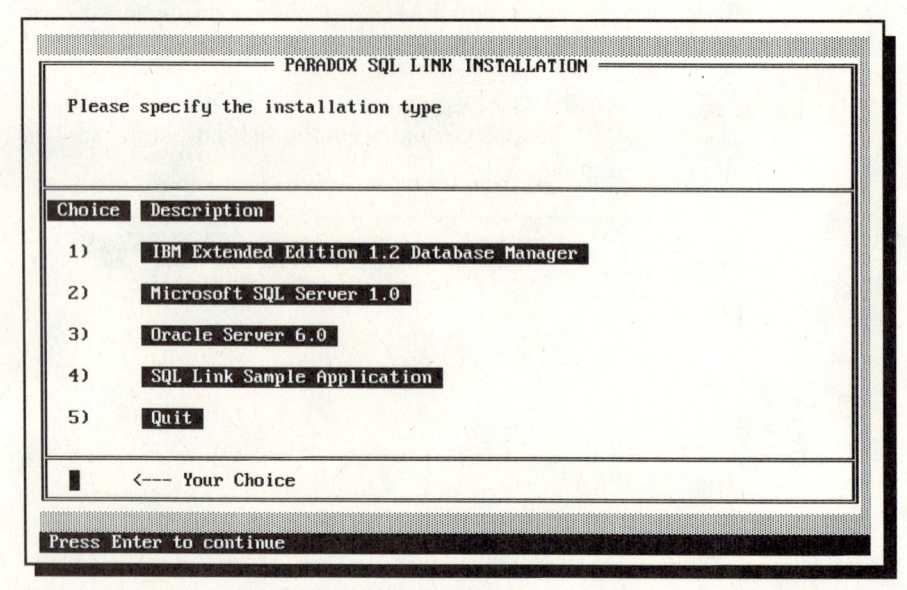

```
╔══════════════════════════════════════════════════════════════════╗
║  ┌──────────────── PARADOX SQL LINK INSTALLATION ──────────────┐ ║
║  │ Please specify the installation type                         │ ║
║  │                                                              │ ║
║  │                                                              │ ║
║  │ ┌────────┬─────────────────────────────────────────────────┐ │ ║
║  │ │ Choice │ Description                                     │ │ ║
║  │ │   1)   │ IBM Extended Edition 1.2 Database Manager       │ │ ║
║  │ │   2)   │ Microsoft SQL Server 1.0                        │ │ ║
║  │ │   3)   │ Oracle Server 6.0                               │ │ ║
║  │ │   4)   │ SQL Link Sample Application                     │ │ ║
║  │ │   5)   │ Quit                                            │ │ ║
║  │ └────────┴─────────────────────────────────────────────────┘ │ ║
║  │ ▌    <--- Your Choice                                        │ ║
║  └──────────────────────────────────────────────────────────────┘ ║
║ Press Enter to continue                                            ║
╚══════════════════════════════════════════════════════════════════╝
```

Figure 13-4 SQL Link installation options screen

The remainder of the installation is similar to that of installing Paradox. A list of the .SOM files updated during the install process is presented. These files will modified with the serial number and count information from SQL Link. You enter the serial number found on the 5.25-inch disk. The remaining screen prompts differ depending on the media size you are using to install SQL Link. The SQL Setup Program and UseSQL utility (discussed later in this chapter) are also installed with the system files. When this process is finished, the product installation screen is re-displayed. At this point you can install the files to support another server, the sample application, or quit. If you want to install the option to access all three database servers, you have to select each one individually and follow the prompts.

If you're working in a network environment, you only need to purchase a single copy of SQL Link and install it on the file server. Any Paradox session started using the system files from the file server has SQL Link capabilities. Each Paradox user reduces the number of available user counts by one.

With SQL Link, you use an additional user count when a connection is made to a database server. SQL Link comes with one user count. The serial number should be added to those in the .SOM file for Paradox. For individual workstations, a separate copy of SQL Link is necessary. Add user counts with the Paradox Multi-Pack (increments of 5), or additional Paradox 3.5 or SQL Link purchases (increments of 1).

There are a few more things you should do before you start SQL Link. The first thing is to read the READSQL file on the installation disk. It contains important information on SQL Link, the servers, and corrections to the documentation. Print a copy of the file and attach it to your *SQL Link User's Guide*, it's a useful reference. Depending on the server(s) you connect to, you're required to load additional software. For instance, SQL Server needs a Named Pipes TSR loaded, Oracle requires you have the correct SQL*Net driver loaded, and IBM EE requires a couple of steps before you connect (these are covered in the READSQL file and printed towards the end of this chapter).

Interactive Access Connecting to a Server

Accessing data on a SQL database server requires you to connect to the server before Paradox can process your request. Figure 13-5 shows the connection screen (with the software to access all three servers loaded) from which you select the product to connect to. This screen varies depending on which of the SQL database server connections have been installed, and the customized connection options added using the SQL Setup Program. The server connection screen is activated by selecting {*Tools*} {*SQL*} {*Connection*} {*Select*}.

Once the type of server is selected, you must provide the appropriate connection information. Each server product has different requirements. Figures 13-6 through 13-8 show the screens for each of the three server products. Appendix A of this book also lists the connection parameters for each server. The user name and password are common among the three product offerings.

Figure 13-9 shows an example of connecting to Microsoft SQL Server. Once the connection is made, data on the server is available for manipulation.

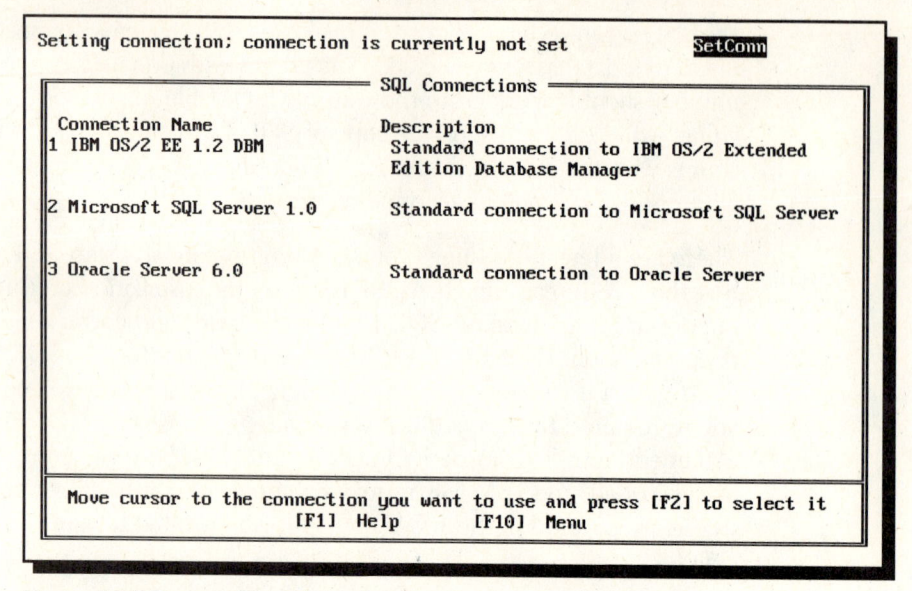

```
Setting connection; connection is currently not set          SetConn
                      ═══ SQL Connections ═══
   Connection Name              Description
   1 IBM OS/2 EE 1.2 DBM         Standard connection to IBM OS/2 Extended
                                 Edition Database Manager

   2 Microsoft SQL Server 1.0    Standard connection to Microsoft SQL Server

   3 Oracle Server 6.0           Standard connection to Oracle Server




   Move cursor to the connection you want to use and press [F2] to select it
                    [F1]  Help        [F10]  Menu
```

Figure 13-5 Server connection selection screen

```
Setting parameters for: IBM OS/2 EE 1.2 DBM                  SetConn
                    ═══ SQL Connection Parameters ═══
   Parameter                    Value
   Remote User Name

   Remote Password

   Server

   Database

   Library Directory             c:






                    [F2]  DO-IT!   [F10]  Menu
              [Esc]  Return to the SQL Connections screen
```

Figure 13-6 IBM server connection parameter screen

Using Paradox SQL Link

```
Setting parameters for: Microsoft SQL Server 1.0              SetConn
                       ─ SQL Connection Parameters ─
 Parameter                    Value
 Remote User Name
 Remote Password
 Server
 Database




                   [F2] DO-IT!   [F10] Menu
             [Esc] Return to the SQL Connections screen
```

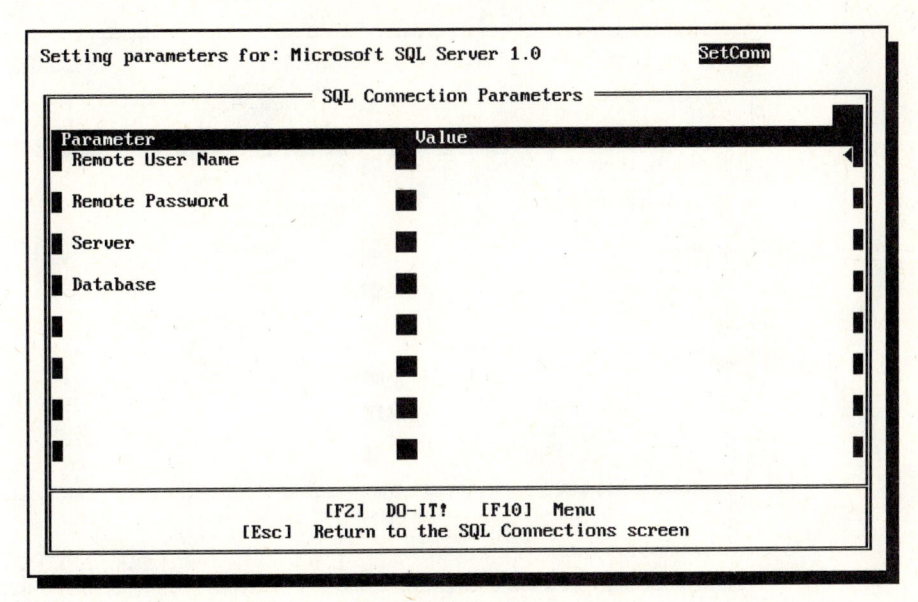

Figure 13-7 Microsoft server connection parameter screen

```
Setting parameters for: Oracle Server 6.0                     SetConn
                       ─ SQL Connection Parameters ─
 Parameter                    Value
 Remote User Name
 Remote Password
 Host




                   [F2] DO-IT!   [F10] Menu
             [Esc] Return to the SQL Connections screen
```

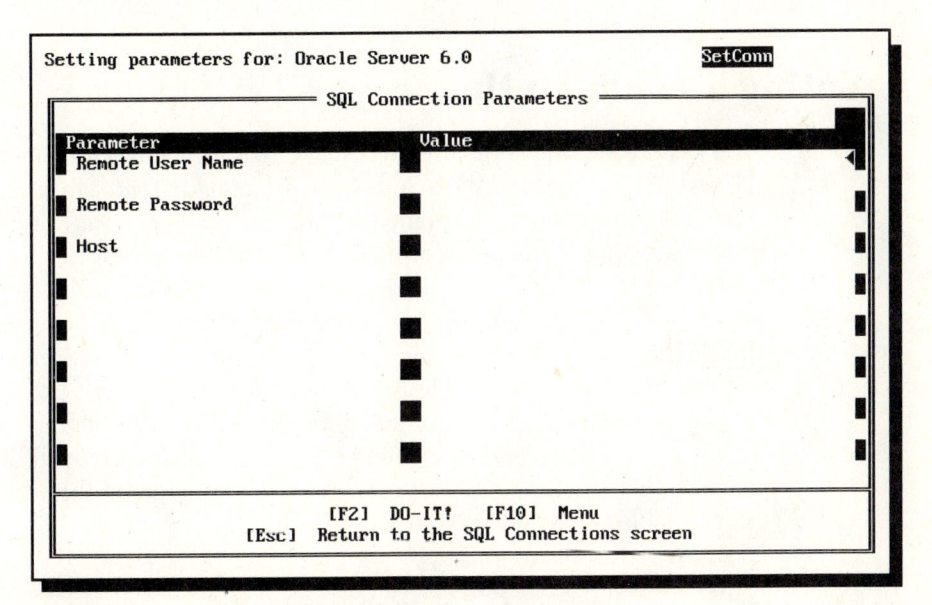

Figure 13-8 Oracle server connection parameter screen

```
Setting parameters for: Microsoft SQL Server 1.0            SetConn
                    ═══ SQL Connection Parameters ═══
Parameter                    Value
Remote User Name             johns2

Remote Password              *******

Server                       srvr241man

Database                     stats










                  [F2]  DO-IT!    [F10]  Menu
            [Esc]  Return to the SQL Connections screen
                        Microsoft SQL Server 1.0 : Opening database...
```

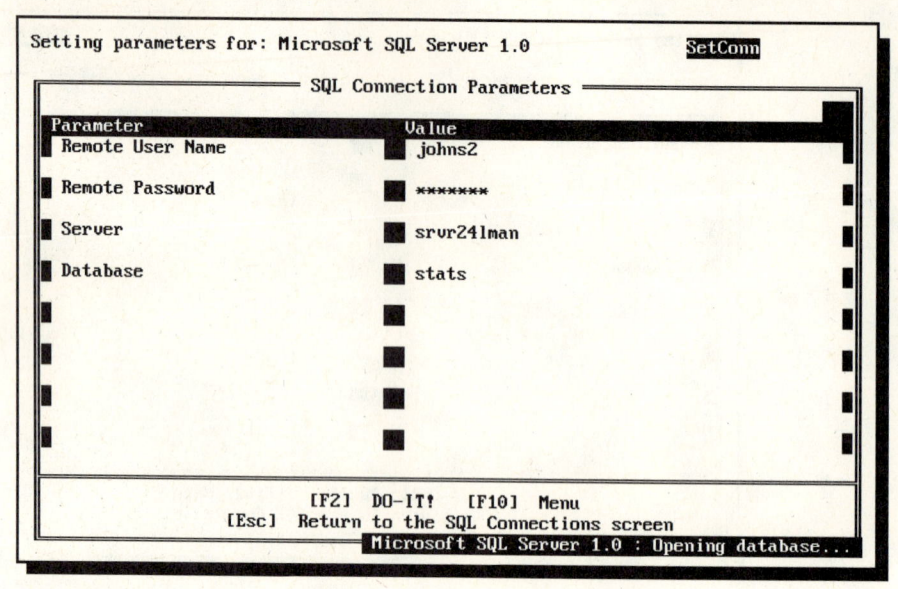

Figure 13-9 Connection example

Creating a Table on the Server

You can create a table on a server using Paradox menus with {Create} or {Tools} {Copy} {Table}. With SQL Link, selecting {Create} from the Main menu displays a second-level menu asking to create a {Local} or {Remote} table. Selecting {Remote} informs Paradox that the new table is to reside on the server and must follow the database server's naming and data type conventions. Appendix A of this book contains information on the naming rules for the fields and a comparison of data types across servers. Some of this information is also included in Appendix B of the *SQL Link User's Guide*. Creating the structure for a remote table is the same as creating a local Paradox table. If you violate any naming rules, Paradox won't let you save the table. If the structure has no syntax errors, it is created on the server and a replica table is created on your local workstation.

You can copy an existing table to a new table on the server using {Tools} {Copy}. The existing data can reside either on your workstation or on the database server. Like {Create}, there is a {Local} {Remote} menu selection to inform Paradox where the existing table resides and where the new table is to be created.

NOTE: *Database servers do not allow spaces in field names. Any Paradox table that contains a field name with spaces must be changed. The most common approach is to replace the space with an underscore.*

Entering Data into a Server Table

The {*DataEntry*} option can be used to add data to a remote table. You can even use a form if you've created one on the replica table. All data is entered into an Entry table, which has the same structure as the replica table. Key violations are automatically detected if the remote table has an index when the data is saved (a local Keyviol table is created containing the duplicate records). If a record doesn't pass a database server data validation rule, it is placed in a local Problems table. If you don't want to commit the records but you want to save them, use the {*KeepEntry*} selection in DataEntry mode. The data is saved in Entry until another DataEntry session is started, you change directories, or you leave Paradox.

You design a form for a remote table just as you do for a local table with one exception: you cannot create a multitable form. Paradox will let you walk through the menu choices and select the option to add an embedded form up to where the table name is selected. At that point, Paradox displays the message:

Remote table form is not allowed.

Multirecord forms are supported, as are expressions that use PAL functions and global variables.

You can also use {*Tools*} {*More*} {*Add*} to enter new records in a remote table or to update the remote table's data. If the target table is indexed, the {*NewEntries*} {*Update*} menu is displayed. Any records added that duplicate a key are placed into a Keyviol table. If there are server-enforced rules that the data violates, the offending records are placed in a Problems table. Any record that is changed is placed into a Changed table. The Add operation works the same on remote tables as on local tables. It can be used to add data in the combinations of

- Local table to local table
- Local table to remote table
- Remote table to local table
- Remote table to remote table

When using the last option, remote to remote, the tables don't have to be in the same database. The data can reside on different servers. If the remote table is locked, the records are added when the lock is released.

Querying a Server Table

Paradox's QBE provides the same easy access to remote data as it does to local data. Once you've selected the name of the remote table to query, Paradox prompts you for your user name and password if you have not logged on to the database containing the table. When the query form is displayed, you fill it out and press [F2] to execute the query. At this point the query is validated, translated into the correct SQL dialect for the server you are connected to, and the SQL statement is sent to the database server. The result is stored in an Answer table and placed on the workspace for you to view. This is the same result as querying a local Paradox table. The Answer table can be renamed, saved, copied, sorted, and so forth.

You can see the SQL statement Paradox creates by pressing [Alt][F2]. Figure 13-10 shows the SELECT command generated from a single table query. Multitable queries are allowed as long as all the tables in the query have the same connection. You cannot mix local tables with remote tables or combine remote tables with different connections. If you need to do this, query the data from the remote tables to an Answer table and use the Answer table in combination with local tables. If your data resides in two different connections, you need to rename the Answer table before you execute the successive remote queries. Figure 13-11 shows a three-table query on remote tables and Figure 13-12 shows the SQL statement Paradox generates.

Not all of the query operations available for local tables are supported for remote tables. Certain reserved words, special operators, and query types are excluded. The restrictions/exclusions are:

1. No SET queries

    The ONLY, NO, EVERY, and EXACTLY operators cannot be used. Attempting a SET query displays the following message, preceded by the title of the connection:

    : SET operation is not supported

2. GroupBy, [Shift][F6] cannot be used

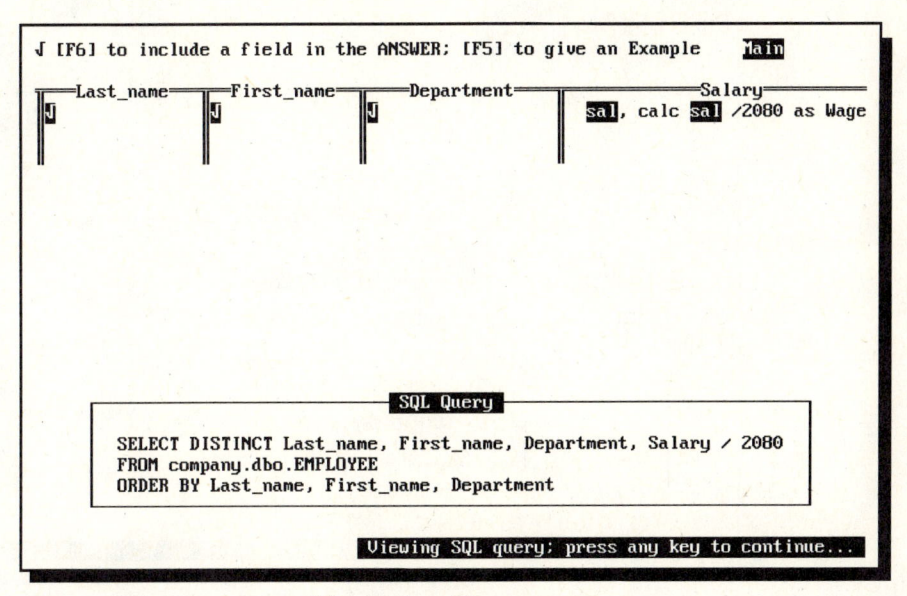

```
┌─ √ [F6] to include a field in the ANSWER; [F5] to give an Example   Main ─┐
│    ┌─Last_name─┬─First_name─┬─Department─┬──────Salary──────────────┐     │
│    │ √         │ √          │ √          │ sal, calc sal /2080 as Wage│   │
│                                                                           │
│                         ┌──── SQL Query ────┐                             │
│                         │ SELECT DISTINCT Last_name, First_name, Department, Salary / 2080
│                         │ FROM company.dbo.EMPLOYEE                       │
│                         │ ORDER BY Last_name, First_name, Department      │
│                         └──────────────────────────────────────────────┘  │
│                               Viewing SQL query; press any key to continue...│
└───────────────────────────────────────────────────────────────────────────┘
```

Figure 13-10 SQL generated for single-table query

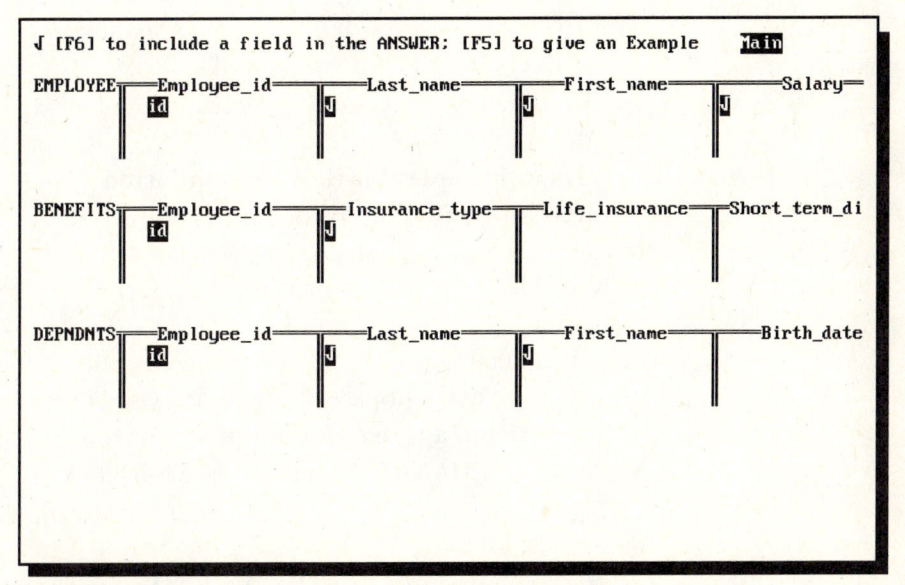

```
┌─ √ [F6] to include a field in the ANSWER; [F5] to give an Example   Main ─┐
│  EMPLOYEE─┬─Employee_id─┬─Last_name─┬─First_name─┬─Salary─┐               │
│           │ id          │ √         │ √          │ √      │               │
│                                                                           │
│  BENEFITS─┬─Employee_id─┬─Insurance_type─┬─Life_insurance─┬─Short_term_di  │
│           │ id          │                │                │               │
│                                                                           │
│  DEPNDNTS─┬─Employee_id─┬─Last_name─┬─First_name─┬─Birth_date              │
│           │ id          │ √         │ √          │                        │
└───────────────────────────────────────────────────────────────────────────┘
```

Figure 13-11 Three-table query

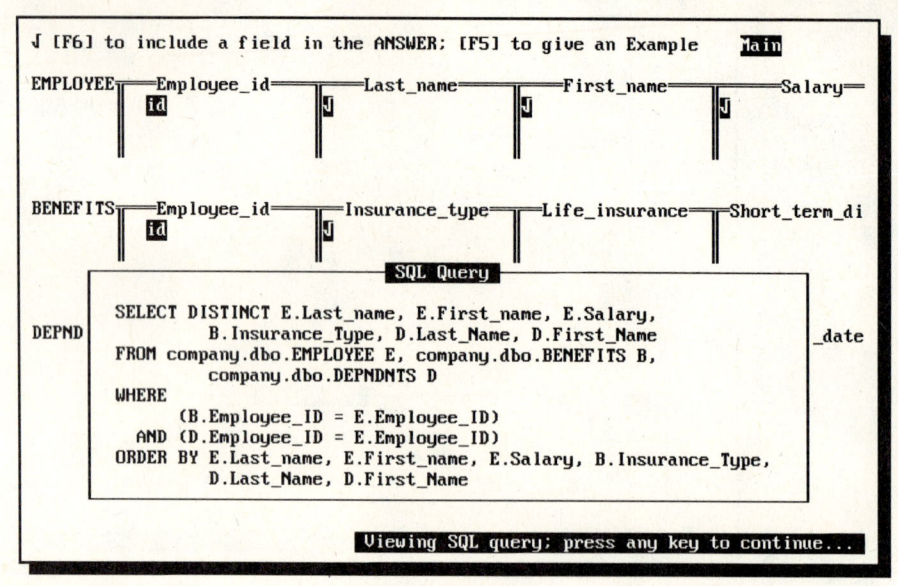

```
√ [F6] to include a field in the ANSWER; [F5] to give an Example    Main
EMPLOYEE┬──Employee_id──┬┬──Last_name──┬┬──First_name──┬┬──Salary─
        │      id       ││      √      ││      √       ││     √

BENEFITS┬──Employee_id──┬┬──Insurance_type──┬┬──Life_insurance──┬┬──Short_term_di
        │      id       ││         √        ││                  ││
                                ┌─────────── SQL Query ───────────┐
DEPND                           │ SELECT DISTINCT E.Last_name, E.First_name, E.Salary,     │_date
                                │       B.Insurance_Type, D.Last_Name, D.First_Name        │
                                │ FROM company.dbo.EMPLOYEE E, company.dbo.BENEFITS B,     │
                                │      company.dbo.DEPNDNTS D                              │
                                │ WHERE                                                    │
                                │     (B.Employee_ID = E.Employee_ID)                      │
                                │ AND (D.Employee_ID = E.Employee_ID)                      │
                                │ ORDER BY E.Last_name, E.First_name, E.Salary, B.Insurance_Type,│
                                │          D.Last_Name, D.First_Name                       │
                                │                                                          │
                                │             Viewing SQL query; press any key to continue...│
                                └──────────────────────────────────────────────────────────┘
```

Figure 13-12 SQL generated for three-table query

3. No FIND queries. They display the following message

    : FIND query is not supported

4. Special operators ! (inclusion) and LIKE are not allowed. They display the error messages

    : Inclusive operator (!) is not supported

    : Paradox LIKE operator is not supported

5. No selection based on the aggregates SUM, COUNT, AVERAGE, MIN, or MAX.

    The expressions CALC SUM or CALC MAX are okay. A selection of SUM > 100000 or COUNT > 10 cannot be used. Attempting to use these in a query displays the following error message

    : Restricted aggregation is not supported

6. Multiple line CHANGETO queries are prohibited.

    If you attempt a multiple line CHANGETO query, the following message is displayed

    SQL : Only single line CHANGETO queries are supported

> **NOTE:** *The SQL Link User's Guide states that multiple-line DELETE queries are not supported. This is not the case for all servers. The READSQL file on the installation disk has a note that multiple-line DELETE queries are not allowed for IBM EE. A multiple-line query is shown later in this chapter for Microsoft SQL Server.*

7. Multiple table queries for DELETE and CHANGETO operations are prohibited. Attempting to perform either of these displays the following message

    SQL : Cannot link rows in CHANGETO and DELETE queries

8. Wildcard operators in date or numeric fields are not allowed. In Paradox you can use 4/../90 to get all of the records for April of 1990. With a remote table, you need to use >=4/1/90,<5/1/90. The following error message is displayed when you attempt to use wildcards

    : Patterns are supported only for Alphanumeric column

To get around these limitations, you have to perform multiple queries or use the result of a query to perform another query (using the Answer table).

Paradox has implemented a nice feature to save queries for remote tables. You can use {*QuerySave*} to save the data in the same format as a local table query, or you can save the SQL statements Paradox generates using {*Tools*} {*SQL*} {*SQLSave*}. The SELECT statements are saved in a script you name. Using the three-table query from the previous example, Figure 13-13 shows the result of a {*QuerySave*} and Figure 13-14 shows the result of a {*SQLSave*}. Saving the SQL statement lets you use QBE to generate as much of the SQL statement as possible using Paradox and therefore ensure accuracy. Any additional SQL requirement not supported by Paradox can easily be added to the saved statement, provided you understand the dialect for the connection.

> **TIP:** *If you're going to be using the same query to process data against different database servers, it's best to save the query using {QuerySave}. Each time Paradox executes a query via QBE, the correct SQL dialect is used to translate the query. If you use {SQLSave} to capture the query, it saves the SELECT statement for the dialect of the current connection (the same SELECT as shown with [Alt][F2]).*

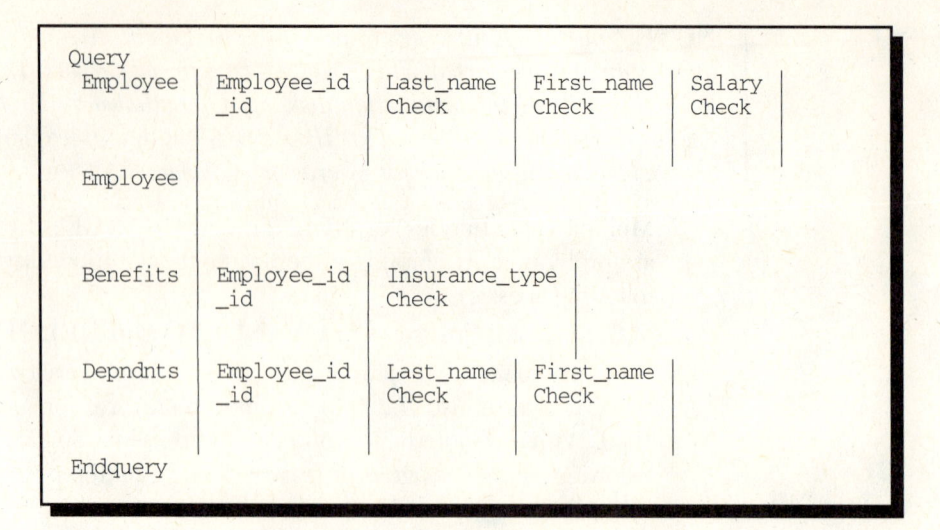

```
Query
  Employee   | Employee_id | Last_name  | First_name | Salary
             | _id         | Check      | Check      | Check

  Employee

  Benefits   | Employee_id | Insurance_type
             | _id         | Check

  Depndnts   | Employee_id | Last_name  | First_name
             | _id         | Check      | Check

Endquery
```

Figure 13-13 QuerySave for three-table remote query

```
SQL
    SELECT DISTINCT E.Last_name, E.First_name, E.Salary,
             B.Insurance_Type, D.Last_Name, D.First_Name
    FROM company.dbo.EMPLOYEE E, company.dbo.BENEFITS B,
             company.dbo.DEPNDNTS D
    WHERE
         (B.Employee_ID = E.Employee_ID)
      AND (D.Employee_ID = E.Employee_ID)
    ORDER BY E.Last_name, E.First_name, E.Salary,
 B.Insurance_Type,
             D.Last_Name, D.First_Name
EndSQL
```

Figure 13-14 SQLSave for three-table remote query

If you try to perform a query saved with either of these methods without setting a connection, you'll get a script error. For example, if you don't have a connection set and you try to execute a saved query on the remote Employee table, a {QuerySave} script displays the message

RUN error: Unknown connection parameter for replica Employee

A {SQLSave} query displays the message

RUN error: Connection is not set

In either case, it's best to ensure a connection is set before executing a query.

QBE supports other SQL Data Manipulation commands besides SELECT. SQL DELETE, UPDATE, and INSERT are all available from QBE using DELETE, CHANGETO, and INSERT queries. Let's look at a couple of examples using Microsoft SQL Server as the server connection. Each example has both the query form and the SQL statement displayed.

Figure 13-15 shows a DELETE query form for the Employee table with multiple-line selection. Paradox SQL Link creates the equivalent SQL DELETE statement based on the selection criteria. This example deletes all the employees in the Finance or MIS departments.

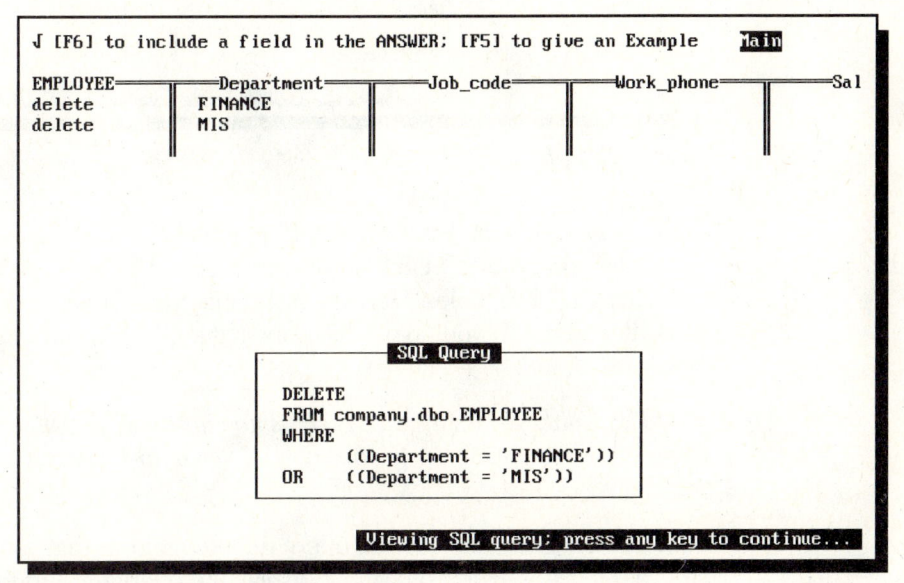

```
√ [F6] to include a field in the ANSWER; [F5] to give an Example    Main
EMPLOYEE========Department========Job_code========Work_phone========Sal
delete          FINANCE
delete          MIS




                          ┌─────SQL Query─────┐
                          │ DELETE            │
                          │ FROM company.dbo.EMPLOYEE
                          │ WHERE             │
                          │      ((Department = 'FINANCE'))
                          │ OR   ((Department = 'MIS'))
                          └───────────────────┘
                          Viewing SQL query; press any key to continue...
```

Figure 13-15 SQL DELETE example

A SQL UPDATE example is shown in Figure 13-16. Here there is a department name change for the employees in the MIS department. The new name is DP.

SQL INSERT statements are generated using the INSERT query in two ways:

- Placing the values directly in the query form
- Using global variables and the tilde (~) character

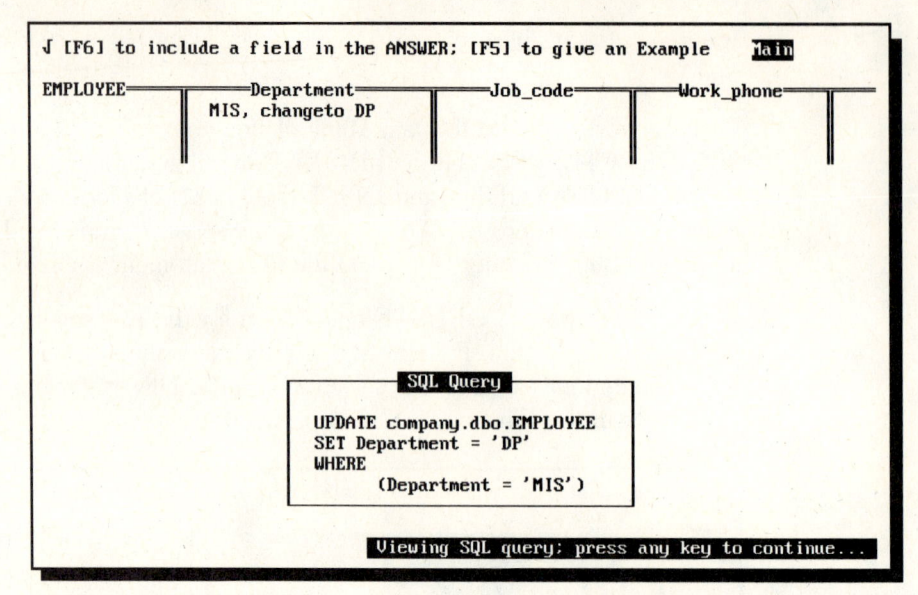

```
┌─────────────────────────────────────────────────────────────────────┐
│ √ [F6] to include a field in the ANSWER; [F5] to give an Example  Main │
│ ┌EMPLOYEE─┬──────Department──────┬──────Job_code──────┬──────Work_phone──────┐ │
│          │ MIS, changeto DP     │                    │                      │ │
│                                                                              │
│                                                                              │
│                                                                              │
│                                                                              │
│                      ┌──────── SQL Query ────────┐                           │
│                      │ UPDATE company.dbo.EMPLOYEE │                         │
│                      │ SET Department = 'DP'       │                         │
│                      │ WHERE                       │                         │
│                      │     (Department = 'MIS')    │                         │
│                      └─────────────────────────────┘                         │
│                            Viewing SQL query; press any key to continue...  │
└─────────────────────────────────────────────────────────────────────┘
```

Figure 13-16 SQL UPDATE example

Figure 13-17 shows the first method. If a field doesn't have a value, the field is not included in the INSERT statement. Figure 13-18 shows the query form using global variables. Here each variable must be defined before the query will execute. If you do not have any data to insert, you must initialize the variable to null.

> **NOTE:** *Unlike local Paradox, there is no audit trail for these types of queries on remote tables. No Inserted, Deleted, or Changed table is created.*

One disadvantage to the way you query remote tables is that you have to be connected to the server. You cannot display the query form for a remote table and save the query in Paradox format or SQL format. You are always prompted for your user name and password before the query form is placed on the workspace. Being able to create queries but not execute them would be a nice feature, especially if you have the structure of the tables on a laptop and want to work on the application away from the office.

Using Paradox SQL Link

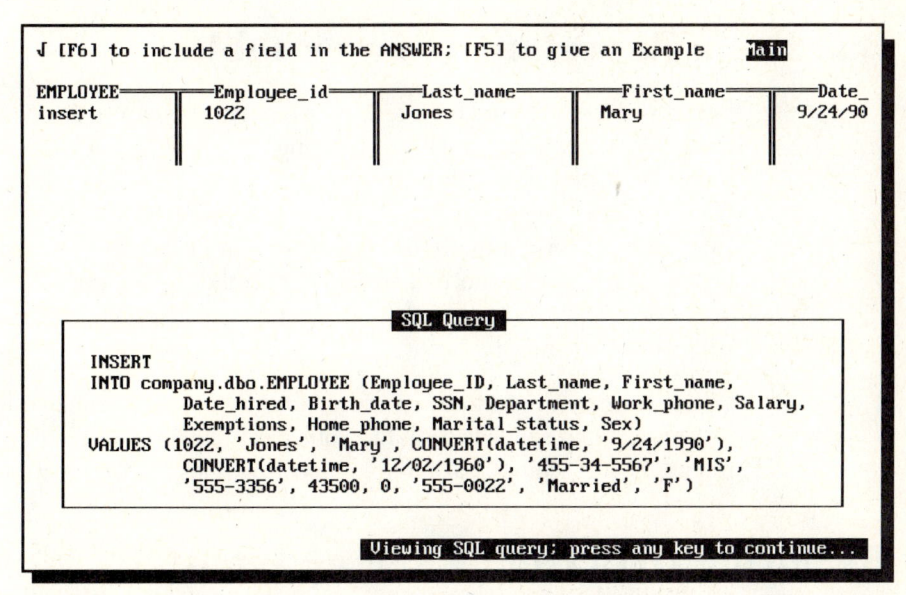

```
√ [F6] to include a field in the ANSWER; [F5] to give an Example    Main
EMPLOYEE───────Employee_id──────Last_name──────First_name──────Date_
insert         1022             Jones          Mary            9/24/90




                              ┌─ SQL Query ─┐
      INSERT
      INTO company.dbo.EMPLOYEE (Employee_ID, Last_name, First_name,
              Date_hired, Birth_date, SSN, Department, Work_phone, Salary,
              Exemptions, Home_phone, Marital_status, Sex)
      VALUES (1022, 'Jones', 'Mary', CONVERT(datetime, '9/24/1990'),
              CONVERT(datetime, '12/02/1960'), '455-34-5567', 'MIS',
              '555-3356', 43500, 0, '555-0022', 'Married', 'F')


                              Viewing SQL query; press any key to continue...
```

Figure 13-17 SQL INSERT example with data values in query form

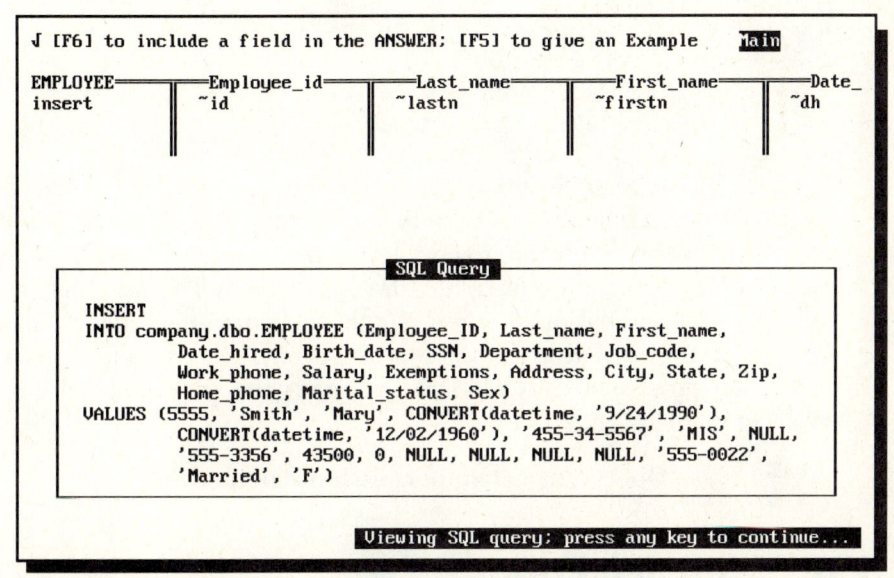

```
√ [F6] to include a field in the ANSWER; [F5] to give an Example    Main
EMPLOYEE───────Employee_id──────Last_name──────First_name──────Date_
insert         ~id              ~lastn         ~firstn         ~dh




                              ┌─ SQL Query ─┐
      INSERT
      INTO company.dbo.EMPLOYEE (Employee_ID, Last_name, First_name,
              Date_hired, Birth_date, SSN, Department, Job_code,
              Work_phone, Salary, Exemptions, Address, City, State, Zip,
              Home_phone, Marital_status, Sex)
      VALUES (5555, 'Smith', 'Mary', CONVERT(datetime, '9/24/1990'),
              CONVERT(datetime, '12/02/1960'), '455-34-5567', 'MIS', NULL,
              '555-3356', 43500, 0, NULL, NULL, NULL, NULL, '555-0022',
              'Married', 'F')

                              Viewing SQL query; press any key to continue...
```

Figure 13-18 SQL INSERT example using variables in query form

Building a Report on a Server Table

Reports can be created on a remote table with certain restrictions. All of the grouping, formatting, functions, totalling, subtotaling, and so on is supported but you cannot create a multitable report. Linking either remote or detail tables is not permitted. If data from the server must be combined with local data, perform a query first, then generate the report. If data from multiple remote tables is necessary to generate the report, perform a multitable query, save the report format saved with a local table, copy it to the Answer table, and then run the report.

When you run a report on a remote table, SQL Link actually queries the server and then sends the data to your local machine before generating the report. This is why global variables and functions work with remote tables.

Removing Data from a Server Table

Using interactive Paradox, there are three ways to delete data in a remote table:

- DELETE query
- {Tools} {More} {Empty}
- {Tools} {Delete} {Table}

Each successive option is more destructive to the table. A DELETE query lets you remove rows from the table using QBE. All records matching the selection criteria are removed from the remote table. Using {Tools} {More} {Empty} removes all of the rows from a table. The last option not only deletes all the data but it removes the table from the server. You need the correct level of database server access privileges to execute any of these data removal options. If you have not been granted delete privileges, you'll see the message

Operation failed; permission is denied

SQL Menu Selection

Paradox SQL Link supports the transaction processing features of SQL database servers. However, each server handles transaction processing differently. Some automatically start a transaction with each activity and others do not. Paradox normally commits each change to a remote table automatically, but you can change this default. You can also group a set of actions into a unit and either commit or rollback the actions.

All of these options are available from the {*Tools*} {*SQL*} menu selection. Figure 13-19 shows the {*SQL*} menu tree. The first level of menus are

Connection	Manages server connections
Transaction	Transaction processing control
ReplicaTools	Copy, delete, rename local replica tables
SQLSave	Save the query on the workspace as a text file of the SELECT statement for the current connection
Preferences	Set how to automatically commit transactions or not and how [Ctrl][Break] works during remote operations

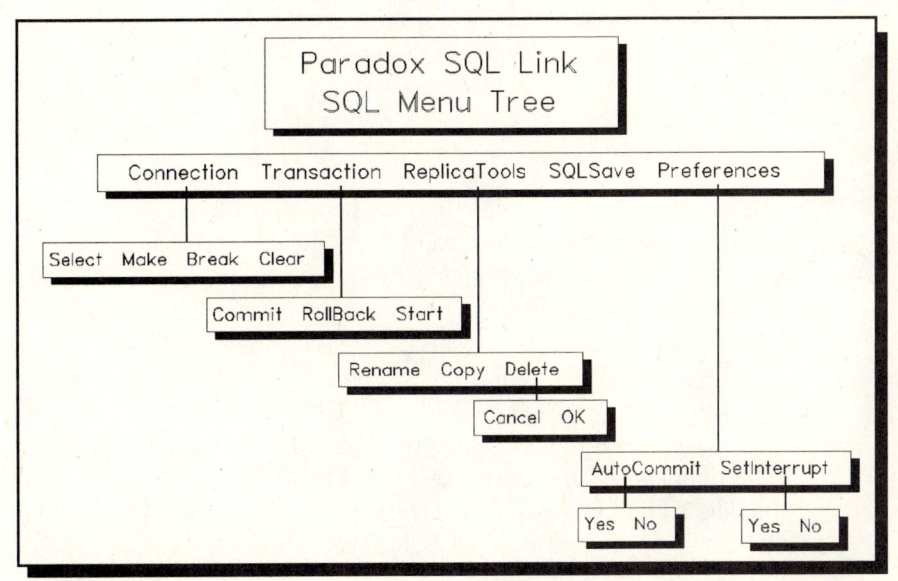

Figure 13-19 SQL menu tree

We've already discussed the {*Select*} option (found on the {*Connection*} menu) used to connect to a server. Any action that supports access to a remote table uses the connection set with {*Select*}. If you create, copy, delete, or empty a remote table, the current connection determines which set of server data to access. Default settings for the connection screen can be set using the SQL Setup Program (discussed later in this chapter).

If a connection is broken, you don't have to use the {Select} option to reconnect. {Make} reconnects to the server using the current connection settings. You can disconnect from the server in six different ways:

- Select {Tools} {SQL} {Connection} {Break}
- Select {Tools} {SQL} {Connection} {Clear}
- Select a table with a different server connection
- Press [Ctrl][Break] during an operation on a remote table
- Execute a DOSBIG, RUN BIG, or press [Alt][O]
- Exit Paradox

When a connection is broken, if there is a current transaction it is rolled back. Paradox also closes remote files and disconnects you from the server. There might be times when you want to explicitly disconnect using the {Break} selection. If a remote resource is no longer needed, you free up server resources when you disconnect. The {Clear} selection disconnects the current connection, clears the workspace, and all remote user names and passwords for any connection. When you're not connected to a server, Paradox doesn't display the {Local} {Remote} menu options.

Transaction processing control is handled with the {Tools} {SQL} {Transaction} menu options. You can {Start}, {Commit}, or {Rollback} a transaction. When you want to group a series of actions and you want all of them to complete or none of them to affect the data, group the actions into a transaction. When all actions are finished, you determine at that time if you want to save the results of the actions by issuing a {Commit} or if you want to undo all the actions by executing a {Rollback}. This is similar to incremental undo capabilities in Edit and DataEntry modes. If you're familiar with the EDITLOG command, {Commit} is like EDITLOG PERMANENT and {Rollback} is like EDITLOG REVERT. If you have {AutoCommit} set to No, you must explicitly commit transactions. This is also true if you use the PAL SQL...ENDSQL construct (discussed later in this chapter).

The {Tools} {SQL} {ReplicaTools} option provides rename, delete, and copy actions that only affect replica tables. If you use the {Tools}, {Copy}, or {Delete} options, they affect both the replica table and the remote table. {ReplicaTools} acts on replica tables only.

As discussed earlier, {Tools} {SQL} {SQLSave} creates a text file of the query on the workspace. The SQL statement for the dialect of the connection is written to the script you name. The SQL...ENDSQL construct is placed around the SQL statement, allowing the script to be played from the

{*Script*} menu or called from within a PAL application. The text written is the same SQL statement as shown with [Alt][F2] when you're in the query form. Remember, this option writes the SQL statement for the current connection. There is no guarantee the SQL statement will run on a different vendor's database server. SQL dialect differences cause this problem. If you want to run the query on different SQL database servers, use {*Scripts*} {*QuerySave*} to save the query (Paradox dynamically translates this type of saved query into the appropriate dialect for the connected server).

The last option off {*Tools*} {*SQL*} is {*Preferences*}. This is where you set if Paradox is to commit transactions automatically after changing remote data. The {*AutoCommit*} option has a {*Yes*} {*No*} submenu. If you select {*Yes*}, Paradox automatically commits any changes you make to remote tables, and doesn't let you rollback your changes. If you select {*No*}, Paradox does not automatically commit changes to remote tables.

Changes are not committed until an explicit commit is executed with

- {*Tools*} {*SQL*} {*Transaction*} {*Commit*}
- PAL SQLCOMMIT
- A command that Paradox automatically commits

Changes are rolled back when {*AutoCommit*} is set to {*No*} and

- You select {*Tools*} {*SQL*} {*Transaction*} {*RollBack*}
- You select a different connection or a table with a different connection
- You execute PAL SQLROLLBACK
- The server executes a implicit rollback
- You select {*Tools*} {*SQL*} {*Connection*} {*Break*}
- You press [Ctrl][Break] or [Alt][O]
- You execute PAL RUN BIG or DOS BIG

NOTE: *Certain commands (Copy, Create, and Delete) are always committed even if {AutoCommit} is set to {No}.*

The {*Preferences*} option also let you set how [Ctrl][Break] affects processing on remote tables. {*SetInterrupt*} has a {*Yes*} {*No*} submenu. If you select {*Yes*} (the default), you can press [Ctrl][Break] and Paradox halts the remote action as soon as possible. It also rolls back the current transaction and the breaks the current connection. If you select {*No*}, [Ctrl][Break] doesn't affect the remote table processing but Paradox halts at the completion of the current PAL command. This is a crucial setting for applications, especially where you don't want the user to cancel an action. You might set {SetInterrupt} on and off within your application. (You can use SQLSETINTERRUPT in a PAL program.)

> **NOTE:** *Password protecting the startup script still protects your user from pressing [Ctrl][Break] and getting the {Cancel} {Debug} message within an application.*

Security

SQL Link does not bypass the access restrictions defined on the server. Centralized data access control is one of the benefits of the client/server architecture. SQL Link adheres to any restriction the database administrator applies for a database or table. You can further restrict your Paradox users from accessing remote data by protecting the replica tables. You can assign passwords on replica tables just like on any other table using the {Tools} {More} {Protect} menu selections. This capability, along with the server's access privileges, provides the highest level of security.

Existing Commands Enhanced by SQL Link

Some of the existing PAL commands have been enhanced to work with SQL Link. Table 13-2 lists these commands. Each of these commands uses the remote table and/or the replica table. Following the chart is a brief explanation of how SQL Link expands each command, along with the PAL syntax and its menu equivalent (if one exists).

ADD

Syntax: ADD TableName1 TableName2
Menu: {Tools} {More} {Add} {TableName1} {TableName2} {Update}

You can use local or remote tables for *TableName1* or *TableName2*. The data is automatically committed if {AutoCommit} or SQLAUTOCOMMIT is set to Yes. Paradox rolls back the ADD if an error occurs. You have to explicitly commit the changes if {AutoCommit} or SQLAUTOCOMMIT is set to No.

**Table 13-2
List of PAL commands used with SQL Link**

ADD	Adds records from one table to another
COPY	Copies a table
CREATE	Creates a table
DELETE	Deletes a table
EMPTY	Removes all the records from a table
PROTECT	Encrypts the table by adding password protection
QUERY...ENDQUERY	Places a query form on the workspace
REPORT	Prints a report from a table to the printer
SHOWFILES	Displays a menu of files to select from
SHOWTABLES	Displays a menu of tables to select from

REMEMBER: *ADD performs an {Update} on the target table if it is keyed. This is true for both local and remote tables.*

COPY

Syntax: COPY *TableName1* [REMOTE] *TableName2*
Menu: {Tools} {Copy} {Table} {*TableName1*} {*TableName2*}

You can use local or remote tables for *TableName1* or *TableName2*. If *TableName1* is keyed, *TableName2* will also be keyed. A replica is created when a copy is made to a remote table. Paradox automatically commits a COPY command so you cannot roll back this statement. Therefore, you should never use COPY in the middle of a transaction. *TableName2* contains a snapshot of the data at the time the copy is made. Make sure the field names of the table you are copying conform to the server field naming conventions. A server connection is required before executing COPY.

CREATE

Syntax 1: CREATE [REMOTE] *TableName FieldNameList*
Menu 1: {Create} {Tablename}

Syntax 2: CREATE [REMOTE] *TableName2* LIKE *TableName1*

Menu 2: {Create} {*TableName2*} MENU {Borrow} {*TableName1*}

Creating a remote table automatically creates a replica table. If the name of the remote table already exists, CREATE fails. Like COPY, Paradox automatically commits CREATE.

DELETE

Syntax: DELETE *TableName*

Menu: {Tools} {Delete} {Table} {*TableName*}

Use DELETE to remove both local and remote tables. When a remote table is deleted, the replica and all objects associated with the replica are also deleted. Paradox automatically commits a DELETE.

EMPTY

Syntax: EMPTY *TableName*

Menu: {Tools} {More} {Empty} {*TableName*}

EMPTY is essentially a delete all query. Every record from the table is removed. Paradox does not automatically commit the changes when EMPTY is finished, it follows the AutoCommit settings. This lets you control the commit and roll back operation of this command.

PROTECT, QUERY...ENDQUERY, REPORT, SHOWFILES, and SHOWTABLES

All of these commands are affected by SQL Link. A replica table can be used in each of them.

New PAL Commands with SQL Link

SQL Link adds fourteen new commands to PAL. Many of them are menu equivalents. Table 13-3 lists the new commands along with a brief description. Following the chart is a brief explanation of each command, along with the PAL syntax and its menu equivalent (if there is one).

Table 13-3
New SQL Link PAL commands

SQL ... ENDSQL	Embedded SQL statements sent directly to the server
SQLAUTOCOMMIT	Specifies whether to automatically commit server activity
SQLBREAKCONNECT	Disconnects the current server connection
SQLCLEARCONNECT	Clears the current server connection
SQLCOMMIT	Commits changes made to remote tables
SQLFETCH	Returns a record to an array from a pending query
SQLMAKECONNECT	Connects to the server using the current server connection values
SQLRELEASE	Releases the pending query
SQLRESTORECONNECT	Restores the server connection saved with SQLSAVECONNECT
SQLROLLBACK	Rolls back the current transaction
SQLSAVECONNECT	Saves the values of the current server connection
SQLSELECTCONNECT	Selects a server connection
SQLSETINTERRUPT	Specifies how [Ctrl][Break] works on remote operations
SQLSTARTTRANS	Starts a transaction on the server

SQL...ENDSQL

Syntax: SQL [NOFETCH]
    { *SQLText* | *~Expression~* } ...
ENDSQL

This command sends embedded SQL statements directly to the current connection. *SQLText* is any valid SQL statement. Syntax checking is done by the server, not Paradox. PAL variables and functions can be used within SQL...ENDSQL when enclosed in tildes (~). The expression is converted to an alphanumeric string before the statement is sent to the server. Query results are placed in an Answer table. Unlike queries on local tables, the Answer table isn't placed on the workspace. You need to view the table to have it visible on the workspace. The NOFETCH keyword tells Paradox not to create an Answer table. It is used in conjunction with SQLFETCH (discussed below).

The system variable *retval* is set to True if the SQL statement returns a result, and False if no results are returned. SELECT statements always return a result (in some cases it's just an empty table). Therefore, *retval* is always True for a SELECT statement.

You must be in Main mode to execute a SQL...ENDSQL statement that returns a value. You can use the NOFETCH option with a SELECT in a mode other than Main.

Remote changes made with SQL...ENDSQL are not automatically committed no matter what the Autocommit setting is. You decide whether to commit or roll back the transaction.

Any errors that result from a SQL...ENDSQL command are trapped using SQLERRORCODE and SQLERRORMESSAGE.

SQLAUTOCOMMIT

    Syntax: SQLAUTOCOMMIT { Yes | No }
    Menu: {Tools} {SQL} {Preferences} {AutoCommit}

SQLAUTOCOMMIT performs the same function as its menu equivalent (discussed earlier).

SQLBREAKCONNECT

    Syntax: SQLBREAKCONNECT
    Menu: {Tools} {SQL} {Connection} {Break}

SQLBREAKCONNECT performs the same function as its menu equivalent (discussed earlier).

SQLCLEARCONNECT

    Syntax: SQLCLEARCONNECT
    Menu: {Tools} {SQL} {Connection} {Clear}

SQLCLEARCONNECT performs the same function as its menu equivalent (discussed earlier).

SQLCOMMIT

    Syntax: SQLCOMMIT
    Menu: {Tools} {SQL} {Transaction} {Commit}

SQLCOMMIT performs the same function as its menu equivalent (discussed earlier).

SQLFETCH

    Syntax: SQLFETCH *ArrayName*

SQLFETCH is used in conjunction with the SQL NOFETCH...ENDSQL command. When NOFETCH is used, the results of the SQL statement are not placed in an Answer table. SQL NOFETCH retrieves the next record from the results and places it into *ArrayName*. It is similar to the COPYTOARRAY command with the exception that SQLFETCH doesn't place a table name in array element 1, it places a null value there instead. The system variable *retval* is True if SQLFETCH returns a record and False if there are no more records. This is like SQL CURSOR statements.

You don't have to be in Main mode to execute SQLFETCH. You can use it in Edit or CoEdit to retrieve records and populate a local table. An example is discussed later using SQLFETCH to edit data from the server in a multitable form and to allow forward and backward scrolling in a multitable form with real time data access. Another use of SQLFETCH is to validate data in a column against a table residing on the server. You can execute a query to see if a row exists in a remote table for the value entered in a field.

The SQLRELEASE command must be used to cancel a pending query where SQLFETCH has been used.

SQLMAKECONNECT

    Syntax: SQLMAKECONNECT

    Menu: {Tools} {SQL} {Connection} {Make}

SQLMAKECONNECT performs the same function as its menu equivalent (discussed earlier).

SQLRELEASE

    Syntax: SQLMAKECONNECT

SQLRELEASE releases resources used by SQLFETCH. You must execute SQLRELEASE before you execute another query. A script error occurs if you don't release the pending query and attempt another query. The following error message is displayed when this occurs

    Run error: SQL NOFETCH .. ENDSQL command is pending

SQLRESTORECONNECT

    Syntax: SQLRESTORECONNECT

You restore the saved connection using SQLRESTORECONNECT. You save a connection using SQLSAVECONNECT (discussed below). The SQL Link documentation says that when no connection is saved, SQLRESTORECONNECT clears the current connection and removes it from memory but we didn't find this to be true; our connection was not cleared.

SQLROLLBACK

    Syntax: SQLROLLBACK

    Menu: {Tools} {SQL} {Transaction} {RollBack}

SQLROLLBACK performs the same function as its menu equivalent (discussed earlier).

SQLSAVECONNECT

    Syntax: SQLSAVECONNECT

You save the current connection in memory using SQLSAVECONNECT. It lets you save the current connection, connect to another server, then reconnect back to the original connection with SQLRESTORECONNECT. If you've already saved a connection, it is overwritten with each SQLSAVECONNECT command. If you have not established a connection, SQLSAVECONNECT doesn't do anything and no errors occur.

SQLSELECTCONNECT

Syntax: SQLSELECTCONNECT [{PRODUCT *ProductName* | TITLE *Title*} VALUES *ParameterList*]
Menu: {Tools} {SQL} {Connection} {Select}

When you execute SQLSELECTCONNECT without any parameters, it works the same as its menu equivalent. (The connections setting screen for you to choose from the list of installed SQL server products and then the connection parameter screen is displayed.) The system variable *retval* is set to True if you choose a connection and False if you cancel. Using this in an application lets your users establish a connection to any server with their name and password.

Use the PRODUCT keyword to connect to a server based on the server code name. The code names are

    IBMEE   IBM Extended Edition Database Manager 1.2
    MSSQL   Microsoft SQL Server 1.0 and 1.1
    ORACLE   Oracle Server 6.0

Using the TITLE keyword lets you specify the product title:

IBM Extended Edition 1.2 Database Manager
Microsoft SQL Server 1.0
Oracle Server 6.0

Use the *ParameterList* to enter the connection parameters. The parameters for each server are (optional parameters are shown in italics)

    IBMEE   user name, password, server, database, *directory*
    MSSQL   user name, *password*, server, *database*
    ORACLE   user name, password, *host*

SQLSETINTERRUPT

    Syntax: SQLSETINTERRUPT {Yes | No}
    Menu: {Tools} {SQL} {Preferences} {SetInterrupt}

SQLSETINTERRUPT performs the same function as its menu equivalent (discussed earlier). If you interrupt a remote operation, and SQLSETINTERRUPT is set to Yes, error code 1003 is set, the transaction is rolled back, and Paradox breaks the server connection.

You probably don't want to interrupt a transaction. Therefore, it is best to set SQLSETINTERRUPT to No before starting the transaction. Once the transaction is completed, you can turn it back on if you want that option in your application.

SQLSTARTTRANS

    Syntax: SQLSTARTTRANS
    Menu: {Tools} {SQL} {Transaction} {Start}

SQLSTARTTRANS performs the same function as its menu equivalent (discussed earlier).

New PAL Functions with SQL Link

SQL Link adds eight new PAL functions to Paradox. Table 13-4 lists these functions, along with a brief description. Following the chart is an explanation of each function and the PAL syntax.

ISSQL

    Syntax: ISSQL()

ISSQL returns True if SQL Link is installed and enabled, otherwise it returns False. SQL access is automatically available once SQL Link is installed. It can be turned off with the **-sql off** command-line parameter. ISSQL is the only SQL Link function available even when SQL Link is not installed or enabled. This function is typically used at the beginning of an application to determine if SQL capabilities are available.

**Table 13-4
New SQL Link PAL functions**

ISSQL	Tells you if SQL Link is running
SQLCONNECTINFO	Returns connection or replica information
SQLERRORCODE	Returns the error code of the most recent server action
SQLERRORMESSAGE	Returns the error message of the most recent server action
SQLISCONNECT	Tests if SQL Link is currently connected to a server
SQLISREPLICA	Tests if a table is a replica
SQLMAPINFO	Returns structural information on a remote table
SQLVAL	Returns the SQL value of a Paradox expression

SQLCONNECTINFO

Syntax: SQLCONNECTINFO(*OptionName* [,*ReplicaName*])

Use SQLCONNECTINFO to get connection information on a remote table or on the current server connection. Four different pieces of information can be returned by using one of the following text strings for *OptionName*

"TITLE"	Title of the connection
"DESCRIPTION"	Connection description
"PRODUCT"	Product code
"DIALECT"	Code name for the SQL dialect

You can also use SQLCONNECTINFO to get the connection information on a replica table using the *ReplicaName* parameter. If the table name is not a replica, a null string is returned.

NOTE: *These options are not case sensitive but you do need to enclose the values used for* OptionName *in double quotes.*

SQLERRORCODE

Syntax: SQLERRORCODE()

Use SQLERRORCODE to return the error code of the most recent database server error. If no error is active, a null string is returned. Both runtime and syntax errors are trapped.

> **NOTE:** *ERRORCODE returns a numeric value, SQLERRORCODE returns a text string.*

SQLERRORMESSAGE

Syntax: SQLERRORMESSAGE()

SQLERRORMESSAGE returns the text of the most recent database server error. These messages are generated by the server, they are not Paradox error messages. A null string is returned if there is no error.

SQLISCONNECT

Syntax: SQLISCONNECT()

Use SQLISCONNECT to determine if you are currently connected to a server and if the connection is active. This function returns True if the connection is active, otherwise it returns False.

SQLISREPLICA

Syntax: SQLISREPLICA(*TableName*)

You can test if a table is a replica using SQLISREPLICA. This function returns True if *TableName* is a replica, otherwise it returns False.

SQLMAPINFO

Syntax: SQLMAPINFO(*OptionName*, *TableName* [,*ColumnNumber*])

SQLMAPINFO returns information about a remote table's structure. The type of information returned is specified by *OptionName*

"TABLENAME" Returns name of remote table
"COLUMNNAME" Returns the column name specified by *ColumnNumber*
"COLUMNTYPE" Returns the data type of the column specified by *ColumnNumber*

Specify the name of the replica table with *TableName*. If you use COLUMNNAME or COLUMNTYPE for *OptionName*, *ColumnNumber* is required.

NOTE: *These options are not case sensitive but you do need to enclose the values used for* OptionName *in double quotes.*

SQLVAL

Syntax: SQLVAL(*Expression*)

Use SQLVAL to determine the correct dialect to use in SQL...ENDSQL commands. This function returns the correct string needed for the SQL dialect of the current connection. You must have an active connection for this function to work. The translation of expressions to SQL strings is

- Blank expressions return "NULL"
- Alphanumeric expressions are surrounded by single quotes (')
- N, $, and S expression data types are returned as strings
- Date expressions are returned as a dialect-specific dates

Error Handling in SQL Link

SQL Link expands Paradox's error-handling feature with the SQLERRORCODE and SQLERRORMESSAGE functions. Any error code or message returned by the server is available using these two functions. The error codes and messages differ between server products. Use the manuals provided with your server as a guide to the error codes, messages, and their meaning. Additionally, ERRORCODE has been changed. When a SQL database server error occurs, the numeric value returned by ERRORCODE is 1000 or greater. Table 13-5 lists the values and descriptions of the new ERRORCODE values.

You need to update your error procedure to handle these conditions. Test for error codes of 1000 or more at the beginning of the error procedure to determine if the error is from Paradox or the database server.

Table 13-5
Error codes for SQL environment

Error Code	Description
1000	General SQL error, SQLERRORMESSAGE contains server message
1001	Network error
1002	Deadlock on the server
1003	User aborted process with [Ctrl][Break]
1004	Not enough memory to complete operation
1005	Communication error
1006	Connection failed
1007	Insufficient access privileges or incompatible locks
1008	Object already exists
1009	Object name invalid
1010	General create error
1011	Database or disk full
1012	Object does not exist
1013	Column type or usage invalid
1014	Remote key violations (only when SQL...ENDSQL is used)
1015	Syntax error (only when SQL...ENDSQL is used)
1016	Copy failed
1017	Number of authorized users exceeded
1018	Replica inconsistent with remote table

The SQL Setup Program

The SQL Setup Program (SSP) included with SQL Link is a utility program that lets you customize your Paradox environment to work with SQL database servers. SSP features include

- Create replicas to provide access to server tables
- Customize server connections
- Create and execute SQL statements

SSP is a script that is stored in the same directory as the Paradox system files. The script name is SQLSETUP. If you're in a directory other than the one containing SQLSETUP.SC, use the full path name to play the script. Figure 13-20 shows the SSP splash screen.

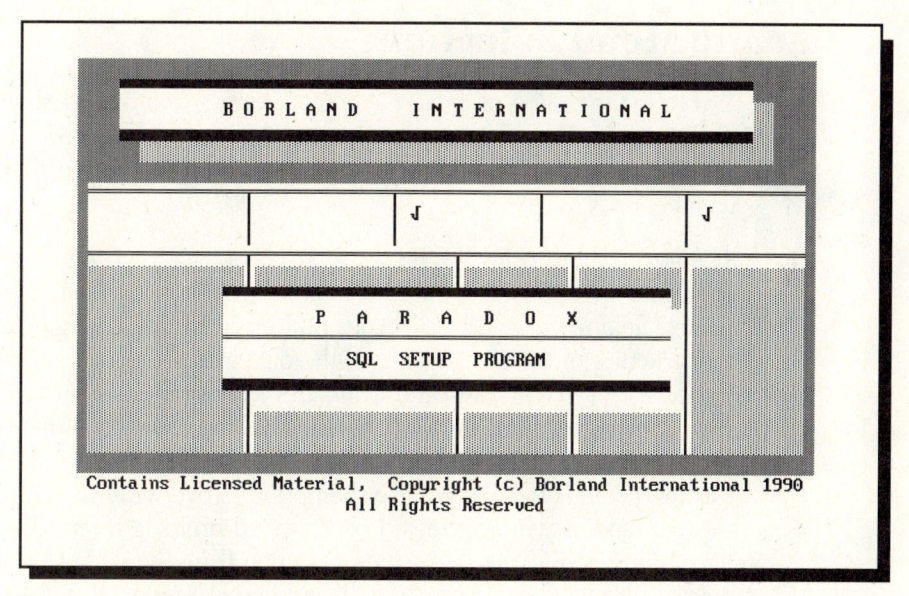

Figure 13-20 SQL Setup splash screen

After the splash screen is displayed you'll see the SSP Main menu as shown in Figure 13-21. The function each menu option provides is

Automatic	Automatically steps you through the process of creating replica tables and the local dictionary
Manual	Lets you control each step of the process

UseSQL Loads the SQL Editor so that you can create and execute SQL commands

ConnectList Lets you add, modify, and delete entries in the server connection list

Help Gives you access to the SSP Help system

Exit Exits SSP and returns to Paradox

```
Automatic    Manual    UseSql    ConnectList    Help    Exit
Let SQL Setup guide you through the process of creating replicas.
```

Figure 13-21 SQL Setup Main menu

Automatic Menu Selection

You have the option of using the current connection or choosing a new connection when you select {*Automatic*} or {*Manual*}. If no connection is set, the connection screen is displayed and you are prompted to choose a server connection.

The next prompt is for the name of the dictionary. SSP stores replica information in a dictionary (a Paradox table). The dictionary contains table names, field names, and field types of the remote tables. Figure 13-22 shows the structure of the dictionary and the data actually stored in the Company dictionary. (Two copies of the Company dictionary are shown. The second copy displays columns not displayed in the first copy.) The dictionary is always created in the current directory. If the name you enter duplicates an existing Paradox table, you have the option to overwrite the table, unless the existing table is write-protected or password-protected. In either case, you have to exit SSP and remove the protection from the table (SSP cannot replace tables that are protected). The table that SSP creates as the dictionary is write-protected.

While SSP is generating the dictionary, informational messages are displayed on the screen, indicating the status of operations. Figure 13-23 shows the initial message screen. If a server error occurs, the error message is displayed and you are returned to the SSP Main menu. Use the error message to resolve the problem.

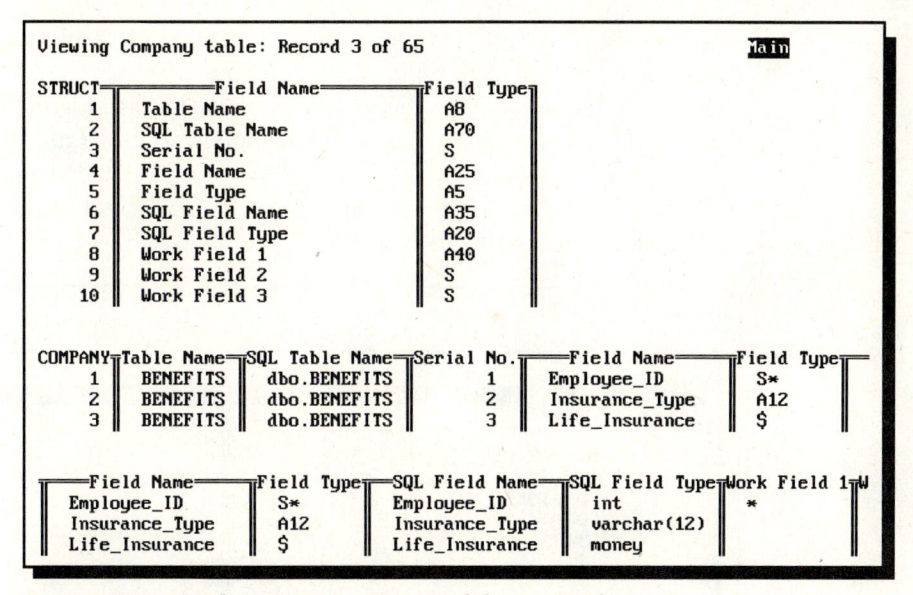

```
Viewing Company table: Record 3 of 65                        Main
STRUCT         Field Name        Field Type
   1    Table Name                A8
   2    SQL Table Name            A70
   3    Serial No.                S
   4    Field Name                A25
   5    Field Type                A5
   6    SQL Field Name            A35
   7    SQL Field Type            A20
   8    Work Field 1              A40
   9    Work Field 2              S
  10    Work Field 3              S

COMPANY  Table Name   SQL Table Name   Serial No.   Field Name       Field Type
   1     BENEFITS     dbo.BENEFITS         1        Employee_ID        S*
   2     BENEFITS     dbo.BENEFITS         2        Insurance_Type     A12
   3     BENEFITS     dbo.BENEFITS         3        Life_Insurance     $

       Field Name      Field Type   SQL Field Name    SQL Field Type  Work Field 1
       Employee_ID        S*        Employee_ID       int              *
       Insurance_Type     A12       Insurance_Type    varchar(12)
       Life_Insurance     $         Life_Insurance    money
```

Figure 13-22 SSP dictionary structure and data example

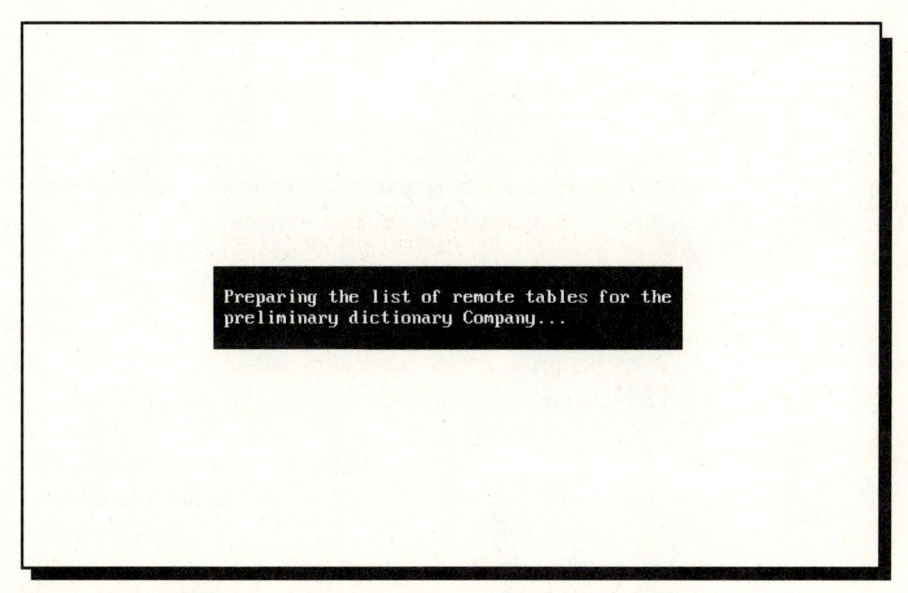

```
Preparing the list of remote tables for the
preliminary dictionary Company...
```

Figure 13-23 SSP processing message during dictionary creation

Once the list of remote tables is created, the tables are displayed for you to select the tables to create replicas for. Only the table names that your password gives you access to on the server appear in the list. Figure 13-24 shows an example of the table selection screen. Initially all tables are checked because SSP assumes you want access to all the remote tables. To remove a table from the list, move the cursor to the table name and press the space bar. A dash replaces the checkmark.

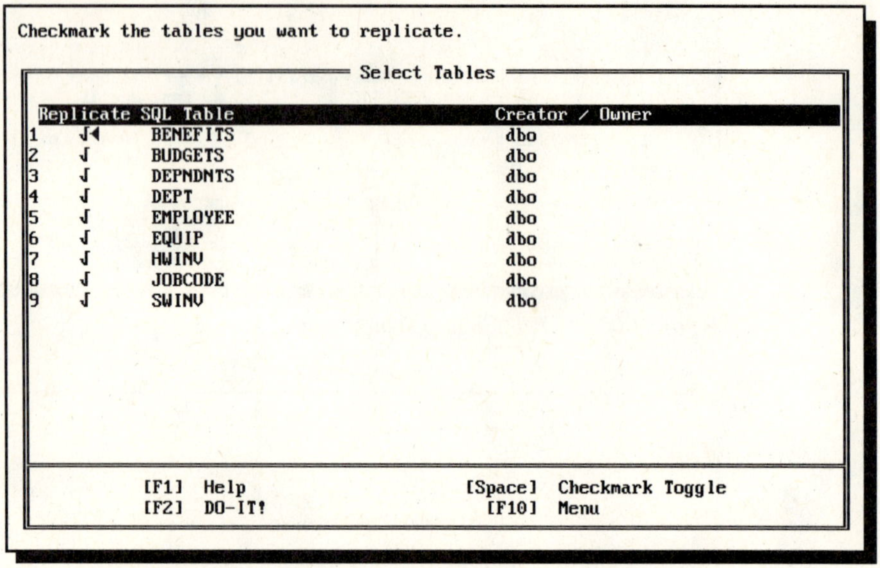

```
Checkmark the tables you want to replicate.
                          ═══════════════ Select Tables ═══════════════
      Replicate SQL Table                     Creator / Owner
   1      √◄      BENEFITS                    dbo
   2      √       BUDGETS                     dbo
   3      √       DEPNDNTS                    dbo
   4      √       DEPT                        dbo
   5      √       EMPLOYEE                    dbo
   6      √       EQUIP                       dbo
   7      √       HWINV                       dbo
   8      √       JOBCODE                     dbo
   9      √       SWINV                       dbo




               [F1]  Help                  [Space]  Checkmark Toggle
               [F2]  DO-IT!                [F10]    Menu
```

Figure 13-24 SSP remote table selection screen

Press [F2] after you have selected the tables. Potential errors are checked in table names, field names, and field types. All errors must be corrected before the dictionary is created. Sometimes two or more tables will have the same Paradox name because of the eight character DOS limitation for file names. SSP resolves this problem by abbreviating the table name and appending a dash and sequential number. The same technique is used if there are any server tables that duplicate any of Paradox's temporary table names (Answer, Changed, Entry, and so on). This is the same result as when you have two or more duplicate column names in the result of a query. A remote table cannot be replicated if

- It has more than 255 columns
- It has a record size greater than 1350 characters for keyed tables or 4000 characters for non-keyed tables

Figure 13-25 shows the Exception Replica List screen that displays remote tables that SSP had problems replicating. The first entry has the replica name changed to ANSWER-1 because the remote table duplicates one of Paradox's temporary table names. The SQL table Long_rcd has two dashes in the Replica column because the size of the record was greater than 1350 and has a key defined on the table.

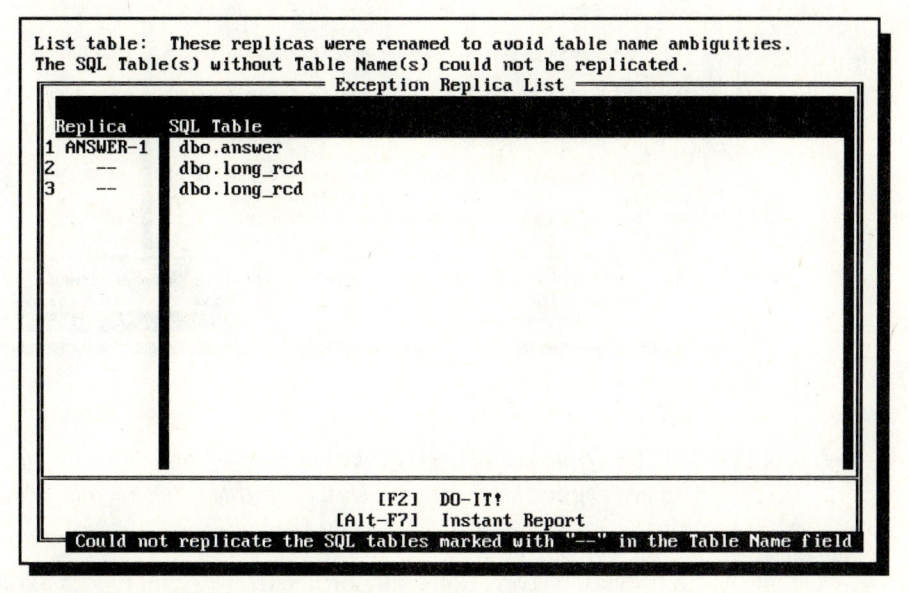

```
List table:  These replicas were renamed to avoid table name ambiguities.
The SQL Table(s) without Table Name(s) could not be replicated.
============================= Exception Replica List =============================

  Replica     SQL Table
1 ANSWER-1    dbo.answer
2 --          dbo.long_rcd
3 --          dbo.long_rcd




                              [F2]    DO-IT!
                            [Alt-F7]  Instant Report
  Could not replicate the SQL tables marked with "--" in the Table Name field
```

Figure 13-25 SSP Exception Replica List

It's also possible that field names will be duplicated in a table. In both Oracle and SQL Server, 30 characters is the maximum length for a field name. Paradox only supports 25-character field names. If the first 25 characters are not unique, a screen is displayed with the cursor on the problem and SSP asks for you to correct the problem. Figure 13-26 shows an example using test data with field names larger than 25 characters. The entries in the first Field Name column are the column names Paradox has created for the replica table, and the values in the second Field Name column are those of the SQL table. You can see each replica table entry is max_text_field_of_charact. Because the server field names are not unique at the 25th character, SSP requires the Paradox field name to be modified. This is not a problem with the IBM Database Manager because 18 characters is the maximum for field names.

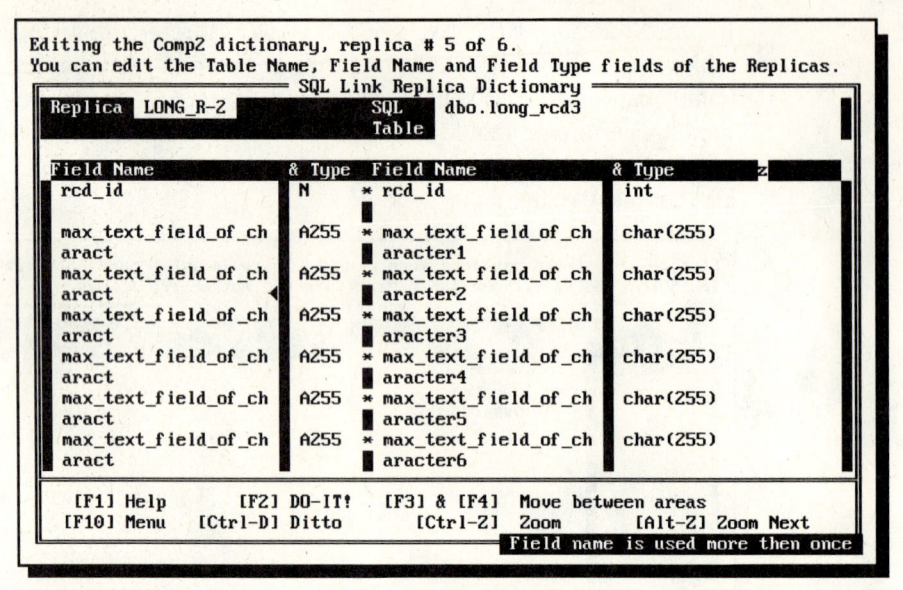

```
Editing the Comp2 dictionary, replica # 5 of 6.
You can edit the Table Name, Field Name and Field Type fields of the Replicas.
═══════════════════ SQL Link Replica Dictionary ═══════════════════
 Replica  LONG_R-2            SQL      dbo.long_rcd3
                              Table

 Field Name            & Type  Field Name            & Type
 rcd_id                  N    * rcd_id                int

 max_text_field_of_ch   A255  * max_text_field_of_ch  char(255)
 aract                         aracter1
 max_text_field_of_ch   A255  * max_text_field_of_ch  char(255)
 aract               ◄         aracter2
 max_text_field_of_ch   A255  * max_text_field_of_ch  char(255)
 aract                         aracter3
 max_text_field_of_ch   A255  * max_text_field_of_ch  char(255)
 aract                         aracter4
 max_text_field_of_ch   A255  * max_text_field_of_ch  char(255)
 aract                         aracter5
 max_text_field_of_ch   A255  * max_text_field_of_ch  char(255)
 aract                         aracter6

 [F1] Help        [F2] DO-IT!   [F3] & [F4]  Move between areas
 [F10] Menu   [Ctrl-D] Ditto    [Ctrl-Z] Zoom       [Alt-Z] Zoom Next
                                         Field name is used more then once
```

Figure 13-26 Field duplication resolution screen

NOTE: *While in the SQL Link Replica Dictionary form you can move between replica table entries. However, this is not recommended. Change only the information SSP asks you to modify.*

Some database servers don't support a currency data type. SSP converts these fields to numeric (N) field types but also gives you the option to change the data type to currency ($). Figure 13-27 shows an example from the Oracle sample database. Use the space bar on any field to toggle between N and $ data types.

Even after all this error checking, problems might still exist if the names of any of the replica tables to be created conflict with an existing local table or an existing replica table. When this occurs, SSP prompts you to correct the problem. A menu is displayed with four choices:

View   If the conflict is a local table, you can display it. This is only displayed if there is a conflict with a local table.

Rename   Rename the local or replica table (provided you have sufficient access rights).

Delete   You can delete a local table (provided you have sufficient access rights).

Cancel   Stops SSP and cancels processing.

Using Paradox SQL Link **429**

```
┌─────────────────────────────────────────────────────────────────────┐
│ Convert field types from numeric to currency.                       │
│ ══════════════════════════ Type Convert ═══════════════════════════ │
│ Replica                        SQL                                  │
│ Name        Field Name  & Type Table Name     Field Name    & Type  │
│ BONUS       SAL         N  ◄   SCOTT.BONUS    SAL           NUMBER(38)│
│                                                                     │
│ BONUS       COMM        N      SCOTT.BONUS    COMM          NUMBER(38)│
│                                                                     │
│ CUSTOMER    CUSTID      N      SCOTT.CUSTO    CUSTID        NUMBER(6)│
│                                MER                                  │
│                                                                     │
│ CUSTOMER    CREDITLIMIT N      SCOTT.CUSTO    CREDITLIMIT   NUMBER(9)│
│                                MER                                  │
│                                                                     │
│ DUMMY       DUMMY       N      SCOTT.DUMMY    DUMMY         NUMBER(38)│
│                                                                     │
│                                                                     │
│         [F1]  Help                    [Space]  Numeric Field Toggle │
│         [F2]  DO-IT!                  [F10]    Menu                 │
└─────────────────────────────────────────────────────────────────────┘
```

Figure 13-27 SSP data type conversion example

If duplicate replica tables exist, a message is not displayed as long as no forms or reports are associated with the replica. When the replica does have associated forms or reports, a message and menu is displayed as shown in Figure 13-28. At this point you must rename the existing replica, delete the replica, or cancel the Automatic setup process.

Problem resolution continues until all problems are corrected or until you cancel the process. When all conflicts are resolved, SSP creates the dictionary. The time it takes to create the dictionary depends on the number of tables and fields. SSP displays processing information during dictionary creation. Figure 13-29 shows the second step of the three-part process. When the dictionary is created, you return to the SSP Main menu.

Manual Menu Selection

Selecting {*Manual*} from the SSP Main menu displays the menu shown in Figure 13-30. The menu selections are

    Create   Create a preliminary dictionary.
    SelectTables   Select remote tables from a preliminary or existing dictionary.

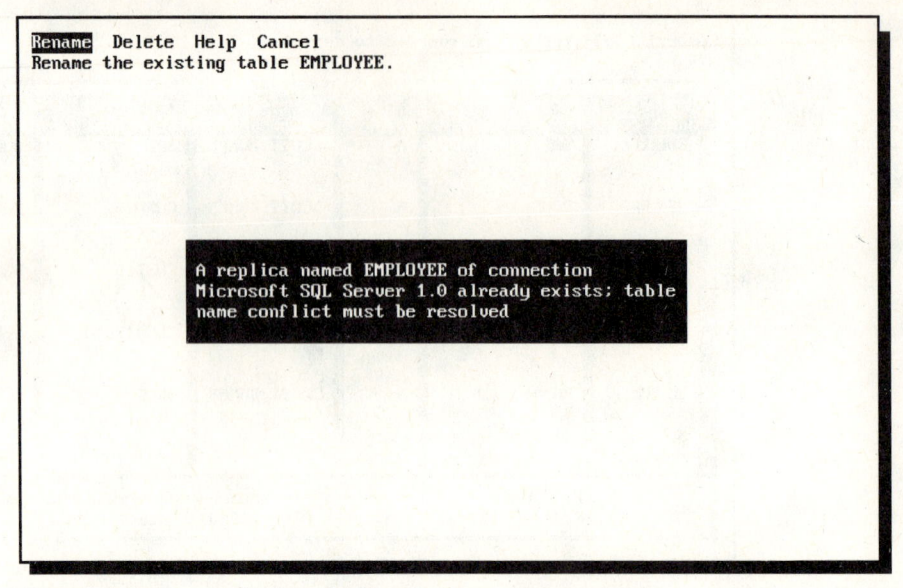

```
Rename  Delete  Help  Cancel
Rename the existing table EMPLOYEE.




                A replica named EMPLOYEE of connection
                Microsoft SQL Server 1.0 already exists; table
                name conflict must be resolved
```

Figure 13-28 Screen displayed when duplicate replica exists

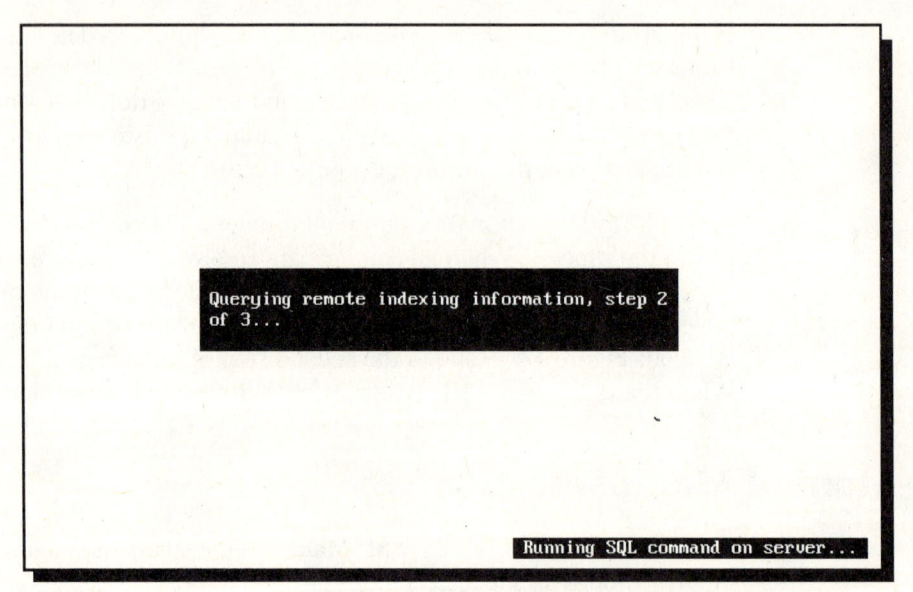

```
                Querying remote indexing information, step 2
                of 3...




                                        Running SQL command on server...
```

Figure 13-29 Dictionary creation information screen example

TypeConvert	Select fields to convert from N data type to $ data type.
Edit	Revise the replica table names, field names, and field data types.
ModifyName	Resolve local and replica table name conflicts.
Replicate	Create the replica tables.
Delete	Remove a dictionary from the directory.
Help	Access the Help system.

For each option except {*Help*}, you need to establish a connection and identify a dictionary. When you use {*Manual*}, you control each step as the dictionary is created or modified. The options are the same actions offered when you select {*Automatic*} from the SSP Main menu.

```
Create  SelectTables  TypeConvert  Edit  ModifyName  Replicate  Delete  Help
Create a preliminary dictionary.
```

Figure 13-30 SQL Setup Manual menu

> **NOTE:** *If you edit the dictionary and change the field names or data types of any replica table, SSP does not change the structure of the replica table. Your dictionary will not represent the true state of your tables. Therefore, it is best not to modify the dictionary directly.*

UseSQL Menu Selection

The {*UseSQL*} SSP Main menu selection loads the SQL Command Editor, where you can create SQL statements and sends them directly to the server. Figure 13-31 shows the command editor's window. {*UseSQL*} lets you test SQL statements before you include them in your application. (You can also do this with the PAL menu {*MiniScript*} option but in that case you have to use SQL...ENDSQL.) In the SQL Command Editor you can enter multiple SQL statements, but only one at a time is sent to the server for execution. SQL Command Editor options are discussed in more detail later in this chapter.

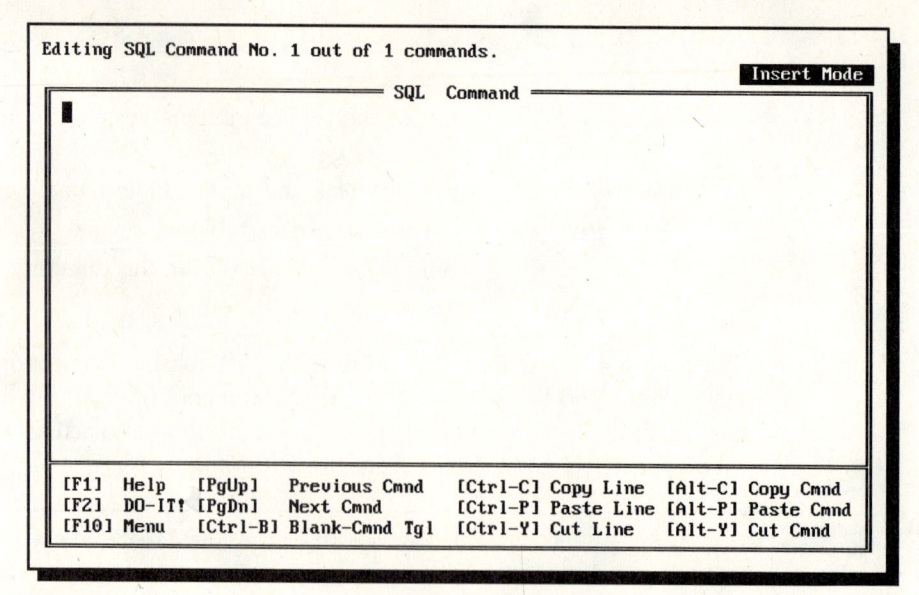

```
┌─────────────────────────────────────────────────────────────────┐
│ Editing SQL Command No. 1 out of 1 commands.                    │
│                       ═ SQL  Command ═           │ Insert Mode │ │
│ ▌                                                               │
│                                                                 │
│                                                                 │
│                                                                 │
│                                                                 │
│                                                                 │
│                                                                 │
│                                                                 │
│                                                                 │
│                                                                 │
│                                                                 │
│   [F1]  Help    [PgUp]  Previous Cmnd   [Ctrl-C] Copy Line  [Alt-C] Copy Cmnd │
│   [F2]  DO-IT!  [PgDn]  Next Cmnd       [Ctrl-P] Paste Line [Alt-P] Paste Cmnd│
│   [F10] Menu    [Ctrl-B] Blank-Cmnd Tgl [Ctrl-Y] Cut Line   [Alt-Y] Cut Cmnd  │
└─────────────────────────────────────────────────────────────────┘
```

Figure 13-31 {UseSQL} command editor window

ConnectList Menu Selection

Selecting {*ConnectList*} from the SSP Main menu lets you modify your server connection list. Each supported product has default connection settings. The connection information is stored in a file named PARADOX.DSQ. Multiple .DSQ files can exist. SSP looks for a .DSQ file in the same manner as Paradox looks for a .CFG file. The current directory is searched first. If no .DSQ file is found, the DOS path is used. SSP uses the first .DSQ file it finds. If none is found, the default server connections are used.

Connection information is displayed using the SQL Connection form. Figure 13-32 shows the screen for IBM Extended Edition Database Manager. Initially there is one entry for each installed product. Each connection in the list is treated as a single record and the form displays the information for one connection at a time. You can add, modify, and delete connections from this form. If you add an entry, some of the information for the currently displayed connection is duplicated as a new connection. The SQL Product, SQL Dialect, and all of the Connection Information Parameters are copied. The Connection Name and Description are left blank. You can enter up to 28 characters for the Connection Name and up to 80 characters for the Description. The combination of each of these must be unique and both fields must be entered. You can use [Ctrl][D] to ditto the values from the entry you copied. The Connection Name is used in the connection selection list displayed when you select {*Tools*} {*SQL*} {*Connection*} {*Select*}. The Connection Information Parameters differ based on the product the connection is based upon.

```
Editing the Connection Data Table.
Editing Connection No. 1, out of 3 connections.
═══════════════════════ SQL Connection ═══════════════════════
        SQL Product  IBMEE            SQL Dialect  IBMEE

   Connection Name  IBM OS/2 EE 1.2 DBM
       Description  Standard connection to IBM OS/2 Extended Edition Database
                    Manager
─────────────────── Connection Information Parameters ───────────────────
   Parameter                        Value
   1. Remote User Name
   2. Remote Password
   3. Server
   4. Database
   5. Library Directory             c:


   [F1]  Help           [F2] DO-IT!    [F3] & [F4] Move between areas   [F10] Menu
   [Ins] New Entry      [Del] Del Entry    [Ctrl-D] Ditto               [Alt-F7] Report
   [PgUp] & [PgDn] Scroll connections up and down
```

Figure 13-32 SQL Connection modification screen

If you press [F10] while in the SQL Connection screen, the ConnectList menu is displayed, as shown in Figure 13-33. The options are

Report	Print a report of the current server connection information.
Password	Define, modify, or remove the password for PARADOX.DSQ.
Help	Access the Help system.
DO-IT!	Save the server connection information after validation.
Cancel	Cancel changes to the server connection information.

```
 Report    Password    Help    DO-IT!    Cancel
Print a report on the current contents of PARADOX.DSQ
```

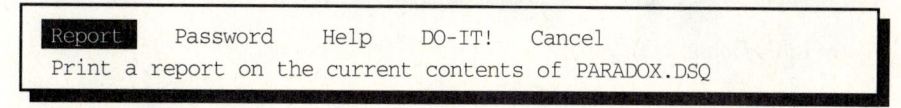

Figure 13-33 ConnectList Menu

Selecting {*Report*} from the ConnectList menu prints a report with all the current server connection information. Figure 13-34 shows an example of the report output when SQL Link support for all three products have been installed.

```
10/1/90                   Connection Data Report                    Page    1
                          ========================
Product: IBMEE          Dialect: IBMEE
======                  =======
Title:       IBM OS/2 EE 1.2 DBM
Description: Standard connection to IBM OS/2 Extended Edition Database
             Manager
             Parameter         Value
             ---------         -----
             Database
             Directory         c:
             Server
             User
             password
=============================================================================
Product: MSSQL          Dialect: MSSQL
======                  =======
Title:       Microsoft SQL Server 1.0
Description: Standard connection to Microsoft SQL Server
             Parameter         Value
             ---------         -----
             Database
             Password
             Server
             User
=============================================================================
Product: ORACLE         Dialect: ORACLE
======                  =======
Title:       Oracle Server 6.0
Description: Standard connection to Oracle Server
             Parameter         Value
             ---------         -----
             Host
             Password
             User
=============================================================================
```

Figure 13-34 ConnectList report

NOTE: *If you include the password for any connection, it is included in the printed output. This report is something you want to keep confidential otherwise you could compromise server security.*

To protect information in the PARADOX.DSQ file, select {Password} from the ConnectList menu. You are then asked for a master password and for confirmation of this password. The auxiliary password screen is then displayed. If you password protect a PARADOX.DSQ file, the first time an attempt is made to select a server connection from the list, a prompt is displayed asking for a password to access the connection list. If you don't want every user to have the ability to modify the connection list parameters, you need to assign a read-only password to the PARADOX.DSQ. Distribute only the read-only password to your users. The master password should be given only to those who have authorization to modify the connection list information.

You have the option to store the PARADOX.DSQ file in the directory as the Paradox system files, or in any other directory. The menu {HardDisk} {Network} is displayed when you save the connection list. If you select {HardDisk}, the file is stored in the same directory as the Paradox system files. The {Network} selection prompts you for the directory to store the file.

TRAP: *SSP looks in the current directory first for PARADOX.DSQ, then searches the DOS path. Paradox relies solely on the path when it needs to find the connection list information. It's best to keep one PARADOX.DSQ file in the directory with the Paradox system files unless you create a method for managing multiple copies.*

The SQL Command Editor

Start the SQL command editor by playing the UseSQL script or by selecting {UseSQL} from the SSP Main menu. The UseSQL script is installed in the same directory as the Paradox system files and can be executed from any directory by including the full path name.

The command editor lets you enter and execute SQL statements without having to use SQL...ENDSQL. In the editor, multiple SQL statements can be entered but each command is executed separately. The editor provides a scratch pad to store and test multiple SQL statements. You can view the results of a SQL statement if it returns data to Paradox. The splash screen shown in Figure 13-35 is displayed when you execute SQL, then you are

436 PC World Paradox 3.5—Power Programming Techniques

placed in the editor window shown in Figure 13-36. If a connection is not currently set, you are prompted to select a server connection.

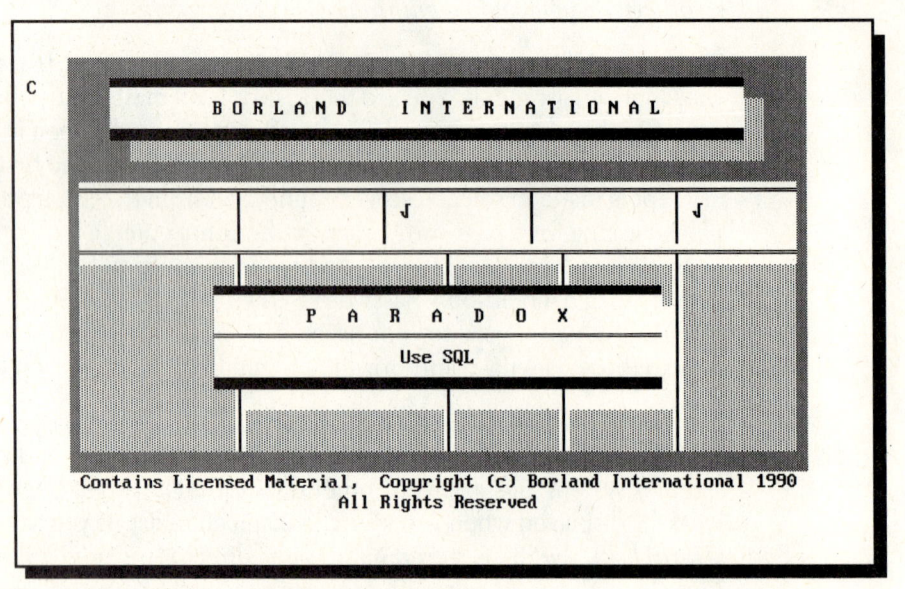

Figure 13-35 SQL command editor splash screen

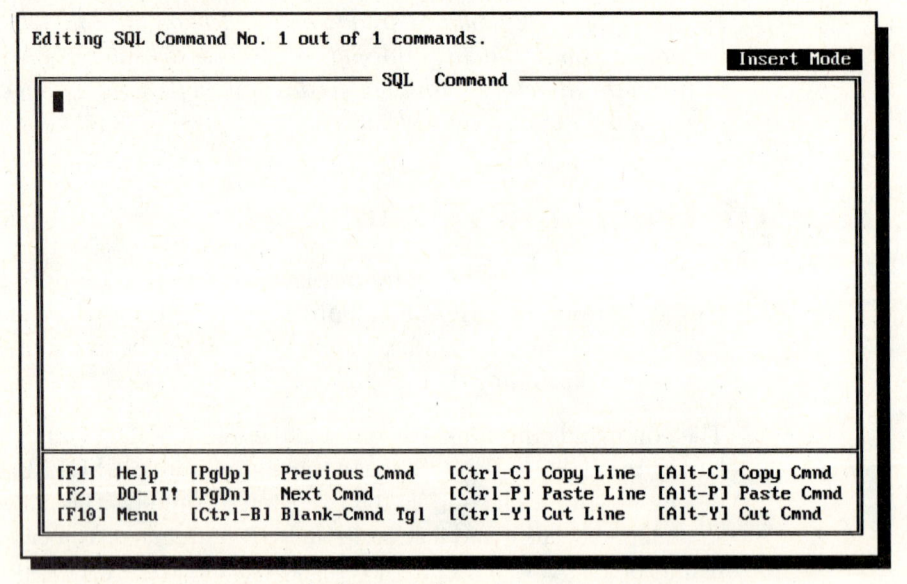

Figure 13-36 SQL command editor window

Using Paradox SQL Link **437**

The SQL command editor has better editing support than the Paradox script editor. Beyond the basic cursor movement keys, you can move between words, cut, copy, and paste commands and lines, move between commands, and more. SQL statements entered in the editor can be saved to a script or stored for use the next time the editor is used. Figure 13-37 shows the editor window on the second of two SQL statements.

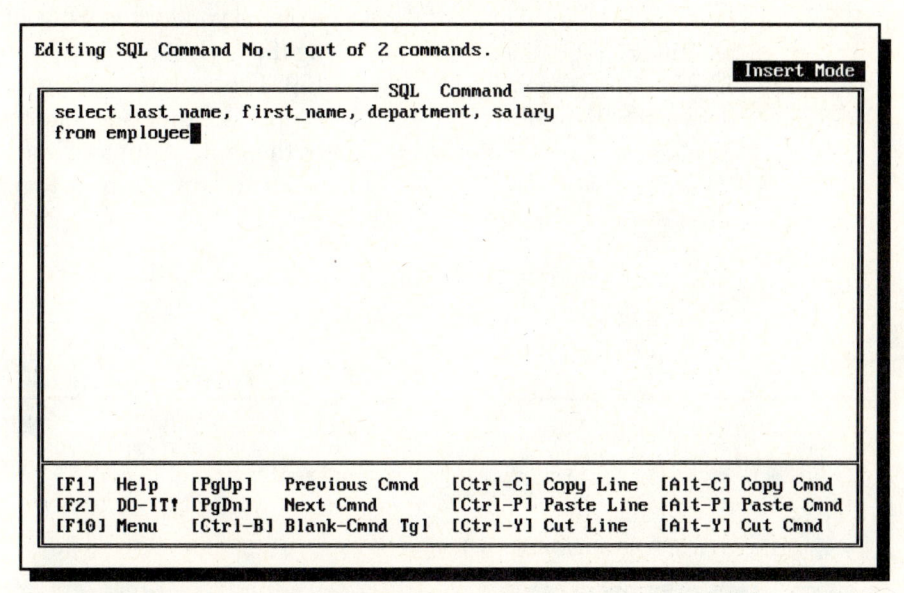

```
Editing SQL Command No. 1 out of 2 commands.
                                                        Insert Mode
                       ══════ SQL   Command ══════
  select last_name, first_name, department, salary
  from employee█




















 [F1]  Help    [PgUp]  Previous Cmnd    [Ctrl-C] Copy Line   [Alt-C] Copy Cmnd
 [F2]  DO-IT!  [PgDn]  Next Cmnd        [Ctrl-P] Paste Line  [Alt-P] Paste Cmnd
 [F10] Menu    [Ctrl-B] Blank-Cmnd Tgl  [Ctrl-Y] Cut Line    [Alt-Y] Cut Cmnd
```

Figure 13-37 SQL command editor screen with SQL statement entered

The SQL command editor menu is shown in Figure 13-38. The menu options are

SQLSave	Saves the SQL statements in the editor window as a Paradox script.
ChangeConnection	Displays a list of available servers to select from.
Erase	Deletes all SQL statements currently in the editor.
DO-IT!	Executes the SQL statement in the editor window on the server.
Help	Accesses the Help system.
Exit	Leaves the SQL command editor and saves the SQL statements currently in the editor.

```
┌─────────────────────────────────────────────────────────────────┐
│ SQLSave    ChangeConnection    Erase    DO-IT!   Help    Exit   │
│ Save the current SQL command in a PAL script                    │
└─────────────────────────────────────────────────────────────────┘
```

Figure 13-38 SQL command editor menu

If you select {*SQLSave*}, SQL Link prompts you for the name of the script to write the SQL statements to. Saving the SQL statements shown in Figure 13-37 creates the script in Figure 13-39. The SQL statements are placed between SQL and ENDSQL in the script. The time and date the script was created are also included. This creates the same script as {*Tools*} {*SQL*} {*SQLSave*} with the exception of the date and time information. If the script already exists, a menu is displayed asking if you want to

- Append the SQL command to the end of the script.
- Replace the existing script.
- Cancel the action.

```
; Script name: Usesql01.sc - SQL command saved at 09:37:30, Fri., 9/28/90
SQL
    select last_name, first_name, department, salary
    from employee
ENDSQL
; End of saving SQL command
```

Figure 13-39 Script saved from SQL command editor

Results of a SQL statement are stored in an Answer table. When data is returned, the editor displays the results. Figure 13-40 shows the screen after executing the SQL statement shown in Figure 13-39. Pressing [F10] displays a menu that allows you to

- View data in other local tables for the current directory.
- Rename the current table. This includes the Answer table or any other local table that you are viewing.
- Quit viewing the data and return to the command editor.

Exiting from the SQL command editor saves all the SQL commands in the scratch pad. A file called PARADOX.SQ1 is stored in your private directory and used to store the commands. If the scratch pad is empty, the file is not created.

```
Press [F10] Menu; [F3] UpImage; [F4] DownImage.
[F8] ClearImage; [Esc] Return to UseSQL work area.
ANSWER    Last_name        First_name     Department     Salary
   1    Charles          Anthony        MARKETING      42,200.00
   2    Garth            Timothy        MFG            26,050.00
   3    Williams         Bill           MARKETING      23,500.00
   4    McCarthy         Jennifer       MARKETING      22,100.00
   5    Jones            Mike II        MFG            32,000.00
   6    Brown            John II        MIS            46,400.00
   7    Barnes           Dorothy        FINANCE        22,000.00
   8    Owens            Lucy           MIS            27,400.00
   9    Harris           Jean           FINANCE        32,000.00
  10    Barnaby          Raymond        SALES          32,000.00
  11    Barth            Jim            MIS            43,000.00
  12    Smith            Peter          FINANCE        28,000.00
  13    Adams            Jerry          MFG            45,700.00
  14    Brown, Jr.       Bubba          MFG            31,500.00
  15    Walls II         Ingrid 11      SALES          44,550.00
```

Figure 13-40 Results of a SQL statement

Notes From READSQL Covering Each SQL Database Server Product

The following is an excerpt from the READSQL file on the Borland Paradox SQL Link installation disk:

5. ORACLE RDBM

Make sure that you have completely installed your DOS client's Oracle software by running the ORAINST program from the Oracle package. This process will set up the appropriate directories, copy the appropriate drivers and programs, create the configuration file, and set up the correct environment variables. You can verify the correctness of your installation with the SQL*Plus program, also included with the Oracle package.

The SQL Connection Parameters screen for Oracle includes a Host parameter. The Host string is a formatted string like '@p:servername'. It is made up of the '@' sign, the Driver Prefix from your SQL*Net *driver, and the name of your server. You can determine the Driver Prefix by typing REMORA LIST at the DOS prompt after you have loaded your SQL*Net driver.*

Due to a problem with the shipping SPX SQL*Net driver, Paradox may lose the connection during certain operations. If this happens, obtain the newest SPX SQL*Net driver from Oracle or restart Paradox with the following command-line option:

>   PARADOX -SQL ORACLEn

where n is the number 1 if the problem occurred while sending information to the server, 2 if the problem occurred while receiving information, or 3 if it occurred during both operations. With this command line option, server traffic is sent one record at a time, instead of in blocks, so communication will be slower.

To access data on other remote Oracle servers, create a VIEW to that data. The SQL Setup program will not look for tables on servers accessed by synonyms, but will create replicas for tables referenced by VIEWs.

6. IBM Extended Edition Database Manager

After installing the product, the first user to access the remote database must have administrator privileges. During that initial access, the administrator automatically creates an access plan called IBMSQL.

In order for other users to access the remote database, they must have execute privileges on the access plan. The administrator should run the following command from the Query Manager on the server:

>   GRANT EXECUTE ON username.IBMSQL TO username2

where 'user name' is the name of the administrator who created the access plan, and 'username2' is the name of the user or group who will have access to remote data.

The Library Directory prompt on the Paradox SQL Link connection screen indicates the location where the local catalog will be built. If you specify only the drive letter (the default) like 'c:', the catalog will be placed in 'C:\SQLDBDIR'. You can also specify an existing directory by listing the path on the Library Directory prompt. If you do specify a directory other than the root, be sure that the catalog directory is available when you connect to the server with that replica, or you will see the message "Error cataloging remote database." If you share replicas *with other users, be sure that they have a directory for the catalog in the same location on their computer. We recommend that you leave the Library Directory at the default 'c:' unless you don't have a c: drive.*

When you select a connection to the server, SQL Link will look in the directory specified by the Library Directory parameter. If it doesn't find a catalog there, it will build one for the server you have named. If it finds a catalog, it will use that catalog to locate the server containing the database you are requesting. For this reason, don't use the same Database name on different servers. Manually delete the local catalog if the server that the catalog references is no longer available or valid. Paradox SQL Link will then automatically create a new catalog when you next connect to the server.

A query cannot contain a checkmark on an A255 field (an alphanumeric field of 255 characters in length). Use Check Plus [Alt][F6] instead to query A255 fields.

Multi-line INSERT queries based on only one table are not allowed (you cannot insert values from a table into that same table).

Date arithmetic, string concatenation, and range operators on alpha fields are not supported.

7. Microsoft SQL Server

The Microsoft SQL Server 1.0 connection also supports Microsoft SQL Server 1.1.

The Transact-SQL PRINT statement is not supported in SQL...ENDSQL commands.

SQL Server does not support SELECT DISTINCT queries on IMAGE or TEXT fields. Use Check Plus [Alt][F6] instead of Check [F6] to include these fields in queries."

SQL Link Code Examples

The scripts and procedures listed in this section are included to give you a flavor of how to use some of the commands and functions in SQL Link. These scripts include logons, connection, or replica table connection information, transaction processing, and real-time multitable processing with forward and backward browsing through a table. Each of these examples use SQL Server as the server connection.

As stated earlier, before you can access any table on the database server, you need to connect to the server. Listing 13-1 shows a script that always connects to the same server and database each time it is played. Lines 3 through 6 place information on the screen stating that the connection is being initiated. Line 8 performs the connection. SQLSELECTCONNECT is used with a parameter list to prevent the server selection screen from being displayed. The VALUES keyword identifies the user name, password, server, and database connection parameters. If the connection fails, *retval* is set to False. Lines 12 through 22 display the error messages and codes from both Paradox and the server if the connection fails. This type of script is handy to include in your directory so you can quickly attach to the server. Since it has user name and password information in it, it is a good idea to password-protect the script.

```
1)  ; SqlLogin.sc
2)
3)  CURSOR OFF
4)  CLEAR
5)  MESSAGE "Connecting to Microsoft SQL Server, Company database, Please wait!"
6)  CANVAS OFF
7)
8)  SQLSELECTCONNECT PRODUCT "MSSQL"
9)    VALUES "Johns", "xyz5567", "srvr291man", "company"
10)
11) IF retval = False THEN
12)   CLEAR
13)   @ 5,0  ?? "Connection failed, error codes and messages are as follows:"
14)   ? ""
15)   ? "ErrorCode      :" + STRVAL(ERRORCODE())
16)   ? "ErrorMessage   :" + ERRORMESSAGE()
17)   ? "SQLErrorCode   :" + STRVAL(SQLERRORCODE())
18)   ? "SQLErrorMessage:" + SQLERRORMESSAGE()
19)   @ 24,0 ?? "Press any key to continue"
20)   CANVAS ON
21)   kp = GETCHAR()
22)   RELEASE VARS kp
23) ELSE
24)   QUIT "Connection established to SQL Server, Company database!"
25) ENDIF
```

Listing 13-1 Server logon script

A more generalized login procedure is displayed in Listing 13-2. Line 7 tests to see if SQL Link is installed and operating. If it isn't, there is no sense in asking for connection information or trying to connect to a server. If SQL Link is active, the next thing the procedure does is to see if you are already connected using SQLCONNECTINFO("TITLE") in line 10. If this function returns a blank, there is no connection established and the server selection screen is displayed using SQLSELECTCONNECT (line 34). If a connection is already established, you are asked if you would like to change the connection. If the answer is N (no), the procedure ends. If you respond with a Y, the connection selection screen is displayed. If you cancel from the server selection screen or the connection fails, the Paradox and server error messages are displayed (lines 51 through 57). This procedure can be used to connect to any server using any user name and password. It is more flexible than the previous example but does require input.

```
1)  ; Login.sc
2)
3)  ;  This script contains a generic logon procedure
4)
5)  PROC Login()
6)    PRIVATE chngconnect
7)    IF NOT ISSQL() THEN
8)       RETURN True
9)    ELSE
10)      IF NOT ISBLANK(SQLCONNECTINFO("TITLE")) THEN ;  If current connection
11)                                                  ; connection active
12)         @ 24,0 ?? "Current connection: ",SQLCONNECTINFO("Title")+ ". Change it" +
13)            " (Y/N)? "
14)         STYLE REVERSE
15)         ACCEPT "A1" PICTURE "{Y,N}" DEFAULT "N" TO chngconnect
16)         STYLE
17)         @ 24,0 CLEAR EOL
18)         IF chngconnect = "Y" THEN
19)            SQLSELECTCONNECT
20)            IF retval THEN
21)               SQLSAVECONNECT
22)               RETURN False
23)            ELSE
24)               @ 24,0 ?? "Connection not made, press any key to continue"
25)               kp = GETCHAR()
26)               @ 24,0 CLEAR EOL
27)               RETURN True
28)            ENDIF
29)         ELSE
30)            RETURN False
31)         ENDIF
32)      ELSE
33)         MESSAGE "Loading connection screen, Please wait!"
34)         SQLSELECTCONNECT
35)         IF retval THEN
36)            SQLSAVECONNECT
37)            RETURN False
```

Listing 13-2 *Generalized login procedure*

```
38)       ELSE
39)          @ 24,0 ?? "Connection not made, press any key to continue"
40)          kp = GETCHAR()
41)          @ 24,0 CLEAR EOL
42)          RETURN True
43)       ENDIF
44)
45)    ENDIF
46)  ENDIF
47) ENDPROC
48)
49) Login()
50) IF retval = True THEN
51)    CLEAR
52)    @ 5,0
53)    ? "Connection to server failed: "
54)    ? "SQLERRORCODE    : ",SQLERRORCODE()
55)    ? "SQLERRORMESSAGE : ",SQLERRORMESSAGE()
56)    @ 24,0 ?? "Press any key to continue"
57)    kp = GETCHAR()
58)  ELSE
59)    MESSAGE "Connection made"
60) ENDIF
```

Listing 13-2 Generalized login procedure—continued

If you forget which server you're connected to, SQLCONNECTINFO returns four different pieces of connection information. Listing 13-3 is a sample program demonstrating the use of this function to get server information. If a connection is set, the title, description, product code, and dialect are printed to the screen.

```
1) ; ConnInfo.sc
2)
3) ;  This script is an example of how to use SQLCONNECTINFO
4)
5) CLEAR
6) MESSAGE "Getting information on current server connection, Please wait!"
7) CANVAS OFF
8) IF ISBLANK(SQLCONNECTINFO("TITLE")) THEN
9)    BEEP SLEEP 100 BEEP SLEEP 100 BEEP
10)   MESSAGE "Current connection not set!"
11) ELSE
12)    CLEAR
13)    @ 5,0
14)    ?? "Connection Information"
15)    ? ""
```

Listing 13-3 SQLCONNECTINFO example to retrieve information on current connection

```
16)  ?   "Title       : " + SQLCONNECTINFO("TITLE")
17)  ?   "Description: " + SQLCONNECTINFO("DESCRIPTION")
18)  ?   "Product     : " + SQLCONNECTINFO("PRODUCT")
19)  ?   "Dialect     : " + SQLCONNECTINFO("DIALECT")
20) ENDIF
21) @ 24,0 ?? "Press any key to continue"
22) CANVAS ON
23) kp = GETCHAR()
24) RELEASE VARS kp
```

Listing 13-3 *SQLCONNECTINFO example to retrieve information on current connection—cont.*

The next script shows how to get the same information on a replica table. Listing 13-4 is a generic procedure that lets you select any table from the current directory and print the same information as in the previous example. **SHOWTABLES** is used to display a list of tables for the current directory. **SQLISREPLICA** is used to determine if the selected table name is a replica. If it is, **SQLCONNECTINFO** returns the title, description, product, and dialect information.

```
1)  ; Coninfo2
2)
3)  ;  Example of SQLCONNECTINFO for replica tables
4)
5)
6)  CLEAR
7)  WHILE True
8)    SHOWTABLES
9)    DIRECTORY()
10)   "Select table name to get server connect information for, [Esc] to cancel"
11)   TO tblname
12)   IF tblname = "Esc" OR tblname = "None" THEN
13)     CLEAR
14)     MESSAGE("No table selected or none available!")
15)     SLEEP 3000
16)     QUITLOOP
17)   ENDIF
18)
19)   MESSAGE "Getting information on ", tblname," replica table, Please wait!"
20)   CANVAS OFF
21)   IF NOT SQLISREPLICA(tblname) THEN
22)     BEEP SLEEP 100 BEEP SLEEP 100 BEEP
23)     MESSAGE "Table ",tblname," is not a replica table!"
24)   ELSE
25)     CLEAR
26)     @ 5,0
```

Listing 13-4 *SQLCONNECTINFO example to retrieve information on replica tables*

```
27)     ?? "Connection Information for " + tblname + " replica table"
28)     ? ""
29)     ? "Title      : " + SQLCONNECTINFO("TITLE",tblname)
30)     ? "Description: " + SQLCONNECTINFO("DESCRIPTION",tblname)
31)     ? "Product    : " + SQLCONNECTINFO("PRODUCT",tblname)
32)     ? "Dialect    : " + SQLCONNECTINFO("DIALECT",tblname)
33)   ENDIF
34)   @ 24,0 ?? "Press any key to continue"
35)   CANVAS ON
36)   kp = GETCHAR()
37)   @ 24,0 CLEAR EOL
38) ENDWHILE
39) RELEASE VARS kp, tblname
```

Listing 13-4 SQLCONNECTINFO example to retrieve information on replica tables—continued

Transaction processing is one of the selling points of a SQL database. A set of actions can be grouped into a unit of work defined as a transaction. If all the actions are successful, the entire set of actions are committed (saved) in the database. If any one action fails, you have the option to roll back (cancel) the changes. Listing 13-5 contains procedures demonstrating how to use transaction processing during data modification to provide Edit and CoEdit type features while editing data on a server. The process also demonstrates how you can use SQL NOFETCH...ENDSQL and SQLFETCH to move forward and backward in a table.

The technique used here is to create a local table that duplicates the structure of the remote table. The first record of the master table is retrieved from the server. Scrolling forward and backward in a SQL table is not directly supported. Using cursor control, you can get scrolling capability, but you pay a price in performance.

The process starts by retrieving the first Employee record in the EmpOnly procedure (lines 65 through 74). SQL NOFETCH executes the SELECT statement on the server. If there are no records, the command fails and the processing halts.

```
65)   SQL NOFETCH                              ; RETRIEVE THE EMPLOYEE DATA
66)     select * from employee order by employee_id
67)   ENDSQL
68)   IF retval = True THEN
69)     FetchEmp()
70)     IF retval = False THEN
71)       MESSAGE "No employee records, modification cancelled!"
72)       SLEEP 3000
73)       RETURN
74)     ENDIF
```

The next step is to retrieve the record from the pending query. This is done by FetchEmp. SQLFETCH returns the next record into the *employee.data* array. If this is successful, COPYTOARRAY copies the data into the local table for viewing and editing in a WAIT command (line 81).

```
 3) PROC FetchEmp()
 4)   PRIVATE employee.data
 5)   SQLFETCH employee.data            ; Retrieve employee record
 6)   SQLRELEASE                        ; Release pending query
 7)   IF retval THEN                    ; If record retrieved,
 8)     COPYFROMARRAY employee.data     ; place data in Lemp table
 9)     empid = employee.data[2]        ; save Employee Id value
10)     RETURN True
11)   ELSE                              ; Else no record returned from
12)     RETURN False                    ; query
13)   ENDIF
14) ENDPROC
```

When one of the keys in the UNTIL key list is pressed, the procedure calls CheckRcdStat to determine if the record was modified. RECORDSTATUS returns True if there have been changes to the record. If this is the case, the appropriate update procedure is called. In this example there is only one table in the form. The procedure UpdateEmployee executes SQL UPDATE, sending the current value for each field in the local table. The WHERE clause matches the record on the server based on the key field.

```
17) PROC UpdateEmployee()                     ; Start a transaction
18)   SQL
19)     UPDATE employee
20)       SET Last_Name      = ~SQLVAL([Last_Name])~,
21)           First_Name     = ~SQLVAL([First_Name])~,
22)           Date_hired     = ~SQLVAL([Date_hired])~,
23)           Birth_date     = ~SQLVAL([Birth_date])~,
24)           Ssn            = ~SQLVAL([Ssn])~,
25)           Department     = ~SQLVAL([Department])~,
26)           Job_code       = ~SQLVAL([Job_code])~,
27)           Work_phone     = ~SQLVAL([Work_phone])~,
28)           Salary         = ~SQLVAL([Salary])~,
29)           Exemptions     = ~SQLVAL([Exemptions])~,
30)           Address        = ~SQLVAL([Address])~,
31)           City           = ~SQLVAL([City])~,
32)           State          = ~SQLVAL([State])~,
33)           Zip            = ~SQLVAL([Zip])~,
34)           Home_phone     = ~SQLVAL([Home_phone])~,
35)           Marital_Status = ~SQLVAL([Marital_status])~,
36)           Sex            = ~SQLVAL([Sex])~
37)       WHERE Employee_ID = ~[Employee_ID]~
38)   ENDSQL
39)   RETURN retval
40) ENDPROC
```

To go to the next record, the SQL statements in line 112 and 113 are executed to position the cursor on the next record. By selecting the employee_id's greater than the current record's ID and sorting the results by the ID, the next available record on the server is retrieved.

```
112)              select * from employee where employee_id > ~empid~
113)                 order by employee_id
```

Scrolling backward requires a different SQL statement. To get the previous record, the SQL statements in lines 123 and 124 are executed. The major difference here is to retrieve the records less than the current ID and sort the results in descending order.

```
123)              select * from employee where employee_id < ~empid~
124)                 order by employee_id desc
```

Providing the undo capability of Paradox's Edit mode requires that you start the entire session as one transaction. This is done in line 76 with SQLSTARTTRANS. If you press [F2] to save the modifications, the transaction is committed by SQLCOMMIT (line 107). If you press [Esc] and cancel the session, all the changes are rolled back by SQLROLLBACK (line 142).

```
1)  ; EmpOnly.sc
2)
3)  PROC FetchEmp()
4)    PRIVATE employee.data
5)    SQLFETCH employee.data              ; Retrieve employee record
6)    SQLRELEASE                          ; Release pending query
7)    IF retval THEN                      ; If record retrieved,
8)      COPYFROMARRAY employee.data       ; place data in Lemp table
9)      empid = employee.data[2]          ; save Employee Id value
10)     RETURN True
11)   ELSE                                ; Else no record returned from
12)     RETURN False                      ; query
13)   ENDIF
14) ENDPROC
15)
16)
17) PROC UpdateEmployee()                 ; Start a transaction
18)   SQL
19)     UPDATE employee
20)       SET Last_Name    = ~SQLVAL([Last_Name])~,
21)           First_Name   = ~SQLVAL([First_Name])~,
22)           Date_hired   = ~SQLVAL([Date_hired])~,
23)           Birth_date   = ~SQLVAL([Birth_date])~,
24)           Ssn          = ~SQLVAL([Ssn])~,
25)           Department   = ~SQLVAL([Department])~,
```

Listing 13-5 SQL transaction commit and rollback example

```
26)            Job_code         = ~SQLVAL([Job_code])~,
27)            Work_phone       = ~SQLVAL([Work_phone])~,
28)            Salary           = ~SQLVAL([Salary])~,
29)            Exemptions       = ~SQLVAL([Exemptions])~,
30)            Address          = ~SQLVAL([Address])~,
31)            City             = ~SQLVAL([City])~,
32)            State            = ~SQLVAL([State])~,
33)            Zip              = ~SQLVAL([Zip])~,
34)            Home_phone       = ~SQLVAL([Home_phone])~,
35)            Marital_Status   = ~SQLVAL([Marital_status])~,
36)            Sex              = ~SQLVAL([Sex])~
37)        WHERE Employee_ID = ~[Employee_ID]~
38)     ENDSQL
39)     RETURN retval
40) ENDPROC
41)
42)
43) PROC CheckRcdStat()
44)   PRIVATE retprocval
45)   IF RECORDSTATUS("Modified") THEN      ; If the current record has been
46)     SWITCH                              ; modified update server record
47)       CASE tblname = "Lemp"     : retprocval = UpdateEmployee()
48)       CASE tblname = "Lbene"    : retprocval = UpdateBenefits()
49)       CASE tblname = "Ldepndts" : retprocval = UpdateDepndnts()
50)     ENDSWITCH
51)     RETURN retprocval                   ; Return the success or failure
52)   ELSE                                  ; status of the update
53)     RETURN True
54)   ENDIF
55) ENDPROC
56)
57)
58)
59) PROC EmpOnly()
60)   PRIVATE tblname, retkey, msg
61)   COEDIT "lemp"
62)   PICKFORM 2
63)   SQLRELEASE                            ; Release any active SQL NOFETCH
64)   msg     = ""
65)   SQL NOFETCH                           ; RETRIEVE THE EMPLOYEE DATA
66)     select * from employee order by employee_id
67)   ENDSQL
68)   IF retval = True THEN
69)     FetchEmp()
70)     IF retval = False THEN
71)       MESSAGE "No employee records, modification cancelled!"
72)       SLEEP 3000
73)       RETURN
74)     ENDIF
75)
76)     SQLSTARTTRANS                       ; Start a transaction on the server
77)
```

Listing 13-5 SQL transaction commit and rollback example—continued

```
78)        IF retval = True THEN
79)          CANVAS ON
80)          WHILE True
81)            WAIT RECORD
82)              prompt "View Employee Information   [F2]-Exit   [Esc]-Cancel",
83)                     "[PgDn]-Next Record   [PgUp]-Previous Record"
84)              MESSAGE msg
85)              UNTIL "F2","PgUp","PgDn","Esc",
86)                    "DOS","DOSBIG","ZOOM","ZOOMNEXT"
87)            retkey = retval
88)            msg = ""
89)            tblname = TABLE()
90)
91) ; ****************************************************
92) ; *                                                  *
93) ; * Data validation should be done here              *
94) ; *                                                  *
95) ; ****************************************************
96)
97)            CheckRcdStat()           ;  Check to see if the record was
98)                                     ;  was updated, if so, update server
99)            SWITCH
100)             CASE retkey = "F2" :
101)               CLEAR
102)               MESSAGE "Saving data, Please wait!"
103)               CANVAS OFF
104)               DEL
105)               DO_IT!
106)
107)               SQLCOMMIT            ; Commit the modifications
108)
109)               QUITLOOP
110)             CASE retkey = "PgDn" :
111)               SQL NOFETCH
112)                 select * from employee  where employee_id > ~empid~
113)                 order by employee_id
114)               ENDSQL
115)               IF retval = True THEN
116)                 FetchEmp()
117)               ELSE
118)                 msg = "Select failed!"
119)               ENDIF
120)               LOOP
121)             CASE retkey = "PgUp" :
122)               SQL NOFETCH
123)                 select * from employee  where employee_id < ~empid~
124)                 order by employee_id desc
125)               ENDSQL
126)               IF retval = True THEN
127)                 FetchEmp()
128)               ELSE
129)                 msg = "Select failed!"
```

Listing 13-5 *SQL transaction commit and rollback example—continued*

```
130)              ENDIF
131)           CASE retkey = "Esc" :
132)              SHOWMENU
133)                 "No"  :  "Do Not cancel sesssion, Return to form",
134)                 "Yes" :  "Cancel ENTIRE session"
135)              TO cancelchoice
136)              IF cancelchoice = "Yes" THEN
137)                 CLEAR
138)                 MESSAGE "Session cancelled, modifications are being" +
139)                         " rolled back!"
140)                 CANVAS OFF
141)
142)                 SQLROLLBACK       ;  Roll back the transaction
143)
144)                 DEL               ; Delete record in holding table
145)                 DO_IT!
146)                 QUITLOOP
147)              ENDIF
148)              LOOP
149)         ENDSWITCH
150)       ENDWHILE
151)     ELSE
152)       MESSAGE "Could not start transaction: ",SQLERRORMESSAGE()
153)       kp = getchar()
154)     ENDIF
155)   ELSE
156)     MESSAGE "Extract failed: ",SQLERRORMESSAGE()
157)   ENDIF
158)   CLEARALL
159)   CANVAS ON
160) ENDPROC
161)
162)
163) message "Retrieving data and loading form, Please wait"
164) CANVAS ON
165) CANVAS OFF
166)
167) EmpOnly()
```

Listing 13-5 SQL transaction commit and rollback example—continued

The next example demonstrates how to provide multitable and multi-row capability using data from the database server. The same basic technique from the previous example is the foundation for the program. A three-table form with a one-to-one relationship and a one-to-many relationship is the structure of the example. This is the same Employee, Benefits, Dependents example used in earlier chapters of the book. The first record of the master table is retrieved from the server and the key is used to retrieve the records for both detail tables. In this example, each time a record is changed, it is committed.

Each table must have a separate update procedure. CheckRcdStat determines the current table and calls the appropriate SQL UPDATE statement when a record has been modified.

```
140) PROC CheckRcdStat()
141)   PRIVATE retprocval
142)   IF RECORDSTATUS("Modified") THEN        ; If the current record has been
143)     SWITCH                                 ; modified update server record
144)       CASE tblname = "Lemp"     : retprocval = UpdateEmployee()
145)       CASE tblname = "Lbene"    : retprocval = UpdateBenefits()
146)       CASE tblname = "Ldepndts" : retprocval = UpdateDepndnts()
147)     ENDSWITCH
148)     RETURN retprocval                      ; Return the success or failure
149)   ELSE                                     ; status of the update
150)     RETURN True
151)   ENDIF
152) ENDPROC
```

The update procedures are slightly different than in the previous code listing. Using the benefits information as an example, each update is treated as a single transaction. A SQLSTARTTRANS statement precedes the SQL statement. If the update succeeds, the transaction is committed (line 81). If it fails, the transaction is rolled back (line 84). This same process is performed for both employee and dependents data.

```
69) PROC UpdateBenefits()
70)   SQLSTARTTRANS                             ; Start a transaction
71)   SQL                                        ; Send SQL UPDATE statement
72)     UPDATE Benefits
73)       SET Insurance_type   = ~SQLVAL([Insurance_type])~,
74)           Life_insurance   = ~SQLVAL([Life_insurance])~,
75)           Short_term_disab = ~SQLVAL([Short_term_disab])~,
76)           Long_term_disab  = ~SQLVAL([Long_term_disab])~,
77)           Us_saving_bond   = ~SQLVAL([Us_saving_bond])~
78)       WHERE Employee_ID = ~[Employee_ID]~
79)   ENDSQL
80)   IF SQLERRORCODE() = "0" AND ERRORCODE() = 0 THEN  ; If no error occurred
81)     SQLCOMMIT                                        ; commit transaction
82)     RETURN True
83)   ELSE
84)     SQLROLLBACK                                      ; else roll back
85)     RETURN False                                     ; transaction
86)   ENDIF
87) ENDPROC
```

Retrieving records from the server now requires the local table be emptied before the data is inserted. The CleanTables procedure moves to each table and deletes any existing rows. This provides clean master and detail tables for data insertion.

```
 7) PROC CleanTables()
 8)   PRIVATE numofrcds
 9)   MOVETO "Ldepndts"
10)   numofrcds = NIMAGERECORDS()              ; Remove current Depndnts record
11)   FOR i FROM 1 to numofrcds
12)      DEL
13)   ENDFOR
14)   MOVETO "Lbene"                            ; Remove current Depndnts record
15)   DEL
16)   MOVETO "Lemp"                             ; Remove current Employee record
17)   DEL
18) ENDPROC
```

Populating the local table with the dependents data requires a loop process because there could be multiple records returned from the query. In FetchDepndnts, lines 57 through 61 retrieves a record, inserts the data, moves to the next record, and starts the process over again. Because the SQL statement sorted the rows on the dependents SSN, which is the second part of the key, this technique works fine. If the query did not sort the data, an INSERT is used and Paradox puts the data in the correct order.

```
48) PROC FetchDepndnts()
49)   PRIVATE depndnts.data, numofrcds
50)   SQL NOFETCH                               ; Retrieve dependents data
51)     select * from depndnts
52)     where employee_id = ~empid~
53)     order by dependents_ssn
54)   ENDSQL
55)   IF retval = True THEN                     ; If data exists,
56)     SQLFETCH depndnts.data                  ; place each dependents record
57)     WHILE retval = True                     ; in the Ldepnts table
58)        COPYFROMARRAY depndnts.data
59)        DOWN
60)        SQLFETCH depndnts.data
61)     ENDWHILE
62)     DEL                                     ; Delete blank record
63)     HOME                                    ; Move to first record
64)   ENDIF
65)   SQLRELEASE                                ; Release pending query
66)   MOVETO "Lemp"
67) ENDPROC
```

As you can see, providing multitable, forward and backward scrolling with database server data requires a substantial amount of coding. What this code doesn't show you is the amount of time it takes to return the data. In our testing, each forward or backward movement took about 2-3 seconds before the screen was refreshed. If your applications and users need this capability and the data is in remote tables, this is the response time that you'll have to live with until Paradox SQL Link provides built-in support for multitable access.

```
1) ; Fetch.sc
2) CLEARALL CURSOR OFF
3) CLEAR
4) MESSAGE "Defining Procs, Please wait"
5) CANVAS OFF
6)
7) PROC CleanTables()
8)   PRIVATE numofrcds
9)   MOVETO "Ldepndts"
10)  numofrcds = NIMAGERECORDS()       ; Remove current Depndnts record
11)  FOR i FROM 1 to numofrcds
12)     DEL
13)  ENDFOR
14)  MOVETO "Lbene"                    ; Remove current Depndnts record
15)  DEL
16)  MOVETO "Lemp"                     ; Remove current Employee record
17)  DEL
18) ENDPROC
19)
20) PROC FetchEmp()
21)  PRIVATE employee.data
22)  CleanTables()                     ; Empty local tables
23)  SQLFETCH employee.data            ; Retrieve employee record
24)  SQLRELEASE                        ; Release pending query
25)  IF retval THEN                    ; If record retrieved,
26)     COPYFROMARRAY employee.data    ; place data in Lemp table
27)     empid = employee.data[2]       ; save Employee Id value
28)     RETURN True
29)  ELSE                              ; Else no record returned from
30)     RETURN False                   ; query
31)  ENDIF
32) ENDPROC
33)
34) PROC FetchBene()
35)  PRIVATE benefits.data
36)  SQL NOFETCH                       ; Request benefits data
37)     select * from benefits
38)     where employee_id = ~empid~
39)  ENDSQL
40)  IF retval = True THEN             ; If record retrieved,
41)     SQLFETCH benefits.data         ; place record in Lbene record
42)     COPYFROMARRAY benefits.data
43)  ENDIF
44)  SQLRELEASE
45)  MOVETO "Lemp"
46) ENDPROC
47)
48) PROC FetchDepndnts()
49)  PRIVATE depndnts.data, numofrcds
50)  SQL NOFETCH                       ; Retrieve dependents data
51)     select * from depndnts
52)     where employee_id = ~empid~
```

Listing 13-6 Multitable form with three tables from database server

```
53)        order by dependents_ssn
54)      ENDSQL
55)      IF retval = True THEN              ;  If data exists,
56)        SQLFETCH depndnts.data           ;  place each dependents record
57)        WHILE retval = True              ;  in the Ldepnts table
58)          COPYFROMARRAY depndnts.data
59)          DOWN
60)          SQLFETCH depndnts.data
61)        ENDWHILE
62)        DEL                              ;  Delete blank record
63)        HOME                             ;  Move to first record
64)      ENDIF
65)      SQLRELEASE                         ;  Release pending query
66)      MOVETO "Lemp"
67)    ENDPROC
68)
69)    PROC UpdateBenefits()
70)      SQLSTARTTRANS                      ;  Start a transaction
71)      SQL                                ;  Send SQL UPDATE statement
72)        UPDATE Benefits
73)        SET Insurance_type   = ~SQLVAL([Insurance_type])~,
74)            Life_insurance   = ~SQLVAL([Life_insurance])~,
75)            Short_term_disab = ~SQLVAL([Short_term_disab])~,
76)            Long_term_disab  = ~SQLVAL([Long_term_disab])~,
77)            Us_saving_bond   = ~SQLVAL([Us_saving_bond])~
78)        WHERE Employee_ID = ~[Employee_ID]~
79)      ENDSQL
80)      IF SQLERRORCODE() = "0" AND ERRORCODE() = 0 THEN ;  If no error occurred
81)        SQLCOMMIT                                      ;  commit transaction
82)        RETURN True
83)      ELSE
84)        SQLROLLBACK                                    ;  else roll back
85)        RETURN False                                   ;  transaction
86)      ENDIF
87)    ENDPROC
88)
89)    PROC UpdateDepndnts()                ;  Start a transaction
90)      SQLSTARTTRANS                      ;  Send SQL UPDATE statement
91)      SQL
92)        UPDATE depndnts
93)        SET Last_name  = ~SQLVAL([Last_Name])~,
94)            First_name = ~SQLVAL([First_name])~,
95)            Birth_date = ~SQLVAL([Birth_date])~
96)        WHERE Employee_id    = ~SQLVAL([Employee_id])~ AND
97)              Dependents_ssn = ~SQLVAL([Dependents_ssn])~
98)      ENDSQL
99)      IF SQLERRORCODE() = "0" AND ERRORCODE() = 0 THEN ;  If no error occurred
100)       SQLCOMMIT                                      ;  commit transaction
101)       RETURN True
102)     ELSE
103)       SQLROLLBACK                                    ;  else roll back
104)       RETURN False                                   ;  transaction
```

Listing 13-6 Multitable form with three tables from database server—continued

```
105)     ENDIF
106) ENDPROC
107)
108) PROC UpdateEmployee()                    ;  Start a transaction
109)    SQLSTARTTRANS                         ;  Send SQL UPDATE statement
110)    SQL
111)    UPDATE employee
112)       SET Last_Name      = ~SQLVAL([Last_Name])~,
113)           First_Name     = ~SQLVAL([First_Name])~,
114)           Date_hired     = ~SQLVAL([Date_hired])~,
115)           Birth_date     = ~SQLVAL([Birth_date])~,
116)           Ssn            = ~SQLVAL([Ssn])~,
117)           Department     = ~SQLVAL([Department])~,
118)           Job_code       = ~SQLVAL([Job_code])~,
119)           Work_phone     = ~SQLVAL([Work_phone])~,
120)           Salary         = ~SQLVAL([Salary])~,
121)           Exemptions     = ~SQLVAL([Exemptions])~,
122)           Address        = ~SQLVAL([Address])~,
123)           City           = ~SQLVAL([City])~,
124)           State          = ~SQLVAL([State])~,
125)           Zip            = ~SQLVAL([Zip])~,
126)           Home_phone     = ~SQLVAL([Home_phone])~,
127)           Marital_Status = ~SQLVAL([Marital_status])~,
128)           Sex            = ~SQLVAL([Sex])~
129)       WHERE Employee_ID = ~[Employee_ID]~
130)    ENDSQL
131)    IF SQLERRORCODE() = "0" AND ERRORCODE() = 0 THEN ; If no error occurred
132)       SQLCOMMIT                          ; commit transaction
133)       RETURN True
134)    ELSE
135)       SQLROLLBACK                        ; else roll back
136)       RETURN False                       ; transaction
137)    ENDIF
138) ENDPROC
139)
140) PROC CheckRcdStat()
141)   PRIVATE retprocval
142)   IF RECORDSTATUS("Modified") THEN    ; If the current record has been
143)      SWITCH                           ; modified update server record
144)         CASE tblname = "Lemp"    : retprocval = UpdateEmployee()
145)         CASE tblname = "Lbene"   : retprocval = UpdateBenefits()
146)         CASE tblname = "Ldepndts" : retprocval = UpdateDepndnts()
147)      ENDSWITCH
148)      RETURN retprocval                ; Return the success or failure
149)   ELSE                                ; status of the update
150)      RETURN True
151)   ENDIF
152) ENDPROC
153)
154) PROC ViewAndEdit3Tables()
155)   PRIVATE tblname, retkey, msg
156)   COEDIT "Lemp"
```

Listing 13-6 Multitable form with three tables from database server—continued

```
157)     PICKFORM 3                          ; Three table form
158)     SQLRELEASE                          ; Release any active SQL NOFETCH
159)     msg    = ""
160)     SQL NOFETCH                         ; Rretrieve the employee data
161)       select * from employee order by employee_id
162)     ENDSQL
163)     IF retval = True THEN               ; Get first employee record
164)       FetchEmp()
165)       IF retval = False THEN
166)         MESSAGE "No employee records, modification cancelled"
167)         SLEEP 3000
168)         RETURN
169)       ENDIF
170)     MOVETO "Ldepndts"                   ; Get dependents data
171)     FetchDepndnts()
172)     MOVETO "Lbene"                      ; Get benefits data
173)     FetchBene()
174)     IMAGERIGHTS UPDATE                  ; Prevent changes to key fields
175)     CANVAS ON
176)     WHILE True
177)       IMAGERIGHTS UPDATE                ; Prevent changes to key fields
178)       WAIT RECORD
179)         PROMPT "Employee Information   [F2]-Exit   [PgDn]-Next Record  " +
180)             "[PgUp]-Previous Record",
181)             "[F3]-Employee Data   [F4]-Benefits Data   [F5]-Dependents Data"
182)         MESSAGE msg
183)         UNTIL "F2","F3","F4","F5","PgUp","PgDn",
184)             "DOS", "DOSBIG", "ZOOM", "ZOOMNEXT"
185)       retkey = retval
186)       tblname = TABLE()
187)       msg = ""
188)       IMAGERIGHTS                       ;  Need to turn option on to modify
189)                                         ; key fields for COPYFROMARRAY
190)                                         ; command in fetch procs
191)
192) ; ******************************************
193) ; *                                        *
194) ; * Data validation should be done here    *
195) ; *                                        *
196) ; ******************************************
197)
198)      retprocval = CheckRcdStat()    ; Check to see if the record was
199)                                     ; was updated, if so, update server
200)                                     ;  If an error occurred in the
201)      IF retprocval = False THEN     ; update display message and do
202)                                     ; not process keystroke
203)        msg = "Error occurred! SQLERRORMESSAGE: " + SQLERRORMESSAGE() +
204)              "ERRORMESSAGE: " + ERRORMESSAGE()
205)        LOOP
206)      ENDIF
207)      SWITCH
208)        CASE retkey = "F3" :
```

Listing 13-6 Multitable form with three tables from database server—continued

```
209)              MOVETO "Lemp"
210)              LOOP
211)        CASE retkey = "F4" :
212)              MOVETO "Lbene"
213)              LOOP
214)        CASE retkey = "F5" :
215)              MOVETO "Ldepndts"
216)              LOOP
217)        CASE retkey = "PgDn" :
218)           SWITCH
219)              CASE tblname = "Lemp" :
220)                 SQL NOFETCH
221)                    select * from employee  where employee_id > ~empid~
222)                     order by employee_id
223)                 ENDSQL
224)                 IF retval = True THEN
225)                    FetchEmp()
226)                    IF retval = True THEN
227)                       MOVETO "Lbene"
228)                       FetchBene()
229)                       MOVETO "Ldepndts"
230)                       FetchDepndnts()
231)                    ELSE
232)                       BEEP SLEEP 100 BEEP
233)                       msg = "No more data!"
234)                    ENDIF
235)                 ELSE
236)                    msg = "Select failed!"
237)                 ENDIF
238)                 LOOP
239)              CASE tblname = "Lbene" :
240)                 BEEP
241)                 LOOP
242)              CASE tblname = "Ldepndts" :
243)                 IF NOT ATLAST() THEN
244)                    DOWN CTRLHOME
245)                 ELSE
246)                    BEEP
247)                 ENDIF
248)                 LOOP
249)           ENDSWITCH
250)        CASE retkey = "PgUp" :
251)           SWITCH
252)              CASE tblname = "Lemp" :
253)                 SQL NOFETCH
254)                    select * from employee  where employee_id < ~empid~
255)                     order by employee_id desc
256)                 ENDSQL
257)                 IF retval = True THEN
258)                    FetchEmp()
259)                    IF retval THEN
260)                       MOVETO "Lbene"
```

Listing 13-6 Multitable form with three tables from database server—continued

```
261)                        FetchBene()
262)                        MOVETO "Ldepndts"
263)                        FetchDepndnts()
264)                    ELSE
265)                        BEEP SLEEP 100 BEEP
266)                        msg = "No more data!"
267)                    ENDIF
268)                ELSE
269)                   msg = "Select failed!"
270)                ENDIF
271)                LOOP
272)            CASE tblname = "Lbene" :
273)                BEEP
274)                LOOP
275)            CASE tblname = "Ldepndts" :
276)                IF NOT ATFIRST() THEN
277)                    UP CTRLHOME
278)                ELSE
279)                    BEEP
280)                ENDIF
281)                LOOP
282)            ENDSWITCH
283)        CASE retkey = "F2" :
284)            CLEAR
285)            MESSAGE "Saving data, Please wait!"
286)            CANVAS OFF
287)            MOVETO "Lbene"
288)            DEL
289)            MOVETO "Ldepndts"
290)            WHILE NIMAGERECORDS() > 1
291)                DEL
292)            ENDWHILE
293)            DEL
294)            MOVETO "Lemp"
295)            DEL
296)            DO_IT!
297)            QUITLOOP
298)        OTHERWISE :
299)            BEEP
300)        ENDSWITCH
301)     ENDWHILE
302)   ELSE
303)     MESSAGE "Extract failed: ",SQLERRORMESSAGE()
304)   ENDIF
305)   CLEARALL
306) ENDPROC
307)
308) message "Retrieving data and loading form, Please wait"
309) CANVAS ON
310) CANVAS OFF
311)
312) ViewAndEdit3Tables()
```

Listing 13-6 Multitable form with three tables from database server—continued

Summary

SQL Link lets you access data in SQL databases. At the same time, it offers the familiar interface used to access Paradox data. SQL Link buffers you from having to know SQL by creating statements in the appropriate dialect using QBE. Integrating SQL database information into an existing application doesn't require extensive modification provided you don't duplicate your current application. Taking an existing Paradox application, moving it entirely into the client/server architecture, and expecting the same features and functionality but faster performance isn't always realistic. Think of SQL Link as another tool, just like adding the Paradox Engine to your toolbox.

14 Using the Paradox Engine

C is the language of choice for PC developers. Few database products on the market support an Applications Programming Interface (API) for C or any other language. This limits MIS departments when thinking seriously about production applications on personal computers. The Paradox Engine opens the door for these developers.

The Paradox Engine lets you integrate Paradox data into your C applications. The Engine is the core of the data handling and multiuser features of the Paradox kernel. The Paradox Engine offers over 70 functions that give you the ability to create and manipulate Paradox tables. The Engine doesn't replace PAL, but augments PAL.

The Paradox Engine is the cornerstone of Borland's product strategy. The Engine furnishes interoperability at the data level between Paradox, Quattro Pro, C applications, and SideKick for Presentation Manager. Borland has announced support for C++, Pascal, and Windows in the next release of the Engine, possibly by the end of 1990.

This chapter is a brief introduction to the Paradox Engine and is presented from the Paradox developer's viewpoint. This isn't an in-depth coverage of the Engine's capabilities. It is not intended to cover basic C programming concepts. If you're a Paradox developer, you'll gain a basic understanding of the features of the Engine and how it complements PAL. If you're a C programmer, the material presented here will be minimally useful. The following areas are covered:

- Engine overview
- Engine requirements

- Using Turbo C and Microsoft C with the Engine
- Comparison of PAL and Engine features
- Basic description of Engine functions by category
- Two simple programs to list data in a table

Engine Overview

The Paradox Engine is the nucleus of Paradox. All table creation, manipulation, encryption, and multiuser concurrency technology is available in the form of a C library. Any C programmer can now use Paradox's format to store data, including complete file compatibility with existing Paradox tables. Following are the basic Paradox features supported by the Engine:

- Read, write, and create tables
- File and record locking (concurrent with any other Borland application based on the Engine)
- Table encryption and password protection
- Create, use, and update key and index files
- Record searching

You don't have to pay any royalties for applications you create with the Engine. You can distribute the .EXE files to run standalone, in a network environment, or from within a PAL application (using the RUN command). If you're a C programmer, you don't have to own a copy of Paradox.

Why use the Engine? To handle application requirements that PAL cannot handle, such as: direct manipulation of the serial port, downloading or uploading data, using a scanner, using a bar code reader for data input, importing and exporting to file formats not supported by Paradox, creating a character-oriented window interface with mouse support, or any other requirement not available in PAL. You can combine your own favorite C library functions with Engine functions to incorporate Paradox into your repertoire.

Engine Requirements

The Engine supports two C compilers, Microsoft C 5.1 or higher and Borland's Turbo C 2.0 or higher. Disk space and RAM requirements are the same as for the compilers themselves, with additional disk space to load the

Engine library, source code, and compiled programs. You need DOS 3.0 or higher. At this time, the Engine supports only DOS (OS/2 is a future enhancement). To install the Engine, run the INSTALL program on the Engine disk and follow the prompts. Table 14-1 lists the database limitations of the Engine.

Table 14-1
Database limitations using the Engine

Number of open tables	64
Maximum swap buffer	256K
Maximum record buffer	128K
Maximum number of file locks	128
Records per table	2 billion
Fields per record	255
Characters per record	4000 for non-keyed table and 1350 for keyed table

Multiple code examples come with the Engine. There are two programs included with the Engine which form the base for describing how to use the various functions. One is an import program and the other is a phone list. Also included are small code examples for each function and for groups of functions used to perform specific tasks. We use the same code examples as those used in the Engine product.

PAL and the Engine: Major Differences

When comparing Engine features to PAL features, you'll see that you gain some capabilities and you lose some capabilities. It's important to know what you can and cannot do with the Engine. PAL offers a high-level language in which keystroke recording, QBE, and multitable forms and reports let you prototype the design without a great amount of effort. Writing an application in C requires a greater amount of time. It's like building a house with nothing but hand tools and even having to cut the trees yourself. C gives you more flexibility but increases the time it takes to create programs.

When using the Engine, you cannot access the following Paradox objects:

- Forms
- Reports
- Graphs
- ValChecks
- Image settings
- QBE
- All interactive features

The Engine gives you the following features that are not available in PAL:

- Hardware and operating system access
- Utilization of third-party C libraries
- Creation of .EXE files for distributing applications
- Efficiencies of compiled programs
- Ability to traverse the table in index order
- Backwards ZOOM

Many PAL commands, functions, and interactive Paradox menu choices have Engine-equivalent functions. Table 14-2 lists the Engine calls by category, along with the corresponding Paradox commands, functions, and menu choices (if one exists).

Table 14-2
Engine functions with PAL command/function and menu equivalents

Engine Function	PAL Command or Function	Menu Equivalent
Table Functions		
PXTblCreate	CREATE	{Create}
PXTblEmpty	EMPTY	{Tools} {More} {Empty}
PXTblDelete	DELETE	{Tools} {Delete} {Table}
PXTblCopy	COPY	{Tools} {Copy} {Table}
PXTblRename	RENAME	{Tools} {Rename} {Table}
PXTblAdd	ADD	{Tools} {More} {Add}
Record Functions		
PXRecAppend	INS	
PXRecInsert	INS	

Table 14-2—continued

Engine Function	PAL Command or Function	Menu Equivalent
PXRecGoto	MOVETO RECORD	
PXRecNext	SKIP +1	
PXRecPrev	SKIP -1	
PXRecDelete	DEL	

Password Functions

PXTblProtected	ISENCRYPTED	
PXPswAdd	PASSWORD	
PXPswDel	UNPASSWORD	
PXTblEncrypt	PROTECT	{Tools} {Protect} {Password}
PXTblDecrypt		{Tools} {Protect} {ClearPasswords}

Informational Functions

PXTblExist	ISTABLE	
PXTBlName	TABLE	
PXRecNum	RECNO	
PXTblNRecs	NRECORDS	
PXRecNFlds	NFIELDS	
PXKeyNflds	NKEYFIELDS	
PXFldHandle	FIELDNO	
PXFldType	FIELDTYPE	
PXFldName	FIELD	
PXTblMaxSize	SETMAXSIZE	

Network/Concurrency Functions

PXNetUserName	USERNAME	
PXNetFileLock	LOCK	{Tools} {Net} {Lock}
PXNetFileUnlock	UNLOCK	{Tools} {Net} {Lock}
PXNetTblLock	LOCK	{Tools} {Net} {Lock}
PXNetTblUnlock	UNLOCK	{Tools} {Net} {Lock}
PXNetTblRefresh	REFRESH	
PXNetRecLock	LOCKRECORD	
PXNetRecUnlock	UNLOCKRECORD	

Error Functions

PXErrMsg	ERRORMESSAGE	
PXNetErrUser	ERRORUSER	

Compiling with Turbo C or Microsoft C

You can use the Engine with both Turbo C 2.0 (or higher) and Microsoft C 5.1 (or higher). Each compiler has different requirements and offers different ways to compile and link your programs. Both compilers support the large memory model only, for Engine applications.

Using Turbo C, you can compile from the command line or in the integrated development environment. Use the following statement to compile and link from the command line:

    TCC -ml <source> PXENGTCL.LIB

The -ml switch tells the compiler to use the large memory model, and PXENGTCL.LIB is the library for the Engine. Turbo C must know the location of the include and library files. You specify this at install time and then it is stored in TURBOC.CFG.

The other Turbo C option is to use the integrated development environment. Load the Editor by entering TC at the command line. Then create a project file containing the location of the Engine library and the source file name (or the names of the files you want to compile and link). Figure 14-1 shows the Editor with a project identified and loaded in the window.

With Microsoft C you must use DOS environment variables to identify the include and library files. These variables must be set to the drive and directory where you installed the Engine files. The following examples assume the Engine is installed on the C drive:

    SET INCLUDE=C:\PXENGINE;%INCLUDE%
    SET LIB=C:\PXENGINE;%LIB%

To compile and link your Engine programs, you either:

1. Use one CL command to compile and link
2. Compile with CL and link with LINK

If you choose the first option, you need to enter the following command at the DOS prompt:

    CL /AL /F D00 [options] <Source1> [SourceN] [-link options]
       PXENGMSL.LIB

Using the Paradox Engine

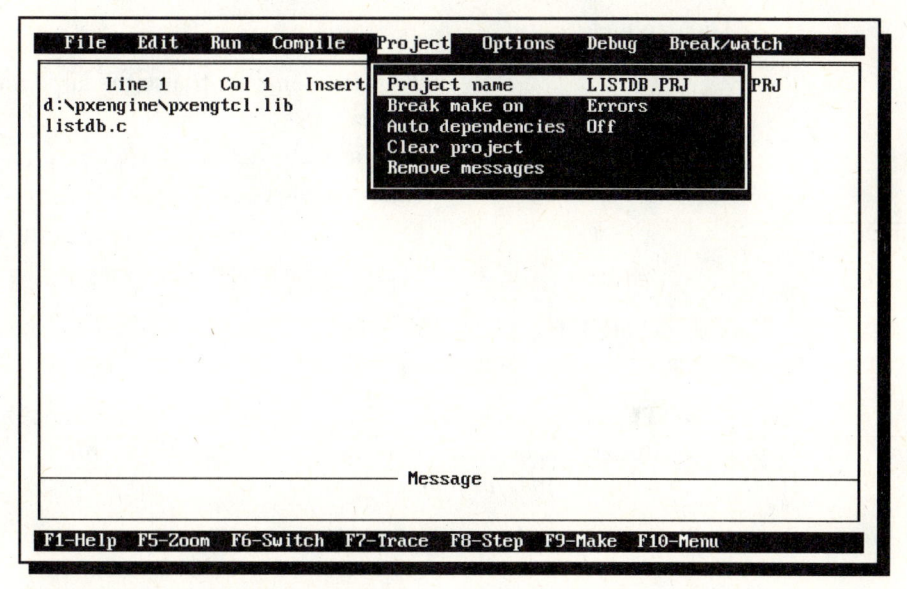

```
┌─────────────────────────────────────────────────────────────────┐
│  File    Edit    Run    Compile   Project  Options  Debug  Break/watch │
│      Line 1      Col 1     Insert │ Project name      LISTDB.PRJ │PRJ
│ d:\pxengine\pxengtcl.lib          │ Break make on     Errors     │
│ listdb.c                          │ Auto dependencies Off        │
│                                   │ Clear project                │
│                                   │ Remove messages              │
│                                   └──────────────────────────────┘
│
│
│
│
│
│                         ──── Message ────
│
│ F1-Help  F5-Zoom  F6-Switch  F7-Trace  F8-Step  F9-Make  F10-Menu │
└─────────────────────────────────────────────────────────────────┘
```

Figure 14-1 Turbo C Editor window

The parameters are:

/AL	Tells the compiler to use the large memory model
/F D00	Increased the default stack size
[options]	Optional parameters supplied to the compiler
<Source1>	Name of the first program to compile
<SourceN>	Names of any additional program files to be compiled
[-link options]	Optional parameters supplied to the linker
PXENGMSL.LIB	Paradox Engine library for Microsoft compiler

If you compile and link in separate steps, use make files and the compile statement as follows:

CL /AL /F D00 /C [options] <Source>

The parameters are:

/AL	Tells the compiler to use the large memory model
/F D00	Increases the default stack size
/C	Instructs the compiler to create an object file
[options]	Optional parameters supplied to the compiler
<Source>	Name of the program to compile

The second step is to link the object modules using the LINK command. This is where you specify PXENGMSL.LIB and one of the library files.

> **NOTE:** *No matter which compiler or option you use to compile and link your program, you must add the Engine's header file along with any other header files, as follows:*
>
> *#include "pxengine.h"*

Engine Functions

The Engine functions are categorized into eleven groups:

- Initialization and finalization functions
- Table functions
- Record functions
- Field functions
- Index functions
- Date functions
- Search functions
- Password functions
- Informational functions
- Network/concurrency functions
- Error functions

There are over 70 functions in the Engine. Table 14-3 lists the functions by category with a brief description. Some of the functions are listed more than once because they cross boundaries.

**Table 14-3
Engine functions by category**

Initialization and Finalization Functions

PXExit	Closes single user or multiuser Engine environment
PXGetDefaults	Returns the internal defaults used by the Engine
PXInit	Non-network Engine initialization
PXNetInit	Network Engine initialization
PXSetDefaults	Sets the internal defaults used by the Engine
PXSetHWHandler	Enables/disables hardware error handler

Table Functions

PXRecNFlds	Returns the number of fields in a table
PXRecNum	Returns the current record number
PXTblAdd	Adds data in one table to another table
PXTblClose	Closes a table
PXTblCopy	Copies a table and its family to another table name
PXTblCreate	Creates a table
PXTblDelete	Deletes a table and its family
PXTblEmpty	Deletes all records from a table
PXTblExist	Tests if a table exists
PXTblMaxSize	Sets the block size for a table
PXTblName	Returns the name of the table for a table handle
PXTblOpen	Opens a table
PXTblRecs	Returns the number of records in a table
PXTblRename	Renames a table and its family

Record Functions

PXRecAppend	Appends a record to a table
PXRecBufClose	Closes the record transfer buffer
PXRecBufCopy	Copies source record buffer to destination record buffer
PXRecBufEmpty	Clears a record transfer buffer
PXRecBufOpen	Creates a record transfer buffer
PXRecDelete	Deletes the current record from a table
PXRecInsert	Inserts a record into the table

Table 14-3—continued

PXRecFirst	Moves to the first record of a table
PXRecGet	Transfers the current record into the record transfer buffer
PXRecGoto	Moves to a specified record
PXRecLast	Moves to the last record of a table
PXRecNext	Moves to the next record
PXRecNum	Returns the current record number
PXRecPrev	Moves the previous record in a table
PXRecUpdate	Updates the current record in a table
Field Functions	
PXFldBlank	Tests if a field is blank
PXFldHandle	Gets field handle for specified field name
PXFldName	Name of a field for specified field handle
PXFldType	Data type for a specified field handle
PXGetAlpha	Retrieves a string from an alphanumeric field
PXGetDate	Retrieves a long date value from a field
PXGetDoub	Retrieves a double value from a field
PXGetLong	Retrieves a long value from a field
PXGetShort	Retrieves a short value from a field
PXPutAlpha	Assigns a string value to a field
PXPutBlank	Assigns a blank to a field
PXPutDate	Assigns a long date value to a field
PXPutDoub	Assigns a double value to a field
PXPutLong	Assigns a long integer value to a field
PXPutShort	Assigns a short integer value to a field
Index Functions	
PXKeyAdd	Primary or secondary index creation
PXKeyDrop	Deletes a primary or secondary index
PXKeyNFlds	Number of key fields
Date Functions	
PXDateDecode	Converts internal date to calendar date
PXDateEncode	Converts calendar date to internal format

Table 14-3—continued

Search Functions

PXSrchFld	Searches a table on a specified field
PXSrchKey	Searches a table based on the primary index

Password Functions

PXPswAdd	Enters a password into the system
PXPswDel	Removes a password from the system
PXTblDecrypt	Decrypts a password-protected table
PXTblEncrypt	Encrypts a password-protected table
PXTblProtected	Tells if a table is password protected

Informational Functions

PXFldBlank	Tests if a field is blank
PXFldHandle	Gets field handle for specified field name
PXFldName	Name of a field for specified field handle
PXFldType	Data type for a specified field handle
PXGetDefaults	Returns the internal defaults used by the Engine
PXKeyNFlds	Number of key fields
PXNetRecLocked	Tests if a record is locked
PXNetTblChanged	Tests if a table has been changed by other users
PXNetUserName	Returns network user name
PXRecNFlds	Returns the number of fields in a table
PXRecNum	Returns the current record number
PXTblExist	Tests if a table exists
PXTblNRecs	Returns the number of records in a table
PXTblProtected	Tests if a table is password protected

Network/Concurrency Functions

PXNetErrUser	Name of user with resource locked
PXNetFileLock	Locks a file
PXNetFileUnlock	Unlocks a file
PXNetRecGotoLock	Goes to a previously locked record
PXNetRecLock	Locks a record
PXNetRecLocked	Tests if a record is locked
PXNetRecUnlock	Unlocks a record

	Table 14-3—continued
PXNetTblChanged	Tests if a table has been changed by other users
PXNetTblLock	Locks a table
PXNetTblRefresh	Refreshes internal cache if table changed by another user
PXNetTblUnlock	Unlocks a table
PXNetUserName	Returns network user name
Error Functions	
PXErrMsg	Reports error message for current error code
PXNetErrUser	Name of user with resource locked
PXSetHWHandler	Enables/disables hardware error handler

Structure of an Engine Program

Writing a C program using the Engine requires that you always perform certain function calls at the start of the program and at the end of the program. In between these calls, the functions used depend on the type of processing being performed. The type of program used here is a simple table listing program. The following basic steps are required to start the Engine, read data from a table, write it to the screen, and close the Engine. Some of the steps are optional.

1. Get Engine environment defaults and change any if necessary. This is an optional step.
2. Initialize the Engine to either a standalone or network environment.
3. Open a table. This also requires that you
    a. Open a record buffer.
    b. Get the table structure.
    c. Determine the number of records.
    d. Determine the number of fields.
    e. Get the field names.
    f. Get the field types.

4. Print the column headings. This is optional depending on the output format.
5. Print the records. This requires that you
    a. Go to a record.
    b. Place the record in the buffer.
    c. Print the record. This requires that you determine the data type of each field in order to print it.
6. Close the record buffer and table.
7. End the program.

As you can see, many steps are required to print the contents of a table, and this is just the basics. There is no handling for records wider than 80 characters, outputting to a printer or file, formatting the screen page, and so on. Let's look at each step in a little more detail.

Getting the Engine Defaults

At the start of an Engine program, it is important to know what internal defaults the Engine is using. This isn't mandatory but, depending on the intensity and size of your program, you might want to make adjustments accordingly. The PXGetDefaults function returns the values of six default settings:

swapSize	Internal swap buffer size
maxTabls	Maximum number of tables that can be simultaneously open
maxRecBufs	Maximum number of record buffers
maxLocks	Maximum number of record locks per table
maxFiles	Maximum number of file handles that can be used
sortTable	Address of the current sort table

Listing 14-1 is the example program GETDEF.C which prints the defaults to the screen. The PXSetDefaults function modifies the current defaults based on the values passed as arguments. In GETDEF.C, the defaults are set to the maximum options defined in PXENGINE.H.

```c
/*
    getdef.c
*/
#include <stdio.h>
#include "pxengine.h"
main(void)
{
    int pxErr;
    char *sortTable;
    int maxSwapsize,maxTableHandles,maxRecBufs,
        maxLockHandles,maxFileHandles;
    PXSetDefaults(MAXSWAPSIZE,MAXTABLEHANDLES, PXDEFAULT,
        MAXLOCKHANDLES,MAXFILEHANDLES, PXDEFAULT);
    /* Retrieve the current defaults. */
    if ((pxErr = PXGetDefaults(&maxSwapsize,&maxTableHandles,&maxRecBufs,
                            &maxLockHandles,&maxFileHandles,&sortTable))
                    != PXSUCCESS)
        printf("%s\n",PXErrMsg(pxErr));
    else
    {
        printf("Swap Size: %d\nTable Handles: %d\nRecord Buffers: %d\n",
            maxSwapsize,maxTableHandles,maxRecBufs);
        printf("Lock Handles: %d\nFile Handles: %d\nSort Table: %s\n",
                maxLockHandles,maxFileHandles,
            sortTable == DEFSORTORDER ? "System Default":sortTable);
    }
    return (pxErr);
}
```

Listing 14-1 Getting Engine internal defaults

Initializing the Engine

You need to initialize the Engine environment at the start of your program. Configuration includes internal data structures, memory buffers, and internal defaults. If the program is for a standalone environment, use PXInit, which doesn't require any other parameters. Listing 14-2 is a sample program (INIT.C) that initializes a standalone environment.

If the program is for a network environment, you need to establish the values for

- The location of the PARADOX.NET file.
- The type of network being used.
- The network user name.

```
/*
    init.c
*/
#include <stdio.h>
#include "pxengine.h"
int main(void)
{
    int pxErr;
    /* Attempt to initialize the Engine */
    if ((pxErr = PXInit()) != PXSUCCESS)
        printf("%s\n", PXErrMsg(pxErr));
    else
        PXExit();
    return(pxErr);
}
```

Listing 14-2 Initializing a standalone environment

Listing 14-3 is a sample program (NETINIT.C) that initializes a network environment but does not specify a network connection. The NETTYPE parameter is actually an integer value. The PXENGINE.H file has the following mnemonics defined to increase program readability:

Mnemonic	*Value*	*Network Type*
NOTONET	1	User not on a network
NOVELLNET	2	Novell
THREECOMNET	3	3Com
IMBPCNET	4	IBM PC
OTHERNET	5	DOS 3.1 compatible network
TOURUSNET	6	Torus version 1.4
STARLANNET	7	StarLAN
BANYANNET	8	Banyan

Other Engine functions will not work until your environment is properly initialized. It is crucial that you provide the correct network information so your Engine program can coexist with other Borland products accessing the same data.

```c
/*
    netinit.c
*/
#include <stdio.h>
#include "pxengine.h"
#define NETDIR            ""
#define NETTYPE           NOTONNET
int main(void)
{
    int pxErr;
    /* Attempt to initialize Engine */
    if ((pxErr = PXNetInit(NETDIR,NETTYPE,DEFUSERNAME))
    != PXSUCCESS)
        printf("%s\n", PXErrMsg(pxErr));
    else
        PXExit();

    return(pxErr);
}
```

Listing 14-3 Initializing a network environment

Opening a Table

To access a Paradox table you need a table handle. All references to the table are made using the table handle instead of the table name. Executing PXTblOpen returns the table handle (which is a number) as shown in Listing 14-4 (TBLOPEN.C). This is just the beginning—you must also execute the following function calls before you get the data:

PXRecBufOpen	Open a record buffer

Get the table structure with:

PXTblNRecs	Determine the number of records
PXRecNFlds	Determine the number of fields
PXFldName	Get the field names
PXFldType	Get the field types

Each of these functions is shown later in this chapter in the sample program.

```
/*
    tblopen.c
*/
#include <stdio.h>
#include "pxengine.h"
#define TABLENAME       "table"
int main(void)
{
    TABLEHANDLE tblHandle;
    int pxErr;
    PXInit();
    /* Open a table */
    if ((pxErr = PXTblOpen(TABLENAME, &tblHandle, 0, 0)) != PXSUCCESS)
        printf("%s\n", PXErrMsg(pxErr));
    else
        PXTblClose(tblHandle);
    PXExit();
    return(pxErr);
}
```

Listing 14-4 *Open a table*

Printing Column Headings

There is no Engine function call that prints column headers for you. (That's interface.) Using the field name information retrieved during the table open step, the following statements provide a simple method of printing column headers with virtually no formatting (tabs are used between field names).

```
for(i = 0; i < nFields; i++)
    printf("%s\t", fieldNames[i]);
putchar('\n');
```

The variable *nFields* is set by calling PXRecNFlds. The array *fieldNames* is set in a loop using PXFldName. The second list table sample program shown later in this chapter demonstrates an enhanced table heading formatting process.

Printing Records in a Table

Printing the records requires two loops: one for each record and one for each field. The first loop is obvious—each record has to be processed separately. The second loop requires that you determine the data type of each field in the record and execute the appropriate Engine function for the field. Following are the steps and functions necessary to print records in a table:

PXRecGoto	Go to a record
PXRecGet	Place the record in the buffer

Print the record by using different functions for each data type:

PXGetDouble	For numeric (N) and currency ($) data types
PXGetAlpha	For alphanumeric (A*nnn*) data types
PXGetDate	For date data types
PXDateDecode	To convert internal date to calendar date
PXGetShort	For short (S) data types

Listing 14-5 is the sample program GETALPHA.C. It shows the calls to open a table, open a buffer, get a record, and print the field. Examples of handling all data types are provided later in the list table sample program.

```
/*
    getalpha.c
*/
#include <stdio.h>
#include "pxengine.h"
#define TABLENAME       "table"
int main(void)
{
    TABLEHANDLE tblHandle;
    RECORDHANDLE recHandle;
    FIELDHANDLE fldHandle;
    char avalue[BUFSIZ];
    int pxErr;
    PXInit();
    PXTblOpen(TABLENAME, &tblHandle, 0, 0);
    PXRecBufOpen(tblHandle, &recHandle);
    PXFldHandle(tblHandle,"Alpha Field",&fldHandle);
    PXRecGet(tblHandle, recHandle);
    /* Get an alphanumeric value out of a field */
    if ((pxErr = PXGetAlpha(recHandle, fldHandle, BUFSIZ, avalue))
        != PXSUCCESS)
        printf("%s\n", PXErrMsg(pxErr));
    else
        printf("Field number %d contents: %s\n", fldHandle,avalue);
    PXRecBufClose(recHandle);
    PXTblClose(tblHandle);
    PXExit();
    return(pxErr);
}
```

Listing 14-5 *Example of retrieving an alpha field from a record*

Closing the Record Buffer and the Table

When you're finished with table and record processing, use PXRecBufClose to release the record transfer buffer and PXTblClose to release the table handle and all associated memory. Listing 14-6 is the sample program BUFCLOSE.C that shows how to use each of these functions.

```c
/*
    bufclos.c
*/
#include <stdio.h>
#include "pxengine.h"
#define TABLENAME       "table"
int main(void)
{
    RECORDHANDLE recHandle;
    TABLEHANDLE tblHandle;
    int pxErr;
    PXInit();
    PXTblOpen(TABLENAME, &tblHandle, 0, 0);
    PXRecBufOpen(tblHandle, &recHandle);
    /* Close a record buffer */
    if ((pxErr = PXRecBufClose(recHandle)) != PXSUCCESS)
        printf("%s\n", PXErrMsg(pxErr));
    PXTblClose(tblHandle);
    PXExit();
    return(pxErr);
}
```

Listing 14-6 Record buffer and table closure

Terminating the Program

At the end of your Engine program, you must terminate the Paradox environment. Calling PXExit clears the buffer areas, data structures, and internal tables created at the start of the program. PXExit also removes you from the PARADOX.NET file if the program is running in a network environment. Listing 14-7 is the sample program PXEXIT.C that terminates the program and closes the Paradox environment.

```c
/*
    pxexit.c
*/
#include <stdio.h>
#include "pxengine.h"
int main(void)
{
    int pxErr;
    PXInit();
    /* Try and close Paradox environment */
    if ((pxErr = PXExit()) != PXSUCCESS)
        printf("%s\n", PXErrMsg(pxErr));
    else
        printf("Engine terminated.\n");
    return(pxErr);
}
```

Listing 14-7 *Program termination*

List Table Examples

Using the outline discussed above, let's create a program that gets the name of a table and prints it to the screen. The first example prints the data for each field on a separate line. The second example outputs a single line for each row. Figure 14-2 shows the structure of the table and the data.

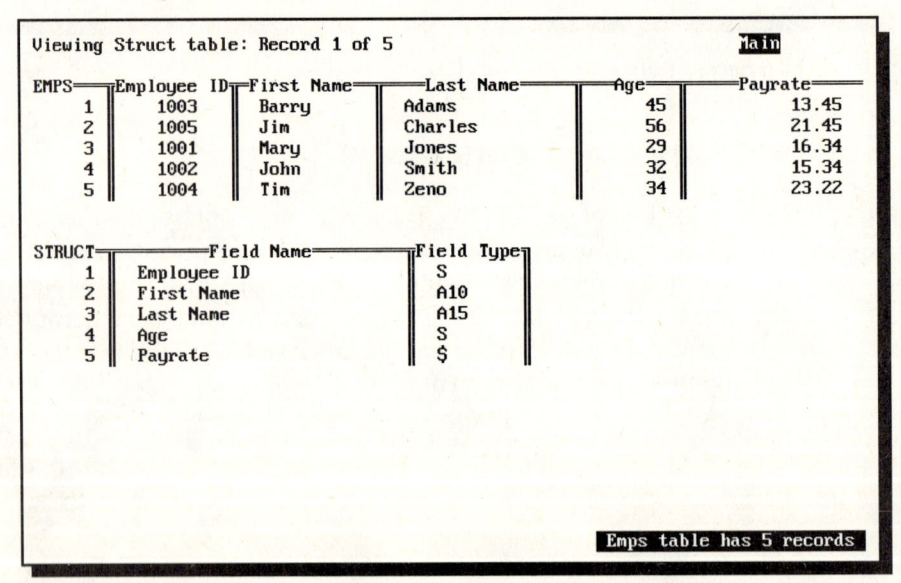

```
 Viewing Struct table: Record 1 of 5                                Main
 EMPS──┬─Employee ID─┬─First Name─┬─Last Name─┬─Age─┬─Payrate═══
     1 │    1003     │   Barry    │   Adams   │  45 │  13.45
     2 │    1005     │   Jim      │   Charles │  56 │  21.45
     3 │    1001     │   Mary     │   Jones   │  29 │  16.34
     4 │    1002     │   John     │   Smith   │  32 │  15.34
     5 │    1004     │   Tim      │   Zeno    │  34 │  23.22


 STRUCT─┬──────────Field Name──────┬─Field Type─
      1 │    Employee ID           │    S
      2 │    First Name            │    A10
      3 │    Last Name             │    A15
      4 │    Age                   │    S
      5 │    Payrate               │    $


                                              Emps table has 5 records
```

Figure 14-2 *Table structure and data used in listing program*

The first example is shown in Listing 14-8 (we'll step through the code before showing the complete program). Separate functions are defined for each of the following and called from the main funciton.

- Initializing the Engine
- Displaying the introduction text screen
- Opening the table
- Getting the structure of the table
- Looping through the records
- Looping through the fields
- Closing the table
- Terminating the Engine

Since examples of initializing the environment and opening the table were discussed above, let's start with defining the table structure. There isn't an Engine function to define the structure of a table in a single call. The technique used in this example is to create two arrays, one to hold the field name (*fieldNames*) and another to hold the field types (*fieldTypes*). Having retrieved the number of records in the table with PXTblNRecs, and the number of fields with PXRecNFlds, the program knows how many times to loop to get each field's information. The number of records is used later to print out the data.

```
void GetTableStructure(void)
{
    int i;
    PXTblNRecs(tableHandle, &nRecs);
    PXRecNFlds(tableHandle, &nFields);
    for(i = 0; i < nFields; i++)
    {
        PXFldName(tableHandle, (FIELDHANDLE) i + 1,
              MAX_BUFFER_SIZE, fieldNames[i]);
        PXFldType(tableHandle, (FIELDHANDLE) i + 1,
              MAX_BUFFER_SIZE, fieldTypes[i]);
    }
}
```

The next step is to print the data (PrintTable). A FOR loop is used to get each record from the table. You first have to move to the record using PXRecGoto, then return the record to the buffer using PXRecGet. At this point, you're ready to print the data for a record by calling PrintTableRecord.

```
void PrintTable(void)
{
    int i;
    for(i = 0; i < nRecs; i++)
    {
```

```
            PXRecGoto(tableHandle, i + 1);
            PXRecGet(tableHandle, recHandle);
            PrintTableRecord(i);
        }
    }
```

A second loop is used to retrieve each field. This is where a SWITCH statement is necessary to process the different data types. Depending on the data type of the current field (based on the value in *fieldTypes*) a call is made to the appropriate PXGet function. If you look at the CASE statement for date fields, you'll notice there are actually two calls, one to get the data and one to convert it from an internal format to a calendar format. In this example, each field is printed on a separate line preceded by the field name. Because Paradox allows a maximum of 25 characters for a field name, the format for field name output is %-25. This left justifies the field name in a 25-character space.

```
void PrintTableRecord(int rcdnum)
{
    int i;
    double dvalue;
    char avalue[BUFSIZ];
    int mo, da, yr;
    long lvalue;
    short svalue;
    printf("%-25s: %d\n", "Record #", rcdnum);
    for(i = 0; i < nFields; i++)
    {
        switch(fieldTypes[i][0])
        {
            case 'N':
            case '$':
                PXGetDoub(recHandle, i + 1, &dvalue);
                printf("%-25s: %g\n", fieldNames[i], dvalue);
                break;
            case 'A':
                PXGetAlpha(recHandle, i + 1, BUFSIZ, avalue);
                printf("%-25s: %s\n", fieldNames[i], avalue);
                break;
            case 'D':
                PXGetDate(recHandle, i + 1, &lvalue);
                PXDateDecode(lvalue, &mo, &da, &yr);
                printf("%-25s: %d/%d/%d\n", fieldNames[i], mo, da, yr);
                break;
            case 'S':
                PXGetShort(recHandle, i + 1, &svalue);
                printf("%-25s: %d\n", fieldNames[i], svalue);
                break;
            default:
                printf("unknown\n");
```

```
                        break;
                }
        }
        putchar('\n');
}
```

When all the records are printed, the table and buffers are closed and the program ends. The output of this program is shown in Figure 14-3. As you can see, not many records fit on the screen. That leads us to the second example.

```
Payrate                         : 21.45

Record #                        : 2
Employee ID                     : 1001
First Name                      : Mary
Last Name                       : Jones
Age                             : 29
Payrate                         : 16.34

Record #                        : 3
Employee ID                     : 1002
First Name                      : John
Last Name                       : Smith
Age                             : 32
Payrate                         : 15.34

Record #                        : 4
Employee ID                     : 1004
First Name                      : Tim
Last Name                       : Zeno
Age                             : 34
Payrate                         : 23.22


D:\TC\ENGTEST>
```

Figure 14-3 List table sample output

```
/* listdb.c
    This code example lists the contents of a table. The table name can
    be include along with the program name. If it is not, the program
    prompts for the name of a table.
*/
#include <stdio.h>
#include "pxengine.h"
#define NET_NAME_PATH           "c:\\apps\\paradox3"
#define NET_TYPE                NOTONNET
#define USER_NAME               "demoprog"
#define SUCCESS                 0
#define MAX_FIELDS              255
#define MAX_BUFFER_SIZE         26
```

Listing 14-8 Table listing program example 1

```
int main(int, char **);
void Intro();
int Initialize(void);
void OpenTable(char *);
void GetTableStructure(void);
void PrintTable(void);
void PrintTableRecord(int);
void CloseTable(void);
void Terminate(void);
TABLEHANDLE tableHandle;
RECORDHANDLE recHandle;
char fieldNames[MAX_FIELDS][MAX_BUFFER_SIZE];
char fieldTypes[MAX_FIELDS][MAX_BUFFER_SIZE];
int nFields;
RECORDNUMBER nRecs;
int main(int argc, char **argv)
{
    char filename[MAX_FILENAME_SIZE + 1];
    int pxErr=0;
    system("cls");                          /* clear the screen          */
    if (Initialize() == SUCCESS)            /* initialize system         */
        {
        if (argc > 1)                       /* if table name included at */
            OpenTable(argv[1]);             /* startup open the table    */
        else
        {
            Intro();                        /* display introduction text */
            printf("Enter table name: ");   /* prompt for table name     */
            scanf("%s",filename);
            OpenTable(filename);            /* attemp to open table      */
        }
        GetTableStructure();                /* determines table structure*/
        PrintTable();                       /* prints records            */
        CloseTable();                       /* closes table              */
        Terminate();                        /* terminates the engine     */
        }
    else
        printf("%s\n", PXErrMsg(pxErr));    /* print error message if    */
                                            /* the Engine could not be   */
                                            /* initialized               */
    return(pxErr);                          /* exit and return value of  */
                                            /* Engine error code         */
}
int Initialize(void)
{
    return(PXNetInit(NET_NAME_PATH, NET_TYPE, USER_NAME));
}
void Intro()
{
    printf("\nThis is a program that reads from a Paradox table,\n"
           "and prints the data to the screen, each field on a \n"
           "separate line.\n\n");
```

Listing 14-8 *Table listing program example 1—continued*

```c
}
void OpenTable(char *tableName)
{
    if(PXTblOpen(tableName, &tableHandle, 0, 0))
    {
        printf("Cannot open table %s\n", tableName);
        exit(1);
    }
    PXRecBufOpen(tableHandle, &recHandle);       /* don't forget error chk */
}
void GetTableStructure(void)
{
    int i;
    PXTblNRecs(tableHandle, &nRecs);
    PXRecNFlds(tableHandle, &nFields);
    for(i = 0; i < nFields; i++)
    {
        PXFldName(tableHandle, (FIELDHANDLE) i + 1,
                  MAX_BUFFER_SIZE, fieldNames[i]);
        PXFldType(tableHandle, (FIELDHANDLE) i + 1,
                  MAX_BUFFER_SIZE, fieldTypes[i]);
    }
}
void PrintTable(void)
{
    int i;
    for(i = 0; i < nRecs; i++)
    {
        PXRecGoto(tableHandle, i + 1);
        PXRecGet(tableHandle, recHandle);
        PrintTableRecord(i);
    }
}
void PrintTableRecord(int rcdnum)
{
    int i;
    double dvalue;
    char avalue[BUFSIZ];
    int mo, da, yr;
    long lvalue;
    short svalue;
    printf("%-25s: %d\n", "Record #", rcdnum);
    for(i = 0; i < nFields; i++)
    {
        switch(fieldTypes[i][0])
        {
            case 'N':
            case '$':
                PXGetDoub(recHandle, i + 1, &dvalue);
                printf("%-25s: %g\n", fieldNames[i], dvalue);
                break;
            case 'A':
```

Listing 14-8 Table listing program example 1—continued

```
                    PXGetAlpha(recHandle, i + 1, BUFSIZ, avalue);
                    printf("%-25s: %s\n", fieldNames[i], avalue);
                    break;
                case 'D':
                    PXGetDate(recHandle, i + 1, &lvalue);
                    PXDateDecode(lvalue, &mo, &da, &yr);
                    printf("%-25s: %d/%d/%d\n", fieldNames[i], mo, da, yr);
                    break;
                case 'S':
                    PXGetShort(recHandle, i + 1, &svalue);
                    printf("%-25s: %d\n", fieldNames[i], svalue);
                    break;
                default:
                    printf("unknown\n");
                    break;
            }
        }
        putchar('\n');
}
void CloseTable(void)
{
    PXRecBufClose(recHandle);
    PXTblClose(tableHandle);
}
void Terminate(void)
{
    PXExit();
}
```

Listing 14-8 Table listing program example 1—continued

The second example is essentially the same as the previous example except that each row of the table is printed on a single row of the screen. Figure 14-4 shows the output from this program. Listing 14-9 shows the complete program (we'll step through the added code first).

To align each field, the maximum number of characters used for the column name is compared to the number of characters required by the data type. The largest of these two numbers is the space required for the column. The size for each field is stored in the array *fieldSize*, established at the same time as the field names and data types. The following code has been added to GetTableStructure.

```
switch(fieldTypes[i][0])
{                                       /* determine the maximum    */
    case 'N' :                          /* width a field needs to be */
    case '$' :                          /* on ouput by comparing the */
    case 'D' :                          /* data type to field name   */
        fieldSize[i] =  (int) max(10, strlen(fieldNames[i]));
```

Using the Paradox Engine   **487**

```
Employee ID  First Name  Last Name       Age      Payrate
      1003   Barry       Adams            45       13.45
      1005   Jim         Charles          56       21.45
      1001   Mary        Jones            29       16.34
      1002   John        Smith            32       15.34
      1004   Tim         Zeno             34       23.22

D:\TC\ENGTEST>
```

Figure 14-4 List table sample output

```
      break;
   case 'S' :
      fieldSize[i] = (int) max(5, strlen(fieldNames[i]));
      break;
   case 'A' :
      fieldSize[i] = (int) max(atoi(&fieldTypes[i][1]),
         strlen(fieldNames[i]));
      break;
}
```

If the data type is N, $, or D, the column width is either 10 characters or the size of the field name. The column length for S data type is either 5 or the column name width. The size of alpha fields is either the length of the field name or the number of characters the field can contain.

One additional change is made to the field output code. The printf statement now dynamically determines the width of the output column, based on the values in *fieldSize*. Using an asterisk (*) informs C that the output width is based on an argument. This technique is the initial step in improving the output.

```
   case 'N':
   case '$':
      if (pxErr = PXGetDoub(recHandle, i + 1, &dvalue))
         PXErrMsg(pxErr);
      printf("%*g  ", fieldSize[i], dvalue);
      break;
```

```c
/* listdb2.c
   This code example lists the contents of a table. The table name can
   be include along with the program name. If it is not, the program
   prompts for the name of a table.
*/
#include <stdio.h>
#include <string.h>
#include <stdlib.h>
#include "pxengine.h"
#define NET_NAME_PATH          "c:\\apps\\paradox3"
#define NET_TYPE               NOTONNET
#define USER_NAME              "demoprog"
#define SUCCESS                0
#define MAX_FIELDS             255
#define MAX_BUFFER_SIZE        26
#define MAX_FILENAME_SIZE      40
int main(int, char **);
void Intro();
int Initialize(void);
void OpenTable(char *);
void GetTableStructure(void);
void PrintTableHeader(void);
void PrintTable(void);
void PrintTableRecord(void);
void CloseTable(void);
void Terminate(void);
TABLEHANDLE tableHandle;
RECORDHANDLE recHandle;
char  fieldNames[MAX_FIELDS][MAX_BUFFER_SIZE];
char  fieldTypes[MAX_FIELDS][MAX_BUFFER_SIZE];
int   fieldSize[MAX_FIELDS];
int nFields;
RECORDNUMBER nRecs;
int main(int argc, char **argv)
{
    char filename[MAX_FILENAME_SIZE + 1];
    int pxErr=0,i;
    system("cls");                          /* clear the screen          */
    if (Initialize() == SUCCESS)            /* initialize system         */
    {
        if (argc > 1)                       /* if table name included at */
            OpenTable(argv[1]);             /* startup open the table    */
        else
        {
            Intro();                        /* display introduction text */
            printf("Enter table name: ");   /* prompt for table name     */
            scanf("%s",filename);
            OpenTable(filename);            /* attemp to open table      */
        }
        GetTableStructure();                /* determines table structure*/
        PrintTableHeader();                 /* prints column headings    */
        PrintTable();                       /* prints records            */
```

Listing 14-9 Table listing program example 2

```
            CloseTable();                          /* closes table             */
            Terminate();                           /* terminates the engine    */
    }
    else
        printf("%s\n", PXErrMsg(pxErr));   /* print error message if   */
                                           /* the Engine could not be  */
                                           /* initialized              */
    return(pxErr);                         /* exit and return value of */
                                           /* Engine error code        */
}
int Initialize(void)
{
    return(PXNetInit(NET_NAME_PATH, NET_TYPE, USER_NAME));
}
void Intro()
{
    printf("\nThis is a program that reads from a Paradox table,\n"
           "and prints the data to the screen, each record on a \n"
           "separate line.\n\n");
}
void OpenTable(char *tableName)
{
    int pxErr;
    if (PXTblOpen(tableName, &tableHandle, 0, 0))
    {
        printf("Cannot open table %s\n", tableName);
        exit(1);
    }
    if (pxErr = PXRecBufOpen(tableHandle, &recHandle))
        PXErrMsg(pxErr);
}
void GetTableStructure(void)
{
    int i, pxErr;
    if (pxErr = PXTblNRecs(tableHandle, &nRecs))
        PXErrMsg(pxErr);
    if (pxErr = PXRecNFlds(tableHandle, &nFields))
        PXErrMsg(pxErr);
    for(i = 0; i < nFields; i++)
    {
        PXFldName(tableHandle, (FIELDHANDLE) i + 1,  /* field names   */
                  MAX_BUFFER_SIZE, fieldNames[i]);
        PXFldType(tableHandle, (FIELDHANDLE) i + 1,  /* field types   */
                  MAX_BUFFER_SIZE, fieldTypes[i]);
        switch(fieldTypes[i][0])
        {                                      /* determine the maximum */
            case 'N' :                         /* width a field needs to be */
            case '$' :                         /* on ouput by comparing the */
            case 'D' :                         /* data type to field name   */
                fieldSize[i] =  (int) max(10, strlen(fieldNames[i]));
                break;
            case 'S' :
```

Listing 14-9 Table listing program example 2—continued

```
                    fieldSize[i] = (int) max(5, strlen(fieldNames[i]));
                    break;
            case 'A' :
                    fieldSize[i] = (int) max(atoi(&fieldTypes[i][1]),
                    strlen(fieldNames[i]));
                    break;
        }
    }
}
void PrintTableHeader(void)
{
    int i;                                      /* print the column names   */
    for(i = 0; i < nFields; i++)
        printf("%-*s  ", fieldSize[i], fieldNames[i]);
    putchar('\n');
}
void PrintTable(void)
{
    int i, pxErr;                               /* print the data for each  */
                                                /* record                   */
    for(i = 0; i < nRecs; i++)
    {
        if (pxErr = PXRecGoto(tableHandle, i + 1))
            PXErrMsg(pxErr);
        if (pxErr = PXRecGet(tableHandle, recHandle))
            PXErrMsg(pxErr);
        PrintTableRecord();
    }
}
void PrintTableRecord(void)
{
    double dvalue;
    char avalue[BUFSIZ];
    int mo, da, yr, i, pxErr;
    long lvalue;
    short svalue;
    for(i = 0; i < nFields; i++)
    {
        switch(fieldTypes[i][0])
        {
            case 'N':
            case '$':
                if (pxErr = PXGetDoub(recHandle, i + 1, &dvalue))
                    PXErrMsg(pxErr);
                printf("%*g  ", fieldSize[i], dvalue);
                break;
            case 'A':
                if (pxErr = PXGetAlpha(recHandle, i + 1, BUFSIZ, avalue))
                    PXErrMsg(pxErr);
                printf("%-*s  ", fieldSize[i], avalue);
                break;
            case 'D':
                if ( pxErr = PXGetDate(recHandle, i + 1, &lvalue))
```

Listing 14-9 Table listing program example 2—continued

```
                        PXErrMsg(pxErr);
                if ( pxErr = PXDateDecode(lvalue, &mo, &da, &yr))
                        PXErrMsg(pxErr);
                printf("%-02d/%-02d/%-04d  ", mo, da, yr);
                break;
            case 'S':
                if ( pxErr = PXGetShort(recHandle, i + 1, &svalue))
                    PXErrMsg(pxErr);
                printf("%*d  ", fieldSize[i], svalue);
                break;
            default:
                printf("unknown\t");
                break;
            }
    }
    putchar('\n');
}
void CloseTable(void)
{
    int pxErr;
    if (pxErr = PXRecBufClose(recHandle))
        PXErrMsg(pxErr);
    if (pxErr = PXTblClose(tableHandle))
        PXErrMsg(pxErr);
}
void Terminate(void)
{
    int pxErr;
    if (pxErr = PXExit())
        PXErrMsg(pxErr);
}
```

Listing 14-9 *Table listing program example 2—continued*

What's Missing

The programs shown in this chapter are just beginning code examples of what it takes to use the Engine. Actually, most Paradox developers would never use the Engine to print data from a single table. The time it takes to write the code and maintain it is too high a price to pay. There is also little to no error handling in the programs. They work well only if the data is 80 characters wide or less. There is no provision to handle more data than will fit on the width of a screen. If a record is wider, it wraps around the screen. Even though this is a trivial example, it demonstrates some of the basic requirements necessary to work with tables.

Summary

Adding the Engine to your developer's toolbox expands your opportunities to better meet the needs of your users. Like building a house, the better the tools, the faster and better the house is built. Including the Engine with SQL Link, Quattro Pro, and SideKick for PM gives you a range of tools to select from based on the application's requirements.

At the same time, don't think that the Engine is the solution to improve performance. For example, if you have a query that is taking excessively long to complete, look towards making improvements within PAL before trying to create an Engine program, especially on multitable joins. Remember, Paradox has built-in optimization for queries that would take considerable effort to include in an Engine program. Use the Engine to perform tasks PAL cannot. Let the Engine complement PAL, not replace it.

15   Some Performance Tips

This chapter is a paradox in itself, in that it provides as many questions as it does answers. Ensuring optimum performance in an application can be tedious and is certainly not a foolproof process. The first step is gathering a significant amount of information and then analyzing and balancing your system's overall needs. In this chapter, we present the questions you need to answer before you can determine how to fine-tune your system's performance.

Memory

We discuss memory management and Paradox's provisions for utilizing memory in greater detail in Chapter 19, but here we need to first consider the memory mix. The memory mix consists of a system's total RAM and disk space. Total RAM available is the combination of conventional memory, expanded memory, and extended memory. Total disk space is the amount of usable DOS disk storage at any given time during Paradox operations. Remember, Paradox has built-in VMM (Virtual Memory Management) capabilities. Whenever Paradox doesn't have enough space to perform a procedure, work with a table, or display information, it uses space on your working disk drive to extend available RAM resources. However, Paradox can still run out of RAM and when it does, you get the veritable:

> **Resource Limit Exceeded: Insufficient memory to complete operation**

Paradox can and does extend its RAM capabilities by utilizing your disk storage device to run larger, more complex procedures. Because it uses the disk, the disk's operating speed becomes extremely important to your application's performance. You should have no less than a 28MS fixed system, preferably with at least 32K of disk cache. Disk cache is hardware memory that stores requested information and all information that surrounds that data on the disk. Disk caching programs do with software what hardware caches do with chips. If you don't have a hardware cache, use a disk caching product such as Super PC Qwik to improve your disk's performance. Of course, running any program requires some memory and disk caching programs are no exception. The most popular disk caching programs let you run a large portion of the cache in expanded memory, taking from conventional only what's needed to start and control the program. Hardware and software disk caching programs can improve system performance by 10 to 60 percent.

> **REMEMBER:** *Disk caching software or hardware caching are loaded when you boot your PC. Every DOS product you run that accesses your fixed disk can benefit from these programs.*

> **TRAP:** *To avoid possible conflicts with a disk cache, turn off Paradox's internal cache (use CCP or run Paradox from the command line with* **paradox -cachek 0**).

The next memory item you should consider is how much total RAM you have. We recommend that 8088 and 8086 systems have 640K of conventional memory plus an expanded memory board with 2MB. Paradox cannot use more than 48-208K of this expanded memory (this goes for all platforms) but you can employ the leftover memory as an electronic disk. If your system is a network workstation, you can improve performance by copying the PARADOX*.EXE and *.OV* (overlay files) from your Paradox directory on the network server to your local workstation. Copying everything except PARADOX.EXE, *.HLP and *.MSG to a RAM disk greatly speeds up applications.

> **REMEMBER:** *If you have a 286 or higher CPU and have at least 1.5MB of memory, it's best to run Paradox in protected mode.*

In addition to these items, you need to review the speed of the RAM installed in your machine. First, any memory you add should match the speed of the chips already installed (speed of chips are rated in nanoseconds). You should have at least 120ns chips, preferably 80-100ns chips.

> **REMEMBER:** *The lower the nanosecond number, the faster the chip.*

Some Performance Tips   495

TRAP: *Never mix faster and slower chips. Never have faster chips on an expanded memory board than those that reside on your motherboard.*

Back to your fixed disk for a moment. Make sure that your application has enough storage space to perform the task you require. If you have a Paradox table that is 2MB in DOS file size and you try to restructure the table with less than 6.5MB of available space, you're asking for trouble and frustration. Make sure that you're running a 1:1 interleaf and using DOS 3.3 or higher.

If you have only 40MB of hard disk storage (we remember when having 10MB seemed like more than we'd ever need!), think about adding another 40MB half-height to your system. Then you can make your application use a drive that should always have plenty of space to work with.

Memory questions

- How much available disk space do you have?
- How much total RAM is on your system?
- Will running a cache improve your disk access?
- If you have a 286 or higher, can you run in protected mode? (There are few reasons why you can't, such as if you're going to run Windows.)
- If you have a network workstation, do you already have or can you add extended/expanded memory to the system? What about setting up the application to copy the Paradox files down to the network workstation to improve performance? Could you obtain disk caching software to speed disk access?

TIP: *If you have a PS/2, use FASTOPEN to speed up tracking and access of tables.*

- Do you have a large enough disk? Could you add more disk space and make it available to Paradox?

REMEMBER: *There are two Paradox functions that help you monitor how much memory is available to Paradox. The first is MEMLEFT(). It returns the amount of working memory (RAM memory available at that point to your application), rounded to the nearest 2K. (You can get the same result by accessing the memory utilization screen. Press [ALT][=]. The amount of memory available is shown on the second line from the bottom in the form Memleft48, where 48K is the amount of RAM memory available to Paradox.)*

The other function is RMEMLEFT(). It returns the amount of memory remaining in a special place in memory called the code pool. If an application runs out of working memory and starts using the code pool, it's ready to run out of memory. Use MEMLEFT() and RMEMLEFT() to fine-tune your application.

TIP: *To ensure that the maximum amount of memory is available to your applications, use RESET CLEARALL and/or the new SAVETABLES. Each table you place on the workspace takes at least 2K of memory to display. Clear tables that you don't need from the workspace before starting a query.*

TIP: *Reuse variables, use closed procedures, and use the PRIVATE provision for procedures. As PRIVATE variables are no longer needed, as closed procedures are completed and exited, the memory they occupied returns to your application.*

```
Proc Closed GoodProc()
Private answer
if answer = "Y" then
  rv = "Yes"
else
  rv = "No"
endif
return rv
EndProc
```

TIP: *Keep your procedures small. Use INFOLIB("LIBRARYNAME") to find the size of each procedure in a certain library. If a procedure is larger than 6 to 8K, review it and see if you can divide it into two procedures or re-engineer it so that it's smaller in some way.*

Table Design

If there is one sure way to quick performance improvements in your system, it's redesigning your table structures so that they're as efficient as possible. Remember, high (many records) and narrow (as few fields as possible) tables are better than wide (many fields) tables. Let's review how Paradox allocates its disk space.

Field lengths (in bytes) follow these rules:

A	Alphanumeric	1 byte per char
N	Numeric	8 bytes
D	Date	4 bytes
S	Short Number	2 bytes
$	Currency (Numeric)	8 bytes

For example:

Field Name	*Type*
Customer ID	N
Last Name	A20
First Name	A15
MI	A3
Honorific	A6
Address 1	A35
Address 2	a35
City	A20
State	A2
Country	A15
Zip	A15
Current Balance	$
Customer Date	D

This record has a total record size of 186 bytes.

> **REMEMBER:** *The maximum record size for a non-keyed table is 4000 bytes. The maximum record size for a keyed table is 1350 bytes.*
>
> *Deleted records are usually not removed physically from tables until you restructure, unless Paradox determines that it needs the deleted space to store more information.*
>
> *When you do restructure, the table is completely rewritten. Therefore, once a restructure occurs, there are no gaps in a table due to deleted records. (The more gaps in a table, the slower the table's performance under edits, views, and queries.)*

Paradox uses a very flexible algorithm to determine file allocation for a table. Paradox assigns blocks of disk space in either 1K, 2K, 3K, or 4K block sizes. Following is a discussion of how Paradox allocates disk space for tables.

> **NOTE:** *Paradox 3.5 is generally compatible with previous versions of Paradox. Although tables from previous versions of Paradox are completely compatible with Paradox 3.5, tables created in Paradox 3.5 are blocked in a way that gives better performance in almost all cases. For best performance in Paradox 3.5, you should restructure existing tables in Paradox 3.5. To do this, restructure the table without making any changes to it (access Modify/Restructure and simply press Do-It! to exit). However, if some users will continue to use these tables with earlier versions of Paradox, be aware that these restructured tables will require more memory when placed on the workspace (up to 2K more for each table and for each index on the table).*

Non-keyed tables

Paradox will choose the smallest block size that will hold exactly one record.

Example:

Record Size	Block Size	Recs/Block
100 bytes	1K	10
800 bytes	1K	1
500 bytes	1K	2
3450 bytes	4K	1

Keyed tables

Paradox selects the smallest block that will hold exactly three records.

Example:

Record Size	Block Size	Recs/Block
100 bytes	1K	10
200 bytes	1K	5
350 bytes	2K	5
513 bytes	2K	3
1350	4K	3

TIP: *If you could restructure the 350 byte table so that it was only 300 bytes, you could reduce the block size to 1K. The smaller the block, the faster the access.*

Other Tips

- Create key tables with additional indexes to speed query and report operations.
- When you create indexes, stay away from MAINTAINED indexes. Unless you need access *now*, maintaining a tremendous number of indexes only slows an application down.
- Use CoEdit instead of Edit. Remember that Edit keeps log of all changes while CoEdit keeps only the previous record's changes.
- Make sure that your DOS directories don't have too many file entries. Try to keep the number of files in any one directory under 132. (Target it to be less than 90 since Paradox creates temporary tables on the fly). If necessary, divide your files into script, data, and master table directories.

TRAP: *Remember that Paradox tags forms and reports with the DOS path they reside in. Therefore, avoid the RDA problem (relative directory address): create your forms and reports in the directories they will be used in and then copy them to a different directory.*

- If your application is networked, decrease refresh time or turn it off altogether.
- On network queries and reports, "snap-shot" data to a private location and perform your query or report from the snapshot. This alleviates the problem with query and report restarts.
- Be extremely careful when using SETSWAP. Make sure you have enough memory to complete your operations but be sure you don't set SETSWAP too high or you'll wait forever for certain procedures and routines to complete.
- PRINT FILE:
    - PAL's PRINT FILE command is much faster now because Paradox keeps the file open as long as possible and buffers the output. If you previously optimized PRINT FILE by concatenating output into long strings, it is no longer necessary to do

so. Paradox knows to write the buffer and close the file almost any time it could be necessary.
- If you use a filename as a semaphore to other network users, and you want to close the file before Paradox does so automatically, try

    DUMMY = ISFILE("filename.txt")

(where "filename.txt" is the name of your file) to force it closed.

Summary

In this chapter, we've covered issues regarding performance that are not covered in other chapters. For related topics, see Chapters 7, 10, and 19. In the next chapter, we'll look at a sample application and the code that actually performs the tasks.

16 Sample Applications

In this chapter, we show you how to put some of our concepts and tools together. The sample applications in this chapter include many of the concepts discussed earlier, so you may want to look back at the following chapters: "Building Procedures and Libraries," "Setting up a Multiuser Environment," "Creating and Enhancing the Paradox Interface," and "Prototyping Paradox Applications."

You shouldn't view the applications in this chapter as shrink-wrapped, ready-to-go products. Rather, you should approach these systems as you brainstorm your own applications. They are presented to help you decide what style of PAL programming you want or need to employ. The two sample systems in this chapter include a retail store application and a personnel application.

REMEMBER: *Like all of the scripts and procedures referenced in this book, these applications are included on disk as well; after installation, they'll be in /POWERDOX/16.*

ABC Music Store

The first application is the ABC Music Store application. The ABC Music Store is a fictitious music store in the equally fictitious city of Anywhere, Washington. This application illustrates a modular approach to program design and delivery. It incorporates multiple libraries and scripts to deliver a fully menu-driven system that can invoice customers for products as well as track students who take music lessons from the store. Application features include:

- Pop-up menus, including context-sensitive help.
- An Administration module that features invoicing, customer and account maintenance, and product verification.
- A Music Lesson module that forecasts upcoming classes and shows current openings.
- Reports:
    Class schedules
    Aging of accounts
    Statement generation
    Product listing
    Invoices on demand
- A multiuser environment (uses a variation of the shadow table technique shown in Chapter 12).

Like most applications, this one starts by playing a script that brings up the Main menu. The Main menu is shown in Figure 16-1.

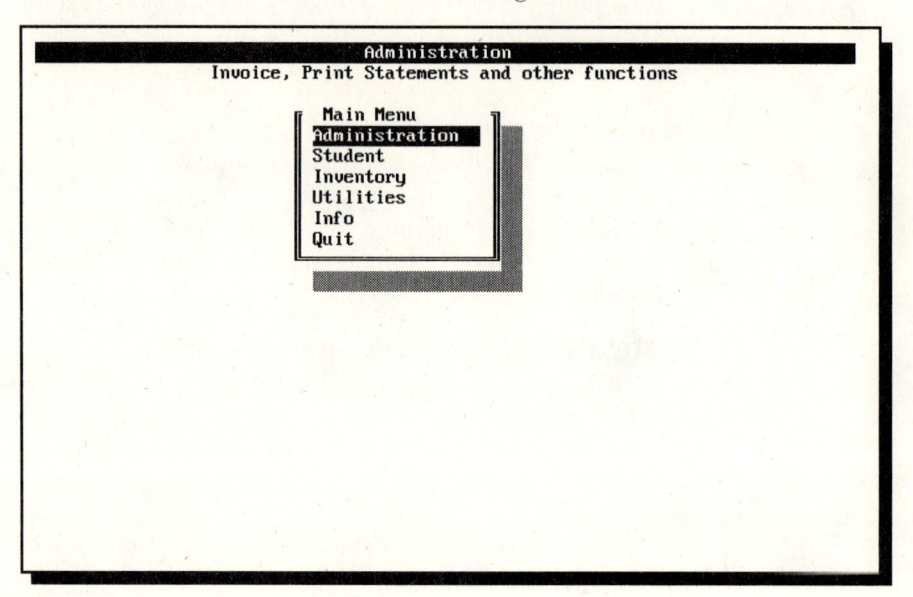

Figure 16-1 The ABC Music Store Main menu (MMAIN.SC)

> **NOTE:** *Start the MMAIN script with Menu {Script} {Play} {Mmain}. Of course you could also launch the application by creating an INIT.SC with:*
>
> ### play "MMAIN"

You've already looked at the pop-up style menus in Chapter 8, but let's look at ABC's Main menu to get oriented with the system.

The MMAIN script starts by setting [Shift][F1] to play the MMAIN script in the event that you left the application and wanted to return at some point to the application's Main menu. The complete code for this section of the application is shown in Listing 16-1.

MMAIN.SC

```
;****************************************************************
;Script:MMain
;Description:Main Menu for the ABC Music Store
;
;Created [9/15/90] By [G.Salcedo ]
;****************************************************************
AutoLib = "MMenus,MMesgLib,MMenuHlp"
Color = 31
shadow = privdir()+"shadow"
play "preptabl"
setkey "F11" play "MMain"
While (true)
CANVAS OFF
Release Procs All
Release Vars All
Reset
Clear
ClearAll
shadow = privdir()+"shadow"
Autolib = "MMenus,MMesgLib,MMenuHlp"
Array   Prevx[4]
Array   Prevy[4]
Array PrevNC[4]
Array PrevPW[4]
Array PrevCL[4]
Array   PrevN[4]
Array PrevML[4]
Level = 1                  ; Set Menu level to 1
    n = 1                  ; Set first menu choice
 Prevx[Level] = 3          ; Upper Left 'X' coordinate
 Prevy[Level] = 25         ; Upper Left 'Y' coordinate
```

Listing 16-1 MMAIN.SC

```
PrevNC[Level] = 6                       ; Number of menu choices
PrevPW[Level] = 20                      ; Width of the PopUp Menu
PrevCL[Level] = 31                      ; Color of the Menu
PrevML[Level] = "   Main Menu      "; Menu Name
       BeginX = Prevx[Level]
       BeginY = Prevy[Level]
NumberChoices = PrevNC[Level]
     Popwidth = PrevPW[Level]
        Color = PrevCL[level]
     MenuName = PrevML[level]
; the following arrays set up all the menu choices and their
; corresponding messages
;
;         C[n] = menu items (the possible choices)
;         D[n] = descriptions of the menu items
;        SC[n] = "top bar" representation of menu item
;        SD[n] = "top bar"      "            "  "   description
;      NICK[n] = first letter of menu items
Array            C[NumberChoices]
Array            D[NumberChoices]
Array           SC[NumberChoices]
Array           SD[NumberChoices]
Array         NICK[NumberChoices]
```

Listing 16-1 MMAIN.SC—continued

The following arrays set up all the menu choices and their corresponding messages:

C[n]   Menu items (the possible choices) to appear in the pop-up menu box. These are one-word selections.

D[n]   Descriptions of the menu items. These descriptions are limited to 79 characters in length and provide more information on the current selection.

SC[n]   Top bar representation of menu items. Provides the same information as the *C[n]* array of data but appears at the top of the screen. This particular style of menus allows for the tastes of both the pop-up and top bar preferences.

SD[n]   Top bar descriptions are the same as their *D[n]* counterparts except they appear at the top of the screen, directly below the *SC[n]* information.

NICK[n]   Records first letter of menu items so that you can press the first letter of the menu choice to start a procedure (rather than using [Up Arrow] and [Down Arrow]), highlighting the selection and pressing [Enter]. These are the actual menu choices and the corresponding "wide" bar (top) display.

> **NOTE:** *Be sure to enclose the menu item in quotes. The number of characters in the menu items should not exceed the PopWidth-2 parameter.*

```
C[1] = "Administration"
D[1] = "Invoice, Print Statements and other functions"
C[2] = "Student"
D[2] = "Go the the MUSIC lesson menu"
C[3] = "Inventory"
D[3] = "Go to the Inventory Menu"
C[4] = "Utilities"
D[4] = "Go to the Utilities Menu"
C[5] = "Info"
D[5] = "More information on system"
C[6] = "Quit"
D[6] = "Exit the System"
if isassigned(n) = false then
     n = 1
else
     n = n
endif
last = arraysize(c)
CANVAS ON
```

Listing 16-1 MMAIN.SC—continued

In this next section, the FILLMENU and SELMENU scripts are read from the MMENUS library. These procedures gather in all the variables declared previously and then display the Main menu as a pop-up style menu.

```
FillMenu()
SelMenu()
Reset
if sel = "Esc" then
     @24,0 Clear EOL ?? format("w79,ac","One moment please ...")
     quitloop
else
```

Listing 16-1 MMAIN.SC—continued

Finally, this last section processes the selection. If you press [Esc], you return to interactive Paradox. If you make a selection via the direction and [Enter] keys, or by pressing the proper first letter of your desired menu selection, SWITCH...ENDSWITCH launches the next step in the process.

> **NOTE:** *You can eliminate the option of returning to interactive Paradox by replacing QUITLOOP with* **EXIT** *for case sel = c[6]. Doing so causes Paradox to exit and return to DOS.*

```
switch
          case sel = "Esc" : level = level -1
                             quitloop
          case sel = c[1]  : play "Modimenu"
          case sel = c[2]  : play "lesnmenu"
          case sel = c[3]  : play "invtmenu"
          case sel = c[4]  : play "utilmenu"
          case sel = c[5]  : HelpMenu(sel)
          case sel = c[6]  : play "chekdata"
                             if dataexists = "Yes" then
                                 MessgBox(100)
                                 loop
                             endif
                             quitloop
OtherWise:loop
EndSwitch
endif
EndWhile
```

Listing 16-1 MMAIN.SC—*continued*

When you're in any of the menus, help is available by pressing [F1]. Like the examples shown in Chapter 8, you must enter the specific help message you want to appear in the help library. In this application, the help library is called **MMENUHLP**. Figure 16-2 shows a help message.

The Administration menu lists all of the retail business functions available, except for purchase ordering. Figure 16-3 shows how the menu appears.

As Figure 16-3 shows, you can view the Customer and Products table, create an invoice, edit the customer's account, and produce reports, including aging activity and account statements. Figure 16-4 shows the Report menu, Figure 16-5 the Customer screen, and Figure 16-6 the Product screen.

You access the Products and Customer tables through two scripts, VIEWCUST and VIEWPROD. Both scripts work the same except that one is called specifically for Customer and the other for Products. Listing 16-2 shows the VIEWCUST script.

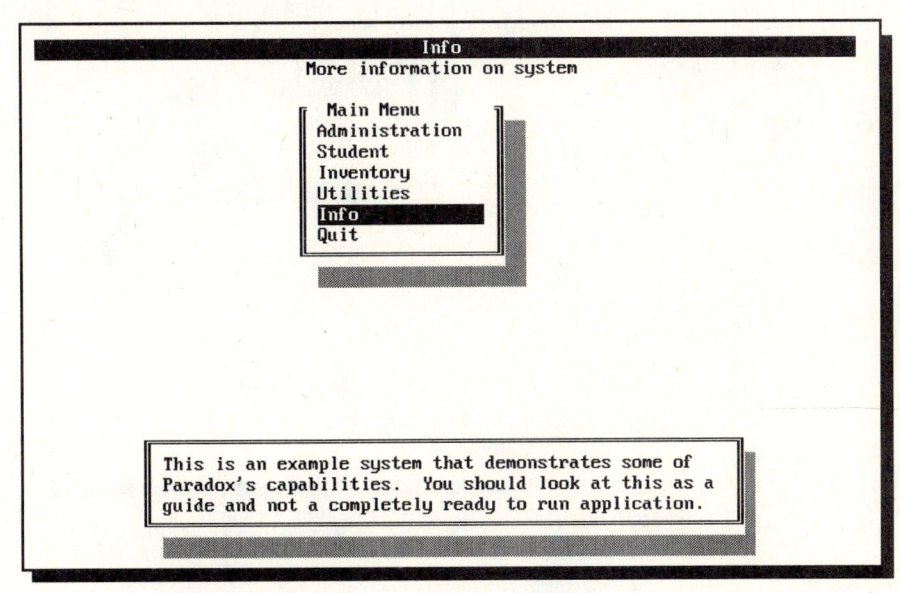

```
┌──────────────────────────── Info ────────────────────────────┐
│                    More information on system                │
            ┌─Main Menu─────────┐
            │ Administration    │
            │ Student           │
            │ Inventory         │
            │ Utilities         │
            │ Info              │
            │ Quit              │
            └───────────────────┘




            ┌──────────────────────────────────────────┐
            │ This is an example system that demonstrates some of │
            │ Paradox's capabilities.  You should look at this as a │
            │ guide and not a completely ready to run application. │
            └──────────────────────────────────────────┘
```

Figure 16-2 Built-in help facility

```
┌──────────────────────────── Customer ────────────────────────┐
│                    View/Edit/Enter CUSTOMER table            │
            ┌─Main Menu─────────┐
            │ ┌Administration───┐
            │ │ Customer        │
            │ │ Products        │
            │ │ Reports         │
            │ │ Invoice         │
            │ │ Accounts        │
            │ │ Quit            │
            │ └─────────────────┘
```

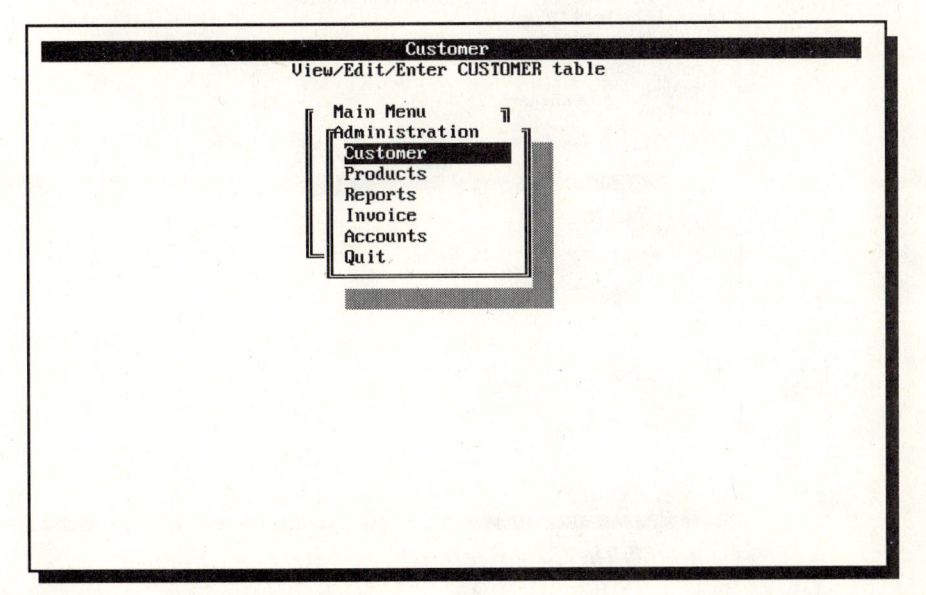

Figure 16-3 The Administration menu

```
              Statements
           Print Statements
      ┌─────────────────────┐
      │ Main Menu        ⇓ │
      │┌Administration   ⇓─┐│
      ││┌Report Menu       ││
      │││ Statements       ││
      │││ Aging            ││
      │││ Product Report   ││
      │││ Quit             ││
      └└└──────────────────┘┘┘
```

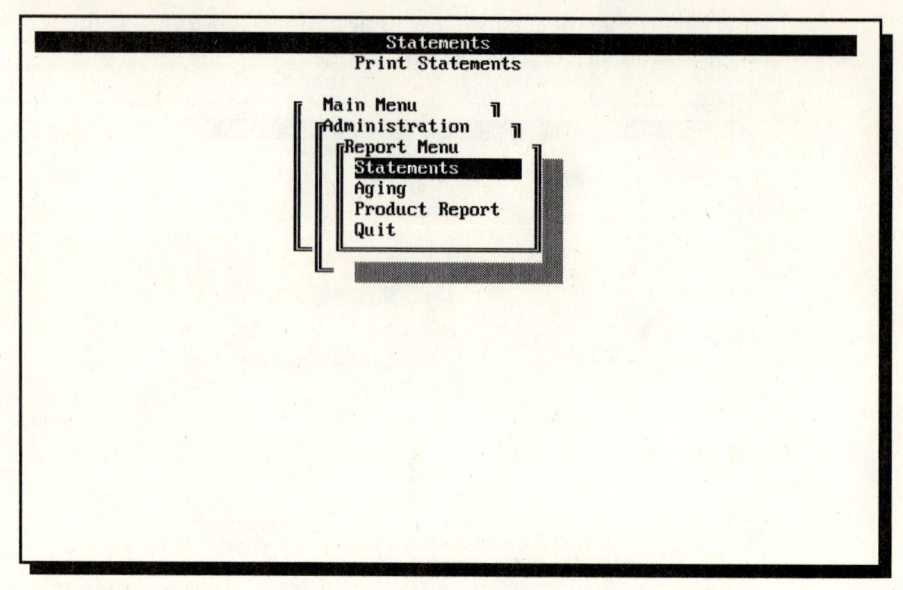

Figure 16-4 The Reports menu

```
Press [F2] Save ...    [F5] LookUp CUSTOMER #...   [F6] LookUp Last Name  Main
Press [F7] Form Toggle ....                        [F10] Edit Record
  Customer/Accounts       CUSTOMER # [      15200     ]
  Name       [John                       ] [Parker                      ]
  Street #   [              12345        ]
  Address 1  [Grandpere St               ]
  Address 2  [                           ]
  C/S/Z/Phone[Anywhere                   ] [WA ] [12346-1234 ] [555-124-9876 ]
  Balance    [              2,645.00     ]
```

Figure 16-5 The Customer screen

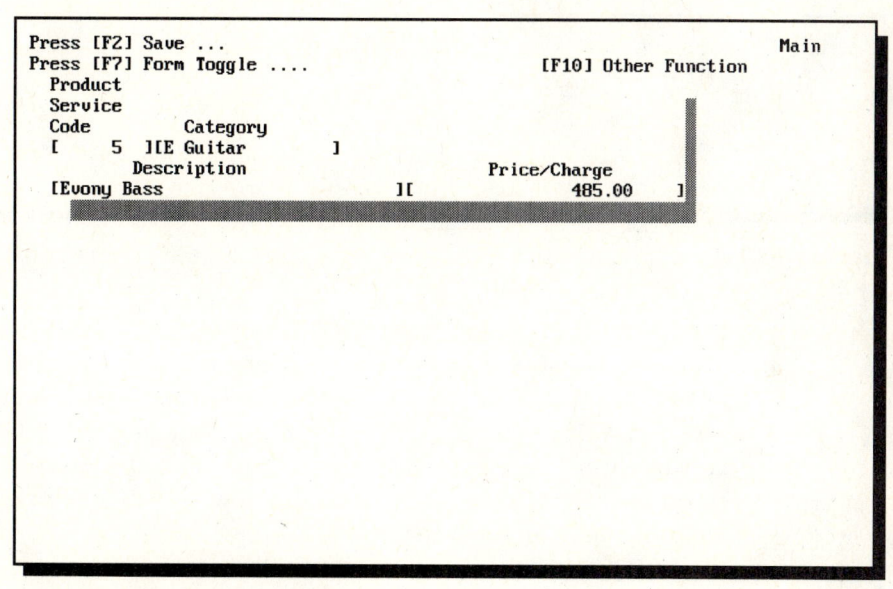

```
Press [F2] Save ...                                              Main
Press [F7] Form Toggle ....              [F10] Other Function
  Product
  Service
  Code       Category
  [    5 ][E Guitar         ]
        Description                   Price/Charge
        [Evony Bass                ][        485.00    ]
```

Figure 16-6 The Product screen

VIEWCUST.SC

The VIEWCUST script lets you update the customer's balance before viewing the Customer table, or view the Customer screen directly. Notice that the Customer table is locked with a Prevent Full Lock where necessary.

```
;***********************************************************************
;Script [ViewCust]
;Description [Edit or enter information based on the CUSTOMER table linked
;             to the ACCOUNTS table (1-M)]
;Created [05/26/90] By [G.Salcedo ]
;***********************************************************************
MessgBox(97)
ShowMenu
        "Update Total" : "Update the customer totals",
        "Go"           : "View the Customer table without updating the totals"
        Until "F2" keyto keyvar
        to answer
                Switch
                        case answer = "Update Total":    play "UpdtTotl"
                        case answer = "Go" :
                OtherWise:loop
                EndSwitch
```

Listing 16-2 VIEWCUST.SC

```
While (true)
        Lock "Customer" PFL
        if retval = true then
                quitloop
        endif
EndWhile
```

Listing 16-2 VIEWCUST.SC—continued

Notice that in this section, you aren't allowed to exit to DOS with [Ctrl][O] or [ALT][O] (DOS or DOSBIG). Another interesting feature is the way FIELDVIEW (-108) is trapped and accounted for. While this particular script is a VIEW, the routine for trapping and handling FIELDVIEW works very nicely in EDIT or COEDIT. This approach lets you have a DELETE record function without being hassled by it when you're in FIELDVIEW and you want to delete a character.

```
While (true)
View tablename
Pickform pform
While (true)   ; Keep doing UNTIL
Wait Table
Prompt "Press [F2] Save ... [F5] LookUp CUSTOMER #... [F6] LookUp Last Name
"+sysmode(),
       "Press [F7] Form Toggle ....                            [F10] Edit Record"
Until  "F2", "F7", -108, "Del", "DOS","DOSBIG","F10","F3","F4","F5","F6"
lookretval = retval
if lookretval = "DOS" or lookretval = "DOSBIG" then
        NoDosExit("Top")
        loop
endif
```

Listing 16-2 VIEWCUST.SC—continued

This IF...ENDIF allows you to jump back and forth from the top and bottom of the form.

```
if lookretval = "F3" or lookretval = "F4" then
        keypress lookretval
        loop
endif
```

Listing 16-2 VIEWCUST.SC—continued

The next two IF...ENDIFs handle looking up a Customer # or Last Name.

```
if lookretval = "F5" then
      @1,0 Clear EOL
      @0,0 Clear EOL ?? "Customer # ? "
      accept "n" to answer
      if isassigned(answer) = false then
            loop
      endif
      if answer = "Esc" then
            loop
      endif
      moveto field "customer number"
      ZOOM select answer
      loop
endif
if lookretval = "F6" then
      @1,0 Clear EOL
      @0,0 Clear EOL ?? "Last Name ? "
      accept "a35" to answer
      if isassigned(answer) = false then
            loop
      endif
      if answer = "Esc" then
            loop
      endif
      moveto field "Last Name"
      ZOOM select answer
      loop
endif
if lookretval = -108 then
      keypress -108
      While (true)
      WAIT FIELD
      Prompt "Press [F2] or [ENTER] to leave FIELDVIEW"
      UNTIL "F2","Enter","DOS","DOSBIG"
      fieldretval = retval
      if fieldretval = "DOS" or fieldretval = "DOSBIG" then
           NoDosExit("Bottom")
           loop
      endif
      if fieldretval = "F2" or fieldretval = "Enter" then
           quitloop
      endif
      EndWhile
      release vars fieldretval
      loop
endif
```

Listing 16-2 VIEWCUST.SC—*continued*

This IF...ENDIF lets you toggle from FORMVIEW to TABLEVIEW and then proceed with viewing the table.

```
if lookretval = "F7" then
     Formkey
          loop
endif
```

Listing 16-2 VIEWCUST.SC—continued

It's always a good idea to make an application as flexible as possible. In this case, the following IF...ENDIF lets you edit a record even though you selected View.

```
if lookretval = "F10" then
     CoEditKey
     Wait Record
     Prompt "Make Changes ... press [F2] to continue"
     Until "F2","Esc"
     if retval = "F2" then
          Do_it!
     else
          UNDO
          Do_it!
     endif
     loop
endif
UNLOCK "CUSTOMER" FL
Reset
ClearAll
ReDrawPopBox(level)
Release procs ReDrawPopBox
reset
quitloop
Endwhile
quitloop
Endwhile
```

Listing 16-2 VIEWCUST.SC—continued

This application's features include the ability to invoice customers, update accounts, and print invoices. Most of these tasks are performed by ENTERINV.SC (Listing 16-3).

ENTERINV.SC

ENTERINV starts out by letting you choose for an existing customer or a new customer. If you select an existing customer, SEL_CUST is played to let you select the customer to invoice. If the customer is new, a random number is assigned (the system checks to ensure that this number isn't assigned already) and then invoicing proceeds. Notice that extra steps are taken to lock the appropriate tables before processing. In addition, a special control table, Invnumb, facilitates entering a new invoice number.

NOTE: *This is one of the routines that uses a variation of the shadow table techniques discussed in Chapter 12.*

```
;****************************************************************
;Script [EntrInv ]
;Description [Enter and print a new invoice
;
;Created [05/26/90] By [G.Salcedo ]
;****************************************************************
Reset
ClearAll
ShowMenu
        "Existing":"Create INVOICE for an existing customer",
        "New"     :"Create NEW CUSTOMER and INVOICE"
        Until "F2" keyto keyvar
        to sel
        Switch
                case sel = "Esc"      : ReDrawPopBox(level) Return
                case sel = "Existing" : ; Select from existing
                case sel = "New"      : ; New customer
        OtherWise:Loop
        EndSwitch
MessgBox(97) ; one moment please
if sel = "Existing" then
        play "Sel_Cust"
endif
counter = 0
if sel = "New" then
While (true)
LOCK "CUSTOMER" PFL
if retval = false then
    loop
endif
View "Customer"
moveto field "customer number"
quitloop
EndWhile
endif
MessgBox(97)
counter = counter+1
```

Listing 16-3 ENTERINV.SC

This section calculates a new invoice number. If the number hasn't been assigned, the procedure continues.

```
if sel = "New" then
While (true)
      newnumber = round(rand()*100000,-2)  ;assign arbitrary cust#
      locate newnumber
      if retval = false then
           Reset
           quitloop
      endif
EndWhile
endif
Reset
view "Invnumb"
pform = "2"
IMAGERIGHTS
```

Listing 16-3 ENTERINV.SC—continued

If the customer being invoiced is a current customer, the information picked up in the SEL_CUST routine is transferred to this invoicing session; otherwise the new customer number is assigned to the invoice record and processing continues.

```
if sel = "Existing" then
      CoEdit shadow+"\\custmstr"
      Menu {Image} {PickForm} select pform
      COPYFROMARRAY TRANCUST
      IMAGERIGHTS UPDATE
else
      EMPTY shadow+"\\custmstr"
      CoEdit shadow+"\\custmstr"
      Menu {Image} {PickForm} select pform
      [customer number] = newnumber
      IMAGERIGHTS UPDATE
endif
While (true)
goback = ""
FIRSTSHOW
MessgBox(97)
While (true)   ; Keep doing UNTIL
Wait Table
           Prompt "Press [F2] Save... [F5] LookUp CUSTOMER #... [F6] LookUp
           Last Name"+sysmode(),
      "Press [F7] Add Cust# [F9] Calc Total ... [F10] Create Inv#"
Until  "F2", -108, "Del", "DOS","DOSBIG","F10","F3","F4","F9","F5","F6"
lookretval = retval
```

Listing 16-3 ENTERINV.SC—continued

```
        if lookretval = "DOS" or lookretval = "DOSBIG" then
             NoDosExit("Top")
             loop
endif
if lookretval = "F3" or lookretval = "F4" then
        keypress lookretval
        loop
endif
if lookretval = "F5" then
        @1,0 Clear EOL
        @0,0 Clear EOL ?? "Customer # ? "
        accept "n" to answer
        if isassigned(answer) = false then
                loop
        endif
        if answer = "Esc" then
                loop
        endif
        moveto 2
        moveto field "customer number"
        ZOOM select answer
        loop
endif
if lookretval = "F6" then
        @1,0 Clear EOL
        @0,0 Clear EOL ?? "Last Name ? "
        accept "a35" to answer
        if isassigned(answer) = false then
                loop
        endif
        if answer = "Esc" then
                loop
        endif
        moveto 2
        moveto field "Last Name"
        ZOOM select answer+".."
        loop
endif
if lookretval = -108 then
        keypress -108
        While (true)
        WAIT FIELD
        Prompt "Press [F2] or [ENTER] to leave FIELDVIEW"
        UNTIL "F2","Enter","DOS","DOSBIG"
        fieldretval = retval
        if fieldretval = "DOS" or fieldretval = "DOSBIG" then
              NoDosExit("Bottom")
              loop
        endif
        if fieldretval = "F2" or fieldretval = "Enter" then
              quitloop
        endif
        EndWhile
```

Listing 16-3 ENTERINV.SC—continued

```
        release vars fieldretval
        loop
endif
if lookretval = "Del" then
        @24,0 Clear EOL ?? "Do you really want to delete (Y/N) ? "
        Accept "A1" picture "{Y,N}" default "N" to answer
        if answer = "Y" then
                Del
                loop
        else
                loop
        endif
endif
```

Listing 16-3 ENTERINV.SC—continued

Product look-up is available for the Code field (see Figure 16-10 later in this chapter). Once the item has been entered, press [F9] to calculate and extend the item to be invoiced. If the item is a product or service and the Quantity field is blank, an error message is displayed and you are asked to enter a quantity value. If the item is a payment or credit, or if the quantity field is filled in properly, the next IF...ENDIF updates the record.

```
if lookretval = "F9" then
        FFlag = isformview()
        if FFlag = false then
        FormKey
        endif
        here = imageno()
        here2 = field()
        here3 = recno()
        moveto 2
        [invoice balance] = 0
        moveto 3
        stop = nimagerecords()
        MessgBox(97)
        for counter from 1 to stop
                if [product/service code] < 10000 then
                        if isblank([quantity]) = true then
                                MessgBox(3)
                                quitloop
                        endif
                        [line total] = [quantity]*[amount]
                        [debit/credit] = "D"
                else
                        [line total] = [amount]*-1
                        [debit/credit] = "C"
```

Listing 16-3 ENTERINV.SC—continued

```
            endif
            if [line total] > 0 then
                    [debit/credit] = "D"
            else
                    [debit/credit] = "C"
            endif
        endfor
        moveto field "line total"
        down up
        total = imagecsum()
        moveto 2
        moveto field "invoice balance"
        [] = total
        moveto here
        moveto field here2
        home up
        moveto record here3
        CtrlHome
        Down
        if FFlag = false then
            FormKey
        endif
        loop
endif
```

Listing 16-3 ENTERINV.SC—continued

This IF...ENDIF lets you assign one or more invoice numbers to the current transaction.

```
if lookretval = "F10" then
    lockrecord
    FormKey
    moveto 3
    play "invnumb"
    if newnumber <> 0 then
        FormKey
        moveto 3
        if isblank([invoice number]) = true or
                [invoice number] = -9999 then
                [invoice number] = newnumber
        endif
    else
        FormKey
    endif
    CANVAS ON
    loop
endif
```

Listing 16-3 ENTERINV.SC—continued

Before you leave this routine by selecting [F2], all records are calculated and assigned debit/credit flags. If a quantity field is blank for an inventory item, the routine sends you back to the top and prompts you to enter the quantity.

```
    if lookretval = "F2" then
         Do_it!
         if nrecords(shadow+"\\invoice") > 0 then
         CoEdit shadow+"\\invoice"
         MessgBox(97)
         Scan
                    if [product/service code] > 9999 then
                        [line total] = [amount]*-1
                        [debit/credit] = "C"
                    else
                        if isblank([quantity]) = false then
                            [line total] = [quantity]*[amount]
                            [debit/credit] = "D"
                        else
                            here3 = recno()
                            goback = "Yes"
                        endif
                    endif
         EndScan
         Do_it!
         if goback = "Yes" then
                 goback = ""
                 MessgBox(3)
                 moveto 2
                 FormKey

                 moveto 3
                 moveto record here3
                 moveto field "quantity"
                 CoEditKey
                 loop
         endif
         endif
counter = 0
printit = ""
;In this section you put the information back in the the CUSTOMER
;and ACCOUNTS tables.
While (true)
MessgBox(97)
counter = counter+1
LOCK "ACCOUNTS" PFL
if retval = true then
      ADD   shadow+"\\invoice"  "ACCOUNTS"
else
      if counter < 10 then
            loop
      else
```

Listing 16-3 ENTERINV.SC—*continued*

```
                MessgBox(91)
                printit = "No"
        endif
endif
UNLOCK "ACCOUNTS" PFL
quitloop
EndWhile
While (true)
MessgBox(97)
counter = counter+1
LOCK "CUSTOMER" PFL
if retval = true then
        ADD shadow+"\\custmstr" "Customer"
else
    if counter < 10 then
            loop
    else
            MessgBox(91)
            printit = "No"
    endif
endif
UNLOCK "CUSTOMER" PFL
quitloop
EndWhile
endif
While (true)
```

Listing 16-3 ENTERINV.SC—*continued*

This last section lets you print and invoice. Once the invoice has either been printed or skipped, the routine quits and returns to the menu it was launched from, calling a procedure from the MMENUS library to rebuild the menu.

```
if nrecords(shadow+"\\invoice") > 0 and printit <> "No" then
      ShowMenu
                "Print":"Print out the Invoices",
                "Skip" :"Don't print the invoices now"
                to answer
                switch
                        case answer = "Esc"   : quitloop
                        case answer = "Print" : play "prntnewi"
                        case answer = "Skip"  : quitloop
                OtherWise:loop
                EndSwitch
else
      quitloop
endif
quitloop
```

Listing 16-3 ENTERINV.SC—*continued*

```
EndWhile
Reset
ClearAll
ReDrawPopBox(level)
Release procs ReDrawPopBox
reset
quitloop
Endwhile
quitloop
Endwhile
```

Listing 16-3 ENTERINV.SC—continued

The following figures help to illustrate the invoicing process. Figures 16-7 and 16-8 show how to select a customer, Figure 16-9 shows how to assign the invoice number, Figure 16-10 shows how to select a product (using a look-up table), Figure 16-11 shows how to calculate and post the invoice record, and Figure 16-12 shows how to print the invoice.

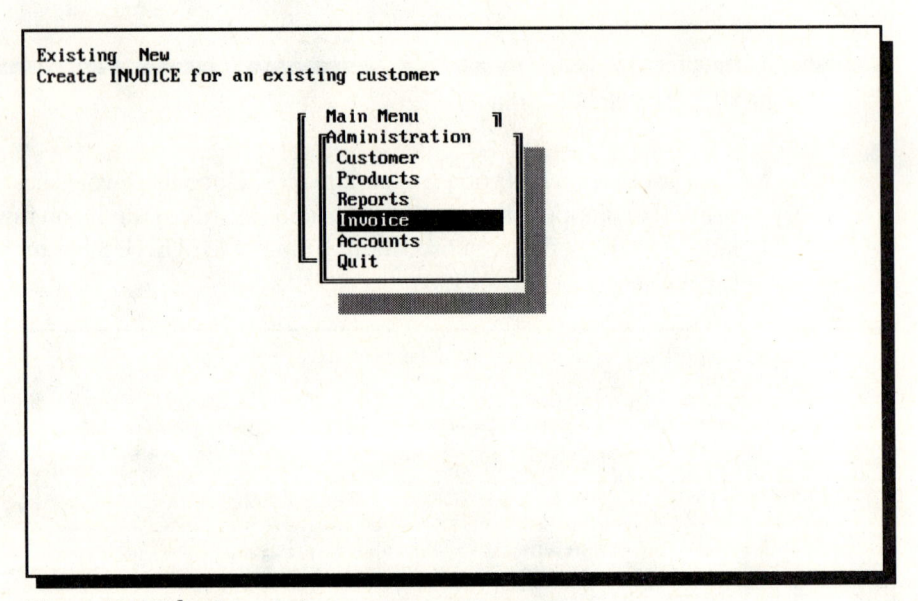

Figure 16-7 Selecting existing versus new customer

```
Move to the CUSTOMER to INVOICE and press [F2], [Esc] to quit
CUSTOMER╤Customer Numb╤════════Last Name═══════╤════════First Name═══════╤═S
    1  ║    15200    ║ Parker                  ║ John                    ║**
    2  ║    17100    ║ Smith                   ║ James                   ║**
    3  ║    19400    ║ Jones                   ║ Mary                    ║**
    4  ║    48400    ║ Salcedo                 ║ Bernard                 ║**
    5  ║    50600    ║ Salcedo                 ║ Greg                    ║**
    6  ║    58400    ║ Reason                  ║ Nina                    ║**
    7  ║    64100    ║ Anthony                 ║ Mario                   ║**
    8  ║    78900    ║ Hall                    ║ Larry                   ║**
    9  ║    84100    ║ Cascade                 ║ Timothy                 ║**
   10  ║    87800    ║ Rudy                    ║ Martin                  ║**
   11  ║    99900    ║ Smith                   ║ James                   ║**
```

Figure 16-8 Selecting an existing customer

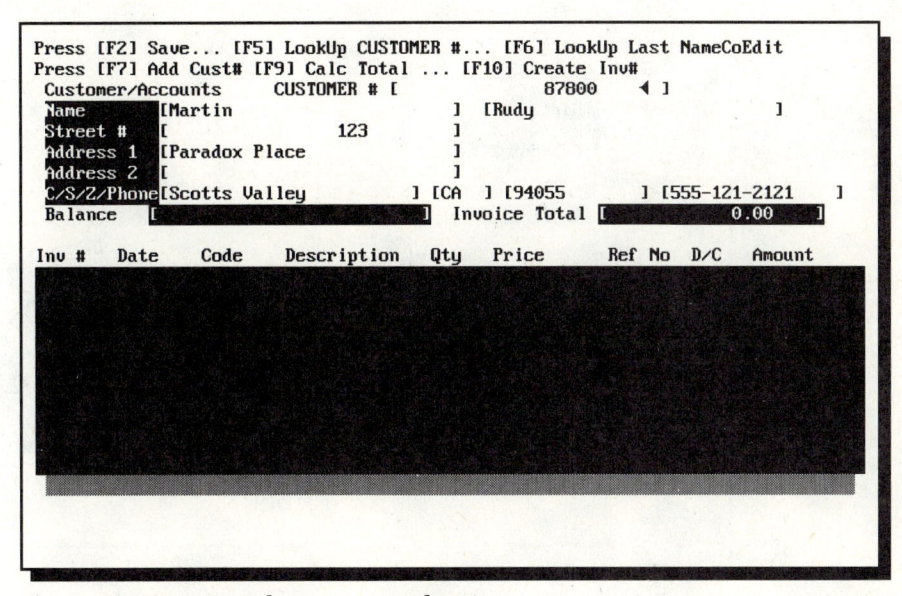

```
Press [F2] Save... [F5] LookUp CUSTOMER #... [F6] LookUp Last NameCoEdit
Press [F7] Add Cust# [F9] Calc Total ... [F10] Create Inv#
  Customer/Accounts      CUSTOMER # [      87800    ◄ ]
  Name      [Martin              ] [Rudy                    ]
  Street #  [          123       ]
  Address 1 [Paradox Place       ]
  Address 2 [                    ]
  C/S/Z/Phone[Scotts Valley      ] [CA ] [94055   ] [555-121-2121   ]
  Balance   [                    ]   Invoice Total [        0.00    ]

  Inv #   Date    Code    Description   Qty    Price    Ref No  D/C   Amount
```

Figure 16-9 Assigning the invoice number

```
Move to the record you want to select
Press [F2] to select the record; [Esc] to cancel; [F1] for help
┌PRODUCTS┬Product Number┬───Category───┬─────────Description─────────┐
│    1   │       5      │ E Guitar     │ Evony Bass                  │ *
│    2   │      10      │ C Guitar     │ Evony Guitar                │ *
│    3   │      15      │ E Guitar     │ Evony Guitar (Tele Copy)    │ *
│    4   │      20      │ C Guitar     │ Movation                    │ *
│    5   │      25      │ E Guitar     │ Movation Humbuckin 2        │ *
│    6   │      30      │ Brass        │ Signor Trumpet              │ *
│    7   │      35      │ Brass        │ Signor Trombone             │ *
│    8   │      40      │ Brass        │ Signor French Horn          │ *
│    9   │      45      │ Brass        │ Signor Clarinet             │ *
│   10   │      50      │ String       │ 3/4 Violin                  │ *
│   11   │      55      │ String       │ Full Violin                 │ *
│   12   │      60      │ Piano        │ Moda Synthesizer            │ *
│   13   │      65      │ Piano        │ Moda Upright                │ *
│   14   │      70      │ Piano        │ Moda B3 Portable            │ *
│   15   │      80      │ PA           │ Paver Sound System T1000    │ *
│   16   │      90      │ PA           │ Paver Sound System T2000    │ *
│   17   │     100      │ PA           │ Paver Sound System T3000    │ *
│   18   │    1000      │ SERVICE      │ Instrument Repair           │ *
│   19   │    2000      │ SERVICE      │ Music Lessons               │ *
│   20   │    3000      │ SERVICE      │ Pro Sound Consulting        │ *
│   21   │    9999      │ SERVICE      │ Miscellaneous Service       │ *
│   22   │   10000      │ PAYMENT      │ PAYMENT CASH                │
```

Figure 16-10 Look-up help for selecting a product or service to invoice

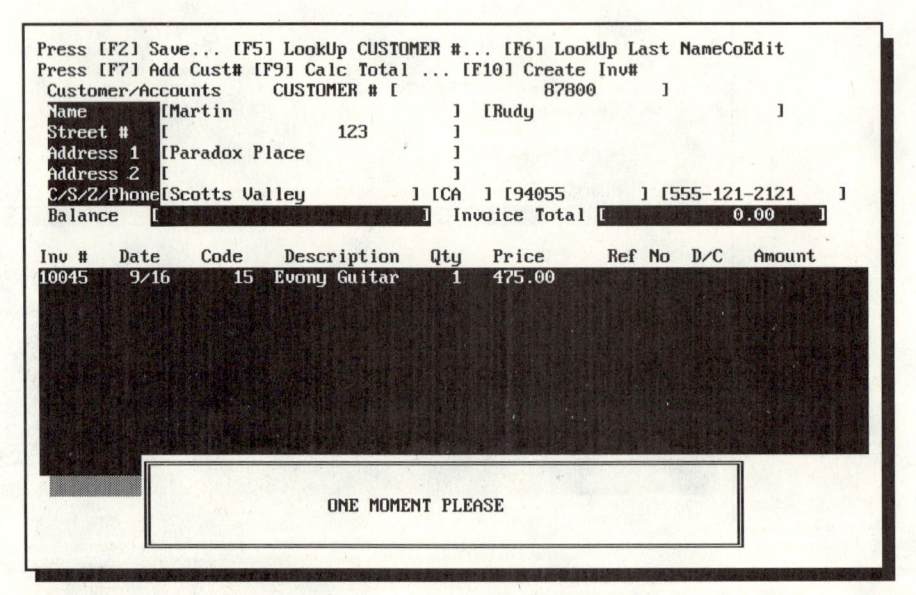

```
Press [F2] Save... [F5] LookUp CUSTOMER #... [F6] LookUp Last NameCoEdit
Press [F7] Add Cust# [F9] Calc Total ... [F10] Create Inv#
 Customer/Accounts      CUSTOMER # [     87800      ]
 Name       [Martin                 ] [Rudy                     ]
 Street #   [              123       ]
 Address 1  [Paradox Place           ]
 Address 2  [                        ]
 C/S/Z/Phone[Scotts Valley          ] [CA ] [94055     ] [555-121-2121    ]
 Balance    [                        ]  Invoice Total [          0.00    ]

 Inv #   Date   Code   Description    Qty    Price     Ref No  D/C   Amount
 10045   9/16    15    Evony Guitar    1    475.00




                         ┌─────────────────────┐
                         │  ONE MOMENT PLEASE  │
                         └─────────────────────┘
```

Figure 16-11 Calculating and posting the entered item

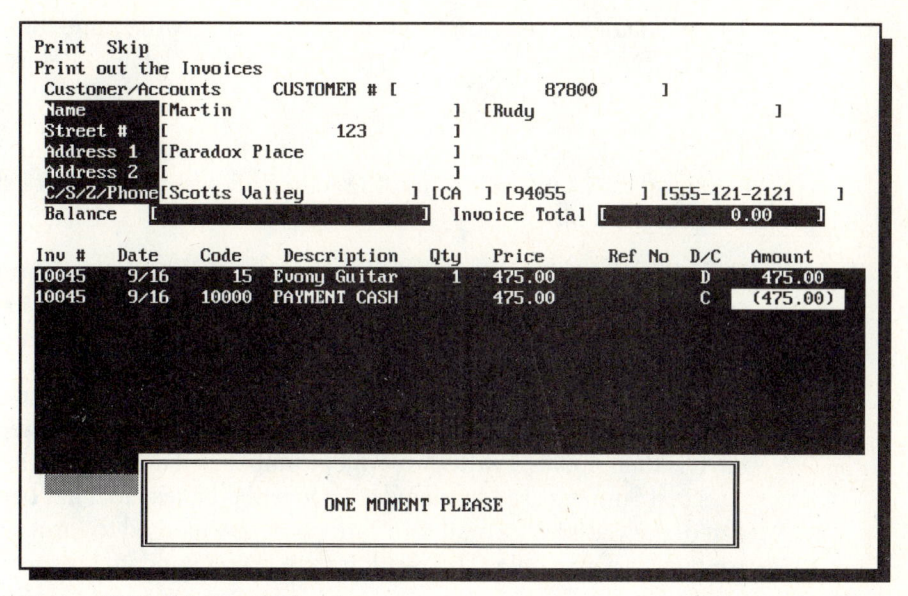

```
Print  Skip
Print out the Invoices
 Customer/Accounts      CUSTOMER # [          87800          ]
 Name       [Martin                ] [Rudy                    ]
 Street #   [              123     ]
 Address 1  [Paradox Place         ]
 Address 2  [                      ]
 C/S/Z/Phone[Scotts Valley         ] [CA ] [94055      ] [555-121-2121     ]
 Balance    [                      ]  Invoice Total [          0.00       ]

 Inv #   Date    Code    Description   Qty    Price    Ref No  D/C   Amount
 10045   9/16      15    Evony Guitar    1   475.00             D    475.00
 10045   9/16   10000    PAYMENT CASH        475.00             C   (475.00)




                        ONE MOMENT PLEASE
```

Figure 16-12 Printing the invoice

This application lets you review and edit customer information by selecting Accounts from the Administration menu. Figure 16-13 shows the Accounts screen.

```
Press [F2] Save ...    [F5] LookUp CUSTOMER #...  [F6] LookUp Last NameCoEdit
Press [F7] Add New Cust#       [F9] Calc Total ... [F10] Other Function
 Customer/Accounts      CUSTOMER # [       15200   ◄ ]
 Name       [John                  ] [Parker                  ]
 Street #   [            12345     ]
 Address 1  [Grandpere St          ]
 Address 2  [                      ]
 C/S/Z/Phone[Anywhere              ] [WA ] [12346-1234 ] [555-124-9876     ]
 Balance    [          2,645.00    ]

 Inv #   Date    Code    Description   Qty    Price    Ref No  D/C   Amount
 10016   9/12       5    Evony Bass      1   485.00             D    485.00
 10016   9/12      15    Evony Guitar    2   475.00             D    950.00
 10018   9/12      30    Signor Trump    1   895.00             D    895.00
 10018   9/12    2000    Music Lesson    2    60.00             D    120.00
 10040   9/15      10    Evony Guitar    1   195.00             D    195.00
```

Figure 16-13 The Accounts screen

The remainder of the Administration scripts follow the same theme set by ENTERINV. They all take extra precautions to lock tables before allowing any process to continue.

The next major section of this application is the module that records, forecasts, and tracks music lessons offered to students. Figure 16-14 shows the Music Lesson menu.

The Music Lesson module includes a number of interesting features, but the heart of the module is the ability to create a forecast of music lessons based on student information. Listing 16-4 shows this forecasting capability.

This script starts by asking how many weeks need to be added to the current schedule. The routine then calculates the current maximum date. The Dates table is then updated with the proper number of dates (notice that Saturdays and Sundays are not included). Once the Dates table has been updated, the Class1 table and the Dates table are merged to form a new, expanded class schedule. The result is then used to update the current schedule table.

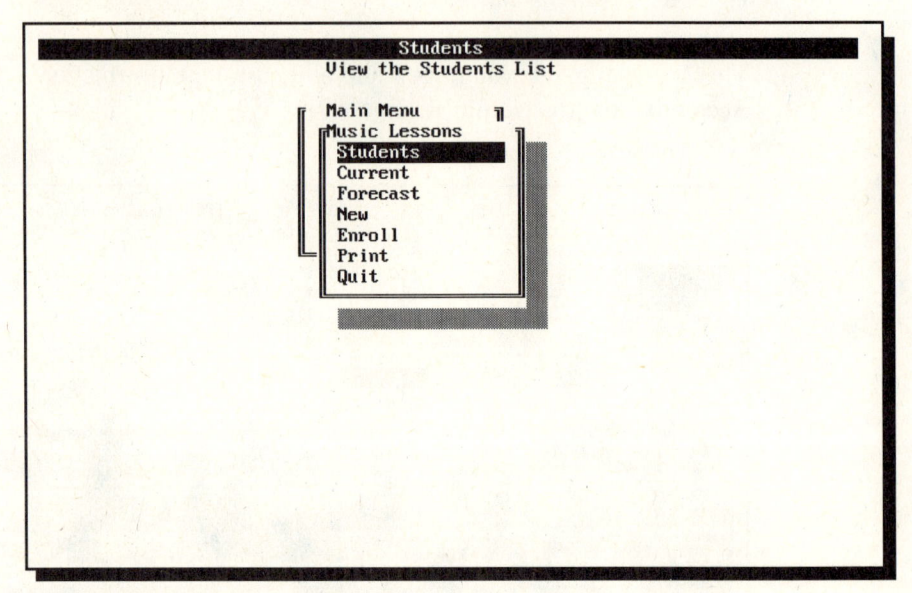

Figure 16-14 The Music Lesson menu

PROJ_SCH.SC

```
While (true)
@24,0 Clear EOL ?? "Schedule how many weeks ? "
accept "s" required default 4 to weeks
ClearMsg()
MessgBox(97)
days = weeks * 7
Reset
Menu {ask} {dates}
moveto[date]
"calc max as maxdate"
Do_it!
if nrecords("answer") > 0 then
     maxdate = [maxdate]
endif
if isassigned(maxdate) = false then
     maxdate = today()
endif
CoEdit "Dates"
End
Down
moveto[date]
for counter from 1 to days step 1
       [] = maxdate+counter
    [dow] = dow([])
        if [dow] = "Sat" or [dow] = "Sun" then
            Del
        endif
        Down
endfor
Do_it!
Reset
Query
  Dates  |   Date     | DOW |
         | CheckPlus  | _d  |
  Class1 |  Category  | Instrument |    Day        | Class Slot     |
         | CheckPlus  | CheckPlus  | CheckPlus _d  | CheckPlus _c   |
  Class1 |    Time    | Student Last Name | Student First Name     |
         | CheckPlus  | CheckPlus         | CheckPlus              |
Endquery
Do_it!
Reset
ADD "ANSWER" "CURRSCH2"
ClearMsg()
quitloop
EndWhile
```

Listing 16-4 PROJ_SCH.SC

The following figures help illustrate the other capabilities of the Music Lesson module. Figure 16-15 shows the Student screen, Figure 16-16 shows the

Current Schedule screen, Figure 16-17 shows the New Student screen, and Figure 16-18 shows the Enroll screen.

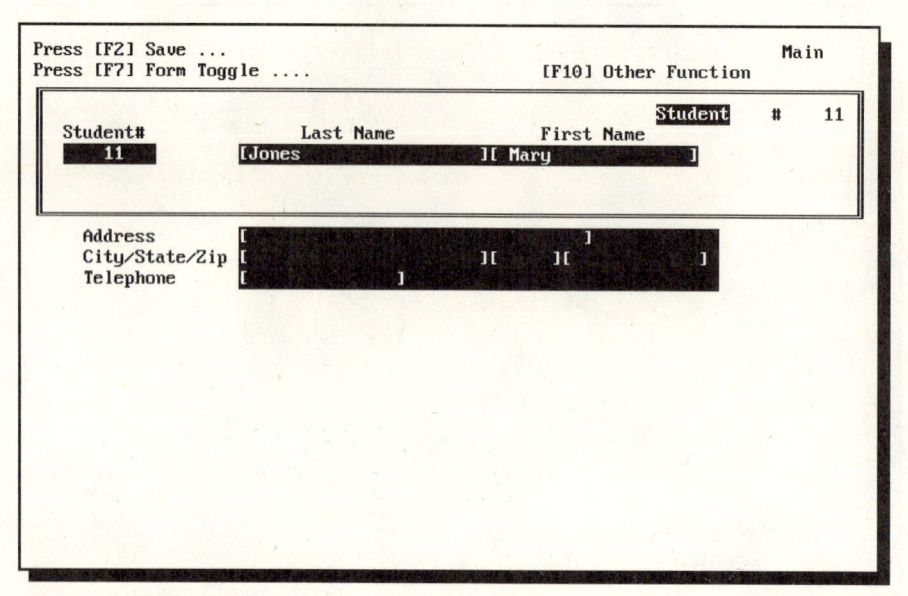

```
Press [F2] Save ...                                              Main
Press [F7] Form Toggle ....              [F10] Other Function
                                                    Student   #   11
     Student#            Last Name           First Name
        11            [Jones            ][ Mary             ]

        Address      [                                       ]
        City/State/Zip [                    ][   ][          ]
        Telephone    [                ]
```

Figure 16-15 *The Student screen*

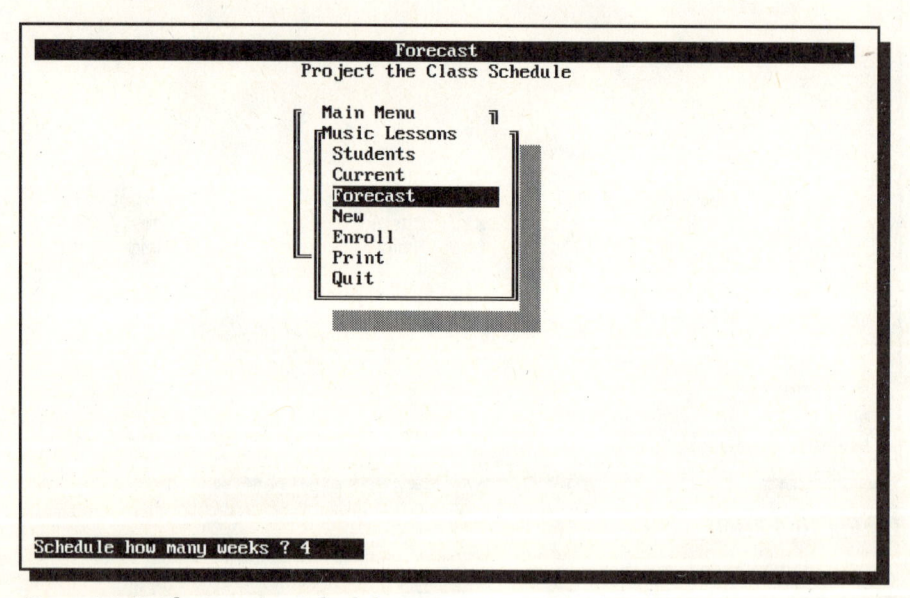

```
                              Forecast
                       Project the Class Schedule
                         ┌── Main Menu ──┐
                         │ Music Lessons │
                         │ Students      │
                         │ Current       │
                         │ Forecast      │
                         │ New           │
                         │ Enroll        │
                         │ Print         │
                         │ Quit          │
                         └───────────────┘


 Schedule how many weeks ? 4
```

Figure 16-16 *The Current Schedule screen*

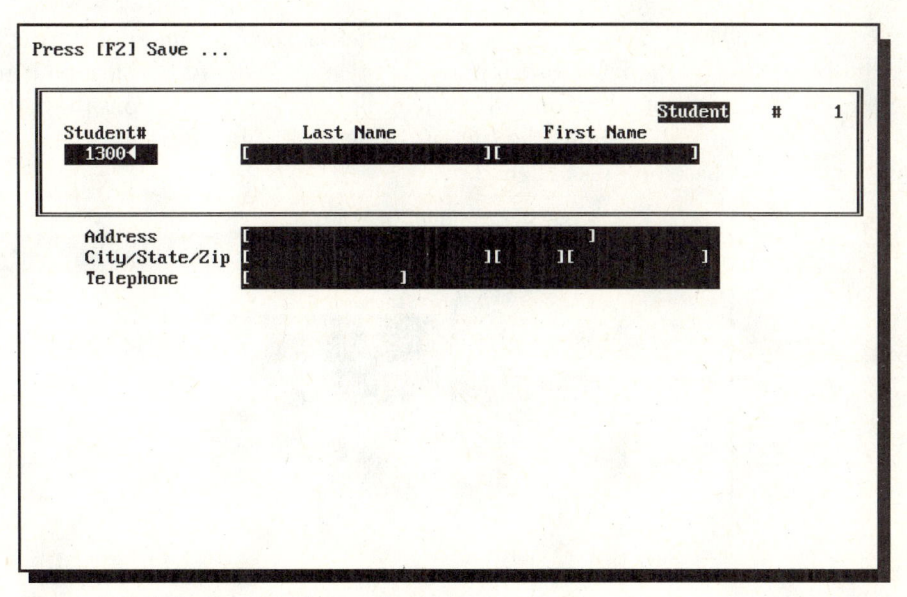

```
Press [F2] Save ...

                                                       Student    #    1
      Student#          Last Name            First Name
       1300◄         [              ][              ]


        Address      [                              ]
        City/State/Zip [                  ][    ][        ]
        Telephone    [              ]
```

Figure 16-17 The New Student screen

```
Schedule Class,      Press [F2] Save ...

  DOW#    Slot    Day    Category      Instrument      Time
    2      2     Tue    String         Intermediate    PM 03:30

  * Student#        Last Name          First Name
  [     ◄ ][              ][                  ]










  * Student List Available (press [F1])
```

Figure 16-18 The Enroll screen

The Inventory module provides a basic product and purchasing facility. The code in this section follows the style set in its Administration counterparts, with some obvious differences dictated by the functions they address. Figure 16-19 shows the Inventory menu. Listing 16-5 shows how a new purchase order is assigned.

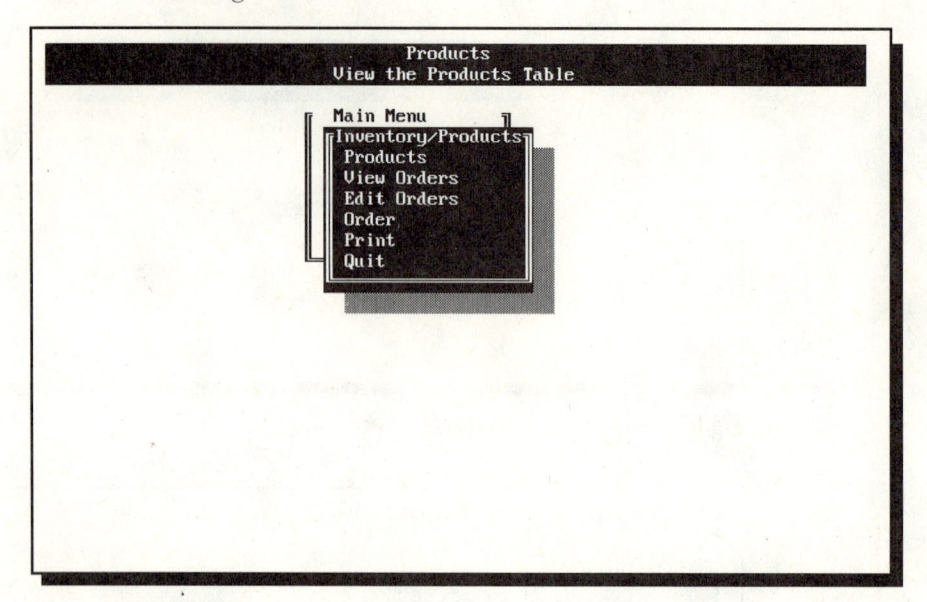

```
              Products
         View the Products Table

            Main Menu
         ┌Inventory/Products┐
          Products
          View Orders
          Edit Orders
          Order
          Print
          Quit
```

Figure 16-19 The Inventory menu

This script does not work with the actual purchase master table (Prchmstr) or purchase detail table (Prcdetl) initially, other than to assign a new purchase order number. This routine also makes use of the shadow table techniques to set up a "private" entry of the purchase order at hand. Once the purchase has been entered, the information is transferred back to the master table counterpart and the purchase order is printed.

No system is complete without utilities. This system includes a menu for utilities but only one of the menu choices is active. The Backup menu choice provides a very simple backup facility using the DOS BACKUP program. Figure 16-20 shows the Utilities menu and Listing 16-6 shows how to call the DOS BACKUP program.

```
;******************************************************************
;Script [PrchOrd ]
;Description [Enter and print a purchase order
;
;Created [05/26/90] By [G.Salcedo ]
;******************************************************************
Reset
ClearAll
MessgBox(97)
nextnumber = cmax("prchmstr","purchase order #")+1
if nextnumber = "Error" then
     nextnumber = 1
endif
color = color+128
MessgBox(97)
color = color-128
tablename = shadow+"\\prchmstr"
pform = "F"
EMPTY tablename
EMPTY shadow+"\\prchdetl"
CoEdit tablename
Menu {Image} {PickForm} select pform
[purchase order #] = nextnumber
IMAGERIGHTS UPDATE
While (true)
goback = ""
FIRSTSHOW
MessgBox(97)
While (true)   ; Keep doing UNTIL
Wait Table
Prompt "Press [F2] Save ...                                    "+sysmode()
Until  "F2", -108, "Del", "DOS","DOSBIG","F3","F4"
lookretval = retval
if lookretval = "DOS" or lookretval = "DOSBIG" then
       NoDosExit("Top")
       loop
endif
if lookretval = "F3" or lookretval = "F4" then
     keypress lookretval
     loop
endif
if lookretval = -108 then
       keypress -108
       While (true)
       WAIT FIELD
       Prompt "Press [F2] or [ENTER] to leave FIELDVIEW"
       UNTIL "F2","Enter","DOS","DOSBIG"
       fieldretval = retval
       if fieldretval = "DOS" or fieldretval = "DOSBIG" then
            NoDosExit("Bottom")
            loop
       endif
```

Listing 16-5 PRCHORD.SC

```
            if fieldretval = "F2" or fieldretval = "Enter" then
                quitloop
            endif
        EndWhile
        release vars fieldretval
        loop
endif
if lookretval = "Del" then
        @24,0 Clear EOL ?? "Do you really want to delete (Y/N) ? "
        Accept "A1" picture "{Y,N}" default "N" to answer
        if answer = "Y" then
                Del
                loop
        else
                loop
        endif
endif
if lookretval = "F2" then
     Do_it!
     Messgbox(97)
     While (true)
     Lock "PrchMstr" FL
     if retval = true then
            ADD tablename "PrchMstr"
            UNLOCK "PrchMstr" FL
            quitloop
     endif
     quitloop
     EndWhile
     While (true)
     Lock "Prchdetl" FL
     if retval = true then
            ADD shadow+"\\prchdetl" "PrchDetl"
            UNLOCK "prchdetl" FL
            quitloop
     endif
     EndWhile
     play "prntpurc"
endif
Reset
ReDrawPopBox(level)
Release procs ReDrawPopBox
reset
quitloop
Endwhile
quitloop
Endwhile
```

Listing 16-5 PRCHORD.SC—continued

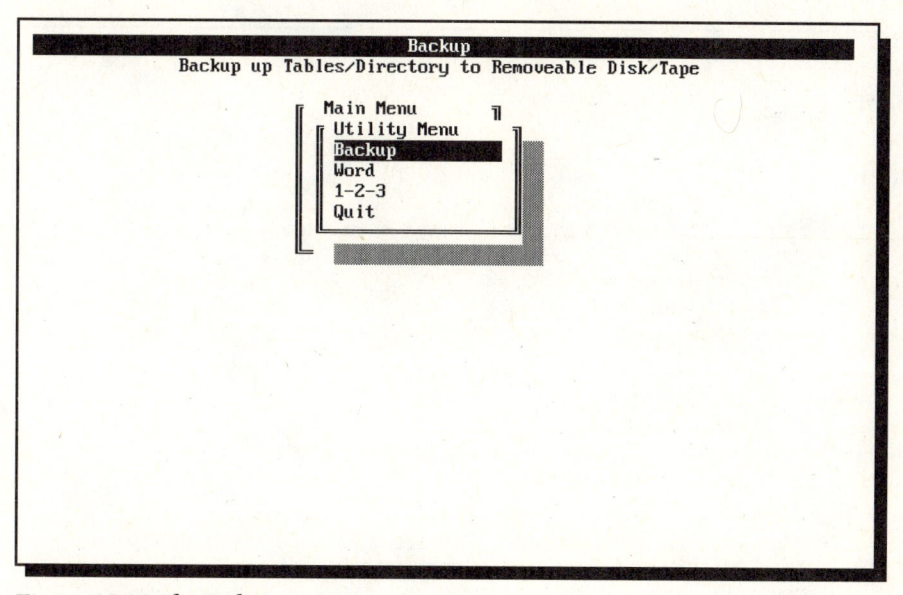

```
                           Backup
              Backup up Tables/Directory to Removeable Disk/Tape
                        ┌─Main Menu──┐
                        │┌Utility Menu─┐
                        ││ Backup      │
                        ││ Word        │
                        ││ 1-2-3       │
                        ││ Quit        │
                        └─            ─┘
```

Figure 16-20 The Utilities menu

```
;*************************************************************************
;Script:      Backup
;Description: Performs simple DOS backup
;
;Created [5/26/90 ] By [G.Salcedo ]
;*************************************************************************
path=directory()
RUN "backup "+path+"*.* a:"
```

Listing 16-6 BACKUP.SC

PRCHORD.SC

The final section of this application that we'll inspect is the AGING script (Listing 16-7), invoked from the Reports menu. It's of particular interest because it uses Paradox's Crosstab feature to create an activity report of invoices across certain time spans (currents, 30, 60, 90, and 120 days overdue).

```
MessgBox(97)
play "updttotl"
ClearMsg()
While (true)
MessgBox(97)
ClearMsg()
agedate=today()-day(today())
@24,0 Clear EOL ?? "Print Statements thru date ? "
Accept "D" required default agedate to agedate
if isassigned(agedate) = false then
     @24,0 Clear EOL
     quitloop
endif
if retval = "Esc" then
     @24,0 Clear EOL
     quitloop
endif
ClearMsg()
MessgBox(97)
Query
 Accounts | Customer Number | Invoice Number | Date    |
          | Check           | Check          | Check   |
 Accounts |       Line Total        |
          | calc sum as Invoice Total |
Endquery
Do_it!
Rename "Answer" "Entry400"
balance = csum("entry400","invoice total")
Reset
Query
 Customer | Customer Number | Last Name    | First Name |
          | CheckPlus _a    | CheckPlus    | CheckPlus  |
 Customer | Current Balance |
          | CheckPlus       |
 Entry400 | Customer Number | Invoice Number | Date      |Invoice Total             |
          | _a              | CheckPlus      | CheckPlus | CheckPlus calc ""
 as Aging |
Endquery
Do_it!
Reset
nr = nrecords("answer")
ClearMsg()
CURSOR OFF
@24,0 Clear EOL ?? "SCANNING and marking aging of Invoices"
style blink ?? "..." style
CoEdit "Answer"
moveto[aging]
Scan
     days = agedate - [date]
     agecolumn = days/30
     if agecolumn <1                              then [] =     "00-30"      endif
     if agecolumn >1 and agecolumn <= 2 then [] =     "31-60"      endif
```

Listing 16-7 AGING.SC

```
            if agecolumn >2 and agecolumn <= 3 then [] =    "61-90"     endif
            if agecolumn >3 and agecolumn <= 4 then [] =    "91-120"    endif
            if agecolumn >4                    then [] = "Over 120"     endif
             here = int((([#]/nr) * 100)
             if mod(here,5) = 0 then
                 @24,65 ?? here," % complete"
            endif
EndScan
Do_it!
CURSOR NORMAL
Reset
ClearAll
@24,0 Clear EOL ?? "Creating Aging"
style blink ?? "..."
style
Menu {View} {Answer}
Menu {Image} {Zoom} {Field} {Invoice Total} Rotate
Menu {Image} {Zoom} {Field} {Aging}
Left
CrosstabKey
Reset
ClearMsg()
MessgBox(97)
EMPTY "AGEMSTR"
Reset
excount = nfields("crosstab")
Menu {ask} {crosstab}
Menu {ask} {agemstr}
moveto "crosstab"
Right
for counter from 1 to excount-1 step 1
      fieldname =  field()
      Example typein counter
      DownImage
      moveto field fieldname
      Example typein counter
      UpImage
      Right
endfor
fieldname = field()
Example typein counter
DownImage
moveto field fieldname
Example typein counter
CtrlHome
typein "Insert"
Do_it!
echo off
Reset
ClearAll
ClearMsg()
@24,0 Clear EOL ?? "Clearing ZERO's from ACCOUNT information " style blink ??
"..." style
```

Listing 16-7 AGING.SC—continued

```
CoEdit "AgeMstr"
Scan
        if [00-30]    = 0 then [00-30]    = blanknum() endif
        if [31-60]    = 0 then [31-60]    = blanknum() endif
        if [61-90]    = 0 then [61-90]    = blanknum() endif
        if [91-120]   = 0 then [91-120]   = blanknum() endif
        if [Over 120] = 0 then [Over 120] = blanknum() endif
EndScan
Do_it!
ClearMsg()
@0,0 Clear EOL ?? "Checking PRINTER" style blink ?? "..." style
While (true)
        MessgBox(97)
        Style
        @24,0 Clear EOL
        if printerstatus() = false then
            Style Attribute 192
            @0,0 Clear EOL ?? "Printer Not Ready ..."
            ShowMenu
                    "Quit" : "Stop printing process",
                    "Retry": "Try printer again"
                    to answer
                    Switch
                            case answer = "Quit"  : ClearMsg()
                                                    @0,0 Clear EOL
                                                    quitloop
                            case answer = "Retry" : loop
                        OtherWise:Loop
                        EndSwitch
        endif
        @0,0 Clear EOL
        Style
        @0,0 Clear EOL ?? "PRINTING AGING" style blink ?? "..." style
        ClearMsg()
        MessgBox(97)
        REPORT "AgeMstr" "R"
Reset
ClearAll
quitloop
EndWhile
ClearMsg()
quitloop
EndWhile
```

Listing 16-7 AGING.SC—continued

The ABC Music Store is a nice application to use as a starting point for your own multiuser application. However, not all pieces are shown or included. If you want to use this application as a starting point for your own application, you'll want to add the ability to receive inventory, and improve how the inventory is managed.

You can improve performance in this system if you don't have to deal with the multiuser portion of the system. If you want to use these scripts on a standalone system, you can omit all the locking provisions and eliminate the shadow table approach. The scripts will work fine on a standalone workstation, but performance improves if you make these changes.

Next, we'll look at another approach, using a personnel system to illustrate some ideas.

Personnel Application

The Personnel application consists of tables typical for tracking information in a small company. The core information centers around employees (their benefits, dependents, college education, and internal training). Also included are department budgets and actuals, which demonstrate comparative analysis. The Personnel application is not a complete application and cannot be used to support human resource department, but is included here for illustration purposes.

Figure 16-21 shows the Main menu. You'll notice it isn't a typical Paradox-style menu. Menu options are listed vertically and the highlight bar moves forward or backward as you press [Up Arrow] and [Down Arrow]. You can also enter the number next to the menu choice to select the option.

```
              Paradox  Application

              Personnel  System

                  1. View
                  2. Enter Data
                  3. Modify Data
                  4. Queries
                  5. Reports
                  6. Graphs
                  7. Maintenance
                  8. Exit
```

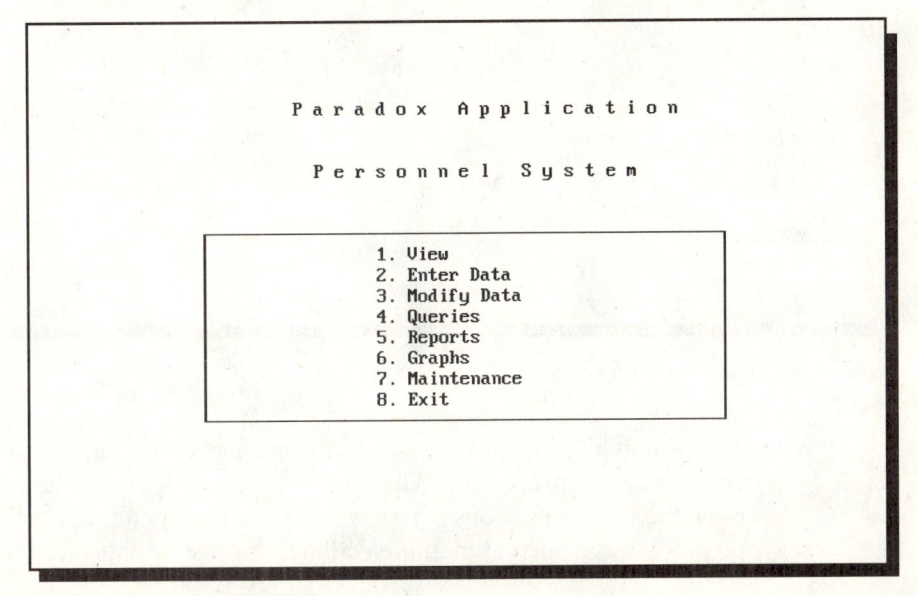

Figure 16-21 Personnel Main menu

The vertical menu technique used here has three parts:

- Text section
- Keystroke processor
- Conditional calling based on selection

The text section is shown in Listing 16-8. It consists of initializing the variables used to position the menu and define the menu's colors. The TEXT...ENDTEXT command places menu options on the canvas (this is faster than using the ? or ?? commands).

```
PROC MainMenuSplash()
  CANVAS OFF
  numofitems = 8
  startrow = 10
  endrow = startrow + numofitems - 1
  currow = startrow
  begcol = 32
  endcol = 45
  menumargin = 32
  slctclr    = 31
  nonslctclr = 121
  FillWindow(startrow-1,endrow+1,15,65,nonslctclr,"S","Y","Y")
  @ startrow,0
  SETMARGIN  begcol
  STYLE ATTRIBUTE nonslctclr
  TEXT
1. View
2. Enter Data
3. Modify Data
4. Queries
5. Reports
6. Graphs
7. Maintenance
8. Exit
  ENDTEXT
  STYLE
  SETMARGIN OFF
  CANVAS ON
ENDPROC
```

Listing 16-8 Main menu text section

The second block of code processes the key movement in the menu. Listing 16-9 shows this procedure. Whenever you press [Up Arrow] or [Down Arrow], the next or previous option is highlighted (depending on the key pressed). If the current menu selection is the first option and [Up Arrow] is pressed, the highlight bar moves to the last option. This lets you move forward or backward to a menu option. The vertical bar menu is dependent on the GETCHAR function. The procedure waits for you to press a key and then acts on that keystroke. If you press a number that is within the range of available menu options, the highlight bar moves directly to the selection and the program executes that option.

```
PROC  VertMenu(startrow,endrow,begcol,endcol,currow,slctclr,nonslctclr)
 PRIVATE kp
  PAINTCANVAS ATTRIBUTE slctclr currow,begcol,currow,endcol
  WHILE TRUE
    SYNCCURSOR
    kp = GETCHAR()
    SWITCH
      CASE kp = -80 :    ; Down arrow
           PAINTCANVAS ATTRIBUTE nonslctclr currow,begcol,currow,endcol
           IF currow <> endrow THEN
              currow = currow + 1
           ELSE
              currow = startrow
           ENDIF
           PAINTCANVAS ATTRIBUTE slctclr currow,begcol,currow,endcol
      CASE kp = -72 :    ; Up arrow
           PAINTCANVAS ATTRIBUTE nonslctclr currow,begcol,currow,endcol
           IF currow <> startrow THEN
              currow = currow -1
           ELSE
              currow = endrow
           ENDIF
           PAINTCANVAS ATTRIBUTE slctclr currow,begcol,currow,endcol
      CASE kp = 13 :
            RETURN currow - startrow + 1
      CASE kp = -59 :            ; F1 pressed
           ShowHelp()
      CASE kp = 27  :
           RETURN 0       OTHERWISE  :
           IF kp >= 49 AND kp <= 49 + numofitems -1 THEN
              PAINTCANVAS ATTRIBUTE nonslctclr currow,begcol,currow,endcol
              PAINTCANVAS ATTRIBUTE slctclr currow,begcol,currow,endcol
              currow = startrow + (kp - 49)
              RETURN currow - startrow + 1
           ELSE
              Beeps()
           ENDIF
    ENDSWITCH
  ENDWHILE
ENDPROC
```

Listing 16-9 Processing key movement

The last of the three components of this application is the processing section. Once you make a selection, the appropriate procedure executes. Listing 16-10 shows the procedure for the Main menu. The number of the menu item selected is passed to MainMenu where a SWITCH statement executes the appropriate procedure.

```
PROC MainMenu(menunum)
  PRIVATE menuitem, kp, choice
  SWITCH
    CASE menunum = 1 :    ViewMenu()
    CASE menunum = 2 :    EnterMenu()
    CASE menunum = 3 :    ModifyMenu()
    CASE menunum = 4 :    QueryMenu()
    CASE menunum = 5 :    ReportMenu()
    CASE menunum = 6 :    GraphMenu()
    CASE menunum = 7 :
         MaintSplash()
         menuitem = VertMenu(startrow,endrow,begcol,endcol,currow,
                     slctclr,nonslctclr)
         MaintMenu(menuitem)
    CASE menunum = 8 :    SHOWMENU
              "Yes"   :   "Exit application",
              "No"    :   "Return to menu, do not leave app"
           TO choice
           IF choice = "Yes" THEN
              QUIT "Thanks for testing the app"
           ENDIF
  ENDSWITCH
ENDPROC
```

Listing 16-10 Main menu selection procedure

If Option 1, View, is selected, the screen looks as shown in Figure 16-22. View displays a Paradox-style menu at the top of the screen. SHOWMENU is the most common implementation of this type of menu. The Main menu is still displayed showing which option was selected.

Vertical menus can be stacked as shown in Figure 16-23. The Maintenance menu is a second-level vertical menu and uses the same process as the View menu. Separate procedures are used for text and for processing. The keystroke control procedure is the same as described previously. (This generic procedure is used for all vertical menu key movement.)

Figure 16-24 displays the Query menu. You select options from this menu by entering the letter next to the menu option. While the system is waiting for you to make a selection, it displays the time in the upper-right corner.

Like the vertical menu technique, GETCHAR is used to accept the menu selection.

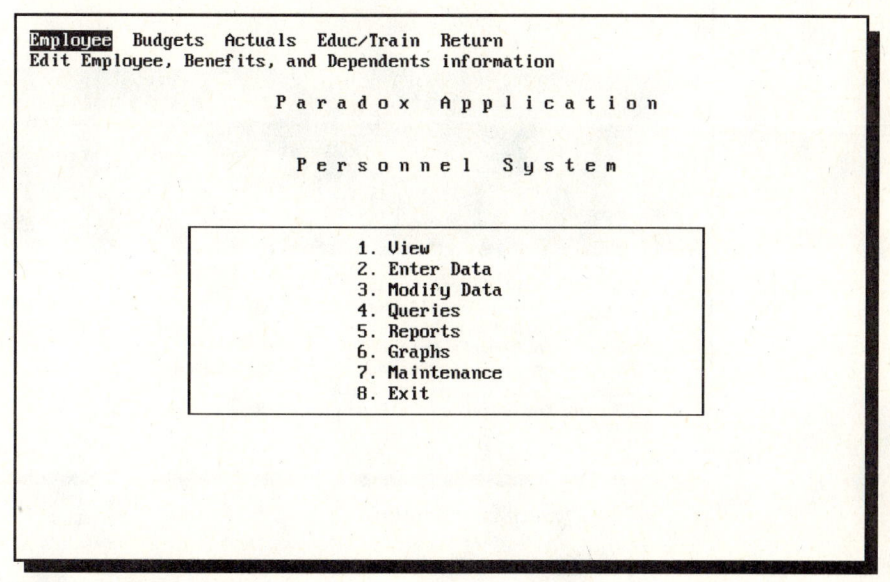

```
Employee  Budgets  Actuals  Educ/Train  Return
Edit Employee, Benefits, and Dependents information

              Paradox   Application

              Personnel   System

                   1. View
                   2. Enter Data
                   3. Modify Data
                   4. Queries
                   5. Reports
                   6. Graphs
                   7. Maintenance
                   8. Exit
```

Figure 16-22 View option

```
              Paradox   Application

              Personnel   System

              1.
              2.  1. Backup
              3.  2. SelectBackup
              4.  3. Pack
              5.  4. Return
              6.
              7. Maintenance
              8. Exit
```

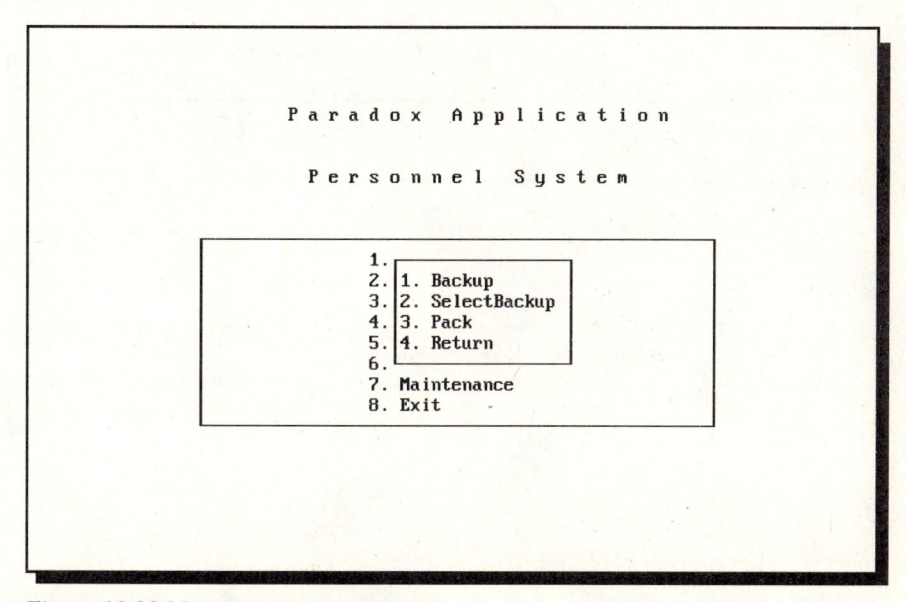

Figure 16-23 Maintenance menu option

```
                                                                  19:43:47



                        Queries Menu Description


              This menu allows users to select from the list of available
                 queries to answer questions asked on a routine basis.



           A - One Year Dept Budget Summary
           B - Budget Summary For All Years
           C - Actuals to Budgets Dept/Category
           D - Actuals to Budgets Dept only
           E - Select Emp/Benefits Records          Q - Dynamic Queries
           F - Select Emp/Educ/Training Records
           G - Courses for Selected Category        X - Return to Main Menu
```

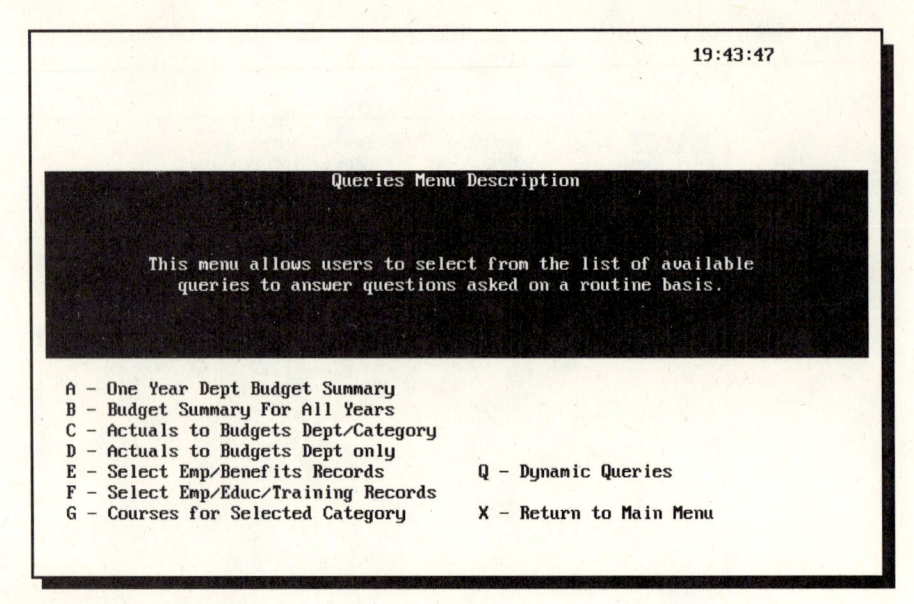

Figure 16-24 Query menu option

The QueryMenu procedure tests if a keystroke has been entered. If there are no characters in the keyboard buffer, the time display is updated. This continues until you press a key. If you enter a key that is in the range of available menu selections, the program takes the indicated action.

```
WHILE (TRUE)
   CLEAR
   ScrnInfo()
   TEXT
A - One Year Dept Budget Summary
B - Budget Summary For All Years
C - Actuals to Budgets Dept/Category
D - Actuals to Budgets Dept only
E - Select Emp/Benefits Records          Q - Dynamic Queries
F - Select Emp/Educ/Training Records
G - Courses for Selected Category        X - Return to Main Menu
   ENDTEXT
   CURSOR OFF
   WHILE (TRUE)
      IF CHARWAITING() THEN
         vi = GETCHAR()
         IF vi < 0 THEN
            LOOP
         ENDIF
```

Listing 16-11 The QueryMenu (keystroke interaction) procedure

```
        IF SEARCH(CHR(vi),"ABCDEFGHQX") > 0 THEN  ; NOTE: SEARCH not case
           QUITLOOP                                ; sensitive.
        ENDIF
     ENDIF
     vtime = TIME()
     @ 0,63  ?? vtime
  ENDWHILE
  vci = UPPER(CHR(vi))
  IF vci = "X" THEN
     QUITLOOP
  ENDIF
  CURSOR NORMAL
```

Listing 16-11 *The QueryMenu (keystroke interaction) procedure—continued*

There is more to the Personnel application than just menu styles. Generic code is used for viewing and modifying a table. For both of these options, the name of the table and the form number (if a form is to be used) are passed as parameters. This reduces the number of procedures necessary in the application. The form used to view and edit college education history and internal training for employees is shown in Figure 16-25.

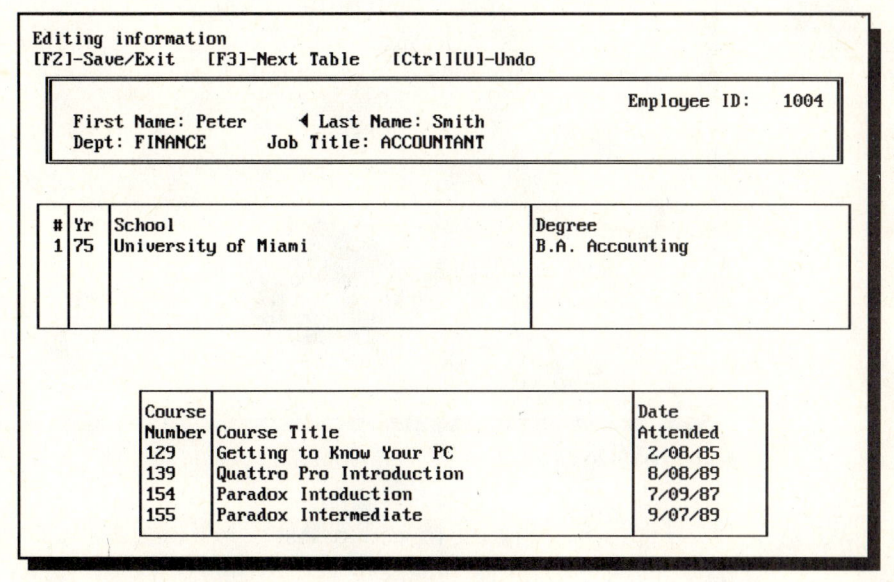

Figure 16-25 *Employee education and training form*

An option on the Query menu lets you perform a query on any table in the current directory. To provide this capability as though you're using interactive Paradox, use the ECHO NORMAL command. (However, you cannot use this option in Paradox Runtime.) This option provides free-form queries that are difficult to program in an application.

Graphs are used as visual representations of queried data. The graphs in this application cover salaries by department as well as gender, budgets, and actuals. Figure 16-26 shows a graph displaying the percentage of the total budget allocated to each department for a selected year.

As an application is developed, you know that certain menu options are required but often the full requirements of each action are not defined. Instead of modifying the application after the module is finished, an alternative is to place menu items in your code but don't have them do anything. The Personnel application has a few of these menu options.

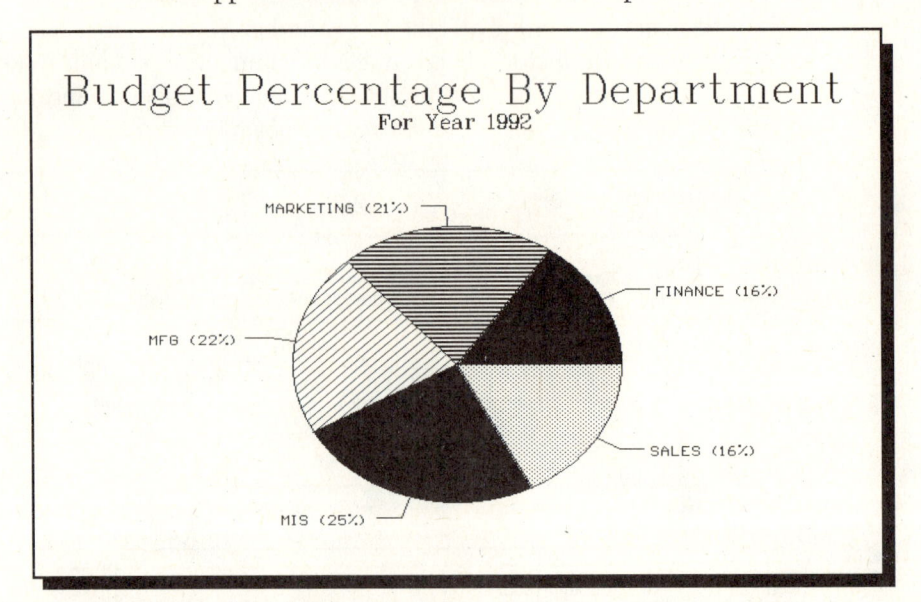

Figure 16-26 Graph for budget distribution

Listing 16-12 shows the procedure that is used for these situations. This simple, two-line procedure sounds the system bell and displays a message for two seconds, stating that the current selection is not defined. This is a handy procedure to include in your toolbox.

```
PROC NotDefined()
  Beeps()
  ShowMsg("Current selection is not defined!","OFF","Y",2000)
ENDPROC
```

Listing 16-12 Procedure used when menu items are not defined

The remainder of this application includes entry, modification, and report modules typical of any application. Data validation techniques used are those that we discussed in Chapter 6 and 7. Password protection is not implemented in this system. Give serious thought to your overall objectives before encrypting tables.

Summary

In this chapter we looked at some real application code to illustrate the concepts and ideas we have discussed so far. It's important to remember that these applications should be viewed as a good starting point, not a commercial system. You can run it as it stands, but of course you'll want to customize it to your own situation.

In the next chapter, we'll look at items you can add to your development arsenal to make your applications easier to create and to save you some valuable time.

17 Creating and Using Development Tools

Now let's add some tools to our bag of development tricks.

How often have you asked yourself "Why doesn't the Paradox editor have features like cut and paste, search and replace, and the ability to print a script with line numbers?" In this chapter, we'll look at adding these tools to your development toolbox. What makes this especially interesting is that all of these tools are provided by Paradox itself. Besides providing extra capabilities, these tools serve as potential building blocks for handling text, presenting menus, and manipulating system information. All of the programs presented in this chapter are available on the enclosed disk.

Creating Paradox Tools

You can add a tremendous amount of functionality to the development of your applications as well as to your applications themselves with features found right in Paradox. For example, suppose you want to see the structure of a table. In interactive Paradox, you would simply press *Menu* {*Tools*} {*More*}{*Info*}{*Structure*} *tablename* and press [Enter]. This isn't too tedious if you only have to do it a few times, but if you had to get a series of table structures, it wouldn't be very efficient. Listing 17-1 shows you how to automate this process.

```
1    SetKey "F30" play "getflds"   ; use the [Ctrl][F10] keys
2
3    Proc Get_Fields(tablename)
4    Private gc,answer
5
6    if istable(tablename) = true then
7
8        Menu {Tools} {Info} {Structure} select tablename
9        tablestru = substr(tablename,1,5)+"str"
10       if istable(tablestru) = true then
11           @0,0 Clear EOL ?? "Structure table aleady exists...[O]verwrite or [Q]uit?"
12           Accept "A1" picture "{O,Q}" required to answer
13           if answer = "Q" then
14               Return
15           endif
16       endif
17       rename "struct" tablestru
18       nn = nrecords(tablestru)
19       Array Names[nn]
20       Array Types[nn]
21       moveto[field name]
22
23       for counter from 1 to nn step 1
24           Names[counter] = []
25           Types[counter] = [Field Type]
26           Down
27       endfor
28       ShowArray
29              Names Types
30       to sel
31   else
32       message "Table ",tablename," does not exist ... press   any key"
33       gc = getchar()
34   endif
35   endproc
36
37   ShowTables
38          directory()
39          "Use your - or - keys to select table, then press ⏎"
40          Until "F2"
41          keyto keyvar
42
43          to tablename
44
45   if tablename = "Esc" then
46       quit
47   endif
48
49
50   Get_Fields(tablename)
```

Listing 17-1 GETFLDS.SC

Get_Fields is the procedure invoked when the user either plays the GETFLDS script or, having played GETFLDS once, presses [F30] ([ALT][F10]).

This procedure lets you select a table from the current directory. Once the table is selected, it calculates a structure named Tablestru. Tablestru consists of the first five letters of the table name plus the letters "str." The procedure checks to see if the structure table already exists and asks the user to confirm overwriting the existing table.

Once the structure is retrieved, the procedure scans the structure and presents the field names and the corresponding types in a SHOWARRAY.

You can use these structure tables to help document your system. This script is also very useful for creating a table that the report generator can use to write some of your PAL code. PAL code? We'll look at that next.

Using the Report Generator to write PAL

The table structure you obtained using the GETFLDS script can be put to a number of uses. One of the more interesting twists is using the report generator to write a script that will edit a table's fields directly. The structure tables consist of two fields—name and type. You can use the name field to create some nice PAL statements in a fraction of the time it would take you to enter the same code.

Figure 17-1 shows how the Statsstr table is used in just such a manner. The standard report is used to write the main body of a script that will update the Stats table. In this particular case, the script uses PAL functions to return information to the Stats table on such items as available memory, printer status, and so on. Here are the steps to follow:

1. Make the report page length continuous.
2. Eliminate any unnecessary lines (header, footer, and so forth).
3. Place COEDIT "STATS" at the report header position.
4. Place "[" and "]" brackets around the field name.
5. Type in "=" next to the field name and place a calculated [name]+"()" next to the "=".
6. At the report footer, type in "Do_It!"

7. Finally, OUTPUT the report to a file called STATSCRP.SC. The result is similar to Listing 17-2 (unnecessary fields were deleted from the script).

```
Changing report R for Statsstr table                          Report    1/1
Report Header
....+...10....+...20....+...30....+...40....+...50....+...60....+...70....+...8*
CoEdit "Stats"
—▼page—————————————————————————————————————————————————————————————————————————
—▼form—————————————————————————————————————————————————————————————————————————
[AAAAAAAAAAAAAAAAAAAAAAAA]=AAAAAAAAAAAAAAAAAAAAAAAAAA
—▲form—————————————————————————————————————————————————————————————————————————
—▲page—————————————————————————————————————————————————————————————————————————
Do_it!
```

Figure 17-1 *Using the Report Generator to create PAL*

```
CoEdit "Stats"
[Memleft] = Memleft()
[Rmemleft] = Rmemleft()
[Drivespace] = Drivespace()
[Nettype] = Nettype()
[Directory] = Directory()
[Privdir] = Privdir()
[Today] = Today()
[Time] = Time()
[DriveStatus] = DriveStatus()
[IsRuntime] = IsRuntime()
[Monitor] = Monitor()
[Printerstatus] = Printerstatus()
[QueryOrder] = QueryOrder()
[Retryperiod] = Retryperiod()
[Sortorder] = Sortorder()
[Syscolor 0] = Syscolor(0)
[Syscolor 2] = Syscolor(2)
[Syscolor 3] = Syscolor(3)
[Syscolor 4] = Syscolor(4)
[Syscolor 5] = Syscolor(5)
```

Listing 17-2 *STATSCRP.SC*

```
[Syscolor 6]  = Syscolor(6)
[Syscolor 7]  = Syscolor(7)
[Syscolor 8]  = Syscolor(8)
[Syscolor 9]  = Syscolor(9)
[Syscolor 11] = Syscolor(11)
[Syscolor 12] = Syscolor(12)
[Syscolor 13] = Syscolor(13)
[Syscolor 15] = Syscolor(15)
[Syscolor 16] = Syscolor(16)
[Syscolor 17] = Syscolor(17)
[Syscolor 18] = Syscolor(18)
[Syscolor 19] = Syscolor(19)
[Syscolor 21] = Syscolor(21)
[Syscolor 22] = Syscolor(22)
[Syscolor 23] = Syscolor(23)
[Syscolor 24] = Syscolor(24)
[Syscolor 25] = Syscolor(25)
[Syscolor 27] = Syscolor(27)
[Syscolor 28] = Syscolor(28)
[Syscolor 29] = Syscolor(29)
[UserName] = UserName()
[Version] = Version()
Do_it!
```

Listing 17-2 STATSCRP.SC—*continued*

Once the STATSCRP script has been created, you can edit it as necessary to complete the process. If you need to manipulate data at the field level of a table, using the report generator to create PAL code can save you a lot of time.

Database Selection Menu

In Paradox, the concept of a database is presented by storing all the tables defining a database in the same DOS directory. This isn't a requirement, but distinguishing between different groupings of tables is much easier if they're separated into different directories. By doing this, each directory name becomes the database name. Using the {*Tools*}{*More*}{*Directory*} menu selection, it's easy to move between directories as long as you remember the directory names. Creating a script to bring up a menu of the available databases/directories remedies this.

The first step is to determine the keystroke combination to bring up the database selection menu. Appendix B in the PAL User's Guide, "Keycodes Recognized by Paradox," lists all available keycodes, the ASCII code, and if it is used in Paradox. Keycode –32, [Alt][D], is available and is used in this example.

To initialize the keycode sequence, put the following command into INIT.SC, embed it in a start-up script, or enter it from the {Miniscript} option on the PAL Menu:

SETKEY -32 PLAY "DBSelect"

This command sets [Alt][D] to execute the DBSelect script. Figure 17-2 shows the content of the screen when [Alt][D] is pressed.

```
Scripts  Dvlpment  Company  Finance  ToDoList  Wishlist  ActItems  Status ▶
Special scripts directory

            Database Selection Menu - Main Title Screen

        The current directory is: d:\PDXAPPL\ZDB\
```

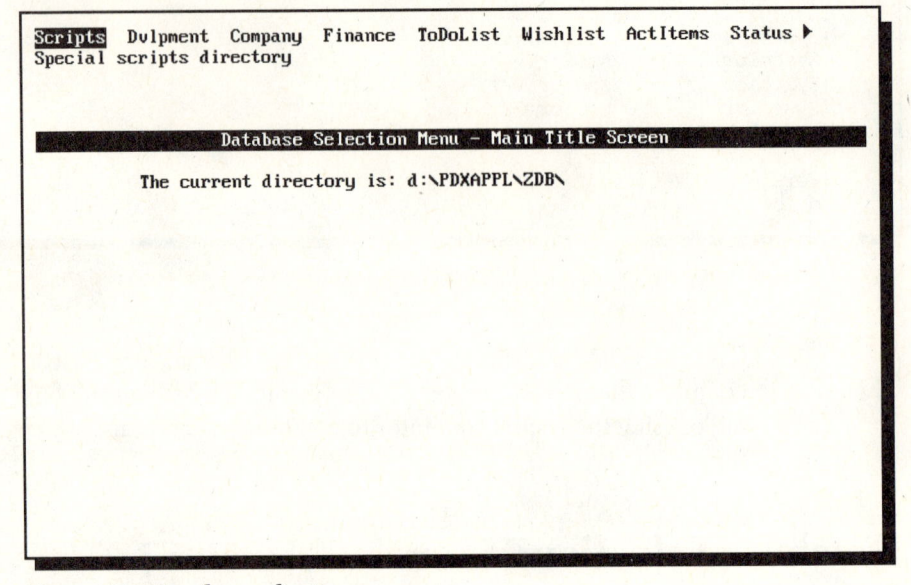

Figure 17-2 Database selection menu

This menu works exactly like the Paradox Main menu. Cursor movement keys, [Enter], pressing the first letter of an option, and so on can be used to select an option. If a "W" is pressed, the WISHLIST directory is selected and the screen looks like Figure 17-3.

The script used to display the database selection menu is shown in Listing 17-3. It contains two major sections: a SHOWMENU section to display the menu options and a SWITCH section to change to the appropriate directory. In the SHOWMENU command, each directory to be displayed on the menu must be included. The option description (the second line of the menu) is optional but recommended to fully explain the content of the directory. Only the directory name needs to be included; the drive and any possible parent directories are specified in the SWITCH command.

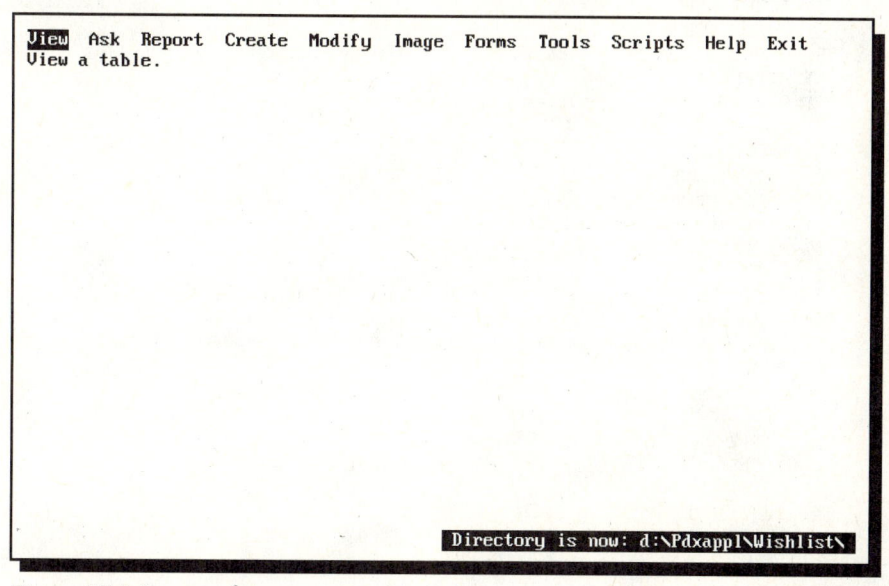

```
View  Ask  Report  Create  Modify  Image  Forms  Tools  Scripts  Help  Exit
View a table.




                                                  Directory is now: d:\Pdxappl\Wishlist\
```

Figure 17-3 Screen after execution

Depending on how the disk and directories are set up, each directory may or may not require a separate CASE statement. In this example, most of the directories are on the C: drive under the \PDXDATA directory. The Company, Wishlist, and Gantt options reside on the D: drive under the \PDXAPPL directory. All three of these have a separate line in the SWITCH command (lines 29, 30, and 31). The Receivables/Payables option resides on the C: drive but the directory name is \RECPAY and is handled in line 32. The rest of the options are handled by the statements in line 33. The key to this statement is using the exact name of the directory for the menu options in the SHOWMENU command. If a different name is used, a separate CASE statement is required as shown with the Receivables/Payables option. Line 37 displays a message in reverse video indicating the current directory in the lower-right corner of the Main menu.

NOTE: *Remember to use "\\" as shown in lines 29 through 33. In Paradox, a backslash is a special character used to indicate a numeric ASCII sequence or to indicate that the next character is a literal. A double backslash is required to be interpreted by Paradox as a single backslash.*

```
 1) ; DBSelect.sc
 2)
 3) RESET                                                ; Put Paradox in Main Mode
 4) STYLE REVERSE
 5) @ 5,0 ?? FORMAT("w80,ac","Database Selection Menu - Main Title Screen")
 6) STYLE
 7) @ 7,10  ?? "The current directory is: " + DIRECTORY()
 8)
 9) SHOWMENU
10)    "Scripts"                 : "Special scripts directory",
11)    "Dvlpment"                : "Special scripts being development",
12)    "Company"                 : "Company sample application",
13)    "Finance"                 : "Finance application",
14)    "ToDoList"                : "Personal TO DO Lists",
15)    "Wishlist"                : "Paradox wish list",
16)    "ActItems"                : "Action item database",
17)    "Status"                  : "Status system database",
18)    "Demo"                    : "Database used to do demos",
19)    "Info"                    : "General Information",
20)    "Gantt"                   : "Gantt chart example - in work",
21)    "Receivables/Payables"    : "Account payable and receivables",
22)    "Budgets"                 : "Current year budget database"
23) TO choice
24) IF choice = "Esc" THEN
25)    RETURN
26) ENDIF
27)
28) SWITCH
29)   CASE choice = "Company"                 : SETDIR "D:\\Pdxappl\\Company"
30)   CASE choice = "Gantt"                   : SETDIR "D:\\Pdxappl\\Gantt"
31)   CASE choice = "Wishlist"                : SETDIR "D:\\Pdxappl\\Wishlist"
32)   CASE choice = "Receivables/Payables"    : SETDIR "C:\\Pdxdata\\RecPay"
33)   OTHERWISE                               : SETDIR "C:\\Pdxdata\\" + choice
34) ENDSWITCH
35) CLEAR
36) RELEASE VARS choice
37) QUIT  "Directory is now: " + DIRECTORY()
```

Listing 17-3 Database selection program

Beeps

Listing 17-4 is a utility procedure to sound the system bell with three distinct beeps. Use **SLEEP** 100 between the **BEEP** commands to get three distinct beeps instead of one long beep.

```
1) ; Beeps.sc
2)
3) PROC Beeps()
4)    BEEP SLEEP 100 BEEP SLEEP 100 BEEP
5) ENDPROC
```

Listing 17-4 Beep utility program

Display Paradox-Style Message in Window

All applications require that you display status and informational messages to users. Listing 17-5 is a procedure to display messages onscreen. It has four parameters:

inmsg	Text of the display message
ca	Flag to turn canvas on or off
clrscrn	Flag indicating if the screen should be cleared before the message is displayed
slp	Number of seconds to pause after message is displayed

The MESSAGE command is used to display the text, and gives the look and feel of interactive Paradox. If *clrscrn* equals "Y", the screen is cleared before the message is displayed. The message window remains on the canvas until a command or menu option is selected that clears it from the workspace. To prevent the message from leaving the screen, CANVAS OFF is executed, which leaves the canvas at the current state. This occurs if the value of *ca* is "OFF". In some instances it is necessary to pause further program execution. Line 20 executes a SLEEP with the number of seconds in *slp*.

```
1) ; ShowMsg.sc
2)
3) PROC ShowMsg(inmsg,ca,clrscrn,slp)
4)  ;
5)  ; Procedure arguments
6)  ;
7)  ; inmsg    - message to be displayed
8)  ; ca       - after message CANVAS option
9)  ; clrscrn  - if = Y then CLEAR before message
10) ; slp      - number for use with SLEEP command
11)   CANVAS ON
```

Listing 17-5 Procedure to display messages

```
12)    IF clrscrn = "Y" THEN
13)       CLEAR
14)    ENDIF
15)    MESSAGE inmsg
16)    IF ca = "OFF" THEN
17)       CANVAS OFF
18)    ENDIF
19)    SLEEP slp
20) ENDPROC
```

Listing 17-5 Procedure to display messages—continued

Clearing Query Images on the Workspace

Images are placed on the workspace and removed from the workspace many times in an application. ClrQry in Listing 17-6 is a generic procedure that removes all query images from the workspace. The first image on the workspace is always image number one. Paradox places query images before any tables, which makes it easy to remove any query image. Line 4 moves to the first workspace image. The IMAGETYPE function returns the image type of the current table. While it returns "Query," the image is cleared (lines 5 through 7). If there are any images on the workspace after the completion of this procedure, they are tables.

```
1) ; ClrQry.sc
2)
3) PROC ClearQueryImages()
4)    MOVETO 1
5)    WHILE IMAGETYPE() = "Query"
6)       CLEARIMAGE
7)    ENDWHILE
8) ENDPROC
```

Listing 17-6 Procedure to clear query images

Exploding Window

Cosmetics in an application goes a long way towards user acceptance. One such flashy item is exploding windows. Listing 17-7 is an example of how to add this capability to your systems.

ExplodeWindow takes seven parameters:

sr	Top row position of the window
er	Bottom row position of the window
sc	Left column position of the window
ec	Right column position of the window
clr	Attribute number for the color of the window
brdr	Flag for the type of border. If the value is "S" then a single-line border is drawn. If the value is "D" then a double-line border is drawn. Any other value is interpreted to mean no border is to be used.
shdw	Flag indicating a shadow is to be painted. If the value is "Y" a shadow for the painted area is displayed.

The algorithm used in this procedure is to calculate the midpoint for both the row values and column values. These values indicate the starting position for painting the canvas. The ratio of row to column determines the number of columns from the midpoint to paint in relationship to each row painted. The calculations for these values are performed in lines 23 through 26. The first area painted is the midpoint, line 28. A FOR loop expands the window based on the current row, column, and row/column ratio aspect. There is no error checking for values between 0 (zero) and 79 to reduce the size of the procedure.

If a border is requested, it is painted in lines 33 through 54. A shadow for the window is painted by lines 56 and 57. (There is no check to see if there is room to paint the border, and, to keep the procedure size down, it is assumed the calling procedure or script doesn't have values too large to support a shadow.) On some machines this procedure works too fast to see the window explode. In those cases, you might want to add another argument (the number to use with SLEEP to generate an artificial slowdown). This command should be placed after line 30.

```
1) ; ExpldWin.sc
2)
3) PROC ExplodeWindow(sr,er,sc,ec,clr,brdr,shdw)
4)   PRIVATE i, midr, midc, rcaspect, numofsteps
5) ;
6) ; Private variables
7) ;    i          - counter variable
8) ;    midr       - row midpoint value
```

Listing 17-7 Exploding window procedure

```
 9) ;    midc      - column midpoint value
10) ;    rcaspect  - row and column aspect ratio
11) ;    numofsteps - number of steps to explode window
12) ;
13) ; Argument list
14) ;
15) ;    sr   - starting row position
16) ;    er   - ending row position
17) ;    sc   - starting column position
18) ;    ec   - ending column position
19) ;    clr  - color to use for the window
20) ;    brdr - border flag, "S" for single line, "D" for double line border
21) ;    shdw - shadow flag, "Y" to include shadow
22) ;
23)   midr = ROUND((sr + er)/2,0)
24)   midc = ROUND((sc + ec)/2,0)
25)   rcaspect = ROUND(((ec - sc)/(er - sr)) + 1 ,0)
26)   numofsteps = ROUND((midc - sc)/rcaspect,0)
27)
28)   PAINTCANVAS ATTRIBUTE clr midr,midc,midr,midc
29)   FOR i FROM 1 TO numofsteps  - 1
30)      PAINTCANVAS ATTRIBUTE clr midr-i,midc-rcaspect*i,midr+i,midc+i*rcaspect
31)   ENDFOR
32)   PAINTCANVAS ATTRIBUTE clr sr,sc,er,ec
33)   STYLE ATTRIBUTE clr
34)   SWITCH
35)     CASE brdr = "S" :
36)         PAINTCANVAS FILL "-" ATTRIBUTE clr sr,sc+1,sr,ec-1
37)         PAINTCANVAS FILL "-" ATTRIBUTE clr er,sc+1,er,ec-1
38)         PAINTCANVAS FILL "|" ATTRIBUTE clr sr,sc,er,sc
39)         PAINTCANVAS FILL "|" ATTRIBUTE clr sr,ec,er,ec
40)         @ sr,sc ?? "┌"
41)         @ sr,ec ?? "┐"
42)         @ er,sc ?? "└"
43)         @ er,ec ?? "┘"
44)     CASE brdr = "D" :
45)         PAINTCANVAS FILL "=" ATTRIBUTE clr sr,sc+1,sr,ec-1
46)         PAINTCANVAS FILL "=" ATTRIBUTE clr er,sc+1,er,ec-1
47)         PAINTCANVAS FILL "‖" ATTRIBUTE clr sr,sc,er,sc
48)         PAINTCANVAS FILL "‖" ATTRIBUTE clr sr,ec,er,ec
49)         @ sr,sc ?? "╔"
50)         @ sr,ec ?? "╗"
51)         @ er,sc ?? "╚"
52)         @ er,ec ?? "╝"
53)   ENDSWITCH
54)   STYLE
55)   IF shdw = "Y" THEN
56)      PAINTCANVAS ATTRIBUTE 7 er+1,sc+2,er+1,ec+2
57)      PAINTCANVAS ATTRIBUTE 7 sr+1,ec+1,er,ec+2
58)   ENDIF
59) ENDPROC
```

Listing 17-7 *Exploding window procedure—continued*

Filled Window

There are instances when you need to paint an area of the screen and have the text on the canvas removed. This is commonly used for pull-down or pop-up menus, or help screens. The PAINTCANVAS command includes the FILL option to provide this capability. The procedure FillWin in Listing 17-8 supports this requirement. It is similar to ExplodeWindow (Listing 17-7) and has the same parameter list plus one additional argument:

> *fillspc*   Flag indicating if the painted window should clear the text on the canvas within the borders of the window. If the value is "Y", all text is cleared. Any other value leaves the text on the canvas.

No midpoints or ratio aspects have to be calculated as they are in ExplodeWindow. This procedure paints the box specified by the procedure arguments. Line 18 uses PAINTCANVAS FILL " " to clear any text on the canvas at the same time the window is painted. This makes it easy to "clear" a space for text or a pop-up menu without having existing text included in the display.

```
1)  ; FillWin.sc
2)
3)  PROC FillWindow(sr,er,sc,ec,clr,brdr,shdw,fillspc)
4)  ;
5)  ; Argument list
6)  ;
7)  ;    sr   - starting row position
8)  ;    er   - ending row position
9)  ;    sc   - starting column position
10) ;    ec   - ending column position
11) ;    clr  - color to use for the window
12) ;    brdr - border flag, "S" for single line, "D" for double line border
13) ;    shdw    - shadow flag, "Y" to include shadow
14) ;    fillspc - FILL flag, "Y" indicates the area to be painted is to be
15) ;              cleared using the FILL option with PAINTCANVAS
16) ;
17)    IF fillspc = "Y" THEN
18)       PAINTCANVAS FILL " " ATTRIBUTE clr sr,sc,er,ec
19)    ELSE
20)       PAINTCANVAS ATTRIBUTE clr sr,sc,er,ec
21)    ENDIF
22)    STYLE ATTRIBUTE clr
23)    SWITCH
24)      CASE brdr = "S" :
25)           PAINTCANVAS FILL "-" ATTRIBUTE clr sr,sc+1,sr,ec-1
26)           PAINTCANVAS FILL "-" ATTRIBUTE clr er,sc+1,er,ec-1
```

Listing 17-8 Color-filled window

```
27)         PAINTCANVAS FILL "|" ATTRIBUTE clr sr,sc,er,sc
28)         PAINTCANVAS FILL "|" ATTRIBUTE clr sr,ec,er,ec
29)         @ sr,sc ?? "┌"
30)         @ sr,ec ?? "┐"
31)         @ er,sc ?? "└"
32)         @ er,ec ?? "┘"
33)      CASE brdr = "D" :
34)         PAINTCANVAS FILL "=" ATTRIBUTE clr sr,sc+1,sr,ec-1
35)         PAINTCANVAS FILL "=" ATTRIBUTE clr er,sc+1,er,ec-1
36)         PAINTCANVAS FILL "‖" ATTRIBUTE clr sr,sc,er,sc
37)         PAINTCANVAS FILL "‖" ATTRIBUTE clr sr,ec,er,ec
38)         @ sr,sc ?? "╔"
39)         @ sr,ec ?? "╗"
40)         @ er,sc ?? "╚"
41)         @ er,ec ?? "╝"
42)   ENDSWITCH
43)   STYLE
44)   IF shdw = "Y" THEN
45)      PAINTCANVAS ATTRIBUTE 7 er+1,sc+2,er+1,ec+2
46)      PAINTCANVAS ATTRIBUTE 7 sr+1,ec+1,er,ec+2
47)   ENDIF
48) ENDPROC
```

Listing 17-8 Color-filled window—continued

Procedure to Test if Printer is Ready

Any printer output should test to see if the printer is ready before sending the report or graph. Listing 17-9 is a procedure that gives your user a maximum of four tries to get the printer online before it returns False to the calling program. Using the PRINTERSTATUS function, a FOR loop is executed, displaying a message if the status of the printer is False (printer not ready). If PRINTERSTATUS returns True, the procedure returns to the calling program indicating the printer is online. A call using this procedure looks like:

```
printeronline = PrinterOn()
IF printeronline THEN
   printreport()
ELSE
   PrintMessage("Report cancelled, printer not ready")
ENDIF
```

```
 1) ; PrntrOn.sc
 2)
 3) PROC PrinterOn()
 4)   PRIVATE i,kp
 5)   FOR i FROM 1 TO 4
 6)     ShowMsg("Checking to see if the printer is ready, Please wait!",
 7)             "Off","N",0)
 8)     IF PRINTERSTATUS() THEN
 9)       CLEAR
10)       RETURN True
11)     ELSE
12)       IF i = 4 THEN
13)         RETURN False
14)       ELSE
15)         BEEP SLEEP 100 BEEP SLEEP 100 BEEP
16)         ShowMsg("Printer not on, press any key after turning printer on",
17)                 "Off","N",0)
18)         kp = GETCHAR()
19)       ENDIF
20)     ENDIF
21)   ENDFOR
22) ENDPROC
```

Listing 17-9 Printer test procedure

ValCheck Reporting Program

Paradox doesn't provide a built-in menu selection or command to report the ValChecks defined for a table, but the capability can be achieved by writing a PAL program. The VCPGM.SC script included on the disk is an example. This script is the basic code necessary to create Paradox tables containing the tables, fields, and ValChecks for tables in a directory. The Main menu is shown in Figure 17-4.

The ValCheck Catalog program has three Main menu selections:

    View   Form display of data in the catalog
    Report Reports for the data in the catalog
    Create Create a new catalog for the current directory

Two tables form the basis for the application design. A master table, Vctbls, contains all the tables in the catalog. Vccatlg is a detail table containing the fields and ValChecks for each table. This one-to-many relationship is used to view the data via a multitable form. Selecting {View} from the menu displays the data as shown in Figure 17-5.

```
View  Reports  Create  Exit
View the ValCheck Catalog
```

	ValCheck Catalog Program	
View	View the ValCheck Catalog	
Reports	Reports Menu	
Create	Create a ValCheck Catalog for the current directory	
Exit	Leave the ValCheck Catalog Program	

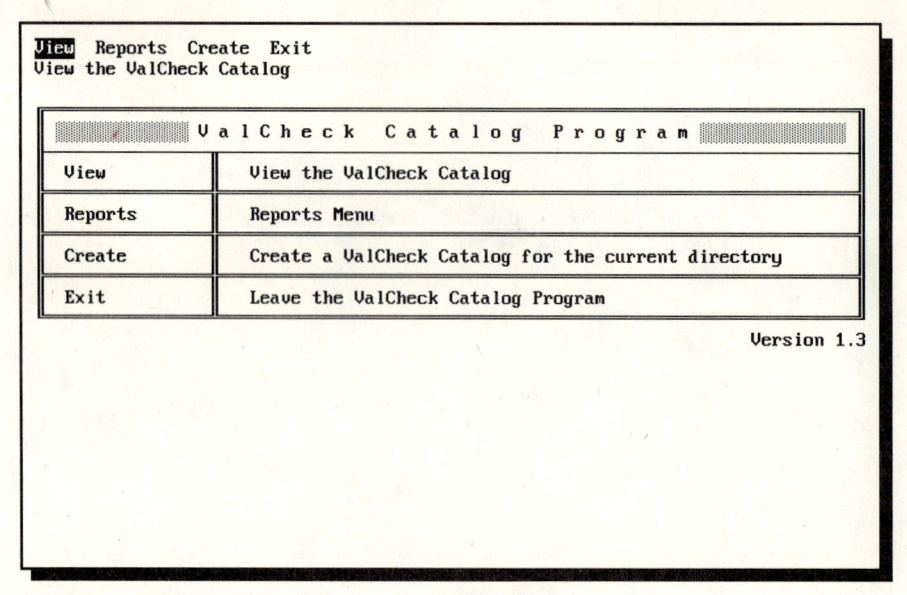

Version 1.3

Figure 17-4 ValCheck Catalog Program Main menu

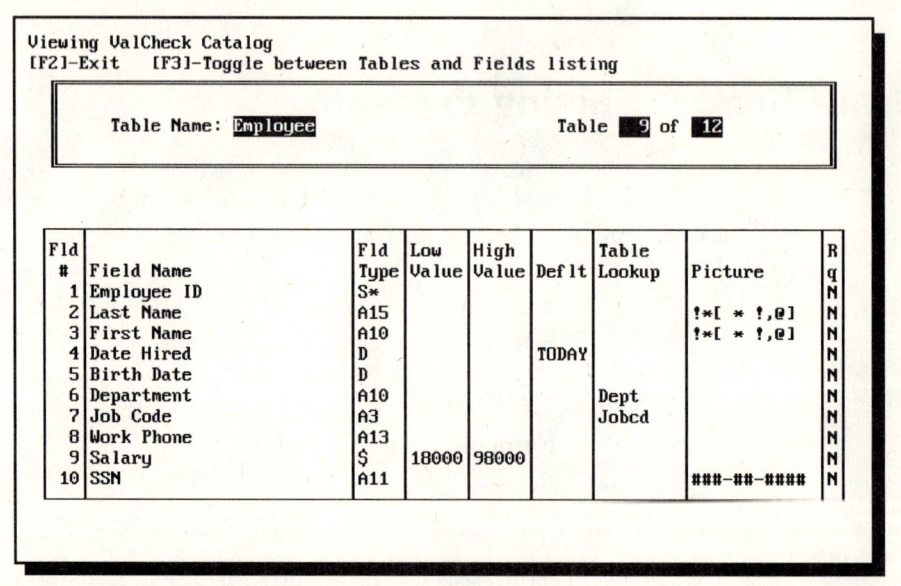

```
Viewing ValCheck Catalog
[F2]-Exit   [F3]-Toggle between Tables and Fields listing

     Table Name: Employee                    Table  9 of  12
```

Fld #	Field Name	Fld Type	Low Value	High Value	Deflt	Table Lookup	Picture	R q
1	Employee ID	S*						N
2	Last Name	A15					!*[* !,@]	N
3	First Name	A10					!*[* !,@]	N
4	Date Hired	D			TODAY			N
5	Birth Date	D						N
6	Department	A10				Dept		N
7	Job Code	A3				Jobcd		N
8	Work Phone	A13						N
9	Salary	$	18000	98000				N
10	SSN	A11					###-##-####	N

Figure 17-5 ValCheck Catalog Program Main menu

Reports come in three flavors:

Tables	Listing of all the tables
Fields	Alphabetical listing of fields, including data type and table.
ValChecks	Listing by table of the fields and ValChecks for each field.

Figure 17-6 shows the reports menu and Figure 17-7 shows the screen output for the ValChecks report.

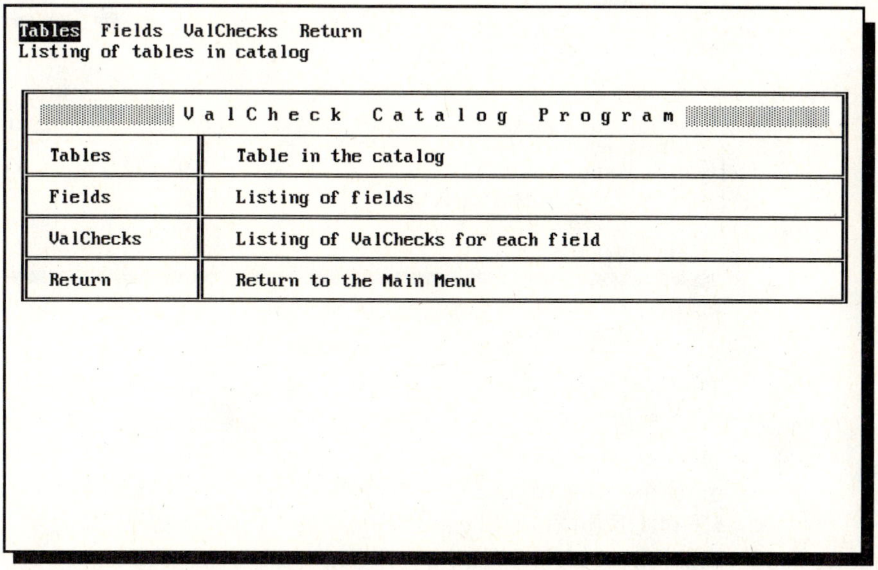

```
Tables  Fields  ValChecks  Return
Listing of tables in catalog
            ┌──────────────────────────────────────────────┐
            │           ValCheck  Catalog  Program         │
            ├────────────────┬─────────────────────────────┤
            │ Tables         │ Table in the catalog        │
            │ Fields         │ Listing of fields           │
            │ ValChecks      │ Listing of ValChecks for each field │
            │ Return         │ Return to the Main Menu     │
            └────────────────┴─────────────────────────────┘
```

Figure 17-6 ValCheck Catalog Program Report menu

All existing data in the catalog is replaced when {*Create*} is selected from the Main menu. A list of tables in the current directory is displayed from which you select the tables to add to the catalog. Figure 17-8 shows the selection screen.

From here the program checks if any of the tables are encrypted. For each password-protected table, the master password is requested. This is necessary to gain access to the ValCheck option during Edit mode. These tables can be selectively dropped from the selection list if the password is not known.

```
Now viewing Page 1 of Page Width 1
Press any key to continue...

 9/09/90                  Fields and ValChecks by Table                    Page  1

                           Field  Low    High            Table                       R
 #  Field Name             Type   Value  Value Default  Lookup   Picture             q
 --- ---------------------- -----  -----  ----- -------- -------- --------------- -
 Table Name: Benefits

  1 Employee ID            S                                                         N
  2 Insurance Type         A12                 Aetna             Aetna,King          N
                                                                 County,Group
                                                                 Health
  3 Life Insurance         $                   0.00              {50000,1{0000      N
                                                                 0,50000},2{00
                                                                 000,50000}}
  4 Short Term Disab       A1                  N                 Y,N                 N
  5 Long Term Disab        A1                  N                 Y,N                 N
  6 US Saving Bond         $                   0.00              {2{5[0]},1{00      N
                                                                 ,50},50[0]}

 Table Name: Budctgy
```

Figure 17-7 ValCheck report screen output

The technique used to provide ValCheck reporting is to capture the settings during an Edit session of each ValCheck menu option. The nucleus of this process is shown in Listing 17-10. Once in Edit mode for the table, the program interrogates each ValCheck menu setting and uses the MENU-CHOICE function to capture the current setting. The only ValCheck option that is a problem is {Required}. This option must be turned off during this process or the program will halt if the field doesn't have an entry (REQUIREDCHECK OFF). Starting with version 3.01a, this also sets the {Required} selection to {No}. Therefore, before recording the setting for {Required}, REQUIREDCHECK ON is executed to turn checking on, the setting is recorded, then required checking is turned back off. This process successfully captures the ValCheck setting.

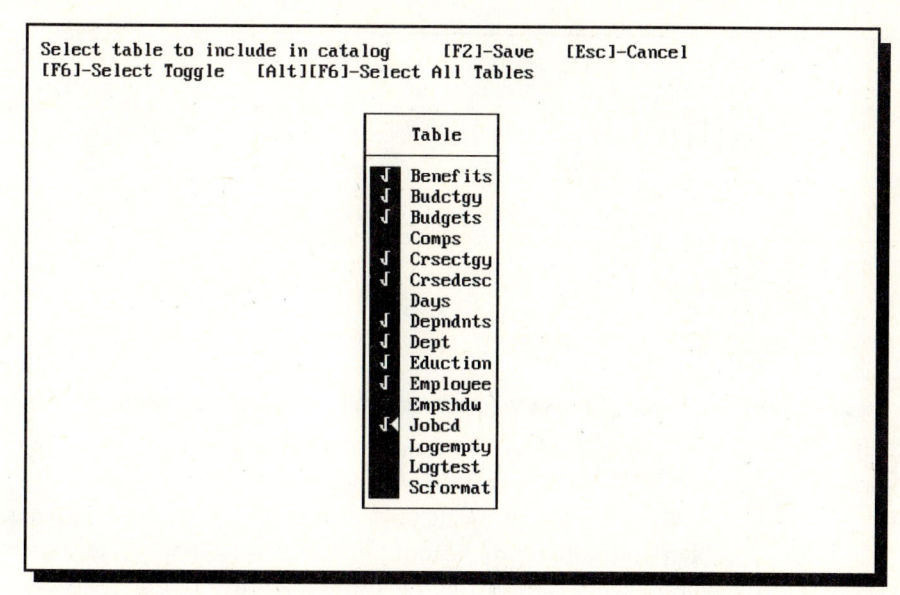

```
Select table to include in catalog    [F2]-Save    [Esc]-Cancel
[F6]-Select Toggle    [Alt][F6]-Select All Tables
```

```
                    ┌──────────┐
                    │  Table   │
                    ├──────────┤
                    │√ Benefits│
                    │√ Budctgy │
                    │√ Budgets │
                    │  Comps   │
                    │√ Crsectgy│
                    │√ Crsedesc│
                    │  Days    │
                    │√ Depndnts│
                    │√ Dept    │
                    │√ Eduction│
                    │√ Employee│
                    │  Empshdw │
                    │√◄ Jobcd  │
                    │  Logempty│
                    │  Logtest │
                    │  Scformat│
                    └──────────┘
```

Figure 17-8 Table selection screen

```
numfields = NFIELDS(TABLE())
numkeyfields = NKEYFIELDS(tblname)
FOR i FROM 1 TO numfields
  RIGHT
  [Vccatlg->Table Name] = tblname
  [Vccatlg->Field #]    = FIELDNO(FIELD(),tblname)
  IF [Vccatlg->Field #] <= numkeyfields THEN
     [Vccatlg->Field Type] = FIELDTYPE() + "*"
  ELSE
     [Vccatlg->Field Type] = FIELDTYPE()
  ENDIF
  [Vccatlg->Field Name] = FIELD()
  IF ISFILE(TABLE() + ".VAL") THEN
     MENU {ValCheck} {Define} Enter {LowValue}
     [Vccatlg->LowValue]      = MENUCHOICE()
     ESC {HighValue}
     [Vccatlg->HighValue]     = MENUCHOICE()
     ESC {Default}
     [Vccatlg->Default]       = MENUCHOICE()
     ESC {TableLookup}
     [Vccatlg->TableLookup]   = MENUCHOICE()
     ESC {Picture}
```

Listing 17-10 Code to capture ValCheck settings

```
        [Vccatlg->Picture]        = MENUCHOICE()
        REQUIREDCHECK ON
        ESC {Required}
        [Vccatlg->Required]       = MENUCHOICE()
        REQUIREDCHECK OFF
        MENU ESC
    ELSE
        [Vccatlg->Required] = "N"
    ENDIF
    MOVETO "Vccatlg"
    DOWN
    MOVETO tblname
ENDFOR
```

Listing 17-10 *Code to capture ValCheck settings—continued*

As we said earlier, the ValCheck Catalog Program is the foundation for a full-system catalog application. It is included here to give you an idea of how to create your own. If you don't want to write your own catalog system, try ParaLex from Zenreich Systems—an excellent tool to document your applications.

Another Information Tool

Earlier we discussed how the report generator can write PAL code. Let's see how the STATSCRP.SC evolves to provide you with more system information.

The STATSPEC script (Listing 17-11) is further refinement of the STATSCRP script. The first part of the script looks basically the same, with the addition of some release statements to ensure that we clear the system environment as much as possible. Next, PAL functions that require parameters are edited to allow them to function.

NOTE: *The DRIVESTATUS function returns a logical value of True or False. If you want to record the returned value to a table, you must first make it a string value with the STRVAL function.*

```
Release procs all
release vars all
Reset
Clearall
While (true)
mem = memleft()
rmem = rmemleft()
CoEdit "Stats"
[Memleft]=Mem
[Rmemleft]=Rmem
[Drivespace]=Drivespace(substr(directory(),1,1))
[Nettype]=Nettype()
[Directory]=Directory()
[Privdir]=Privdir()
[Today]=Today()
[Time]=Time()
[drivestatus]=strval(drivestatus(substr(directory(),1,1)))
[IsRuntime]=strval(IsRuntime())
[Monitor]=Monitor()
[Printerstatus]=strval(Printerstatus())
[QueryOrder]=QueryOrder()
[Retryperiod]=Retryperiod()
[Sortorder]=Sortorder()
[Syscolor 0]=Syscolor (0)
[Syscolor 2]=Syscolor (2)
[Syscolor 3]=Syscolor (3)
[Syscolor 4]=Syscolor (4)
[Syscolor 5]=Syscolor (5)
[Syscolor 6]=Syscolor (6)
[Syscolor 7]=Syscolor (7)
[Syscolor 8]=Syscolor (8)
[Syscolor 9]=Syscolor (9)
[Syscolor 11]=Syscolor(11)
[Syscolor 12]=Syscolor(12)
[Syscolor 13]=Syscolor(13)
[Syscolor 15]=Syscolor(15)
[Syscolor 16]=Syscolor(16)
[Syscolor 17]=Syscolor(17)
[Syscolor 18]=Syscolor(18)
[Syscolor 19]=Syscolor(19)
[Syscolor 21]=Syscolor(21)
[Syscolor 22]=Syscolor(22)
[Syscolor 23]=Syscolor(23)
[Syscolor 24]=Syscolor(24)
[Syscolor 25]=Syscolor(25)
[Syscolor 27]=Syscolor(27)
[Syscolor 28]=Syscolor(28)
[Syscolor 29]=Syscolor(29)
[UserName]=UserName()
[Version]=Version()
Do_it!
Quitloop
EndWhile
```

Listing 17-11 *STATSPEC.SC*

Once the system environment has been read and the Stats table updated, the next part of the script looks up the numerical codes for the system color settings and fills in an "English" description of the color code. It does so by jumping back and forth from a Colrchrt table and the Stats table. For example:

TopTwoLines=31
Color setting is white foreground characters on a blue background.

```
Reset
ClearAll
View "ColrChrt"
CoEdit "Stats"
While (true)
look = [Syscolor 0]
moveto[colrchrt->ascii number/ext code]
locate look
foundit = [background/foreground]
moveto[stats->syscolor 0 Color]
[] = foundit
look = [Syscolor 2]
moveto[colrchrt->ascii number/ext code]
locate look
foundit = [background/foreground]
moveto[stats->syscolor 2 Color]
[] = foundit
look = [Syscolor 3]
moveto[colrchrt->ascii number/ext code]
locate look
foundit = [background/foreground]
moveto[stats->syscolor 3 Color]
[] = foundit
look = [Syscolor 4]
moveto[colrchrt->ascii number/ext code]
locate look
foundit = [background/foreground]
moveto[stats->syscolor 4 Color]
[] = foundit
look = [Syscolor 5]
moveto[colrchrt->ascii number/ext code]
locate look
foundit = [background/foreground]
moveto[stats->syscolor 5 Color]
[] = foundit
look = [Syscolor 6]
moveto[colrchrt->ascii number/ext code]
locate look
foundit = [background/foreground]
moveto[stats->syscolor 6 Color]
[] = foundit
look = [Syscolor 7]
moveto[colrchrt->ascii number/ext code]
locate look
```

```
foundit = [background/foreground]
moveto[stats->syscolor 7 Color]
[] = foundit
look = [Syscolor 8]
moveto[colrchrt->ascii number/ext code]
locate look
foundit = [background/foreground]
moveto[stats->syscolor 8 Color]
[] = foundit
look = [Syscolor 9]
moveto[colrchrt->ascii number/ext code]
locate look
foundit = [background/foreground]
moveto[stats->syscolor 9 Color]
[] = foundit
look = [Syscolor 19]
moveto[colrchrt->ascii number/ext code]
locate look
foundit = [background/foreground]
moveto[stats->syscolor 19 Color]
[] = foundit
look = [Syscolor 11]
moveto[colrchrt->ascii number/ext code]
locate look
foundit = [background/foreground]
moveto[stats->syscolor 11 Color]
[] = foundit
look = [Syscolor 12]
moveto[colrchrt->ascii number/ext code]
locate look
foundit = [background/foreground]
moveto[stats->syscolor 12 Color]
[] = foundit
look = [Syscolor 13]
moveto[colrchrt->ascii number/ext code]
locate look
foundit = [background/foreground]
moveto[stats->syscolor 13 Color]
[] = foundit
look = [Syscolor 15]
moveto[colrchrt->ascii number/ext code]
locate look
foundit = [background/foreground]
moveto[stats->syscolor 15 Color]
[] = foundit
look = [Syscolor 16]
moveto[colrchrt->ascii number/ext code]
locate look
foundit = [background/foreground]
moveto[stats->syscolor 16 Color]
[] = foundit
look = [Syscolor 17]
moveto[colrchrt->ascii number/ext code]
locate look
foundit = [background/foreground]
moveto[stats->syscolor 17 Color]
[] = foundit
```

```
          look = [Syscolor 18]
          moveto[colrchrt->ascii number/ext code]
          locate look
          foundit = [background/foreground]
          moveto[stats->syscolor 18 Color]
          [] = foundit
          look = [Syscolor 21]
          moveto[colrchrt->ascii number/ext code]
          locate look
          foundit = [background/foreground]
          moveto[stats->syscolor 21 Color]
          [] = foundit
          look = [Syscolor 22]
          moveto[colrchrt->ascii number/ext code]
          locate look
          foundit = [background/foreground]
          moveto[stats->syscolor 22 Color]
          [] = foundit
          look = [Syscolor 23]
          moveto[colrchrt->ascii number/ext code]
          locate look
          foundit = [background/foreground]
          moveto[stats->syscolor 23 Color]
          [] = foundit
          look = [Syscolor 24]
          moveto[colrchrt->ascii number/ext code]
          locate look
          foundit = [background/foreground]
          moveto[stats->syscolor 24 Color]
          [] = foundit
          look = [Syscolor 25]
          moveto[colrchrt->ascii number/ext code]
          locate look
          foundit = [background/foreground]
          moveto[stats->syscolor 25 Color]
          [] = foundit
          look = [Syscolor 27]
          moveto[colrchrt->ascii number/ext code]
          locate look
          foundit = [background/foreground]
          moveto[stats->syscolor 27 Color]
          [] = foundit
          look = [Syscolor 28]
          moveto[colrchrt->ascii number/ext code]
          locate look
          foundit = [background/foreground]
          moveto[stats->syscolor 28 Color]
          [] = foundit
          look = [Syscolor 29]
          moveto[colrchrt->ascii number/ext code]
          locate look
          foundit = [background/foreground]
          moveto[stats->syscolor 29 Color]
          [] = foundit
          Do_it!
          Quitloop
        EndWhile
```

Creating and Using Development Tools 569

The end result is shown in Figures 17-9 through 17-11. This is a nice way to give you a quick look at the environment that Paradox is dealing with. In addition, you can create a customized report to print out the data.

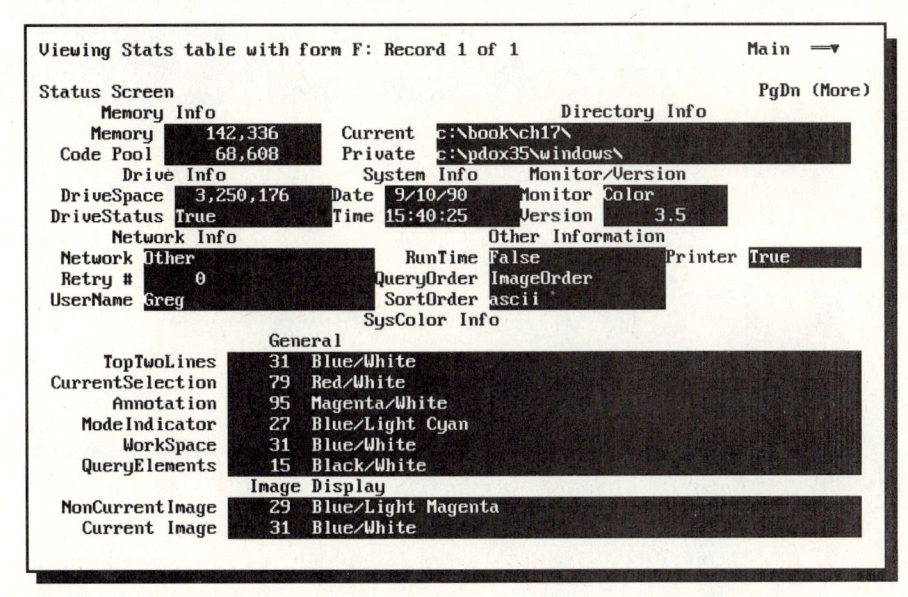

```
Viewing Stats table with form F: Record 1 of 1                Main    ═▼
Status Screen                                                 PgDn (More)
         Memory Info                        Directory Info
        Memory    142,336       Current   c:\book\ch17\
     Code Pool     68,608       Private   c:\pdox35\windows\
         Drive Info              System Info      Monitor/Version
    DriveSpace  3,250,176       Date     9/10/90   Monitor Color
    DriveStatus True            Time    15:40:25   Version     3.5
         Network Info                        Other Information
      Network Other                       RunTime False       Printer True
      Retry #      0                   QueryOrder ImageOrder
     UserName Greg                      SortOrder ascii
                              SysColor Info
                          General
       TopTwoLines         31  Blue/White
  CurrentSelection         79  Red/White
        Annotation         95  Magenta/White
     ModeIndicator         27  Blue/Light Cyan
         WorkSpace         31  Blue/White
     QueryElements         15  Black/White
                       Image Display
   NonCurrentImage         29  Blue/Light Magenta
      Current Image        31  Blue/White
```

Figure 17-9 Stats table information Page 1

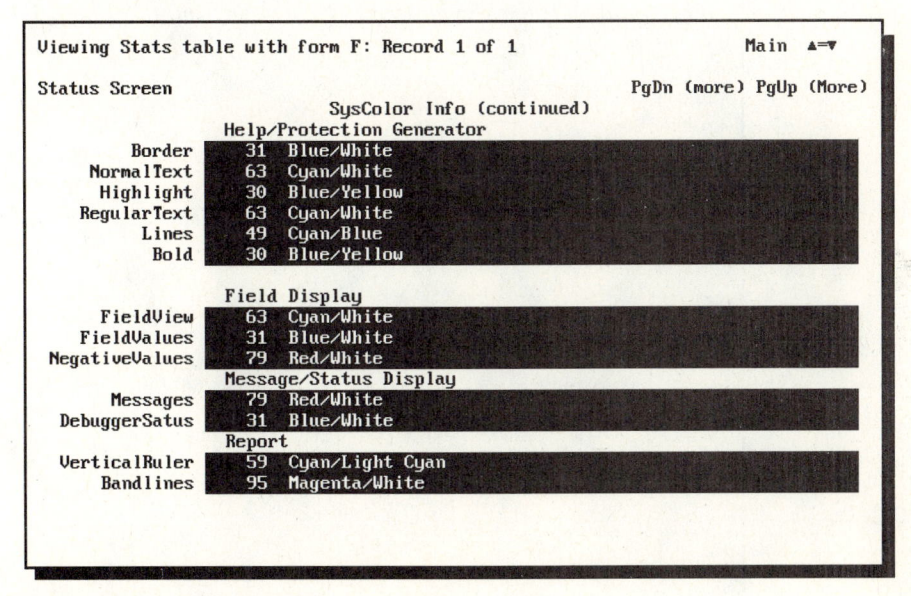

```
Viewing Stats table with form F: Record 1 of 1                Main    ▲═▼
Status Screen                                       PgDn (more) PgUp (More)
                       SysColor Info (continued)
                  Help/Protection Generator
             Border    31  Blue/White
         NormalText    63  Cyan/White
          Highlight    30  Blue/Yellow
        RegularText    63  Cyan/White
              Lines    49  Cyan/Blue
               Bold    30  Blue/Yellow
                       Field Display
          FieldView    63  Cyan/White
        FieldValues    31  Blue/White
     NegativeValues    79  Red/White
                    Message/Status Display
           Messages    79  Red/White
      DebuggerSatus    31  Blue/White
                       Report
       VerticalRuler   59  Cyan/Light Cyan
           Bandlines   95  Magenta/White
```

Figure 17-10 Stats table information Page 2

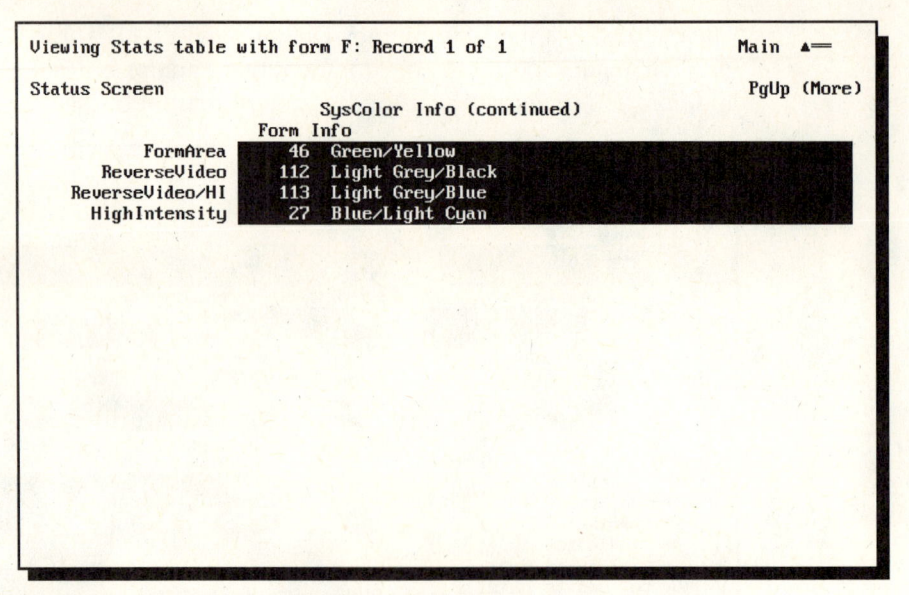

```
Viewing Stats table with form F: Record 1 of 1        Main  ▲═
Status Screen                                         PgUp (More)
                        SysColor Info (continued)
                    Form Info
         FormArea     46   Green/Yellow
      ReverseVideo   112   Light Grey/Black
    ReverseVideo/HI  113   Light Grey/Blue
     HighIntensity    27   Blue/Light Cyan
```

Figure 17-11 Stats table information Page 3

NOTE: *The script used to create the "English" phrases for the Stats table is interesting in itself. It uses the PAL MOD (modulus) function to determine which number in a set of 16 is the current ASCII code and to return a remainder. If the remainder is 0, the foreground is black, if it's 1 the foreground is blue, and so on. Here's the code:*

```
Reset
ClearAll
CoEdit "ColrChrt"
Scan
if [ascii number/ext code] > 0 then
if mod([ascii number/ext code],16) = 0   then
    [foreground] = "Black"
endif
if mod([ascii number/ext code],16) = 1   then
    [foreground] = "Blue"
endif
if mod([ascii number/ext code],16) = 2   then
    [foreground] = "Green"
endif
if mod([ascii number/ext code],16) = 3   then
    [foreground] = "Cyan"
endif
if mod([ascii number/ext code],16) = 4   then
    [foreground] = "Red"
endif
if mod([ascii number/ext code],16) = 5   then
    [foreground] = "Magenta"
```

```
endif
if mod([ascii number/ext code],16) = 6 then
    [foreground] = "Brown"
endif
if mod([ascii number/ext code],16) = 7 then
    [foreground] = "Light Grey"
endif
if mod([ascii number/ext code],16) = 8 then
    [foreground] = "Dark Grey"
endif
if mod([ascii number/ext code],16) = 9 then
    [foreground] = "Light Blue"
endif
if mod([ascii number/ext code],16) = 10 then
    [foreground] = "Light Green"
endif
if mod([ascii number/ext code],16) = 11 then
    [foreground] = "Light Cyan"
endif
if mod([ascii number/ext code],16) = 12 then
    [foreground] = "Light Red"
endif
if mod([ascii number/ext code],16) = 13 then
    [foreground] = "Light Magenta"
endif
if mod([ascii number/ext code],16) = 14 then
    [foreground] = "Yellow"
endif
if mod([ascii number/ext code],16) = 15 then
    [foreground] = "White"
endif
if [ascii number/ext code] >= 0 and [ascii number/ext code] <15
then
    [background] = "Black"
endif
if [ascii number/ext code] >= 16 and [ascii number/ext code] <32
then
    [background] = "Blue"
endif
if [ascii number/ext code] >= 32 and [ascii number/ext code] <48
then
    [background] = "Green"
endif
if [ascii number/ext code] >= 48 and [ascii number/ext code] <64
then
    [background] = "Cyan"
endif
if [ascii number/ext code] >= 64 and [ascii number/ext code] <80
then
    [background] = "Red"
endif
if [ascii number/ext code] >= 80 and [ascii number/ext code] <96
then
    [background] = "Magenta"
```

```
    endif
    if [ascii number/ext code] >= 96 and [ascii number/ext code] <112
    then
        [background] = "Brown"
    endif
    if [ascii number/ext code] >= 112 and [ascii number/ext code]
    <128 then
        [background] = "Light Grey"
    endif
    if [ascii number/ext code] >= 128 and [ascii number/ext code]
    <144 then
        [background] = "Black"
    endif
    if [ascii number/ext code] >= 144 and [ascii number/ext code]
    <160 then
        [background] = "Blue"
    endif
    if [ascii number/ext code] >= 160 and [ascii number/ext code]
    <176 then
        [background] = "Green"
    endif
    if [ascii number/ext code] >= 176 and [ascii number/ext code]
    <192 then
        [background] = "Cyan"
    endif
    if [ascii number/ext code] >= 192 and [ascii number/ext code]
    <208 then
        [background] = "Red"
    endif
    if [ascii number/ext code] >= 208 and [ascii number/ext code]
    <224 then
        [background] = "Magenta"
    endif
    if [ascii number/ext code] >= 224 and [ascii number/ext code]
    <240 then
        [background] = "Brown"
    endif
    if [ascii number/ext code] >= 240  and [ascii number/ext code]
    <256 then
        [background] = "Light Grey"
    endif
    endif
    [background/foreground] = [background]+"/"+[foreground]
    if mod([#],10)=0 then
        message [#]
    endif
    EndScan
    Do_it!
```

Enhancing the PAL Editor

The built-in PAL editor is spartan at best, but you can do a few things to spruce it up.

Listing 17-12, KEYEDIT.SC, sets [Shift][F7] to copy a line starting at your current cursor position. [Shift][F8] pastes the line in scrap at your current cursor position. [Shift][F9] copies the line at the cursor position and then deletes the line (only the partial line if the cursor is not at column 0). [Shift][F10] pastes the line back.

In addition, [Ctrl][F1],[Ctrl][F2],[Ctrl][F3], [Ctrl][F4], [Ctrl][F5], [Ctrl][F6], and [Ctrl][F7] have been set to type in characters below ASCII code 32. Without a special setup, such as this script provides, it is impossible to type these characters into the screen.

```
;These keys let you first copy the current line and then paste that
;line anywhere. Note that cursor position is taken into account
;so that a "line" is from the current cursor position to the end.
setkey "F17" lin = substr(cursorline(),colno(),len(cursorline()))
setkey "F18" typein lin
;The following keys copys and pastes a line.
setkey "F19" lin = substr(cursorline(),colno(),len(cursorline())) Deleteline
setkey "F20" CtrlHome Enter typein lin
;The following keys allow you to type in these otherwise silent
;characters into your PAL scripts.
setkey "F21" "\016"              ; this is a left arrowhead
setkey "F22" "\017"              ; this is a right arrowhead
setkey "F23" "\030"              ; this is an up character
setkey "F24" "\031"              ; this is a down character
setkey "F25" "\017\196"          ; this is a left direction key
setkey "F26" "\196\016"          ; this is a right direction
setkey "F27" "\017\217"          ; this is the [ENTER] key
```

Listing 17-12 KEYEDIT.SC

KEYEDIT.SC gives your PAL editor some simple additional capabilities. Next, let's look at some scripts included on disk with this book that give you a great deal more.

EDITOR3

EDITOR3 (Listing 17-13) is a system that supplements PAL's editor functions. Other editors can be used, but this editing supplement lets you stay entirely in Paradox 3.0 or greater and also lets you work in more than just the Script mode of Paradox.

EDITOR3 and GO_EDIT3 are written entirely in PAL. We have tried to take caution and not be a memory hog, so that developers can produce their applications and keep EDITOR3 working in the background. We suggest that you *RELEASE PROCS ALL RELEASE VARS ALL RESET* if you appear not to have sufficient memory to complete your program.

To INSTALL EDITOR3:

1. Install the enclosed disk on your hard drive, following the instructions in INSTALL.BAT
2. Start Paradox 3.5.
3. Run SETEDIT3.

    SETEDIT3 asks you in which directory your EDITOR3 resides. It will default to your current directory. Enter the location of EDITOR3 as appropriate (it starts out in /POWERDOX/17). EDITOR3 will then start up.

4. Press [Esc] to return to Paradox Main mode.

    EDITOR3 has now been loaded and will pop-up by simply pressing [Alt][F1].

> **NOTE:** *EDITOR3 works in Script, Form, and Report modes.*

Once you've installed EDITOR3 it is at your service anytime Paradox is running. Once installed, call EDITOR3 from any directory you're currently working in. Simply do a *Menu {Scripts} {Play} dospath\GO_EDIT3*, answer EDITOR3, tell it which directory to make its calls from, and press [Enter]. Now EDITOR3 will pop up anytime you press [Alt][F1] simultaneously.

> **NOTE:** *EDITOR3 has help built into it. The SHOWMENU portion of each menu in EDITOR3 makes use of the UNTIL clause to set the current menu selection to a help variable. When you press [F1], and if help text is available, the help information is returned to the screen (see Figure 17-12).*

```
Style Attribute 192
@24,0 Clear EOL ?? "Compiling Editor_Menu..."
proc closed Editor_Menu()
usevars editorlib
while (true)
```

Listing 17-13 EDITOR3

```
ShowMenu
         "Draw"   : "Draw a LINE or BOX",
         "ASCII"  : "Reference ASCII Chart and place ASCII characters",
         "Block"  : "Block operations, COPY, MOVE & PASTE",
       "Replace"  : "Search & Replace",
         "File"   : "Save current script",
         "Print"  : "Print current script",
  "Special Characters":"Place a special ASCII character",
         "Quit"   : "Quit EDITOR 3 and release memory"
        Until "F1"
         keyto keyvar
         to editorsel
         if keyvar = "F1" then
              helpsub = editorsel
              ReadLib EditorLib Editor_Help
                       Editor_Help(helpsub)
              loop
         endif
         Switch
          case editorsel = "Draw" :While (true)
                                    ShowMenu
                                     "Line":"Draw a Line",
                                     "Box" :"Draw a Box"
                                        Until "F1"
                                        keyto keyvar
                                        to editorsel
                     if keyvar = "F1" then
                          helpsub = editorsel
                          ReadLib EditorLib Editor_Help
                          Editor_Help(helpsub)
                          loop
                     endif
Switch
  case editorsel = "Esc"  : quitloop
 case editorsel = "Line" : ReadLib EditorLib Draw_Line
                           Draw_Line()
                           Return
 case editorsel = "Box"  : ReadLib EditorLib Draw_Box
                           Draw_Box()
                           Return
EndSwitch
                                   EndWhile
                                   loop
 case editorsel = "ASCII" : Readlib EditorLib Editor_Ref
                Editor_Ref()
                  case editorsel = "Block" : While (true)
                                    ShowMenu
                                    "Copy" : "Copy Area",
                                    "Paste": "Paste Area"
      Until "F1"
            keyto keyvar
            to editorsel
```

Listing 17-13 EDITOR3—continued

```
                if keyvar = "F1" then
                    helpsub = editorsel
                    ReadLib EditorLib Editor_Help
                    Editor_Help(helpsub)
                    loop
                endif
              Switch
                    case editorsel = "Esc"  :Quitloop
                    case editorsel = "Copy": ReadLib EditorLib Copy_Area
Copy_Area()
Return
                    case editorsel = "Paste":Readlib EditorLib Paste_Area
Paste_Area()
Return
                                                     OtherWise:Loop
                                                     EndSwitch
 EndWhile
 loop
case editorsel = "Replace":ReadLib EditorLib Search_Replace
                                           Search_Replace()
            case editorsel = "File"    :ReadLib EditorLib Save_Script
                                         Save_Script()
            case editorsel = "Print"   :ReadLib EditorLib Print_It
                                         Print_It()
            case editorsel = "Special Characters"  :ReadLib EditorLib
Special_Char
                                                    Special_Char()
            case editorsel = "Quit"    :Savevars editorpath,editorlib
                                         Release Vars All
                                         play "savevars"
                                         Return
         OtherWise:Loop
         EndSwitch
quitloop
EndWhile
EndProc
writelib EditorLib Editor_Menu
```

Listing 17-13 EDITOR3—continued

Here's a quick overview of the functions included in EDITOR3. Figure 17-13 shows EDITOR's Main menu. Again, EDITOR3, with its source code, is on the disk accompanying this book.

```
┌Copy─────────────────────┐
│Copy allows you to copy in a│
│Script, Form or Report.  │
│You can even copy screens│
│from your PAL scripts to your│
│reports or from the headings│
│from one report to another│
│table with a totally differ-│
│nt structure.  First move to│
│the upper left-hand ...  │
│                         │
│ [PgDn] ▼ ... more ⏎ = Quit│
└─────────────────────────┘
```

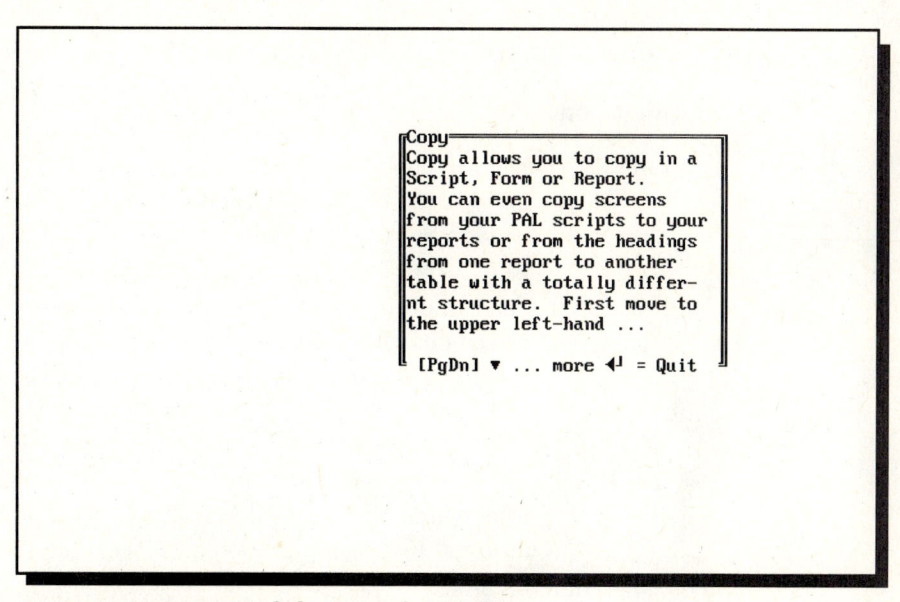

Figure 17-12 EDITOR3 help screen for COPY

```
Draw  ASCII  Block  Replace  File  Print  Special Characters  Quit
Draw a LINE or BOX
```

Figure 17-13 EDITOR3 Main menu

Explanation of EDITOR3 features

Draw Functions

- Line: You can choose single, double, or any other ASCII character by using [Alt] + ASCII code (see your *PAL User's Guide*). Start drawing by pressing your arrow keys. Press your [Enter] key to stop.
- Box: You can draw a box with single, double, or any other ASCII character (see your *PAL User's Guide*). Move to the upper-left corner of where you want to start your box and press [F6]. Next, move to the lower-right corner of where you want your box to stop and press [F6] again.
- ASCII: ASCII is a reference to the ASCII codes from 1 to 255 and what characters result from typing in the ASCII code number. For example, a left arrow is entered as \017\196.

Block Operations

- Copy: Copy lets you copy in a script, form, or report. You can even copy screens from your PAL scripts to your reports, or from the headings of one report to another table with a totally different structure. First, move to the upper-left corner of the area you want to copy and press [F6].

  Now move to the lower-right corner of the area you want to copy and press [F6] again. Finally, move to the starting point of where you want to copy and press [F6].
- Paste: Paste lets you paste a previously copied area into a form, report, or script. For example, you can create a form in the form designer, use COPY, and then PASTE it into the report generator to avoid re-keying the form.

Search and Replace

- Replace: Search lets you find any set of characters and replace them with another.

▽ **WARNING:** *Do not search for thisvar and replace with thisvarx or you'll be in an endless loop. As an alternative, make two passes. First replace thisvar with xxxxx, then replace xxxxx with thisvarx.*

File: File lets you save a script without exiting to Paradox Main mode. It can also be used to get a snapshot of a form or report. (Use Print and choose File if you're trying to document your system.)

Print: Print lets you print the current script, form, or report to the printer or to a file. You can choose to print with or without numbers. This scripts assumes that you have an IBM ProPrinter or compatible.

Special Keys: This selection lets you place ASCII characters below ASCII code 32 on a form, script, or report.

Summary

In this chapter, we created a number of tools using Paradox to help us develop Paradox applications more easily and with more accuracy. There are hundreds of ways you can enhance your development efforts merely by fully exploiting Paradox's potential. The examples in this chapter shouldn't be taken as definitive ways to perform the processes they address. They should be viewed as idea generators; that is, let these examples motivate you to create your own tools. You might want to start with the functions shown here and expand or customize them, but by all means, add a few of these to your repertoire.

In Chapter 20, we'll look at some third-party products that can also boost your development capabilities. Meanwhile, we'll delve into ways of getting data in and out of Paradox as well as take a stab at using Quattro Pro as a tool to create Paradox tables.

18   Integrating Data

Working with other programs and their data formats is an essential component of any good application. Paradox sports a wide array of supported Import/Export file formats. Unfortunately, there are no PAL commands for importing and exporting data, so a good understanding of Paradox's {*Tools*} {*ExportImport*} menu sequences is required.

In addition to Paradox's built-in import and export features, you can get information to and from Paradox in a number of other ways. In fact, you have tools available to you right now that could help you create a Paradox application without ever using Paradox itself.

First, let's take a look at the menu commands that let you import data into and export data from Paradox.

Importing Information

Paradox imports the following file formats:

- Quattro Pro
- Lotus 1-2-3
- Lotus Symphony
- dBASE
- PFS
- Reflex
- VisiCalc (DIF)
- ASCII

```
Quattro/PRO  1-2-3  Symphony  Dbase  Pfs  Reflex  Visicalc  Ascii   Main
Import a .WKQ or .WQ1 file.
```

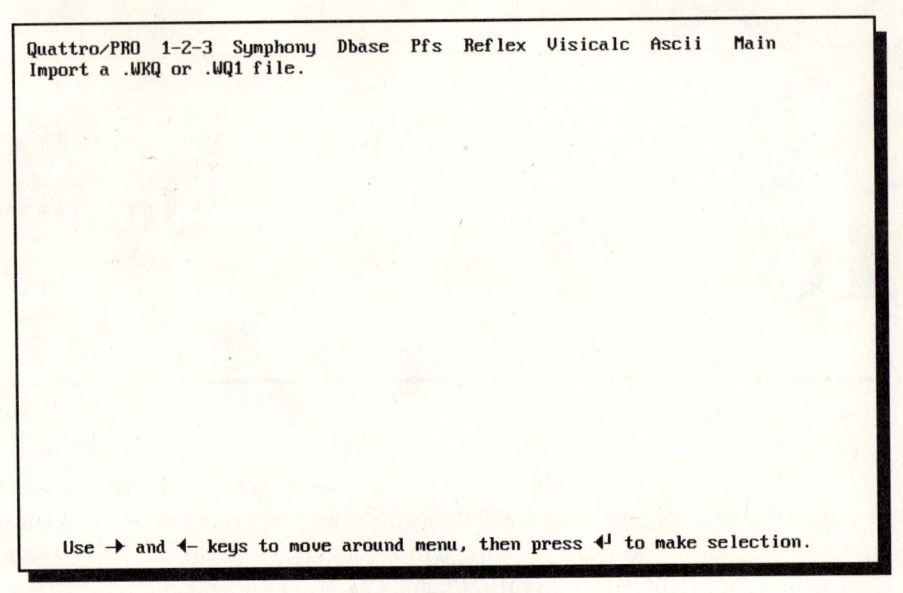

```
Use → and ← keys to move around menu, then press ↵ to make selection.
```

Figure 18-1 The Paradox Select File Format screen

Following are a few special rules for importing data from other sources, depending on the source of the imported information.

First, do not type a file extension when asked for a filename to import from. The file extension is designated by your menu choice. Simply supply the filename you want to import.

Next, regarding certain file formats, you should be aware of the following special provisions and cautions.

Spreadsheets

Imported spreadsheet data should consist of a row of column labels and data. The row of column labels should rest directly on the data, without any underline or other characters beneath the labels.

dBASE

Although Paradox can import dBASE II, III Plus, and IV data files, if the file contains memo fields, Paradox truncates the memo field after the first 255 characters.

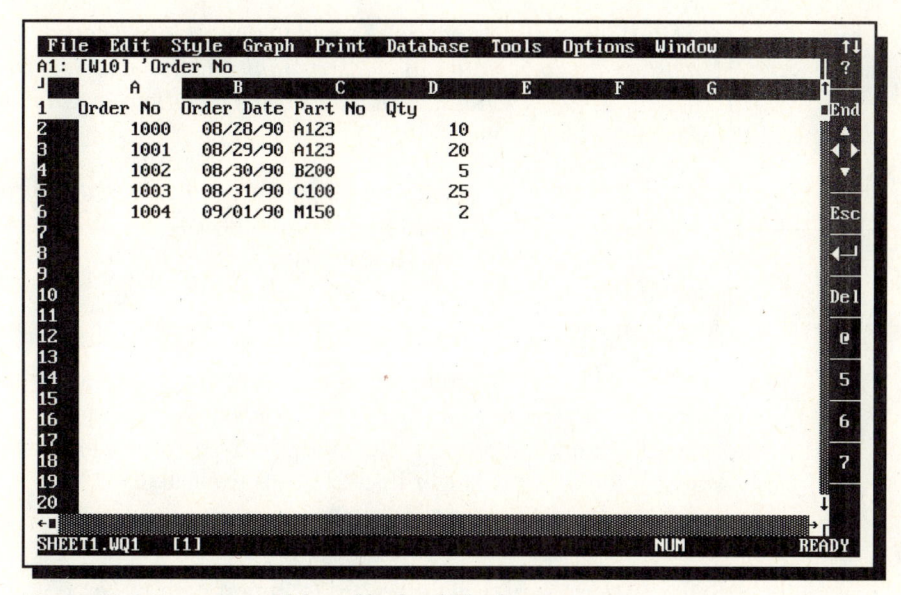

Figure 18-2 How a spreadsheet file should look prior to import

VisiCalc

The problem you might run into with DIF (Data Interchange Format, a supposed standard in the marketplace) files is that not all DIFs are truly DIF files. If you have problems importing a DIF file, try translating it to some other format before importing it into Paradox.

ASCII

You can import three types of ASCII files:

- Delimited
- AppendDelimited
- Text

Delimited and AppendDelimited look to the delimiter specified in the CCP to know how to parse the ASCII file into fields. AppendDelimited works just like Delimited except that it lets you append records to an existing Paradox table. Delimited always creates a new Paradox table.

TIP: *When using AppendDelimited to import into a keyed table, you must designate whether the imported information will be NewEntries or merely Updates. Choose Update. Any key violations are then placed in a Keyviol table.*

NOTE: *Anytime there are problems with any data in a record being imported, the entire record is placed in a table called Problems, with an explanation (as best Paradox can discern at the time) of why the record could not be imported.*

The Text option creates a new Paradox table with a single field of up to 132 characters. If you need to import a text string longer than 132 characters and if there are no commas in any of the records to be imported, you can use AppendDelimited to import a text file with a string no longer than 255 characters. If the string is longer than 255, it is truncated.

Reflex

Reflex files are very straightforward to import with the exception of fields that don't have a designated field type. Because Paradox isn't given an indication of what field type to create, the undesignated field is simply ignored. This is particularly true of Reflex long text fields. The other restriction is that you must save your data in 1.1 format before importing the data to Paradox.

Examples of Keystroke Sequences for Import

NOTE: *The following examples assume that Mstr is both the import name and the new (or existing) Paradox table name.*

Quattro Pro

Version 1

Menu {Tools} {ExportImport} {Import} {Quattro/PRO} {1} Quattro Release 1.X} {Mstr} {Mstr}

Version 2

Menu {Tools} {ExportImport} {Import} {Quattro/PRO} {2} Quattro PRO} {Mstr} {Mstr}

Lotus 1-2-3

Version 1A
Menu {Tools} {ExportImport} {Import} {1-2-3} {1} 1-2-3 Release 1A} {Mstr} {Mstr}

Version 2
Menu {Tools} {ExportImport} {Import} {1-2-3} {2} 1-2-3 Release 2} {Mstr} {Mstr}

Lotus Symphony

Version 1
Menu {Tools} {ExportImport} {Export} {Symphony} {1} Symphony Release 1.0} {Mstr} {Mstr}

Version 1.1
Menu {Tools} {ExportImport} {Import} {Symphony} {2} Symphony Release 1.1} {Mstr} {Mstr}

dBASE

dBASE II, III, IV
Menu {Tools} {ExportImport} {Import} {Dbase} {Mstr} {Mstr}

PFS
Menu {Tools} {ExportImport} {Import} {Pfs} {Mstr} {Mstr}

Reflex

Version 1
Menu {Tools} {ExportImport} {Import} {Reflex} {1} Reflex Release 1.0} {Mstr} {Mstr}

Version 1.1
Menu {Tools} {ExportImport} {Import} {Reflex} {2} Reflex Release 1.1} {Mstr} {Mstr} Esc {Mstr2}

VisiCalc (DIF)

Menu {Tools} {ExportImport} {Import} {Visicalc} {Mstr} {Mstr}

ASCII

Delimited

Menu {Tools} {ExportImport} {Import} {Ascii} {Delimited} {Test.txt} {Test}

AppendDelimited

Menu {Tools} {ExportImport} {Import} {Ascii} {AppendDelimited} {Test.txt} {Test}

Text

Menu {Tools} {ExportImport} {Import} {Ascii} {Text} {Test.txt}{Test}

Flimport

Another way to import data into Paradox is with the FLIMPORT (Fixed-length Import) utility that ships with Paradox. FLIMPORT is installed into the UTILS directory if you request that the utility programs be installed. There is also a text file with documentation on how to use it. Its basic function is to let you create a parsing specification for a fixed-length ASCII text file. Once you enter the specification, you can save it for future use. When you tell FLIMPORT to start importing, it reports any problems back via the screen and/or the printer. This utility is especially helpful when importing information downloaded from a large mainframe or minicomputer system. Figure 18-3 shows the Main FLIMPORT screen, and Figure 18-4 shows FLIMPORT's specification screen.

Integrating Data **587**

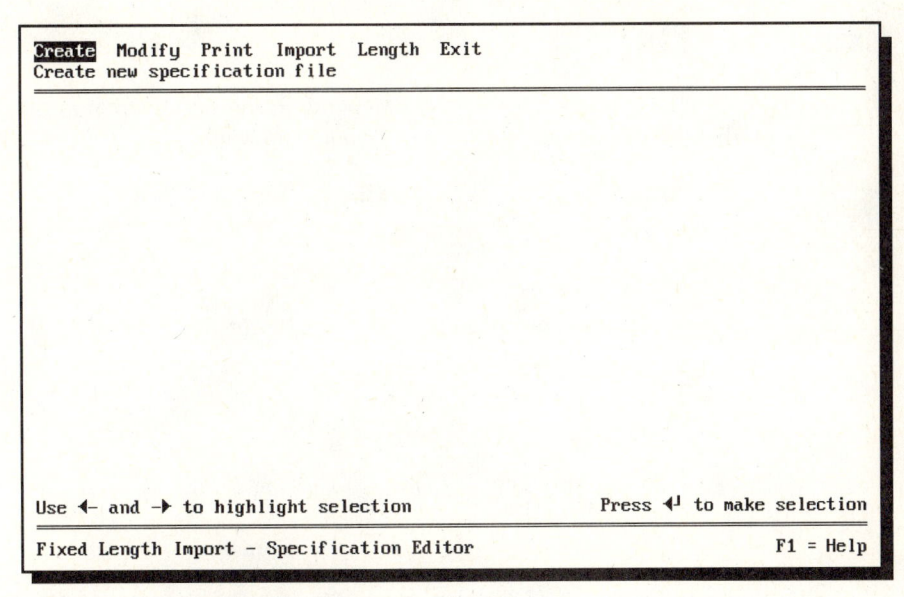

```
Create  Modify  Print  Import  Length  Exit
Create new specification file




















Use ← and → to highlight selection        Press ↵ to make selection
Fixed Length Import - Specification Editor              F1 = Help
```

Figure 18-3 Main FLIMPORT screen

```
Save  Cancel  Print  Import  Resume
Save current specification to disk

         Table Name: test                              Table/Source Specs
             Action: create      (Create, Append, Overwrite)
   Source File Name: \pdox35\book\test.rpt
      Record Length: 150
 Field Spec #  1 of  1
         Field Name: CUSTOMER                                   Field Spec
         Field Type: A20
   Starting Position: 1
       Field Length: 20

                                                              Creating t
      F1 = Help   F2 = Save   F3 = UpImage   F4 = DownImage   F10 = Menu
```

Figure 18-4 FLIMPORT specification screen

Exporting Data

Paradox exports information pretty much the same way it imports it except that instead of reading the file formats, it creates them.

Paradox can export to the following file formats:

- Quattro Pro
- Lotus 1-2-3
- Lotus Symphony
- dBASE
- PFS
- Reflex
- VisiCalc (DIF)
- ASCII

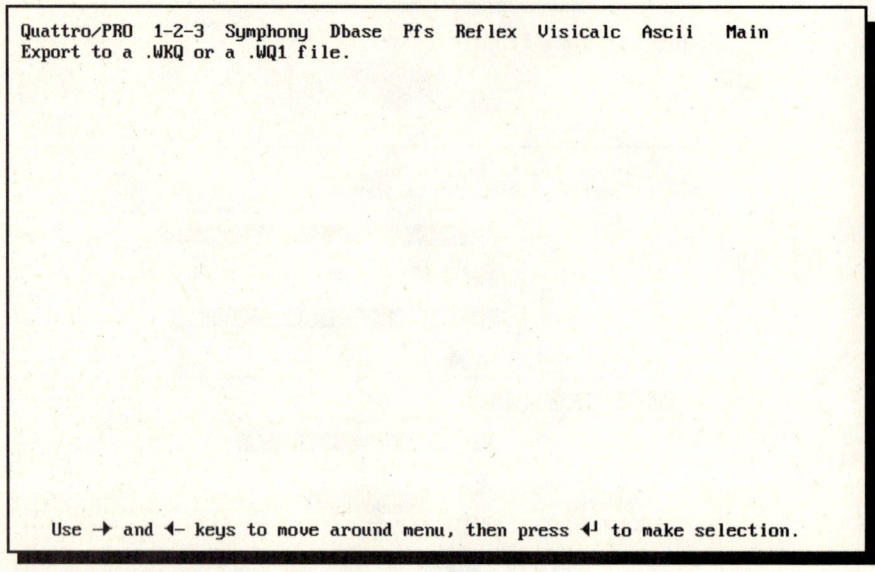

```
Quattro/PRO  1-2-3  Symphony  Dbase  Pfs  Reflex  Visicalc  Ascii   Main
Export to a .WKQ or a .WQ1 file.




















     Use → and ← keys to move around menu, then press ↵ to make selection.
```

Figure 18-5 The Paradox Select File Format screen

Following are a few special rules for exporting data from Paradox to other programs, depending on which program you are exporting to.

First, do not type in a file extension when asked for a filename to export to. The file extension is designated by your menu choice. Simply supply the Paradox filename you want to export to.

Next, regarding certain file formats, be aware of the following special provisions and cautions.

Spreadsheets

Exported Paradox information is translated as row and column information where each column represents a field name and each row represents a record.

VisiCalc

Although DIF is supposed to be an industry-standard format, this isn't always the case. You'll have to consult the target program's manual if problems arise when reading data exported from Paradox in DIF format.

ASCII

You can export two types of ASCII files:

- Delimited
- Text

Delimited looks to the delimiter specified in the CCP to know how to parse the ASCII file into fields.

Text creates an ASCII file with a single row length of 132 characters. If you need to create a fixed-length flat file with more than 132 characters per record, use the report generator and print the table's data to a file. Remember to set your page length to continuous ("C") and remove any unnecessary blank lines with [Ctrl][Y] (DELETELINE).

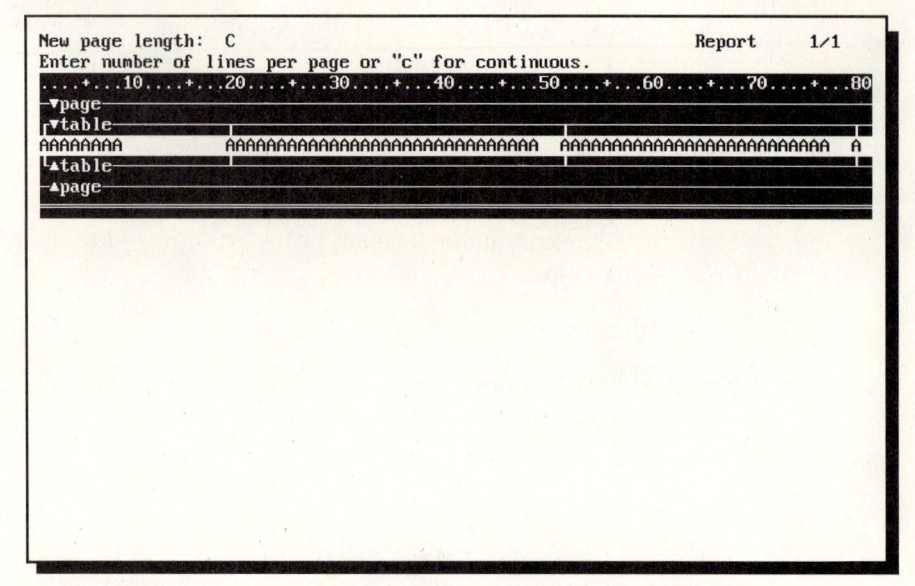

```
New page length:  C                                                Report    1/1
Enter number of lines per page or "c" for continuous.
....+...10....+...20....+...30....+...40....+...50....+...60....+...70....+...80
▼page
▼table
AAAAAAAA         AAAAAAAAAAAAAAAAAAAAAAAAAA    AAAAAAAAAAAAAAAAAAAAAAAA   A
▲table
▲page
```

Figure 18-6 Using the report generator to export fixed-length records

Examples of Keystroke Sequences for Export

NOTE: *The following examples assume that Mstr is both the export table name and the existing Paradox table name.*

Quattro Pro

Version 1

Menu {Tools} {ExportImport} {Export} {Quattro/PRO} {1} Quattro Release 1.X} {Mstr} {Mstr}

Version 2

Menu {Tools} {ExportImport} {Export} {Quattro/PRO} {2} Quattro PRO} {Mstr} {Mstr}

Lotus 1-2-3

Version 1A

Menu {Tools} {ExportImport} {Export} {1-2-3} {1) 1-2-3 Release 1A} {Mstr} {Mstr}

Version 2

Menu {Tools} {ExportImport} {Export} {1-2-3} {2} 1-2-3 Release 2}
{Mstr} {Mstr}

Lotus Symphony

Version 1

Menu {Tools} {ExportImport} {Export} {Symphony}
{1) Symphony Release 1.0} {Mstr} {Mstr}

Version 1.1

Menu {Tools} {ExportImport} {Export} {Symphony}
{2) Symphony Release 1.1} {Mstr} {Mstr}

dBASE

dBASE II

Menu {Tools} {ExportImport} {Export} {Dbase} {1) dBase II} {Mstr} {Mstr}

dBASE III

Menu {Tools} {ExportImport} {Export} {Dbase} {2) dBase III} {Mstr}
{Mstr}

dBASE IV

Menu {Tools} {ExportImport} {Export} {Dbase} {3) dBase IV} {Mstr}
{Mstr}

PFS

Menu {Tools} {ExportImport} {Export} {Pfs} {Mstr} {Mstr}

Reflex

Version 1

Menu {Tools} {ExportImport} {Export} {Reflex} {1) Reflex Release 1.0}
{Mstr} {Mstr}

Version 1.1

Menu {Tools} {ExportImport} {Export} {Reflex} {2) Reflex Release 1.1}
{Mstr} {Mstr} Esc {Mstr2}

VisiCalc (DIF)

Menu {Tools} {ExportImport} {Export} {Visicalc} {Mstr} {Mstr}

ASCII

Delimited
Menu {Tools} {ExportImport} {Export} {Ascii} {Delimited} {Test.txt} {Test}

AppendDelimited
Menu {Tools} {ExportImport} {Export} {Ascii} {AppendDelimited} {Test.txt} {Test}

Text
Menu {Tools} {ExportImport} {Export} {Ascii} {Text} {Test.txt}{Test}

Running Other Programs from Paradox

The key to transferring data between various products is knowing the format requirements of each product.

Using Paradox's RUN and RUN BIG commands, you can launch other programs right from within Paradox. By combining the export techniques above, you can further automate sending data back and forth by invoking AUTOEXEC or other macros from within the other programs.

Here are a few examples:

Launching Microsoft Word and passing it a filename

```
RUN BIG "c:\\word5\\word "+filename
Where filename is the name of a document in the current Paradox
directory.
```

Quattro Pro

Although Quattro Pro can automatically load a table based on how it's configured, you might want to load different files at different times. The following process involves a query, translating the answer to Quattro Pro file format, launching Quattro Pro, and invoking a Quattro Pro macro.

```
MENU {ASK} {ORDERS}
moveto[customer]
Check
moveto[month]
Check
moveto[amount]
typein "calc sum all as TOTAL"
Do_it!
```

```
moveto[customer]
CROSSTABKEY
RESET CLEARALL
Menu {Tools} {ExportImport} {Export} {Quattro/PRO} {2} Quattro
PRO} {crosstab} {QPANS}
MACRONAME = "RUN_REGRESSION"
FILENAME  = "QPANS.WQ1"
RUN BIG "Q "+FILENAME+" "+MACRONAME
```

Lotus 1-2-3

This same process is available to 1-2-3 users except that Paradox cannot read or write version 3 files nor can 1-2-3 accept a filename or macro as it is being launched. (To get the same effect as Quattro Pro, you need to create an Autoexec macro in 1-2-3 that loads a file named "123ANS" and launches the Regression macro.)

```
MENU {ASK} {ORDERS}
moveto[customer]
Check
moveto[month]
Check
moveto[amount]
typein "calc sum all as TOTAL"
Do_it!
moveto[customer]
CROSSTABKEY
RESET CLEARALL
Menu {Tools} {ExportImport} {Export} {1-2-3} {2} 1-2-3 Release 2}
{crosstab} {123ANS}
RUN BIG "\123\123 "
```

Data Modeling with Quattro Pro

Paradox users seeking time-saving and innovative ways to create information systems can look to Borland's Quattro Pro for some dynamic capabilities.

NOTE: *The following techniques can be used with any spreadsheet program that can save its information in Lotus 1-2-3 format. Quattro Pro, however, integrates this process unlike any other spreadsheet.*

One of the difficulties in creating new tables in Paradox is its lack of data modeling functions. For example, when creating table A, you might want to view the structure of table B so that table A can be properly entered. Quattro Pro provides Paradox users with an easy-to-use, visual, data modeling tool.

Data modeling is a process that analyzes and builds the theoretical data structures of an information system prior to actually creating the databases. True data modeling provides rules and methods for fine-tuning and verifying the relationships within data structures. Using data modeling, a developer can ensure the creation of optimum database structures that efficiently store and manipulate a system's information. While the following isn't a full-blown data modeling process, it does provide some useful tools and a methodology for creating your Paradox systems.

Quattro Pro can actually create Paradox tables faster than native Paradox! At the same time, Quattro Pro helps develop the data model by creating the Paradox tables.

If you are not familiar with Quattro Pro, don't worry. If you have used 1-2-3 or the original Quattro, you'll have no trouble with creating quick data models and precise Paradox tables. Quattro Pro has many versatile functions and features but you need to master only a few in order to create data models and Paradox tables.

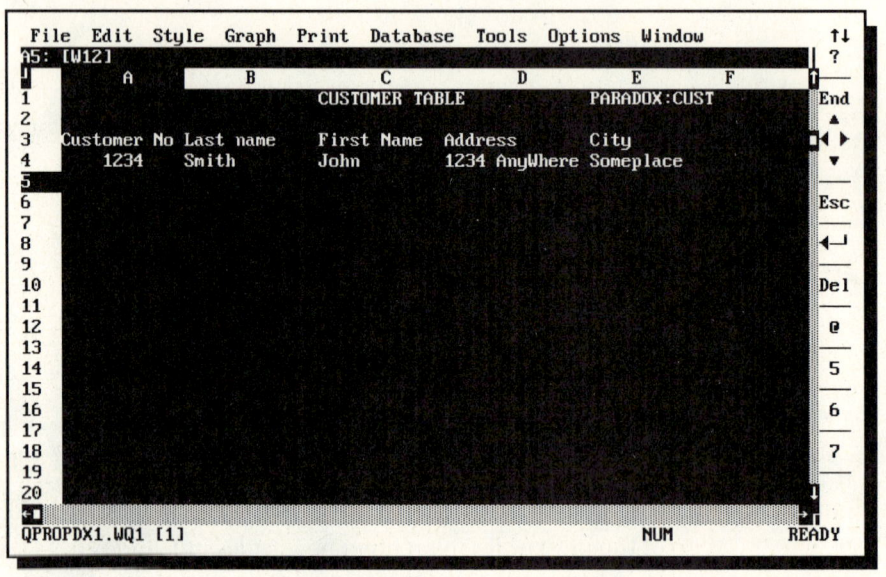

Figure 18-7 The electronic sheet of paper

The Quattro Pro spreadsheet provides the electronic sheet of paper in which to enter the data model. Once you have entered the data model, you transfer the model to Paradox, creating the Paradox tables in the process.

To build the data model:

- Write down the tables you need to create.
- Enter the fields in the table that contain the information to be recorded.
- Add example information to the table's data model to further identify what type of information is to be contained in each field.

Next, identify the different tables in the model using Quattro Pro's Range Name Create function, naming each area on the electronic sheet of paper as the name corresponding to the DOS filename you will give each Paradox table.

Finally, use Quattro Pro's Extract facility to extract each range to a separate file. It is during this process that the Paradox table is actually created.

Step-by-Step: Creating A Data Model Using Quattro Pro

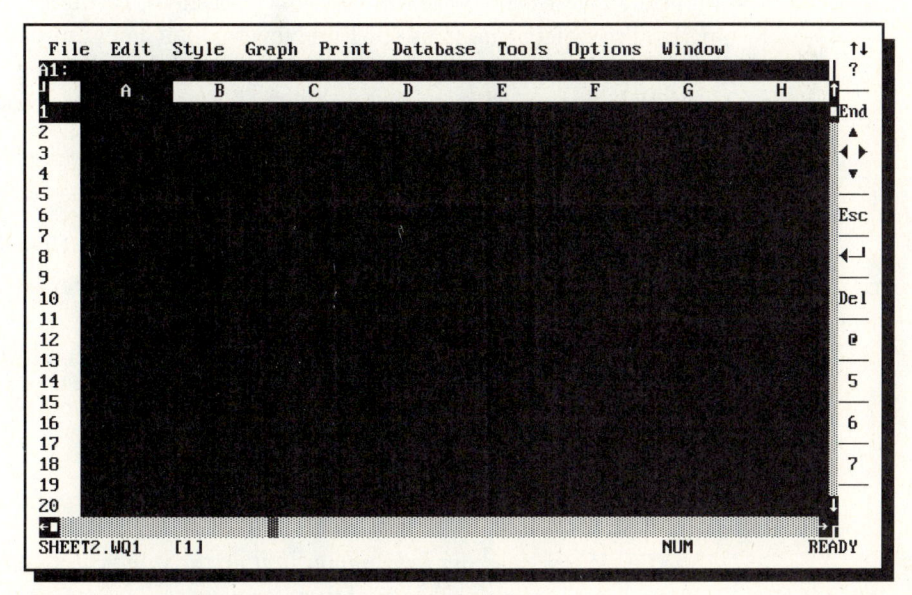

Figure 18-8 Step 1—Start with a new spreadsheet

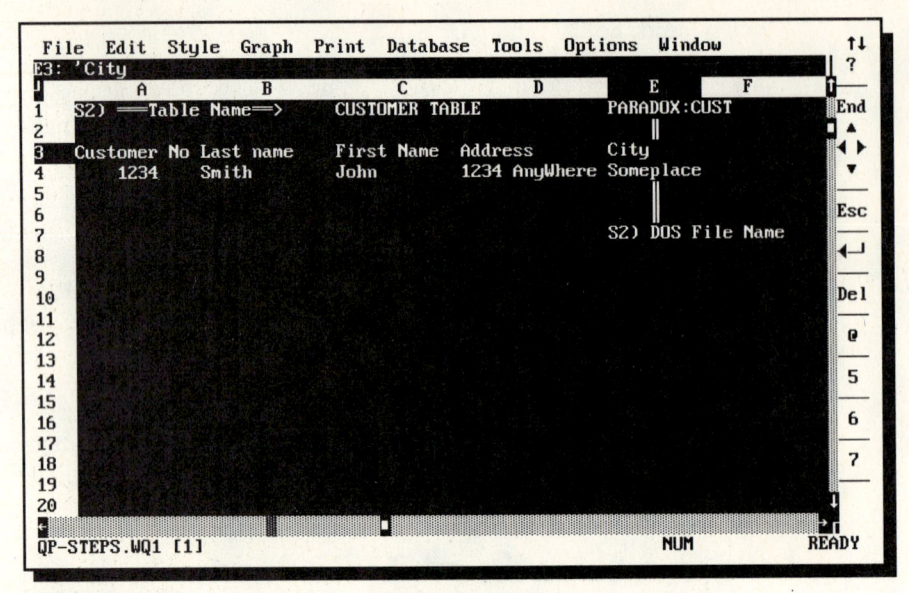

PC World Paradox 3.5—Power Programming Techniques

```
  File   Edit   Style   Graph   Print   Database   Tools   Options   Window        ↑↓
E3: 'City                                                                           ?
       A          B              C              D             E          F       End
1    S2) ══Table Name══>     CUSTOMER TABLE              PARADOX:CUST
2                                                             ║
3    Customer No  Last name   First Name    Address       City                    ◄►
4       1234      Smith       John          1234 AnyWhere Someplace                ▼
5
6                                                                                 Esc
7                                                             S2) DOS File Name
8                                                                                  ↵
9
10                                                                                Del
11
12                                                                                 @
13
14                                                                                 5
15
16                                                                                 6
17
18                                                                                 7
19
20
QP-STEPS.WQ1 [1]                                                    NUM        READY
```

Figure 18-9 Step 2—Enter table and DOS filename

First, start Quattro Pro with a clean, new worksheet. If you're already in Quattro Pro, select File Erase or File New to open a new spreadsheet. (Use the keyboard or mouse to perform these or any of the following commands.) This is the electronic sheet of paper that will record the data model.

It is recommended that you work in the upper-left hand corner of the worksheet.

- Enter the table name in your model, for example: **Customer table**
- Enter the DOS filename (8 characters or less, no spaces), for example: **CUST**
- Drop down two lines and enter the names of the fields to be contained in the table. The field names must be:

   Unique
   25 characters or less
   Entered on one row

NOTE: *When entering field names, follow the same rules and procedures as when you create a table in native Paradox.*

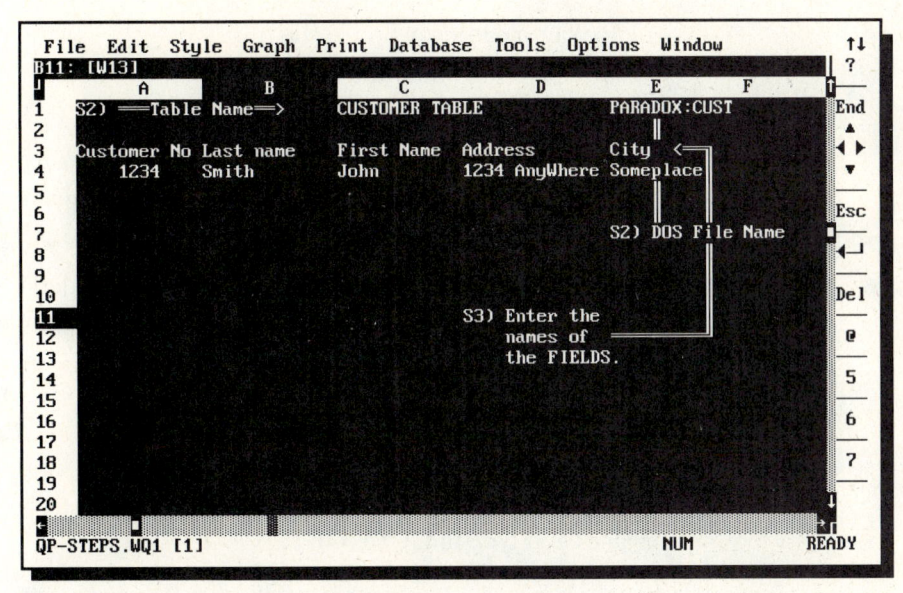

Figure 18-10 Step 3—Enter field names

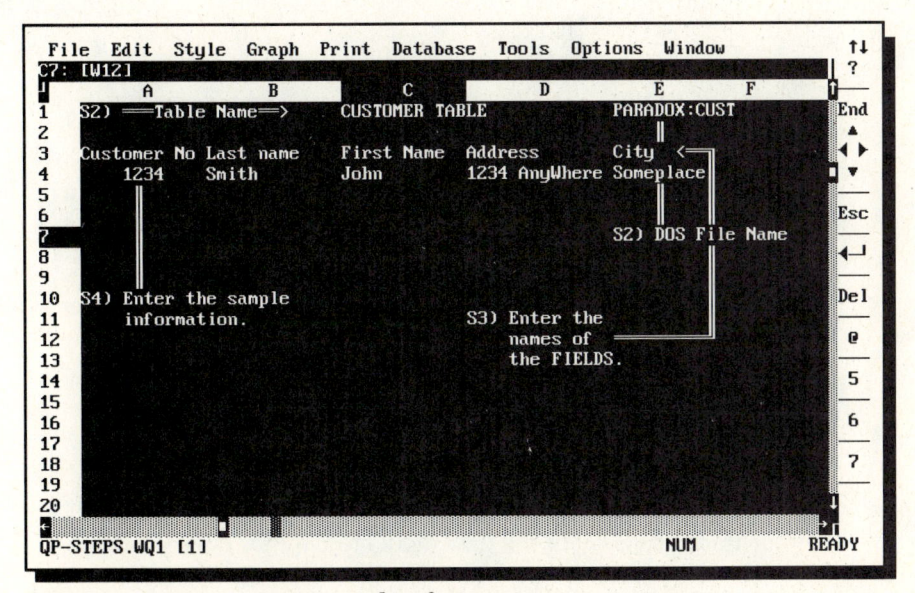

Figure 18-11 Step 4—Enter sample information

- Enter sample information in the row directly below the field names.
- Do not place an underline beneath the field names. The field names (labels) must "sit on" the data they describe.

NOTE: *When creating a Date field (D) in Paradox, be sure to format the sample information as a date field. The result should be an acceptable date format such as 1/1/89.*

- Create a range name for the table. It is recommended that the range name be the same name as the DOS filename previously designated for the table. For example:
    - Select Menu Edit Name Create, type in **Cust**, and press [Enter].
    - Highlight the area containing the field names and the single row of example data, then press [Enter].
- Extract the range and create a Paradox table (select Tools Extract Values and type in **CUST.DB**).

NOTE: *It's important to type in the .DB extension so Quattro Pro will know to create a Paradox table.*

- Press [Enter].
- When Quattro Pro asks for the area to Extract, press [F3] and select the Range Name created for the table (specifically, Cust), and press [Enter].
- Quattro Pro analyzes the requested Extract. It then displays a pop-up menu that:
    - Includes a View of the data structure.
    - Lets you proceed with the Write of the Extract as a Paradox table.
- In View, Quattro Pro lets you view and/or change the Paradox structure before creating the Paradox table.
- For this example, select Write.

Repeat Steps 1 through 7 as many times as needed in order to complete the transformation of the data model to Paradox tables.

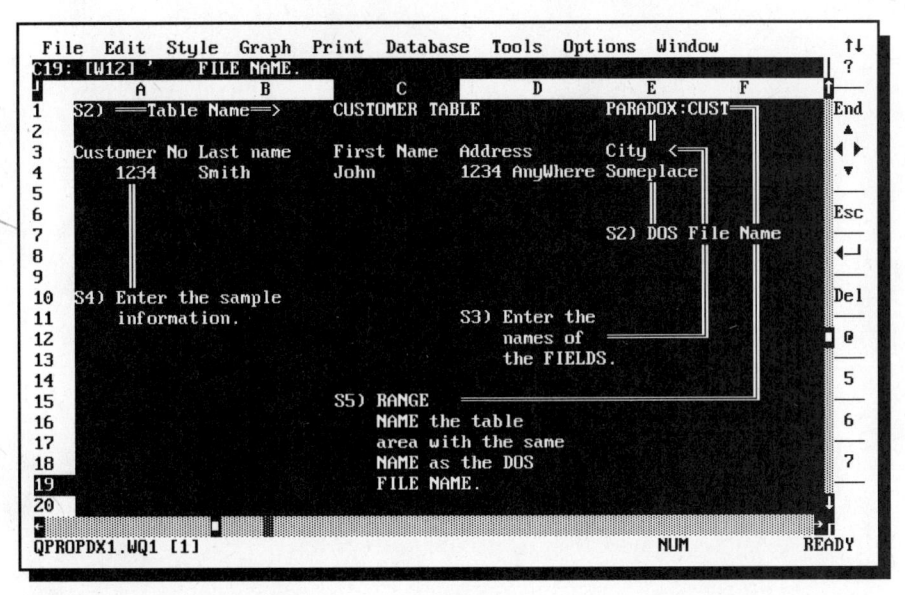

Figure 18-12 Step 5—Create a range name

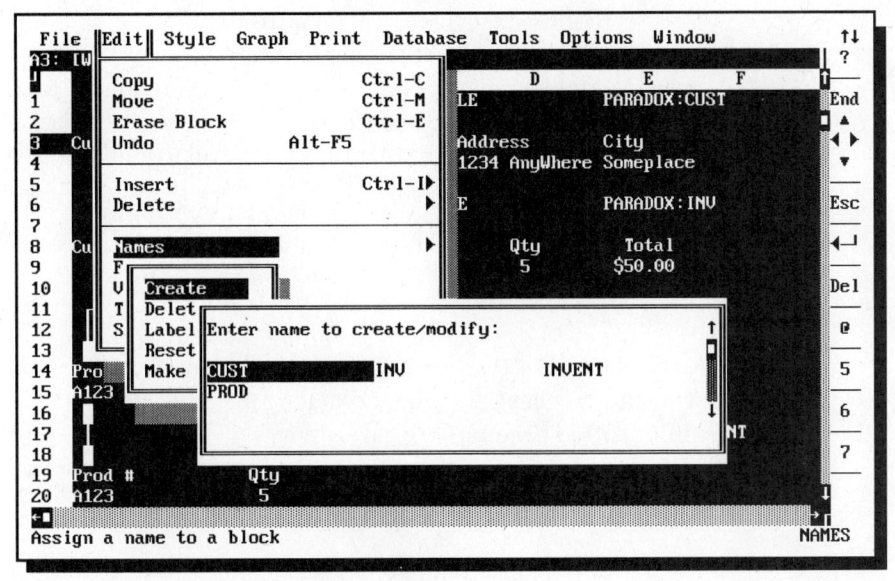

Figure 18-13 Step 6—Extract the range

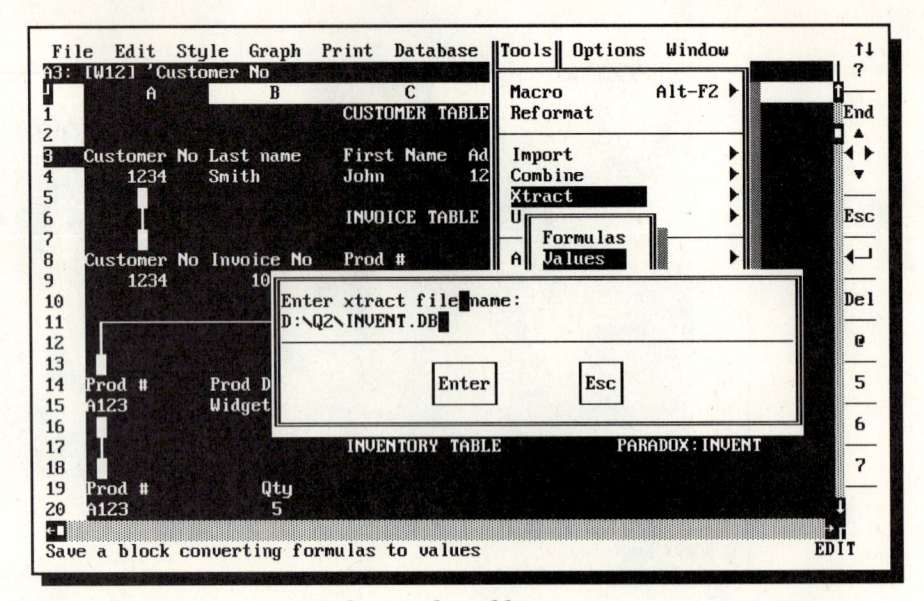

Figure 18-14 Step 7—Create the Paradox table

Figure 18-15 illustrates the use of Quattro Pro's data modeling capabilities by creating a data model containing four tables. To highlight the relationship between the tables, characters from the ASCII extended character set are used to show the links between the tables. Reviewing the data model for its links between tables ensures that the model will work the way you expect it to in the Paradox environment.

To speed up the process of creating tables, wait until the model looks correct and then Extract all of the Range Names, creating the Paradox tables all at the same time.

After your model is completed and your tables are created, Quattro Pro provides an excellent document detailing the table structures contained in the information system.

For those wishing additional information, the Quattro Pro manual goes into the following subjects in greater detail:

- Edit Range Name
- Style Numeric-format
- Tools Extract Range

Integrating Data **601**

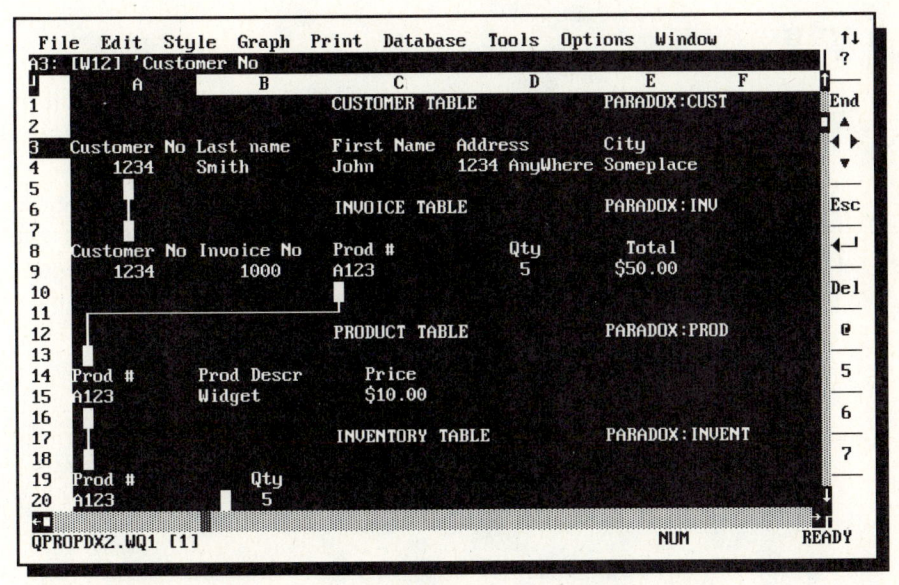

Figure 18-15 Data model for four tables showing links between tables

Here are some final hints to help you with data modeling using Quattro Pro.

TIPS:

- *Don't worry about the column widths while creating the data model. Remember, as each range is extracted, Quattro Pro provides the opportunity to change the Name and Type of each field. Or, if preferred, the data structure can always be restructured in Paradox.*

- *Range name your tables on your worksheet to be the same name as the DOS filename you will give each table. This naming convention will help you keep track of where you are in the data modeling process.*

- *Use the line draw or ASCII extended character set to map the relationship of one table to another.*

Summary

In this chapter, you have examined how you can transfer information to and from Paradox. In addition, you have seen a data modeling technique that uses a tool most PC users have on each and every machine—a spreadsheet. There are many ways to get various products to work with each other and we have covered only a few. The hope is that this discussion prompts you to think of different ways to exchange data and use other programs. In the next chapter we take an in-depth look at how Paradox views memory and how you can take advantage of it.

19 Understanding and Managing Paradox Memory

When the tide has turned in a game or when momentum shifts from one side to another, you'll often here an announcer remark "Folks, it's a whole new ball game!" Such is the case with Paradox 3.5 and how it provides and manages memory. Unless you have at least a rudimentary understanding of how Paradox manages memory, you are doomed to rely on its ability to know what resources your applications and the machines using your applications require. Paradox simply cannot do the job alone. You need to step in and help it along. Table 19-1 lists some terms we will address in this chapter.

Table 19-1
Key Terms and Concepts

VROOMM	Extended	Expanded
Cache	Command line	Buffers
Temporary space	MEMLEFT	RMEMLEFT
Protected mode	Real mode	Windows
Shadow RAM	Graphic memory	

Because Borland has included VROOMM (Virtual Runtime Object-Oriented Memory Manager), Paradox 3.5 heralds a big change for Paradox developers. VROOMM lets Paradox optimize application memory resources by allowing it to swap itself and its application code in and out of memory.

Paradox can run in either protected or real mode. If you have a 286, 386, or 486 machine, Paradox addresses up to 16MB of extended memory. This means that you don't have to buy a special version of Paradox (Paradox 386) to gain better performance on your 386 or higher platforms, while your 286's are left to wallow with less memory and poorer performance. Paradox can now take full advantage of all of the memory on your 286 or higher platforms. We say *can* because, depending on your application's requirements, you might want to use only a portion of those memory resources for Paradox.

If you run other programs from within Paradox (such as Lotus 1-2-3, Microsoft Word, or Quattro Pro), you'll want to leave enough memory for those programs to run as expected. If you plan to run Paradox under DESQview or Windows 3.0, you'll need to take special care in how you start Paradox. Without any restrictions or parameters on how it should run, Paradox takes over all available resources. To keep it from clobbering some other vital application capability, you need to tackle 3.5's new memory management scheme and tune your system for optimum *overall* performance.

How Paradox Looks at Memory

Now that Paradox can run on 286 or higher platforms, let's take a moment to understand the difference between expanded and extended memory.

Expanded and extended memory are often confused because they sound the same and they both deal with your PC's memory. But they provide you with two very different ways of handling programs and data, which can result in a very confusing situation.

Extended memory is only available on 286 or higher platforms. Unless you configure a RAM disk (an electronic form of a disk drive), a 286 can only access this memory while it's running in *protected* mode. Programs that can access extended memory out-perform those that don't because they can utilize the extended memory for whatever purpose they desire.

In contrast, expanded memory exists only if an EMS driver (for example, EMS, REMM, QEMM, or 386/Max) is configured in your CONFIG.SYS when your machine is booted. This driver creates a control page that manipulates up to 16MB of expanded memory, in the form of 16K pages.

Expanded memory is a fine place to store temporary data but it is no place to put program code. Another name for expanded memory is bank-switched memory because banks of memory are switched on and off. No program wants to be halted by an on/off memory mechanism. Even if this could work, performance would suffer. Expanded memory is great to extend a spreadsheet's resources or even a flat-file database manager, but its uses are limited.

If you have both expanded *and* extended memory, it's generally best to run Paradox in extended or protected mode. Even though running in protected mode is preferred, the next best thing is to run in real mode with expanded memory.

> **NOTE:** *Paradox 3.5 doesn't care where it gets its extended memory. If you use an XMS-conforming product such as QEMM from Quarterdeck or Qualista's 386 to the Max, Paradox will run in protected mode. Currently, Paradox has a conflict with the way HIMEM.SYS (used for Windows 3.0), allocates and controls extended memory. If you plan to run in Windows, it's best to run Paradox in real mode until this issue is resolved.*

Protected Mode versus Real Mode

Protected mode and real mode are features that depend on the processor of your computer. 8086 and 8088 processors can run Paradox in real mode only (with expanded memory if you desire). An AT-class (80286) or higher processor can run in real or protected mode.

Paradox 3.5 runs in protected mode if it can. If you have a system with only 640K of conventional memory and 1MB as shadow RAM, then you'll need to add at least 512K of extended memory. If you're adding memory to your machine, we suggest that you go for 2 to 4MB (for your 286 or higher). This way you'll have a machine that can run any of today's DOS programs, but will also be capable of running environments such as Windows and DESQview.

Paradox chooses to run in real mode if:

- You're running Paradox on an 8086 or 8088 machine.
- You have a 286 or higher platform but you have less than 1MB of memory.
- You have a 286 or higher that Paradox can't recognize.
- You load conflicting software with your hardware setup.

> **NOTE:** *Systems with shadow RAM can use this memory as extended memory only if it is absolutely free (not allocated for any other purpose such as caching or video memory). Some machines will copy ROM's to shadow RAM to improve performance. If your machine falls into this category, add more extended memory to avoid possible conflicts.*

Paradox Graphics and Expanded Memory Conflicts

Paradox will access your video graphics memory in the adapter segment of your PC's memory according to the type of graphics card in your system. You should make sure that any expanded memory driver avoids overlapping these graphic memory positions. Exclude the following video memory addresses in your CONFIG.SYS:

Type of video graphics	Exclude
EGA/VGA	A000-AFFF
CGA	B800-BFFF
Hercules (or emulated)	B000-BFFF
MCGA	A000-AFFF
AT&T	B800-BFFF
3270 PC	B800-BFFF
Tandy 1000	B800-BFFF

To exclude an adapter memory address in your expanded memory setup, use an exclusion parameter in the statement of your CONFIG.SYS that loads your expanded memory driver.

Intel AboveBoard Example

The following example loads your expanded memory driver, avoids EGA/VGA/MCGA video conflicts, and starts your control page for expanded memory at C800.

DEVICE = EMM.SYS at 258 EXCLUDE=A000-AFFF EXPF=C800 MC

Sometimes you need to exclude more than one area of memory to avoid other hardware conflicts such as network cards and scanning devices. Most expanded memory drivers let you exclude multiple adapter memory address segments.

AST Rampage Example

The following example avoids a network card packet at B000 as well as a possible conflict with CGA/AT&T/3270/TANDY1000 video memory.

DEVICE=REMM.SYS /X=B000-BFFF,B800-BFFF

Getting More Memory Out of your 286

There are three additional ways to get more memory out of 286 or higher platforms, especially the 286. 80386 or higher machines are generally not as much of a problem, but you can use the following techniques to give them maximum memory capabilities.

- Use an adapter segment memory manager such as Quarterdeck's QRAM or Qualista's Move-em.
- Run DOS LAN MAN 2.0 to load the DOS redirector high (network stations).
- Plan on switching to DOS 5.x in the future.

An adapter memory manager is easy to configure and very similar to setting up your expanded memory. Products like QRAM and Move-em let you grab any unallocated memory between 640K and 1MB. Once you grab this memory, you can load special provisions that let you load DOS parameters such as FILES, BUFFERS, mouse drivers, ANSI.SYS, even your network and 3270 keyboard drivers into the adapter segment of your system. Because these programs move these parameters and drivers high, more low memory (under 640K) is made available for other uses.

Even networked PC's gain at least 32K or more of DOS memory. Whether you're running in protected or real mode (especially if you're running Windows) you can highly utilize this extra DOS memory. Think of DOS 640K memory as near memory and expanded/extended as far memory. Whether you run in protected or real mode, the more near memory you have, the better the system and application performance.

These adapter memory managers *are not* expanded memory. In fact, they really need an expanded memory driver and board to be truly effective. Like their expanded memory counterparts, you should load these drivers with exclusion statements to avoid possible conflicts with hardware and software devices.

Intel AboveBoard with QRAM example

To load your expanded memory and adapter memory manager drivers and avoid conflict with a network card located at B000 on a machine with EGA graphics, your CONFIG.SYS should look like this:

CONFIG.SYS

>   **device=emm.sys at 258 X=A000-AFFF-BFFF EXPF=C800 MC**
>   **device=qram.sys X=A000-BFFF**

Now, to load your 3270 keyboard macro driver, mouse, and ANSI.SYS high, add these statements:

>   **device=loadhi.sys \network\kmacdrv.sys -1**
>   **device=loadhi.sys \dos\ansi.sys**
>   **device=loadhi.sys \mouse\mouse.sys**

The final touch is making your CONFIG.SYS take up as little DOS memory as possible. Add these statements:

>   **files=5**
>   **buffers=1**
>   **fcbs=1,0**
>   **stacks=0,0**
>   **lastdrive=d** (where "d" is the highest drive on your workstation)

Next, so that Paradox and your other DOS-based programs can perform, add the following statements to your AUTOEXEC.BAT. These statements pump up your files, buffers, and so forth so your DOS programs can run. You accomplish this by using the COM version of the LOADHI.SYS driver to move these parameters into the memory now allocated to the adapter memory manager.

AUTOEXEC.BAT

>   **loadhi /h files=30**
>   **loadhi /h buffers=20**
>   **loadhi /h fcbs=16,8**
>   **loadhi /h lastdriv = z** (for network stations)

There are other steps you can take with an adapter memory manager to give you back even more DOS 640K memory, though we tend not to use them since they turn off Paradox's ability to view a graph.

DOS LAN MAN 2.0 and loading network drivers high

This is your second option, and is especially good news for network users. With the advent of DOS LAN MAN 2.0, the DOS redirector (30K) can be loaded into extended memory using HIMEM.SYS. To use this you must add:

> **device=himem.sys**

as the very first statement (or directly after your expanded memory driver statement on 286's) in your CONFIG.SYS. If you're loading an MS-NET NetBIOS-compatible network, you can then designate that the DOS redirector be loaded high when the network is loaded.

For Novell users, there are several products and techniques you can use to load network drivers outside of conventional DOS 640K memory. Consult your Novell dealer for details on how you can make use of the loading high capability.

DOS 5.x

Using DOS version 5.x is your third option for maximizing memory resources on a 286 machine. Microsoft must have thought that third-party vendors like Qualistas and Quarterdeck had the right idea because they're packing similar capabilities in their next release of DOS. DOS will take up less conventional memory and you'll be able to load the parameters and follow the techniques listed in the first option to gain even more DOS memory.

Running Caching Programs: Super PC Qwik, Lightning, Paul Mace

Contrary to popular belief, Paradox can use a lot of help when it comes to caching and speeding up disk access. Because of Paradox's VMM provisions (Virtual Memory Manager, now incorporated into their VROOMM technology), even if Paradox has the maximum amount of memory available, it still has to read and write from your disk.

We recommend that unless your machine includes a hardware cache on your controller card of at least 32K, you run Super PC Qwik, Lightning, or Paul Mace's caching programs.

When you do so, be sure to turn Paradox's caching off (set Paradox's cache to 0 in the CCP or start Paradox from the DOS command line with the -cacheK 0 parameter). Also, don't set up a huge disk cache—it's basically a waste of vital DOS memory in return for no better performance than if you set up a smaller disk cache.

We recommend you set your cache in the range of 60-100K. Most of the products discussed in this chapter can run the cache in expanded memory (another reason to have both expanded and extended memory), taking as little as 12K of conventional DOS memory.

Some of the following sections are excerpts from the Paradox 3.5 README.

Running Paradox from Windows

Paradox 3.5 will run under all Windows 3.0 modes—real, protected, and enhanced (386). It does so by running itself in real mode only. VROOMM is still working for you and performance is good but this configuration prevents Paradox 3.5 from running in protected mode, which precludes using the SQL Link add-on product.

Of course, the fastest and best performance can be gained by running Paradox 3.5 outside of Windows where it can run in protected mode and access the extended memory Windows is monopolizing. Both Borland and Microsoft have stated their intent to make their access to XMS-compliant memory more well-behaved with each other. Look for future improvements.

Here are a number of other items you should consider when running Paradox 3.5 under Windows.

You can run Paradox 3.5 and the Paradox Personal Programmer (PPROG) under Windows 3.0. In order to do this you need to take four steps:

Copy the .PIF and .GRP files from the \WINDOWS subdirectory on your Paradox Installation/Sample Tables disk into your Windows di-

rectory (usually C:\WINDOWS). The PARADOX.PIF and PPROG.PIF files allow Paradox and the Personal Programmer to run optimally under Windows. PARADOX.GRP gives Windows a program manager icon for Paradox 3.5 that contains icons for Paradox 3.5 and the Paradox Personal Programmer.

Make sure your Paradox system directory is in your DOS PATH statement, so Windows can find the files.

Run the DOS SHARE program. (Type SHARE at any DOS prompt or add a SHARE statement to your AUTOEXEC.BAT file.) SHARE must be resident to run Paradox 3.5 under Windows.

Set up a program group in Windows to put a Paradox icon on the Windows Program Manager screen. To make this program group,

- Choose File from the Windows Program Manager.
- Choose New, then choose Program Group.
- Fill in a description of the group to appear under the icon (for example, PARADOX 3.5).
- Fill in the full path name of the group file (for example, C:\WINDOWS\PARADOX.GRP).
- Click OK. Two new icons appear in your Paradox 3.5 window: one for Paradox 3.5 and one, PProg, for the Paradox Personal Programmer.

Running Paradox from DESQview

Here are some special provisions for running Paradox and PPROG under DESQview:

- Install Paradox 3.5 according to the installation instructions in the Introduction to Paradox manual or the Upgrade Guide.
- From the DESQview Main menu, choose Open Window.
- If you are upgrading from Paradox 3.0 to 3.5, select Paradox3 from the file list, then choose Change a Program. If you are installing Paradox for the first time, you'll first have to use Add a Program to add the program name to this list.
- Press the F1 function key to see the Standard Options screen. Type the program name, any batch file name you use to invoke it, the full path name (including filename), and any command-line parameters

you use. Set Memory Size (in K) to 440. Set the Standard Option switches as follows:

Writes Text To Screen	[N]*
Displays Graphics Info	[Y]
Virtualize Text/Graphics	[N]**
Uses Serial Ports	[N]
Requires Floppy	[N]

- Press F1 again for the Advanced Options screen. Set the following parameters:

System memory	0
Max Program Size (in K)	640
Script Buffer Size	1000
Max Expanded Memory	1024***

- Set the switches as follows:

Close On Exit	[ ](blank)
Allow Close Window Command	[N]
Uses Math Coprocessor	[Y]
Share CPU When Foreground	[Y]
Can Be Swapped Out	[ ](blank)
Use Its Own Colors	[Y]
Run In Background	[ ](blank)
Keyboard Conflict	[0]
Share EGA When Foreground	[Y]
Protection Level	[0]

* On 286 machines, set this switch to Yes.

** On a 286 machine or on a 386 or higher machine running in protected mode, set this switch to Yes.

*** Max Expanded Memory can be set higher, if you have more.

- Exit Change a Program or Add a Program and start Paradox in the usual way under DESQview.

Use the same procedure to configure DESQview to run the Paradox Personal Programmer.

If you want to run multiple Paradox sessions under DESQview, you should make the Paradox program files read-only. Also note that you'll need one Paradox serial number for each session. Be sure you run the DOS SHARE program prior to entering DESQview and be sure that you load Paradox with the -share option.

Special Troubleshooting Notes

Not every installation is quite the same, and often you'll run into incompatibilities as hardware and software go through normal progressive changes. Here is a list of known Paradox configuration problems, excerpted from the Paradox 3.5 README:

Paradox conforms to the major standards that do exist: the VDISK standard for RAM disks, the VCPI standard for EMS emulation, and the XMS standard for extended memory. If you use software that conforms to some other standard, you may have to make adjustments to run Paradox.

- *If you're running your machine in fast mode, it may be running faster than the hardware was designed to run. This may cause it to drop instructions occasionally at its fastest speed. While some of your software may run okay, Paradox sometimes makes heavier demands on the hardware than other software packages. If you experience difficulty, try running Paradox in slower or "safe" mode. (This is not to say that all machines offering a choice of speeds are suspect; Paradox will not have trouble on any machine's highest speed as long as all the machine's components are designed to run at that speed.) Machines that may experience this problem include 6MHz IBM ATs that have been sped up to 8MHz or faster, the WYSEpc 286 in its 12.5MHz mode, and the Rose Hill 286 at its faster speed.*
- *The Tall Tree JRAM EMS card is not supported by Paradox.*
- *286 machines with old BIOSs might not be able to run in protected mode. Because there were initially no real-world applications to test those BIOSs, they sometimes have bugs.*
- *A disk cache called VCache is known to be incompatible with Paradox. Do not run VCache with Paradox.*
- *Some EMS emulators can run without allocating an EMS page frame. This lets you use their many extra features, particularly the*

ability to relocate drivers above 640K, even if you don't want to use EMS. QEMM's FRAME=NONE option has this effect, as does 386Max's NOFRAME option. If you use your EMS emulator this way, you must run Paradox in real mode (this is the mode it will run in by default). Attempting to force Paradox into protected mode in this situation might hang your machine.

- If you use a version of PC LAN that includes a cache and you locate the cache in the network server's extended memory, you cannot run Paradox on the server—there isn't enough memory below 640K left for Paradox to run in real mode, and the PC LAN cache does not allow any other program to use extended memory.
- The AST REX.SYS driver, which converts EEMS expanded memory back to extended memory, is not compatible with Paradox 3.5. To obtain extended memory with an EEMS board, don't let the REMM.SYS expanded memory driver use some or all of the memory on the board. (In some cases, you will have to set switches on the board to accomplish this.)
- Under DOS 2.x, Paradox 3.5 runs only in real mode, not in protected mode.

Testing Your CPU and EMS

Intermittent failures may be due to a processor that's running too fast or memory that is defective or runs too slowly. Paradox includes two small programs to test for problems of this sort. Although they cannot detect all machine problems, they do test machine components that Paradox 3.5 stresses; as a result, they often help pinpoint problem areas. The programs are CPUTEST.EXE and EMSTEST.COM. Both are installed in your Paradox 3.5 program directory automatically. If you have any reason to suspect that your hardware may not be able to keep up with Paradox, you should run both programs (run only CPUTEST if you don't have expanded memory). Even if your computer is running flawlessly, feel free to try them out. CPUTEST runs just a few seconds, and EMSTEST just a few minutes.

To run CPUTEST, just move to your Paradox directory (usually \PDOX35) and type:

```
CPUTEST
```

You should see the message "This CPU Tests OK." A message like "2 instructions skipped" probably indicates that your computer's processor is running too fast.

To run EMSTEST, move to your Paradox directory, type:

>   *EMSTEST*

... and press keys as instructed. The test will verify that your Expanded Memory Specification (EMS) hardware and software are working correctly. You should see descriptions of a number of tests, each followed by the status "OK." Any other status message indicates a probable EMS failure.

Summary

Managing memory is a key component in ensuring maximum system performance. There are a number of ways to improve performance. When in doubt, let's face it—the best way to enhance your system may be to throw a little money at it. In the long run, a small investment in expanded and extended memory and adapter segment memory managers can go a long way in providing your systems and applications optimal performance. In the next chapter, we'll look at a number of products that can enhance your development capabilities, including ways to manipulate Paradox without loading it.

20

Getting More out of Paradox

If Paradox had every tool you'd ever need built into it, you wouldn't need third-party products. However, you'd have to give up trivial items such as data integrity and performance in order to gain these capabilities. Paradox doesn't include every feature you can think of, but it does include the essentials and a lot more. And, thankfully, there are a number of excellent add-on products for Paradox and the Paradox development environment. The products described in this chapter are by no means the only ones available, but they are either our personal favorites, or simply interesting programs.

In addition to the products we'll discuss, there are several organizations that provide excellent training. We mention only a few, and concentrate on training seminars we've found beneficial in gaining valuable Paradox knowledge.

Finally, there are a number of ways to get help with Paradox. Third-party books, such as this one, are certainly one way. We recommend a number of books, and also tell you how to get online support from Borland for a mere hook-up and use charge.

Paradox Add-ons and Utilities

The Paradox add-ons and utilities we will discuss can be divided into the following categories:

- Script editors
- Documentation tools

- Value-added Paradox functions/capabilities
- Training organizations
- Books, newsletters, and support

Script Editors

Besides your trusty old word processor (sorry Microsoft and WordPerfect) and EDIT3 included with this book, there are a number of text editors that greatly enhance your development efforts. The three we use most often are:

- PlayRight Pro
- PAL-EDIT
- QEDIT

PlayRight Pro

PlayRight Pro, from The Burgiss Group, is an excellent text editor that was designed specifically for the Paradox environment. PlayRight Pro sports a Paradox-like menu system that goes out of its way to use the same naming and procedural conventions that Paradox uses. The product can be run stand-alone or integrated into Paradox (designate it as your editor in the Paradox Custom Configuration Program). One of the more useful features of PlayRight Pro is the ability to view table structures from within the editor. You don't have to exit your script and perform a *Menu* {*Tools*} {*Info*} {*Structure*} *tablename*—PlayRight Pro shows you the structure of any table from anywhere in your application.

Product Summary

PRODUCT:	PlayRight Pro
VENDOR:	The Burgiss Group One Newark Street Suite 5B Hoboken, NJ 07030 (800)-262-8069 (Orders only)
CATEGORY:	Editor

FEATURES:	Run from within Paradox
	Paradox-style menus
	View a structure from within editor
	Script formatting
	Multifile capability
	Reserved word checks
	Search, Replace, Copy, Erase block
COMMENTS:	For developer who doesn't use the Paradox Engine.

PAL-EDIT

PAL-EDIT (Kallista, Inc., Chicago) is a customized version of the very popular Multi-Edit (American Cybernetic). Like PlayRight Pro, it too can display the structure of a table while editing a script. It also has the capability to display procedure declarations with a few keystrokes. It features a lexicon that includes all Paradox commands and key codes. With a flick of the wrist and a keypress, you can instantly insert Paradox commands, functions, and keycodes into your scripts.

You can fully customize PAL-EDIT. Any key or favorite macro can be set up fairly easily. PAL-EDIT does have a different menu style so Paradox users might need a few hours to get used to the way the product thinks. If you program in other languages (such as C) and your aren't married to your current text editor, you'll find PAL-EDIT a delight.

Product Summary

PRODUCT:	PAL-EDIT
VENDOR:	Kallista, Inc.
	600 South Dearborn Street
	Suite 504
	Chicago, IL 60605
	(312)-663-0101
CATEGORY:	Editor
FEATURES:	Run from within Paradox
	View a structure from within editor
	Script formatting

Multifile capability
Reserved word checks
Search, Replace, Copy, Erase block
Communication add-on
Macro source code available

COMMENTS: Great value for developer looking for a Paradox-specific or general text editor.

QEDIT

QEDIT (the "quick editor") is a shareware editor available on most Bulletin Board Systems (BBS). Published by SemWare, QEDIT is primarily for programmers. It requires 96K of system memory and cannot be called directly from Paradox (specifically, you can't Cancel/Debug right into QEDIT at the line where your error occurred). Programmers working on large systems should find QEDIT familiar as it has the look and feel of XEDIT. QEDIT is very inexpensive and a very good editor for the price. One of the more cumbersome aspects of QEDIT is its lack of a robust macro capability. Still, many Paradox developers find that QEDIT gives them all the editing power they need.

Product Summary

PRODUCT: QEDIT

VENDOR: SemWare c/o Sammy Mitchell
136 Mark Lane
Smyrna, GA 30080
Available on popular BBS's

CATEGORY: Editor

FEATURES: Script formatting
Multifile capability
Search, Replace, Copy, Erase block

COMMENTS: Simple to use, inexpensive editor. Good if you haven't yet decided on PlayRight Pro or PAL-EDIT.

Documentation Tools

Aside from our own documentor, included on disk with this book, there are a number of products that bring tremendous documentation capabilities to your Paradox projects. Following are brief discussions of just a few of these products.

ScriptView

ScriptView is an absolute must for any Paradox programmer. ScriptView is not an editor, but it can format your scripts in seconds, changing Paradox keywords and your own user-defined procedures into capitalized or proper word format. ScriptView sports a wide array of reports, including:

- Action diagrams
- Call reports
- Cross reference reports
- Procedure reports
- User-defined reports
- Family object reports
- Formatted script output

ScriptView allows you to work with a single script or with multiple scripts. It does this by giving you the capability to form a list of scripts into a project. This project file can then produce any of these reports, and output either to a printer or to a file (it even allows you to view its reports to the screen prior to outputting a report). ScriptView can be called from Paradox and can be fully customized to your specific needs.

If you're not big on using tools, make ScriptView one of the tools you will use. It saves a great deal of time compiling system documentation and it produces quality report output.

Product Summary

PRODUCT: ScriptView

VENDOR: FarPoint Systems Corp.
           Washington & York Streets
           P.O. Box 13093
           Jersey City, NJ 07303

CATEGORY: Documentation tool

FEATURES: Run from within Paradox
Script formatting
Multifile capability
Reserved word and user dictionary checks
Variety of reports available

COMMENTS: Great value, every Paradox developer should have a copy of this program.

ParaLex

ParaLex, from Zenreich Systems, is another tool no developer should be without. Alan Zenreich has created some of the tightest, well-behaved PAL code that does a fantastic job of documenting your Paradox tables and system. ParaLex is the closest thing the Paradox developer has to a data dictionary. ParaLex reports on your table's structures, fields, field types, validity checks, indexes, and even user rights. ParaLex has a host of reports that can be sent to the printer, screen, or to a file. ParaLex is totally menu-driven, easy-to-use, and includes information every developer can use to enhance their projects.

Product Summary

PRODUCT: ParaLex

VENDOR: Zenreich Systems
208 Kinderkamack Road
Oradell, NJ 97649
(201)-261-3325

CATEGORY: Documentation tool

FEATURES: Data dictionary
Variety of reports

COMMENTS: Excellent value. Along with ScriptView, a must for every developer.

ParaTrak

ParaTrak, from Financial Modeling Specialists, is a procedure-tracking program somewhat similar to, though more limited than, ScriptView. This is a nice little utility to have if you don't need a tool with all the capabilities of ScriptView.

Product Summary

PRODUCT:	ParaTrak
VENDOR:	Financial Modeling Specialists, Inc. P.O. Box 1251 Arlington, VA 22210 (703)-356-4700
CATEGORY:	Documentation tool
FEATURES:	Documents relationships between procedures in an application.
COMMENTS:	Nice product. Not a ScriptView, but provides a nice documentation and diagnostic capability.

Other Paradox Add-ons

K-MEMO

K-MEMO is another product from Kallista. This product uses the Paradox Engine and provides long text capability (128 rows per comment/note). The data is actually stored in a Paradox table. Easy to integrate into your existing applications, K-MEMO is a very useful add-on for a number of Paradox applications. Paradox SQL users should note that K-MEMO employs RUN BIG, which breaks your SQL connection. You'll need to write a mechanism to re-attach to your database server once you exit your K-MEMO routine.

Product Summary

PRODUCT:	K-MEMO

VENDOR:	Kallista, Inc. 600 South Dearborn Street Suite 504 Chicago, IL 60605 (312)-663-0101
CATEGORY:	Long text add-on utility
FEATURES:	Run from within Paradox Simple word processing capability
COMMENTS:	Nice product. SQL users will need to make special provisions for using this product.

TextView

TextView is another long text product for Paradox. It is produced by The Burgiss Group. Unlike K-MEMO, TextView does not store its long text in a Paradox table. The K-MEMO advantage of storing information in Paradox tables is somewhat offset by TextView's speed and ease of use. You can easily print information and export your long text document to an ASCII file. TextView does not require RUN BIG, although you can increase the program's capability by invoking it with RUN BIG versus RUN.

Product Summary

PRODUCT:	TextView
VENDOR:	The Burgiss Group One Newark Street, Suite 5B Hoboken, NJ 07030 (800)-262-8069 (Orders only)
CATEGORY:	Long text add-on utility
FEATURES:	Run from within Paradox Paradox-style menus Fast, easy-to-use Search, Replace, Copy, Erase block

COMMENTS: If you want to query your text data then K-MEMO is for you; for speed and word processing, TextView is your ticket.

DeskTop for Paradox

DeskTop for Paradox is a compilation of more than 30 useful add-in functions for your development environment. Some of its features include a simple MiniNotePad, Calculator, Calendar, ASCII table, and Box Draw functions. DeskTop's pop-up reference is especially helpful. Other functions help you reduce keystrokes and automate the more repetitive functions of using Paradox. Source code is available. (See the vendor information for Kallista for ordering details.)

pTools

pTools is a very interesting collection of Paradox tools. pTools includes Browse, List, Append, Query, Import, Compare, Export, and inventory capabilities to work with objects. It also has a crosstab capability for Paradox 2.0 users. All of these functions are available without entering Paradox itself. This is a very nice utility to use in conjunction with other programs such as word processors, spreadsheets, and communication programs. The vendor is CompuMethods Company, P.O. Box 338, Westminster, CA 94684; (714) 893-6838.

OverDrive 2 for Microsoft Word

OverDrive 2 for Microsoft Word is a mail-merge utility that does not require Paradox to run. This product lets you query a Paradox table directly and export its information to a merge document created in Microsoft Word. You can automate the merge of up to twenty tables and letters in just a few keystrokes. This product has a full-blown document capability, so it's not for the faint of heart. If you produce a lot of mailings, this product can solve a number of headaches and streamline your process at the same time.

Product Summary

PRODUCT: OverDrive 2

VENDOR: OverDrive Systems, Inc.
23811 Chagrin Blvd
Suite 260
Cleveland, OH 44122
(216)-292-3425, (800) 284-7600

CATEGORY: Mail-merge utility/Documentation tool

FEATURES: Run from within Paradox
Data dictionary
Library reports
Query by form
Multiple document assembly

COMMENTS: A hidden treasure for most Paradox users. Great value for large mailing-house applications.

Training Organizations and Seminars

You can never know too much about Paradox. There are a number of Paradox/PAL training and consultation outfits, but for our money, the following organizations are the best of the best.

Softbite International, Ltd.
33 North Addison Road
Suite 206
P.O. Box 1401
Addison, IL 60101
(708) 833-0006

Brian J. Smith and Associates
901-A North Pacific Coast Highway
Suite 200
Redondo Beach, CA 90277
(213) 374-0151

Kallista, Incorporated
600 South Dearborn Street
Suite 504
Chicago, IL 60605
(312) 663-0101

Other Books, Newsletters, and Support

In addition to all these tools and training organizations, here are a number of other resources that you have at your fingertips. Especially useful are the following books:

Interactive user:	Elementary Paradox
	Greg Salcedo and Rusel DeMaria
	Compute!, 1990
Supplement to manual:	Best Book of Paradox
	Celeste Robinson
	Howard W. Sams and Co., 1990
Programming:	Paradox Programmer's Guide, PAL by Example
	Alan Zenreich and James M. Kocis
	Scott Foresman and Co., 1990

In addition to these books, there are a number of newsletters (both commercial and user group) that can provide some important information for power users.

Newsletters

Paradox User's Journal and Paradox Developer's Journal
The COBB Group
P.O. Box 24412
Louisville, KY 40244-9960
1-800-223-8720

LAPALS (Los Angeles/San Diego User Group Newsletter)
LAPALS Membership Director
2149 N. Fairview
Santa Ana, CA 92706
(714) 740-1521

PNPUG (Pacific Northwest Paradox User's Group Newsletter)
Pacific Northwest Paradox User's Group
1075 Bellevue Way NE #156
Bellevue, WA 98004

Last but not least, for the cost of a modem and some communication software, you can have Borland's Paradox support team at your fingertips. In addition, you get the very best Paradox developers to assist you with your programming questions and problems. CompuServe has a special forum devoted to Paradox and Reflex users, named BORDB. There's a Borland support team monitoring BORDB every business day. You can leave a message for Borland support or throw a problem out to the myriad of Paradox listeners. You can also download libraries of PAL code, technical papers, and group discussions. Every Borland product is shipped with a $15 credit towards a CompuServe membership. If you don't have one of these coupons, write to:

> CompuServe
> P.O. Box 20212
> Dept F02C8
> 5000 Arlington Centre Blvd.
> Columbus, OH 43220

These are some formidable additions to your current Paradox resources. Add-on products, utilities, books, newsletters, and training seminars all bring you the information you need to understand and use Paradox effectively. If you're looking for ways to improve your development capabilities, check into these resources.

21

More Information on PAL

Throughout this book we've used a wide variety of PAL commands and functions. In this chapter we look at those functions and commands that need further explanation, and provide examples of how to use these commands and functions in context.

PAL Commands and Functions

ACCEPT

TYPE
COMMAND

PAL SYNTAX
ACCEPT DataType PICTURE Picture MIN MinValue MAX MaxValue LOOKUP TableName DEFAULT DefaultValue REQUIRED TO VarName

CONTEXT
Input/Output

DESCRIPTION
When PAL executes an ACCEPT statement, it opens an invisible window at the current cursor position to accept the requested value. Its input field extends to the necessary width to allow for input of the value.

You can implement automatic validity checking with any combination of PICTURE, MIN, MAX, or LOOKUP parameters. These validity checks work the same as they do with their MENU VALCHECKS counterparts, except that [F1] will not let you view and select a record from the LOOKUP table.

EXAMPLE

```
While (true)   ; Set up looktable as the next ACCEPT lookup table.
; Clear any previous assignment to the thisvar variable.
looktable= "ch21mstr"
thisvar = ""
```

Especially in multiuser applications, check to see that the lookup table Looktable is available. Grab retval when you issue the LOCK command and assign it to a variable *lockretval*. Set up a counter and try to lock the Looktable ten times. If unsuccessful, tell the user and return.

```
counter = 0
While counter < 10
        counter = counter + 1
        lock looktable pfl
        lockretval = retval
        if lockretval = false then
                message lockretval "unable to lock table...retrying"
                loop
        else
                quitloop
        endif
EndWhile
if counter > 10 then
      message "Unable to grab table"
      RETURN
endif
```

The next section is the ACCEPT statement. This example sets a variable *thisvar* to accept up to 26 alphanumeric characters. The PICTURE statement allows any characters and ensures that they are converted to uppercase. LOOKUP checks the user's input against the first key field in the LOOKUP table. If multiple keys exist, LOOKUP will not function correctly.

```
if istable(looktable) = true then
     @0,0 Clear EOL ?? "Which keyword ?"
     ACCEPT "a26" PICTURE "{*!}" LOOKUP looktable TO thisvar
     if retval = true then
             mesg = "Input was made successfully..."
     else
             mesg = "Incorrect input made...value has not been as-
signed..."
```

```
        endif
        message mesg," RETVAL=",retval," VARIABLE=",thisvar
        gc = getchar()
endif
quitloop
EndWhile
```

Note that the ACCEPT statement has three possible scenarios:

- ◆ The user inputs a correct value.
- ◆ The user presses [Enter] and the ACCEPT statement assigns "" to the variable.
- ◆ The user presses [Esc] and the variable is not set.

ARRAYSIZE

TYPE
FUNCTION

PAL SYNTAX
ARRAYSIZE(ArrayName)

CONTEXT
Information

DESCRIPTION
Returns the dimension of ARRAYNAME.

EXAMPLE
```
ARRAY ThisArray[20]
asize = arraysize(thisarray)
message asize   ; display 20
```

ATFIRST

TYPE
FUNCTION

PAL SYNTAX
ATFIRST()

CONTEXT

Workspace/Canvas/Status

DESCRIPTION

If the current record equals the first record, ATFIRST() returns True, otherwise it returns False.

ATLAST

TYPE

FUNCTION

PAL SYNTAX

ATLAST()

CONTEXT

Workspace/Canvas/Status

DESCRIPTION

If the current record equals the last record, ATLAST() returns True, otherwise it returns False.

EXAMPLE

```
if atlast() = true then
      24,0 Clear EOL ?? "Done"
else
      @24,0 Clear EOL ?? "Working "
      style blink ?? "..." style
endif
```

BLANKDATE

TYPE

FUNCTION

PAL SYNTAX

BLANKDATE()

CONTEXT

Date/Time

DESCRIPTION

Gives you back a blank date.

EXAMPLE

```
CoEdit tablename
moveto[date]
Scan
     if [date] < today()-30 then
          [] = blankdate()
     endif
EndScan
```

BLANKNUM

TYPE

FUNCTION

PAL SYNTAX

BLANKNUM()

CONTEXT

Mathematical

DESCRIPTION

Gives you back a blank number.

EXAMPLE

```
CoEdit tablename
moveto[age]
Scan
     [] = blanknum()
EndScan
```

BOT

TYPE

FUNCTION

PAL SYNTAX

BOT()

CONTEXT

Canvas/Information

DESCRIPTION

If MOVETO and/or SKIP action would bring you to the last record, BOT() returns True, otherwise it returns False.

CALCDEBUG

TYPE

COMMAND

PAL SYNTAX

CALCDEBUG {ON|OFF} "Debug String"

CONTEXT

Abbreviated Menu Command

DESCRIPTION

Lets you turn off or change system CALCDEBUG message. This command works like the CCP equivalent PAL|CALCDEBUG command.

EXAMPLE

```
CALCDEBUG OFF ""
CALCDEBUG ON "NA" ; sets NA as the error message.
```

CANCELEDIT

TYPE

COMMAND

MENU COMMAND

Menu {Image} {Cancel} {No,Yes}

PAL SYNTAX

CANCELEDIT

CONTEXT
Abbreviated Menu Command

DESCRIPTION
This command actually works in any mode where the menu commands Cancel|Yes exist. This means that a CANCELEDIT will work in Edit, Form, Report, and DataEntry modes.

If no Cancel|Yes menu command exists, a script error occurs.

EXAMPLE
```
Edit tablename
While (true)
Wait Table
Prompt "Press [F2] to save or [Esc] to cancel"
Until "F2", "Esc"
lookretval = retval
Switch
      case lookretval = "F2": Do_it!
      case lookretval = "Esc": CANCELEDIT
OtherWise:loop
EndSwitch
quitloop
EndWhile
```

CANVAS

TYPE
COMMAND

PAL SYNTAX
CANVAS {ON|OFF}

CONTEXT
Input/Output

DESCRIPTION
This is one of the commands that controls the PAL canvas. CANVAS ON|OFF gives you the capability to build a screen behind the scenes and display it when it is ready.

EXAMPLE

```
CANVAS OFF ; turn of the CANVAS
;Build a screen in the background.
CANVAS ON  ; display what you built
```

CLEAR

TYPE

COMMAND

PAL SYNTAX

CLEAR [EOL|EOS]

CONTEXT

Input/Output

DESCRIPTION

CLEAR actually works in three contexts:

- CLEAR by itself clears the current PAL canvas.
- CLEAR EOL clears the current line from the current cursor position to the end of the current line.
- CLEAR EOS clears the screen from the current cursor position to the end of the screen.

CLEARALL

TYPE

COMMAND

PARADOX Key

[Alt][F8]

ASCII Code

-111

PAL SYNTAX

CLEARALL

CONTEXT

Key/Workspace

DESCRIPTION

CLEARALL clears the workspace of all query, table, and form images. CLEARALL does not clear the PAL canvas—CLEAR does.

EXAMPLE

```
CLEARALL   ; clear the workspace images
CLEAR      ; clear the PAL canvas
```

COPYFORM

TYPE

COMMAND

MENU COMMAND

Menu {Tools} {Copy} {Form} {SameTable,DifferentTable} {SourceTable} {Form} {DifferentTable} {Form}

PAL SYNTAX

COPYFORM SourceTable SourceForm TargetTable TargetForm

CONTEXT

Abbreviated Menu Command

DESCRIPTION

COPYFORM was added in version 3.0 and is very handy. Many Paradox users still perform a query, empty a target report table, add their Answer table to a table that contains the proper form, and then view the data.

A faster, more efficient way of accomplishing the same thing (especially in a multiuser environment) is to perform the query and just COPYFORM the proper form to the Answer table.

COPYREPORT

TYPE

COMMAND

MENU COMMAND

Menu {Tools} {Copy} {Report} {SameTable,DifferentTable} {Source TableName} {Source Report} {Target TableName} {Target Report}

PAL SYNTAX

COPYREPORT SourceTable SourceReport TargetTable TargetReport

CONTEXT

Abbreviated Menu Command

DESCRIPTION

COPYREPORT was added in version 3.0 and is very handy. Many Paradox users still perform a query, empty a target report table, add their Answer table to a table that contains the proper report, and then print the report.

A faster, more efficient way of accomplishing the same thing (especially in a multiuser environment) is to perform the query, COPYREPORT to the Answer table, and then print the report.

CREATE

TYPE

COMMAND

MENU COMMAND

Menu {Create} {TableName}

PAL SYNTAX

CREATE TableName FieldsDefinition

or

CREATE TableName1 LIKE TableName2

CONTEXT

Abbreviated Menu Command

DESCRIPTION

CREATE lets you build a Paradox table on the fly in a PAL script. CREATE lets you specify the table name, field names, and field types.

In addition, Paradox lets you BORROW a structure of another table to create the new table.

EXAMPLE

```
CREATE "PARTS"
        "Part Number" : "S*" Key Field
        "Description" : "A40"
        "On Hand"     : "N"
        "On Order"    : "N"
        "Cost"        : "$"
        "Inspected"   : "D"
CREATE "newpart" LIKE "parts"
```

CURSOR

TYPE
COMMAND

PAL SYNTAX
CURSOR {BAR|BOX|NORMAL|OFF}

CONTEXT
Input/Output

DESCRIPTION

The CURSOR command lets you change the appearance of the CURSOR (or hide it if desired) on the PAL canvas.

CURSOR OFF turns the cursor off, whereas CURSOR NORMAL turns it back on in its normal state.

CURSOR BOX makes the cursor appear as a box and CURSOR BAR gives you a thicker, horizontal-bar cursor.

CURSORCHAR

TYPE
FUNCTION

PAL SYNTAX
CURSORCHAR()

CONTEXT

Workspace/Canvas/Status

DESCRIPTION

Returns the character that the cursor is resting on in the Form, Report, or Script Editor. Returns an error if used outside one of these modes.

CURSORLINE

TYPE

FUNCTION

PAL SYNTAX

CURSORLINE()

CONTEXT

Workspace/Canvas/Status

DESCRIPTION

Returns the current line of text on the Paradox workspace/canvas. Valid only in Form, Report, or Script Editor modes.

DATEVAL

TYPE

FUNCTION

PAL SYNTAX

DATEVAL(String)

CONTEXT

Date/Time

DESCRIPTION

Converts an alphanumeric date string to an actual date value. Returns an error if the string is not in proper date format.

DEBUG

TYPE
COMMAND

PAL SYNTAX
DEBUG

CONTEXT
System Control PAL/Paradox

DESCRIPTION
DEBUG pauses script execution and places you in the PAL debugger. To step through a script from the DEBUG point, press [Ctrl][S]. To resume script execution and leave the Debugger, press [Ctrl][G] or select Go from the DEBUGGER menu.

DIREXISTS

TYPE
FUNCTION

PAL SYNTAX
DIREXISTS(DOSPath)

CONTEXT
Information

DESCRIPTION
Tests whether a string (DOSPath) is a directory or not. Returns 1 if true, 0 if false, and -1 if there is a syntax error.

ECHO

TYPE
COMMAND

PAL SYNTAX

ECHO {FAST|SLOW|OFF|NORMAL}

CONTEXT

Input/Output

DESCRIPTION

ECHO lets you reveal to the user what is normally a background function or procedure.

ECHO provides three speeds:

SLOW	; works very slow
FAST	; works at medium speed
NORMAL	; works at fastest ECHO possible
OFF	; turns the ECHO command off

You can use ECHO as an alternative to DEBUG to observe a script as it runs.

EOT

TYPE

FUNCTION

PAL SYNTAX

EOT()

CONTEXT

Information

DESCRIPTION

Tests if the next MOVETO, SKIP, or LOCATE will position the cursor at the end of the table. Returns True if the cursor is positioned at the end of the table, otherwise returns False.

FAMILYRIGHTS

TYPE

FUNCTION

PAL SYNTAX

FAMILYRIGHTS(TableName,String)

CONTEXT

Information

DESCRIPTION

Tests the user's right to create or modify a table's family of objects. Strings equal F, R, S, or V.

FIELDRIGHTS

TYPE

FUNCTION

PAL SYNTAX

FIELDRIGHTS(TableName,FieldName,String)

CONTEXT

Information

DESCRIPTION

Returns True or False, based on PASSWORD—you can test only if a user has READONLY or ALL rights.

Returns True if the user has the right to modify the record (including the key fields), otherwise it returns False.

EXAMPLE

```
FIELDRIGHTS("Customer","Cust ID","ALL")
```

FIELDSTR

TYPE
FUNCTION

PAL SYNTAX
FIELDSTR()

CONTEXT
String

DESCRIPTION
Returns the contents of the current field as an alphanumeric string.

FIELDSTR is especially good for lifting the value of the current field as it is entered, before any validity checks have been applied.

FIELDTYPE

TYPE
FUNCTION

PAL SYNTAX
FIELDTYPE()

CONTEXT
Workspace/Canvas/Status

DESCRIPTION
Returns A*n* (where *n* is the field length), N, D, S, or $.

FORMTABLES

TYPE
COMMAND

PAL SYNTAX
FORMTABLES TableName Form StoreInArray

CONTEXT
Variable/Array

DESCRIPTION
FORMTABLES returns a list of the tables that are embedded in a master form. To record these values you must provide FORMTABLES with a table name, a form number, and an array to store the names of the tables that have been embedded in the form.

EXAMPLE
```
FormTables "Ch21Mstr" "F1" tables
RETURNS tables[1]="Ch21Detl"
```

FORMTYPE

TYPE
FUNCTION

PAL SYNTAX
FORMTYPE(String)

CONTEXT
Information

DESCRIPTION
FORMTYPE indicates whether the type of form being tested is the form being used. You can test for four form types:

> MultiRecord
> Linked
> Detail
> DisplayOnly

IMAGERIGHTS

TYPE
COMMAND

PAL SYNTAX
IMAGERIGHTS [UPDATE|READONLY]

CONTEXT

Workspace, Input/Output

DESCRIPTION

IMAGERIGHTS lets you restrict access to all data in a record or prevent any key changes to the record.

Issuing an IMAGERIGHTS by itself revokes any IMAGERIGHTS [UPDATE|READONLY] issued previously.

EXAMPLE

```
CoEdit tablename
if username() <> = "Suzy" then
      IMAGERIGHTS READONLY;No one but suzy can
else                     ;modify the record
      IMAGERIGHTS UPDATE   ;Suzy can update all
endif                    ;data except the key(s).
While (true)
Wait Table
if username() <> "Suzy" then
     Prompt "Press [F2] to stop viewing records"
else Prompt "Make changes, press [F2] to save."
endif
Until "F2"
lookretval = retval
if lookretval = "F2" then
     Do_it!
endif
IMAGERIGHTS
EndWhile
```

LOCKSTATUS

TYPE

FUNCTION

PAL SYNTAX

LOCKSTATUS(TableName,LockType)

CONTEXT

WorkSpace/Canvas/Status

DESCRIPTION

LOCKSTATUS returns the number of times that you've placed a certain lock type on a table.

```
LOCKSTATUS(TABLENAME,"FL")     ; Full Lock
LOCKSTATUS(TABLENAME,"WL")     ; Write Lock
LOCKSTATUS(TABLENAME,"PWL")    ; Prevent Write Lock
LOCKSTATUS(TABLENAME,"PFL")    ; Prevent Full Lock
LOCKSTATUS(TABLENAME,"ANY")    ; ANY Locks on table
```

EXAMPLE

```
LOCK "Customer" PFL
LOCK "Customer" PWL
MESSAGE LOCKSTATUS("Customer","ANY") ; returns 2
MESSAGE LOCKSTATUS("Customer","PWL") ; returns 1
MESSAGE LOCKSTATUS("Customer","PFL") ; returns 1
MESSAGE LOCKSTATUS("Customer","FL")  ; returns 0
UNLOCK ALL
MESSAGE LOCKSTATUS("Customer","ANY") ; returns 0
```

LOOP

TYPE

COMMAND

PAL SYNTAX

LOOP

CONTEXT

Control (Programming) Structure

DESCRIPTION

LOOP directs control to the top of the current LOOP command. Commands following LOOP are ignored—the routine goes back to the top of the current control structure and continues processing.

> **NOTE:** *Placing a loop in an IF...ENDIF, SCAN...FOR...ENDFOR and WHILE...ENDWHILE can help optimize your routines. If you have a series of IF statements in a SCAN where only one of the IF statements will be acted upon (True), then place a LOOP before the ENDIF to tell PAL to skip the rest of the code, go to the next record, and start processing the information from the top (first) set of code after the SCAN statement.*

EXAMPLE

```
CoEdit tablename
moveto[state]
Scan
    if mod([#],10) = 0 then
        message [#]
    endif
    if [] = "CA" then
        [sales tax] = "Yes"
        loop
    endif
    if [] = "WA" then
        [sales tax] = "Yes"
        loop
    endif
    if [] = "OR" then
        [sales tax] = "No"
        loop
    endif
    if [] = "NY" then
        [sales tax] = "Yes"
        loop
    endif
    ; Place an IF/ENDIF for every state, etc.
EndScan
Do_it!
```

Execution of this routine is improved by placing the explicit LOOP rather than relying on ENDSCAN to return to the top of processing. In addition, the script can be optimized by placing the IF for the most-often found [State] in the table. In other words, the routine will most often find the State that occurs the most frequent times in the table, it will then process that record, ignore the balance of the code, and move on to the next record.

MATCH

TYPE
FUNCTION

PAL SYNTAX
MATCH(String,PatternString,VarNameList)

CONTEXT
String

DESCRIPTION

MATCH compares a string with a designated pattern and lets you assign the matching string values to variables. MATCH returns True if the PATTERNSTRING is found in the STRING, otherwise it returns False.

EXAMPLE

```
; Eval date is alpha date in the form year month day yymmdd
Reset
startmatch =  time()
CoEdit "dates"
moveto[baddate]
Scan
        evaldate = []
                yy =  substr(evaldate,1,2)
                mm =  substr(evaldate,3,2)+"/"
                dd =  substr(evaldate,5,2)+"/"
        [substr] = mm+dd+yy
        if mod([#],10) = 0 then
                message [#]
        endif
EndScan
Do_it!
endsubstr = time()
Reset
startmatch =  time()
CoEdit "dates"
moveto[baddate]
Scan
        evaldate = []
        y = match(evaldate,"@@@@@@..",y1,y2,m1,m2,d1, d2
        [match] = m1+m2+"/"+d1+d2+"/"+y1+y2
        if mod([#],10) = 0 then
                message [#]
        endif
EndScan
Do_it!
endmatch = time()
savevars endsubstr,startsubstr,endmatch,startmatch
```

MEMLEFT

TYPE

FUNCTION

PAL SYNTAX

MEMLEFT()

CONTEXT

WorkSpace/Canvas/Status

DESCRIPTION

MEMLEFT() returns a numeric value of the amount of RAM that is available to your application. MEMLEFT() returns all available memory for the central memory pool, including all memory allocated to the cache.

EXAMPLE

```
if MEMLEFT() < 12000 then
    @24,0 Clear EOL ?? "Not enough memory to edit"
    beep sleep 1000
    return
endif
```

PAINTCANVAS

TYPE

COMMAND

PAL SYNTAX

PAINTCANVAS [BORDER][FILL String]
{MonoChromeOptions|ATTRIBUTE|BACKGROUND}
Row1, Col1, Row2, Col2

CONTEXT

Input/Output

DESCRIPTION

PAINTCANVAS is very powerful, requires little memory, and simplifies many programming tasks involved with building a screen in PAL. When combined with CANVAS ON/CANVAS OFF, PAINTCANVAS is a very useful tool.

Row1	Top row of the area to be painted
Col1	Upper-left column of the area to be painted
Row2	Bottom row of the area to be painted
Col2	Lower-right column of the area to be painted

Rows must be an integer between 0 and 24.

Columns must be an integer between 0 and 79.

BORDER — Creates a one-character wide border around the area designated by Row1, Col1, Row2, Col2. If no FILL statement is present, the area's current contents are not overwritten.

FILL — Takes a String argument and then fills the area with the string.

You can use BLINK, INTENSE, and REVERSE style text in any combination to produce the desired effect.

ATTRIBUTE — Sets colors on the PAL canvas covered by PAINTCANVAS according to the values found in Appendix B of this book.

BACKGROUND — Picks up the color and style attributes from the current PAL screen values, changing only the values involved in the FILL parameter.

EXAMPLE

The following example creates a box with a shadow border.

```
CANVAS OFF                ; turn off canvas
PAINTCANVAS FILL "▓"
        ATTRIBUTE 15 ; black w/white foreground
        5,11,21,41
PAINTCANVAS FILL "▓"
        ATTRIBUTE 48 ; cyan w/black foreground
        4,10,20,40
CANVAS ON
gc = getchar()
```

NOTE: *If you want the shadow to have a background effect, place it before the PAINTCANVAS that needs to lay on top of the screen.*

REPORTTABLES

TYPE
COMMAND

PAL SYNTAX
REPORTTABLES Tablename ReportName StoreInArray

CONTEXT

Variable/Array

DESCRIPTION

REPORTTABLES returns a list of the tables that are embedded in a report. To record these values you must provide REPORTTABLES with a table name, a form number, and an array to store the names of the tables that have been embedded in the report.

EXAMPLE

```
ReportTables "Ch21Det1" "R1" tables
RETURNS tables[1]="Ch21SMstr"
```

RESYNCKEY

TYPE

COMMAND

PARADOX KEY

[Ctrl][L]

ASCII Code

12

PAL SYNTAX

RESYNCKEY

CONTEXT

Key

DESCRIPTION

RESYNCKEY is the PAL equivalent of pressing [Ctrl][L]. RESYNCKEY rescynchronizes the display of detail records whenever you change a master record key that the detailed records depend on.

In a multitable form (1-M or M-M), the master record does not automatically change the key field in the detail record when the master key is changed. RESYNCKEY lets you update the detail records to the new key and redisplay the row(s).

RMEMLEFT

TYPE

FUNCTION

PAL SYNTAX

RMEMLEFT()

CONTEXT

Information

DESCRIPTION

RMEMLEFT is a new PAL function that returns the amount of RAM left in the code pool. Even though it can hurt application performance, you can cross over the allowable upper area of memory allotted to the code pool and enter the low area. As you do so, error code 44 is set. As you further decrement the amount of memory in the code pool, RMEMLEFT() won't trigger another error 44.

SAVETABLES

TYPE

COMMAND

PAL SYNTAX

SAVETABLES

CONTEXT

System Control PAL/Paradox

DESCRIPTION

SAVETABLES is a new (3.5) command. When an application changes a non-shared table, the changes made to the table are made in memory (in the table buffer), not to disk. SAVETABLES lets you force the changes to disk without issuing a RESET (which clears the workspace).

A related command parameter is the -Tablek option you can invoke when you start Paradox. The -Tablek option lets you set the minimum BUFFER size for reading Paradox table blocks (including indexes). Paradox's default buffer size is 24K. Once memory for table buffers has been allocated, you cannot reclaim it.

The -Tablek option is useful for improving performance to those applications that make maximum use of multitable forms and reports. With -Tablek set to the minimum buffer size to read the maximum number of blocks necessary for good performance, Paradox can maintain more blocks in memory and thus improve performance.

NOTE: *Be sure to allocate only the minimum memory needed. If Paradox needs more buffer space than the default or -Tablek has allowed, it will grab it.*

SEARCH

TYPE
FUNCTION

PAL SYNTAX
SEARCH(Substring,String)

CONTEXT
String

DESCRIPTION
SEARCH returns a number between 0 and 255 that states the position of the first character of the search string within the substring being analyzed.

EXAMPLE
```
here=search(",","Rudy, Mathew"); here = 5
here=search("x","Rudy, Mathew"); here = 0
here=search("r","Rudy, Terri") ; here = 1 (finds the first
occurrence  of "r" - ignores case)
```

SETPRIVDIR

TYPE
COMMAND

MENU COMMAND
Menu {Tools} {Net} {Setprivate} {DOSPath} {Cancel,Ok}

PAL SYNTAX
SETPRIVDIR DOSPath

CONTEXT
Abbreviated Menu Command

DESCRIPTION
SETPRIVDIR sets the Paradox private directory for the current Paradox session.

EXAMPLE
```
SETPRIVDIR "c:\\user\\kevin"
```
is the same as ...
```
Menu {Tools}{Net}{Setprivate}{C:\\User\\Kevin}{Ok}
```

SETQUERYORDER

TYPE
COMMAND

PAL SYNTAX
SETQUERYORDER {TABLEORDER|IMAGEORDER}

CONTEXT
Workspace

DESCRIPTION
Paradox operates on queries in TABLEORDER by default (you can modify this in the CCP).

However, sometimes it is useful to have a query that rotates fields into a certain order and then produce an Answer that appears in the same order as the query request. This can be especially helpful when you want to run a report right after running the query. It also helps you avoid inserting records into a table in order to use a particular report for printing.

Using SETQUERYORDER, you can produce a query such that the fields are in the same order as the tables containing the report, and when the Answer table is produced, you then COPYREPORT the report name to the Answer table and print.

SETRECORDPOSITION

TYPE
COMMAND

PAL SYNTAX
SETRECORDPOSITION Number Row

CONTEXT
Workspace

DESCRIPTION
SETRECORDPOSITION lets you control the scrolling region of multirecord forms. Number is the record number of the record in the multirecord portion of the form (1-n). Row is the position on the screen where you want the record to appear.

EXAMPLE
```
Reset
findit = "Example.."
View "Ch21Mstr"
PickForm "1"
While (true)
Wait Table
Prompt "Press [F2] to return ... [F3] TopForm",
       "[F5] to find the example [F4] Detail"
Until  "F2","F5","F3","F4"
lookretval = retval
if lookretval = "F3" or lookretval = "F4" then
    keypress lookretval
    loop
endif
if lookretval = "F2" then
    quitloop
endif
if lookretval = "F5" then
    imagehere = imageno()
    fieldhere = field()
    moveto 2
    moveto field "text"
    locate pattern findit
    if retval = true then
        SETRECORDPOSITION recno() 1
    else
        message "No example available"
        beep sleep 1000
    endif
    moveto 1                    ;This syncs the screen.
```

```
        moveto imagehere      ;This goes back to
        moveto field fieldhere ;where you were.
        loop
endif
EndWhile
```

SORTORDER

TYPE
FUNCTION

PAL SYNTAX
SORTORDER()

CONTEXT
WorkSpace/Canvas/Status

DESCRIPTION
SORTORDER() returns one of the following values:

    ascii

    intl

    nordan

    swedfin

The SORTORDER is determined when you install Paradox and is maintained in the PARADOX.SOR file.

STRVAL

TYPE
FUNCTION

PAL SYNTAX
STRVAL(expression)

CONTEXT
String

DESCRIPTION

Converts a value of any data type to a string.

EXAMPLE

```
datemsg = strval(1/1/91)
```

... returns "1/1/91"

```
datemsg = strval(1/1/91 + 15)
```

... returns "1/16/91"

```
here = strval([#]) ;current record number
```

... message "Record #"+here

```
totalrecs = nrecords(tablename)
View
Scan
     here = [#]
     percent=strval(round((here/totalrecs)*100),2)
     message percent+" % complete"
EndScan
```

SUBSTR

TYPE
FUNCTION

PAL SYNTAX
SUBSTR(String,Number1,Number2)

CONTEXT
String

DESCRIPTION

SUBSTR lets you grab a portion of a string of characters.

EXAMPLE

To convert a column of information stored as an A8 field into the form YYMMDD so that the data reads MM/DD/YY (in order to convert the column into a date through restructure), you could do the following:

```
Coedit tablename
moveto[baddate]
Scan
     mm = substr([],3,2)  ;start at 3rd chr, read 2
```

```
    dd = substr([],5,2) ;start at 5th chr, read 2
    yy = substr([],1,2) ;start at 1st chr, read 2
    [] = mm+"/"+dd+"/"+yy
    message [#] ; show the user where you are
EndScan
Do_it!
```

SYSMODE

TYPE

FUNCTION

PAL SYNTAX

SYSMODE()

CONTEXT

WorkSpace/Canvas/Status

DESCRIPTION

SYSMODE() returns the value of the current Paradox environment mode.

SYSMODE() returns:

    Main

    Create

    DataEntry

    Edit

    CoEdit

    Form

    Graph

    Password

    Report

    Restructure

    Script

    Sort

EXAMPLE

```
Menu {Report} {Change} Select tablename Select repno ENTER
Echo normal
While (true)
gc = getchar()
if gc = -60 then
     Do_it!
else
     Keypress gc
endif
loop
echo off
quit loop
end while
```

TABLERIGHTS

TYPE
FUNCTION

PAL SYNTAX
TABLERIGHTS(TableName,String)

CONTEXT
Information

DESCRIPTION
TABLERIGHTS lets you determine whether you can perform a certain function on a given table, before you actually attempt that function.

TABLERIGHTS(TableName,String) returns True if you do have the right, or False if you don't have the particular right to the table.

EXAMPLE
`TableRights(Customer,"ReadOnly")`

Returns True if ReadOnly rights to Customer.

`TableRights(Customer,"Update")`

Returns True if updates to all fields except the key fields are allowed.

`TableRights(Customer,"Entry")`

Returns True if you can enter or change data but are not allowed to insert or delete.

`TableRights(Customer,"InsDel")`

Returns True if you have the rights to perform all tasks except restructure the table.

`TableRights(Customer,"All")`

Returns True if you have the rights to perform all tasks including restructuring the table.

```
Wait Table
Prompt "[F2] to save , [INS] to add a record"
Until "F2","Ins"
lookretval = retval
if lookretval = "Ins" then
    checkrights = tablerights(tablename,"InsDel")
        if checkrights = true then
            keypress -82 ;press [INS]
        else
            Message "INSERT not ALLOWED"
            beep sleep 1000
        endif
    loop
endif
```

> **NOTE:** *All has higher rights than InsDel, InsDel has higher rights than Entry, and so on. TABLERIGHTS always returns True for a user who requests a function at a lower level than they have already been designated.*

TOQPRO

TYPE
COMMAND

PARADOX KEY
[Ctrl][F10]

ASCII Code
-103

PAL SYNTAX
TOQPRO

CONTEXT
Key

DESCRIPTION

Lets you pass control of Paradox to Quattro Pro. In order to leave Paradox and enter Quattro Pro with the TOQPRO or [Ctrl][F10] commands, you must have at least 2MB of memory and you must start Paradox with:

    c> paradox -qpro

In addition, you must load the DOS SHARE program to access Quattro from Paradox (add the SHARE command to your AUTOEXEC.BAT).

> **NOTE:** *To toggle back and forth (without exiting) from Paradox and Quattro Pro, press [Ctrl][F10] in either product. In addition, if you quit Paradox while Quattro Pro is still active, Paradox performs the exit and then toggles you into Quattro Pro. If you have open files in Quattro, you can save the tables or files before exiting to DOS.*

Pressing [Ctrl][F10] or performing TOQPRO sets or doesn't set *retval* to one of three states, depending on how you've configured your system and how you designate Paradox to start. For example:

- Did not start Paradox with -qpro parameter:

    Retval equals the last *retval*, or Cancel/Debug if this is the first activity you perform in the current Paradox session.

- Quattro Pro is not on your PATH, or there is not enough memory to load Quattro Pro:

    Retval is set to -1.

    (If Quattro Pro is not on your path, exit Paradox, correct your PATH statement, reload Paradox, and try again.)

- Loads Quattro Pro successfully:

    Retval is set to 768.

UNPASSWORD

TYPE
COMMAND

MENU COMMAND
Menu {Tools} {More} {Protect} {Clear Passwords}

PAL SYNTAX
UNPASSWORD PasswordList

CONTEXT
Abbreviated Menu Command

DESCRIPTION
UNPASSWORD revokes a password but does not unprotect the table(s). UNPASSWORD leaves the tables open, so you'll want to issue a RESET CLEARALL after UNPASSWORD.

> **NOTE:** *UNPASSWORD is not always a reliable way of revoking access to a table and/or function. Use the {Tools} {Protect}{ClearPassword} menu commands to ensure that access is totally revoked.*

USERNAME

TYPE
FUNCTION

PAL SYNTAX
USERNAME()

CONTEXT
WorkSpace/Canvas/Status

DESCRIPTION
USERNAME() returns the value of the current user's name as it is set by the CCP, SETUSERNAME, or with the DOS command line startup -User.

EXAMPLE
```
    CCP="Greg"
                USERNAME() = "Greg"
    SETUSERNAME() = "Greg Salcedo"
                USERNAME() = "Greg Salcedo"
c> paradox -user "Greg 555-1212"
                USERNAME() = "Greg 555-1212"
```

VERSION

PAL SYNTAX
VERSION()

CONTEXT

WorkSpace/Canvas/Status

DESCRIPTION

VERSION returns the Paradox version number, either 1, 1.1, 2, 3, or 3.5.

If you have users who have different versions of Paradox, you'll have to compile different sets of libraries for your application.

EXAMPLE

```
ver = version()
Switch
        case sel = 3    : play "comp_30"
                          beep message "One moment"
        case sel = 3.5  : message "Version Ok"
                          sleep 1000
EndSwitch
```

WINDOW

TYPE

FUNCTION

PAL SYNTAX

WINDOW()

CONTEXT

WorkSpace/Canvas/Status

DESCRIPTION

WINDOW returns a string that consists of the current contents of the Paradox window message. WINDOW messages are only available through a script. An example of window messages is **Press Edit [F9] or CoEdit [Alt][F9] to make changes**.

EXAMPLE

```
Query
Ch21mstr |
         |
         |
         |
Endquery
Do_it!
msg=WINDOW()
msg=Nothing to process now
```

Special Functions

The following PAL functions have a number of aspects and return values that warrant special attention.

FORMAT

With Paradox 3.5, FORMAT has taken on an even greater role. Table 21-1 is a chart of the FORMAT types and how they function.

Table 21-1
Format Types

Format type	Spec	Explanation	Data types supported
Width	Wn	Set allowable width	All
Width	Wn.d	Set width and decimal places	All
Alignment	AL	Left-justify value	All
Alignment	AR	Right-justify value	All
Alignment	AC	Center-justify value	All
Case	CU	Convert and display in uppercase	All
Case	CL	Convert and display in lowercase	All
Case	CC	Convert and display in initial capitals	All
Edit	E$	Floating dollar sign preceding value	N,S,$
Edit	EC	Use commas as whole number separators	N,S,$
Edit	EZ	Leading zeros preceding value	N,S,$
Edit	E*	Leading asterisk (*) preceding value	N,S,$
Edit	EI	Convert and display in internal format	N,S,$
Sign	S+	Leading + or - sign preceding value	N,S,$
Sign	S-	Leading - sign preceding negative value	N,S,$
Sign	SP	Parentheses on negative values	N,S,$
Sign	SD	DB or CR following value	N,S,$
Sign	SC	CR following negative value	N,S,$
Date	D1	Format date as mm/dd/yy	D
Date	D2	Format date as Month dd, yyyy	D
Date	D3	Format date as mm/dd	D
Date	D4	Format date as mm/yy	D
Date	D5	Format date as dd-Mon-yy	D

Table 21-1—continued

Format type	Spec	Explanation	Data types supported
Date	D6	Format date as Mon-yy	D
Date	D7	Format date as dd-Mon-yyyy	D
Date	D8	Format date as mm/dd/yyyy	D
Date	D9	Format date as dd.mm.yy	D
Date	D10	Format date as dd/mm/yy	D
Date	D11	Format date as yy-mm-dd	D
Logical	LY	Use Yes/No when returned True/False	L
Logical	LO	Use On/Off when returned True/False	L

FORMTYPE

FORMTYPE(String) provides you with the capability to test what kind of form is being used. String is the type of form being tested and must be one of the following:

- MultiRecord
- Linked
- Detail
- DisplayOnly

FORMTYPE is a useful function to employ when a user exits a WAIT statement and wants to go on to view another table. Table 21-2 gives you the return value of FORMTYPE(String) in various contexts.

LOCKINFO

In multiuser applications, it's important to know what kind of locking Paradox applies automatically. Table 21-3 shows the automatic locks placed by Paradox when it takes action through its menu commands.

Table 21-2
FORMTYPE

Form type	Multi-record	Linked	Detail	Display Only
Standard form, or master of multitable	False	False	False	False
MultiRecord single table	True	False	False	False
Unlinked detail	False	False	True	False
DisplayOnly Master	False	False	False	True
Unlinked MultiRecord detail	True	False	True	False
Linked detail	False	True	True	False
DisplayOnly unlinked detail	False	False	True	True
MultiRecord linked detail	True	True	True	False
MultiRecord unlinked detail, DisplayOnly	True	False	True	True
Linked detail, DisplayOnly	False	True	True	True

Table 21-3
LOCKINFO

Menu Command	Operation	Effect
View	Table View	PFL on table
View	Form View	PFL on table
Ask	Normal, Find, Set	Snapshot of records
Ask	Insert, Delete	PFL on table
Ask	Changeto	FL on Do_it!
Report	Output	Snapshot of records
Report	RangeOutput	Snapshot of records
Report	Design	PFL table, FL on report object
Report	Change	PFL table, FL on form object
Create	Create	FL on table
Create	Borrow	PFL on table being borrowed
Modify	Sort (new)	WL on source, FL on target
Modify	Sort (same)	FL on table
Modify	Edit	FL on table

Table 21-3—continued

Menu Command	Operation	Effect
Modify	CoEdit	PFL table, PWL on record edited
Modify	DataEntry	PFL source, PWL on source on Do_it!
Modify	MultiEntry	WL source, WL map, PWL target on Do_it!
Modify	Restructure	FL on table
ValCheck	Define/Clear	FL on TableLookup-Edit or DataEntry
ValCheck	TableLookup	PFL on lookup table-Edit or DataEntry
Image	KeepSet	FL while creating settings object
Image	Graph/Crosstab	Snapshot of records
Image	Graph/View	PFL on table
Forms	Design	PFL table, FL on form object
Forms	Change	PFL table, FL on form object
Tools	Rename	FL on source and target table
Tools	QuerySpeedup	Snapshot of records (like ASK)
Tools	ExportImport/Export	WL on source table
Tools	ExportImport/Import	FL on target table
Tools	Copy/Tables	WL on source, FL on target
Tools	Copy/Family Objects	WL on source, FL on target
Tools	Copy/JustFamily	PFL source table, WL source objects-FL target
Tools	Delete Table	FL on table
Tools	Delete Forms,Reports	FL on object, PFL on table
Tools	Delete Settings	FL on on object
Tools	Info/Structure	PFL on table
Tools	Info/Family	WL on table and objects
Tools	Add	WL on source, PWL on target table
Tools	MultiAdd	WL on source, PWL on target table(s)
Tools	FormAdd	PFL all target tables/objects
Tools	FormAdd	PFL all source tables/objects on Do_it!
Tools	FormAdd	UPDATE-PFL all targets, WL all sources
Tools	FormAdd	NEW-PWL all targets, WL all sources
Tools	Subtract	FL on source, FL on target tables
Tools	Empty	FL on table
Tools	Protect	FL on table

PICTURE

A PICTURE statement can be entered as a VALCHECK to a field in a table or can be used to help a user input into an ACCEPT statement. Table 21-4 is a chart of the various PICTURE elements and how each can be used.

Table 21-4
PICTURE

Element	Description
#	Accept only digits (1,2,3,0,-1,-4,...n)
?	Accept letters only either as uppercase or lowercase—no case change
&	Accept letters only and convert letter to uppercase
	Accept any character—no case conversion of letters
!	Accept any character—convert any letter to uppercase
[ ]	Any character without specific picture provision is taken literally
;	Take the very next character in the picture statement literally
*	Repeat value (n) times limited by field width only
[]	Optional input of picture, characters or literals
{}	Grouping operator
,	Used to present a set of alternatives

[(###)-]###-####	Telephone number with optional area code
*3{##:}	Time input
*4&[*4!]	Require 4 characters alpha, other 4 optional any
{SAL-,MKT-,ACC-}*3#	Enter department prefix and three-number suffix
!*[[*?][ ][&]]	Capitalize first character of each sentence

RECORDSTATUS

RECORDSTATUS lets you test the current record's status.

PAL SYNTAX

RECORDSTATUS(String)

String indicates the type of condition to test. The record status must be one of the following strings:

- New
- Locked
- Modified
- KeyViol

Table 21-5 is a chart that lists the expected return values for a given record's status.

Table 21-5
RECORDSTATUS

RecordStatus	New	Locked	Modify	KeyViol
New, blank record	True	False	False	False
New record after input	True	False	True	False
New record, key violation when attempting to post	True	True	True	True
Existing record unchanged	False	False	False	False
Existing record locked but unchanged	False	True	False	False
Existing record modified	False	True	True	False
Existing record modified, key violation when attempting to post	False	True	True	True

Calling RECORD STATUS

Many times you need to know the status of the record your cursor is on. One RECORDSTATUS call might not give you all the information that you need to interpret the current status correctly. Table 21-6 is a matrix of the possible combinations that occur during a given action against a record.

**Table 21-6
Calling RecordStatus**

RecordStatus	New	Locked	Modify	KeyViol
New, blank record	True		False	
New record after input	True	False	True	
New record, key violation attempting to post	True			True
Existing record unchanged	False	False		
Existing record locked but unchanged		True	False	
Existing record modified	False			False
Existing record modified, key violation when attempting to post	False			True

Summary

In this chapter, we have tried to fill in some of the areas that needed extra explanation. Throughout this book we have tried to give you examples and strategies to help you develop Paradox applications. To wrap up the book, the appendixes give you some information on client/server setups as well as a number of reference charts on key codes, colors, and so on. We've had fun presenting this information to you. Dig into the enclosed disk and try out some of these techniques for yourself!

A Database Servers

Setting up your client/server environment is no easy task. We've assembled the following information to help you understand how to set up and manage some of the major database server products. For more information on this subject, consult the Paradox *SQL Link User's Guide*.

Microsoft SQL Server 1.1

Microsoft SQL Server comes with a number of facilities and tools, and there is no limit to the number of nodes per server. MS SQL Server includes facilities for the system administrator, bulk copies, server utilities, and DB-LIBRARY (an API library for DOS).

Hardware and software requirements

To install SQL Server, you need the following hardware and software.

Server requirements

Computer

    80286 or 80386 microprocessor

Memory

    8 megabytes (MB) minimum (more recommended)

Hard disk

> 30MB hard disk drive, 5.25" or 3.5" diskette drive(s) to back up (minimum, more is recommended)

Operating system

> OS/2 1.0 or later
> AT-class PC: MS OS/2 1.0 Server Adaptation-AT Bus
> PS/2-class PC: MS OS/2 1.0 Server Adaptation-PS/2 Bus

Network software

> MS OS/2 LAN Manager 1.0 or network system that supports Named Pipes

Client Requirements

Computer

> 80286 or 80386 microprocessor recommended

Memory

> 2-4MB minimum, 6-8MB recommended

Hard disk

> 30MB hard disk drive, 5.25" or 3.5" diskette drive(s) to back up (minimum, more is recommended)

Operating system

> OS/2 stations: OS/2 1.0 or later
> DOS stations: DOS 3.2 or later

Network software

> MS OS/2 LAN Manager Redirector for OS/2 stations
> MS DOS LAN Manager Enhanced Redirector for DOS stations

Oracle Server for OS/2

Oracle Server for OS/2 comes with an unlimited-use license per server, including DOS and OS/2 versions of SQLdba, the import and export utilities, PRO C, SQL Loader, OS/2 Server Manager, NETBIOS drivers, and support for Named Pipes and SPX.

Hardware and software requirements

To install Oracle Server for OS/2, you need the following hardware and software.

Server requirements

Computer

> 80286 or 80386 microprocessor

Memory

> 12MB minimum (16MB recommended)

Hard disk

> 30MB hard disk drive, 5.25" or 3.5" diskette drive(s) to back up (minimum, more is recommended)

Operating system

> OS/2 1.1 or later
> AT-class PC: MS OS/2 1.0 Server Adaptation-AT Bus
> PS/2-class PC: MS OS/2 1.0 Server Adaptation-PS/2 Bus

Network software

> MS OS/2 LAN Manager 1.0 or later

Client requirements

Computer

> 80286 or 80386 microprocessor recommended

Memory

    4-6MB minimum, 6-8MB recommended

Hard disk

    30MB hard disk drive, 5.25" or 3.5" diskette drive(s) to back up (minimum, more is recommended)

Operating system

    OS/2 stations: OS/2 1.0 or later
    DOS stations: DOS 3.2 or later

Network software

    MS OS/2 LAN Manager Redirector for OS/2 stations
    MS DOS LAN Manager Enhanced Redirector for DOS stations

IBM OS/2 1.2

Comes with Extended Edition Database Manager, Query Manager, and Remote Data Servers via OS/2 Communication Manager. Latest release includes a Presentation Manager interface and application programmer interface (API). API can perform Query Manager functions using C, COBOL, FORTRAN, Pascal, or REXX.

Hardware and software requirements

To install IBM Extended Edition 1.2, you need the following hardware and software.

Server requirements

Computer

    80286 or 80386 microprocessor

Memory

    8-12MB minimum (more recommended)

Hard disk

    60-100MB hard disk drive, 5.25" or 3.5" diskette drive(s) to back up (minimum, more is recommended)

Operating System

    OS/2 1.2 or later
    AT-class PC: IBM OS/2 1.2 Server Adaptation-AT Bus
    PS/2-class PC: IBM OS/2 1.0 Server Adaptation-PS/2 Bus

Network software

    IBM OS/2 LAN Server 1.0

Client Requirements

Computer

    80286 or 80386 microprocessor recommended

Memory

    2-4MB minimum, 6-8MB recommended

Hard disk

    40-60MB hard disk drive, 5.25" or 3.5" diskette drive(s) to back up (minimum, more is recommended)

Operating system

    OS/2 stations: OS/2 1.0 or later
    DOS stations: DOS 3.2 or later

Network software

    OS/2 LAN Server Redirector for OS/2 stations
    DOS LAN Manager Enhanced Redirector for DOS stations

Database Server Comparison

	IBM EE 1.2	SQL Server	Oracle Server
Specific SQLSTARTTRANS	No	Yes	No
SQL Dialect	IBMEE	MSSQL	ORACLE
Case sensitive	Yes	Optional*	Yes
Case sensitive objects	No	Optional*	No

* determined at installation

Server Connection Information

Connection Parameters

IBM EE 1.2

User name, password, server, database, directory*

Example:

>Doug, Jones, ACC_SERVER, ACCOUNTS, D:

Microsoft SQL Server

User name, password*, server, database*

Example:

>Doug, Jones, ACC_SERVER, ACCOUNTS

Oracle Server

User name, password, host*

Example:

>Doug, Jones,@Q:ACC_SERVER

* optional parameters

Field-Naming Conventions

	IBM EE 1.2	SQL Server	Oracle Server
Max length	18	30	30
Invalid characters	"[]{}()->	space,-	space,-
Begin with character	Any valid	Letter,#,_	Letter

SQL Link Queries that Lock Records with Autocommit=OFF

IBM EE 1.2	SQL Server	Oracle Server
All	All	Queries that:
		CheckPlus
		No Check
		No CheckDescending
		No CALC expressions

Supported Data Types

	IBM EE 1.2	SQL Server	Oracle Server
CHAR	Yes	Yes	Yes
VARCHAR	Yes	Yes	Yes
VARCHAR LONG	Yes	Text	Yes
INTEGER	Yes	Yes	No
FLOAT	Yes	Yes	Yes
DECIMAL	Yes	No	Yes
DATETIME	No	Yes	No
DATE	Yes	No	Yes
TIME	Yes	No	No
NUMERIC	No	No	Yes
SMALLINT	Yes	Yes	Yes
TIMESTAMP	Yes	Yes	No

Supported Data Types—continued

	IBM EE 1.2	*SQL Server*	*Oracle Server*
GRAPHICS	DBCS	(Image)	(LONG RAW)
TINYINT	No	Yes	No
BINARY	No	Yes	RAW
VARBINARY	No	Yes	RAW
BIT	No	Yes	No
MONEY	No	Yes	No
SYSNAME	No	Yes	No
USER DEFINED	No	Yes	No
REAL	No	No	Yes
ROWID	No	No	Yes

Database Server Limitations by Product

	IBM EE 1.2	*SQL Server*	*Oracle Server*
Number of databases	None*	32767	**
Bytes per database	None*	None*	None*
Tables per database	None*	2 billion	None
Columns/Row	255	250	254
Bytes per row	4005	2000	128K
Rows per table	None*	None*	None*
Indexes per table	None*	251	**
Columns per index	16	16	16
Tables per join	16	16	**

* Limits are imposed by the physical size of the hard disk only. An IBM EE database cannot span disks or partitions. (OS/2 disk partition limit is 2.046 gigabytes.)

** Information is not known or not applicable.

B Reference Charts

This Appendix includes reference tables you'll find helpful when you're looking for specific values. All of this information can be found in the *PAL User's Guide*, but we've compiled it here for easier access. Table 1 is a compilation of the KeyCode, ASCII Code, Color, and Character Set charts. Table 2 is a Paradox command reference with Key and ASCII code information, grouped by command usage. Table 3 consists of Paradox commands and their interactive menu equivalents, grouped by command usage. Table 4 is a quick function reference chart with PAL syntax, grouped by function usage. Finally, Table 5 is a list of Paradox's reserved words, along with the context in which they are used. If you need further information, glance at Chapter 21 or refer to your *PAL User's Guide*.

Table 1
ASCII Code to KeyCode

ASCII Code	Blink Symbol	Keystrokes	Keycode Name	Background	Foreground	Code
-132		[Ctrl][PgUp]	CtrlPgUp			
-131		[Alt][=]	Net Compatibility			
-130		[Alt][-]	Memory Utilization			
-129		[Alt][0]				
-128		[Alt][9]				
-127		[Alt][8]				
-126		[Alt][7]				
-125		[Alt][6]				
-124		[Alt][5]				

681

Table 1—continued

ASCII Code	Blink Symbol	Keystrokes	Keycode Name	Background	Foreground	Code
-123		[Alt][4]				
-122		[Alt][3]				
-121		[Alt][2]				
-120		[Alt][1]				
-119		[Ctrl][Home]	CtrlHome			
-118		[Ctrl][PgDn]	CtrlPgDn			
-117		[Ctrl][End]	CtrlEnd			
-116		[Ctrl][Right]	CtrlRight			
-115		[Ctrl][Left]	CtrlLeft			
-114		[Ctrl][PrtSc]				
-113		[Alt][F10]	PalMenu	[F40]		
-112		[Alt][F9]	CoEditKey	[F39]		
-111		[Alt][F8]	ClearAll	[F38]		
-110		[Alt][F7]	InstantReport	[F37]		
-109		[Alt][F6]	CheckPlus	[F36]		
-108		[Alt][F5]	FieldView	[F35]		
-107		[Alt][F4]	InstantPlay	[F34]		
-106		[Alt][F3]	InstantRecord	[F33]		
-105		[Alt][F2]	[F32]			
-104		[Alt][F1]	[F31]			
-103		[Ctrl][F10]	[F30]			
-102		[Ctrl][F9]	[F29]			
-101		[Ctrl][F8]	[F28]			
-100		[Ctrl][F7]	[F27]			
-99		[Ctrl][F6]	[F26]			
-98		[Ctrl][F5]	[F25]			
-97		[Ctrl][F4]	[F24]			
-96		[Ctrl][F3]	[F23]			
-95		[Ctrl][F2]	[F22]			
-94		[Ctrl][F1]	[F21]			
-93		[Shift][F10]	[F20]			
-92		[Shift][F9]	[F19]			
-91		[Shift][F8]	[F18]			
-90		[Shift][F7]	[F17]			
-89		[Shift][F6]	[F16]			
-88		[Shift][F5]	[F15]			
-87		[Shift][F4]	[F14]			

Table 1—continued

ASCII Code	Blink Symbol	Keystrokes	Keycode Name	Background	Foreground	Code
-86		[Shift][F3]	[F13]			
-85		[Shift][F2]	[F12]			
-84		[Shift][F1]	[F11]			
-83		[Del]	Delete			
-82		[Ins]	Insert			
-81		[PgDn]	Page Down			
-80		Down	Down			
-79		End	End			
-77		Right	Right			
-75		Left	Left			
-73		PgUp	Page Up			
-72		Up	Up			
-71		Home	Home			
-68		[F10]	Menu			
-67		[F9]	EditKey			
-66		[F8]	ClearImage			
-65		[F7]	FormKey			
-64		[F6]	Check			
-63		[F5]	Example			
-62		[F4]	Down Image			
-61		[F3]	Up Image			
-60		[F2]	Do_it!			
-59		[F1]	Help			
-50		[Alt][M]				
-49		[Alt][N]				
-48		[Alt][B]				
-47		[Alt][V]				
-46		[Alt][C]	PaletteToggle			
-45		[Alt][X]	Crosstab			
-44		[Alt][Z]	ZoomNext			
-38		[Alt][L]	Record Lock			
-37		[Alt][K]	KeyLookUp			
-36		[Alt][J]				
-35		[Alt][H]				
-34		[Alt][G]				
-33		[Alt][F]	FieldView			
-32		[Alt][D]				

Table 1—continued

ASCII Code	Blink Symbol	Keystrokes	Keycode Name	Background	Foreground	Code
-31		[Alt][S]				
-30		[Alt][A]				
-25		[Alt][P]				
-24		[Alt][O]	DosBig			
-23		[Alt][I]				
-22		[Alt][U]				
-21		[Alt][Y]				
-20		[Alt][T]				
-19		[Alt][R]	RefreshKey			
-18		[Alt][E]				
-17		[Alt][W]				
-16		[Alt][Q]				
-15		ENTER	[Ctrl][M]	Enter		
-3		(NULL)				
0		[Ctrl][2]				
1		[Ctrl][A]		Black	Blue	129
2		[Ctrl][B]		Black	Green	130
3		[Ctrl][C]		Black	Cyan	131
4	Ditto	[Ctrl][D]	Ditto	Black	Red	132
5		[Ctrl][E]		Black	Magenta	133
6	FieldView	[Ctrl][F]	FieldView	Black	Brown	134
7		[Ctrl][G]		Black	L. Grey	135
8	BackSpace	[Ctrl][H]	BackSpace	Black	Dark Grey	136
9		[Ctrl][I]	Tab,"\\t"	Black	L. Blue	137
10		[Ctrl][J]	NewLine,"\\n"	Black	L. Green	138
11		[Ctrl][K]		Black	L. Cyan	139
12	PageBreak	[Ctrl][L]	Lock,FormFeed,"\\f"	Black	L. Red	140
13	Enter	[Ctrl][M]	Enter,Menu,CR,"\\r"	Black	L. Magenta	141
14		[Ctrl][N]		Black	L. Yellow	142
15		[Ctrl][O]	DOS	Black	Black	143
16		[Ctrl][P]		Blue	Blue	144
17		[Ctrl][Q]		Blue	Green	145
18		[Ctrl][R]	Rotate	Blue	Cyan	146
19		[Ctrl][S]		Blue	Red	147
20		[Ctrl][T]		Blue	Magenta	148
21		[Ctrl][U]		Blue	Brown	149
22		[Ctrl][V]	VertRuler	Blue	L. Grey	150

Table 1—continued

ASCII Code	Blink Symbol	Keystrokes	Keycode Name	Background	Foreground	Code
23		[Ctrl][W]		Blue	Dark Grey	151
24		[Ctrl][X]		Blue	L. Blue	152
25		[Ctrl][Y]	DeleteLine	Blue	L. Green	153
26		[Ctrl][Z]	Zoom	Blue	L. Cyan	154
27	Esc	[Ctrl][[]	Esc,Shift,Ctrl,Esc	Blue	L. Red	155
28		[Ctrl][\]		Blue	L. Magenta	156
29		[Ctrl][]]		Blue	L. Yellow	157
30		[Ctrl][6]		Blue	Black	158
31		[Ctrl][-]		Blue	Blue	159
32	Space	[SpaceBar]	Shift,Ctrl,Alt	Green	Green	160
33	!	!		Green	Cyan	161
34	"	"		Green	Red	162
35	#	#		Green	Magenta	163
36	$	$		Green	Brown	164
37	%	%		Green	L. Grey	165
38	&	&		Green	Dark Grey	166
39	'	'		Green	L. Blue	167
40	(	(		Green	L. Green	168
41	)	)		Green	L. Cyan	169
42	*	*		Green	L. Red	170
43	+	+		Green	L. Magenta	171
44	,	,		Green	L. Yellow	172
45	-	-		Green	Black	173
46	.	.		Green	Blue	174
47	/	/		Green	Green	175
48	0	0		Cyan	Cyan	176
49	1	1		Cyan	Red	177
50	2	2		Cyan	Magenta	178
51	3	3		Cyan	Brown	179
52	4	4		Cyan	L. Grey	180
53	5	5		Cyan	Dark Grey	181
54	6	6		Cyan	L. Blue	182
55	7	7		Cyan	L. Green	183
56	8	8		Cyan	L. Cyan	184
57	9	9		Cyan	L. Red	185
58	:	:		Cyan	L. Magenta	186
59	;	;		Cyan	L. Yellow	187

Table 1—continued

ASCII Code	Blink Symbol	Keystrokes	Keycode Name	Background	Foreground	Code
60	<	<		Cyan	Black	188
61	=	=		Cyan	Blue	189
62	>	>		Cyan	Green	190
63	?	?		Cyan	Cyan	191
64	@	@		Red	Red	192
65	A	A		Red	Magenta	193
66	B	B		Red	Brown	194
67	C	C		Red	L. Grey	195
68	D	D		Red	Dark Grey	196
69	E	E		Red	L. Blue	197
70	F	F		Red	L. Green	198
71	G	G		Red	L. Cyan	199
72	H	H		Red	L. Red	200
73	I	I		Red	L. Magenta	201
74	J	J		Red	L. Yellow	202
75	K	K		Red	Black	203
76	L	L		Red	Blue	204
77	M	M		Red	Green	205
78	N	N		Red	Cyan	206
79	O	O		Red	Red	207
80	P	P		Magenta	Magenta	208
81	Q	Q		Magenta	Brown	209
82	R	R		Magenta	L. Grey	210
83	S	S		Magenta	Dark Grey	211
84	T	T		Magenta	L. Blue	212
85	U	U		Magenta	L. Green	213
86	V	V		Magenta	L. Cyan	214
87	W	W		Magenta	L. Red	215
88	X	X		Magenta	L. Magenta	216
89	Y	Y		Magenta	L. Yellow	217
90	Z	Z		Magenta	Black	218
91	[	[		Magenta	Blue	219
92	\	\		Magenta	Green	220
93	]	]		Magenta	Cyan	221
94	^	^		Magenta	Red	222
95	_	_		Magenta	Magenta	223
96	`	`		Brown	Brown	224

Table 1—continued

ASCII Code	Blink Symbol	Keystrokes	Keycode Name	Background	Foreground	Code
97	a	a		Brown	L. Grey	225
98	b	b		Brown	Dark Grey	226
99	c	c		Brown	L. Blue	227
100	d	d		Brown	L. Green	228
101	e	e		Brown	L. Cyan	229
102	f	f		Brown	L. Red	230
103	g	g		Brown	L. Magenta	231
104	h	h		Brown	L. Yellow	232
105	i	i		Brown	Black	233
106	j	j		Brown	Blue	234
107	k	k		Brown	Green	235
108	l	l		Brown	Cyan	236
109	m	m		Brown	Red	237
110	n	n		Brown	Magenta	238
111	o	o		Brown	Brown	239
112	p	p		L. Grey	L. Grey	240
113	q	q		L. Grey	Dark Grey	241
114	r	r		L. Grey	L. Blue	242
115	s	s		L. Grey	L. Green	243
116	t	t		L. Grey	L. Cyan	244
117	u	u		L. Grey	L. Red	245
118	v	v		L. Grey	L. Magenta	246
119	w	w		L. Grey	L. Yellow	247
120	x	x		L. Grey	Black	248
121	y	y		L. Grey	Blue	249
122	z	z		L. Grey	Green	250
123	{	{		L. Grey	Cyan	251
124	|	|		L. Grey	Red	252
125	}	}		L. Grey	Magenta	253
126	~	~		L. Grey	Brown	254
127				L. Grey	L. Grey	255
128	é	[Alt][128]		Black	Dark Grey	
129	f	[Alt][129]		Black	L. Blue	
130	Ä	[Alt][130]		Black	L. Green	
131	ë	[Alt][131]		Black	L. Cyan	
132	è	[Alt][132]		Black	L. Red	
133	ê	[Alt][133]		Black	L. Magenta	

Table 1—continued

ASCII Code	Blink Symbol	Keystrokes	Keycode Name	Background	Foreground Code
134	å	[Alt][134]		Black	L. Yellow
135	ç	[Alt][135]		Black	Black
136	ê	[Alt][136]		Black	Blue
137	ë	[Alt][137]		Black	Green
138	è	[Alt][138]		Black	Cyan
139	ï	[Alt][139]		Black	Red
140	î	[Alt][140]		Black	Magenta
141	ì	[Alt][141]		Black	Brown
142	Ä	[Alt][142]		Black	L. Grey
143	Å	[Alt][143]		Black	Dark Grey
144	É	[Alt][144]		Blue	L. Blue
145	æ	[Alt][145]		Blue	L. Green
146	Æ	[Alt][146]		Blue	L. Cyan
147	ô	[Alt][147]		Blue	L. Red
148	ö	[Alt][148]		Blue	L. Magenta
149	ò	[Alt][149]		Blue	L. Yellow
150	û	[Alt][150]		Blue	Black
151	ù	[Alt][151]		Blue	Blue
152	ÿ	[Alt][152]		Blue	Green
153	Ö	[Alt][153]		Blue	Cyan
154	Ü	[Alt][154]		Blue	Red
155	¢	[Alt][155]		Blue	Magenta
156	£	[Alt][156]		Blue	Brown
157	¥	[Alt][157]		Blue	L. Grey
158	₧	[Alt][158]		Blue	Dark Grey
159	ƒ	[Alt][159]		Blue	L. Blue
160	á	[Alt][160]		Green	L. Green
161	í	[Alt][161]		Green	L. Cyan
162	ó	[Alt][162]		Green	L. Red
163	ú	[Alt][163]		Green	L. Magenta
164	ñ	[Alt][164]		Green	L. Yellow
165	Ñ	[Alt][165]		Green	Black
166	ª	[Alt][166]		Green	Blue
167	º	[Alt][167]		Green	Green
168	¿	[Alt][168]		Green	Cyan
169	⌐	[Alt][169]		Green	Red
170	¬	[Alt][170]		Green	Magenta

Table 1—continued

ASCII Code	Blink Symbol	Keystrokes	Keycode Name	Background	Foreground	Code
171	½	[Alt][171]		Green	Brown	
172	¼	[Alt][172]		Green	L. Grey	
173	⊥	[Alt][173]		Green	Dark Grey	
174	╟	[Alt][174]		Green	L. Blue	
175	╚	[Alt][175]		Green	L. Green	
176	░	[Alt][176]		Cyan	L. Cyan	
177	▒	[Alt][177]		Cyan	L. Red	
178	▓	[Alt][178]		Cyan	L. Magenta	
179	│	[Alt][179]		Cyan	L. Yellow	
180	┤	[Alt][180]		Cyan	Black	
181	╡	[Alt][181]		Cyan	Blue	
182	╢	[Alt][182]		Cyan	Green	
183	╖	[Alt][183]		Cyan	Cyan	
184	╕	[Alt][184]		Cyan	Red	
185	╣	[Alt][185]		Cyan	Magenta	
186	║	[Alt][186]		Cyan	Brown	
187	╗	[Alt][187]		Cyan	L. Grey	
188	╝	[Alt][188]		Cyan	Dark Grey	
189	╜	[Alt][189]		Cyan	L. Blue	
190	╛	[Alt][190]		Cyan	L. Green	
191	┐	[Alt][191]		Cyan	L. Cyan	
192	└	[Alt][192]		Red	L. Red	
193	┴	[Alt][193]		Red	L. Magenta	
194	┬	[Alt][194]		Red	L. Yellow	
195	├	[Alt][195]		Red	Black	
196	─	[Alt][196]		Red	Blue	
197	┼	[Alt][197]		Red	Green	
198	╞	[Alt][198]		Red	Cyan	
199	╟	[Alt][199]		Red	Red	
200	╚	[Alt][200]		Red	Magenta	
201	╔	[Alt][201]		Red	Brown	
202	╩	[Alt][202]		Red	L. Grey	
203	╦	[Alt][203]		Red	Dark Grey	
204	╠	[Alt][204]		Red	L. Blue	
205	═	[Alt][205]		Red	L. Green	
206	╬	[Alt][206]		Red	L. Cyan	
207	╧	[Alt][207]		Red	L. Red	

Table 1—continued

ASCII Code	Blink Symbol	Keystrokes	Keycode Name	Background	Foreground Code
208	╨	[Alt][208]		Magenta	L. Magenta
209	╤	[Alt][209]		Magenta	L. Yellow
210	╥	[Alt][210]		Magenta	Black
211	╙	[Alt][211]		Magenta	Blue
212	╘	[Alt][212]		Magenta	Green
213	╒	[Alt][213]		Magenta	Cyan
214	╓	[Alt][214]		Magenta	Red
215	╫	[Alt][215]		Magenta	Magenta
216	╪	[Alt][216]		Magenta	Brown
217	┘	[Alt][217]		Magenta	L. Grey
218	┌	[Alt][218]		Magenta	Dark Grey
219	█	[Alt][219]		Magenta	L. Blue
220	▄	[Alt][220]		Magenta	L. Green
221	>	[Alt][221]		Magenta	L. Cyan
222	<	[Alt][222]		Magenta	L. Red
223	▀	[Alt][223]		Magenta	L. Magenta
224	α	[Alt][224]		Brown	L. Yellow
225	ß	[Alt][225]		Brown	Black
226	Γ	[Alt][226]		Brown	Blue
227	π	[Alt][227]		Brown	Green
228	Σ	[Alt][228]		Brown	Cyan
229	σ	[Alt][229]		Brown	Red
230	µ	[Alt][230]		Brown	Magenta
231	τ	[Alt][231]		Brown	Brown
232	Φ	[Alt][232]		Brown	L. Grey
233	Θ	[Alt][233]		Brown	Dark Grey
234	Ω	[Alt][234]		Brown	L. Blue
235	δ	[Alt][235]		Brown	L. Green
236	∞	[Alt][236]		Brown	L. Cyan
237	φ	[Alt][237]		Brown	L. Red
238	ε	[Alt][238]		Brown	L. Magenta
239	∩	[Alt][239]		Brown	L. Yellow
240	≡	[Alt][240]		L. Grey	Black
241	±	[Alt][241]		L. Grey	Blue
242	≥	[Alt][242]		L. Grey	Green
243	≤	[Alt][243]		L. Grey	Cyan
244	⌠	[Alt][244]		L. Grey	Red

Table 1—continued

ASCII Code	Blink Symbol	Keystrokes	Keycode Name	Background	Foreground	Code
245	‖	[Alt][245]		L. Grey	Magenta	
246	π	[Alt][246]		L. Grey	Brown	
247	≑	[Alt][247]		L. Grey	L. Grey	
248	ı	[Alt][248]		L. Grey	Dark Grey	
249	ñ	[Alt][249]		L. Grey	L. Blue	
250	Ñ	[Alt][250]		L. Grey	L. Green	
251	⊦	[Alt][251]		L. Grey	L. Cyan	
252	ⁿ	[Alt][252]		L. Grey	L. Red	
253	²	[Alt][253]		L. Grey	L. Magenta	
254	■	[Alt][254]		L. Grey	L. Yellow	
255	BLANK	[Alt][255]		L. Grey	Black	

Table 2
Paradox Commands with Paradox Keys and ASCII Codes

Command	Paradox Key(s)	ASCII Code
Abbreviated Menu Commands		
ADD		
CALCDEBUG		
CANCELEDIT		
COEDIT	[F9]	-67
COPY		
COPYFORM		
COPYREPORT		
CREATE		
DELETE		
EDIT		
EMPTY		
EXIT		
INDEX		
LOCK		
PICKFORM		
PLAY		
PRINT		
PROTECT		

Table 2—continued

Command	Paradox Key(s)	ASCII Code
QUERY		
RENAME		
REPORT		
SETDIR		
SETPRIVDIR		
SETUSERNAME		
SORT		
SUBTRACT		
UNPASSWORD		
VIEW		
LIKE (CREATE)		
MAINTAINED (INDEX)		
ENDQUERY (QUERY)		
ON (SORT)		

Control (Programming) Structure Commands

Command	Paradox Key(s)	ASCII Code
FOR		
IF		
LOOP		
QUIT		
QUITLOOP		
RETURN		
SCAN		
SWITCH		
ENDFOR (FOR)		
FROM (FOR)		
STEP (FOR)		
TO (FOR)		
ELSE (IF)		
ENDIF (IF)		
THEN (IF)		
BIG (RUN)		
ENDSCAN (SCAN)		
FOR (SCAN)		
FOREGROUND (SESSION)		
ENDSWITCH (SWITCH)		
OTHERWISE (SWITCH)		
ENDWHILE (WHILE)		
WHILE		

Table 2—continued

Command	Paradox Key(s)	ASCII Code

Input/Output Commands
= (assignment operator)
?
??
@
ACCEPT
BEEP
CANVAS
CLOSE PRINTER
CURSOR
ECHO
KEYPRESS
MESSAGE
OPEN
PAINTCANVAS
PRINT FILE
PRINTER
PROMPT
SETPRINTER
SHOWARRAY
SHOWFILES
SHOWMENU
SHOWTABLES
STYLE
STYLE ATTRIBUTE
SYNCCURSOR
WAIT
TO (ACCEPT)
OFF (CANVAS)
ON (CANVAS)
EOL (CLEAR)
EOS (CLEAR)
PRINTER (CLOSE)
BAR (CURSOR)
BOX (CURSOR)
NORMAL (CURSOR)
OFF (CURSOR)

Table 2—continued

Command	Paradox Key(s)	ASCII Code
FAST (ECHO)		
NORMAL (ECHO)		
OFF (ECHO)		
SLOW (ECHO)		
PRINTER (OPEN)		
ATTRIBUTE (PAINTCANVAS)		
BLINK (PAINTCANVAS)		
BORDER (PAINTCANVAS)		
FILL (PAINTCANVAS)		
INTENSE (PAINTCANVAS)		
REVERSE (PAINTCANVAS)		
FILE (PRINT)		
OFF (PRINTER)		
ON (PRINTER)		
OFF (SETMARGIN)		
ON (SETMARGIN)		
AUX (SETPRINTER)		
COM1 (SETPRINTER)		
LPT1 (SETPRINTER)		
TABLEORDER (SETQUERYORDER)		
DEFAULT (SHOWARRAY)		
KEYTO (SHOWARRAY)		
TO (SHOWARRAY)		
UNTIL (SHOWARRAY)		
KEYTO (SHOWFILES)		
NOEXT (SHOWFILES)		
TO (SHOWFILES)		
UNTIL (SHOWFILES)		
DEFAULT (SHOWMENU)		
KEYTO (SHOWMENU)		
TO (SHOWMENU)		
UNTIL (SHOWMENU)		
KEYTO (SHOWTABLES)		
TO (SHOWTABLES)		
UNTIL (SHOWTABLES)		
ATTRIBUTE (STYLE)		
BLINK (STYLE)		
INTENSE (STYLE)		

Table 2—continued

Command	Paradox Key(s)	ASCII Code
REVERSE (STYLE)		
ENDTEXT (TEXT)		
TEXT		
FIELD (WAIT)		
MESSAGE (WAIT)		
PROMPT (WAIT)		
RECORD (WAIT)		
TABLE (WAIT)		
UNTIL (WAIT)		

Key Equivalent Commands

Command	Paradox Key(s)	ASCII Code
BACKSPACE	[BACKSPACE]	8
CLEAR		
CLEARALL	[ALT][F8]	-111
CLEARIMAGE	[F8]	-66
COEDITKEY	[ALT][F9]	-112
CROSSTABKEY	[CTRL][X]	-45
CTRLBACKSPACE	[CTRL][BS]	127
CTRLBREAK	[CTRL][BREAK]	
CTRLEND	[CTRL][END]	-117
CTRLHOME	[CTRL][HOME]	-119
CTRLLEFT	[CTRL][LEFT]	-115
CTRLPGDN	[CTRL][PGDN]	-118
CTRLPGUP	[CTRL][PGUP]	-132
CTRLRIGHT	[CTRL][RIGHT]	-116
DEL	[DEL]	-83
DELETELINE	[CTRL][Y]	25
DITTO	[CTRL][D]	4
DOS	[CTRL][O]	15
DOSBIG	[ALT][O]	-24
DOWN	[DOWN]	-80
DOWNIMAGE	[F4]	-62
DO_IT!	[F2]	-60
EDITKEY	[F9]	-67
EDITOR	[CTRL][E]	5
END		-79
ENTER	[ENTER]	13
ESC	[ESC]	27

Table 2—continued

Command	Paradox Key(s)	ASCII Code
EXAMPLE	[F5]	-63
FIELDVIEW	[CTRL][F]	6
FORMKEY	[F7]	-65
GRAPHKEY		-100
HELP	[F1]	-59
HOME	[HOME]	-71
INS	[INS]	-82
INSTANTPLAY	[ALT][F4]	-107
INSTANTRECORD	[ALT][F3]	-106
INSTANTREPORT	[ALT][F7]	-110
KEYLOOKUP	[ALT][K]	-37
LEFT	[LEFT]	-75
LOCKKEY	[ALT][L]	-38
REFRESHKEY	[ALT][R]	-19
RESYNCKEY	[CTRL][L]	12
REVERSETAB	[SHIFT][TAB]	-15
RIGHT	[RIGHT]	-77
ROTATE	[CTRL][R]	18
TAB	[TAB]	9
TOQPRO	[CTRL][F10]	-103
UNDO	[CTRL][U]	21
UP	[UP]	-72
UPIMAGE	[F3]	-61
VERTRULER	[CTRL][V]	22
ZOOM	[CTRL][Z]	26
ZOOMNEXT	[ALT][Z]	-44
MENU	[F10]	-68

SQL Commands
SQL
SQLAUTOCOMMIT
SQLBREAKCONNECT
SQLCLEARCONNECT
SQLCOMMIT
SQLCONNECT
SQLCONNECTINFO
SQLERRORCODE
SQLERRORMESSAGE

Table 2—continued

Command	Paradox Key(s)	ASCII Code
SQLFETCH		
SQLISREPLICA		
SQLMAKECONNECT		
SQLMAPINFO		
SQLRELEASE		
SQLRESTORECONNECT		
SQLROLLBACK		
SQLSAVECONNECT		
SQLSELECTCONNECT		
SQLSETINTERRUPT		
SQLSTARTTRANS		
SQLVAL		

Multiuser Commands
IMAGERIGHTS
LOCKRECORD
PRIVTABLES
REFRESH
SETRETRYPERIOD
UNLOCK
UNLOCKRECORD
READONLY (IMAGERIGHTS)
UPDATE (IMAGERIGHTS)
ALL (UNLOCK)

Procedure and Procedure Library Commands
CREATELIB
EXECPROC
INFOLIB
PROC
READLIB
RELEASE
SETSWAP
WRITELIB
SIZE (CREATELIB)
CLOSED (PROC)
ENDPROC (PROC)
USEVARS (PROC)

Table 2—continued

Command	Paradox Key(s)	ASCII Code
IMMEDIATE (READLIB)		
ALL (RELEASE)		
PROCS (RELEASE)		
VARS (RELEASE)		
ALL (SAVEVARS)		
System Control Commands		
DEBUG		
EDITLOG		
EXECUTE		
NOSHELL		
RESET		
RUN		
SAVETABLES		
SESSION		
SETKEY		
SETMAXSIZE		
SLEEP		
INDEX (EDITLOG)		
MARK (EDITLOG)		
PERMANENT (EDITLOG)		
REVERT (EDITLOG)		
PRIVATE (PROC)		
NOREFRESH (RUN)		
NORESTORE (RUN)		
SLEEP (RUN)		
Variable/Array Commands		
ARRAY		
COPYFROMARRAY		
COPYTOARRAY		
FORMTABLES		
REPORTTABLES		
SAVEVARS		
Workspace Commands		
CHECK	[F6]	-64
CHECKDESCENDING	[CTRL][F6]	-99

Table 2—continued

ASCII CODE	Command	Paradox Key(s)
CHECKPLUS	[ALT][F6]	-109
FIRSTSHOW		
GROUPBY	[SHIFT][F6]	-89
LOCATE		
MOVETO		
PASSWORD		
PGDN	[PGDN]	-81
PGUP	[PGUP]	-73
REQUIREDCHECK		
SELECT		
SETMARGIN		
SETNEGCOLOR		
SETQUERYORDER		
SETRECORDPOSITION		
SKIP		
TYPEIN		
NEXT (LOCATE)		
PATTERN (LOCATE)		
FIELD (MOVETO)		
RECORD (MOVETO)		
OFF (REQUIREDCHECK)		
ON (REQUIREDCHECK)		
BOTH (SETNEGCOLOR)		
CURRENCY (SETNEGCOLOR)		
NUMERIC (SETNEGCOLOR)		
OFF (SETNEGCOLOR)		
ON (SETNEGCOLOR)		
IMAGEORDER (SETQUERYORDER)		
INVENTORY		

Table 3
Paradox Commands with Equivalent Menu Commands

Command	Menu Equivalent Command(s)
Abbreviated Menu Commands	
ADD	MENU{TOOLS}{MORE}{ADD}{SOURCETABLE}{TARGETTABLE}
CANCELEDIT	MENU{IMAGE}{CANCEL}{NO,YES}
COEDIT	MENU{MODIFY}{COEDIT}{TABLENAME}
COPYREPORT	MENU{TOOLS}{COPY}{REPORT}{SAMETABLE, DIFFERENTTABLE} {SOURCE TABLENAME}{SOURCE REPORT}{TARGETTABLENAME} {TARGET REPORT}
CREATE	MENU{CREATE}{TABLENAME}
DELETE	MENU{TOOLS}{MORE}{DELETE}{TABLENAME}{CANCEL,OK}
EDIT	MENU{MODIFY}{EDIT}{TABLENAME}
EMPTY	MENU{TOOLS}{MORE}{EMPTY}{TABLENAME}{CANCEL,OK}
EXIT	MENU{EXIT}{NO,YES}
INDEX	MENU{TOOLS}{QUERYSPEED}
LOCK	MENU{TOOLS}{INFO}{LOCK}{TABLENAME}
PICKFORM	MENU{IMAGE}{PICKFORM}{FORMNUMBER}
PLAY	MENU{SCRIPTS}{PLAY}{SCRIPTNAME}
PRINT	MENU{REPORT}{OUTPUT}{TABLENAME}{REPORTNUMBER}{PRINTER,FILE(FILENAME),SCREEN}
PROTECT	MENU{TOOLS}{MORE}{PROTECT}{PASSWORD}{PASSWORD}{CLEAR PASSWORD}{WRITE-PROTECT}
QUERY	MENU{ASK}{TABLENAME}
RENAME	MENU{TOOLS}{RENAME}{TABLE,SCRIPT,REPORT,FORM,GRAPH}
REPORT	MENU{REPORT}{OUTPUT,DESIGN,CHANGE,RANGEOUTPUT,SETPRINTER}{TABLENAME}{REPORTNUMBER}{PRINTER,SCREEN,FILE}
SETDIR	MENU{TOOLS}{MORE}{DIRECTORY}{DOSPATH}{CANCEL,OK}
SETPRIVDIR	MENU{TOOLS}{NET}{SETPRIVATE}{DOSPATH}{CANCEL,OK}
SETUSERNAME	MENU{TOOLS}{NET}{USERNAME}{NAME}
SORT	MENU{MODIFY}{SORT}{SAME,NEW}{SORTORDER}
SUBTRACT	MENU{TOOLS}{MORE}{SUBTRACT}{SOURCETABLE}{TARGETTABLE}
UNPASSWORD	MENU{TOOLS}{MORE}{PROTECT}{CLEAR PASSWORDS}
VIEW	MENU{VIEW}{TABLENAME}
LIKE (CREATE)	MENU{CREATE}{TABLENAME}{MENU}{BORROW}{TABLENAME}

Table 3—continued

Command	Menu Equivalent Command(s)
MAINTAINED (INDEX)	MENU{TOOLS}{QUERYSPEED}
ENDQUERY (QUERY)	MENU{ASK}{TABLENAME}
ON (SORT)	MENU{MODIFY}{SORT}{TABLENAME}{SAME,NEW}{ENTER SORT ORDER}{DO_IT!,CANCEL}

Key Commands

Command	Menu Equivalent Command(s)
CROSSTABKEY	MENU{IMAGE}{GRAPH}{CROSSTAB}{SUM,COUNT,MIN,MAX}{ROWVAL,COLVAL,CROSSVAL}
DOS	MENU{TOOLS}{MORE}{TODOS}{EXIT}
DOSBIG	MENU{TOOLS}{MORE}{TODOS}{EXIT}
DO_IT!	MENU{DO_IT!}
EDITOR	MENU{SCRIPTS}{EDITOR}{WRITE,EDIT}{SCRIPTNAME}

Workspace Commands

Command	Menu Equivalent Command(s)
MOVETO	MENU{IMAGE}{ZOOM}{FIELD,RECORD,VALUE}

Table 4
Quick Function Reference

Function	PAL Syntax
Canvas/Information Functions	
BOT	BOT()
CHECKMARKSTATUS	CHECKMARKSTATUS()
Date/Time Functions	
BLANKDATE	BLANKDATE()
DATEVAL	DATEVAL(string)
DAY	DAY(Date)
DOW	DOW(tablename,fieldname)
MONTH	MONTH(date)
MOY	MOY(date)
TIME	TIME()
TODAY	TODAY()
YEAR	YEAR(date)

Table 4—continued

Function	PAL Syntax
Financial Functions	
FV	FV(number1,number2,number3)
PMT	PMT(number1,number2,number3)
PV	PV(number1,number2,number3)
Information Functions	
ARRAYSIZE	ARRAYSIZE(arrayname)
CHARWAITING	CHARWAITING()
DIREXISTS	DIREXISTS(dospath)
EOT	EOT()
ERRORCODE	ERRORCODE()
ERRORMESSAGE	ERRORMESSAGE()
ERRORUSER	ERRORUSER()
FAMILYRIGHTS	FAMILYRIGHTS(tablename,string)
FIELDRIGHTS	FIELDRIGHTS(tablename,fieldname,string)
FILESIZE	FILESIZE(filename)
FORMTYPE°	FORMTYPE(string)
GETCHAR	GETCHAR()
HELPMODE	HELPMODE()
ISBLANK	ISBLANK(expression)
ISEMPTY	ISEMPTY(tablename)
ISENCRYPTED	ISENCRYPTED(tablename)
ISFILE	ISFILE(string)
ISSHARED	ISSHARED(tablename)
ISSQL	ISSQL()
ISTABLE	ISTABLE(tablename)
ISVALID	ISVALID()
RMEMLEFT°	RMEMLEFT()
TABLERIGHTS	TABLERIGHTS(tablename,string)
TYPE	TYPE(expression)
Functions Used in Various Contexts	
FORMAT	FORMAT(FormatSpec,String)
Mathematical Functions	
ABS	ABS(number)
ACOS	ACOS(number)

Table 4—continued

Function	PAL Syntax
ASC	ASC(char)
ASIN	ASIN(number)
ATAN	ATAN(number)
ATAN2	ATAN2(number)
BLANKNUM	BLANKNUM()
COS	COS(number)
EXP	EXP(number)
INT	INT(number)
LN	LN(number)
LOG	LOG(number)
MOD	MOD(number1,number2)
PI	PI()
POW	POW(number1,number2)
RAND	RAND()
ROUND	ROUND(number1,round precision)
SIN	SIN(number)
SQRT	SQRT(number)
TAN	TAN(number)

Statistical Functions

Function	PAL Syntax
CAVERAGE	CAVERAGE(tablename,fieldname)
CCOUNT	CCOUNT(tablename,fieldname)
CMAX	CMAX(tablename,fieldname)
CMIN	CMIN(tablename,fieldname)
CNPV	CNPV(tablename,fieldname,number)
CSTD	CSTD(tablename,fieldname)
CSUM	CSUM(tablename,fieldname)
CVAR	CVAR(tablename,fieldname)
IMAGECAVERAGE	IMAGECAVERAGE()
IMAGECCOUNT	IMAGECCOUNT()
IMAGECMAX	IMAGECMAX()
IMAGECMIN	IMAGECMIN()
IMAGECSUM	IMAGECSUM()
MAX	MAX(number1,number2)
MIN	MIN(number1,number2)

Table 4—continued

Function	PAL Syntax
String Functions	
CHR	CHR(number)
FIELDSTR	FIELDSTR()
FILL	FILL(expression,number)
ISASSIGNED	ISASSIGNED(string)
LEN	LEN(expression)
LOWER	LOWER(expression)
MATCH	MATCH(string,patternstring,varnamelist)
NUMVAL	NUMVAL(string)
SEARCH	SEARCH(substring,string)
SPACES	SPACES(number)
STRVAL	STRVAL(expression)
SUBSTR	SUBSTR(string,number1,number2)
UPPER	UPPER(string)
WorkSpace/Canvas/Status Functions	
TABLE	TABLE(tablename)
ISBLANKZERO	ISBLANKZERO()
ISFIELDVIEW	ISFIELDVIEW()
ISFORMVIEW	ISFORMVIEW()
ISINSERTMODE	ISINSERTMODE()
ISLINKLOCKED	ISLINKLOCKED()
ISMULTIFORM	ISMULTIFORM(tablename,formname)
ISMULTIREPORT	ISMULTIREPORT(tablename,reportname)
ISRUNTIME	ISRUNTIME()
LINKTYPE	LINKTYPE()
LOCKSTATUS	LOCKSTATUS(tablename,locktype)
MEMLEFT	MEMLEFT()
MENUCHOICE	MENUCHOICE()
MONITOR	MONITOR()
NETTYPE	NETTYPE()
NFIELDS	NFIELDS(tablename)
NIMAGERECORDS	NIMAGERECORDS()
NIMAGES	NIMAGES()
NKEYFIELDS	NKEYFIELDS(tablename)
NPAGES	NPAGES()
NRECORDS	NRECORDS(tablename)

Table 4—continued

Function	PAL Syntax
NROWS	NROWS()
PAGENO	PAGENO()
PAGEWIDTH	PAGEWIDTH()
PRINTERSTATUS	PRINTERSTATUS()
PRIVDIR	PRIVDIR()
QUERYORDER	QUERYORDER()
RECNO	RECNO()
RECORDSTATUS*	RECORDSTATUS()
RETRYPERIOD	RETRYPERIOD()
ROW	ROW()
ROWNO	ROWNO()
SDIR	SDIR()
SORTORDER	SORTORDER()
SYSCOLOR	SYSCOLOR()
SYSMODE	SYSMODE()
USERNAME	USERNAME()
VERSION	VERSION()
WINDOW	WINDOW()

Workspace/Canvas/Status (Other) Functions

Function	PAL Syntax
ATFIRST	ATFIRST()
ATLAST	ATLAST()
BANDINFO	BANDINFO()
COL	COL()
COLNO	COLNO()
CURSORCHAR	CURSORCHAR()
CURSORLINE	CURSORLINE()
DIRECTORY	DIRECTORY()
DRIVESPACE	DRIVESPACE(string)
DRIVESTATUS	DRIVESTATUS(string)
FIELD	FIELD()
FIELDINFO	FIELDINFO()
FIELDNO	FIELDNO(fieldname,tablename)
FIELDTYPE	FIELDTYPE()
FORM	FORM()
GRAPHTYPE	GRAPHTYPE()
IMAGENO	IMAGENO()
IMAGETYPE	IMAGETYPE()

Table 5
Paradox Reserved Words

Reserved Word	Type	Context Use
?	COMMAND	Input/Output
??	COMMAND	Input/Output
@	COMMAND	Input/Output
ABS	FUNCTION	Mathematical
ACCEPT	COMMAND	Input/Output
ACOS	FUNCTION	Mathematical
ADD	COMMAND	Abbrev Menu Command
ALL (RELEASE)	COMMAND	Proc/Proc Library
ALL (SAVEVARS)	COMMAND	Proc/Proc Library
ALL (UNLOCK)	COMMAND	Multiuser
ARRAY	COMMAND	Variable/Array
ARRAYSIZE	FUNCTION	Information
ASC	FUNCTION	Mathematical
ASIN	FUNCTION	Mathematical
ATAN	FUNCTION	Mathematical
ATAN2	FUNCTION	Mathematical
ATFIRST	FUNCTION	Workspace/Canvas/Status
ATLAST	FUNCTION	Workspace/Canvas/Status
ATTRIBUTE	COMMAND	Input/Output
AUX (SETPRINTER)	COMMAND	Input/Output
BACKSPACE	COMMAND	Key
BANDINFO	FUNCTION	Workspace/Canvas/Status
BAR (CURSOR)	COMMAND	Input/Output
BEEP	COMMAND	Input/Output
BIG (RUN)	COMMAND	Control (Programming) Structure
BLANKDATE	FUNCTION	Date/Time
BLANKNUM	FUNCTION	Mathematical
BLINK (PAINTCANVAS)	COMMAND	Input/Output
BLINK (STYLE)	COMMAND	Input/Output
BORDER (PAINTCANVAS)	COMMAND	Input/Output
BOT	FUNCTION	Canvas/Information
BOTH (SETNEGCOLOR)	COMMAND	Workspace
BOX (CURSOR)	COMMAND	Input/Output
CALCDEBUG	COMMAND	Abbrev Menu Command
CANCELEDIT	COMMAND	Abbrev Menu Command
CANVAS	COMMAND	Input/Output
CAVERAGE	FUNCTION	Statistical

Table 5—continued

Reserved Word	Type	Context Use
CCOUNT	FUNCTION	Statistical
CHARWAITING	FUNCTION	Information
CHECK	COMMAND	Workspace
CHECKDESCENDING	COMMAND	Workspace
CHECKMARK	FUNCTION	Canvas/Information
CHECKPLUS	COMMAND	Workspace
CHR	FUNCTION	String
CLEAR	COMMAND	Key
CLEARALL	COMMAND	Key
CLEARIMAGE	COMMAND	Key
CLOSE PRINTER	COMMAND	Input/Output
CLOSED (PROC)	COMMAND	Proc/Proc Library
CMAX	FUNCTION	Statistical
CMIN	FUNCTION	Statistical
CNPV	FUNCTION	Statistical
COEDIT	COMMAND	Abbrev Menu Command
COEDITKEY	COMMAND	Key
COL	FUNCTION	Workspace/Canvas/Status
COLNO	FUNCTION	Workspace/Canvas/Status
COM1 (SETPRINTER)	COMMAND	Input/Output
COPY	COMMAND	Abbrev Menu Command
COPYFORM	COMMAND	Abbrev Menu Command
COPYFROMARRAY	COMMAND	Variable/Array
COPYREPORT	COMMAND	Abbrev Menu Command
COPYTOARRAY	COMMAND	Variable/Array
COS	FUNCTION	Mathematical
CREATE	COMMAND	Abbrev Menu Command
CREATELIB	COMMAND	Proc/Proc Library
CROSSTABKEY	COMMAND	Key
CSTD	FUNCTION	Statistical
CSUM	FUNCTION	Statistical
CTRLBACKSPACE	COMMAND	Key
CTRLBREAK	COMMAND	Key
CTRLEND	COMMAND	Key
CTRLHOME	COMMAND	Key
CTRLLEFT	COMMAND	Key
CTRLPGDN	COMMAND	Key
CTRLPGUP	COMMAND	Key

Table 5—continued

Reserved Word	Type	Context Use
CTRLRIGHT	COMMAND	Key
CURSOR	COMMAND	Input/Output
CURSORCHAR	FUNCTION	Workspace/Canvas/Status
CURSORLINE	FUNCTION	Workspace/Canvas/Status
CVAR	FUNCTION	Statistical
DATEVAL	FUNCTION	Date/Time
DAY	FUNCTION	Date/Time
DEBUG	COMMAND	System Control PAL/Paradox
DEFAULT(SHOWARRAY)	COMMAND	Input/Output
DEFAULT(SHOWMENU)	COMMAND	Input/Output
DEL	COMMAND	Key
DELETE	COMMAND	Abbrev Menu Command
DELETELINE	COMMAND	Key
DIRECTORY	FUNCTION	Workspace/Canvas/Status
DIREXISTS	FUNCTION	Information
DITTO	COMMAND	Key
DOS	COMMAND	Key
DOSBIG	COMMAND	Key
DOW	FUNCTION	Date/Time
DOWN	COMMAND	Key
DOWNIMAGE	COMMAND	Key
DO_IT!	COMMAND	Key
DRIVESPACE	FUNCTION	Workspace/Canvas/Status
DRIVESTATUS	FUNCTION	Workspace/Canvas/Status
ECHO	COMMAND	Input/Output
EDIT	COMMAND	Abbrev Menu Command
EDITKEY	COMMAND	Key
EDITLOG	COMMAND	System Control PAL/Paradox
EDITOR	COMMAND	Key
ELSE (IF)	COMMAND	Control (Programming) Structure
EMPTY	COMMAND	Abbrev Menu Command
END	COMMAND	Key
ENDFOR (FOR)	COMMAND	Control (Programming) Structure
ENDIF (IF)	COMMAND	Control (Programming) Structure
ENDPROC (PROC)	COMMAND	Proc/Proc Library
ENDQUERY (QUERY)	COMMAND	Abbrev Menu Command
ENDSCAN (SCAN)	COMMAND	Control (Programming) Structure
ENDSWITCH (SWITCH)	COMMAND	Control (Programming) Structure

Table 5—continued

Reserved Word	Type	Context Use
ENDTEXT (TEXT)	COMMAND	Input/Output
ENDWHILE (WHILE)	COMMAND	Control (Programming) Structure
ENTER	COMMAND	Key
EOL (CLEAR)	COMMAND	Input/Output
EOS (CLEAR)	COMMAND	Input/Output
EOT	FUNCTION	Information
ERRORCODE	FUNCTION	Information
ERRORMESSAGE	FUNCTION	Information
ERRORUSER	FUNCTION	Information
ESC	COMMAND	Key
EXAMPLE	COMMAND	Key
EXECPROC	COMMAND	Proc/Proc Library
EXECUTE	COMMAND	System Control PAL/Paradox
EXIT	COMMAND	Abbrev Menu Command
EXP	FUNCTION	Mathematical
FAMILYRIGHTS	FUNCTION	Information
FAST (ECHO)	COMMAND	Input/Output
FIELD	FUNCTION	Workspace/Canvas/Status
FIELD (MOVETO)	COMMAND	Workspace
FIELD (WAIT)	COMMAND	Input/Output
FIELDINFO	FUNCTION	Workspace/Canvas/Status
FIELDNO	FUNCTION	Workspace/Canvas/Status
FIELDRIGHTS	FUNCTION	Information
FIELDSTR	FUNCTION	String
FIELDTYPE	FUNCTION	Workspace/Canvas/Status
FIELDVIEW	COMMAND	Key
FILE (PRINT)	COMMAND	Input/Output
FILESIZE	FUNCTION	Information
FILL	FUNCTION	String
FILL (PAINTCANVAS)	COMMAND	Input/Output
FIRSTSHOW	COMMAND	Workspace
FOR	COMMAND	Control (Programming) Structure
FOR (SCAN)	COMMAND	Control (Programming) Structure
FOREGROUND (SESSION)	COMMAND	Control (Programming) Structure
FORM	FUNCTION	Workspace/Canvas/Status
FORMAT	FUNCTION	Many Contexts
FORMKEY	COMMAND	Key
FORMTABLES	COMMAND	Variable/Array

Table 5—continued

Reserved Word	Type	Context Use
FORMTYPE*	FUNCTION	Information
FROM (FOR)	COMMAND	Control (Programming) Structure
FV	FUNCTION	Financial
GETCHAR	FUNCTION	Information
GRAPHKEY	COMMAND	Key
GRAPHTYPE	FUNCTION	Workspace/Canvas/Status
GROUPBY	COMMAND	Workspace
HELP	COMMAND	Key
HELPMODE	FUNCTION	Information
HOME	COMMAND	Key
IF	COMMAND	Control (Programming) Structure
IMAGECAVERAGE	FUNCTION	Statistical
IMAGECCOUNT	FUNCTION	Statistical
IMAGECMAX	FUNCTION	Statistical
IMAGECMIN	FUNCTION	Statistical
IMAGECSUM	FUNCTION	Statistical
IMAGENO	FUNCTION	Workspace/Canvas/Status
IMAGEORDER	COMMAND	Workspace
IMAGERIGHTS	COMMAND	Multiuser
IMAGETYPE	FUNCTION	Workspace/Canvas/Status
IMMEDIATE (READLIB)	COMMAND	Proc/Proc Library
INDEX	COMMAND	Abbrev Menu Command
INDEX (EDITLOG)	COMMAND	System Control PAL/Paradox
INFOLIB	COMMAND	Proc/Proc Library
INS	COMMAND	Key
INSTANTPLAY	COMMAND	Key
INSTANTRECORD	COMMAND	Key
INSTANTREPORT	COMMAND	Key
INT	FUNCTION	Mathematical
INTENSE (STYLE)	COMMAND	Input/Output
INVENTORY	MENU	Workspace
ISASSIGNED	FUNCTION	String
ISBLANK	FUNCTION	Information
ISBLANKZERO	FUNCTION	Workspace/Canvas/Status
ISEMPTY	FUNCTION	Information
ISENCRYPTED	FUNCTION	Information
ISFIELDVIEW	FUNCTION	Workspace/Canvas/Status
ISFILE	FUNCTION	Information

*Paradox 3.5 command

Table 5—continued

Reserved Word	Type	Context Use
ISFORMVIEW	FUNCTION	Workspace/Canvas/Status
ISINSERTMODE	FUNCTION	Workspace/Canvas/Status
ISLINKLOCKED	FUNCTION	Workspace/Canvas/Status
ISMULTIFORM	FUNCTION	Workspace/Canvas/Status
ISMULTIREPORT	FUNCTION	Workspace/Canvas/Status
ISRUNTIME	FUNCTION	Workspace/Canvas/Status
ISSHARED	FUNCTION	Information
ISSQL	FUNCTION	Information
ISTABLE	FUNCTION	Information
ISVALID	FUNCTION	Information
KEYLOOKUP	COMMAND	Key
KEYPRESS	COMMAND	Input/Output
KEYTO (SHOWARRAY)	COMMAND	Input/Output
KEYTO (SHOWFILES)	COMMAND	Input/Output
KEYTO (SHOWMENU)	COMMAND	Input/Output
KEYTO (SHOWTABLES)	COMMAND	Input/Output
LEFT	COMMAND	Key
LEN	FUNCTION	String
LIKE (CREATE)	COMMAND	Abbrev Menu Command
LINKTYPE	FUNCTION	Workspace/Canvas/Status
LN	FUNCTION	Mathematical
LOCATE	COMMAND	Workspace
LOCK	COMMAND	Abbrev Menu Command
LOCKKEY	COMMAND	Key
LOCKRECORD	COMMAND	Multiuser
LOCKSTATUS	FUNCTION	Workspace/Canvas/Status
LOG	FUNCTION	Mathematical
LOOP	COMMAND	Control (Programming) Structure
LOWER	FUNCTION	String
LPT1 (SETPRINTER)	COMMAND	Input/Output
MAINTAINED (INDEX)	COMMAND	Abbrev Menu Command
MARK (EDITLOG)	COMMAND	System Control PAL/Paradox
MATCH	FUNCTION	String
MAX	FUNCTION	Statistical
MEMLEFT	FUNCTION	Workspace/Canvas/Status
MENU	MENU	Key
MENUCHOICE	FUNCTION	Workspace/Canvas/Status
MESSAGE	COMMAND	Input/Output

Table 5—continued

Reserved Word	Type	Context Use
MESSAGE (WAIT)	COMMAND	Input/Output
MIN	FUNCTION	Statistical
MOD	FUNCTION	Mathematical
MONITOR	FUNCTION	Workspace/Canvas/Status
MONTH	FUNCTION	Date/Time
MOVETO	COMMAND	Workspace
MOY	FUNCTION	Date/Time
NETTYPE	FUNCTION	Workspace/Canvas/Status
NEXT (LOCATE)	COMMAND	Workspace
NFIELDS	FUNCTION	Workspace/Canvas/Status
NIMAGERECORDS	FUNCTION	WorkSpace/Canvas/Status
NIMAGES	FUNCTION	Workspace/Canvas/Status
NKEYFIELDS	FUNCTION	Workspace/Canvas/Status
NOEXT (SHOWFILES)	COMMAND	Input/Output
NOREFRESH (RUN)	COMMAND	System Control PAL/Paradox
NORESTORE (RUN)	COMMAND	System Control PAL/Paradox
NORMAL (CURSOR)	COMMAND	Input/Output
NORMAL (ECHO)	COMMAND	Input/Output
NOSHELL	COMMAND	System Control PAL/Paradox
NPAGES	FUNCTION	Workspace/Canvas/Status
NRECORDS	FUNCTION	Workspace/Canvas/Status
NROWS	FUNCTION	Workspace/Canvas/Status
NUMVAL	FUNCTION	String
OFF (CANVAS)	COMMAND	Input/Output
OFF (CURSOR)	COMMAND	Input/Output
OFF (ECHO)	COMMAND	Input/Output
OFF (PRINTER)	COMMAND	Input/Output
OFF (REQUIREDCHECK)	COMMAND	Workspace
OFF (SETMARGIN)	COMMAND	Input/Output
OFF (SETNEGCOLOR)	COMMAND	Workspace
ON (CANVAS)	COMMAND	Input/Output
ON (PRINTER)	COMMAND	Input/Output
ON (REQUIREDCHECK)	COMMAND	Workspace
ON (SETMARGIN)	COMMAND	Input/Output
ON (SETNEGCOLOR)	COMMAND	Workspace
ON (SORT)	COMMAND	Abbrev Menu Command
OPEN	COMMAND	Input/Output
OTHERWISE (SWITCH)	COMMAND	Control (Programming) Structure

Table 5—continued

Reserved Word	Type	Context Use
PAGENO	FUNCTION	Workspace/Canvas/Status
PAGEWIDTH	FUNCTION	Workspace/Canvas/Status
PAINTCANVAS	COMMAND	Input/Output
PASSWORD	COMMAND	Workspace
PATTERN (LOCATE)	COMMAND	Workspace
PERMANENT (EDITLOG)	COMMAND	System Control PAL/Paradox
PGDN	COMMAND	Workspace
PGUP	COMMAND	Workspace
PI	FUNCTION	Mathematical
PICKFORM	COMMAND	Abbrev Menu Command
PLAY	COMMAND	Abbrev Menu Command
PMT	FUNCTION	Financial
POW	FUNCTION	Mathematical
PRINT	COMMAND	Abbrev Menu Command
PRINT FILE	COMMAND	Input/Output
PRINTER	COMMAND	Input/Output
PRINTER (CLOSE)	COMMAND	Input/Output
PRINTER (OPEN)	COMMAND	Input/Output
PRINTERSTATUS	FUNCTION	Workspace/Canvas/Status
PRIVATE (PROC)	COMMAND	System Control PAL/Paradox
PRIVDIR	FUNCTION	Workspace/Canvas/Status
PRIVTABLES	COMMAND	Multiuser
PROC	COMMAND	Proc/Proc Library
PROCS(RELEASE)	COMMAND	Proc/Proc Library
PROMPT	COMMAND	Input/Output
PROMPT(WAIT)	COMMAND	Input/Output
PROTECT	COMMAND	Abbrev Menu Command
PV	FUNCTION	Financial
QUERY	COMMAND	Abbrev Menu Command
QUERYORDER	FUNCTION	Workspace/Canvas/Status
QUIT	COMMAND	Control (Programming) Structure
QUITLOOP	COMMAND	Control (Programming) Structure
RAND	FUNCTION	Mathematical
READLIB	COMMAND	Proc/Proc Library
RECNO	FUNCTION	WorkSpace/Canvas/Status
RECORD(MOVETO)	COMMAND	Workspace
RECORD (WAIT)	COMMAND	Input/Output

Table 5—continued

Reserved Word	Type	Context Use
RECORDSTATUS°	FUNCTION	Workspace/Canvas/Status
REFRESH	COMMAND	Multiuser
REFRESHKEY	COMMAND	Key
RELEASE	COMMAND	Proc/Proc Library
RENAME	COMMAND	Abbrev Menu Command
REPORT	COMMAND	Abbrev Menu Command
REPORTTABLES	COMMAND	Variable/Array
REQUIREDCHECK	COMMAND	Workspace
RESET	COMMAND	System Control PAL/Paradox
RESYNCKEY	COMMAND	Key
RETRYPERIOD	FUNCTION	Workspace/Canvas/Status
RETURN	COMMAND	Control (Programming) Structure
REVERSE (STYLE)	COMMAND	Input/Output
REVERSETAB	COMMAND	Key
REVERT (EDITLOG)	COMMAND	System Control PAL/Paradox
RIGHT	COMMAND	Key
RMEMLEFT°	FUNCTION	Information
ROTATE	COMMAND	Key
ROUND	FUNCTION	Mathematical
ROW	FUNCTION	Workspace/Canvas/Status
ROWNO	FUNCTION	Workspace/Canvas/Status
RUN	COMMAND	System Control PAL/Paradox
SAVETABLES°	COMMAND	System Control PAL/Paradox
SAVEVARS	COMMAND	Variable/Array
SCAN	COMMAND	Control (Programming) Structure
SDIR	FUNCTION	Workspace/Canvas/Status
SEARCH	FUNCTION	String
SELECT	COMMAND	Workspace
SESSION	COMMAND	System Control PAL/Paradox
SETDIR	COMMAND	Abbrev Menu Command
SETKEY	COMMAND	System Control PAL/Paradox
SETMARGIN	COMMAND	Workspace
SETMAXSIZE	COMMAND	System Control PAL/Paradox
SETNEGCOLOR	COMMAND	Workspace
SETPRINTER	COMMAND	Input/Output
SETPRIVDIR	COMMAND	Abbrev Menu Command
SETQUERYORDER	COMMAND	Workspace

°Paradox 3.5 command

Table 5—continued

Reserved Word	Type	Context Use
SETRECORDPOSITION	COMMAND	Workspace
SETRETRYPERIOD	COMMAND	Multiuser
SETSWAP	COMMAND	Proc/Proc Library
SETUSERNAME	COMMAND	Abbrev Menu Command
SHOWARRAY	COMMAND	Input/Output
SHOWFILES	COMMAND	Input/Output
SHOWMENU	COMMAND	Input/Output
SHOWTABLES	COMMAND	Input/Output
SIN	FUNCTION	Mathematical
SIZE (CREATELIB)	COMMAND	Proc/Proc Library
SKIP	COMMAND	Workspace
SLEEP	COMMAND	System Control PAL/Paradox
SLEEP (RUN)	COMMAND	System Control PAL/Paradox
SLOW (ECHO)	COMMAND	Input/Output
SORT	COMMAND	Abbrev Menu Command
SORTORDER	FUNCTION	Workspace/Canvas/Status
SPACES	FUNCTION	String
SQL°	MENU	Managing SQL
SQLAUTOCOMMIT°	MENU	Managing SQL
SQLBREAKCONNECT°	MENU	Managing SQL
SQLCLEARCONNECT°	MENU	Managing SQL
SQLCOMMIT°	MENU	Managing SQL
SQLCONNECT°	MENU	Managing SQL
SQLCONNECTINFO°	MENU	Managing SQL
SQLERRORCODE°	MENU	Managing SQL
SQLERRORMESSAGE°	MENU	Managing SQL
SQLFETCH°	MENU	Managing SQL
SQLISREPLICA°	MENU	Managing SQL
SQLMAKECONNECT°	MENU	Managing SQL
SQLMAPINFO°	MENU	Managing SQL
SQLRELEASE°	MENU	Managing SQL
SQLRESTORECONNECT°	MENU	Managing SQL
SQLROLLBACK°	MENU	Managing SQL
SQLSAVECONNECT°	MENU	Managing SQL
SQLSELECTCONNECT°	MENU	Managing SQL
SQLSETINTERRUPT°	MENU	Managing SQL
SQLSTARTTRANS°	MENU	Managing SQL

°Paradox 3.5 command

Table 5—continued

Reserved Word	Type	Context Use
SQLVAL°	MENU	Managing SQL
SQRT	FUNCTION	Mathematical
STEP (FOR)	COMMAND	Control (Programming) Structure
STRVAL	FUNCTION	String
STYLE	COMMAND	Input/Output
STYLE ATTRIBUTE	COMMAND	Input/Output
SUBSTR	FUNCTION	String
SUBTRACT	COMMAND	Abbrev Menu Command
SWITCH	COMMAND	Control (Programming) Structure
SYNCCURSOR	COMMAND	Input/Output
SYSCOLOR	FUNCTION	Workspace/Canvas/Status
SYSMODE	FUNCTION	Workspace/Canvas/Status
TAB	COMMAND	Key
TABLE	COMMAND	Workspace/Canvas/Status
TABLE (WAIT)	COMMAND	Input/Output
TABLERIGHTS	FUNCTION	Information
TAN	FUNCTION	Mathematical
TEXT	COMMAND	Input/Output
THEN (IF)	COMMAND	Control (Programming) Structure
TIME	FUNCTION	Date/Time
TO (ACCEPT)	COMMAND	Input/Output
TO (FOR)	COMMAND	Control (Programming) Structure
TO (SHOWARRAY)	COMMAND	Input/Output
TO (SHOWFILES)	COMMAND	Input/Output
TO (SHOWMENU)	COMMAND	Input/Output
TO (SHOWTABLES)	COMMAND	Input/Output
TODAY	FUNCTION	Date/Time
TOQPRO°	COMMAND	Key
TYPE	FUNCTION	Information
TYPEIN	COMMAND	Workspace
UNDO	COMMAND	Key
UNLOCK	COMMAND	Multiuser
UNLOCKRECORD	COMMAND	Multiuser
UNPASSWORD	COMMAND	Abbrev Menu Command
UNTIL (SHOWARRAY)	COMMAND	Input/Output
UNTIL (SHOWFILES)	COMMAND	Input/Output
UNTIL (SHOWMENU)	COMMAND	Input/Output

°Paradox 3.5 command

Table 5—continued

Reserved Word	Type	Context Use
UNTIL (SHOWTABLES)	COMMAND	Input/Output
UNTIL (WAIT)	COMMAND	Input/Output
UP	COMMAND	Key
UPDATE (IMAGERIGHTS)	COMMAND	Multiuser
UPIMAGE	COMMAND	Key
UPPER	FUNCTION	String
USERNAME	FUNCTION	Workspace/Canvas/Status
USEVARS (PROC)	COMMAND	Proc/Proc Library
VARS (RELEASE)	COMMAND	Proc/Proc Library
VERSION	FUNCTION	Workspace/Canvas/Status
VERTRULER	COMMAND	Key
VIEW	COMMAND	Abbrev Menu Command
WAIT	COMMAND	Input/Output
WHILE	COMMAND	Control (Programming) Structure
WINDOW	FUNCTION	Workspace/Canvas/Status
WRITELIB	COMMAND	Proc/Proc Library
YEAR	FUNCTION	Date/Time
ZOOM	COMMAND	Key
ZOOMNEXT	COMMAND	Key

Glossary

!

The inclusion operator. Used in conjunction with an example element, the inclusion operator specifies that all rows (records) from one table should be returned in the Answer table, regardless if they match the linking field's information in the other table.

=

The assignment operator. Assigns a value to a variable, array element, or field (if the image and field are both present on the workspace). Example:

1. VariableName = Expression

    x = 123.45

2. ArrayName[Element Number] = Expression

    Array TestVal[10]

    TestVal[1] = "Martin"

    TestVal[2] = "Terry"

    TestVal[3] = "Mathew"

    TestVal[4] = "Debbie"

    TestVal[5] = "Kevin"

    TestVal[6] = "Brian"

    .

    .

    .

    TestVal[10] = "George"

3. FieldSpec = Expression

    if [State] = "WA" then

    [long state] = "Washington"

    endif

    moveto[date]

    [] = today()

?

Writes a message on the PAL canvas on the line below the current cursor position (new cursor position becomes one row down).

??

Writes a message on the canvas at the current cursor position. (New cursor position becomes the last character of the message on the same row).

@

Positions the cursor on the PAL canvas at a declared row and column. Example:

@10,20

ASCII

ASCII is an acronym for the American Standard Code for Information Interchange. It represents a seven-bit series of codes that define 128 standard characters, letters, numbers, and symbols.

The extended ASCII codes are an extension of this standard and consist of eight-bit codes that include special characters.

Abbreviated menu command

A type of PAL command that performs the equivalent series of menu sequences. Example:

PAL COMMAND:
SORT <tablename> ON <fieldname>

MENU COMMAND:
Menu {Modify}{Sort}{Tablename} {Same,New} ; select a field(s) to sort on

Do_it! ; press [F2]

Alphanumeric field

A field containing letters, numbers, and special characters (in any combination).

Argument

Information passed to a command or function.

Array

A special kind of variable. Arrays can have up to 15,000 elements. Each element can contain a different data type.

Array element

One component of an array. You can refer to an array element by addressing the element number. Example:

Data[4] (where Data is the name of an array)

Asymmetrical outer join

A type of query in which an inclusive link is specified in one table so that all of that table's records are included in the Answer table, regardless if they find a match with any other tables.

Backslash

A special Paradox character that tells Paradox to take the next character literally. For example, to designate a directory with the SETDIR command:

setdir "c:\\tables"

Band

A horizontal section of a report specification. There are a number of bands:

Report Header band

Page Header band

Group Header band

Table or Form band

Report Footer band

Page Footer band

Group Footer band

Blank

Usually refers to a field that contains no value (NULL). Blank numeric fields do not equal zero.

Borrow

To copy all or part of a table's structure while creating or restructuring another table.

Braces {}

The {} symbols are used to enclose Paradox menu selections in recorded scripts. Do not confuse these symbols with brackets [], which specify a field or array element.

Calculated field

A field that can perform simple arithmetic or that can concatenate alphanumeric phrases and fields. Calculated fields exist only in a report or form and are not stored by Paradox.

Canvas

The screen you see when running a PAL script or procedure.

CheckMark

Query key command that presses the [F6] key to select a field or fields for inclusion in the Answer table.

Closed procedure

A self-contained procedure. As it completes, it releases the memory and variables it has been allocated. To import a variable into a closed procedure, you must invoke USEVARS or pass the closed procedure as an argument.

Closed script

A script called from the DOS prompt and returning to DOS upon exit. Example:

    C:\>paradox <scriptname>

CoEdit

To edit a table concurrently with other users. CoEdit maintains a one-record change log (only the last change can be backed out).

Command

A PAL instruction to perform a certain task. Example:

    VIEW <tablename>

Concatenate

To join two or more strings to form a single string.

Control structure

A sequence of statements such as IF...THEN...ELSE...ENDIF or SWITCH...CASE...ENDSWITCH.

Current

The field, image, record, or table that the workspace cursor is currently resting on.

Cursor

The visual marker that indicates your current position on the screen.

Data integration

The process of combining, sending, and receiving information from other programs (in this case, programs other than Paradox).

Data integrity

The assurance that the values in a table are protected from corruption.

Data structure

The physical arrangement of fields and records in a table.

Data type

The type of data that is contained in a field or array element. The available data types are:

Type	Description	Physical Storage
A[#]	Alphanumeric #=length	1 byte/char
N	Number	8 bytes
$	Currency	8 bytes
D	Date	4 bytes
S	Short number +/- 32767	2 bytes
L	Logical (PAL only)	

Debugger

A built-in Paradox facility that lets you interactively test, trace, and correct your PAL scripts and procedures.

Display image

A view of a table onscreen that shows the information in the table.

Dynamic scoping

A scheme that assigns the value of a variable depending on whether the variable is global or private.

EMS

Expanded Memory Specification. See expanded memory.

Encrypt

To translate a table or script into code that cannot be read unless you have the proper password.

Example element

An arbitrary sequence of characters entered after you press [F5] to signify to the query or link on that example.

Expanded memory

Also known as EMS memory. Paradox uses expanded memory to provide more resources to an application. Paradox can address up to 16MB of expanded memory.

Export

To translate information from the Paradox environment to a file format that other programs can understand.

Expression

A group of characters that can include data values, variables, arrays, operators, field specifiers, and functions. An expression must represent either an actual value, a logical state, or a return code.

Extended memory

Memory available on 80286 and higher machines. Extended memory starts at 1MB. Paradox can address up to 16MB of extended memory.

Family

A Paradox table and its set of related objects:

  Forms

  Reports

  Indexes

  Validity checks

  Settings

Field

A single element (column) in a table.

Field assignment

Use of a field specifier [], to assign a value to a field. Example:

  [customer id] = 1900

  [state] = "WA"

  [birth date] = "7/5/52"

Field specifier [] or [fieldname]

A special PAL provision that lets you represent the value of a certain field. Example:

  string=[last name]

Field type

The type of information that can be entered into a specific field of a table.

Field value

The data contained in one field of a Paradox table. If no data resides in the field, the field is blank (NULL).

Field view

A Paradox mode that lets you view or edit the contents of the current field. FieldView is invoked by pressing [Alt][F5] or [Ctrl][F]. To exit FieldView, press [Enter].

File

A collection of information stored under one name on a disk. Paradox tables, forms, reports, and scripts are all files.

Form view

To view a table using a Paradox form. Form view shows one record at a time.

Format

The way a field value is displayed on the screen, sent to a printer, or presented in a form. PAL can format a value in numerous ways.

Function

A PAL or user-defined formula that performs computations or returns the status of PAL, Paradox, or your system.

Function keys

The ten to twelve keys located at the far left of the IBM PC keyboard or at the top row of AT-compatible machines. These keys are labeled F or PF 1 through 12. You can extend their meaning by using them in combination with the [Ctrl], [Alt], and [Shift] keys. Example:

[F11] = [Shift]+[F1]
[F21] = [Ctrl]+[F1]
[F31] = [Alt]+[F1]

Global variable

A variable that is assigned in the main portion of a PAL script or procedure and remains active until specifically released.

IBM extended keycodes

Keys or combinations of keys on the keyboard that do not correspond to standard ASCII character codes. These extended codes are designated with numbers ranging from -1 to -132.

Image

A representation of a Paradox table or query form on the workspace. Images on the workspace are numbered from top to bottom starting with 1.

Image type

The type of image on the Paradox workspace. There are two types of images: table and query.

Import

To accept data from another program into Paradox. For example, to accept a *.WK1 file from 1-2-3 or an ASCII text file downloaded from a large-scale system.

Index

A special file used to determine the location of records in a table. Indexes are used to speed operations such as searching for a name in a [last name] field. There are two types of indexes supported by Paradox, primary and secondary.

Key field

One or more contiguous fields that identify unique records. Records are maintained in sorted order. A primary index is created to make retrieval of records easier and faster.

Link

A logical association of two tables based on the values of corresponding or "linking" fields.

Link key

In a linked multitable form, the part of the detail table's key that is linked or matched to fields in the master table.

Logical operator

One of three operators—AND, OR, and NOT—that are used on logical data. For example, an AND between logical values states that both of the values must be true in order for the value True to be returned.

Logical value

A value assigned to an expression after it has been tested to see if it is true or false. The value assigned will be either True or False.

Menu

You can display a menu by pressing [F10]. The PAL Menu is displayed by pressing [Alt][F10]. If the Debugger is active, the Debugger Menu is displayed with [Alt][F10].

Menu selection

An option chosen from a menu. Menu selections in this book are shown as {*View*}.

Message

A string expression that is displayed in the message window.

MiniScript

A selection in the PAL Menu that lets you type in a sequence of commands (number of characters not to exceed 175). After typing in the characters, press [Enter] to execute the miniscript. You can edit the last miniscript executed in your current Paradox session by bringing up the PAL Menu, selecting {*Miniscript*}, and pressing [Ctrl][E].

Mode

The current Paradox state. Paradox modes are:

    Main
    Edit
    CoEdit
    Restructure
    Sort
    Form
    Report
    Create
    DataEntry
    Password
    Script

The current mode is always shown at the top of the screen to the right of the menu line.

Normalized table structure

An optimized database structure that ensures the data's efficient use. Normalized table structures let relationships between different tables be created very easily.

Object

Paradox objects include:

    Tables
    Forms
    Reports
    Indexes
    Validity checks
    Settings
    Libraries
    Scripts

Outer join

A type of query which uses the inclusion operator (!) to retrieve all of the records in a table, regardless of whether the linked values match or not.

Primary index

An index on key fields used to determine the location and order of records in a table.

Private directory

A personal directory where your Answer tables (and other Paradox objects) are stored to avoid conflicts with other Paradox users in a network environment.

Procedure

A program module consisting of PAL commands and functions created to perform a particular task. There are basically two types of procedures: regular procedures and closed procedures.

Prompt

A message in the menu area that explains what the current highlighted selection will do or what activity or input is needed.

Prototyping

The process of application development in which small parts or the general structure of the application are designed interactively. Prototypes are sometimes built to provide a model for a more in-depth application and sometimes move straight from prototype to production application.

QBE (Query By Example)

Paradox's non-procedural query language that lets you ask questions about the data residing in a table by giving it a series of examples, checkmarks, and selection criteria.

Query

A question put to a Paradox table via a query form either through PAL or interactively.

QuerySave

An option on the {Scripts} menu that saves a query statement to a script for later use.

QuerySpeedup

An option on the {Tools} menu that creates a secondary index on a table based on the query form(s) present on the workspace.

Record

A horizontal row in Paradox table that contains at least one and no more than 255 fields of related information.

Relational database

A database system that arranges data in tables.

Restricted view

A detail table on a multitable form, linked to the master table on a one-to-one or one-to-many basis. This type of view limits the records shown to those that match the master record.

Restructure

To change the physical order, name, or type of the fields in an existing table.

Row

The horizontal component of a table.

Run-time error

A script error that occurs when a valid command cannot be completed in the current context.

Script

Any sequence of PAL commands stored in a script file. A PAL script is Paradox's equivalent to a program or database application.

Secondary index

An index that is used to keep track of and speed up queries. Secondary indexes search based on non-key fields in a table.

Slash sequence

A backslash followed by one or more characters which represent an ASCII character. Example:

    setdir "c:\\direct"

The first "\" tells Paradox to take the next character "\" literally so Paradox can properly change the directory.

Symmetrical outer join

A query involving two or more tables that returns all values whether the linking values match or not.

Syntax error

A script or procedure error that occurs when an improperly coded set of functions or commands are presented to Paradox to process.

Table

A structure made up of records (rows) and fields (columns) that contain information.

Table view

The representation of a Paradox table in row and column format. Also known as a spreadsheet view.

Tilde variable

A PAL variable used in a query form. It must be preceded by the tilde character (~).

Transaction

A group of related changes, additions, or subtractions to a database.

Transaction log

A list of changes that have been made to a table that can be undone.

Variable

A place in memory to store data temporarily. A variable exists until it is released or until you exit Paradox.

Working directory

The directory set either in the CCP, PAL, or by selecting {Tools} {More} {Directory} {directoryname}.

Index

! (inclusion operator), 719
10-PB-1 listing, 324
10-PB-2 listing, 325
10-PB-3 listing, 326
= (assignment operator), 719
?, 719
??, 719
@, 719

A

abbreviated menu command, 720
ABC Music Store application, 501-535
    Aging module, 531-534
    Backup module, 531
    Inventory module, 528-530
    invoicing customers, 513-523
    Main menu, 502-509
    Music Lessons module, 524-527
    viewing customer balance, 509-512
ACCEPT command, 629-631
ADD command, 410-411
add-on programs
    DeskTop for Paradox, 625
    K-MEMO, 623-624
    OverDrive 2 for Microsoft Word, 625-626
    pTools, 625
    TextView, 624-625
AddBlankLines utility procedure, 339

AddLineNumber utility procedure, 339
advanced
    graphs, 331, 347-357
    queries, 293-330
    reports, 331-352
AGING.SC listing, 532-534
alphanumeric field, 720
applications
    see also program listings
    ABC Music Store, 501-535
    Beep utility, 552-553
    disk caching, 494
    documenting, 33-38
    DOS and, 292
    examples, 29
    implementation, 35-38
    life cycle, 17-38
    memory, 493-496
    performance improvement, 493-500
    Personnel, 535-543
    program design, 26-38
    prototyping, 53-76
    RAM and, 493-495
    requirements, 18-25
    sample, 501-543
    table design, 496-499
    testing, 31-32
Applications Programming Interface (API), 461

arguments, 720
arrays, 720
    element, 720
    forms, 272
    reports, 341-346
ARRAYSIZE function, 631
ASCII (American Standard Code for Information Interchange), 719-720
    exporting text, 589
    importing text, 583-584
ASCII code to KeyCode reference chart, 681-691
AST Rampage, 607
asymmetrical outer join, 720
ATFIRST function, 631-632
ATLAST function, 632
autoloading procedures from libraries, 156-157
AVERAGE summary operator (query-by-example (QBE)), 296

B

backslash (\) key, 720
BACKUP.SC listing, 531
bands, 720
basic multitable data entry listing, 123-124
beep procedure, 149
Beeps.sc listing, 553
blank, 720
BLANKDATE function, 632-633
BLANKNUM function, 633
Borland product interoperability, 85
borrow, 720
BOT function, 633-634
braces ({}), 721
BUFCLOSE.C listing, 479

C

C applications integrating with Paradox, 461
cache *see* disk caching *and* caching programs
caching programs, 609-610
    Lightning, 610
    Paul Mace's, 610
    Super PC Qwik, 610
CALCDEBUG command, 86-90, 634
CALCTIM7 listing, 321-322
calculated field, 721
CANCELEDIT command, 250, 634-635
canvas, 721
CANVAS command, 635-636
CFG file, 432
CheckMark command, 721
CheckRcdStat procedure listing, 452
CirQry.sc listing, 554
CleanTables procedure listing, 453
CLEAR command, 636
ClearAll command, 295, 636-637
client/server architecture, 386-390
CLOSED procedure listing, 152
closed procedures, 152-154, 170-173, 721
closed script, 721
code to capture ValCheck settings listing, 563-564
coding, modular, 27-38
CoEdit mode, 246-252, 721
    vs. Edit mode, 249-252

Index **731**

column headings, printing, 477
command-line override options, 96-98
commands, 721
    abbreviated menu, 720
    ACCEPT, 629-631
    ADD, 410-411
    CALCDEBUG, 86-90, 634
    CANCELEDIT, 250, 634-635
    CANVAS, 635-636
    characteristics for data entry, 251-252
    CheckMark, 721
    CLEAR, 636
    ClearAll, 295, 636-637
    COPY, 411
    COPYFORM, 637
    COPYFROMARRAY, 90, 249, 278, 282, 375
    COPYREPORT, 637-638
    COPYTOARRAY, 248, 282, 375, 447
    CREATE, 411-412, 638-639
    CREATELIB, 153-155
    CURSOR, 639
    DEBUG, 641
    DELETE, 412
    Do_it!, 295
    ECHO, 641-642
    EDITLOG, 252-258
    EMPTY, 412
    ENDPROC, 147-149
    EXIT, 91
    FIELD VIEW, 291
    FILESIZE, 91
    FILL, 348, 350
    FORMTABLES, 644-645
    IMAGERIGHTS, 645-646
    INFOLIB, 157
    KEYLOOKUP, 282
    LOCATE, 252-253, 259, 261, 268-269, 272, 289
    LOCK, 371
    LOCKRECORD, 277
    LOOP, 647-648
    modified, 90-91
    new, 85-91
    PAINTCANVAS, 557-558, 650-651
    PRINT, 91
    PRINT FILE, 90
    PROC, 147-149
    QUIT, 140
    READLIB, 156
    RECORDSTATUS, 279, 282
    REPORTTABLES, 651-652
    Reset, 295
    RESYNCKEY, 86-90, 282, 652
    RETURN, 150
    RUN, 90-91
    SAVETABLES, 89, 653-654
    SCAN FOR, 263-265
    SELECT, 398
    SETPRIVDIR, 654-655
    SETQUERYORDER, 655
    SETRECORDPOSITION, 656-657
    SHOW, 90, 92-94
    SHOWARRAY, 91
    SHOWFILES, 91
    SHOWMENU, 91, 193-194, 255
    SHOWTABLES, 91, 445

SQL NOFETCH, 446
SQL...ENDSQL, 413-414
SQLAUTOCOMMIT, 414
SQLBREAKCONNECT, 414
SQLCLEARCONNECT, 415
SQLCOMMIT, 415, 448-451
SQLCONNECTINFO, 443-445
SQLFETCH, 415, 446-447
SQLISREPLICA, 445
SQLMAKECONNECT, 416
SQLRELEASE, 416
SQLRESTORECONNECT, 416
SQLROLLBACK, 416, 448-451
SQLSAVECONNECT, 416-417
SQLSELECTCONNECT, 417, 442-443
SQLSETINTERRUPT, 418
SQLSTARTTRANS, 418, 448
SWITCH, 125-126
TOQPRO, 661-662
TYPEIN, 351
UNDO, 86-90
UNLOCKRECORD, 277
UNPASSWORD, 662-663
used in procedures, 145
WAIT, 124, 130-140, 243, 255, 291-292, 447
ZOOM, 252-253
company roster report, 346-350
composite keys, 47
concatenation, 721
conceptual design, 73
concurrency rules, 106
CONFIG.SYS file, 606

configuration problems (README file), 613-614
Coninfo2 listing, 445-446
Connection SQL menu, 407
connectivity, enhanced, 78
ConnectList SSP menu selection, 432
ConnInfo.sc listing, 444-445
contents of RqdFlds listing, 137-139
context-sensitive help system, 237-240
control structure, 721
COPY command, 411
COPYFORM command, 637
COPYFROMARRAY command, 90, 249, 278, 282, 375
COPYREPORT command, 637-638
COPYTOARRAY command, 248, 282, 375, 447
core capabilities, 3
COUNT summary operator (query-by-example (QBE)), 297
CPU, testing (README file), 614-615
CPUTEST.EXE file, 614
CREATE command, 411-412, 638-639
CreateID procedure listing, 150-151
CREATELIB command, 153-155
CREATELIB listing, 174-175
current, 721
cursor, 721
  changing to box, 244
CURSOR command, 639
CURSORCHAR function, 639-640
CURSORLINE function, 640
custom configuration program, 94-98
Customize Graph for Printing screen, 357

Index 733

D

data
    denormalizing, 50-52
    editing, 241, 253-272, 290-291
    exporting, 588-592, 722
    importing, 581-587, 724
    integrating, 581-601, 721
    integrity, 103-106, 722
    normalizing, 40-49
    structure, 722
    types, 106, 722
    viewing, 241-245
data entry, 241, 246-252
    command characteristics, 251-252
    multitable, 122-124
    requirements, 246-249
    running program, 127-128
    validating, 107-144
Data Entry Tool Kit (DETK), 5-6
data modeling with Quattro Pro, 593-601
database servers, 387-406, 673-680
    building reports, 406
    comparison, 678
    connection data, 678
    field naming conventions, 679
    IBM Extended Edition Database Manager, 440-441
    IBM OS/2 1.2, 676-677
    interactive access connecting, 393-396
    Microsoft SQL Server, 441, 673-674
    modifying connection list, 432-435
    Oracle, 439-440
    Oracle Server for OS/2, 675-676
    product limitations, 680
    querying, 398-405
    SQL link queries, 679
    supported data types, 679-680
    tables, 396
        entering data, 397-398
        removing data, 406
databases
    denormalizing, 50-52
    development, 6-15
    environment, 3-6
    logical, 21-25
    menu selection, 549-552
    normalizing, 39-52
    physical database design, 21-25
    relational, 40-52, 726
DataEntry mode, 246-249
DATEVAL function, 640
dBASE, importing, 582
DBSelect.sc listing, 552
DEBUG command, 641
debugger, 3, 722
debugging, libraries, 158-160
defaults, Paradox Engine, 473-474
DELETE command, 412
denormalizing databases, 50-52
designing
    conceptual design, 73
    databases, 21-25
    physical design, 74
    programs, 26-38
DeskTop for Paradox add-on program, 625
DESQview, running Paradox, 611-613

DETK (Data Entry ToolKit), 5-6, 208
developers, 7-9
development
    conceptual design, 73
    physical design, 74
    decision process and strategy, 10-15
    gathering requirements, 18-25
    installation, 75-76
    internal vs. third-party, 7-9
    KISS versus LAW approaches, 57-58
    logical database design, 21-25
    program, 74
    rapid, 9-15
    realistic vs. theoretical, 6-7
    tools, 545-579
        see also Paradox tools
    traditional method, 54-58
    training, 75-76
devices, outputting graphs to specified, 356
directories
    private, 360-361, 726
    working, 360, 373, 727
DIREXISTS function, 641
disk caching, 494
display image, 722
DisplayMsg procedure listing, 150
documentation tools
    ParaLex, 622
    ParaTrak, 623
    ScriptView, 621-622
documenting programs, 33-38
domain integrity rules, 106

DOS
    applications and, 292
    BACKUP program, 528
DOS LAN MAN (DOS redirector), 609
DOS SHARE program, 611
DOS-based networks, PARADOX.NET file and, 369
DOW function, 345
Do_it! command, 295
DSQ file, 432
dynamic scoping, 722

E

ECHO command, 641-642
Edit mode, 246-258
    controlling transaction log, 253-258
    vs. CoEdit mode, 249-252
Edit Script listing, 63-64
Edit/CoEdit effect, keys and, 290
EditDeptData procedure listing, 260-261
EditEmpByDept procedure listing, 264-269
editing
    data, 253, 290-291
    fields, 290-291
    query subset, 265
    subset of table, 259-272
EDITLOG command, 252-258
EditLogAnyTbl procedure listing, 253-255
EDITOR3 listing, 574-576
    code explanations, 578-579
EmpOnly.sc listing, 448-451
EMPTY command, 412

EMS, 722
    testing (README file), 614-615
EMSTEST.COM file, 614
encryption, 722
ENDPROC command, 147-149
Engine *see* Paradox Engine
Enter2 Procedure listing, 132-135
ENTERINV.SC listing, 513-520
EntrComp.sc listing, 287-289
EOT function, 642
ErrHndler.sc listing, 188
error codes
    list, 179-180
    SQL Link, 422
error log printing routine, 184-189
error-handling, SQL Link, 421-422
ERRORCODE function, 91, 421-422
errors
    procedures, 178, 181-189
        code list, 179-180
        key violation handler, 284-285
    run-time, 727
    syntax, 727
    Unexpected condition, 370
ErrPrnt.sc listing, 184-187
ErrProc procedure listing, 284-285
Errproc.sc listing, 181-182
example element, 722
examples *see* program listings, programs *and* applications
EXIT command, 91
expanded memory, 604-605, 722
    AST Rampage, 607
    graphics conflicts, 606-607
    Intel AboveBoard, 606

ExpldWin.sc listing, 555-556
ExplodeWindow procedure, 37
exporting data, 588-722
    ASCII text, 589
    keystroke sequence examples, 590-592
    spreadsheets, 589
    VisiCalc, 589
expressions, 722
extended memory, 604-605, 723

F

family, 723
FAMILYRIGHTS function, 643
Fetch.sc listing, 454-459
FetchDepndnts procedure listing, 453
FetchEmp procedure listing, 447
Field view, 723
    keys and, 290-291
FIELD VIEW command, 291
FIELDINFO function, 345
FIELDRIGHTS function, 643
fields, 723
    alphanumeric, 720
    assignment, 723
    calculated, 721
    editing, 290-291
    key, 724
    specifier, 723
    subset editing
        select key, 269-272
        with query, 265-267
    type, 723
    validating data entry, 129-140
    value, 723

FIELDSTR function, 644
FIELDTYPE function, 644
file locking on networks, 364-365
file server, 387-388
    networks, 363-364
files, 723
    .OV, 494
    .CFG, 432
    .DSQ, 432
    .GRP, 610
    .HLP, 494
    .LCK, 365-368, 370
    .MSG, 494
    .PIF, 610
    .SOM, 392-393
    calculated for printer control characters, 350-351
    CONFIG.SYS, 606
    CPUTEST.EXE, 614
    EMSTEST.COM, 614
    index, 724
    locking, automatic vs. explicit, 371
    PARADOX*.EXE, 494
    PARADOX.CFG, 360, 363
    PARADOX.DSQ, 432, 435
    PARADOX.EXE, 494
    PARADOX.GRP, 611
    PARADOX.LCK, 360-361, 366-369
    PARADOX.NET, 360, 365-366, 368-370, 479
    PARADOX.PIF, 611
    PARADOX.SOM, 365, 368-369
    PARADOX.SQ1, 438
    PPROG.PIF, 611

PXENGINE.H, 473, 475
    READSQL, 393, 401, 439-441
    SQLSETUP.SC, 423
FILESIZE command, 91
FILL command, 348, 350
FillWin.sc listing, 557-558
First Normal Form (1NF), 42-46
FLIMPORT utility, 6, 586-587
Form Lock, 375-379
    shadow keys and tables workaround, 375-379
    theory vs. reality, 375
Form view, 723
FORMAT function, 665-666
formats, 106, 723
forms
    arrays, 272
    functions, 272-285
    global variables, 272
    multitable, 82-84
FORMTABLES command, 644-645
FORMTYPE function, 87-90, 645, 666-667
full spelling for days and months report, 344-346
function keys, 723-724
functions, 723
    ARRAYSIZE, 631
    ATFIRST, 631-632
    ATLAST, 632
    BLANKDATE, 632-633
    BLANKNUM, 633
    BOT, 633-634
    CURSORCHAR, 639-640

CURSORLINE, 640
DATEVAL, 640
DIREXISTS, 641
DOW, 345
EOT, 642
ERRORCODE, 91, 421-422
FAMILYRIGHTS, 643
FIELDINFO, 345
FIELDRIGHTS, 643
FIELDSTR, 644
FIELDTYPE, 644
FORMAT, 665-666
FORMTYPE, 87-90, 645, 666-667
in forms, 272-285
ISSQL, 418
lack of in query-by-example (QBE), 323
LOCKINFO, 666-668
LOCKSTATUS, 646-647
MATCH, 648-649
MEMLEFT, 91, 495-496, 649-650
MENUCHOICE, 562
modified, 91-94
MONTH, 344
PAL, 80-84
    see also PAL commands and functions
Paradox Engine, 468-472
PICTURE, 669
PRINTERSTATUS, 558
PXDateDecode, 478
PXExit, 479
PXFldName, 476-477
PXFldType, 476
PXGetAlpha, 478

PXGetDate, 478
PXGetDefaults, 473
PXGetDouble, 478
PXGetShort, 478
PXInit, 474
PXRecBufClose, 479
PXRecBufOpen, 476
PXRecGet, 478, 481
PXRecGoto, 478, 481
PXRecNFlds, 476-477, 481
PXSetDefaults, 473
PXTblClose, 479
PXTblNRecs, 476, 481
PXTblOpen, 476
RECORDSTATUS, 87-89, 275-277, 669-671
reference charts, 701-705
REMEMLEFT, 653
reports, 341-347
RMEMLEFT, 87, 90, 496
SEARCH, 654
SORTORDER, 657
SQLCONNECTINFO, 419
SQLERRORCODE, 91, 420-421
SQLERRORMESSAGE, 420-421
SQLISCONNECT, 420
SQLISREPLICA, 420
SQLMAPINFO, 420-421
SQLVAL, 421
STRVAL, 657-658
SUBSTR, 658-659
SYSMODE, 659-660
TABLERIGHTS, 660-661
used in procedures, 145

USERNAME, 663
VERSION, 663-664
WINDOW, 664

G

Generators, 4
Generic Query Script listing, 65-66
GETALPHA.C listing, 478
GETDEF.C listing, 474
GetDept procedure listing, 262
GetEmpByDept procedure listing, 270-272
GETFIELDS.SC listing, 546
GetOneDept procedure listing, 261
GetSubSet procedure listing, 266, 270
global variables, 151-152, 272, 724
    printer control characters, 352
    reports, 341, 348, 350
glossary, 719-727
graphics, expanded memory conflicts, 606-607
graphs
    advanced, 331, 347-357
    outputting to specified devices, 356
    Personnel application, 542
    printing multiple per page, 356-357
    specification, 25
    titles, 354-355
    types, 352-353
    Y-axis scaling, 355
GRP files, 610
GrphAxis.sc listing, 355
GrphDev.sc listing, 355
GrphTit1.sc listing, 354

H

handles for tables, 476
help, 4
    library, MMENUHLP, 506
    systems, developing, 237-240
HLP files, 494

I

IBM Extended Edition Database Manager database server, 440-441
IBM extended keycodes, 724
IBM OS/2 Extended Edition Database Manager version 1.2, 390, 676-677
IMAGERIGHTS command, 645-646
images, 724
importing data, 581-587, 724
    ASCII text, 583-584
    dBASE, 582
    keystroke sequence examples, 584-586
    Reflex, 584
    spreadsheets, 582
    VisiCalc, 583
index file, 724
INFOLIB command, 157
INIT.C listing, 475
initializing Paradox Engine, 474-476
installing
    Paradox, 75-76
    Paradox Engine, 463
    SQL Link, 391-393
InstantRecord, 27-28
InstantScripts, 28
integrating data, 581-601, 721

integrity
    checking program, 140-144
    data, 103-106
    types, 104
Intel AboveBoard, 606
    QRAM memory manager and, 608-609
interactive
    mode, 27-32
    Paradox, 84-91
interface, 191-240
internal
    developers, 7-9, 13
    tools, 4
Intgrty library listing, 140
Inventory menu, 528
ISSQL function, 418

K

K-MEMO add-on program, 623-624
key fields, 724
    subset editing to select, 269-272
keyed tables, 498
KEYEDIT.SC listing, 573
KEYLOOKUP command, 282
keys
    composite, 47
    Edit/CoEdit effect and, 290
    Field view and, 290-291
    menu prompt and, 290
    multifield, 47
    primary, 48-49
    system-assigned, 379-383
    table violations, 275-285
    trapping, 290
    values in networks, 373-375
    violation handler, 283-285
        and error procedures, 284-285
keystroke sequence examples
    exporting data, 590-592
    importing data, 584-586
KeyViol2.sc listing, 283
KeyVioln.sc listing, 279-280
KISS vs. LAW approaches to development, 57-58

L

LAW vs. KISS approaches to development, 57-58
LCK files, 365-370
    interaction with PARADOX.NET files, 368
libraries, 153-155, 173-177
    see also procedures and libraries
    autoloading procedures, 156-157
    building, 145-189
    debugging, 158-160
    displaying information about, 157
    error procedures, 178-189
    loading, 156
    multiple scripts listing, 176
    multiple small vs. single large, 177
    scripts queries vs., 301-323
    storing procedures in, 154-155
Lightning, 610
link key, 724
linking, 724
LISTDB.C listing, 483-486
LISTDB2.C listing, 488-491

local tables, 390
LOCATE command, 252-253, 259, 261, 268-269, 272, 289
LOCK command, 371
LOCKINFO function, 666-668
locking files, automatic vs. explicit, 371
LOCKRECORD command, 277
locks, 361
    logical, 365-367
LOCKSTATUS function, 646-647
logical
    locks, 365-367
    operators, 724
    values, 724
Login.sc listing, 443-444
LOOP command, 647-648
Lotus 1-2-3, running from Paradox, 593

M

Main Menu listing, 59-61
MAIN.SC listing, 195-196
MainMenu procedure listing, 538
MainMenuSplash procedure listing, 536
MAINMENU.SC listing, 221-214, 218-221
MAKELIB.SC listing, 177
Master Picture table, 116-126
MATCH function, 648-649
matching patterns (query-by-example (QBE)), 295
MAX summary operator (query-by-example (QBE)), 298
MEMLEFT function, 91, 495-496, 649-650

memory, 493-496
    286 maximum operating capabilities, 607-609
    caching programs and, 609-610
    expanded, 604-605, 722
    extended, 604-605, 723
    management, 77-79, 83-84, 603-613
    mix, 493
    operating system 5.x and, 609
    requirements for Paradox Engine, 462-463
memory managers
    DOS LAN MAN, 609
    Move-em, 607
    QRAM, 607-609
menu prompt and keys, 290
MENUCHOICE function, 562
MENUHELP.SC listing, 237-240
menus, 4, 725
    automatic selection in SQL Setup Program (SSP), 424-429
    building system, 193-240
    equivalents with Paradox Engine, 464-465
    MAIN.SC (main menu), 195-196
    manual selection in SQL Setup Program (SSP), 429-431
    Paradox-style, 192
    pop-up, 192
    selection, 725
    SQL, 406-410
    static-style, 192
MENUS.SC listing, 225-232
MESGLIBR.SC listing, 233-237

messages, 725
    displaying Paradox-style, 553-554
Microsoft C, compiling Paradox Engine, 466-468
Microsoft SQL Server, 441
    version 1.1, 673-674
    Version 1.0 and 1.1, 390
Microsoft Word, running from Paradox, 592
MIN summary operator (query-by-example (QBE)), 299
MiniScript, 725
MMAIN.SC listing, 503-506
MMENUHLP help library, 506
models, prototyping, 58-76
modes, 725
    CoEdit, 246-252
    DataEntry, 246-249
    Edit, 246-258
Modtbl.sc listing, 280-281
modular coding, 27-38
MONTH function, 344
Move-em memory manager, 607
MSARRAY.SC listing, 197-198
MSFILE.SC listing, 199
MSG files, 494
MSPALSH.SC listing, 196
MTRpts.sc listing, 334-337
Multi-Pack, 100-101
multifield keys, 47
multitable
    forms and reports, 82-84
    programs, running, 127-128

multiuser environment, 359-383
    Editing/CoEditing issues, 371-379
Music Lesson menu, 524

N

NETINIT.C listing, 476
networks
    attempting to edit tables while in use, 372
    configuring for workstations, 360
    file locking, 364-365
    file server, 363-364
    form lock theory vs. reality, 375
    installing Paradox, 361-371
    key values, 373
    locks, 361
    overview, 359-361
    Paradox system files, 362
    private directories, 360-363
        editing, 317-372
        local and network, 363
        tracking access, 360-361
    supported non-dedicated servers, 370-371
    system-assigned keys, 379-383
    table access, 365-367
    user lists, 360
    working directories, 360
        multiple-user editing, 373
        tracking access, 360-361
    workstation configuration, 363
NEXTMENU.SC listing, 215-218, 222-223
NO keyword, 327-330

non-dedicated servers, 370-371
non-keyed tables, 498
normalized table, 42-47
normalizing, 42-49
   Paradox databases, 39-41
NotDefined procedure listing, 543
Novell networks and PARADOX.NET file, 368

O

objects, 4-5, 725
one-to-many relationship, 25, 346-350
one-to-one table relationships, 375
operating system
   5.x and memory, 609
   Paradox Engine requirements, 463
Oracle database server, 390, 439-440
Oracle Server for OS/2, 675-676
outer join, 725
OV* files, 494
OverDrive 2 for Microsoft Word add-on program, 625-626

P

PAINTCANVAS command, 557-558, 650-651
PAL (Paradox Application Language), 3
   changes in version 3.5, 92-97
   commands, 629-671
   equivalents with Paradox Engine, 464-465
   functions, 80-84, 273-274, 629-671
      new with SQL Link, 418-421
   interactive processes, 28-32
   vs. Paradox Engine, 463-465
   written by report generator, 547-549
PAL commands, 629-671
   enhanced by SQL Link, 410-412
   new with SQL Link, 412-418
   query-by-example (QBE) and, 295-300
PAL editor, enhancing, 572-579
PAL-EDIT script editor, 619-620
Paradox
   add-ons and utilities, 617-626
      add-on programs, 623-626
      DETK, 5-6
      documentation tools, 621-623
      FLIMPORT, 6
      PPROG, 5
      script editors, 618-620
      TUTILITY, 5
   application life cycle, 17-38
   books, newsletters, and support, 627-628
   building procedures and libraries, 145-189
   commands and equivalent menu commands reference chart, 700-701
   commands, keys, and ASCII codes reference chart, 691-699
   compatibility with earlier releases, 99-101
   configuring for workstations, 360
   core, 3
   data
      viewing, entering, and editing, 241-291
      integrity, 103-106

databases
- development, 10-15
- environment, 3-6
- normalizing, 39-52

features supported by Paradox Engine, 462

integrating into C applications, 461

interactive, 27-91

interface, 191-240

memory management, 603-613

Multi-Pack, 78

network installation, 361-371

new features, 77-98

non-dedicated servers, 370-371

objects, 4-5

prototyping, 53-76

reserved words reference charts, 706-717

running
- DESQview, 611-613
- other programs, 592
    - Lotus 1-2-3, 593
    - Microsoft Word, 592
    - Quattro Pro, 592-593
    - Windows, 610-611

SQL link, 78, 385-438

system files and networks, 362

training organizations and seminars, 626

user interface, 4

ValChecks, 107-144

Paradox Application Language *see* PAL

Paradox Engine, 461-491
- Borland Turbo C 2.0 or higher compiler, 462
- closing record buffer and table, 479
- compiling with Turbo C or Microsoft C, 466-468
- functions, 468-472
- initializing, 474-476
- installing, 463
- listing table examples, 480-491
- memory requirements, 462-463
- Microsoft C 5.1 or higher compiler, 462
- opening tables, 476-477
- operating system requirements, 463
- overview, 462
- PAL and menu equivalents, 464-465
- Paradox features supported, 462
- printing
    - column headings, 477
    - records in tables, 477-478
- program structure, 472-473
- setting defaults, 473-474
- terminating program, 479-480
- vs. PAL, 463-465

Paradox Personal Programmer (PPROG), 5

Paradox tools, 545-579
- Beep utility program, 552-553
- clearing
    - query images from workspace, 554
    - system environment and writing PAL code, 564-572
- database menu selection, 549-552

displaying Paradox-style message, 553-554
enhancing PAL editor, 572-579
exploding window, 554-556
filling window, 557-558
report generator writing PAL, 547-549
testing if printer ready, 558-559
ValCheck reporting program, 559-564
PARADOX®.EXE files, 494
Paradox-style menus
   MAIN.SC, 195-196
   MSARRAY.SC, 197-198
   MSFILE.SC, 199-200
PARADOX.CFG file, 360, 363
PARADOX.DSQ file, 432, 435
PARADOX.EXE file, 494
PARADOX.GRP file, 611
PARADOX.LCK file, 360-361, 366-369
PARADOX.NET file, 360, 365-366, 368-370, 479
   DOS-based networks and, 369-370
   errors and problems, 368-370
   interaction with .LCK files, 368
   Novell networks and, 368
PARADOX.PIF file, 611
PARADOX.SOM file, 365, 368-369
PARADOX.SQ1 file, 438
ParaLex documentation tool, 564, 622
ParaTrak documentation tool, 623
Parts listing, 373-375
Paul Mace's caching programs, 610
Personal Programmer (PPROG), 98
Personnel application, 535-543
   graphs, 542

Main menu, 535-538
Maintenance menu, 538-539
Query menu, 538-542
picture format symbols, 116
PICTURE function, 669
PIF files, 610
PlayRight Pro script editor, 618-619
pop-style menus
   MAINMENU.SC, 218-221
   MENUS.SC, 223-232
   NEXTMENU.SC, 218, 222-223
pop-up menus, 192
   DETK, 208
   MAINMENU.SC, 209-214
   stacking/tiling, 214
PPROG (Paradox Personal Programmer), 5, 98
PPROG.PIF file, 611
PRCHORD.SC listing, 529-530
Preferences SQL menu, 407
primary index, 726
primary keys, 48-49
PRINT command, 91
PRINT FILE command, 90
PrintBenefits procedure, 340
PrintDriver procedure, 338
printer control characters, 350-352
   calculated fields, 350-351
   global variables, 352
   TYPEIN command, 351
printers, testing if ready, 558-559
PRINTERSTATUS function, 558
printing
   column headings, 477

Index

multiple graphs per page, 356-357
records in tables, 477-478
PrintDepndnts procedure, 340
private directories, 360-361, 726
    editing, 371-372
    local and network, 363
    tracking access, 360-361
private variables, 151-152
PrntrOn.sc listing, 559
PROC command, 147-149
Procedure Library listing, 69
procedures, 726
    see also program listings *and* procedures and libraries
    autoloading, 156-157
    beep, 149
procedures and libraries, 145-189
    closed, 152-154, 721
    comparing
        good and bad procedures, 165-169
        regular and closed, 170-173
    defined, 146-150
    displaying information, 157
    error, 178-189
    ExplodeWindow, 37
    libraries, 153-160
    optimal size, 169-170
    PrintBenefits, 340
    PrintDepndnts, 340
    PrintDriver, 338
    releasing from memory, 161-164
    size of queries stored, 308-319
    terms, 145
    variables, 151-152

Product Line, 101
program listings
    10-PB-1, 324
    10-PB-2, 325
    10-PB-3, 326
    AGING.SC, 532-534
    BACKUP.SC, 531
    basic multitable data entry, 122-124
    Beeps.sc, 553
    BUFCLOSE.C, 479
    CALCTIM7, 321-322
    CheckRcdStat procedure, 452
    CirQry.sc, 554
    CleanTables procedure, 453
    CLOSED procedure, 152
    code to capture ValCheck settings, 563-564
    Coninfo2, 445-446
    ConnInfo.sc, 444-445
    contents of RqdFlds, 137-139
    CreateID procedure, 150-151
    CREATELIB, 174-175
    DBSelect.sc, 552
    DisplayMsg procedure, 150
    Edit Script, 63-64
    EditDeptData procedure, 260-261
    EditEmpByDept procedure, 264-269
    EditLogAnyTbl procedure, 253-255
    EDITOR3, 574-576
    EmpOnly.sc, 448-451
    Enter2 Procedure, 132-135
    ENTERINV.SC, 513-520
    EntrComp.sc, 287-289
    error log printing routine, 184-189

error procedure script, 181-182
ErrHndlr.sc, 188
ErrPrnt.sc, 184-187
ErrProc procedure, 284-285
Errproc.sc, 181-182
ExpldWin.sc, 555-556
Fetch.sc, 454-459
FetchDepndnts procedure, 453
FetchEmp procedure, 447
field- and record-level validation, 129-140
FillWin.sc, 557-558
Generic Query Script, 65-66
GETALPHA.C, 478
GETDEF.C, 474
GetDept procedure, 262
GetEmpByDept procedure, 270-272
GETFLDS.SC, 546
GetOneDept procedure, 261
GetSubSet procedure, 266-270
GrphAxis.sc, 355
GrphDev.sc, 355
GrphTit1.sc, 354
INIT.C, 475
integrity checking program, 140-144
Intgrty library, 140
KEYEDIT.SC, 573
KeyViol2.sc, 283
KeyVioln.sc, 279-280
library with multiple scripts, 176
LISTDB.C, 483-486
LISTDB2.C, 488-491
Login.sc, 443-444
Main Menu, 59-61

MAIN.SC (main menu), 195-196
MainMenu procedure, 538
MAINMENU.SC, 212-214, 218-221
MainMenuSplash procedure, 536
MAKELIB.SC, 177
MENUHELP.SC, 237-240
MENUS.SC, 225-232
MESGLIBR.SC, 233-237
MMAIN.SC, 503-506
Modtbl.sc, 280-281
MSARRAY.SC, 197-198
MSFILE.SC, 199-200
MSPALSH.SC, 196
MTRpts.sc, 334-337
NETINIT.C, 476
NEXTMENU.SC, 215-218, 222-223
NotDefined procedure, 543
Parts, 373-375
PRCHORD.SC, 529-530
PrntrOn.sc, 559
Procedure Library, 69
PROJ_SCH.SC, 525
PXEXIT.C, 480
Qry3Tbls2 procedure, 168
Qry3Tbls3 procedure, 168
Qry3Tbls4 procedure, 169
QueryLb1, 302-308
QueryMenu procedure, 540-541
Report Menu, 61-62
Report Script, 67-68
REPORTS.SC, 206-208
RptFnct1.sc, 347
RUN_TEST.SC, 309

shadow keys and tables Form Lock workaround, 376
shadow keys workaround #2, 377-378
ShowMsg.sc, 553-554
SMAIN.SC, 201-202, 204-205
SqlLogin.sc, 442
Statscrp.sc, 548-549
STATSPEC.SC, 565
system assigning keys method #1, 379-381
system assigning keys method #2, 381-383
system color codes, 566-568
system environment report, 570-572
TBLOPEN.C, 477
TESTCAL1, 311-312
TESTCAL2, 313-314
TestCal3.SC, 318-319
TESTCALC.SC, 310-311
UpdateBenefits procedure, 452
UpdateEmployee procedure, 447
ValidityChecks Procedure, 136
VertMenu procedure, 537
VIEWCUST.SC, 509-512
ViewTbls procedure, 242-243
ViewTblsMenu procedure, 245
programming
   see also program listings
   development, 74
   merging scripts, 30-31
   security, 31
   testing, 31-32, 74
programs
   see also applications *and* program listings

custom configuration, 94-98
designing, 26-38
documenting, 33-38
DOS BACKUP, 528
DOS SHARE, 611
examples, 29
implementation, 35-38
integrity checking program, 140-144
MAINMENU.SC. 209-211
MENUS.SC, 223-224
MESGLIB.SC, 232
MSFILE.SC, 200
NEXTMENU.SC, 219, 223
ParaLex, 564
running
   multitable, 127-128
   other from Paradox, 592
structure in Paradox Engine, 472-473
Super PC Qwik, 494
termination in Paradox Engine, 479-480
PROJ_SCH.SC listing, 525
prompts, 726
protected mode vs. real mode, 605-606
prototyping, 53-76, 726
   model, 58-76
pTools add-on program, 625
PXDateDecode function, 478
PXENGINE.H file, 473, 475
PXExit function, 479
PXEXIT.C listing, 480
PXFldName function, 476-477
PXFldType function, 476
PXGetAlpha function, 478
PXGetDate function, 478

PXGetDefaults function, 473
PXGetDouble function, 478
PXGetShort function, 478
PXInit function, 474
PXRecBufClose function, 479
PXRecBufOpen function, 476
PXRecGet function, 478, 481
PXRecGoto function, 478, 481
PXRecNFlds function, 476-477, 481
PXSetDefaults function, 473
PXTblClose function, 479
PXTblOpen function, 476
PXTblRecs function, 476, 481

Q

QBE *see* query-by-example
QEDIT script editor, 620
QRAM memory manager, 607-609
    Intel AboveBoard and, 608-609
Qry3Tbls2 procedure listing, 168
Qry3Tbls3 procedure listing, 168
Qry3Tbls4 procedure listing, 169
Quattro Pro
    data modeling, 593-601
    running from Paradox, 592-593
queries
    see also query-by-example (QBE)
    advanced, 293-330
    recording, 295-300
    scripts vs. libraries, 301-323
    SET, 327-330
    size when stored in procedures, 308-319

    text analysis and summary of storing, 322-323
Query language, 726
query-by-example (QBE), 294-300, 726
    see also queries
    concepts, 293
    functions, 323
    matching patterns, 295
    PAL commands and, 295-300
    PAL queries, 326
    peanut butter theory of programming, 323-327
    querying database server, 398-405
    QuerySave statements, 295-300
    reserved words, 295
    saving remote table queries, 401-402
    set operators, 295
    special operators, 295
    SQL Link, 390
    summary operators, 294-300
    table discards, 323
    testing results, 326-327
    three-level queries, 324
    three-step queries, 325
    tips, 327-330
QueryLb1 listing, 302-308
QueryMenu procedure listing, 540-541
QuerySave, 27-28, 726
    query-by-example (QBE), 295-300
QuerySpeedup, 726
questionnaire for end user, 72
QUIT command, 140

Index **749**

R

RAM and applications, 493-495
rapid development projects, 9-15
READLIB command, 156
README file
    configuration problems, 613-614
    testing CPU and EMS, 614-615
READSQL file, 393, 401, 439-441
    notes on database server products, 439-441
real mode vs. protected mode, 605-606
realistic development vs. theoretical, 6-7
record buffer, closing, 479
records, 726
    finding, 268-269
    searching in sequence, 263-265
    status
        resetting, 278
        values, 276-277
    validating data entry, 129-140
RECORDSTATUS function, 87-89, 275-277, 279, 282, 669-671
reference charts, 681-717
    ASCII code to KeyCode, 681-691
    functions, 701-705
    Paradox commands and equivalent menu commands, 700-701
    Paradox commands, keys, and ASCII codes, 691-699
    Paradox reserved words, 706-717
Reflex, importing, 584
relational databases, 40-52, 726
    terms, 41

relationships, 25
REMEMLEFT function, 653
remote tables, 390
    entering data, 397
    querying, 398-405
    saving queries, 401-402
replica tables, 390, 426-431
ReplicaTools SQL menu, 407
report generator writing PAL, 547-549
Report Menu listing, 61-62
Report Script listing, 67-68
reports
    advanced, 331-352
    arrays, 341-346
    bands, 720
    building on database server, 406
    company roster, 346-350
    entire table, 332
    full spelling for days and months, 344-346
    functions, 341-347
    generating, 331-341
    global variables, 341-350
    multitable, 82-84, 332-341
    one-to-many relationship, 346-350
    printer control characters, 350-352
    subsets of tables, 332
    system environment, 569-572
REPORTS.SC listing, 206-208
REPORTTABLES command, 651-652
Reset command, 295
Restricted view, 726

restructuring, 726
RESYNCKEY command, 86-90, 282, 652
RETURN command, 150
RMEMLEFT function, 87, 90, 496
rows, 727
RptFnct1.sc listing, 347
RUN command, 90-91
run-time error, 727
RUN_TEST.SC listing, 309

S

sample applications, 501-543
SAVETABLES command, 86-90, 653-654
SCAN FOR command, 263-265
SQLROLLBACK command, 416
script editors
    PAL-EDIT, 619-620
    PlayRight Pro, 618-619
    QEDIT, 620
scripts, 727
    see also program listings
    closed, 721
    ensuring data integrity, 128
    error log printing routine, 184-189
    error procedure, 181-182
    examples, 59-72
    interactive, 28-32
    merging, 30-31
    modifying, 128
    viewing tables, 242-245
    vs. libraries queries, 301-323
ScriptView documentation tool, 621-622
SEARCH function, 654

searching records in sequence, 263-265
Second Normal Form (2NF), 47
secondary index, 727
security
    in programming, 31
    SQL Link, 410
SELECT command, 398
server, 386-387
    see also file server and database server
set operators (query-by-example (QBE)), 295
SET queries, 327-330
SETPRIVDIR command, 654-655
SETQUERYORDER command, 655
SETRECORDPOSITION command, 656-657
shadow key
    Form Lock workaround, 375-379
    tables Form Lock workaround listing, 376
    workaround #2 listing, 377-378
SHOW command, 90-94
SHOWARRAY command, 91
SHOWARRAY procedure, 196
SHOWFILE procedure, 198
SHOWFILES command, 91
SHOWMENU command, 91, 193-194, 255
ShowMsg.sc listing, 553-554
SHOWTABLES command, 91, 445
slash sequence, 727
SMAIN.SC listing, 204-205
SOM files, 392-393
SORTORDER function, 657

Index 751

special operators (query-by-example (QBE)), 295
spreadsheets
    exporting, 589
    importing, 582
SQL, 385-459
    database server, 393-406
    entering statements and sending directly to server, 431
    link code examples, 441-459
    menu selection, 406-410
SQL command editor, 435-438
    loading, 431
SQL Connection form, 432-435
SQL link, 3, 78, 385-438
    see also database servers
    automatic transactions, 409
    broken connection, 408
    client/server architecture, 386-390
    database servers
        IBM OS/2 Extended Edition Database Manager version 2.1, 390
        Microsoft SQL Server Version 1.0 and 1.1, 390
        Oracle, 390
    error-handling, 421-422
    installing, 391-393
    local tables, 390
    overview, 390-391
    PAL
        enhancing commands, 410-412
        new commands, 412-418
        new functions, 418-421

query-by-example (QBE), 390
remote tables, 390
replica tables, 390, 408
security, 391, 410
text file of query, 408-409
transaction processing control, 408
SQL NOFETCH command, 446
SQL Setup Program (SSP), 423-435
    automatic menu selection, 424-429
    ConnectList selection, 432
    manual menu selection, 429-431
    modifying server connection list, 432-435
    UseSQL selection, 431
SQL...ENDSQL command, 413-414
SQLAUTOCOMMIT command, 414
SQLBREAKCONNECT command, 414
SQLCLEARCONNECT command, 415
SQLCOMMIT command, 415, 448-451
SQLCONNECTINFO command, 419, 443-445
SQLERRORCODE function, 91, 420-421
SQLERRORMESSAGE function, 420-421
SQLFETCH command, 446-447
SQLFETCH command, 415
SQLISCONNECT function, 420
SQLISREPLICA command, 420, 445
SqlLogin.sc listing, 442
SQLMAKECONNECT command, 416
SQLMAPINFO function, 420-421
SQLRELEASE command, 416
SQLRESTORECONNECT command, 416

SQLROLLBACK command, 448-451
SQLSAVECONNECT command, 416-417
SQLSELECTCONNECT command, 417, 442-443
SQLSETINTERRUPT command, 418
SQLSETUP.SC file, 423
SQLSTARTTRANS command, 418, 448
SQLVAL function, 421
static-style menus, 192
    NEXTMENU.SC, 215-217
    REPORTS.SC, 206-208
    SMAIN.SC, 201-202, 204-205
Statscrp.sc listing, 548-549
STATSPEC.SC listing, 565
STRVAL function, 657-658
Structured Query Language *see* SQL *and* SQL Link
SUBSTR function, 658-659
SUM summary operator (query-by-example (QBE)), 300
summary operators (query-by-example (QBE)), 294-300
    AVERAGE, 296
    COUNT, 297
    MAX, 298
    MIN, 299
    SUM, 300
Super PC Qwik, 494, 610
swapping, 161-164
SWITCH command, 125-126
symmetrical outer join, 727
syntax error, 727
SYSMODE function, 659-660

system assigning keys method #1 listing, 379-381
system assigning keys method #2 listing, 381-383
system color codes listing, 566-568
system environment report, 569-572
    listing, 570-572
system files and networks, 362
system testing, 31-32

T

Table view, 727
TABLERIGHTS function, 660-661
tables, 727
    access on networks, 365-367
    attempting to edit while in use, 372
    borrow, 720
    closing, 479
    creating on database server, 396
    denormalizing, 50-52
    design, 496-499
    editing in private directories, 372
    editing subset, 259-272
    entering data in database server, 397-398
    finding records, 268-269
    Form Lock workaround, 375-376
    handles, 476
    key violations, 275-285, 397
    keyed, 498
    lack of discards in query-by-example (QBE), 323
    listing examples, 480-491
    local, 390

logical locks, 365-367
Master Picture, 116-126
non-keyed, 498
normalized, 39-49, 725
one-to-many relationships, 375
one-to-one relationships, 375
opening with Paradox Engine, 476-477
printing records, 477-478
relationships, 25
remote, 390-405
removing data on database server, 406
replica, 390, 426-431
reports of subsets or entire, 332
reports on multiple, 332-341
subsets
    editing, 259-272
        fields with query, 265-267
        querying, 265
        select key fields, 269-272
    uniqueness *not* based on key field, 286-290
    viewing, 242-245, 545-547
TBLOPEN.C listing, 477
TESTCAL1 listing, 311-312
TESTCAL2 listing, 313-314
TESTCALC.SC listing, 310-311
testing
    programming, 74
    systems, 31-32
TextCal3.SC listing, 318-319
TextView add-on program, 624-625

theoretical development compared to realistic, 6-7
Third Normal Form (3NF), 48-49
third-party developers, 7-9
Tilde (~) variable, 727
TOQPRO command, 661-662
training, 75-76
transaction log, 727
    Edit mode, 253-258
Transaction SQL menu, 407
Turbo C compiling Paradox Engine, 466-468
TurboDrive, 78-79
TUTILITY, 5
TYPEIN command printer control characters, 351

U

UNDO command, 86-90
Unexpected condition errors, 370
UNLOCKRECORD command, 277
UNPASSWORD command, 662-663
UpdateBenefits procedure listing, 452
UpdateEmployee procedure listing, 447
user interface, 4
USERNAME function, 663
UseSQL SSP menu selection, 431
utilities
    FLIMPORT, 586-587
    procedures
        AddBlankLines, 339
        AddLineNumber, 339
    SQL Setup Program (SSP), 423-435

V

ValChecks, 107-114
    entering, 115-144
    reporting program, 559-564
    visibility reporting, 142-144
validating
    data entry, 107-144
    field entries, 129-140
    record entries, 129-140
ValidityChecks procedure listing, 136
values
    logical, 724
    record status, 276-277
variables, 727
    autolib, 161-164
    global, 272, 724
    global and private, 151-152
    new, 78-84
    Tilde (~), 727
vendor support, 13
Version 3.5
    compatibility with earlier releases, 99-101
    new features, 77-98
VERSION function, 663-664
VertMenu procedure listing, 537
view script for multiple tables, 242-245
VIEWCUST.SC listing, 509-512
ViewTbls procedure listing, 242-243
ViewTblsMenu listing, 245
Virtual Memory Management (VMM), 493
visibility reporting, 142-144
VisiCalc
    exporting, 589
    importing, 583
VROOMM (Virtual Runtime Object-Oriented Memory Manager), 78, 603

W

WAIT command, 124, 130-140, 243, 255, 291-292, 447
WINDOW function, 664
windows
    exploding, 554-556
    filling, 557-558
Windows, running Paradox, 610-611
working directories, 360, 727
    multiple-user editing, 373
    tracking access, 360-361
workspace, 727
    clearing query images, 554
workstations, 386-387
    configuration on networks, 363
WRITELIB statement, 174-177

Z

ZOOM command, 252-253

More from the New World of Computer Books...
IDG Books Worldwide

The only *in-depth*, complete guides to buying software & computers!

InfoWorld Test Center Software Buyer's Guide

▲ More comprehensive, up-to-date, and authoritative than any other guide

▲ Covers: word processors, spreadsheets, databases, desktop publishing (high-end and low-end), and Windows 3!

▲ With definitive, unbiased reviews that really help you evaluate the right software for the job you need done

$14.95
from the Editors of *InfoWorld* Magazine, with a special preface by Michael Miller, Editor-in-Chief, *InfoWorld* Magazine
1-878058-11-8, 356 pp., 5 1/2 x 8 1/2"

InfoWorld Test Center Computer Buyer's Guide

▲ From InfoWorld's $3 million Test Center--the industry's most respected testing facility!

▲ Covers: 16 MHz '386s, 33 MHr '386s, '486 supermachines, and portable computers, too!

▲ With definitive, unbiased reviews that really help you evaluate the right computer for your needs

$14.95
from the Editors of *InfoWorld* Magazine, with a special preface by Michael Miller, Editor-in-Chief, *InfoWorld* Magazine
1-878058-12-6, 254 pp., 5 1/2 x 8 1/2"

The authorized edition--for a bestselling hard disk utility!

The Official XTree MS-DOS & Hard Disk Companion

▲ The definitive, authorized guide to XTree, and the new XTreeGold 2!

▲ Two-books-in-one: every feature of XTree and a guide to hard disk management, too!

▲ "If you have a hard disk you NEED this book"!
    --Don Crabb, Chicago Sun-Times

$15.95
by Beth Woods, with a special preface by Jeffrey C. Johnson, co-creator of XTree
1-878058-22-3, 288 pp., 5 1/2 x 8 1/2"

▲▼▲
Available at your local bookstore or computer/software store.
Or call (800) 28BOOKS.
(That's 800-282-6657)

Other Valuable Guides from the New World of Computer Books...IDG Books Worldwide

Finally--a practical guide to portable computing!

Portable Computing Official Laptop Field Manual

▲ A complete, take-it-with-you-on-the-road-manual:
with printer codes, software keystroke references, on-line access phone numbers, individual hardware references, DOS summaries, and more
▲ Leave your manuals at home--everything you need is in this one handy-sized book!
▲ From Portable Computing Magazine--the mobile professional's monthly bible

$14.95
by Sebastian Rupley, with a foreword by Jim McBrian, Group Publisher, *Portable Computing* Magazine
1-878058-10-X, 224 pp., 5 1/2 x 8 1/2"

The authorized edition--with inside information from the developer!

The Official SpinRite II & Hard Disk Companion

▲ The authorized, inside guide to SpinRite, from Gibson Research
▲ With valuable, "insider" tips never before revealed
▲ With a section on how hard disks die--and how to prevent those problems on your computer

$14.95
by John M. Goodman, Ph.D., with a foreword by Steve Gibson, President of Gibson Research
1-878058-08-8, 280 pp., 5 1/2 x 8 1/2"

▲▼▲

Available at your local bookstore or computer/software store.
Or call (800) 28BOOKS.
(That's 800-282-6657)

IDG Books Worldwide Registration Card --
PC World Paradox 3.5 Power Programming Techniques

Fill this out—and hear about updates to this book & other IDG Books Worldwide products!

Name _____

Company/Title _____

Address _____

City/State/Zip _____

What is the single most important reason you bought this book? _____
_____

Where did you buy this book?
    ❐ Bookstore (Name _____)
    ❐ Electronics/Software Store (Name _____)
    ❐ Advertisement (If magazine, which? _____)
    ❐ Mail Order
    ❐ Other: _____

How did you hear about this book?
    ❐ Book review in: _____
    ❐ Advertisement in: _____
    ❐ Catalog
    ❐ Found in store
    ❐ Other: _____

How many computer books do you purchase a year?
    ❐ 1   ❐ 6-10
    ❐ 2-5   ❐ More than 10

How would you rate the overall content of this book?
    ❐ Very good   ❐ Satisfactory
    ❐ Good   ❐ Poor
Why? _____

What chapters did you find most valuable? _____

What did you find least useful? _____

What kind of chapter or topic would you add to future editions of this book?
_____

Please give us any additional comments. _____
_____

Thank you for your help.

❐ I liked this book! By checking this box, I give you permission to use my name and quote me in future IDG Books Worldwide promotional materials.

Fold Here

Place stamp here

IDG Books Worldwide, Inc.
155 Bovet Road, Ste. 730
San Mateo, CA 94402

Attn: Reader Response

About the Authors

Greg Salcedo is a Systems Analyst with a major Northwest computing services corporation. Mr. Salcedo has worked in the information processing arena for the past 10 years, specializing in finance systems for more than seven of those years. Prior to entering the information systems area, Mr. Salcedo was an accountant/controller for several large firms. Mr. Salcedo has been a beta tester for such firms as Lotus, Intel, Microsoft, and Borland. He's currently a member of the Borland Advisory Board as well as president, and one of the founders, of the Pacific Northwest Paradox User's Group.

Martin Rudy is a Systems Analyst and Paradox database product manager for a major Northwest computing services corporation. He received a Bachelor of Science degree in Computer Science in 1980 from Western Washington University and a Certificate in Data Processing in 1986. He was an advisory board member of the first *International Paradox User's Conference* in 1990, and in addition is the vice president, and one of the founders of the Pacific Northwest Paradox User's Group. Mr. Rudy has worked for over 10 years as a systems analyst on mainframe and microcomputer database applications.

5-1/4 INCH DISK FORMAT AVAILABLE

The enclosed disk is in 3-1/2 inch 1.44 megabyte format. If you don't have a drive in that size and format, and cannot arrange to transfer the data to the disk size you need, you can obtain the code on three 5-1/4 inch 360K disks by sending $7.95 to: IDG Books Worldwide, Attn: Paradox Disks, c/o IDG Peterborough, 80 Elm Street Peterborough, NH 03458. Or call 1-800-28-BOOKS. Please allow 3-4 weeks for delivery.

DISCLAIMER AND COPYRIGHT NOTICE

NOTE

IDG Books Worldwide, Inc., warrants that the physical diskette that accompanies this book is free from defects in materials and workmanship for a period of 60 days from the date of purchase of this book. If IDG Books receives notification within the warranty period of defects in material or workmanship, IDG Books will replace the defective diskette. The remedy for the breach of this warranty will be limited to replacement and will not encompass any other damages, including but not limited to loss of profit, and special, incidental, consequential, or other claims.

IDG Books Worldwide, Inc., PCW Communications Inc., and the authors specifically disclaim all other warranties, express or implied, including but not limited to implied warranties of merchantability and fitness for a particular purpose with respect to defects in the diskette, the programs and source code contained therein, the program listings in the book, and/or the techniques described in the book, and in no event shall IDG Books, Worldwide, Inc., PCW Communications, Inc., and/or the authors be liable for any loss of profit or any other commercial damage, including but not limited to special, incidental, consequential or other damages.

Licensing Agreement

Do not open the accompanying diskette package until you have read and unless you agree with the terms of this licensing agreement. If you disagree and do not wish to be bound by the terms of this licensing agreement, return the book to the source from which you purchased it.

The entire contents of this diskette are copyrighted and protected by both U.S. copyright law and international copyright treaty provisions. There are two kinds of material on the diskette: Paradox source code, which are PAL listings in ASCII (text) format; and utilities, which are executable standalone programs that do not require Paradox to operate. The executable utilities may not be copied (except that a single backup copy may be made, and the program may be copied to a single machine's hard disk), and may not be distributed, modified, or resold, at any time and for any reason. On the other hand, you may copy, modify for your own purposes, embed portions in your own code, and distribute the results for NONCOMMERCIAL PURPOSES ONLY the Paradox source code from this disk, under the following limitations: First, as noted above, we make no warranties of any kind as to the merchantability or fitness of the code for any particular purpose; second, you assume full responsibility and liability for the resulting code and the publishers and authors shall in no event be liable for any damages or loss of profit or any other commercial damages, as noted in the paragraphs above, for the resulting code or for the portions of that code taken from this book or diskette; and third, in all cases any distribution of any kind must include a copyright notice to wit: "Copyright 1990 by IDG Books Worldwide, Inc." or "Portions copyright 1990 by IDG Books Worldwide, Inc.," as appropriate. Absolutely none of the material on this disk or listed in this book may ever be distributed, in original or modified form, for commercial purposes.